Understanding the Theory and Design of Organizations

Understanding the Theory and Design of Organizations

TENTH EDITION

Richard L. Daft

VANDERBILT UNIVERSITY

SOUTH-WESTERN
CENGAGE Learning™

Australia • Brazil • Japan • Korea • Mexico • Singapore • Spain • United Kingdom • United States

SOUTH-WESTERN
CENGAGE Learning™

Understanding the Theory and Design of Organizations, Tenth Edition

Richard L. Daft

With the Assistance of Patricia G. Lane

Vice President of Editorial, Business: Jack W. Calhoun

Vice President/Editor-in-Chief: Melissa Acuña

Publisher: Joe Sabatino

Developmental Editor: Erin Guendelsberger

Executive Marketing Manager: Kimberly Kanakas

Marketing Manager: Clint Kernen

Marketing Coordinator: Sarah Rose

Senior Content Project Manager: Colleen A. Farmer

Media Editor: Rob Ellington

Frontlist Buyer, Manufacturing: Doug Wilke

Production Service and Compositor: S4Carlisle Publishing Services

Senior Art Director: Tippy McIntosh

Internal Designer: Craig Ramsdell, Ramsdell Design

Cover Image: ©Shutterstock

For product information and technology assistance, contact us at **Cengage Learning Customer & Sales Support,** 1-800-354-9706
For permission to use material from this text or product, submit all requests online at **www.cengage.com/permissions**
Further permissions questions can be emailed to **permissionrequest@cengage.com**

Cengage Learning WebTutor™ is a trademark of Cengage Learning.

Library of Congress Control Number: 2009921278

International Student Edition ISBN-13: 978-0-324-59888-9
International Student Edition ISBN-10: 0-324-59888-2

Cengage Learning International Offices

Asia
cengageasia.com
tel: (65) 6410 1200

Australia/New Zealand
cengage.com.au
tel: (61) 3 9685 4111

Brazil
cengage.com.br
tel: (011) 3665 9900

India
cengage.co.in
tel: (91) 11 30484837/38

Latin America
cengage.com.mx
tel: +52 (55) 1500 6000

UK/Europe/Middle East/Africa
cengage.co.uk
tel: (44) 207 067 2500

Represented in Canada by Nelson Education, Ltd.
nelson.com
tel: (416) 752 9100 / (800) 668 0671

For product information: **www.cengage.com/international**
Visit your local office: **www.cengage.com/global**
Visit our corporate website: **www.cengage.com**

Printed in China by China Translation & Printing Services Limited
1 2 3 4 5 6 7 13 12 11 10 09

Richard L. Daft, Ph.D., is the Brownlee O. Currey, Jr., Professor of Management in the Owen Graduate School of Management at Vanderbilt University. Professor Daft specializes in the study of organization theory and leadership. Professor Daft is a Fellow of the Academy of Management and has served on the editorial boards of *Academy of Management Journal, Administrative Science Quarterly*, and *Journal of Management Education*. He was the Associate Editor-in-Chief of *Organization Science* and served for three years as associate editor of *Administrative Science Quarterly*.

Professor Daft has authored or co-authored twelve books, including *New Era of Management, International Edition* (Cengage/South-Western, 2010), *The Leadership Experience, International Edition* (Cengage/South-Western, 2008), and *What to Study: Generating and Developing Research Questions* (Sage, 1982). He also published *Fusion Leadership: Unlocking the Subtle Forces That Change People and Organizations* (Berrett-Koehler, 2000, with Robert Lengel). He has authored dozens of scholarly articles, papers, and chapters. His work has been published in *Administrative Science Quarterly, Academy of Management Journal, Academy of Management Review, Organizational Dynamics, Strategic Management Journal, Journal of Management, Accounting Organizations and Society, Management Science, MIS Quarterly, California Management Review*, and *Organizational Behavior Teaching Review*. Professor Daft has been awarded several government research grants to pursue studies of organization design, organizational innovation and change, strategy implementation, and organizational information processing.

Professor Daft is also an active teacher and consultant. He has taught management, leadership, organizational change, organizational theory, and organizational behavior. He has been involved in management development and consulting for many companies and government organizations, including Allstate Insurance, American Banking Association, Bell Canada, Bridgestone, National Transportation Research Board, NL Baroid, Nortel, TVA, Pratt & Whitney, State Farm Insurance, Tenneco, Tennessee Emergency Pediatric Services, the United States Air Force, the United States Army, J. C. Bradford & Co., Central Parking System, USAA, United Methodist Church, Entergy Sales and Service, Bristol-Myers Squibb, First American National Bank, and the Vanderbilt University Medical Center.

Brief Contents

Contents

Bettina Anzeletti

Part 4: Managing Organizational Processes　　　　　　257

My vision for the Tenth Edition of *Understanding the Theory and Design of Organizations* is to integrate contemporary problems about organization design with classic ideas and theories in a way that is engaging and enjoyable for students. Significant changes in this edition include two new features—"Managing by Design Questions" and "How Do You Fit the Design?"—along with updates to every chapter that incorporate the most recent ideas, new case examples, new book reviews, and new end-of-book integrative cases. The research and theories in the field of organization studies are rich and insightful and will help students and managers understand their organizational world and solve real-life problems. My mission is to combine the concepts and models from organizational theory with changing events in the real world to provide the most up-to-date view of organization design available.

DISTINGUISHING FEATURES OF THE TENTH EDITION

Many students in a typical organization theory course do not have extensive work experience, especially at the middle and upper levels, where organization theory is most applicable. Moreover, word from the field is that many students today often do not read the chapter opening examples or boxed examples, preferring instead to focus on chapter content. To engage students in the world of organizations, the Tenth Edition adds two significant features. First, "Managing by Design Questions" start each chapter to engage students in thinking and expressing their beliefs and opinions about organization design concepts. Second, a new in-chapter feature, "How Do You Fit the Design?" engages students in how their personal style and approach will fit into an organization. Other student experiential activities that engage students in applying chapter concepts are new "In Practice" examples and new integrative cases for student analysis. The total set of features substantially expands and improves the book's content and accessibility. These multiple pedagogical devices are used to enhance student involvement in text materials.

How Do You Fit the Design? The "How Do You Fit the Design?" feature presents a short questionnaire in each chapter about the student's own style and preferences to quickly provide feedback about how they fit particular organizations or situations. For example, questionnaire topics include: "What Size Organization for You?" "Are You Ready to Fill an International Role?" "The Pleasure/Pain of Working on a Team," "How Innovative Are You?" and "How Do You Make Important Decisions?" These short feedback questionnaires connect the student's personal preferences to chapter material to heighten interest and show relevance of the concepts.

Managing by Design Questions Each chapter now opens with three short opinion questions that engage students in clarifying their thoughts about upcoming material and concepts. These questions are based on the idea that when students express their opinions first, they are more open to and interested in receiving material relevant to the questions. Example questions, which ask students to agree or disagree, include:

The primary role of managers in business organizations is to achieve maximum efficiency.

Managers should use the most objective, rational process possible when making a decision.

If management practices and coordination techniques work well for a company in its home country, they probably will be successful in the company's international divisions as well.

A certain amount of conflict is good for an organization.

As a follow-up to the three "Managing by Design" questions, each chapter contains three "Assess Your Answer" inserts that allow students to compare their original opinions with the "correct" or most appropriate answers based on chapter concepts. Students learn whether their mental models and beliefs about organizations align with the world of organizations.

In Practice This edition contains many new "In Practice" examples that illustrate theoretical concepts in organizational settings. Many examples are international, and all are based on real organizations. New "In Practice" cases used within chapters include Samsung Electronics, eBay, the Salvation Army, Axiom Global, Univision, Google, Semco, AT&T, the World Bank, Threadless, Carilion Health System, Apple, Matsushita Electric, Herman Miller, and Great Ormand Street Hospital for Children.

Manager's Briefcase Located in the chapter margins, this feature tells students how to use concepts to analyze cases and manage organizations.

Text Exhibits Frequent exhibits are used to help students visualize organizational relationships, and the artwork has been redone to communicate concepts more clearly.

Design Essentials This summary and interpretation section tells students how the essential chapter points are important in the broader context of organization theory.

Case for Analysis These cases are tailored to chapter concepts and provide a vehicle for student analysis and discussion.

Integrative Cases The integrative cases at the end of each part have been expanded and positioned to encourage student discussion and involvement. The new cases

include Rondell Data Corporation and The Plaza Inn. Previous cases that have
been retained include Royce Consulting; Custom Chip Inc.; and Empire Plastics.

NEW CONCEPTS

Many concepts have been added or expanded in this edition. New material has
been added on organizational configuration and Mintzberg's organization forms;
strategic intent, core competence and competitive advantage; Porter's competitive
forces and strategies; using the balanced scorecard to measure effectiveness; using
strategy maps; the trend toward outsourcing; supply chain management; intelligence
teams; collaborative versus operations management roles; applying Web 2.0 tools
for internal and external coordination; behavior versus outcome control; executive dashboards; interpreting and shaping culture through organization structures,
control systems, and power systems; corporate social responsibility; values-based
leadership; collaborative teams for innovation; prospect theory; groupthink; overcoming cognitive biases in decision making; and the power of empowerment. Many
ideas are aimed at helping students learn to design organizations for an environment
characterized by uncertainty; a renewed emphasis on innovation; public demands
for stronger ethics and social responsibility; and the need for a speedy response to
change, crises, or shifting customer expectations. In addition, coping with the complexity of today's global environment is explored thoroughly in Chapter 5.

CHAPTER ORGANIZATION

Each chapter is highly focused and is organized into a logical framework. Many
organization theory textbooks treat material in sequential fashion, such as "Here's
View A, Here's View B, Here's View C," and so on. *Understanding the Theory
and Design of Organizations* shows how they apply in organizations. Moreover,
each chapter sticks to the essential point. Students are not introduced to extraneous
material or confusing methodological squabbles that occur among organizational
researchers. The body of research in most areas points to a major trend, which is
reported here. Several chapters develop a framework that organizes major ideas into
an overall scheme.

This book has been extensively tested on students. Feedback from students and
faculty members has been used in the revision. The combination of organization
theory concepts, book reviews, examples of leading organizations, self-insight questionnaires, case illustrations, experiential exercises, and other teaching devices is
designed to meet student learning needs, and students have responded favorably.

SUPPLEMENTS

Instructor's Resource Guide The Instructor's Resource Guide includes an Instructor's
Manual and Test Bank. The Instructor's Manual contains chapter overviews, chapter
outlines, lecture enhancements, discussion questions, discussion of workbook activities, discussion of chapter cases, and case notes for integrative cases. The Test Bank
consists of multiple choice, true/false, and essay questions.

PowerPoint Lecture Presentation Available on the Web site (www.cengage.com/international), the PowerPoint Lecture Presentation enables instructors to customize their own multimedia classroom presentations. Prepared in conjunction with the text and instructor's resource guide, the package contains approximately 150 slides. It includes figures and tables from the text, as well as outside materials to supplement chapter concepts. Material is organized by chapter and can be modified or expanded for individual classroom use. PowerPoint presentations are also easily printed to create customized transparency masters.

ExamView A computerized version of the Test Bank is available on the text Web site (www.cengage.com/international). ExamView contains all of the questions in the printed test bank. This program is easy-to-use test creation software. Instructors can add or edit questions, instructions, and answers and can select questions (randomly or numerically) by previewing them on the screen. Instructors can also create and administer quizzes online, whether over the Internet, a local area network (LAN), or a wide area network (WAN).

WebTutor™ Toolbox WebTutor is an interactive, Web-based student supplement on WebCT and/or BlackBoard that harnesses the power of the Internet to deliver innovative learning aids that actively engage students. The instructor can incorporate WebTutor as an integral part of the course, or the students can use it on their own as a study guide.

Web Site (www.cengage.com/international) The Daft Web site is a comprehensive, resource-rich location for both instructors and students to find pertinent information. The Instructor Resources section contains an Instructor's Manual download, Test Bank download, and PowerPoint download.

Video/DVD This DVD includes video segments related to organization design concepts. They're designed to visually reinforce key concepts.

Experiential Exercises in Organization Theory and Design, Second Edition By H. Eugene Baker III and Steven K. Paulson of the University of North Florida.

Tailored to the table of contents in Daft's *Understanding the Theory and Design of Organizations,* Tenth Edition, the core purpose of *Experiential Exercises in Understanding the Theory and Design of Organizations* is to provide courses in organizational theory with a set of classroom exercises that will help students better understand and internalize the basic principles of the course. The chapters of the book cover the most basic and widely covered concepts in the field. Each chapter focuses on a central topic, such as organizational power, production technology, or organizational culture, and provides all necessary materials to fully participate in three different exercises. Some exercises are intended to be completed by individuals, others in groups, and still others can be used either way. The exercises range from instrumentation-based and assessment questionnaires to actual creative production activities.

ACKNOWLEDGMENTS

Textbook writing is a team enterprise. The Tenth Edition has integrated ideas and hard work from many people to whom I am grateful. Reviewers and focus group participants made an especially important contribution. They praised many features, were critical of things that didn't work well, and offered valuable suggestions.

David Ackerman
University of Alaska, Southeast

Michael Bourke
Houston Baptist University

Suzanne Clinton
Cameron University

Jo Anne Duffy
Sam Houston State University

Cheryl Duvall
Mercer University

Patricia Feltes
Missouri State University

Robert Girling
Sonoma State University

John A. Gould
University of Maryland

Ralph Hanke
Pennsylvania State University

Bruce J. Hanson
Pepperdine University

Guiseppe Labianca
Tulane University

Jane Lemaster
University of Texas–Pan American

Steven Maranville
University of Saint Thomas

Rick Martinez
Baylor University

Janet Near
Indiana University

Julie Newcomer
Texas Woman's University

Asbjorn Osland
George Fox University

Laynie Pizzolatto
Nicholls State University

Samantha Rice
Abilene Christian University

Richard Saaverda
University of Michigan

W. Robert Sampson
University of Wisconsin, Eau Claire

Amy Sevier
University of Southern Mississippi

W. Scott Sherman
Pepperdine University

Thomas Terrell
Coppin State College

Jack Tucci
Southeastern Louisiana University

Judith White
Santa Clara University

Jan Zahrly
University of North Dakota

    Among my professional colleagues, I am grateful to my friends and colleagues at Vanderbilt's Owen School—Bruce Barry, Ray Friedman, Neta Moye, Rich Oliver, David Owens, Ranga Ramanujam, and Bart Victor—for their intellectual stimulation and feedback. I also owe a special debt to Dean Jim Bradford and Associate Deans Bill Christie and Dawn Iocabucci for providing the time and resources for me to stay current on the organization design literature and develop the revisions for the text.

I want to extend special thanks to my editorial associate, Pat Lane. She skillfully wrote materials on a variety of topics and special features, found resources, and did an outstanding job with the copyedited manuscript and page proofs. Pat's personal enthusiasm and care for the content of this text enabled the Tenth Edition to continue its high level of excellence.

The team at South-Western also deserves special mention. Joe Sabatino did a great job of designing the project and offering ideas for improvement. Erin Guendelsberger and Emma Guttler were superb to work with during their respective turns as Developmental Editor, keeping the people and project on schedule while solving problems creatively and quickly. Colleen Farmer, Senior Content Project Manager, provided superb project coordination and used her creativity and management skills to facilitate the book's on-time completion. Clint Kernen, Marketing Manager, provided additional support, creativity, and valuable market expertise.

Finally, I want to acknowledge the love and contributions of my wife, Dorothy Marcic. Dorothy has been very supportive of my textbook projects and has created an environment in which we can grow together. She helped the book take a giant step forward with her creation of the Workbook and Workshop student exercises. I also want to acknowledge the love and support of my daughters, Danielle, Amy, Roxanne, Solange, and Elizabeth, who make my life special during our precious time together.

Richard L. Daft

Nashville, Tennessee

March 2009

Understanding the Theory and Design of Organizations

Part 1

Introduction to Organization Theory and Design

Chapter 1
Introduction to Organizations

Chris Ho - www.chrisho.net

Chapter 1

Introduction to Organizations

1 An organization can be understood primarily by understanding the people who make it up.

1	2	3	4	5
STRONGLY AGREE				STRONGLY DISAGREE

2 The primary role of managers in business organizations is to achieve maximum efficiency.

1	2	3	4	5
STRONGLY AGREE				STRONGLY DISAGREE

3 A CEO's top priority is to make sure the organization is designed correctly.

1	2	3	4	5
STRONGLY AGREE				STRONGLY DISAGREE

Managing
by Design
Questions

A LOOK INSIDE

XEROX CORPORATION

On the eve of the twenty-first century, Xerox Corporation seemed on top of the world, with fast-rising earnings, a soaring stock price, and a new line of computerized copier-printers that were technologically superior to rival products. Less than two years later, many considered Xerox a has-been, destined to fade into history. Consider the following events:

- Sales and earnings plummeted as rivals caught up with Xerox's high-end digital machines, offering comparable products at lower prices.
- Xerox's losses for the opening year of the twenty-first century totaled $384 million, and the company continued to bleed red ink. Debt mounted to $18 billion.
- The stock fell from a high of $64 to less than $4, amid fears that the company would file for federal bankruptcy protection. Over an 18-month period, Xerox lost $38 billion in shareholder wealth.
- Twenty-two thousand Xerox workers lost their jobs, further weakening the morale and loyalty of remaining employees. Major customers were alienated, too, by a restructuring that threw salespeople into unfamiliar territories and tied billing up in knots, leading to mass confusion and billing errors.
- The company was fined a whopping $10 million by the Securities and Exchange Commission (SEC) for accounting irregularities and alleged accounting fraud.

What went wrong at Xerox? The company's deterioration is a classic story of organizational decline. Although Xerox appeared to fall almost overnight, the organization's problems were connected to a series of organizational blunders over a period of many years.

BACKGROUND

Xerox was founded in 1906 as the Haloid Company, a photographic supply house that developed the world's first xerographic copier, introduced in 1959. Without a doubt, the 914 copier was a money-making machine. By the time it was retired in the early 1970s, the 914 was the best-selling industrial product of all time, and the new name of the company, Xerox, was listed in the dictionary as a synonym for photocopying.

A LOOK INSIDE *(continued)*

Joseph C. Wilson, Haloid's longtime chairman and president, created a positive, people-oriented culture continued by his successor, David Kearns, who steered Xerox until 1990. The Xerox culture and its dedicated employees (sometimes called "Xeroids") were the envy of the corporate world. In addition to values of fairness and respect, Xerox's culture emphasized risk taking and employee involvement. Wilson wrote the following for early recruiting materials: "We seek people who are willing to accept risk, willing to try new ideas and have ideas of their own...who are not afraid to change what they are doing from one day to the next, and from one year to the next..." Xerox continued to use these words in its recruiting efforts, but the culture the words epitomize had eroded.

"BUROX" TAKES HOLD

Like many profitable organizations, Xerox became a victim of its own success. Leaders no doubt knew that the company needed to move beyond copiers to sustain its growth, but they found it difficult to look beyond the 70 percent gross profit margins of the 914 copier.

Xerox's Palo Alto Research Center (PARC), established in 1970, became known around the world for innovation— many of the most revolutionary technologies in the computer industry, including the personal computer, graphical user interface, Ethernet, and laser printer, were invented at PARC. But the copier bureaucracy, or *Burox* as it came to be known, blinded Xerox leaders to the enormous potential of these innovations. While Xerox was plodding along selling copy machines, younger, smaller, and hungrier companies were developing PARC technologies into tremendous money-making products and services.

The dangers of Burox became dramatically clear when the company's xerography patents began expiring. Suddenly, Japanese rivals such as Canon and Ricoh were selling copiers at the cost it took Xerox to make them. Market share declined from 95 percent to 13 percent by 1982. And with no new products to make up the difference, the company had to fight hard to cut costs and reclaim market share by committing to Japanese-style techniques and total quality management. Through the strength of his leadership, CEO Kearns was able to rally the troops and rejuvenate the company by 1990. However, he also set Xerox on a path to future disaster. Seeing a need to diversify, Kearns moved the company into insurance and financial services on a large scale. When he turned leadership over to Paul Allaire in 1990, Xerox's balance sheet was crippled by billions of dollars in insurance liabilities.

ENTERING THE DIGITAL AGE

Allaire wisely began a methodical, step-by-step plan for extricating Xerox from the insurance and financial services business. At the same time, he initiated a mixed strategy of cost cutting and new-product introductions to get the stodgy company moving again. Xerox had success with a line of digital presses and new high-speed digital copiers, but it fumbled again by underestimating the threat of the inkjet printer. By the time Xerox introduced its own line of desktop printers, the game was already over.

Desktop printers, combined with increasing use of the Internet and e-mail, cut heavily into Xerox's sales of copiers. People didn't need to make as many photocopies, but there was a huge increase in the number of documents being created and shared. Rebranding Xerox as "The Document Company," Allaire pushed into the digital era, hoping to remake Xerox in the image of the rejuvenated IBM, offering not just "boxes (machines)" but complete document management solutions.

As part of that strategy, Allaire picked Richard Thoman, who was then serving as Louis Gerstner's right-hand man at IBM, as his successor. Thoman came to Xerox as president, chief operating officer, and eventually CEO, amid high hopes that the company could regain the stature of its glory years. Only 13 months later, as revenues and the stock price continued to slide, he was fired by Allaire, who had remained as Xerox chairman.

PLAYING POLITICS

Allaire and Thoman blamed each other for the failure to successfully implement the digital strategy. Outsiders, however, believe the failure had much more to do with Xerox's dysfunctional culture. The culture was already slow to adapt, and some say that under Allaire it became almost totally paralyzed by politics. Thoman was brought in to shake things up, but when he tried, the old guard rebelled. A management struggle developed, with the outsider Thoman and a few allies on one side lined up against Allaire and his group of insiders who were accustomed to doing things the Xeroid way. Recognized for his knowledge, business experience, and intensity, Thoman was also considered to be somewhat haughty

and unapproachable. He was never able to exert substantial influence with key managers and employees, nor to gain the support of board members, who continued to rally behind Allaire.

The failed CEO succession illustrates the massive challenge of reinventing a century-old company. By the time Thoman arrived, Xerox had been going through various rounds of restructuring, cost cutting, rejuvenating, and reinventing for nearly two decades, but little had really changed. Many believe Thoman tried to do too much too soon. He saw the urgency for change but was unable to convey that urgency to others within the company and inspire them to take the difficult journey real transformation requires.

Others doubted that anyone could fix Xerox, because the culture had become too dysfunctional and politicized. "There was always an in-crowd and an out-crowd," says one former executive. "They change the branches, but when you look closely, the same old monkeys are sitting in the trees."

THE INSIDER'S INSIDER

Enter Anne Mulcahy, the consummate insider. In August 2001, Allaire turned over the CEO reins to the popular twenty-four-year veteran, who had started at Xerox as a copier saleswoman and worked her way up the hierarchy. Despite her insider status, Mulcahy proved that she was more than willing to challenge the status quo at Xerox. Since she took over, Mulcahy has surprised skeptical analysts, stockholders, and employees by engineering one of the most extraordinary business turnarounds in recent history.

How did she do it? One key success factor was giving people vision and hope. Mulcahy wrote a fictitious *Wall Street Journal* article describing Xerox five years in the future, outlining the things Xerox wanted to accomplish as if they had already been achieved and presenting the company as a thriving, forward-thinking organization. And although few people thought Mulcahy would take the tough actions Xerox needed to survive, she turned out to be a strong decision maker. She quickly launched a turnaround plan that included massive cost cutting and closing of several money-losing operations, including the division she had previously headed. She was brutally honest about "the good, the bad, and the ugly" of the company's situation, as one employee put it, but she also showed that she cared about what happened to employees. After major layoffs, she walked the halls to tell people she was sorry and let them vent their anger. She personally negotiated the settlement of a long investigation into fraudulent accounting practices, insisting that her personal involvement was necessary to signal a new commitment to ethical business practices and corporate social responsibility. She appealed directly to creditors begging them not to pull the plug until a new management team could make needed changes.

Mulcahy transferred much of production to outside contractors and refocused Xerox on innovation and service. Two areas she refused to cut were research and development and customer contact. Since 2005, Xerox has introduced more than 100 new products and moved into high-growth areas such as document management services, IT consulting, and digital press technology. A series of acquisitions enabled the company to enter new markets and expand its base of small- and medium-sized business customers. Sales in 2007 rose to more than $17 billion, and in November of that year, Xerox announced its first quarterly cash dividend in six years. Mulcahy has also responded to global stakeholders with a firm commitment to human rights and sustainable business practices. "By doing the right thing for our stakeholders and the global community, we're also doing what is right for our business," she said.

Mulcahy was belittled in the press when she took over as CEO, but she has proved the pundits wrong and regularly shows up on various "best manager" lists. In 2008, she became the first woman CEO selected by her peers to receive *Chief Executive* magazines's "CEO of the Year" award, which she promptly declared to "represent the impressive accomplishments of Xerox people around the world." But Mulcahy knows Xerox can't afford to rest on its laurels. The technology industry is tough, and she has to keep her management team focused on growth while also maintaining the cost controls that stabilized the company.

Eight years after this American icon almost fell, Xerox is once again admired in the corporate world. Has the "perfect storm" of troubles been replaced with a "perfect dawn"? Mulcahy and her top management team believe Xerox is positioned to be resilient in the face of the current economic slowdown, but in the rapidly changing world of organizations, nothing is ever certain.[1]

Welcome to the real world of organization theory. The shifting fortunes of Xerox illustrate organization theory in action. Xerox managers were deeply involved in organization theory each day of their working lives—but many never realized it. Company managers didn't fully understand how the organization related to the environment or how it should function internally. Organization theory concepts have helped Anne Mulcahy and her management team analyze and diagnose what is happening and the changes needed to keep the company competitive. Organization theory gives us the tools to explain the decline of Xerox and understand Mulcahy's turnaround.

Similar problems have challenged numerous organizations. Consider the dramatic organizational missteps illustrated by the 2008 crises in the mortgage industry and finance sector in the United States. Lehman Brothers Holdings, a pillar in the investment banking industry for more than 150 years, filed for Chapter 11 bankruptcy, unable to weather the storm sweeping through the industry. American International Group (AIG) sought a bailout from the U.S. government. And another icon, Merrill Lynch, was saved by becoming part of Bank of America, which had already snapped up struggling mortgage lender Countrywide Financial Corporation. The Merrill Lynch acquisition gave Bank of America a vast reach into nearly every part of the finance industry, from credit cards and auto loans to stock underwriting, wealth management, and merger advice. Power in the industry took a decided shift away from huge investment firms back toward the basic business of commercial banking, making companies such as Bank of America and Wells Fargo & Company in the United States, Germany's Deutsche Bank AG, and Banco Santander SA of Spain key players in a new financial landscape.[2] The 2008 crisis in the U.S. financial sector represented change and uncertainty on an unprecedented scale, and it would, to some extent, affect managers in all types of organizations and industries around the world.

ORGANIZATION THEORY IN ACTION

Organization theory gives us the tools to analyze and understand how a huge, powerful firm like Lehman Brothers can die and a company like Bank of America can emerge almost overnight as a giant in the industry. It enables us to comprehend how a band like the Rolling Stones, which operates like a highly sophisticated global business organization, can enjoy phenomenal success for nearly half a century, while some musical groups with equal or superior talent don't survive past a couple of hit songs. Organization theory helps us explain what happened in the past, as well as what may happen in the future, so that we can manage organizations more effectively.

Topics

Each of the topics to be covered in this book is illustrated in the Xerox case. Indeed, managers at companies such as Xerox, Lehman Brothers, Bank of America, and even the Rolling Stones are continually faced with a number of challenges. For example:

- How can the organization adapt to or control such external elements as competitors, customers, government, and creditors in a fast-paced environment?
- What strategic and structural changes are needed to help the organization attain effectiveness?

- How can the organization avoid management ethical lapses that could threaten its viability?
- How can managers cope with the problems of large size and bureaucracy?
- What is the appropriate use of power and politics among managers?
- How should internal conflict be managed?
- What kind of corporate culture is needed to enhance rather than stifle innovation and change, and how can that culture be shaped by managers?

These are the topics with which organization theory is concerned. Organization theory concepts apply to all types of organizations in all industries. Managers at Burger King revitalized the once-floundering fast-food chain by revising its menu and marketing approach based on customer analysis. Nokia underwent a major reorganization to improve the organization's flexibility and adaptability. Hewlett-Packard acquired Electronic Data Systems Corporation to move H-P more aggressively into the technology services industry.[3] All of these companies are using concepts based in organization theory. Organization theory also applies to nonprofit organizations such as the United Way, the American Humane Association, local arts organizations, colleges and universities, and the Make-A-Wish Foundation, which grants wishes to terminally ill children.

Organization theory draws lessons from organizations such as Xerox, Bank of America, and United Way and makes those lessons available to students and managers. As our opening example of Xerox shows, even large, successful organizations are vulnerable, lessons are not learned automatically, and organizations are only as strong as their decision makers. Organizations are not static; they continuously adapt to shifts in the external environment. Today, many companies are facing the need to transform themselves into dramatically different organizations because of new challenges in the environment.

Briefcase

As an organization manager, keep these guidelines in mind:

Do not ignore the external environment or protect the organization from it. Because the environment is unpredictable, do not expect to achieve complete order and rationality within the organization. Strive for a balance between order and flexibility.

Current Challenges

Research into hundreds of organizations provides the knowledge base to make Xerox and other organizations more effective. For example, challenges facing organizations today are different from those of the past, and thus the concept of organizations and organization theory is evolving. The world is changing more rapidly than ever before, and managers are responsible for positioning their organizations to adapt to new needs. Some specific challenges today's managers and organizations face are globalization, intense competition, rigorous ethical scrutiny, the need for rapid response, the digital workplace, and increasing diversity.

Globalization. The cliché that the world is getting smaller is dramatically true for today's organizations. With rapid advances in technology and communications, the time it takes to exert influence around the world from even the most remote locations has been reduced from years to only seconds. Markets, technologies, and organizations are becoming increasingly interconnected.[4] Today's successful organizations feel "at home" anywhere in the world. Companies can locate different parts of the organization wherever it makes the most business sense: top leadership in one country, technical brainpower and production in other locales.

Related trends are global *outsourcing*, or contracting out some functions to organizations in other countries, and *strategic partnering* with foreign firms to gain a global advantage. In Bain & Company's 2007 survey of managers, nearly

50 percent said they saw cross-border acquisitions as crucial to their future competitiveness. Moreover, U.S. managers believe developing relationships in India and China will be vital to business success.[5] Already, numerous companies from all over the world, including Home Depot, CNA Life, and Sony, use India's Wipro Ltd. to develop sophisticated software applications, design semiconductors, and manage back-office solutions.[6] Other companies turn to China, which is the world's largest maker of consumer electronics and is rapidly and expertly moving into biotechnology, computer manufacturing, and semiconductors.[7]

Intense Competition. This growing global interdependence creates new advantages, but it also means that the environment for companies is becoming extremely competitive. Customers want low prices for goods and services. Outsourcing firms in low-wage countries can often do work for 50 to 60 percent less than companies based in the United States, for instance, so U.S. firms that provide similar services have to search for new ways to compete or go into new lines of business.[8] In recent years, though, rising fuel costs cut into the cost advantage many manufacturers enjoyed from what has been called the "China price."[9] The higher cost of shipping goods from China or other low-wage countries counteracted the lower cost of production, leaving U.S. manufacturers searching for ways to make up the difference without exorbitant price increases.

Companies in all industries are feeling pressure to drive down costs and keep prices low, yet at the same time they are compelled to invest in research and development or get left behind in the global drive for innovation. In the United States, high oil prices, the housing slump, mortgage meltdown, crisis in the financial sector, and the soaring costs of materials and supplies created a tough environment for companies in all industries. Consider McDonald's. Even as managers were seeking ways to expand the menu and draw in new customers, McDonald's labs were testing how to cut the cost of making basic items on the Dollar Menu. With the price of ingredients such as cheese, beef, and buns going up, McDonald's had to cut internal costs or lose money on its dollar-menu items.[10] Auto insurers searched for new ways to compete as drivers faced with steep gas prices looked for ways to cut their transportation costs.[11] Casual restaurant chains battled to draw in customers as people cut back on eating out. Grocers, too, felt the sting. Managers at Supervalu, the second largest supermarket company in the United States, quickly learned that they couldn't just pass on their higher costs to shoppers. Sales and profits plunged in early 2008 before managers adjusted their strategy to promote cheaper store brands, work with manufacturers to design innovative promotions and coupons, and introduce new lines of products at lower prices.[12]

Ethics and Social Responsibility. Today's managers face tremendous pressure from the government and the public to hold their organizations and employees to high ethical and professional standards. Following widespread moral lapses and corporate financial scandals, organizations are under scrutiny as never before. The pervasiveness of ethical lapses in the early 2000s was astounding. Once-respected firms such as Enron, Arthur Andersen, Tyco, and HealthSouth became synonymous with greed, deceit, and financial chicanery. No wonder a public poll found that 79 percent of respondents in the United States believe questionable business practices are widespread. Fewer than one-third said they think most CEOs are honest.[13] The sentiment is echoed in other countries. Recent investigations of dozens of top executives in Germany for tax evasion, bribery, and other forms of corruption have destroyed the high level of public trust business leaders there once enjoyed, with just

15 percent of respondents in Germany now saying they consider business leaders trustworthy.[14]

The climate of suspicion has spread to nonprofit organizations and colleges and universities as well. For example, the student loan industry has come under close scrutiny after an investigation found that Student Loan Xpress paid financial aid directors at three universities a total of $160,000 in consulting fees, personal tuition reimbursement, and other payments as a gateway to being placed on the universities' preferred lenders lists. Investigators are seeking to determine whether lenders are being recommended to students because of the hidden payments university officials are receiving rather than the fact that they offer the best lending terms to students.[15]

Speed and Responsiveness. A third significant challenge for organizations is to respond quickly and decisively to environmental changes, organizational crises, or shifting customer expectations. For much of the twentieth century, organizations operated in a relatively stable environment, so managers could focus on designing structures and systems that kept the organization running smoothly and efficiently. There was little need to search for new ways to cope with increased competition, volatile environmental shifts, or changing customer demands. Today, globalization and advancing technology have accelerated the pace at which organizations in all industries must roll out new products and services to stay competitive. Today's customers want products and services tailored to their exact needs, and they want them *now*. Manufacturing firms that relied on mass production and distribution techniques must be prepared with new computer-aided systems that can produce one-of-a-kind variations and streamlined distribution systems that deliver products directly from the manufacturer to the consumer. Service firms, as well, are searching for new ways to provide value. Allstate Insurance, for example, enhanced responsiveness to customers with its Your Choice Auto program, which gives drivers the opportunity to choose the insurance perks they want. Allstate managers recognize that what appeals to drivers can change quickly as gasoline prices shift.[16]

Considering the turmoil and flux inherent in today's world, the mindset needed by organizational leaders is to expect the unexpected and be prepared for rapid change and potential crises. Crisis management has moved to the forefront in light of devastating natural disasters and terrorist attacks all over the world; a tough economy, rocky stock market, growing unemployment, and weakening consumer confidence; widespread ethical scandals; and, in general, an environment that may shift dramatically at a moment's notice.

The Digital Workplace. Many traditional managers feel particularly awkward in today's technology-driven workplace. Organizations have been engulfed by information technology that affects how they are designed and managed. In today's workplace, many employees perform much of their work on computers and may work in virtual teams, connected electronically to colleagues around the world. In addition, rather than competing as independent entities, organizations are becoming enmeshed in electronic networks. More and more of today's business takes place by digital processes over a computer network rather than in physical space. Some companies have taken e-business to very high levels to achieve amazing performance. The use of end-to-end digital supply-chain networks to keep in touch with customers, take orders, buy components from suppliers, coordinate with manufacturing partners, and ship customized products directly to consumers has spread to all industries.[17] These advances mean that organizational leaders not only need to be technologically

savvy but are also responsible for managing a web of relationships that reaches far beyond the boundaries of the physical organization, building flexible e-links between a company and its employees, suppliers, contract partners, and customers.[18]

Diversity. As organizations increasingly operate on a global playing field, the workforce—as well as the customer base—grows increasingly diverse. Many of today's leading organizations have an international face. Look at the makeup of consulting firm McKinsey & Company. In the 1970s, most consultants were American, but by the turn of the century, McKinsey's chief partner was a foreign national (Rajat Gupta from India), only 40 percent of consultants were American, and the firm's foreign-born consultants came from forty different countries.[19]

In addition to coping with global diversity, managers in the United States realize the nation's domestic population is changing dramatically. The minority population of the United States is now more than 100 million, making about one in three U.S. residents a minority. Roughly 32 million people speak Spanish at home, and nearly half of these people say they don't speak English very well.[20] Today's average employee is older, and many more women, people of color, and immigrants are seeking job and advancement opportunities. By 2050, it is estimated that 85 percent of entrants into the workforce will be women and people of color. Already, white males, the majority of workers in the past, represent less than half of the workforce.[21] This growing diversity brings a variety of challenges, such as maintaining a strong corporate culture while supporting diversity, balancing work and family concerns, and coping with the conflict brought about by varying cultural styles.

Purpose of This Chapter

The purpose of this chapter is to explore the nature of organizations and organization theory today. Organization theory has developed from the systematic study of organizations by scholars. Concepts are obtained from living, ongoing organizations. Organization theory has a practical application, as illustrated by the Xerox case. It helps managers understand, diagnose, and respond to emerging organizational needs and problems.

The next section begins with a formal definition of organization and then explores introductory concepts for describing and analyzing organizations. Next, the scope and nature of organization theory are discussed more fully. Succeeding sections examine the history of organization theory and design, a framework for understanding organizational forms, the development of new organizational forms in response to changes in the environment, and how organization theory can help people manage complex organizations in a rapidly changing world. The chapter closes with a brief overview of the themes to be covered in this book.

WHAT IS AN ORGANIZATION?

Organizations are hard to see. We see outcroppings, such as a tall building, a computer workstation, or a friendly employee, but the whole organization is vague and abstract and may be scattered among several locations, even around the world. We know organizations are there because they touch us every day. Indeed, they are so common that we take them for granted. We hardly notice that we are born in a hospital, have our birth records registered in a government agency, are educated in schools and universities, are raised on food produced on corporate farms, are treated by doctors engaged in a joint practice, buy a house built by a construction company and sold by a real estate agency, borrow money from a bank, turn to police and fire departments when trouble erupts, use moving companies to change residences, and receive an array of benefits from various government agencies.[22] Most of us spend many of our waking hours working in an organization of one type or another.

Definition

Organizations as diverse as a bank, a corporate farm, a government agency, and Xerox Corporation have characteristics in common. The definition used in this book to describe organizations is as follows: **organizations** are (1) social entities that (2) are goal-directed, (3) are designed as deliberately structured and coordinated activity systems, and (4) are linked to the external environment.

The key element of an organization is not a building or a set of policies and procedures; organizations are made up of people and their relationships with one another. An organization exists when people interact with one another to perform essential functions that help attain goals. Recent trends in management recognize the importance of human resources, with most new approaches designed to empower employees with greater opportunities to learn and contribute as they work together toward common goals.

Managers deliberately structure and coordinate organizational resources to achieve the organization's purpose. However, even though work may be structured into separate departments or sets of activities, most organizations today are striving for greater horizontal coordination of work activities, often using teams of employees from different functional areas to work together on projects. Boundaries between departments, as well as those between organizations, are becoming more flexible and diffuse as companies face the need to respond to changes in the external environment more rapidly. An organization cannot exist without interacting with customers, suppliers, competitors, and other elements of the external environment. Today, some companies are even cooperating with their competitors, sharing information and technology to their mutual advantage.

From Multinationals to Nonprofits

Some organizations are large, multinational corporations, others are small, family-owned businesses, and still others are nonprofit organizations or governmental agencies. Some manufacture products such as automobiles, flat-panel televisions, or lightbulbs, whereas others provide services such as legal representation, Internet and telecommunications services, mental health resources, or car repair. Later in this text, Chapter 13 will look at the distinctions between manufacturing and service technologies. Chapter 12 discusses size and life cycle and describes some differences between small and large organizations.

Another important distinction is between for-profit businesses and *nonprofit organizations*. All of the topics in this text apply to nonprofit organizations such as the Salvation Army, the World Wildlife Fund, the Save the Children Foundation, and Chicago's La Rabida Hospital, which is dedicated to serving the poor, just as they do to such businesses as Xerox, Sirius XM Radio, Dunkin' Donuts, and Nintendo. However, there are some important dissimilarities to keep in mind. The primary difference is that managers in businesses direct their activities toward earning money for the company,

whereas managers in nonprofits direct their efforts toward generating some kind of social impact. The unique characteristics and needs of nonprofit organizations created by this distinction present unique challenges for organizational leaders.[23]

Financial resources for nonprofits typically come from government appropriations, grants, and donations rather than from the sale of products or services to customers. In businesses, managers focus on improving the organization's products and services to increase sales revenues. In nonprofits, however, services are typically provided to nonpaying clients, and a major problem for many organizations is securing a steady stream of funds to continue operating. Nonprofit managers, committed to serving clients with limited funds, must focus on keeping organizational costs as low as possible and demonstrating a highly efficient use of resources.[24] Another problem is that, since nonprofit organizations do not have a conventional "bottom line," managers often struggle with the question of what constitutes organizational effectiveness. It is easy to measure dollars and cents, but nonprofits have to measure intangible goals such as "improve public health," "make a difference in the lives of the disenfranchised," or "enhance appreciation of the arts."

Managers in nonprofit organizations also deal with many diverse stakeholders and must market their services to attract not only clients (customers) but also volunteers and donors. This can sometimes create conflict and power struggles among organizations, as illustrated by the Make-A-Wish Foundation, which is butting heads with small, local wish-granting groups as it expands to cities across the United States. The more kids a group can count as helping, the easier it is to raise funds. Local groups don't want Make-A-Wish invading their turf, particularly at a time when charitable donations in general are declining with the slowing economy. Small groups are charging that Make-A-Wish is abusing the power of its national presence to overwhelm or absorb the smaller organizations. "We should not have to compete for children and money," says the director of the Indiana Children's Wish Fund. "They [Make-A-Wish] use all their muscle and money to get what they want."[25]

Thus, the organization design concepts discussed throughout this book, such as dealing with issues of power and conflict, setting goals and measuring effectiveness, coping with environmental uncertainty, implementing effective control mechanisms, and satisfying multiple stakeholders, apply to nonprofit organizations such as the Indiana Children's Wish Fund just as they do to businesses such as Xerox. These concepts and theories are adapted and revised as needed to fit the unique needs and problems of various small, large, profit, or nonprofit organizations.

Briefcase

As an organization manager, keep this guideline in mind:

Consider the needs and interests of all stakeholders when setting goals and designing the organization to achieve effectiveness.

Importance of Organizations

It may seem hard to believe today, but organizations as we know them are relatively recent in the history of humankind. Even in the late nineteenth century there were few organizations of any size or importance—no labor unions, no trade associations, and few large businesses, nonprofit organizations, or governmental agencies. What a change has occurred since then! The development of large organizations transformed all of society, and, indeed, the modern corporation may be the most significant innovation of the past 100 years.[26]

Organizations are all around us and shape our lives in many ways. But what contributions do organizations make? Why are they important? Exhibit 1.1 lists seven reasons organizations are important to you and to society. First, organizations bring together resources to accomplish specific goals. Consider Northrup

EXHIBIT 1.1
Importance of
Organizations

Organizations exist to do the following:

1. *Bring together resources to achieve desired goals and outcomes*

2. *Produce goods and services efficiently*

3. *Facilitate innovation*

4. *Use modern manufacturing and information technologies*

5. *Adapt to and influence a changing environment*

6. *Create value for owners, customers, and employees*

7. *Accommodate ongoing challenges of diversity, ethics, and the motivation and coordination of employees*

Grumman Newport News (formerly Newport News Shipbuilding), which builds nuclear-powered, Nimitz-class aircraft carriers. Putting together an aircraft carrier is an incredibly complex job involving 47,000 tons of precision-welded steel, more than 1 million distinct parts, 900 miles of wire and cable, and more than seven years of hard work by 17,800 employees.[27] How could such a job be accomplished without an organization to acquire and coordinate these varied resources?

Organizations also produce goods and services that customers want at competitive prices. Bill Gates, who built Microsoft into a global powerhouse, asserts that the modern organization "is one of the most effective means to allocate resources we've ever seen. It transforms great ideas into customer benefits on an unimaginably large scale."[28] Companies look for innovative ways to produce and distribute desirable goods and services more efficiently. Two ways are through e-business and through the use of computer-based manufacturing technologies. Redesigning organizational structures and management practices can also contribute to increased efficiency. Organizations create a drive for innovation rather than a reliance on standard products and outmoded approaches to management and organization design.

Organizations adapt to and influence a rapidly changing environment. Consider Google, provider of the Internet's most popular search engine, which continues to adapt and evolve along with the evolving Internet. Rather than being a rigid service, Google is continually adding technological features that create a better service by accretion. At any time, Google's site features several technologies in development so that engineers can get ideas and feedback from users.[29] Some large businesses have entire departments charged with monitoring the external environment and finding ways to adapt to or influence that environment.

Through all of these activities, organizations create value for their owners, customers, and employees. Managers analyze which parts of the operation create value and which parts do not; a company can be profitable only when the value it creates

is greater than the cost of resources. Vizio Inc., a growing force in the flat-panel television industry, for example, creates value by using existing LCD technology and developing an equity partnership with a contract manufacturer rather than producing televisions in-house. By keeping its costs low, the California-based company has been able to sell flat-panel TVs at about half the cost of those sold by major electronics manufacturers.[30]

Finally, organizations have to cope with and accommodate today's challenges of workforce diversity and growing concerns over ethics and social responsibility, as well as find effective ways to motivate employees to work together to accomplish organizational goals.

DIMENSIONS OF ORGANIZATION DESIGN

Organizations shape our lives, and well-informed managers can shape organizations. The first step for understanding organizations is to look at dimensions that describe specific organizational design traits. These dimensions describe organizations in much the same way that personality and physical traits describe people.

Organizational dimensions fall into two types: structural and contextual, as illustrated in Exhibit 1.2. **Structural dimensions** provide labels to describe the internal characteristics of an organization. They create a basis for measuring and comparing organizations. **Contextual dimensions** characterize the whole organization,

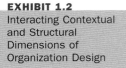

EXHIBIT 1.2
Interacting Contextual and Structural Dimensions of Organization Design

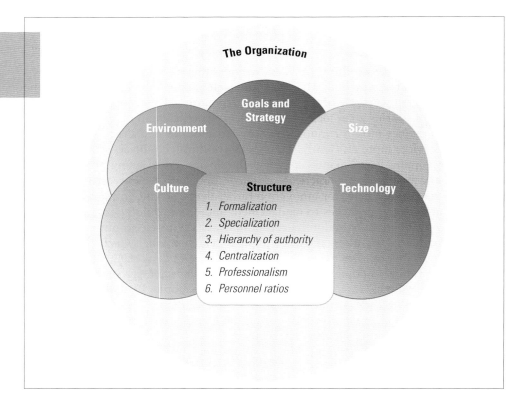

including its size, technology, environment, and goals. They describe the organizational setting that influences and shapes the structural dimensions. Contextual dimensions can be confusing because they represent both the organization and the environment. Contextual dimensions can be envisioned as a set of overlapping elements that underlie an organization's structure and work processes. To understand and evaluate organizations, one must examine both structural and contextual dimensions.[31] These dimensions of organization design interact with one another and can be adjusted to accomplish the purposes listed earlier in Exhibit 1.1.

Structural Dimensions

1. *Formalization* pertains to the amount of written documentation in the organization. Documentation includes procedures, job descriptions, regulations, and policy manuals. These written documents describe behavior and activities. Formalization is often measured by simply counting the number of pages of documentation within the organization. Large state universities, for example, tend to be high on formalization because they have several volumes of written rules for such things as registration, dropping and adding classes, student associations, dormitory governance, and financial assistance. A small, family-owned business, in contrast, may have almost no written rules and would be considered informal.

2. *Specialization* is the degree to which organizational tasks are subdivided into separate jobs. If specialization is extensive, each employee performs only a narrow range of tasks. If specialization is low, employees perform a wide range of tasks in their jobs. Specialization is sometimes referred to as the *division of labor.*

3. *Hierarchy of authority* describes who reports to whom and the span of control for each manager. The hierarchy is depicted by the vertical lines on an organization chart, as illustrated in Exhibit 1.3. The hierarchy is related to span of control (the number of employees reporting to a supervisor). When *spans of control* are narrow, the hierarchy tends to be tall. When spans of control are wide, the hierarchy of authority will be shorter.

4. *Centralization* refers to the hierarchical level that has authority to make a decision. When decision making is kept at the top level, the organization is centralized. When decisions are delegated to lower organizational levels, it is decentralized. Examples of organizational decisions that might be centralized or decentralized include purchasing equipment, establishing goals, choosing suppliers, setting prices, hiring employees, and deciding marketing territories.

5. *Professionalism* is the level of formal education and training of employees. Professionalism is considered high when employees require long periods of training to hold jobs in the organization. Professionalism is generally measured as the average number of years of education of employees, which could be as high as twenty in a medical practice and less than ten in a construction company.

6. *Personnel ratios* refer to the deployment of people to various functions and departments. Personnel ratios include the administrative ratio, the clerical ratio, the professional staff ratio, and the ratio of indirect to direct labor employees. A personnel ratio is measured by dividing the number of employees in a classification by the total number of organizational employees.

Briefcase

As an organization manager, keep these guidelines in mind:

Think of the organization as an entity distinct from the individuals who work in it. Describe the organization according to its size, formalization, decentralization, specialization, professionalism, personnel ratios, and the like. Use these characteristics to analyze the organization and to compare it with other organizations.

EXHIBIT 1.3

Organization Chart Illustrating the Hierarchy of Authority for a Community Job Training Program

Level 1

- Board of Directors
- Executive Committee
- Advisory Committees
- Executive Director

Level 2

- Assistant Executive Director for Community Services
- Assistant Executive Director for Human Services

Level 3

- Director Economic Dev.
- Director Regional Planning
- Director Housing
- Director Criminal Justice
- Director Finance
- Director AAA
- Director CETA

Level 4

- Housing Coordinator
- Alcoh. Coordinator
- Public Information Coordinator
- Accountant
- Assistant Director Finance
- Program Spec. AAA
- Program Planner AAA
- CETA Intake & Orient
- CETA Couns. Devs. Title II ABC
- CETA Couns. Devs. Youth IV
- CETA Couns. Devs. Title II D & VI & VII
- Lead Couns.
- Lead Couns.
- Contract Fiscal Mgr.
- CETA Planner

Level 5

- Secretary
- Records Clerk
- Secretary
- Administrative Assistant
- Payroll Clerk
- Secretary
- IT Specialist
- Staff Clerk
- Administrative Assistant

Contextual Dimensions

1. *Size* can be measured for the organization as a whole or for specific components, such as a plant or division. Because organizations are social systems, size is typically measured by the number of employees. Other measures such as total sales or total assets also reflect magnitude, but they do not indicate the size of the human part of the system.

2. *Organizational technology* refers to the tools, techniques, and actions used to transform inputs into outputs. It concerns how the organization actually produces the products and services it provides for customers and includes such things as flexible manufacturing, advanced information systems, and the Internet. An automobile assembly line, a college classroom, and an overnight package delivery system are technologies, although they differ from one another.

3. The *environment* includes all elements outside the boundary of the organization. Key elements include the industry, government, customers, suppliers, and the financial community. The environmental elements that affect an organization the most are often other organizations.

4. The organization's *goals and strategy* define the purpose and competitive techniques that set it apart from other organizations. Goals are often written down as an enduring statement of company intent. A strategy is the plan of action that describes resource allocation and activities for dealing with the environment and for reaching the organization's goals. Goals and strategies define the scope of operations and the relationship with employees, customers, and competitors.

5. An organization's *culture* is the underlying set of key values, beliefs, understandings, and norms shared by employees. These underlying values and norms may pertain to ethical behavior, commitment to employees, efficiency, or customer service, and they provide the glue to hold organization members together. An organization's culture is unwritten but can be observed in its stories, slogans, ceremonies, dress, and office layout.

The eleven contextual and structural dimensions discussed here are interdependent. For example, large organization size, a routine technology, and a stable environment all tend to create an organization that has greater formalization, specialization, and centralization. More detailed relationships among the dimensions are explored in later chapters of this book.

1 **An organization can be understood primarily by understanding the people who make it up.**

ANSWER: *Disagree.* An organization has distinct characteristics that are independent of the nature of the people who make it up. All the people could be replaced over time while an organization's structural and contextual dimensions would remain similar.

ASSESS YOUR ANSWER

These dimensions provide a basis for measuring and analyzing characteristics that cannot be seen by the casual observer, and they reveal significant information about an organization. Consider, for example, the dimensions of Ternary Software compared with those of Wal-Mart and a governmental agency.

IN PRACTICE

Ternary Software Inc.

Brian Robertson is one of the founders of Ternary Software and holds the title of CEO. But as for having the power and authority typically granted to a top executive, forget about it. Consider a recent strategy meeting where a programmer criticized Robertson's plan to replace the company's profit sharing program with an ad hoc bonus system based on performance. After much discussion, the CEO's plan was soundly rejected in favor of keeping the profit sharing program and using monthly bonus incentives.

At Ternary, a company that writes software on contract for other organizations, everyone has a voice in making important decisions. A seven-member policy-setting team that includes two frontline workers elected by their peers consults with other teams throughout the company, ultimately giving every employee a chance to participate in decision making. Meetings are highly informal and people are invited to share feelings as well as business ideas. Any time a new item on the agenda is brought up for discussion, each person is asked for his or her gut reaction. Then, people get to state objections, offer alternative ideas, rework proposals, and perhaps throw out management's suggestions and plans.

Contrast Ternary's approach to that of Wal-Mart, which achieves its competitive edge through internal cost efficiency. A standard formula is used to build each store, with uniform displays and merchandise. Wal-Mart's administrative expenses are the lowest of any chain. The distribution system is a marvel of efficiency. Goods can be delivered to any store in less than two days after an order is placed. Stores are controlled from the top, although store managers have some freedom to adapt to local conditions. Employees follow standard procedures set by management and have little say in decision making. However, performance is typically high, and most employees consider that the company treats them fairly.

An even greater contrast is seen in many government agencies or nonprofit organizations that rely heavily on public funding. Most state humanities and arts agencies, for example, are staffed by a small number of highly trained employees, but workers are overwhelmed with rules and regulations and swamped by paperwork. Employees who have to implement rule changes often don't have time to read the continuous stream of memos and still keep up with their daily work. Employees must require extensive reporting from their clients in order to make regular reports to a variety of state and federal funding sources. Agency workers are frustrated and so are the community-based organizations they seek to serve.[32] ■

Exhibit 1.4 illustrates several structural and contextual dimensions of Ternary Software, Wal-Mart, and the state arts agency. Ternary is a small organization that ranks very low with respect to formalization and centralization and has a medium degree of specialization. Professionalism is high, with a number of staff assigned to nonworkflow activities to do the R&D needed to stay abreast of changes in the software and information technology industries. Wal-Mart is much more formalized, specialized, and centralized. Efficiency is more important than new products, so most activities are guided by standard regulations. Professionalism is low, and the percentage of nonworkflow personnel is kept to a minimum. The arts agency, in contrast to the other organizations, reflects its status as a small part of a large government bureaucracy. The agency is overwhelmed with rules and standard procedures. Rules are dictated from the top. Most employees are assigned to workflow activities, although in normal times a substantial number of people are devoted to administration and clerical support.

Structural and contextual dimensions can thus tell a lot about an organization and about differences among organizations. Organization design dimensions are

EXHIBIT 1.4
Characteristics of Three
Organizations

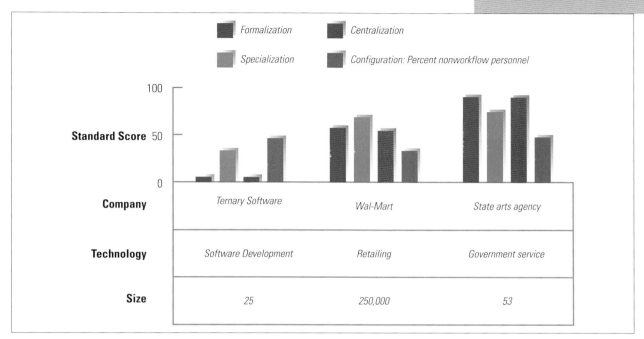

examined in more detail in later chapters to determine the appropriate level of each dimension needed to perform effectively in each organizational setting.

Performance and Effectiveness Outcomes

The whole point of understanding structural and contextual dimensions is to design the organization in such a way as to achieve high performance and effectiveness. Managers adjust structural and contextual dimensions to most efficiently and effectively transform inputs into outputs and provide value. **Efficiency** refers to the amount of resources used to achieve the organization's goals. It is based on the quantity of raw materials, money, and employees necessary to produce a given level of output. **Effectiveness** is a broader term, meaning the degree to which an organization achieves its goals.

To be effective, organizations need clear, focused goals and appropriate strategies for achieving them. Strategy, goals, and approaches to measuring effectiveness will be discussed in detail in Chapter 3. Many organizations are using new technology to improve efficiency and effectiveness. For example, the health care industry is striving to increase efficiency by using information technology to reduce paperwork and streamline procedures. With new technology, one physician's office in Philadelphia says it can now handle more patients with three fewer office employees. Information technology also helps the staff locate information more quickly and reduce mistakes, leading to a higher quality of care and better customer service.[33]

Achieving effectiveness is not always a simple matter because different people want different things from the organization. For customers, the primary concern is high-quality products and services at a reasonable price, whereas employees are mostly concerned with adequate pay, good working conditions, and job satisfaction. Managers carefully balance the needs and interests of various *stakeholders* in setting goals and striving for effectiveness. This is referred to as the **stakeholder approach**, which integrates diverse organizational activities by looking at various organizational stakeholders and what they want from the organization. A **stakeholder** is any group within or outside of the organization that has a stake in the organization's performance. The satisfaction level of each group can be assessed as an indication of the organization's performance and effectiveness.[34]

ASSESS YOUR ANSWER

2 **The primary role of managers in business organizations is to achieve maximum efficiency.**

ANSWER: *Disagree.* Efficiency is important, but organizations must respond to a variety of stakeholders, who may want different things from the organization. Managers strive for both efficiency *and* effectiveness in trying to meet the needs and interests of stakeholders. Effectiveness is often considered more important than efficiency.

Exhibit 1.5 illustrates various stakeholders and what each group wants from the organization. Stakeholder interests sometimes conflict, and organizations often find it difficult to simultaneously satisfy the demands of all groups. A business might have high customer satisfaction, but the organization might have difficulties with creditors or supplier relationships might be poor. Consider Wal-Mart. Customers love its efficiency and low prices, but the low-cost emphasis has caused friction with suppliers. Some activist groups argue that Wal-Mart's tactics are unethical because they force suppliers to lay off workers, close factories, and outsource to manufacturers from low-wage countries. One supplier said clothing is being sold at Wal-Mart so cheaply that many U.S. companies couldn't compete even if they paid their workers nothing. The challenges of managing such a huge organization have also led to strains in relationships with employees and other stakeholder groups, as evidenced by recent gender discrimination suits and complaints about low wages and poor benefits.[35]

Research has shown that the assessment of multiple stakeholder groups is an accurate reflection of organizational effectiveness, especially with respect to organizational adaptability.[36] Moreover, both profit and nonprofit organizations care about their reputations and attempt to shape stakeholders' perceptions of their performance.[37]

In reality, it is unreasonable to assume that all stakeholders can be equally satisfied, but if an organization fails to meet the needs of several stakeholder groups, it is probably not meeting its effectiveness goals. Managers strive to at least minimally satisfy the interests of all stakeholders. When any one group becomes seriously dissatisfied, it may withdraw its support and hurt future organizational performance. Satisfying multiple stakeholders can be challenging, particularly as goals and priorities change, as illustrated by the following example.

EXHIBIT 1.5
Major Stakeholder
Groups and What They
Expect

OWNERS AND STOCKHOLDERS
- *Financial return*

EMPLOYEES
- *Satisfaction*
- *Pay*
- *Supervision*

CUSTOMERS
- *High-quality goods, services*
- *Service*
- *Value*

SUPPLIERS
- *Satisfactory transactions*
- *Revenue from purchases*

CREDITORS
- *Creditworthiness*
- *Fiscal responsibility*

COMMUNITY
- *Good corporate citizen*
- *Contribution to community affairs*

ORGANIZATION

UNION
- *Worker pay*
- *Benefits*

GOVERNMENT
- *Obedience to laws and regulations*
- *Fair competition*

MANAGEMENT
- *Efficiency*
- *Effectiveness*

Few people deny that homeland security should be a top priority for the United States, and since the attacks of September 11, 2001, the Federal Bureau of Investigation

IN PRACTICE

(FBI) has channeled more and more resources into the domestic war on terrorism. Consider the seven-year investigation into the anthrax attacks that occurred weeks after September 11 and killed five people in the United States. The investigation culminated in mid-2008 by identifying the alleged culprit as an Army biological weapons scientist at Fort Detrick in Frederick, Maryland. The suspect committed suicide after being told he would be charged with murder.

Federal Bureau of Investigation

Combatting terrorism sounds good, right? The only problem is, the agency's new priority means hundreds of agents have been pulled off their regular beats, where they investigated everything from drug smuggling to kidnapping to white collar crime. "Just about everyone here is involved in terror cases, one way or another," says agent Ron Buckley. "Everything else is on the back burner."

The FBI's new focus is putting a heavy burden on police departments and other law enforcement agencies around the country. These organizations don't have the personnel, investigative resources, or know-how to fight the kinds of crime FBI agents once handled. For example, even when local departments have adequate manpower, crimes often go unsolved because of lack of access to the FBI's high-tech forensic labs. Local communities are also distressed because they fear more drugs in their neighborhoods and more violent crime on their streets. Although the U.S. public is worried about terrorism, they also want their own little piece of the world protected from criminal activity.

(continued)

> Some FBI agents aren't particularly happy about the change either. An agent who has spent most of his 25-year career poring over financial statements investigating fraud, for example, has to make a huge mental shift to feel comfortable traveling around town in an unmarked car with submachine guns, stun grenades, body armor—and a toothbrush—prepared for the next long stakeout.[38] ■

This example provides a glimpse of how difficult it can be for managers to satisfy multiple stakeholders. In all organizations, managers have to evaluate stakeholder concerns and establish goals that can achieve at least minimal satisfaction for major stakeholder groups.

THE EVOLUTION OF ORGANIZATION THEORY AND DESIGN

Organization theory is not a collection of facts; it is a way of thinking about organizations. Organization theory is a way to see and analyze organizations more accurately and deeply than one otherwise could. The way to see and think about organizations is based on patterns and regularities in organizational design and behavior. Organization scholars search for these regularities, define them, measure them, and make them available to the rest of us. The facts from the research are not as important as the general patterns and insights into organizational functioning. Insights from organization design research can help managers improve organizational efficiency and effectiveness, as well as strengthen the quality of organizational life.[39] One area of insight is how organization design and management practices have varied over time in response to changes in the larger society.

Historical Perspectives

You may recall from an earlier management course that the modern era of management theory began with the classical management perspective in the late nineteenth and early twentieth century. The emergence of the factory system during the Industrial Revolution posed problems that earlier organizations had not encountered. As work was performed on a much larger scale by a larger number of workers, people began thinking about how to design and manage work in order to increase productivity and help organizations attain maximum efficiency. The classical perspective, which sought to make organizations run like efficient, well-oiled machines, is associated with the development of hierarchy and bureaucratic organizations and remains the basis of much of modern management theory and practice. In this section, we will examine the classical perspective, with its emphasis on efficiency and organization, as well as other perspectives that emerged to address new concerns, such as employee needs and the role of the environment. Elements of each perspective are still used in organization design, although they have been adapted and revised to meet changing needs. These different perspectives can also be associated with different ways in which managers think about and view the organization, called manager frame of reference. Complete the questionnaire in the "How Do You Fit the Design?" box on page 23 to understand your frame of reference.

How Do You Fit the Design?

Evolution of Style

This questionnaire asks you to describe yourself. For each item, give the number "4" to the phrase that best describes you, "3" to the item that is next best, and on down to "1" for the item that is least like you.

1. My strongest skills are:
   ___**a.** Analytical skills
   ___**b.** Interpersonal skills
   ___**c.** Political skills
   ___**d.** Flair for drama

2. The best way to describe me is:
   ___**a.** Technical expert
   ___**b.** Good listener
   ___**c.** Skilled negotiator
   ___**d.** Inspirational leader

3. What has helped me the most to be successful is my ability to:
   ___**a.** Make good decisions
   ___**b.** Coach and develop people
   ___**c.** Build strong alliances and a power base
   ___**d.** Inspire and excite others

4. What people are most likely to notice about me is my:
   ___**a.** Attention to detail
   ___**b.** Concern for people
   ___**c.** Ability to succeed in the face of conflict and opposition
   ___**d.** Charisma

5. My most important leadership trait is:
   ___**a.** Clear, logical thinking
   ___**b.** Caring and support for others
   ___**c.** Toughness and aggressiveness
   ___**d.** Imagination and creativity

6. I am best described as:
   ___**a.** An analyst
   ___**b.** A humanist
   ___**c.** A politician
   ___**d.** A visionary

Scoring: Compute your scores according to the following rater. The higher score represents your way of viewing the organization and will influence your management style.

Structure = 1a + 2a + 3a + 4a + 5a + 6a = _____
Human Resource = 1b + 2b + 3b + 4b + 5b + 6b = _____

Political = 1c + 2c + 3c + 4c + 5c + 6c = _____
Symbolic = 1d + 2d + 3d + 4d + 5d + 6d = _____

Interpretation: Organization managers typically view their world through one or more mental frames of reference. (1) The *structural frame* of reference sees the organization as a machine that can be economically efficient with vertical hierarchy and routine tasks that give a manager the formal authority to achieve goals. This manager way of thinking became strong during the era of scientific management when efficiency was everything. (2) The *human resource frame* sees the organization as its people, with manager emphasis given to support, empowerment, and belonging. This manager way of thinking gained importance after the Hawthorne studies. (3) The *political frame* sees the organization as a competition for scarce resources to achieve goals, with manager emphasis on building agreement among diverse groups. This frame of reference reflects the need for organizations to share information, have a collaborative strategy, and to have all parts working together. (4) The *symbolic frame* sees the organization as theater, with manager emphasis on symbols, vision, culture, and inspiration. This manager frame of reference is important for managing an adaptive culture in a learning organization.

Which frame reflects your way of viewing the world? The first two frames of reference—structural and human resource—are important for newer managers at the lower and middle levels of an organization. These two frames usually are mastered first. As managers gain experience and move up the organization, they should acquire political and collaborative skills (Chapter 7) and also learn to use symbols to shape cultural values (Chapter 9). It is important for managers not to be stuck in one way of viewing the organization because their progress may be limited.

Source: Roy G. Williams and Terrence E. Deal, *When Opposites Dance: Balancing the Manage and Leader Within* (Palo Alto, CA: Davies-Black, 2003), pp. 24–28. Reprinted with permission.

Efficiency Is Everything. Pioneered by Frederick Winslow Taylor, **scientific management** emphasizes scientifically determined jobs and management practices as the way to improve efficiency and labor productivity. Taylor proposed that workers "could be retooled like machines, their physical and mental gears recalibrated for better productivity."[40] He insisted that management itself would have to change and emphasized that decisions based on rules of thumb and tradition should be replaced with precise procedures developed after careful study of individual situations.[41] To use this approach, managers develop precise, standard procedures for doing each job, select workers with appropriate abilities, train workers in the standard procedures, carefully plan work, and provide wage incentives to increase output.

Taylor's approach is illustrated by the unloading of iron from railcars and reloading finished steel for the Bethlehem Steel plant in 1898. Taylor calculated that with correct movements, tools, and sequencing, each man was capable of loading 47.5 tons per day instead of the typical 12.5 tons. He also worked out an incentive system that paid each man $1.85 per day for meeting the new standard, an increase from the previous rate of $1.15. Productivity at Bethlehem Steel shot up overnight. These insights helped to establish organizational assumptions that the role of management is to maintain stability and efficiency, with top managers doing the thinking and workers doing what they are told.

The ideas of creating a system for maximum efficiency and organizing work for maximum productivity are deeply embedded in our organizations. A recent *Harvard Business Review* article discussing innovations that shaped modern management put scientific management at the top of its list of twelve influential innovations.[42]

How to Get Organized. Another subfield of the classical perspective took a broader look at the organization. Whereas scientific management focused primarily on the technical core—on work performed on the shop floor—**administrative principles** looked at the design and functioning of the organization as a whole. For example, Henri Fayol proposed fourteen principles of management, such as "each subordinate receives orders from only one superior" (unity of command) and "similar activities in an organization should be grouped together under one manager" (unity of direction). These principles formed the foundation for modern management practice and organization design.

The scientific management and administrative principles approaches were powerful and gave organizations fundamental new ideas for establishing high productivity and increasing prosperity. Administrative principles in particular contributed to the development of **bureaucratic organizations**, which emphasized designing and managing organizations on an impersonal, rational basis through such elements as clearly defined authority and responsibility, formal recordkeeping, and uniform application of standard rules. Although the term *bureaucracy* has taken on negative connotations in today's organizations, bureaucratic characteristics worked extremely well for the needs of the Industrial Age. One problem with the classical perspective, however, is that it failed to consider the social context and human needs.

What about People? Early work on industrial psychology and human relations received little attention because of the prominence of scientific management. However, a major breakthrough occurred with a series of experiments at a Chicago electric company, which came to be known as the **Hawthorne Studies**. Interpretations of these studies at the time concluded that positive treatment of employees improved their motivation and productivity. The publication of these findings led to a revolution in worker treatment and laid the groundwork for subsequent work examining treatment of workers, leadership, motivation, and human resource management. These human relations and behavioral approaches added new and important contributions to the study of management and organizations.

However, the hierarchical system and bureaucratic approaches that developed during the Industrial Revolution remained the primary approach to organization design and functioning well into the 1970s and early 1980s. In general, this approach worked well for most organizations until the past few decades. However, during the 1980s, it began to lead to problems. Increased competition, especially on a global scale, changed the playing field.[43] North American companies had to find a better way.

Can Bureaucracies Be Flexible? The 1980s produced new corporate cultures that valued lean staff, flexibility and learning, rapid response to the customer, engaged employees, and quality products. Organizations began experimenting with teams, flattened hierarchies, and participative management approaches. For example, in 1983, a DuPont plant in Martinsville, Virginia, cut management layers from eight to four and began using teams of production employees to solve problems and take over routine management tasks. The new design led to improved quality, decreased costs, and enhanced innovation, helping the plant be more competitive in a changed environment.[44] Rather than relying on strict rules and hierarchy, managers began looking at the entire organizational system, including the external environment.

Over the past twenty-five years organizations have undergone even more profound and far-reaching changes. More flexible approaches to organization design have become prevalent. Recent influences on the shifting of organization design include the Internet and other advances in communications and information technology; globalization and the increasing interconnection of organizations; the rising educational level of employees and their growing quality-of-life expectations; and the growth of knowledge- and information-based work as primary organizational activities.[45]

Don't Forget the Environment

Many problems occur when all organizations are treated as similar, which was the case with scientific management and administrative principles that attempted to design all organizations alike. The structures and systems that work in the retail division of a conglomerate will not be appropriate for the manufacturing division. The organization charts and financial procedures that are best for an entrepreneurial Internet firm like Google will not work for a large food processing plant at Kraft or Nabisco.

Contingency means that one thing depends on other things, and for organizations to be effective, there must be a "goodness of fit" between their structure and the conditions in their external environment.[46] What works in one setting may not work in another setting. There is no "one best way." Contingency theory means *it depends*. For example, some organizations experience a certain environment, use a routine technology, and desire efficiency. In this situation, a management approach that uses bureaucratic control procedures, a hierarchical structure, and formal communication would be appropriate. Likewise, free-flowing management processes work best in an uncertain environment with a nonroutine technology. The correct management approach is contingent on the organization's situation.

Briefcase

As an organization manager, keep these guidelines in mind:

Be cautious when applying something that works in one situation to another situation. All organizational systems are not the same. Use organization theory to identify the correct structure, goals, strategy, and management systems for each organization.

Today, almost all organizations operate in highly uncertain environments. Thus, we are involved in a significant period of transition, in which concepts of organization theory and design are changing as dramatically as they did with the dawning of the Industrial Revolution.

ORGANIZATIONAL CONFIGURATION

Another important insight from organization design researchers is how organizations are configured—that is, what makes up an organization's parts and how do the various parts fit together?

Mintzberg's Organizational Types

One framework proposed by Henry Mintzberg suggests that every organization has five parts.[47] These parts, illustrated in Exhibit 1.6, include the technical core, top management, middle management, technical support, and administrative support.

Technical Core. The technical core includes people who do the basic work of the organization. This part actually produces the product and service outputs of the organization. This is where the primary transformation from inputs to outputs takes place. The technical core is the production department in a manufacturing firm, the teachers and classes in a university, and the medical activities in a hospital.

Technical Support. The technical support function helps the organization adapt to the environment. Technical support employees such as engineers, researchers, and information technology professionals scan the environment for problems, opportunities, and technological developments. Technical support is responsible for creating innovations in the technical core, helping the organization change and adapt.

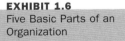
EXHIBIT 1.6
Five Basic Parts of an
Organization

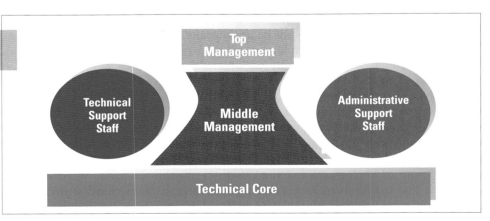

Source: Based on Henry Mintzberg, *The Structuring of Organizations* (Englewood Cliffs, N.J.: Prentice-Hall, 1979), 215–297; and Henry Mintzberg, "Organization Design: Fashion or Fit?" *Harvard Business Review* 59 (January-February 1981), 103–116.

Administrative Support. The administrative support function is responsible for the smooth operation and upkeep of the organization, including its physical and human elements. This includes human resource activities such as recruiting and hiring, establishing compensation and benefits, and employee training and development, as well as maintenance activities such as cleaning of buildings and service and repair of machines.

Management. Management is a distinct function, responsible for directing and coordinating other parts of the organization. Top management provides direction, planning, strategy, goals, and policies for the entire organization or major divisions. Middle management is responsible for implementation and coordination at the departmental level. In traditional organizations, middle managers are responsible for mediating between top management and the technical core, such as implementing rules and passing information up and down the hierarchy.

3 **A CEO's top priority is to make sure the organization is designed correctly.**

ANSWER: *Agree.* Top managers have many responsibilities, but one of the most important is making sure the organization is designed correctly. Organization design organizes and focuses people's work and shapes their response to customers and other stakeholders. Managers consider both structural and contextual dimensions as well as make sure the various parts of the organization work together to achieve important goals.

ASSESS YOUR ANSWER

In real-life organizations, the five parts are interrelated and often serve more than one function. For example, managers coordinate and direct parts of the organization, but they may also be involved in administrative and technical support.

Mintzberg proposed that the five parts could fit together in five basic types of organization, as illustrated in Exhibit 1.7. The five configurations are entrepreneurial structure, machine bureaucracy, professional bureaucracy, diversified form, and adhocracy. The five organizational parts vary in size and importance in each type. This difference is related to the differences in size, goals, and other characteristics of the organization.

1. *Entrepreneurial Structure.* The organization with an **entrepreneurial structure**, as shown in Exhibit 1.7(a), is typically a new, small start-up company. It consists mainly of a top manager and workers in the technical core. The organization is managed and coordinated by direct supervision from the top rather than by middle managers or support departments. Top management is the key part of the structure. Few support staff are needed. The primary goal of the organization is to survive and become established in its industry. There is little formalization or specialization. This form is suited to a dynamic environment because the simplicity and flexibility enable it to maneuver quickly and compete successfully with larger, less adaptable organizations.

2. *Machine Bureaucracy.* The **machine bureaucracy** in Exhibit 1.7(b) is very large, typically mature, and the technical core is often oriented to mass production. It has fully elaborated technical and administrative departments, including engineers, market researchers, and financial analysts who scrutinize, routinize, and

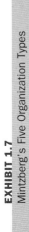

EXHIBIT 1.7
Mintzberg's Five Organization Types

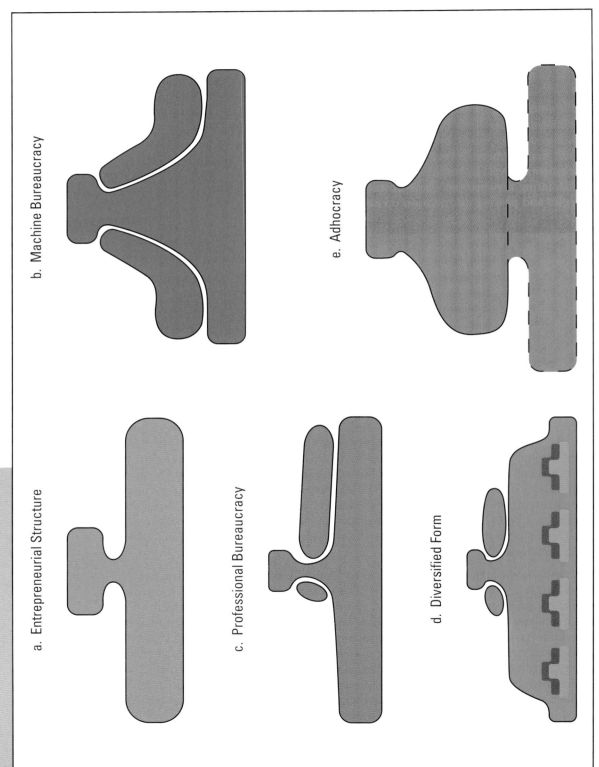

a. Entrepreneurial Structure

b. Machine Bureaucracy

c. Professional Bureaucracy

d. Diversified Form

e. Adhocracy

Source: Mintzberg, Henry. *Structuring of Organizations*, 1st, © 1979. Electronically reproduced by permission of Pearson Education, Inc., Upper Saddle River, New Jersey.

formalize work in the high-volume production center. The narrow middle management area reflects the tall hierarchy for control. This form reflects extensive formalization and specialization, with a primary goal of efficiency. This form is suited to a simple, stable environment. It would not do well in a dynamic environment because the bureaucracy is not adaptable.

3. *Professional Bureaucracy.* The distinguishing feature of the **professional bureaucracy** in Exhibit 1.7(c) is the size and power of the technical core, which is made up of highly skilled professionals, such as in hospitals, universities, law firms, and consulting firms. The technical support staff is small or nonexistent, because professionals make up the bulk of the organization. A large administrative support staff is needed to support the professionals and handle the organization's routine administrative activities. The primary goals are quality and effectiveness, and although there is some specialization and formalization, professionals in the technical core have autonomy. Professional organizations typically provide services rather than tangible goods, and they exist in complex environments.

4. *Diversified Form.* Organizations with a **diversified form** are mature firms that are extremely large and are subdivided into product or market groups, as shown in Exhibit 1.7(d). There is a relatively small top management and a small technical support group for the top level. There is a larger administrative support staff to handle paperwork to and from the divisions. In the exhibit, four independent divisions are shown below the headquarters, and the bulge across the middle indicates that middle management is key. Each of the independent divisions illustrates a machine bureaucracy with its own technical and administrative support staff, but on occasion a division may resemble the entrepreneurial structure, professional bureaucracy, or even adhocracy. The diversified form helps to solve the problem of inflexibility experienced by a too-large machine bureaucracy by dividing it into smaller parts.

5. *Adhocracy.* The **adhocracy** develops in a complex, rapidly changing environment. The design goal is frequent innovation and meeting continually changing needs, as in the aerospace and defense industries. Exhibit 1.7(e) shows the various parts (middle management, technical, and administrative support) merged together into an amorphous mass in the middle. The main structure consists of many overlapping teams rather than a vertical hierarchy. Adhocracies are usually young or middle-aged and can grow quite large. The organization has professional employees, and the technical and administrative support staff are part of the mix of ongoing innovation teams and projects rather than being placed in separate departments. Employees are engaged in the administration and support of their own teams. The production center, illustrated with dashed lines, is separate from the fluid and innovative core above it. If standardized production is done within the organization, it would occur in this operating core quite separate from the ongoing innovation in the professional center above it. In the professional center, the adhocracy is decentralized.

Contemporary Design Ideas

Each of the forms outlined by Mintzberg can be found among today's organizations. To some extent, organizations are still imprinted with the hierarchical, bureaucratic, formalized approach that arose in the nineteenth century. Yet the challenges presented by today's dynamic environment require greater flexibility and adaptability for most

Briefcase

As an organization manager, keep these guidelines in mind:

When designing an organization, consider five basic parts—technical core, technical support, administrative support, top management, and middle management—and how they work together for maximum organizational effectiveness. Design the organization to fit one of Mintzberg's five organizational types.

organizations. Thus, organizations and managers may be seen as shifting from a mindset based on rigid mechanical systems to one based on flexible natural systems.

For most of the twentieth century, Newtonian science, which suggests that the world functions as a well-ordered machine, continued to guide managers' thinking about organizations.[48] The environment was perceived as orderly and predictable and the role of managers was to maintain stability. This mindset worked quite well for the Industrial Age.[49] Growth was a primary criterion for organizational success.

Organizations became large and complex, and boundaries between functional departments and between organizations were distinct. Internal structures grew more complex, vertical, and bureaucratic. Leadership was based on solid management principles and tended to be autocratic; communication was primarily through formal memos, letters, and reports. Managers did all the planning and "thought work," while employees did the manual labor in exchange for wages and other compensation.

The environment for today's companies, however, is anything but stable. With the turbulence of recent years, managers can no longer maintain an illusion of order and predictability. The science of **chaos theory** suggests that relationships in complex, adaptive systems—including organizations—are nonlinear and made up of numerous interconnections and divergent choices that create unintended effects and render the whole unpredictable.[50] The world is full of uncertainty, characterized by surprise, rapid change, and confusion. Managers can't measure, predict, or control in traditional ways the unfolding drama inside or outside the organization. However, chaos theory also recognizes that this randomness and disorder occurs within certain larger patterns of order. The ideas of chaos theory suggest that organizations should be viewed more as natural systems than as well-oiled, predictable machines.

EFFICIENT PERFORMANCE VERSUS THE LEARNING ORGANIZATION

The new mindset has spurred many organizations to shift from strict vertical hierarchies to flexible, decentralized structures that emphasize horizontal collaboration, widespread information sharing, and adaptability. This shift can clearly be seen in the U.S. Army, once considered the ultimate example of a rigid, top-down organization. Today's army is fighting a new kind of war that demands a new approach to how it trains, equips, and uses soldiers. Fighting a fluid, fast-moving, and fast-changing terrorist network means that junior officers in the field who are experts on the local situation have to make quick decisions, learning through trial and error and sometimes departing from standard Army procedures.[51]

Although the stakes might not be as high, business and nonprofit organizations today also need greater fluidity and adaptability. Many managers are redesigning their companies toward something called the **learning organization**. The learning organization promotes communication and collaboration so that everyone is engaged in identifying and solving problems, enabling the organization to continuously experiment, improve, and increase its capability.

Exhibit 1.8 compares organizations designed for efficient performance with those designed for continuous learning by looking at five elements of organization design: structure, tasks, systems, culture, and strategy. As shown in the exhibit, all of these elements are interconnected and influence one another.

EXHIBIT 1.8
Two Organization Design
Approaches

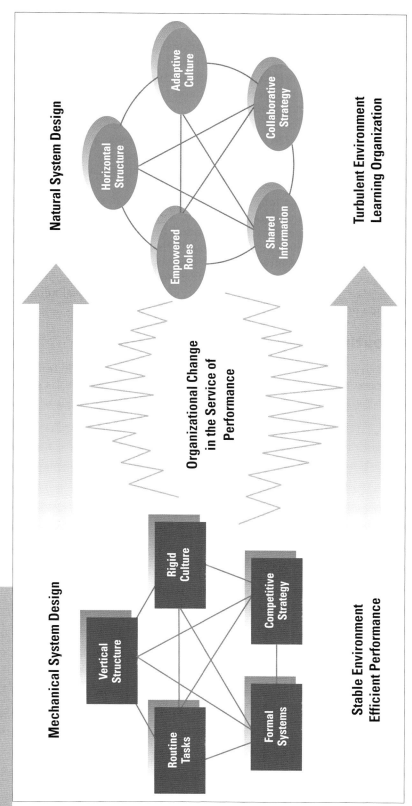

Mechanical System Design

Natural System Design

Adaptive Culture

Horizontal Structure

Collaborative Strategy

Empowered Roles

Shared Information

Turbulent Environment Learning Organization

Organizational Change in the Service of Performance

Rigid Culture

Vertical Structure

Competitive Strategy

Routine Tasks

Formal Systems

Stable Environment Efficient Performance

Source: Adapted from David K. Hurst, *Crisis and Renewal: Meeting the Challenge of Organizational Change* (Boston, Mass.: Harvard Business School Press, 1995).

From Vertical to Horizontal Structure

Traditionally, the most common organizational structure has been one in which activities are grouped together by common work from the bottom to the top of the organization. Generally little collaboration occurs across functional departments, and the whole organization is coordinated and controlled through the vertical hierarchy, with decision-making authority residing with upper-level managers. This structure can be quite effective. It promotes efficient production and in-depth skill development, and the hierarchy of authority provides a sensible mechanism for supervision and control in large organizations. However, in a rapidly changing environment, the hierarchy becomes overloaded. Top executives are not able to respond rapidly enough to problems or opportunities.

In the learning organization, the vertical structure that creates distance between managers at the top of the organization and workers in the technical core is disbanded. Structure is created around horizontal workflows or processes rather than departmental functions. The vertical hierarchy is dramatically flattened, with perhaps only a few senior executives in traditional support functions such as finance or human resources. Self-directed teams are the fundamental work unit in the learning organization. Boundaries between functions are practically eliminated because teams include members from several functional areas.

From Routine Tasks to Empowered Roles

A **task** is a narrowly defined piece of work assigned to a person. In traditional organizations, tasks are broken down into specialized, separate parts, as in a machine. Knowledge and control of tasks are centralized at the top of the organization, and employees are expected to do as they are told. A **role**, in contrast, is a part in a dynamic social system. A role has discretion and responsibility, allowing the person to use his or her discretion and ability to achieve an outcome or meet a goal. In learning organizations, employees play a role in the team or department and roles may be continually redefined or adjusted. There are few rules or procedures, and knowledge and control of tasks are located with workers rather than with supervisors or top executives. Employees are encouraged to take care of problems by working with one another and with customers.

From Formal Control Systems to Shared Information

In young, small organizations (Mintzberg's entrepreneurial structure), communication is generally informal and face-to-face. There are few formal control and information systems because the top leaders of the company usually work directly with employees in the day-to-day operation of the business. However, when organizations grow large and complex, the distance between top leaders and workers in the technical core increases. Formal systems are often implemented to manage the growing amount of complex information and to detect deviations from established standards and goals.[52]

In learning organizations, information serves a very different purpose. The widespread sharing of information keeps the organization functioning at an optimum level. The learning organization strives to return to the condition of a small, entrepreneurial firm in which all employees have complete information about the company so they can act quickly. Ideas and information are shared throughout the organization.

In addition, learning organizations maintain open lines of communication with customers, suppliers, and even competitors to enhance learning capability.

From Competitive to Collaborative Strategy

In traditional organizations designed for efficient performance, strategy is formulated by top managers and imposed on the organization. Top executives think about how the organization can best respond to competition, efficiently use resources, and cope with environmental changes. In the learning organization, in contrast, the accumulated actions of an informed and empowered workforce contribute to strategy development. Since all employees are in touch with customers, suppliers, and new technology, they help identify needs and solutions and participate in strategy making. In addition, strategy emerges from partnerships with suppliers, customers, and other firms. Consider IBM, where top managers used to do all the strategic planning. Now the company invites customers as well as people from nonprofit, business, government, and academic organizations to help, then makes the results public through conferences and reports.[53] Learning companies are willing to share their best ideas. Organizations become collaborators as well as competitors, experimenting to find the best way to learn and adapt. Boundaries between organizations become diffuse, with companies often forming partnerships to compete globally, sometimes joining in modular or virtual network organizations that are connected electronically.

From Rigid to Adaptive Culture

A danger for many organizations is that the corporate culture becomes fixed, as if set in concrete. Organizations that were highly successful in stable environments often become victims of their own success when the environment begins to change dramatically, as we saw illustrated in the opening case of Xerox Corporation. The cultural values, ideas, and practices that helped attain success can be detrimental to effective performance in a rapidly changing environment.

In a learning organization, the culture encourages openness, equality, continuous improvement, and change. People in the organization are aware of the whole system, how everything fits together, and how the various parts of the organization interact with one another and with the environment. This whole-system mindset minimizes boundaries within the organization and with other companies. In addition, activities and symbols that create status differences, such as executive dining rooms or reserved parking spaces, are discarded. Each person is a valued contributor and the organization becomes a place for creating a web of relationships that allows people to develop and apply their full potential. Consider QuikTrip, a chain of convenience stores, where most of the top managers started out at the store level, and everyone is considered a vital part of the chain's success. "The purpose of QuikTrip," says CEO Chester Cadieux II, "is to give our employees the opportunity to grow and succeed."[54] The emphasis on treating everyone with care and respect creates a climate in which people feel safe to experiment, take risks, and make mistakes, all of which encourage learning.

No company represents a perfect example of a learning organization, although many of today's most competitive organizations have shifted toward ideas and forms based on the concept of a living, dynamic system. As illustrated in Exhibit 1.8, today's managers are involved in a struggle as they attempt to change their companies into

learning organizations. The challenge for managers is to maintain some level of stability as they actively promote change toward a new way of thinking, to navigate between order and chaos.

One organization that reflects many of the qualities of a learning organization is Mexico's Cementos Mexicanos (Cemex).

IN PRACTICE

Cementos Mexicanos

Cementos Mexicanos (Cemex), based in Monterrey, Mexico, has been making and delivering concrete for nearly a century. But the organization is on the cutting edge of organization design, a model of what it takes to succeed in the complex environment of the twenty-first century.

Cemex specializes in delivering concrete in developing areas of the world, places where anything can, and usually does, go wrong. Even in Monterrey, Cemex copes with unpredictable weather and traffic conditions, spontaneous labor disruptions, building permit snafus, and arbitrary government inspections of construction sites. In addition, more than half of all orders are changed or canceled by customers, usually at the last minute. Considering that a load of concrete is never more than ninety minutes from spoiling, those chaotic conditions mean high costs, complex scheduling, and frustration for employees, managers, and customers.

To help the organization compete in this environment, managers looked for both techno-logical and organizational innovations. Leaders call their new approach "living with chaos." Rather than trying to change the customers, Cemex resolved to do business on the customers' own terms and design a system in which last-minute changes and unexpected problems are routine.

A core element of this approach is a sophisticated information technology system, including a global positioning satellite system and onboard computers in all delivery trucks, which is fed with streams of day-to-day data on customer orders, production schedules, traf-fic problems, weather conditions, and so forth. Now Cemex trucks head out every morning to cruise the streets. When a customer order comes in, an employee checks the customer's credit status, locates a nearby truck, and relays directions for delivery. If the order is can-celed, computers automatically direct the plant to scale back production.

Cemex also made managerial and organizational changes to support the new approach. The company enrolled all its drivers, who had an average of six years of formal schooling, in weekly secondary-education classes and began training them in delivering not just cement but quality service. In addition, many strict and demanding work rules were abolished so that workers had more discretion and responsibility for identifying and rapidly responding to problems and customer needs. As a result, each Cemex truck now operates as a self-organizing business unit, run by well-trained employees who think like businesspeople. According to Francisco Perez, operations manager at Cemex in Guadalajara, "They used to think of themselves as drivers. But anyone can deliver concrete. Now our people know that they're delivering a service that the competition cannot deliver."[55] ∎

Like most organizations in the construction industry, Cemex has been devas-tated by the recent housing collapse and credit crisis. Yet the company is poised for adaptation to the changing environment due to the combination of extensive networking technology and a new management approach that taps into the mind-power of everyone in the company. People at Cemex are constantly learning—on the job, in training classes, and through visits to other organizations. As a result,

the company has a startling capacity to anticipate customer needs, solve problems, and innovate quickly. In addition, Cemex freely shares what it knows with other organizations, even competitors, believing the widespread sharing of knowledge and information is the best way to keep the organization thriving in a world of complexity and rapid change.

FRAMEWORK FOR THE BOOK

How does a course in organization theory differ from a course in management or organizational behavior? The answer is related to the concept called *level of analysis*.

Levels of Analysis

Each organization is a system that is composed of subsystems. Organization systems are nested within systems, and one **level of analysis** has to be chosen as the primary focus. Four levels of analysis normally characterize organizations, as illustrated in Exhibit 1.9. The individual human being is the basic building block of organizations. The human being is to the organization what a cell is to a biological system. The next higher system level is the group or department. These are collections of individuals who work together to perform group tasks. The next level of analysis is the organization itself. An organization is a collection of groups or departments that combine into the total organization.

Organizations themselves can be grouped together into the next higher level of analysis, which is the interorganizational set and community. The interorganizational set is the group of organizations with which a single organization interacts. Other organizations in the community make up an important part of an organization's environment.

Organization theory focuses on the organizational level of analysis but with concern for groups and the environment. To explain the organization, one should look not only at its characteristics but also at the characteristics of the environment and of

Briefcase

As an organization manager, keep this guideline in mind:

Make yourself a competent, influential manager by using the frameworks that organization theory provides to interpret and understand the organization around you.

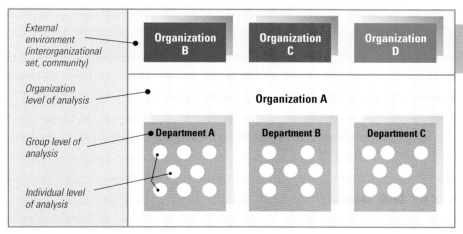

EXHIBIT 1.9

Levels of Analysis in Organizations

Source: Based on Andrew H. Van De Ven and Diane L. Ferry, *Measuring and Assessing Performance* (New York: Wiley, 1980), 8; and Richard L. Daft and Richard M. Steers, *Organizations: A Micro/Macro Approach* (Glenview, Ill.: Scott, Foresman, 1986), 8.

the departments and groups that make up the organization. The focus of this book is to help you understand organizations by examining their specific characteristics, the nature of and relationships among groups and departments that make up the organization, and the collection of organizations that make up the environment.

Are individuals included in organization theory? Organization theory does consider the behavior of individuals, but in the aggregate. People are important, but they are not the primary focus of analysis. Organization theory is distinct from organizational behavior.

Organizational behavior is the micro approach to organizations because it focuses on the individuals within organizations as the relevant units of analysis. Organizational behavior examines concepts such as motivation, leadership style, and personality and is concerned with cognitive and emotional differences among people within organizations.

Organization theory is a macro examination of organizations because it analyzes the whole organization as a unit. Organization theory is concerned with people aggregated into departments and organizations and with the differences in structure and behavior at the organization level of analysis. Organization theory might be considered the sociology of organizations, while organizational behavior is the psychology of organizations.

A new approach to organization studies is called *meso theory*. Most organizational research and many management courses specialize in either organizational behavior or organization theory. **Meso theory** (*meso* means "in between") concerns the integration of both micro and macro levels of analysis. Individuals and groups affect the organization, and the organization in return influences individuals and groups. To thrive in organizations, managers and employees need to understand multiple levels simultaneously. For example, research may show that employee diversity enhances innovation. To facilitate innovation, managers need to understand how structure and context (organization theory) are related to interactions among diverse employees (organizational behavior) to foster innovation, because both macro and micro variables account for innovations.[56]

For its part, organization theory is directly relevant to top- and middle-management concerns and partly relevant to lower management. Top managers are responsible for the entire organization and must set goals, develop strategy, interpret the external environment, and decide organization structure and design. Middle management is concerned with major departments, such as marketing or research, and must decide how the department relates to the rest of the organization. Middle managers must design their departments to fit work-unit technology and deal with issues of power and politics, intergroup conflict, and information and control systems, each of which is part of organization theory. Organization theory is only partly concerned with lower management because this level of supervision is concerned with employees who operate machines, input data, teach classes, and sell goods. Organization theory is concerned with the big picture of the organization and its major departments.

Plan of the Book

The topics within the field of organization theory are interrelated. Chapters are presented so that major ideas unfold in logical sequence. The framework that guides the organization of the book is shown in Exhibit 1.10. Part 1 introduces the basic

Part 1 Introduction to Organization Theory and Design

CHAPTER 1
Introduction to Organizations

EXHIBIT 1.10
Framework for the Book

Part 2 Organizational Strategy and Structure

CHAPTER 2
The Arrangement of Reporting Relationships

CHAPTER 3
Strategy and Effectiveness

Part 3 External Factors and Design

CHAPTER 4
Relationships Between Organizations

CHAPTER 5
Global Organization Design

CHAPTER 6
The Impact of Environment

Part 4 Managing Organizational Processes

CHAPTER 7
Organizational Conflict and Politics

CHAPTER 8
Organizational Decision-Making

CHAPTER 9
Corporate Culture and Values

CHAPTER 10
Organizational Innovation

Part 5 Internal Factors and Design

CHAPTER 11
Information and Control Processes

CHAPTER 12
Organization Size and Life Cycle

CHAPTER 13
Workplace Technology and Design

idea of organizations as social systems and the nature of organization theory. This discussion provides the groundwork for Part 2, which is about strategic management, goals and effectiveness, and the fundamentals of organization structure. Organizations are open systems that exist for a purpose. This section examines how managers help the organization achieve its purpose, including the design of an appropriate structure, such as a functional, divisional, matrix, or horizontal structure. Part 3 looks at the various open system elements that influence organization structure and design, including the external environment, interorganizational relationships, and the global environment.

Parts 4 and 5 look at processes inside the organization. Part 4 shifts to dynamic processes that exist within and between major organizational departments and includes topics such as innovation and change, culture and ethical values, decision-making processes, managing intergroup conflict, and power and politics. Part 5 describes how organization design is related to such factors as manufacturing and service technology, organizational size and life cycle, and information and control systems.

Plan of Each Chapter

Each chapter begins with opening questions to immediately engage the student in the chapter content. Theoretical concepts are introduced and explained in the body of the chapter. Several *In Practice* segments are included in each chapter to illustrate the concepts and show how they apply to real organizations. Each chapter also contains a *How Do You Fit the Design*? questionnaire that draws students more deeply into a particular topic and enables them to experience organization design issues in a personal way. Key points for designing and managing organizations are highlighted in the *Briefcase* items throughout the chapter. Each chapter closes with a *Design Essentials* section that reviews and explains important theoretical concepts.

DESIGN ESSENTIALS

- Turbulence and complexity have replaced stability and predictability as defining traits for today's organizations. Some of the specific challenges managers and organizations face include globalization, intense competition, rigorous ethical scrutiny, the need for rapid response, the digital workplace, and increasing diversity.
- Organizations are highly important, and managers are responsible for shaping organizations to perform well and meet the needs of society. The structural dimensions of formalization, specialization, hierarchy of authority, centralization, professionalism, and personnel ratios, and the contextual dimensions of size, organizational technology, environment, goals and strategy, and culture provide labels for measuring and analyzing organizations. These dimensions vary widely from organization to organization. Subsequent chapters provide frameworks for analyzing organizations with these concepts.
- Many types of organizations exist. One important distinction is between for-profit businesses, in which managers direct their activities toward earning money for the company, and nonprofit organizations, in which managers direct their efforts toward generating some kind of social impact. Managers strive to design organizations to achieve both

efficiency and effectiveness. Effectiveness is complex because different stakeholders have different interests and needs that they want satisfied by the organization.

- Organization design perspectives have varied over time. Managers can understand organizations better by gaining a historical perspective and by understanding basic organizational configurations. Five parts of the organization are the technical core, top management, middle management, technical support, and administrative support. Different configurations of these parts result in five basic organization types: entrepreneurial structure, machine bureaucracy, professional bureaucracy, diversified form, and adhocracy.
- Challenges in today's environment are leading to changes in organization design and management practices. The trend is away from highly structured systems based on a mechanical model toward looser, more flexible systems based on a natural, biological model. Many managers are redesigning companies toward the learning organization, which is characterized by a horizontal structure, empowered employees, shared information, collaborative strategy, and an adaptive culture.
- Finally, most concepts in organization theory pertain to the top- and middle-management levels of the organization. This book is concerned more with the topics of those levels than with the operational-level topics of supervision and motivation of employees, which are discussed in courses on organizational behavior.

Key Concepts

adhocracy
administrative principles
bureaucratic organizations
chaos theory
contextual dimensions
contingency
diversified form
effectiveness
efficiency

entrepreneurial structure
Hawthorne Studies
learning organization
level of analysis
machine bureaucracy
meso theory
organization theory
organizational behavior
organizations

professional bureaucracy
role
scientific management
stakeholder
stakeholder approach
structural dimensions
task

Discussion Questions

1. What is the difference between formalization and specialization? Do you think an organization high on one dimension would also be high on the other? Discuss.
2. Early management theorists believed that organizations should strive to be logical and rational, with a place for everything and everything in its place. Discuss the pros and cons of this approach for today's organizations.
3. Based on what you know about the following organizations, how would you categorize them according to Mintzberg's Five Organizational Types (Exhibit 1.7): General Electric? Facebook? Toyota Motor Corporation? Your college or university? A local consulting firm?
4. What are some differences one might expect among stakeholder expectations for a nonprofit organization versus a for-profit business? Do you think nonprofit managers have to pay more attention to stakeholders than do business managers? Discuss.
5. A handful of companies on the *Fortune* 500 list are more than 100 years old, which is rare. What organizational characteristics do you think might explain 100-year longevity?
6. Why is shared information so important in a learning organization as compared to an efficient-performance organization? Discuss how an organization's approach to information sharing might be related to other

elements of organization design, such as structure, tasks, strategy, and culture.

7. Explain how Mintzberg's five basic parts of the organization (Exhibit 1.6) fit together to perform needed functions. If an organization had to give up one of these five parts, such as during a severe downsizing, which one could it survive the longest without? Discuss.

8. What are the primary differences between an organization designed for efficient performance and one designed for learning and change? Which type of organization do you think would be easier to manage? Discuss.

9. What is the definition of *organization*? Briefly explain each part of the definition.

10. What does *contingency* mean? What are the implications of contingency theory for managers?

Chapter 1 Workbook: Measuring Dimensions of Organizations*

Analyze two organizations along the following dimensions. Indicate where you think each organization would fall on each of the scales. Use an X to indicate the first organization and an * to show the second.

You may choose any two organizations you are familiar with, such as your place of work, the university, a student organization, your church or synagogue, or your family.

Formalization

| Many written rules | 1 2 3 4 5 6 7 8 9 10 | Few rules |

Specialization

| Separate tasks and roles | 1 2 3 4 5 6 7 8 9 10 | Overlapping tasks |

Hierarchy

| Tall hierarchy of authority | 1 2 3 4 5 6 7 8 9 10 | Flat hierarchy of authority |

Technology

| Product | 1 2 3 4 5 6 7 8 9 10 | Service |

External Environment

| Stable | 1 2 3 4 5 6 7 8 9 10 | Unstable |

Culture

| Clear norms and values | 1 2 3 4 5 6 7 8 9 10 | Ambiguous norms and values |

Professionalism

| High professional training | 1 2 3 4 5 6 7 8 9 10 | Low professional training |

Goals

| Well-defined goals | 1 2 3 4 5 6 7 8 9 10 | Goals not defined |

Size

| Small | 1 2 3 4 5 6 7 8 9 10 | Large |

Organizational Mindset

| Mechanical system | 1 2 3 4 5 6 7 8 9 10 | Biological system |

Questions

1. What are the main differences between the two organizations you evaluated?

2. Would you recommend that one or both of the organizations have different ratings on any of the scales? Why?

Case for Analysis: Perdue Farms Inc.: Responding to 21st Century Challenges*

Background and Company History

"I have a theory that you can tell the difference between those who have inherited a fortune and those who have made a fortune. Those who have made their own fortune forget not where they came from and are less likely to lose touch with the common man." (Bill Sterling, Just Browsin' column in Eastern Shore News, *March 2, 1988*)

The history of Perdue Farms is dominated by seven themes: quality, growth, geographic expansion, vertical integration, innovation, branding, and service. Arthur W. Perdue, a Railway Express agent and descendent of a French Huguenot family named Perdeaux, founded the company in 1920 when he left his job with Railway Express and entered the egg business full-time near the small town of Salisbury, Maryland. Salisbury is located in a region immortalized in James Michener's *Chesapeake* that is alternately known as "the Eastern Shore" or "the DelMarVa Peninsula." It includes parts of *Delaware, Maryland* and *Virginia*. Arthur Perdue's only child, Franklin Parsons Perdue, was born in 1920.

A quick look at Perdue Farms' mission statement (Exhibit 1.11) reveals the emphasis the company has always put on quality. In the 1920s, "Mr. Arthur," as he was called, bought leghorn breeding stock from Texas to improve the quality of his flock. He soon expanded his egg market and began shipments to New York. Practicing small economies such as mixing his own chicken feed and using leather from his old shoes to make hinges for his chicken coops, he stayed out of debt and prospered. He tried to add a new chicken coop every year.

By 1940, Perdue Farms was already known for quality products and fair dealing in a tough, highly competitive market. The company began offering chickens for sale when Mr. Arthur realized that the future lay in selling chickens, not eggs. In 1944, Mr. Arthur made his son Frank a full partner in A.W. Perdue & Son Inc.

In 1950, Frank took over leadership of the company, which employed forty people. By 1952, revenues were $6 million from the sale of 2,600,000 broilers. During this period, the company began to vertically integrate, operating its own hatchery, starting to mix its own feed formulations, and operating its own feed mill. Also, in the 1950s, Perdue Farms began to contract with others to grow chickens for them. By furnishing the growers with peeps (baby chickens) and feed, the company was better able to control quality.

In the 1960s, Perdue Farms continued to vertically integrate by building its first grain receiving and storage facilities and Maryland's first soybean processing plant. By 1967, annual sales had increased to about $35 million.

But, it became clear to Frank that profits lay in processing chickens. Frank recalled in an interview for *Business Week* (September 15, 1972) "processors were paying us 10¢ a live pound for what cost us 14¢ to produce. Suddenly, processors were making as much as 7¢ a pound."

A cautious, conservative planner, Arthur Perdue had not been eager for expansion, and Frank Perdue was reluctant to enter poultry processing. But, economics forced his hand and, in 1968, the company bought its first processing plant, a Swift & Company operation in Salisbury.

From the first batch of chickens that it processed, Perdue's standards were higher than those of the federal government. The state grader on the first batch has often told the story of how he was worried that he had rejected too many chickens as not Grade A. As he finished his inspections for that first day, he saw Frank Perdue headed his way and he could tell that Frank was not happy. Frank started inspecting the birds and never argued over one that was rejected. Next, he saw Frank start to go through the ones that the state grader had passed and began to toss some of them over with the rejected birds. Finally, realizing that few met his standards, Frank put all of the birds in the reject pile. Soon, however, the facility was able to process 14,000 Grade A broilers per hour.

From the beginning, Frank Perdue refused to permit his broilers to be frozen for shipping, arguing that it resulted in unappetizing black bones and loss of flavor and moistness when cooked. Instead, Perdue chickens were (and some still are) shipped to market packed in ice, justifying the company's advertisements at that time that it sold only "fresh, young broilers." However, this policy also limited the company's market to those locations that could be serviced overnight from the Eastern Shore of Maryland. Thus, Perdue chose for its primary markets the densely populated towns and cities of the East Coast, particularly New York City, which consumes more Perdue chicken than all other brands combined.

Frank Perdue's drive for quality became legendary both inside and outside the poultry industry. In 1985, Frank and Perdue Farms were featured in the book, *A Passion for Excellence*, by Tom Peters and Nancy Austin.

In 1970, Perdue established its primary breeding and genetic research programs. Through selective breeding, Perdue developed a chicken with more white breast meat than the typical chicken. Selective breeding has been so successful that Perdue Farms chickens are desired by other processors. Rumors have even suggested that Perdue chickens have been stolen on occasion in an attempt to improve competitor flocks.

In 1971, Perdue Farms began an extensive marketing campaign featuring Frank Perdue. In his early advertisements,

EXHIBIT 1.11
Perdue Mission 2000

Stand on Tradition
Perdue was built upon a foundation of quality,
a tradition described in our Quality Policy...

Our Quality Policy

"We shall produce products and provide services at all times which meet or exceed the expectations of our customers."

"We shall not be content to be of equal quality to our competitors."

"Our commitment is to be increasingly superior."

"Contribution to quality is a responsibility shared by everyone in the Perdue organization."

Focus on Today
Our mission reminds us of the purpose we serve...

Our Mission

"Enhance the quality of life with great food and agricultural products."

While striving to fulfill our mission, we use our values to guide our decisions...

Our Values

- **Quality:** We value the needs of our customers. Our high standards require us to work safely, make safe food and uphold the Perdue name.
- **Integrity:** We do the right thing and live up to our commitments. We do not cut corners or make false promises.
- **Trust:** We trust each other and treat each other with mutual respect. Each individual's skill and talent are appreciated.
- **Teamwork:** We value a strong work ethic and ability to make each other successful. We care what others think and encourage their involvement, creating a sense of pride, loyalty, ownership and family.

Look to the Future
Our vision describes what we will become and the qualities
that will enable us to succeed...

Our Vision

"To be the leading quality food company with $20 billion in sales in 2020."

Perdue in the Year 2020

- **To our customers:** We will provide food solutions and indispensable services to meet anticipated customer needs.
- **To our consumers:** A portfolio of trusted food and agricultural products will be supported by multiple brands throughout the world.
- **To our associates:** Worldwide, our people and our workplace will reflect our quality reputation, placing Perdue among the best places to work.
- **To our communities:** We will be known in the community as a strong corporate citizen, trusted business partner and favorite employer.
- **To our shareholders:** Driven by innovation, our market leadership and our creative spirit will yield industry-leading profits.

he became famous for saying things like "If you want to eat as good as my chickens, you'll just have to eat my chickens." He is often credited with being the first to brand what had been a commodity product. During the 1970s, Perdue Farms also expanded geographically to areas north of New York City such as Massachusetts, Rhode Island, and Connecticut.

In 1977, "Mr. Arthur" died at the age of 91, leaving behind a company with annual sales of nearly $200 million, an average annual growth rate of 17 percent compared to an industry average of 1 percent a year, the potential for processing 78 thousand broilers per hour, and annual production of nearly 350 million pounds of poultry per year. Frank Perdue said of his father simply "I learned everything from him."

In 1981, Frank Perdue was in Boston for his induction into the Babson College Academy of Distinguished Entrepreneurs, an award established in 1978 to recognize the spirit of free enterprise and business leadership. Babson College President Ralph Z. Sorenson inducted Perdue into the academy, which, at that time, numbered eighteen men and women from four continents. Perdue had the following to say to the college students:

"There are none, nor will there ever be, easy steps for the entrepreneur. Nothing, absolutely nothing, replaces the willingness to work earnestly, intelligently towards a goal. You have to be willing to pay the price. You have to have an insatiable appetite for detail, have to be willing to accept constructive criticism, to ask questions, to be fiscally responsible, to surround yourself with good people and, most of all, to listen." (Frank Perdue, speech at Babson College, April 28, 1981)

The early 1980s saw Perdue Farms expand southward into Virginia, North Carolina, and Georgia. It also began to buy out other producers such as Carroll's Foods, Purvis Farms, Shenandoah Valley Poultry Company, and Shenandoah Farms. The latter two acquisitions diversified the company's markets to include turkey. New products included value-added items such as "Perdue Done It!," a line of fully cooked fresh chicken products.

James A. (Jim) Perdue, Frank's only son, joined the company as a management trainee in 1983 and became a plant manager. The late 1980s tested the mettle of the firm. Following a period of considerable expansion and product diversification, a consulting firm recommended that the company form several strategic business units, responsible for their own operations. In other words, the firm should decentralize. Soon after, the chicken market leveled off and then declined for a period. In 1988, the firm experienced its first year in the red. Unfortunately, the decentralization had created duplication and enormous administrative costs. The firm's rapid plunge into turkeys and other food processing, where it had little experience, contributed to the losses. Characteristically, the company refocused, concentrating on

efficiency of operations, improving communications throughout the company, and paying close attention to detail.

On June 2, 1989, Frank celebrated fifty years with Perdue Farms. At a morning reception in downtown Salisbury, the governor of Maryland proclaimed it "Frank Perdue Day." The governors of Delaware and Virginia did the same. In 1991, Frank was named chairman of the Executive Committee and Jim Perdue became chairman of the board. Quieter, gentler, and more formally educated, Jim Perdue focused on operations, infusing the company with an even stronger devotion to quality control and a bigger commitment to strategic planning. Frank Perdue continued to do advertising and public relations. As Jim Perdue matured as the company leader, he took over the role of company spokesperson and began to appear in advertisements.

Under Jim Perdue's leadership, the 1990s were dominated by market expansion south into Florida and west to Michigan and Missouri. In 1992, the international business segment was formalized, serving customers in Puerto Rico, South America, Europe, Japan, and China. By fiscal year 1998, international sales were $180 million per year. International markets are beneficial for the firm because U.S. customers prefer white meat, whereas customers in most other countries prefer dark meat.

Food-service sales to commercial customers has also become a major market. New retail product lines focus on value-added items, individually quick-frozen items, home-meal replacement items, and products for the delicatessen. The "Fit & Easy" label continues as part of a nutrition campaign, using skinless, boneless chicken and turkey products.

The 1990s also saw the increased use of technology and the building of distribution centers to better serve the customer. For example, all over-the-road trucks were equipped with satellite two-way communications and geographic positioning, allowing real-time tracking, rerouting if needed, and accurately informing customers when to expect product arrival.

Currently, nearly 20,000 associates have increased revenues to more than $2.5 billion.

Management and Organization

"From 1950 until 1991, Frank Perdue was the primary force behind Perdue Farms growth and success. During Frank's years as the company leader, the industry entered its high growth period. Industry executives had typically developed professionally during the industry's infancy. Many had little formal education and started their careers in the barnyard, building chicken coops and cleaning them out. They often spent their entire careers with one company, progressing from supervisor of grow-out facilities to management of processing plants to corporate executive positions. Perdue Farms was not unusual in that respect. An entrepreneur through and through, Frank lived up to his marketing image of "it takes a tough man to make a tender chicken." He mostly used a centralized management style that kept decision-making authority in his own hands or those of a few trusted, senior executives whom he had known for a lifetime. Workers were expected to do their jobs.

In later years, Frank increasingly emphasized employee (or "associates" as they are currently called) involvement in quality issues and operational decisions. This emphasis on employee participation undoubtedly eased the transfer of power in 1991 to his son, Jim, which appears to have been unusually smooth. Although Jim grew up in the family business, he spent almost fifteen years earning an undergraduate degree in biology from Wake Forest University, a master's degree in marine biology from the University of Massachusetts at Dartmouth, and a doctorate in fisheries from the University of Washington in Seattle. Returning to Perdue Farms in 1983, he earned an EMBA from Salisbury State University and was assigned positions as plant manager, divisional quality control manager, and vice president of Quality Improvement Process (QIP) prior to becoming chairman.

Jim has a people-first management style. Company goals center on the three Ps: People, Products, and Profitability. He believes that business success rests on satisfying customer needs with quality products. It is important to put associates first, he says, because "If [associates] come first, they will strive to assure superior product quality—and satisfied customers." This view has had a profound impact on the company culture, which is based on Tom Peters's view that "Nobody knows a person's 20 square feet better than the person who works there." The idea is to gather ideas and information from everyone in the organization and maximize productivity by transmitting these ideas throughout the organization.

Key to accomplishing this "employees first" policy is workforce stability, a difficult task in an industry that employs a growing number of associates working in physically demanding and sometimes stressful conditions. A significant number of associates are Hispanic immigrants who may have a poor command of the English language, are sometimes undereducated, and often lack basic health care. In order to increase these associates' opportunity for advancement, Perdue Farms focuses on helping them overcome these disadvantages.

For example, the firm provides English-language classes to help non-English-speaking associates assimilate. Ultimately associates can earn the equivalent of a high-school diploma. To deal with physical stress, the company has an ergonomics committee in each plant that studies job requirements and seeks ways to redesign those jobs that put workers at the greatest risk. The company also has an impressive wellness program that currently includes clinics at ten plants. The clinics are staffed by professional medical people working for medical practice groups under contract to Perdue Farms. Associates have universal access to all Perdue-operated clinics and can visit a doctor for

anything from a muscle strain to prenatal care to screening tests for a variety of diseases. Dependent care is available. While benefits to the employees are obvious, the company also benefits through a reduction in lost time for medical office visits, lower turnover, and a happier, healthier, more productive and stable work force.

Marketing

In the early days, chicken was sold to butcher shops and neighborhood groceries as a commodity; that is, producers sold it in bulk and butchers cut and wrapped it. The customer had no idea which firm grew or processed the chicken. Frank Perdue was convinced that higher profits could be made if the firm's products could be sold at a premium price. But, the only reason a product can command a premium price is if customers ask for it by name—and that means the product must be differentiated and "branded." Hence, the emphasis over the years on superior quality, broader-breasted chickens, and a healthy golden color (actually the result of adding marigold petals in the feed to enhance the natural yellow color that corn provided).

Today, branded chicken is ubiquitous. The new task for Perdue Farms is to create a unified theme to market a wide variety of products (e.g., both fresh meat and fully prepared and frozen products) to a wide variety of customers (e.g., retail, food service, and international). Industry experts believe that the market for fresh poultry has peaked while sales of value-added and frozen products continue to grow at a healthy rate. Although domestic retail sales accounted for about 60 percent of Perdue Farms' revenues in the 2000 fiscal year, food service sales now account for 20 percent, international sales account for 5 percent, and grain and oilseed contribute the remaining 15 percent. The company expects food service, international, and grain and oilseed sales to continue to grow as a percentage of total revenues.

Domestic Retail

Today's retail grocery customer is increasingly looking for ease and speed of preparation; that is, value-added products. The move toward value-added products has significantly changed the meat department in the modern grocery store. There are now five distinct meat outlets for poultry:

1. The fresh meat counter—traditional, fresh meat—includes whole chicken and parts
2. The delicatessen—processed turkey, rotisserie chicken
3. The frozen counter—individually quick-frozen items such as frozen whole chickens, turkeys, and Cornish hens
4. Home meal replacement—fully prepared entrees such as Perdue brand "Short Cuts" and Deluca brand entrees (the Deluca brand was acquired and is sold under its own name) that are sold along with salads and desserts so that you can assemble your own dinner
5. Shelf stable—canned products

Because Perdue Farms has always used the phrase "fresh young chicken" as the centerpiece of its marketing, value-added products and the retail frozen counter create a possible conflict with past marketing themes. Are these products compatible with the company's marketing image, and, if so, how does the company express the notion of quality in this broader product environment? To answer that question, Perdue Farms has been studying what the term "fresh young chicken" means to customers who consistently demand quicker and easier preparation and who admit that they freeze most of their fresh meat purchases once they get home. One view is that the importance of the term "fresh young chicken" comes from the customer's perception that "quality" and "freshness" are closely associated. Thus, the real issue may be trust; that is, the customer must believe that the product, whether fresh or frozen, is the freshest, highest quality possible, and future marketing themes must develop that concept.

Operations

Two words sum up the Perdue approach to operations—quality and efficiency—with emphasis on the first over the latter. Perdue, more than most companies, represents the Total Quality Management (TQM) slogan, "Quality, a journey without end." Some of the key events in Perdue's quality improvement process are listed in Exhibit 1.12.

Both quality and efficiency are improved through the management of details. Exhibit 1.13 depicts the structure and product flow of a generic, vertically integrated broiler company. A broiler company can choose which steps in the process it wants to accomplish in-house and which it wants suppliers to provide. For example, the broiler company could purchase all grain, oilseed, meal, and other feed products. Or it could contract with hatcheries to supply primary breeders and hatchery supply flocks.

Perdue Farms chose maximum vertical integration to control every detail. It breeds and hatches its own eggs (19 hatcheries), selects its contract growers, builds Perdue-engineered chicken houses, formulates and manufactures its own feed (12 poultry feedmills, 1 specialty feedmill, 2 ingredient-blending operations), oversees the care and feeding of the chicks, operates its own processing plants (21 processing and further processing plants), distributes via its own trucking fleet, and markets the products (see Exhibit 1.13). Total process control formed the basis for Frank Perdue's early claims that Perdue Farms poultry is, indeed, higher quality than other poultry. When he stated in his early ads that "A chicken is what it eats...I store my own grain and mix my own feed...and give my Perdue chickens nothing but well water to drink...," he knew that his claim was honest and he could back it up.

EXHIBIT 1.12

Milestones in the Quality Improvement Process at Perdue Farms

1924 — Arthur Perdue bought leghorn roosters for $25
1950 — Adopted the company logo of a chick under a magnifying glass
1984 — Frank Perdue attended Philip Crosby's Quality College
1985 — Perdue recognized for its pursuit of quality in *A Passion for Excellence*
     — 200 Perdue managers attended Quality College
     — Adopted the Quality Improvement Process (QIP)
1986 — Established Corrective Action Teams (CAT's)
1987 — Established Quality Training for all associates
     — Implemented Error Cause Removal Process (ECR)
1988 — Steering Committee formed
1989 — First Annual Quality Conference held
     — Implemented Team Management
1990 — Second Annual Quality Conference held
     — Codified Values and Corporate Mission
1991 — Third Annual Quality Conference held
     — Customer Satisfaction defined
1992 — Fourth Annual Quality Conference held
     — How to implement Customer Satisfaction explained to team leaders and Quality Improvement Teams (QIT)
     — Created Quality Index
     — Created Customer Satisfaction Index (CSI)
     — Created "Farm to Fork" quality program
1999 — Launched Raw Material Quality Index
2000 — Initiated High Performance Team Process

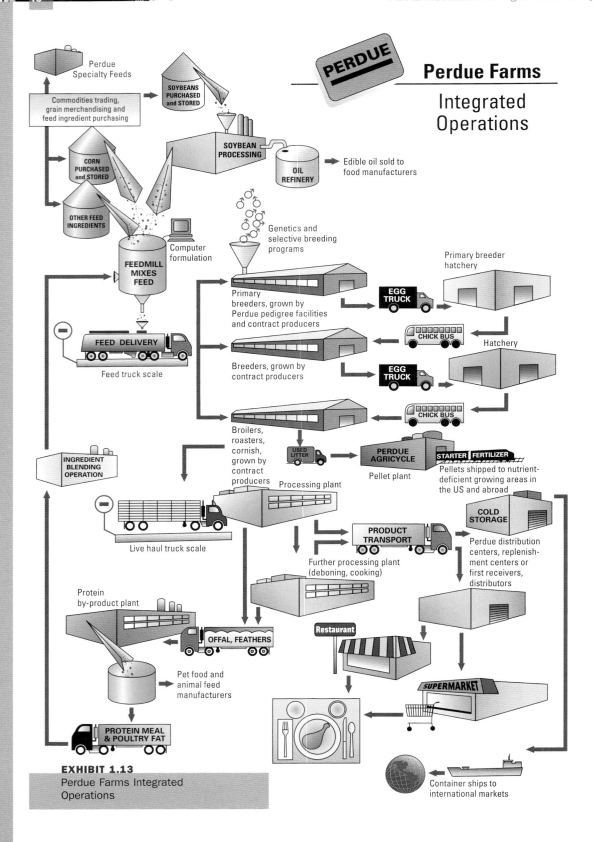

Perdue Farms

Integrated
Operations

EXHIBIT 1.13
Perdue Farms Integrated
Operations

Total process control also enables Perdue Farms to ensure that nothing goes to waste. Eight measurable items—hatchability, turnover, feed conversion, livability, yield, birds per man-hour, utilization, and grade—are tracked routinely.

Perdue Farms continues to ensure that nothing artificial is fed to or injected into the birds. No shortcuts are taken. A chemical-free and steroid-free diet is fed to the chickens. Young chickens are vaccinated against disease. Selective breeding is used to improve the quality of the chicken stock. Chickens are bred to yield more white breast meat because that is what the consumer wants.

To ensure that Perdue Farms poultry continues to lead the industry in quality, the company buys and analyzes competitors' products regularly. Inspection associates grade these products and share the information with the highest levels of management. In addition, the company's Quality Policy is displayed at all locations and taught to all associates in quality training (Exhibit 1.14).

Research and Development

Perdue is an acknowledged industry leader in the use of research and technology to provide quality products and service to its customers. The company spends more on research as a percent of revenues than any other poultry processor. This practice goes back to Frank Perdue's focus on finding ways to differentiate his products based on quality and value. It was research into selective breeding that resulted in the broader breast, an attribute of Perdue Farms chicken that was the basis of his early advertising. Although other processors have also improved their stock, Perdue Farms believes that it still leads the industry. A list of some of Perdue Farms technological accomplishments is given in Exhibit 1.15.

As with every other aspect of the business, Perdue Farms tries to leave nothing to chance in R&D. The company employs specialists in avian science, microbiology, genetics, nutrition, and veterinary science. Because of its R&D capabilities, Perdue Farms is often involved in United States Drug Administration (USDA) field tests with pharmaceutical suppliers. Knowledge and experience gained from these tests can lead to a competitive advantage. For example, Perdue has the most extensive and expensive vaccination program in the industry. Currently, the company is working with and studying the practices of several European producers who use completely different methods.

The company has used research to significantly increase productivity. For example, in the 1950s, it took fourteen weeks to grow a 3 pound chicken. Today, it takes only seven weeks to grow a 5 pound chicken. This gain in efficiency is due principally to improvements in the conversion rate of feed to chicken. Feed represents about 65 percent of the cost of growing a chicken. Thus, if additional research can further improve the conversion rate of feed to chicken by just 1 percent, it would represent estimated additional income of $2.5–3 million per week or $130–156 million per year.

- WE SHALL not be content to be of equal quality to our competitors.
- OUR COMMITMENT is to be increasingly superior.
- CONTRIBUTION TO QUALITY is a responsibility shared by everyone in the Perdue organization.

EXHIBIT 1.14
Quality Policy

- Conducts more research than all competitors combined
- Breeds chickens with consistently more breast meat than any other bird in the industry
- First to use digital scales to guarantee weights to customers
- First to package fully-cooked chicken products in microwaveable trays
- First to have a box lab to define quality of boxes from different suppliers
- First to test both its chickens and competitors' chickens on 52 quality factors every week
- Improved on-time deliveries 20% between 1987 and 1993
- Built state of the art analytical and microbiological laboratories for feed and end product analysis
- First to develop best management practices for food safety across all areas of the company
- First to develop commercially viable pelletized poultry litter

EXHIBIT 1.15
Perdue Farms Technological Accomplishments

Environment

Environmental issues present a constant challenge to all poultry processors. Growing, slaughtering, and processing poultry is a difficult and tedious process that demands absolute efficiency to keep operating costs at an acceptable level. Inevitably, detractors argue that the process is dangerous to workers, inhumane to the poultry, hard on the environment, and results in food that may not be safe. Thus, media headlines such as "Human Cost of Poultry Business Bared," "Animal Rights Advocates Protest Chicken Coop Conditions," "Processing Plants Leave Toxic Trail," or "EPA Mandates Poultry Regulations" are routine.

Perdue Farms tries to be proactive in managing environmental issues. In April 1993, the company created an Environmental Steering Committee. Its mission is ". . . to provide all Perdue Farms work sites with vision, direction, and leadership so that they can be good corporate citizens from an environmental perspective today and in the future." The committee is responsible for overseeing how the company is doing in such environmentally sensitive areas as waste water, storm water, hazardous waste, solid waste, recycling, bio-solids, and human health and safety.

For example, disposing of dead birds has long been an industry problem. Perdue Farms developed small composters for use on each farm. Using this approach, carcasses are reduced to an end-product that resembles soil in a matter of a few days. The disposal of hatchery waste is another environmental challenge. Historically, manure and unhatched eggs were shipped to a landfill. However, Perdue Farms developed a way to reduce the waste by 50 percent by selling the liquid fraction to a pet-food processor that cooks it for protein. The other 50 percent is recycled through a rendering process. In 1990, Perdue Farms spent $4.2 million to upgrade its existing treatment facility with a state-of-the-art system at its Accomac, Virginia, and Showell, Maryland, plants. These facilities use forced hot air heated to 120 degrees to cause the microbes to digest all traces of ammonia, even during the cold winter months.

More than ten years ago, North Carolina's Occupational Safety and Health Administration cited Perdue Farms for an unacceptable level of repetitive stress injuries at its Lewiston and Robersonville, North Carolina, processing plants. This sparked a major research program in which Perdue Farms worked with Health and Hygiene Inc. of Greensboro, North Carolina, to learn more about ergonomics, the repetitive movements required to accomplish specific jobs. Results have been dramatic. Launched in 1991 after two years of development, the program videotapes employees at all of Perdue Farms' plants as they work in order to describe and place stress values on various tasks.

Although the cost to Perdue Farms has been significant, results have been dramatic with workers' compensation claims down 44 percent, lost-time recordables just 7.7 percent of the industry average, an 80 percent decrease in serious repetitive stress cases, and a 50 percent reduction in lost time for surgery for back injuries (Shelley Reese, "Helping Employees get a Grip," *Business and Health*, August 1998).

Despite these advances, serious problems continue to develop. Some experts have called for conservation measures that might limit the density of chicken houses in a given area or even require a percentage of existing chicken houses to be taken out of production periodically. Obviously this would be very hard on the farm families who own existing chicken houses and could result in fewer acres devoted to agriculture. Working with AgriRecycle Inc. of Springfield, Missouri, Perdue Farms has developed a possible solution. The plan envisions the poultry companies processing excess manure into pellets for use as fertilizer. This would permit sales outside the poultry growing region, better balancing the input of grain. Spokesmen estimate that as much as 120,000 tons, nearly one-third of the surplus nutrients from manure produced each year on the DelMarVa Peninsula, could be sold to corn growers in other parts of the country. Prices would be market driven but could be $25 to $30 per ton, suggesting a potential, small profit. Still, almost any attempt to control the problem potentially raises the cost of growing chickens, forcing poultry processors to look elsewhere for locations where the chicken population is less dense.

In general, solving industry environmental problems presents at least five major challenges to the poultry processor:

- How to maintain the trust of the poultry consumer
- How to ensure that the poultry remain healthy
- How to protect the safety of the employees and the process
- How to satisfy legislators who need to show their constituents that they are taking firm action when environmental problems occur
- How to keep costs at an acceptable level

Jim Perdue sums up Perdue Farms' position as follows: ". . . we must not only comply with environmental laws as they exist today, but look to the future to make sure we don't have any surprises. We must make sure our environmental policy statement [see Exhibit 1.16] is real, that there's something behind it and that we do what we say we're going to do."

Logistics and Information Systems

The explosion of poultry products and increasing number of customers during recent years placed a severe strain

EXHIBIT 1.16
Perdue Farms
Environmental Policy
Statement

Perdue Farms is committed to environmental stewardship and shares that commitment with its farm family partners. We're proud of the leadership we're providing our industry in addressing the full range of environmental challenges related to animal agriculture and food processing. We've invested—and continue to invest—millions of dollars in research, new technology, equipment upgrades, and awareness and education as part of our ongoing commitment to protecting the environment.

· Perdue Farms was among the first poultry companies with a dedicated Environmental Services department. Our team of environmental managers is responsible for ensuring that every Perdue facility operates within *100 percent compliance of all applicable environmental regulations and permits.*

· Through our joint venture, Perdue AgriRecycle, Perdue Farms is investing $12 million to build in Delaware a first-of-its-kind pellet plant that will convert surplus poultry litter into a starter fertilizer that will be marketed internationally to nutrient deficient regions. The facility, which will serve the entire DelMarVa region, is scheduled to begin operation in April, 2001.

· We continue to explore new technologies that will reduce water usage in our processing plants without compromising food safety or quality.

· We invested thousands of man-hours in producer education to assist our family farm partners in managing their independent poultry operations in the most environmentally responsible manner possible. In addition, all our poultry producers are required to have nutrient management plans and dead-bird composters.

· Perdue Farms was one of four poultry companies operating in Delaware to sign an agreement with Delaware officials outlining our companies' voluntary commitment to help independent poultry producers dispose of surplus chicken litter.

· Our Technical Services department is conducting ongoing research into feed technology as a means of reducing the nutrients in poultry manure. We've already achieved phosphorous reductions that far exceed the industry average.

· We recognize that the environmental impact of animal agriculture is more pronounced in areas where development is decreasing the amount of farmland available to produce grain for feed and to accept nutrients. That is why we view independent grain *and* poultry producers as vital business partners and strive to preserve the economic viability of the family farm.

At Perdue Farms, we believe that it is possible to preserve the family farm; provide a safe, abundant and affordable food supply; and protect the environment. However, we believe that can best happen when there is cooperation and trust between the poultry industry, agriculture, environmental groups and state officials. We hope Delaware's effort will become a model for other states to follow.

on the existing logistics system, which was developed at a time when there were far fewer products, fewer delivery points, and lower volume. Hence, the company had limited ability to improve service levels, could not support further growth, and could not introduce innovative services that might provide a competitive advantage.

In the poultry industry, companies are faced with two significant problems—time and forecasting. Fresh poultry has a limited shelf life—measured in days. Thus forecasts must be extremely accurate and deliveries must be timely. On one hand, estimating requirements too conservatively results in product shortages. Mega-customers such as Wal-Mart will not tolerate product shortages that lead to empty shelves and lost sales. On the other hand, if estimates are overstated, the result is outdated products that cannot be sold and losses for Perdue Farms. A common expression in the poultry industry is "you either sell it or smell it."

Forecasting has always been extremely difficult in the poultry industry because the processor needs to know approximately eighteen months in advance how many broilers will be needed in order to size hatchery supply flocks and contract with growers to provide live broilers. Most customers (e.g., grocers and food-service buyers) have a much shorter planning window. Additionally, there is no way for Perdue Farms to know when rival poultry processors will put a particular product on special, reducing Perdue Farms sales, or when bad weather and other uncontrollable problems may reduce demand.

In the short run, information technology (IT) has helped by shortening the distance between the customer and Perdue Farms. As far back as 1987, personal computers (PCs) were placed directly on each customer-service associate's desk, allowing the associate to enter customer orders directly. Next, a system was developed to put dispatchers in direct contact with every truck in the system so that they would have accurate information about product inventory and truck location at all times. Now, IT is moving to further shorten the distance between the customer and the Perdue Farms service representative by putting a PC on the customer's desk. All of these steps improve communication and shorten the time from order to delivery.

To control the entire supply chain management process, Perdue Farms purchased a multi-million-dollar information technology system that represents the biggest nontangible asset expense in the company's history. This integrated, state-of-the-art information system required total process re-engineering, a project that took eighteen months and required training 1,200 associates. Major goals of the system were to (1) make it easier and more desirable for the customer to do business with Perdue Farms, (2) make it easier for Perdue Farms associates to get the job done, and (3) take as much cost out of the process as possible.

Industry Trends

The poultry industry is affected by consumer, industry, and governmental regulatory trends. Currently, chicken is the number one meat consumed in the United States, with a 40 percent market share. The typical American consumes about 81 pounds of chicken, 69 pounds of beef, and 52 pounds of pork annually (USDA data). Additionally, chicken is becoming the most popular meat in the world. In 1997, poultry set an export record of $2.5 billion. Although exports fell 6 percent in 1998, the decrease was attributed to Russia's and Asia's financial crisis, and food-industry experts expected this to be only a temporary setback. Hence, the world market is clearly a growth opportunity for the future.

Government agencies whose regulations impact the industry include the Occupational Safety and Health Administration (OSHA) for employee safety and the Immigration and Naturalization Service (INS) for undocumented workers. OSHA enforces its regulations via periodic inspections, and levies fines when noncompliance is found. For example, a Hudson Foods poultry plant was fined more than a million dollars for alleged willful violations causing ergonomic injury to workers. The INS also uses periodic inspections to find undocumented workers. It estimates that undocumented aliens working in the industry vary from 3 to 78 percent of the workforce at individual plants. Plants that are found to use undocumented workers, especially those that are repeat offenders, can be heavily fined.

The Future

The marketplace for poultry in the twenty-first century will be very different from that of the past. Understanding the wants and needs of generation Xers and echo-boomers will be key to responding successfully to these differences.

Quality will continue to be essential. In the 1970s, quality was the cornerstone of Frank Perdue's successful marketing program to "brand" his poultry. However, in the twenty-first century, quality will not be enough. Today's customers expect—even demand—all products to be high quality. Thus, Perdue Farms plans to use customer service to further differentiate the company. The focus will be on learning how to become indispensable to the customer by taking cost out of the product and delivering it exactly the way the customer wants it, where and when the customer wants it. In short, as Jim Perdue says, "Perdue Farms wants to become so easy to do business with that the customer will have no reason to do business with anyone else."

Acknowledgements: The authors are indebted to Frank Perdue, Jim Perdue, and the numerous associates at Perdue Farms, who generously shared their time and information about the company. In addition, the authors would like to thank the anonymous librarians at Blackwell Library, Salisbury State University, who routinely review area newspapers and file articles about the poultry industry—the most important industry on the DelMarVa Peninsula. Without their assistance, this case would not be possible.

*Adapted from George C. Rubenson and Frank M. Shipper, Department of Management and Marketing, Franklin P. Perdue School of Business, Salisbury University. Copyright 2001 by the authors.

Bettina Anzeletti

Part 2

Organizational Strategy and Structure

Chapter 2

The Arrangement of Reporting Relationships

Bettina Anzeletti

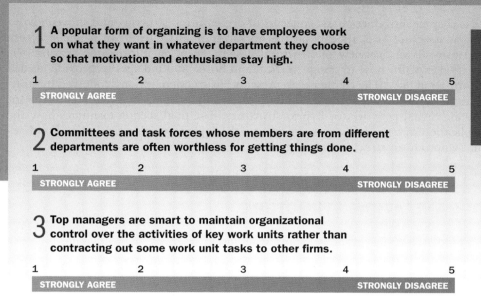

Before reading this chapter, please circle your opinion below for each of the following statements:

1 A popular form of organizing is to have employees work on what they want in whatever department they choose so that motivation and enthusiasm stay high.

1	2	3	4	5
STRONGLY AGREE				STRONGLY DISAGREE

2 Committees and task forces whose members are from different departments are often worthless for getting things done.

1	2	3	4	5
STRONGLY AGREE				STRONGLY DISAGREE

3 Top managers are smart to maintain organizational control over the activities of key work units rather than contracting out some work unit tasks to other firms.

1	2	3	4	5
STRONGLY AGREE				STRONGLY DISAGREE

Managing by Design Questions

Wyeth Pharmaceuticals makes and sells some very powerful drugs, including Effexor for depression, Zosyn to treat infectious diseases, and Telazol, a combined anesthetic/tranquilizer for animals. But Wyeth no longer manages clinical testing of new drugs or vaccines. Outrageous? Shocking? No, just a new reality. In 2004, Wyeth outsourced its entire clinical testing operation—from protocol design to patient recruitment to site monitoring—to Accenture's Health and Life Sciences Practice. Accenture also took over the management of Wyeth's 175 or so clinical data employees and operations. An additional 400 or so people from the Accenture Global Delivery Centers assist in operations.[1] It's all part of Wyeth's drive to improve quality, efficiency, speed, and innovation by outsourcing some of its operations to other firms that can handle them better and faster.

Now, you might wonder how Accenture operates. Let's just say that even CEO Bill Green doesn't have a permanent desk. Accenture doesn't have a formal headquarters, no official branches, no permanent offices. The company's chief technologist is in Germany, its head of human resources in Chicago, the chief financial officer in Silicon Valley, and most of its consultants constantly on the move.[2]

No doubt about it, many organizations are more complex and amorphous than they used to be. Wyeth and Accenture reflect the structural trend among today's organizations toward outsourcing, alliances, and virtual networking. Today's companies also use other structural innovations such as teams and matrix designs to achieve the flexibility they need. Still other firms continue to be successful with traditional functional structures that are coordinated and controlled through the vertical hierarchy. Organizations use a wide variety of structural alternatives to help them achieve their purpose and goals, and nearly every firm needs to undergo reorganization at some point to help meet new challenges. Structural changes are needed to reflect new strategies or respond to changes in other contingency factors introduced in Chapter 3: environment, technology, size and life cycle, and culture.

Purpose of This Chapter

This chapter introduces basic concepts of organization structure and shows how to design structure as it appears on the organization chart. First we define structure and provide an overview of structural design. Then, an information-sharing perspective explains how to design vertical and horizontal linkages to provide needed information flow. The chapter next presents basic design options, followed by strategies for grouping organizational activities into functional, divisional, matrix, horizontal, virtual network, or hybrid structures. The final section examines how the application of basic structures depends on the organization's situation and outlines the symptoms of structural misalignment.

ORGANIZATION STRUCTURE

There are three key components in the definition of **organization structure**:

1. Organization structure designates formal reporting relationships, including the number of levels in the hierarchy and the span of control of managers and supervisors.
2. Organization structure identifies the grouping together of individuals into departments and of departments into the total organization.
3. Organization structure includes the design of systems to ensure effective communication, coordination, and integration of efforts across departments.[3]

These three elements of structure pertain to both vertical and horizontal aspects of organizing. For example, the first two elements are the structural *framework*, which is the vertical hierarchy.[4] The third element pertains to the pattern of *interactions* among organizational employees. An ideal structure encourages employees to provide horizontal information and coordination where and when it is needed.

Organization structure is reflected in the organization chart. It isn't possible to see the internal structure of an organization the way we might see its manufacturing tools, offices, or products. Although we might see employees going about their duties, performing different tasks, and working in different locations, the only way to actually see the structure underlying all this activity is through the organization chart. The organization chart is the visual representation of a whole set of underlying activities and processes in an organization. Exhibit 2.1 shows a simple organization chart for a traditional organization. The organization chart can be quite useful in understanding how a company works. It shows the various parts of an organization, how they are interrelated, and how each position and department fits into the whole.

The concept of an organization chart, showing what positions exist, how they are grouped, and who reports to whom, has been around for centuries.[5] For example, diagrams outlining church hierarchy can be found in medieval churches in Spain. However, the use of the organization chart for business stems largely from the Industrial Revolution. As we discussed in Chapter 1, as work grew more complex and was performed by greater and greater numbers of workers, there was a pressing need to develop ways of managing and controlling organizations. The growth of the railroads provides an example. After the collision of two passenger trains in Massachusetts in 1841, the public demanded better control of the operation. As a result, the board of directors of the Western Railroad took steps to outline "definite responsibilities for

Briefcase

As an organization manager, keep these guidelines in mind:

Develop organization charts that describe task responsibilities, reporting relationships, and the grouping of individuals into departments. Provide sufficient documentation so that all people within the organization know to whom they report and how they fit into the total organization picture.

EXHIBIT 2.1
A Sample Organization Chart

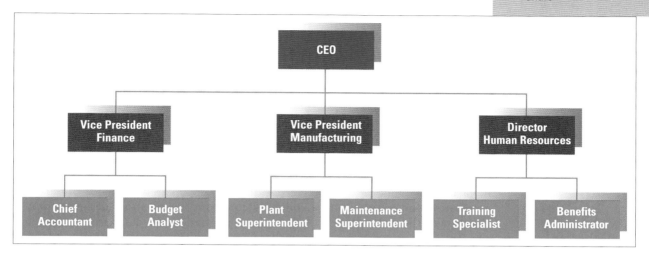

each phase of the company's business, drawing solid lines of authority and command for the railroad's administration, maintenance, and operation."[6]

The type of organization structure that grew out of these efforts in the late nineteenth and early twentieth centuries was one in which the CEO was placed at the top and everyone else was arranged in layers down below, as illustrated in Exhibit 2.1. The thinking and decision making are done by those at the top, and the physical work is performed by employees who are organized into distinct, functional departments. This structure was quite effective and became entrenched in business, nonprofit, and military organizations for most of the twentieth century. However, this type of vertical structure is not always effective, particularly in rapidly changing environments. Over the years, organizations have developed other structural designs, many of them aimed at increasing horizontal coordination and communication and encouraging adaptation to external changes. New approaches to organizing and managing people are crucial for companies to attain durable competitive advantages in the 21st century.

ASSESS YOUR ANSWER

1 A popular form of organizing is to have employees work on what they want in whatever department they choose so that motivation and enthusiasm stay high.

ANSWER: *Disagree.* A small number of firms have tried this approach with some success, but a typical organization needs to structure its work activities, positions, and departments in a way that ensures work is accomplished and coordinated to meet organizational goals. Many managers try to give some consideration to employee choices as a way to keep enthusiasm high.

INFORMATION-SHARING PERSPECTIVE ON STRUCTURE

The organization should be designed to provide both vertical and horizontal information flow as necessary to accomplish the organization's overall goals. If the structure doesn't fit the information requirements of the organization, people either will have too little information or will spend time processing information that is not vital to their tasks, thus reducing effectiveness.[7] However, there is an inherent tension between vertical and horizontal mechanisms in an organization. Whereas vertical linkages are designed primarily for control, horizontal linkages are designed for coordination and collaboration, which usually means reducing control.

Organizations can choose whether to orient toward a traditional organization designed for efficiency, which emphasizes vertical communication and control, or toward a contemporary learning organization, which emphasizes horizontal communication and coordination. Exhibit 2.2 compares organizations designed for efficiency with those designed for learning and adaptation. An emphasis on efficiency and control is associated with specialized tasks, a hierarchy of authority, rules and regulations, formal reporting systems, few teams or task forces, and **centralized** decision making, which means problems and decisions are funneled to top levels of the hierarchy for resolution. Emphasis on learning and adaptation is associated with shared tasks, a relaxed hierarchy, few rules, face-to-face communication, many teams and task forces, and informal, **decentralized** decision making. Decentralized decision making means decision-making authority is pushed down to lower organizational levels.

Organizations may have to experiment to find the correct degree of centralization or decentralization to meet their needs. For example, a study by William Ouchi found that three large school districts that shifted to a more flexible, decentralized structure, giving school principals more autonomy, responsibility, and control over resources, performed better and more efficiently than large districts that were highly centralized.[8] Top executives at New York City Transit are decentralizing the subway system to let managers of individual subway lines make almost every decision about what happens on the tracks, in the trains, and in the

EXHIBIT 2.2
The Relationship of Organization Design to Efficiency versus Learning Outcomes

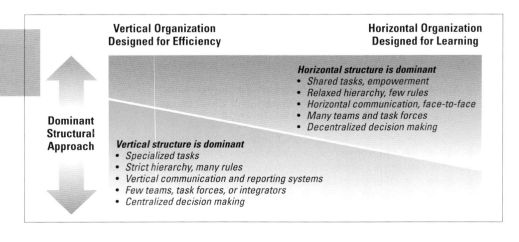

stations. Decentralization helps New York City Transit respond faster and more directly to customer complaints and other problems. Previously, a request to fix a leak causing slippery conditions in a station could languish for years because the centralized system slowed decision making to a crawl.[9] On the other hand, some large decentralized companies sometimes need to build in more centralized communication and control systems to keep these huge, global corporations functioning efficiently. Consider the structural decisions that helped CEO Lewis Campbell revive Textron Inc., a $12 billion industrial conglomerate with headquarters in Providence, Rhode Island.

Textron Inc.

Textron CEO Lewis Campbell was a confirmed believer in decentralization, but in 2001, he took a look at the company's situation and knew something had to change. "We were adrift," says Campbell. "We were doing all the things we used to do but were not getting results." An economic downturn, combined with a steep decline in the industrial and aviation markets from which Textron derived most of its profits, had left Textron in a free fall. Over a two-year period, profits declined 75 percent.

To get the company operating at peak efficiency required some dramatic changes. At the time, Textron's many business units operated autonomously, with each unit handling its own administrative functions and managers making decisions focused on meeting their own division's goals. Many division managers didn't even know what other units of the company did. At the annual management summit, Campbell decreed that the various units would now be required to cooperate and share resources. The new focus would be on how the company as a whole was doing, and bonuses were linked to companywide rather than division performance. To improve efficiency, more than 1,500 payroll systems were cut down to just three, numerous health care plans across the disparate divisions were reduced to just one, and more than a hundred data centers were consolidated into a handful. Managers who had been accustomed to making all their own decisions lost some of their autonomy as companywide decisions, such as a Six Sigma quality improvement program, were centralized to headquarters level and implemented top down.

Taking Textron away from its roots as a decentralized organization to one with a single vision and more centralized decision making didn't lead to overnight success, but the efficiencies soon began to accumulate. Within a few years, Textron's economic health had significantly improved, and Campbell was being hailed as a turnaround artist.[10] ■

It couldn't have been easy, bringing centralization to a company that had thrived on decentralization for its entire existence, but Campbell believed it was necessary for the current situation the company faced. Managers are always searching for the best combination of vertical control and horizontal collaboration, centralization and decentralization, for their own situations.[11]

Vertical Information Sharing

Organization design should facilitate the communication among employees and departments that is necessary to accomplish the organization's overall task. Managers create *information linkages* to facilitate communication and coordination among organizational elements. **Vertical linkages** are used to coordinate activities between

the top and bottom of an organization and are designed primarily for control of the organization. Employees at lower levels should carry out activities consistent with top-level goals, and top executives must be informed of activities and accomplishments at the lower levels. Organizations may use any of a variety of structural devices to achieve vertical linkage, including hierarchical referral, rules, plans, and formal management information systems.[12]

Hierarchical Referral. The first vertical device is the hierarchy, or chain of command, which is illustrated by the vertical lines in Exhibit 2.1. If a problem arises that employees don't know how to solve, it can be referred up to the next level in the hierarchy. When the problem is solved, the answer is passed back down to lower levels. The lines of the organization chart act as communication channels.

Rules and Plans. The next linkage device is the use of rules and plans. To the extent that problems and decisions are repetitious, a rule or procedure can be established so employees know how to respond without communicating directly with their manager. Rules and procedures provide a standard information source enabling employees to be coordinated without actually communicating about every task. At PepsiCo's Gemesa cookie business in Mexico, for example, managers carefully brief production workers on goals, processes, and procedures so that employees themselves do most of the work of keeping the production process running smoothly, enabling the plants to operate with fewer managers.[13] Plans also provide standing information for employees. The most widely used plan is the budget. With carefully designed and communicated budget plans, employees at lower levels can be left on their own to perform activities within their resource allotment.

Vertical Information Systems. A **vertical information system** is another strategy for increasing vertical information capacity. Vertical information systems include the periodic reports, written information, and computer-based communications distributed to managers. Information systems make communication up and down the hierarchy more efficient.

In today's world of corporate financial scandals and ethical concerns, many top managers are considering strengthening their organization's linkages for vertical information and control. The other major issue in organizing is to provide adequate horizontal linkages for coordination and collaboration.

Horizontal Information Sharing

Horizontal communication overcomes barriers between departments and provides opportunities for coordination among employees to achieve unity of effort and organizational objectives. **Horizontal linkage** refers to communication and coordination horizontally across organizational departments. Its importance is articulated by comments made by Lee Iacocca when he took over Chrysler Corporation in the 1980s:

What I found at Chrysler were thirty-five vice presidents, each with his own turf ... I couldn't believe, for example, that the guy running engineering departments wasn't in constant touch with his counterpart in manufacturing. But that's how it was. Everybody worked independently. I took one look at that system and I almost threw up. That's when I knew I was in really deep trouble... Nobody at Chrysler seemed to understand that interaction among the different functions in a company

is absolutely critical. People in engineering and manufacturing almost have to be sleeping together. These guys weren't even flirting![14]

During his tenure at Chrysler, Iacocca pushed horizontal coordination to a high level. Everyone working on a specific vehicle project—designers, engineers, and manufacturers, as well as representatives from marketing, finance, purchasing, and even outside suppliers—worked together on a single floor so they could easily communicate.

Horizontal linkage mechanisms often are not drawn on the organization chart, but nevertheless are a vital part of organization structure. The following devices are structural alternatives that can improve horizontal coordination and information flow.[15] Each device enables people to exchange information.

Information Systems. A significant method of providing horizontal linkage in today's organizations is the use of cross-functional information systems. Computerized information systems enable managers or frontline workers throughout the organization to routinely exchange information about problems, opportunities, activities, or decisions. For example, Siemens uses an organization-wide information system that enables 450,000 employees around the world to share knowledge and collaborate on projects to provide better solutions to customers. The information and communications division recently collaborated with the medical division to develop new products for the health care market.[16]

Some organizations also encourage employees to use the company's information systems to build relationships all across the organization, aiming to support and enhance ongoing horizontal coordination across projects and geographical boundaries. CARE International, one of the world's largest private international relief organizations, enhanced its personnel database to make it easy for people to find others with congruent interests, concerns, or needs. Each person in the database has listed past and current responsibilities, experience, language abilities, knowledge of foreign countries, emergency experiences, skills and competencies, and outside interests. The database makes it easy for people working across borders to seek each other out, share ideas and information, and build enduring horizontal connections.[17]

Direct Contact. A higher level of horizontal linkage is direct contact between managers or employees affected by a problem. One way to promote direct contact is to create a special **liaison role**. A liaison person is located in one department but has the responsibility for communicating and achieving coordination with another department. Liaison roles often exist between engineering and manufacturing departments because engineering has to develop and test products to fit the limitations of manufacturing facilities. Companies also implement other forms of direct contact. At Johnson & Johnson, top executives set up a committee made up of managers from research and development (R&D) and sales and marketing. The direct contact between managers in these two departments enables the company to establish priorities for which new drugs to pursue and market. J & J's CEO also created a new position to oversee R&D, with an express charge to increase coordination with sales and marketing executives.[18]

Task Forces. Liaison roles usually link only two departments. When linkage involves several departments, a more complex device such as a task force is required. A **task force** is a temporary committee composed of representatives from each organizational unit affected by a problem.[19] Each member represents the interest of a department or division and can carry information from the meeting back to that department.

Task forces are an effective horizontal linkage device for temporary issues. They solve problems by direct horizontal coordination and reduce the information load on the vertical hierarchy. Typically, they are disbanded after their tasks are accomplished.

Organizations have used task forces for everything from organizing the annual company picnic to solving expensive and complex manufacturing problems. One example is the Executive Automotive Committee established by Jürgen Schremp when he was CEO of DaimlerChrysler (now Daimler AG) This task force was set up specifically to identify ideas for increasing cooperation and component sharing among Mercedes, Chrysler (which was then owned by Daimler) and Mitsubishi (in which DaimlerChrysler owned a 37 percent stake). The task force started with a product road map, showing all Mercedes, Chrysler, Dodge, Jeep, and Mitsubishi vehicles to be launched over a ten-year period, along with an analysis of the components they would use, so task force members could identify overlap and find ways to share parts and cut time and costs.[20]

ASSESS YOUR ANSWER

2 **Committees and task forces whose members are from different departments are often worthless for getting things done.**

ANSWER: *Disagree.* The point of cross-functional committees and task forces is to share information to coordinate their departmental activities. Meeting, talking, and disagreeing is the work of the committee. These groups should not try to "get things done" in the sense of being efficient.

Full-time Integrator. A stronger horizontal linkage device is to create a full-time position or department solely for the purpose of coordination. A full-time **integrator** frequently has a title, such as product manager, project manager, program manager, or brand manager. Unlike the liaison person described earlier, the integrator does not report to one of the functional departments being coordinated. He or she is located outside the departments and has the responsibility for coordinating several departments. The brand manager for Planters Peanuts, for example, coordinates the sales, distribution, and advertising for that product.

The integrator can also be responsible for an innovation or change project, such as coordinating the design, financing, and marketing of a new product. An organization chart that illustrates the location of project managers for new product development is shown in Exhibit 2.3. The project managers are drawn to the side to indicate their separation from other departments. The arrows indicate project members assigned to the new product development. New Product A, for example, has a financial accountant assigned to keep track of costs and budgets. The engineering member provides design advice, and purchasing and manufacturing members represent their areas. The project manager is responsible for the entire project. He or she sees that the new product is completed on time, is introduced to the market, and achieves other project goals. The horizontal lines in Exhibit 2.3 indicate that project managers do not have formal authority over team members with respect to giving pay raises, hiring, or firing. Formal authority rests with the managers of the functional departments, who have formal authority over subordinates.

EXHIBIT 2.3
Project Manager Location
in the Structure

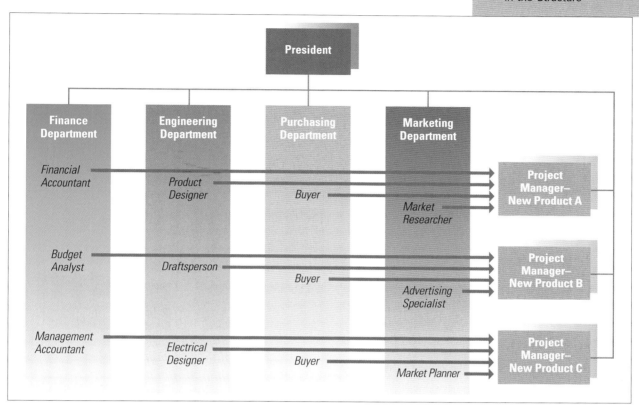

Integrators need excellent people skills. Integrators in most companies have a lot of responsibility but little authority. The integrator has to use expertise and persuasion to achieve coordination. He or she spans the boundary between departments and must be able to get people together, maintain their trust, confront problems, and resolve conflicts and disputes in the interest of the organization.[21]

Teams. Project teams tend to be the strongest horizontal linkage mechanism. **Teams** are permanent task forces and are often used in conjunction with a full-time integrator. When activities among departments require strong coordination over a long period of time, a cross-functional team is often the solution. Special project teams may be used when organizations have a large-scale project, a major innovation, or a new product line. One good example of a special project team comes from Healthwise, a nonprofit organization that works with numerous health care organizations and online health sites like WebMD. The company put together a special project team made up of doctors, other health specialists, writers, and technical people to create a new product line called HealthMastery Campaigns. HealthMastery is a series of programs that e-mails information, surveys, and reminders to consumers on topics such as asthma, back problems, or smoking cessation, fitting with the company's goal of providing information to help consumers make informed health-care decisions.[22]

Hewlett-Packard's Medical Products Group uses *virtual cross-functional teams*, made up of members from various countries, to develop and market medical

Briefcase

As an organization manager, keep these guidelines in mind:

Recognize that the strongest horizontal linkage mechanisms are more costly in terms of time and human resources but are necessary when the organization needs a high degree of horizontal coordination to achieve its goals.

products and services such as electrocardiograph systems, ultrasound imaging technologies, and patient monitoring systems.[23] A **virtual team** is one that is made up of organizationally or geographically dispersed members who are linked primarily through advanced information and communications technologies. Members frequently use the Internet and collaboration software to work together, rather than meeting face to face.[24] IBM's virtual teams, for instance, collaborate primarily via internal websites using wiki technology.[25]

An illustration of how teams provide strong horizontal coordination is shown in Exhibit 2.4. Wizard Software Company develops and markets software for various

EXHIBIT 2.4

Teams Used for
Horizontal Coordination
at Wizard Software
Company

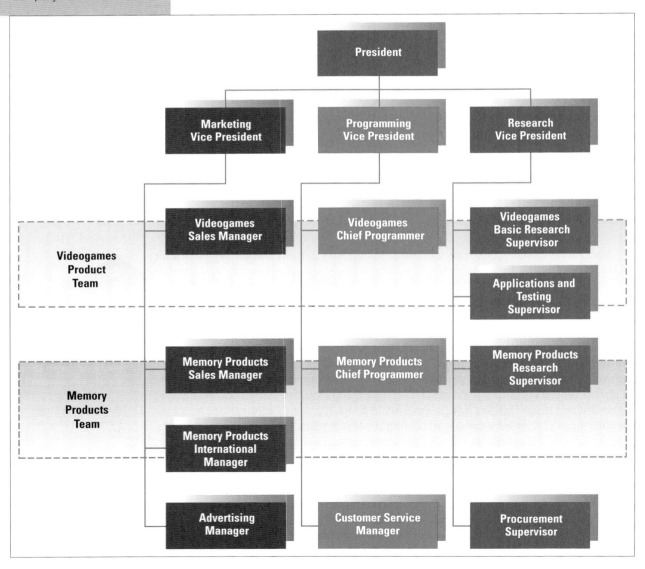

applications, from videogames to financial services. Wizard uses teams to coordinate each product line across the research, programming, and marketing departments, as illustrated by the dashed lines and shaded areas in the exhibit. Members from each team meet at the beginning of each day as needed to resolve problems concerning customer needs, backlogs, programming changes, scheduling conflicts, and any other problem with the product line. Are you cut out for horizontal team work? Complete the questionnaire in the "How Do You Fit the Design?" box to assess your feelings about working on a team.

Exhibit 2.5 summarizes the mechanisms for achieving horizontal linkages. These devices represent alternatives that managers can select to increase horizontal coordination in any organization. The higher-level devices provide more horizontal information capacity, although the cost to the organization in terms of time and human resources is greater. If horizontal communication is insufficient, departments will find themselves out of synchronization and will not contribute to the overall goals

How Do You Fit the Design?

The Pleasure/Pain of Working on a Team

Your approach to your job or schoolwork may indicate whether you thrive on a team. Answer the following questions about your work preferences. Please answer whether each item is Mostly True or Mostly False for you.

	Mostly True	Mostly False
1. I prefer to work on a team rather than do individual tasks.	_____	_____
2. Given a choice, I try to work by myself rather than face hassles of group work.	_____	_____
3. I enjoy the personal interaction when working with others.	_____	_____
4. I prefer to do my own work and let others do theirs.	_____	_____
5. I get more satisfaction from a group victory than an individual victory.	_____	_____
6. Teamwork is not worthwhile when people do not do their share.	_____	_____
7. I feel good when I work with others, even when we disagree.	_____	_____
8. I prefer to rely on myself rather than others to do a job or assignment.	_____	_____

Scoring: Give yourself one point for each odd-numbered item you marked as Mostly True and one point for each even-numbered item you marked Mostly False. Your score indicates your preference for teamwork versus individual work. If you scored 2 or fewer points, you definitely prefer individual work. A score of 7 or above suggests that you prefer working in teams. A score of 3–6 indicates comfort working alone and in a team.

Interpretation. Teamwork can be either frustrating or motivating depending on your preference. On a team you will lose some autonomy and have to rely on others who may be less committed than you. On a team you have to work through other people and you lose some control over work procedures and outcomes. On the other hand, teams can accomplish tasks far beyond what an individual can do, and working with others can be a major source of satisfaction. If you definitely prefer individual work, then you would likely fit better in a functional structure within a vertical hierarchy or in the role of individual contributor. If you prefer teamwork, then you are suited to work in the role of a horizontal linkage, such as on a task force or as an integrator, and would do well in a horizontal or matrix organization structure.

EXHIBIT 2.5
Ladder of Mechanisms
for Horizontal Linkage
and Coordination

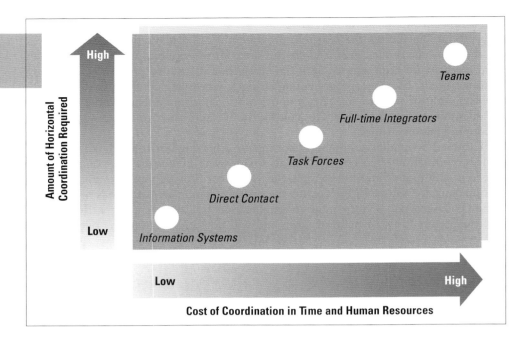

of the organization. When the amount of horizontal coordination needed is high, managers should select higher-level mechanisms.

ORGANIZATION DESIGN ALTERNATIVES

The overall design of organization structure indicates three things—required work activities, reporting relationships, and departmental groupings.

Required Work Activities

Departments are created to perform tasks considered strategically important to the company. For example, in a typical manufacturing company, work activities fall into a range of functions that help the organization accomplish its goals, such as a human resource department to recruit and train employees, a purchasing department to obtain supplies and raw materials, a production department to build products, a sales department to sell products, and so forth. As organizations grow larger and more complex, managers find that more functions need to be performed. Organizations typically define new positions, departments, or divisions as a way to accomplish new tasks deemed valuable by the organization. An interesting example comes from the United States Army, which created a small aviation unit to provide surveillance in Iraq. The new unit was to be focused on detecting and stopping insurgents planting roadside bombs. Previously, the Army had relied totally on air surveillance from the Air Force, but those resources were limited and had to be assigned by top headquarters. The Army's new aviation unit is on call for commanders in the field and fits with the Army's goal of being more responsive to the needs of smaller combat units in direct conflict with adversaries.[26]

Reporting Relationships

Once required work activities and departments are defined, the next question is how these activities and departments should fit together in the organizational hierarchy. Reporting relationships, often called the *chain of command*, are represented by vertical lines on an organization chart. The chain of command should be an unbroken line of authority that links all persons in an organization and shows who reports to whom. In a large organization such as General Electric, Bank of America, or Microsoft, 100 or more charts might be needed to identify reporting relationships among thousands of employees. The definition of departments and the drawing of reporting relationships define how employees are to be grouped into departments.

Departmental Grouping Options

Options for departmental grouping, including functional grouping, divisional grouping, multifocused grouping, horizontal grouping, and virtual network grouping, are illustrated in Exhibit 2.6. **Departmental grouping** affects employees because they share a common supervisor and common resources, are jointly responsible for performance, and tend to identify and collaborate with one another.[27]

Functional grouping places together employees who perform similar functions or work processes or who bring similar knowledge and skills to bear. For example, all marketing people work together under the same supervisor, as do all manufacturing employees, all human resources people, and all engineers. For an Internet company, all the people associated with maintaining the website might be grouped together in one department. In a scientific research firm, all chemists may be grouped in a department different from biologists because they represent different disciplines.

Divisional grouping means people are organized according to what the organization produces. All people required to produce toothpaste—including personnel in marketing, manufacturing, and sales—are grouped together under one executive. In huge corporations, such as Time Warner Corporation, some product or service lines may represent independent businesses, such as Warner Brothers Entertainment (movies and videos), Time Inc. (publisher of magazines such as *Sports Illustrated*, *Time*, and *People*), and AOL (Internet services).

Multifocused grouping means an organization embraces two or more structural grouping alternatives simultaneously. These structural forms are often called *matrix* or *hybrid*. They will be discussed in more detail later in this chapter. An organization may need to group by function and product division simultaneously or might need to combine characteristics of several structural options.

Horizontal grouping means employees are organized around core work processes, the end-to-end work, information, and material flows that provide value directly to customers. All the people who work on a core process are brought together in a group rather than being separated into functional departments. For example, at field offices of the U.S. Occupational Safety and Health Administration, teams of workers representing various functions respond to complaints from American workers regarding health and safety issues, rather than having the work divided up among specialized employees.[28]

Virtual network grouping is the most recent approach to departmental grouping. With this grouping, the organization is a loosely connected cluster of separate components. In essence, departments are separate organizations that are electronically connected for the sharing of information and completion of tasks. Departments can be spread all over the world rather than located together in one geographic location.

EXHIBIT 2.6
Structural Design Options
for Grouping Employees
into Departments

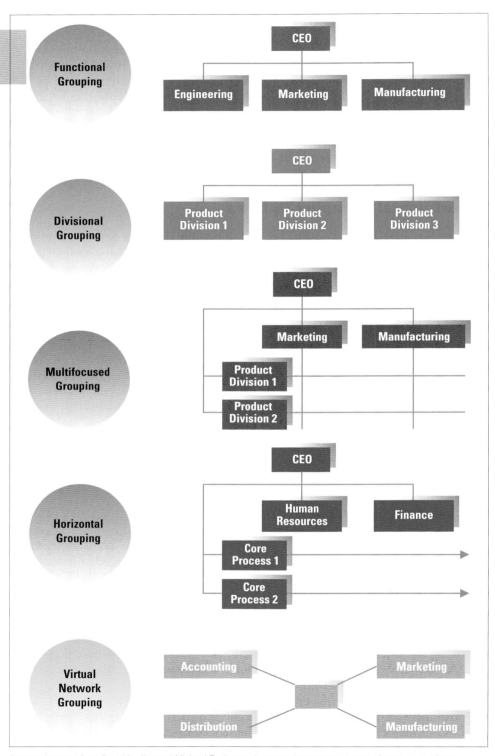

Source: Adapted from David Nadler and Michael Tushman, *Strategic Organization Design* (Glenview, Ill.: Scott Foresman, 1988), 68.

The organizational forms described in Exhibit 2.6 provide the overall options within which the organization chart is drawn and the detailed structure is designed. Each structural design alternative has significant strengths and weaknesses, to which we now turn.

FUNCTIONAL, DIVISIONAL, AND GEOGRAPHIC DESIGNS

Functional grouping and divisional grouping are the two most common approaches to structural design.

Functional Structure

In a **functional structure**, activities are grouped together by common function from the bottom to the top of the organization. All engineers are located in the engineering department, and the vice president of engineering is responsible for all engineering activities. The same is true in marketing, R&D, and manufacturing. An example of the functional organization structure was shown in Exhibit 2.1 earlier in this chapter.

With a functional structure, all human knowledge and skills with respect to specific activities are consolidated, providing a valuable depth of knowledge for the organization. This structure is most effective when in-depth expertise is critical to meeting organizational goals, when the organization needs to be controlled and coordinated through the vertical hierarchy, and when efficiency is important. The structure can be quite effective if there is little need for horizontal coordination. Exhibit 2.7 summarizes the strengths and weaknesses of the functional structure.

One strength of the functional structure is that it promotes economy of scale within functions. Economy of scale results when all employees are located in the same place and can share facilities. Producing all products in a single plant, for example, enables the plant to acquire the latest machinery. Constructing only

EXHIBIT 2.7
Strengths and Weaknesses of Functional Organization Structure

Strengths	Weaknesses
1. Allows economies of scale within functional departments	1. Slow response time to environmental changes
2. Enables in-depth knowledge and skill development	2. May cause decisions to pile on top; hierarchy overload
3. Enables organization to accomplish functional goals	3. Leads to poor horizontal coordination among departments
4. Is best with only one or a few products	4. Results in less innovation
	5. Involves restricted view of organizational goals

one facility instead of separate facilities for each product line reduces duplication and waste. The functional structure also promotes in-depth skill development of employees. Employees are exposed to a range of functional activities within their own department.[29]

The main weakness of the functional structure is a slow response to environmental changes that require coordination across departments. The vertical hierarchy becomes overloaded. Decisions pile up, and top managers do not respond fast enough. Other disadvantages of the functional structure are that innovation is slow because of poor coordination, and each employee has a restricted view of overall goals.

Some organizations perform very effectively with a functional structure. Consider the case of Blue Bell Creameries, Inc.

IN PRACTICE

Blue Bell Creameries, Inc.

It is the third best-selling brand of ice cream in the United States but many Americans have never heard of it. That's because Blue Bell Creameries, with headquarters in Brenham, Texas, sells its ice cream in only seventeen, mostly southern, states. Keeping distribution limited "allows us to focus on making and selling ice cream," says CEO and president Paul Kruse, the fourth generation of Kruses to run Blue Bell. Or, as another family slogan puts it, "It's a cinch by the inch but it's hard by the yard."

The "little creamery in Brenham," as the company markets itself, is obsessed with quality control and doesn't let anyone outside the company touch its product from the plant to the freezer case. "We make it all, we deliver it all in our own trucks, and we maintain all the stock in retailers' freezers," says chairman Ed Kruse. At one time, the company was even buying packages of Oreos at retail prices, cutting open each package by hand, and dumping the cookies into the mixers to make Blue Bell's Cookies 'n Cream flavor. Blue Bell sells more than $400 million in ice cream a year and commands a huge percentage of the ice cream market in Texas, Louisiana, and Alabama. People outside the region often pay $89 to have four half-gallons packed in dry ice and shipped to them. Despite the demand, management refuses to compromise quality by expanding into regions that cannot be satisfactorily serviced or by growing so fast that the company can't adequately train employees in the art of making ice cream.

Blue Bell's major departments are sales, quality control, production, maintenance, and distribution. There is also an accounting department and a small R&D group. Most employees have been with the company for years and have a wealth of experience in making quality ice cream. The environment is stable. The customer base is well established. The only change has been the increase in demand for Blue Bell Ice Cream.[30] ■

The functional structure is just right for Blue Bell Creameries. The organization has chosen to stay medium-sized and focus on making a single product—quality ice cream. However, as Blue Bell expands, it may have problems coordinating across departments, requiring stronger horizontal linkage mechanisms.

Functional Structure with Horizontal Linkages

A recent survey found that organizing by functions is still the prevalent approach to organization design.[31] However, in today's fast-moving world, very few companies can be successful with a strictly functional structure. Organizations compensate for the vertical functional hierarchy by installing horizontal linkages, as described earlier in this chapter. Managers improve horizontal coordination by using information systems, direct contact between departments, full-time integrators or project managers (illustrated in Exhibit 2.3), task forces, or teams (illustrated in Exhibit 2.4). One interesting use of horizontal linkages occurred at Karolinska Hospital in Stockholm, Sweden, which had forty-seven functional departments. Even after top executives cut that down to eleven, coordination was still inadequate. The top executive team set about reorganizing workflow at the hospital around patient care. Instead of bouncing a patient from department to department, Karolinska now envisions the illness to recovery period as a process with "pit stops" in admissions, X-ray, surgery, and so forth. The most interesting aspect of the approach is the new position of nurse coordinator. Nurse coordinators serve as full-time integrators, troubleshooting transitions within or between departments. The improved horizontal coordination dramatically improved productivity and patient care at Karolinska.[32] Karolinska is effectively using horizontal linkages to overcome some of the disadvantages of the functional structure.

Divisional Structure

The term **divisional structure** is used here as the generic term for what is sometimes called a *product structure* or *strategic business units*. With this structure, divisions can be organized according to individual products, services, product groups, major projects or programs, divisions, businesses, or profit centers. The distinctive feature of a divisional structure is that grouping is based on organizational outputs. For example, United Technologies Corporation (UTC), which is among the 50 largest U.S. industrial firms, has numerous divisions, including Carrier (air conditioners and heating), Otis (elevators and escalators), Pratt & Whitney (aircraft engines), and Sikorsky (helicopters).[33]

The difference between a divisional structure and a functional structure is illustrated in Exhibit 2.8. The functional structure can be redesigned into separate product groups, and each group contains the functional departments of R&D, manufacturing, accounting, and marketing. Coordination across functional departments within each product group is maximized. The divisional structure promotes flexibility and change because each unit is smaller and can adapt to the needs of its environment. Moreover, the divisional structure *decentralizes* decision making, because the lines of authority converge at a lower level in the hierarchy. The functional structure, by contrast, is *centralized*, because it forces decisions all the way to the top before a problem affecting several functions can be resolved.

Strengths and weaknesses of the divisional structure are summarized in Exhibit 2.9. The divisional organization structure is excellent for achieving coordination across functional departments. It works well when organizations can no longer be adequately controlled through the traditional vertical hierarchy, and when goals are oriented toward adaptation and change. Giant, complex organizations such as General Electric, Nestlé, and Johnson & Johnson are subdivided into a series of smaller, self-contained organizations for better control and coordination. In these large companies, the units are sometimes called divisions, businesses, or strategic business units. The structure at Johnson & Johnson includes some 250 separate operating units, including McNeil Consumer Products, makers of Tylenol; Ortho Pharmaceuticals, which makes Retin-A and birth-control pills; and J & J Consumer Products, the company that brings us

EXHIBIT 2.8

Reorganization from
Functional Structure to
Divisional Structure at
Info-Tech

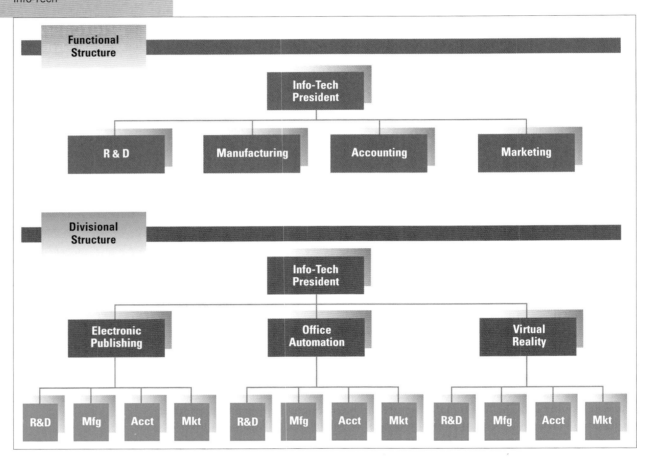

Johnson's Baby Shampoo and Band-Aids. Each unit is a separately chartered, autonomous company operating under the guidance of Johnson & Johnson's corporate headquarters.[34] Some U.S. government organizations also use a divisional structure to better serve the public. One example is the Internal Revenue Service, which wanted to be more customer oriented. The agency shifted its focus to informing, educating, and serving the public through four separate divisions serving distinct taxpayer groups—individual taxpayers, small businesses, large businesses, and tax-exempt organizations. Each division has its own budget, personnel, policies, and planning staffs that are focused on what is best for each particular taxpayer segment.[35]

The divisional structure has several strengths.[36] This structure is suited to fast change in an unstable environment and provides high product or service visibility. Since each product line has its own separate division, customers are able to contact the correct division and achieve satisfaction. Coordination across functions is excellent. Each product can adapt to requirements of individual customers or regions. The divisional structure typically works best in organizations that have

EXHIBIT 2.9
Strengths and
Weaknesses of Divisional
Organization Structure

Strengths	Weaknesses
1. Suited to fast change in unstable environment	1. Eliminates economies of scale in functional departments
2. Leads to customer satisfaction because product responsibility and contact points are clear	2. Leads to poor coordination across product lines
3. Involves high coordination across functions	3. Eliminates in-depth competence and technical specialization
4. Allows units to adapt to differences in products, regions, customers	4. Makes integration and standardization across product lines difficult
5. Best in large organizations with several products	
6. Decentralizes decision making	

Source: *Organizational Dynamics* by Duncan. Copyright 1979 by Elsevier Science & Technology Journals. Reproduced with permission of Elsevier Science & Technology Journals in the format Textbook via Copyright Clearance Center.

multiple products or services and enough personnel to staff separate functional units. Decision making is pushed down to the divisions. Each division is small enough to be quick on its feet, responding rapidly to changes in the market.

One disadvantage of using divisional structuring is that the organization loses economies of scale. Instead of fifty research engineers sharing a common facility in a functional structure, ten engineers may be assigned to each of five product divisions. The critical mass required for in-depth research is lost, and physical facilities have to be duplicated for each product line. Another problem is that product lines become separate from each other, and coordination across product lines can be difficult. As one Johnson & Johnson executive said, "We have to keep reminding ourselves that we work for the same corporation."[37]

Some companies that have a large number of divisions have had real problems with cross-unit coordination. Sony lost the digital media products business to Apple partly because of poor coordination. With the introduction of the iPod, Apple quickly captured 60 percent of the U.S. market versus 10 percent for Sony. The digital music business depends on seamless coordination. Sony's Walkman didn't even recognize some of the music sets that could be made with the company's SonicStage software and thus didn't mesh well with the division selling music downloads.[38] Unless effective horizontal mechanisms are in place, a divisional structure can hurt overall performance. One division may produce products or programs that are incompatible with products sold by another division, as at Sony. Customers can become frustrated when a sales representative from one division is unaware of developments in other divisions. Task forces and other horizontal linkage devices are needed to coordinate across divisions. A lack of technical specialization is also a problem in a divisional structure. Employees identify with the product line rather than with a functional specialty. R&D personnel, for example, tend to do applied research to benefit the product line rather than basic research to benefit the entire organization.

Geographic Structure

Another basis for structural grouping is the organization's users or customers. The most common structure in this category is geography. Each region of the country may have distinct tastes and needs. Each geographic unit includes all functions required to produce and market products or services in that region. Large nonprofit organizations such as the Girl Scouts of the USA, Habitat for Humanity, Make-A-Wish Foundation, and the United Way of America frequently use a type of geographic structure, with a central headquarters and semi-autonomous local units. The national organization provides brand recognition, coordinates fund-raising services, and handles some shared administrative functions, while day-to-day control and decision making is decentralized to local or regional units.[39]

For multinational corporations, self-contained units are created for different countries and parts of the world. Exhibit 2.10 shows a potential geographic structure for a computer company. This structure focuses managers and employees on specific geographic regions and sales targets.[40] Top executives at Citigroup are considering reorganizing to a geographic structure to improve efficiency and give the giant global corporation a more unified face to local customers. The reorganization would put one top manager in charge of all the various banking operations throughout a specific region such as Asia, Europe, or North America.[41]

The strengths and weaknesses of a geographic divisional structure are similar to the divisional organization characteristics listed in Exhibit 2.9. The organization can adapt to the specific needs of its own region, and employees identify with regional goals rather than with national goals. Horizontal coordination within a region is emphasized rather than linkages across regions or to the national office.

EXHIBIT 2.10
Geographic Structure for
Computer Company

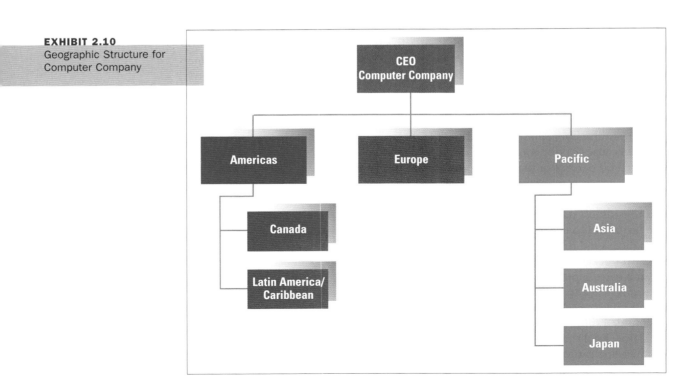

MATRIX STRUCTURE

Sometimes, an organization's structure needs to be multifocused in that both product and function or product and geography are emphasized at the same time. One way to achieve this is through the **matrix structure**. The matrix can be used when both technical expertise and product innovation and change are important for meeting organizational goals. The matrix structure often is the answer when organizations find that the functional, divisional, and geographic structures combined with horizontal linkage mechanisms will not work.

The matrix is a strong form of horizontal linkage. The unique characteristic of the matrix organization is that both product divisions and functional structures (horizontal and vertical) are implemented simultaneously, as shown in Exhibit 2.11. The product managers and functional managers have equal authority within the organization, and employees report to both of them. The matrix structure is similar to the use of full-time integrators or product managers described earlier in this chapter (Exhibit 2.3), except that in the matrix structure the product managers (horizontal) are given formal authority equal to that of the functional managers (vertical).

Conditions for the Matrix

A dual hierarchy may seem an unusual way to design an organization, but the matrix is the correct structure when the following conditions are present:[42]

- *Condition 1.* Pressure exists to share scarce resources across product lines. The organization is typically medium sized and has a moderate number of product lines. It feels pressure for the shared and flexible use of people and equipment across those products. For example, the organization is not large enough to assign engineers full-time to each product line, so engineers are assigned part-time to several products or projects.
- *Condition 2.* Environmental pressure exists for two or more critical outputs, such as for in-depth technical knowledge (functional structure) and frequent new products (divisional structure). This dual pressure means a balance of power is needed between the functional and product sides of the organization, and a dual-authority structure is needed to maintain that balance.
- *Condition 3.* The environmental domain of the organization is both complex and uncertain. Frequent external changes and high interdependence between departments require a large amount of coordination and information processing in both vertical and horizontal directions.

Under these three conditions, the vertical and horizontal lines of authority must be given equal recognition. A dual-authority structure is thereby created so the balance of power between them is equal.

Referring again to Exhibit 2.11, assume the matrix structure is for a clothing manufacturer. Product A is footwear, product B is outerwear, product C is sleepwear, and so on. Each product line serves a different market and customers. As a medium-size organization, the company must effectively use people from manufacturing, design, and marketing to work on each product line. There are not enough designers to warrant a separate design department for each product line, so the

EXHIBIT 2.11
Dual-Authority Structure
in a Matrix Organization

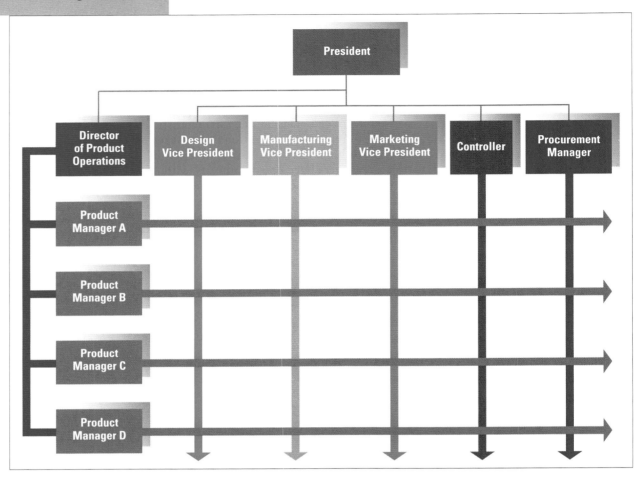

designers are shared across product lines. Moreover, by keeping the manufacturing, design, and marketing functions intact, employees can develop the in-depth expertise to serve all product lines efficiently.

The matrix formalizes horizontal teams along with the traditional vertical hierarchy and tries to give equal balance to both. However, the matrix may shift one way or the other. Many companies have found a balanced matrix hard to implement and maintain because one side of the authority structure often dominates. As a consequence, two variations of matrix structure have evolved—the **functional matrix** and the **product matrix**. In a functional matrix, the functional bosses have primary authority and the project or product managers simply coordinate product activities. In a product matrix, by contrast, the project or product managers have primary authority and functional managers simply assign technical personnel to projects and provide advisory expertise as needed. For many organizations, one of these approaches works better than the balanced matrix with dual lines of authority.[43]

All kinds of organizations have experimented with the matrix, including hospitals, consulting firms, banks, insurance companies, government agencies, and many types of industrial firms.[44] This structure has been used successfully by large, global

organizations such as Procter & Gamble, Unilever, and Dow Chemical, which fine-tuned the matrix to suit their own particular goals and culture.

Strengths and Weaknesses

The matrix structure is best when environmental change is high and when goals reflect a dual requirement, such as for both product and functional goals. The dual-authority structure facilitates communication and coordination to cope with rapid environmental change and enables an equal balance between product and functional bosses. The matrix facilitates discussion and adaptation to unexpected problems. It tends to work best in organizations of moderate size with a few product lines. The matrix is not needed for only a single product line, and too many product lines make it difficult to coordinate both directions at once. Exhibit 2.12 summarizes the strengths and weaknesses of the matrix structure based on what we know of organizations that use it.[45]

The strength of the matrix is that it enables an organization to meet dual demands from customers in the environment. Resources (people, equipment) can be flexibly allocated across different products, and the organization can adapt to changing external requirements.[46] This structure also provides an opportunity for employees to acquire either functional or general management skills, depending on their interests.

One disadvantage of the matrix is that some employees experience dual author-ity, reporting to two bosses and sometimes juggling conflicting demands. This can be frustrating and confusing, especially if roles and responsibilities are not clearly defined by top managers.[47] Employees working in a matrix need excellent interper-sonal and conflict-resolution skills, which may require special training in human

EXHIBIT 2.12
Strengths and Weaknesses of Matrix Organization Structure

Strengths	Weaknesses
1. Achieves coordination necessary to meet dual demands from customers	1. Causes participants to experience dual authority, which can be frustrating and confusing
2. Flexible sharing of human resources across products	2. Means participants need good interpersonal skills and extensive training
3. Suited to complex decisions and frequent changes in unstable environment	3. Is time consuming; involves frequent meetings and conflict resolution sessions
4. Provides opportunity for both functional and product skill development	4. Will not work unless participants understand it and adopt collegial rather than vertical type relationships
5. Best in medium-sized organizations with multiple products	5. Requires great effort to maintain power balance

Source: Adapted from Robert Duncan, "What Is the Right Organization Structure? Decision Tree Analysis Provides the Answer," *Organizational Dynamics* (Winter 1979), 429.

relations. The matrix also forces managers to spend a great deal of time in meet-ings.[48] If managers do not adapt to the information and power sharing required by the matrix, the system will not work. Managers must collaborate with one another rather than rely on vertical authority in decision making. The successful implemen-tation of one matrix structure occurred at a steel company in Great Britain.

Englander Steel

As far back as anyone could remember, the steel industry in England was stable and certain. Then in the 1980s and 1990s, excess European steel capacity, an eco-nomic downturn, the emergence of the mini mill electric arc furnace, and competition from steelmakers in Germany and Japan forever changed the steel industry. By the turn of the century, traditional steel mills in the United States, such as Bethlehem Steel and LTV Corporation, were facing bankruptcy. Mittal Steel in Asia and Europe's leading steelmaker, Arcelor, started acquiring steel companies to become world steel titans. The survival hope of small traditional steel manufacturers was to sell specialized products. A small company could market specialty products aggressively and quickly adapt to customer needs. Complex process settings and operating conditions had to be rapidly changed for each customer's order—a difficult feat for the titans.

Englander Steel employed 2,900 people, made 400,000 tons of steel a year (about 1 percent of Arcelor's output), and was 180 years old. For 160 of those years, a func-tional structure worked fine. As the environment became more turbulent and competitive, however, Englander Steel managers realized they were not keeping up. Fifty percent of Englander's orders were behind schedule. Profits were eroded by labor, material, and energy cost increases. Market share declined.

In consultation with outside experts, the president of Englander Steel saw that the com-pany had to walk a tightrope. It had to specialize in a few high-value-added products tailored for separate markets, while maintaining economies of scale and sophisticated technology within functional departments. The dual pressure led to an unusual solution for a steel company: a matrix structure.

Englander Steel had four product lines: open-die forgings, ring-mill products, wheels and axles, and sheet steel. A business manager was given responsibility for and authority over each line, which included preparing a business plan and developing targets for production costs, product inventory, shipping dates, and gross profit. The managers were given author-ity to meet those targets and to make their lines profitable. Functional vice presidents were responsible for technical decisions. Functional managers were expected to stay abreast of the latest techniques in their areas and to keep personnel trained in new technologies that could apply to product lines. With 20,000 recipes for specialty steels and several hundred new recipes ordered each month, functional personnel had to stay current. Two functional departments—field sales and industrial relations—were not included in the matrix because they worked independently. The final design was a hybrid matrix structure with both matrix and functional relationships, as illustrated in Exhibit 2.13.

Implementation of the matrix was slow. Middle managers were confused. Meetings to coor-dinate orders across functional departments seemed to be held every day. After about a year of training by external consultants, Englander Steel was on track. Ninety percent of the orders were now delivered on time and market share recovered. Both productivity and profitability increased steadily. The managers thrived on matrix involvement. Meetings to coordinate product and functional decisions provided a growth experience. Middle managers began including younger managers in the matrix discussions as training for future management responsibility.[49]

EXHIBIT 2.13
Matrix Structure for
Englander Steel

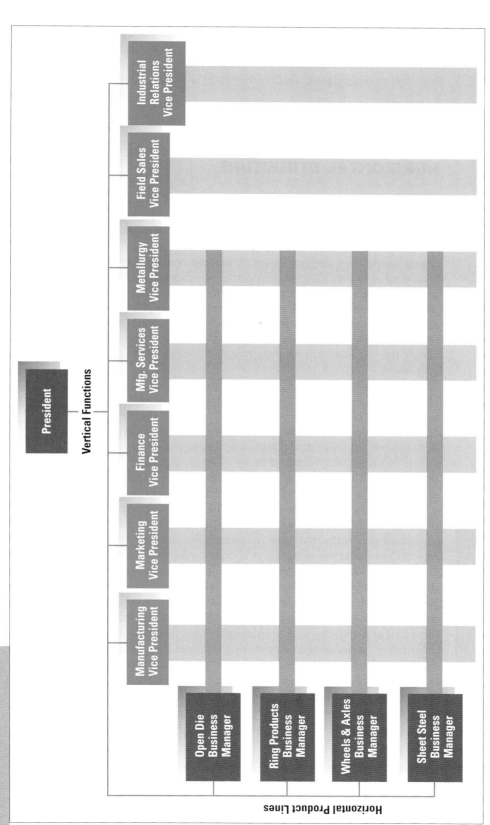

This example illustrates the correct use of a matrix structure. The dual pressure to maintain economies of scale and to market four product lines gave equal emphasis to the functional and product hierarchies. Through continuous meetings for coordination, Englander Steel achieved both economies of scale and flexibility.

HORIZONTAL STRUCTURE

A recent approach to organizing is the **horizontal structure**, which organizes employees around core processes. Organizations typically shift toward a horizontal structure during a procedure called reengineering. **Reengineering**, or *business process reengineering*, basically means the redesign of a vertical organization along its horizontal workflows and processes. A **process** refers to an organized group of related tasks and activities that work together to transform inputs into outputs that create value for customers.[50] Examples of processes include order fulfillment, new product development, and customer service. Reengineering changes the way managers think about how work is done. Rather than focusing on narrow jobs structured into distinct functional departments, they emphasize core processes that cut horizontally across the organization and involve teams of employees working together to serve customers.

A good illustration of process is provided by claims handling at Progressive Casualty Insurance Company. In the past, a customer would report an accident to an agent, who would pass the information to a customer service representative, who, in turn, would pass it to a claims manager. The claims manager would batch the claim with others from the same territory and assign it to an adjuster, who would schedule a time to inspect the vehicle damage. Today, adjusters are organized into teams that handle the entire claims process from beginning to end. One member handles claimant calls to the office while others are stationed in the field. When an adjuster takes a call, he or she does whatever is possible over the phone. If an inspection is needed, the adjuster contacts a team member in the field and schedules an appointment immediately. Progressive now measures the time from call to inspection in hours rather than the seven to ten days it once took.[51]

When a company is reengineered to a horizontal structure, all employees throughout the organization who work on a particular process (such as claims handling or order fulfillment) have easy access to one another so they can communicate and coordinate their efforts. The horizontal structure virtually eliminates both the vertical hierarchy and old departmental boundaries. This structural approach is largely a response to the profound changes that have occurred in the workplace and the business environment over the past fifteen to twenty years. Technological progress emphasizes computer- and Internet-based integration and coordination. Customers expect faster and better service, and employees want opportunities to use their minds, learn new skills, and assume greater responsibility. Organizations mired in a vertical mindset have a hard time meeting these challenges. Thus, numerous organizations have experimented with horizontal mechanisms such as cross-functional teams to achieve coordination across departments or task forces to accomplish temporary projects. Increasingly, organizations are shifting away from hierarchical, function-based structures to structures based on horizontal processes.

Briefcase

As an organization manager, keep these guidelines in mind:

Consider a horizontal structure when customer needs and demands change rapidly and when learning and innovation are critical to organizational success. Carefully determine core processes and train managers and employees to work within the horizontal structure.

Characteristics

An illustration of a company reengineered into a horizontal structure appears in Exhibit 2.14. Such an organization has the following characteristics:[52]

- Structure is created around cross-functional core processes rather than tasks, functions, or geography. Thus, boundaries between departments are obliterated. Ford Motor Company's Customer Service Division, for example, has core process groups for business development, parts supply and logistics, vehicle service and programs, and technical support.
- Self-directed teams, not individuals, are the basis of organizational design and performance. Schwa, a restaurant in Chicago that serves elaborate multicourse meals, is run by a team. Members rotate jobs so that everyone is sometimes a chef, sometimes a dishwasher, sometimes a waiter, or sometimes the person who answers the phone, takes reservations, or greets customers at the door.[53]
- Process owners have responsibility for each core process in its entirety. For Ford's parts supply and logistics process, for example, a number of teams may work on jobs such as parts analysis, purchasing, material flow, and distribution, but a process owner is responsible for coordinating the entire process.
- People on the team are given the skills, tools, motivation, and authority to make decisions central to the team's performance. Team members are cross-trained to perform one another's jobs, and the combined skills are sufficient to complete a major organizational task.

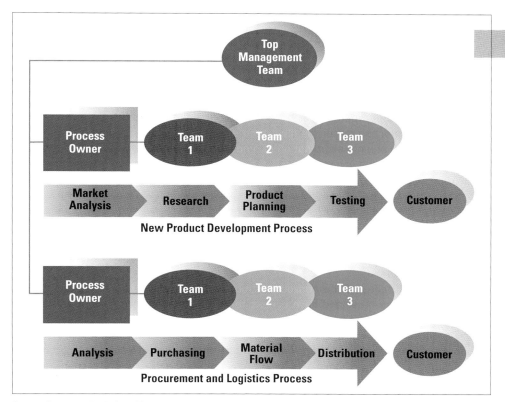

EXHIBIT 2.14
A Horizontal Structure

Source: Based on Frank Ostroff, *The Horizontal Organization* (New York: Oxford University Press, 1999); John A. Byrne, "The Horizontal Corporation," *BusinessWeek* (December 20, 1993), 76–81; and Thomas A. Stewart, "The Search for the Organization of Tomorrow," *Fortune* (May 18, 1992), 92–98.

- Teams have the freedom to think creatively and respond flexibly to new challenges that arise.
- Customers drive the horizontal corporation. Effectiveness is measured by end-of-process performance objectives (based on the goal of bringing value to the customer), as well as customer satisfaction, employee satisfaction, and financial contribution.
- The culture is one of openness, trust, and collaboration, focused on continuous improvement. The culture values employee empowerment, responsibility, and well-being.

General Electric's Salisbury, North Carolina, plant shifted to a horizontal structure to improve flexibility and customer service.

IN PRACTICE

GE Salisbury

General Electric's plant in Salisbury, North Carolina, which manufactures electrical lighting panel boards for industrial and commercial purposes, used to be organized functionally and vertically. Because no two GE customers have identical needs, each panel board has to be configured and built to order, which frequently created bottlenecks in the standard production process. In the mid-1980s, faced with high product-line costs, inconsistent customer service, and a declining market share, managers began exploring new ways of organizing that would emphasize teamwork, responsibility, continuous improvement, empowerment, and commitment to the customer.

By the early 1990s, GE Salisbury had made the transition to a horizontal structure that links sets of multiskilled teams who are responsible for the entire build-to-order process. The new structure is based on the goal of producing lighting panel boards "of the highest possible quality, in the shortest possible cycle time, at a competitive price, with the best possible service." The process consists of four linked teams, each made up of ten to fifteen members representing a range of skills and functions. A production-control team serves as process owner (as illustrated earlier in Exhibit 2.14) and is responsible for order receipt, planning, coordination of production, purchasing, working with suppliers and customers, tracking inventory, and keeping all the teams focused on meeting objectives. The fabrication team cuts, builds, welds, and paints the various parts that make up the steel box that will house the electrical components panel, which is assembled and tested by the electrical components team. The electrical components team also handles shipping. A maintenance team takes care of heavy equipment maintenance that cannot be performed as part of the regular production process. Managers have become *associate advisors* who serve as guides and coaches and bring their expertise to the teams as needed.

The key to success of the horizontal structure is that all the operating teams work in concert with each other and have access to the information they need to meet team and process goals. Teams are given information about sales, backlogs, inventory, staffing needs, productivity, costs, quality, and other data, and each team regularly shares information about its part of the build-to-order process with the other teams. Joint production meetings, job rotation, and cross-training of employees are some of the mechanisms that help ensure smooth integration. The linked teams assume responsibility for setting their own production targets, determining production schedules, assigning duties, and identifying and solving problems.

Productivity and performance have dramatically improved with the horizontal structure. Bottlenecks in the workflow, which once wreaked havoc with production schedules, have been virtually eliminated. A six-week lead time has been cut to two-and-a-half days. More subtle but just as important are the increases in employee and customer satisfaction that GE Salisbury has realized since implementing its new structure.[54] ■

Strengths and Weaknesses

As with all structures, the horizontal structure has both strengths and weaknesses, as listed in Exhibit 2.15.

The most significant strength of the horizontal structure is enhanced coordination, which can dramatically increase the company's flexibility and response to changes in customer needs. The structure directs everyone's attention toward the customer, which leads to greater customer satisfaction as well as improvements in productivity, speed, and efficiency. In addition, because there are no boundaries between functional departments, employees take a broader view of organizational goals rather than being focused on the goals of a single department. The horizontal structure promotes an emphasis on teamwork and cooperation, so that team members share a commitment to meeting common objectives. Finally, the horizontal structure can improve the quality of life for employees by giving them opportunities to share responsibility, make decisions, and contribute significantly to the organization.

A weakness of the horizontal structure is that it can harm rather than help organizational performance unless managers carefully determine which core processes are critical for bringing value to customers. Simply defining the processes around

EXHIBIT 2.15
Strengths and Weaknesses of Horizontal Structure

Strengths	Weaknesses
1. Promotes flexibility and rapid response to changes in customer needs	1. Determining core processes is difficult and time consuming
2. Directs the attention of everyone toward the production and delivery of value to the customer	2. Requires changes in culture, job design, management philosophy, and information and reward systems
3. Each employee has a broader view of organizational goals	3. Traditional managers may balk when they have to give up power and authority
4. Promotes a focus on teamwork and collaboration	4. Requires significant training of employees to work effectively in a horizontal team environment
5. Improves quality of life for employees by offering them the opportunity to share responsibility, make decisions, and be accountable for outcomes	5. Can limit in-depth skill development

Sources: Based on Frank Ostroff, *The Horizontal Organization: What the Organization of the Future Looks Like and How It Delivers Value to Customers* (New York: Oxford University Press, 1999); and Richard L. Daft, *Organization Theory and Design,* 6th ed. (Cincinnati, Ohio: South-Western, 1998), 253.

which to organize can be difficult. In addition, shifting to a horizontal structure is complicated and time consuming because it requires significant changes in culture, job design, management philosophy, and information and reward systems. Traditional managers may balk when they have to give up power and authority to serve instead as coaches and facilitators of teams. Employees have to be trained to work effectively in a team environment. Finally, because of the cross-functional nature of work, a horizontal structure can limit in-depth knowledge and skill development unless measures are taken to give employees opportunities to maintain and build technical expertise.

VIRTUAL NETWORKS AND OUTSOURCING

Recent developments in organization design extend the concept of horizontal coordination and collaboration beyond the boundaries of the traditional organization. The most widespread design trend in recent years has been the outsourcing of various parts of the organization to outside partners.[55] **Outsourcing** means to contract out certain tasks or functions, such as manufacturing, human resources, or credit processing, to other companies.

Companies in almost every industry are jumping on the outsourcing bandwagon. For example, more than 1,000 law enforcement agencies across the United States have turned to PropertyRoom.com to manage the time-consuming business of cataloging and auctioning off unclaimed stolen goods such as cars, computers, jewelry, or paintings.[56] And consider the U.S. military, which increasingly uses private military company contractors to handle just about everything except the core activity of fighting battles and securing defensive positions. Kellogg Brown & Root, a subsidiary of the Halliburton Corporation, for instance, builds and maintains military bases and provides catering and cleaning services. In the business world, Wachovia Corporation transferred administration of its human resources programs to Hewitt Associates, and British food retailer J. Sainsbury's lets Accenture handle its entire information technology department. About 20 percent of drug manufacturer Eli Lilly & Company's chemistry work is done in China by start-up labs such as Chem-Explorer; and companies such as India's Wipro, France's S.R. Teleperformance, and the U.S.-based Convergys manage call center and technical support operations for big computer and cell phone companies around the world. Fiat Auto is involved in multiple complex outsourcing relationships with other companies handling logistics, maintenance, and the manufacturing of some parts.[57]

Once, a company's units of operation "were either within the organization and 'densely connected' or they were outside the organization and not connected at all," as one observer phrased it.[58] Today, the lines are so blurred that it can be difficult to tell what is part of the organization and what is not. IBM handles back-office operations for many large companies, but it also outsources some of its own activities to other firms, which in turn may farm out some of their functions to still other organizations.[59]

A few organizations carry outsourcing to the extreme to create a virtual network structure. With a **virtual network structure**, sometimes called a *modular structure*, the firm subcontracts most of its major functions or processes to separate companies and coordinates their activities from a small headquarters organization.[60]

Briefcase

As an organization manager, keep these guidelines in mind:

Use a virtual network structure for extreme flexibility and rapid response to changing market conditions. Focus on key activities that give the organization its competitive advantage and outsource other activities to carefully selected partners.

How the Structure Works

The virtual network organization may be viewed as a central hub surrounded by a network of outside specialists. Rather than being housed under one roof or located within one organization, services such as accounting, design, manufacturing, marketing, and distribution are outsourced to separate companies that are connected electronically to a central office. Organizational partners located in different parts of the world may use networked computers or the Internet to exchange data and information so rapidly and smoothly that a loosely connected network of suppliers, manufacturers, and distributors can look and act like one seamless company. The virtual network form incorporates a free-market style to replace the traditional vertical hierarchy. Subcontractors may flow into and out of the system as needed to meet changing needs.

With a network structure, the hub maintains control over processes in which it has world-class or difficult-to-imitate capabilities and then transfers other activities—along with the decision making and control over them—to other organizations. These partner organizations organize and accomplish their work using their own ideas, assets, and tools.[61] The idea is that a firm can concentrate on what it does best and contract out everything else to companies with distinctive competence in those specific areas, enabling the organization to do more with less.[62] The network structure is often advantageous for start-up companies, such as TiVo Inc., the company that introduced the digital video recorder.

The market for digital video recorders is hot, and major electronics, cable, and satellite companies are getting in on the action. The company that started it all was TiVo, a small organization based in the San Francisco Bay area.

TiVo Inc.

TiVo's founders developed a technology to allow users to record up to 80 hours of television and replay it at their convenience, without commercial interruption and minus the hassles of digital storage media or videotapes. They knew speed was of the essence if they were to take this new market by storm. The only way to do it was by outsourcing practically everything. TiVo first developed major manufacturing and marketing partnerships with large companies such as Sony, Hughes Electronics, and Royal Philips Electronics. In addition, the company outsourced distribution, public relations, advertising, and customer support. TiVo managers considered the customer support function particularly critical. Because TiVo was a new concept, ordinary call-center approaches wouldn't work. Leaders worked closely with outsourcing partner ClientLogic to develop processes and training materials that would help customer-service agents "think like a TiVo customer."

Using the virtual network structure enabled a small company like TiVo to get the advanced capabilities it needed without having to spend time and limited financial resources building an organization from scratch. TiVo leaders concentrated on technological innovation and developing and managing relationships with outsourcing firms. Today, TiVo has partnership agreements with numerous organizations, including a recent one with YouTube that will allow TiVo subscribers to watch user-generated videos from the website on their televisions, and one with Comcast, the nation's number one cable operator, that will help TiVo reach a larger customer base. The deal with Comcast is critical. Without a cable partner, TiVo would find it difficult to remain a major player in the growing market for digital video recorders.[63] ∎

EXHIBIT 2.16
Partial Virtual Network
Structure at TiVo

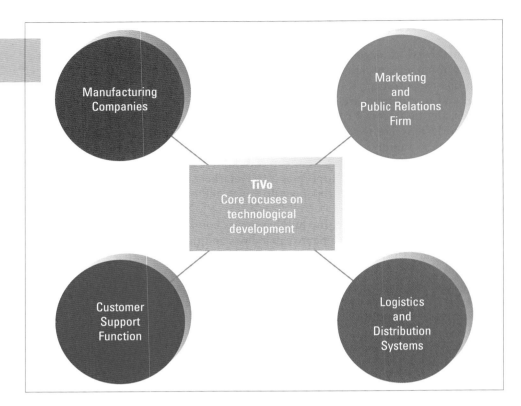

TiVo faces stiff competition, but using the virtual network structure enabled it to get established and survive in the growing industry. TiVo is marketing itself as a premium DVR service to compete with the fast-growing and less expensive options offered by satellite and cable providers. Exhibit 2.16 illustrates a simplified network structure for TiVo, showing some of the functions that are outsourced to other companies.

Strengths and Weaknesses

Exhibit 2.17 summarizes the strengths and weaknesses of the virtual network structure.[64] One of the major strengths is that the organization, no matter how small, can be truly global, drawing on resources worldwide to achieve the best quality and price and then selling products or services worldwide just as easily through subcontractors. The network structure also enables a new or small company to develop products or services and get them to market rapidly without huge investments in factories, equipment, warehouses, or distribution facilities. The ability to arrange and rearrange resources to meet changing needs and best serve customers gives the network structure extreme flexibility and rapid response. New technologies can be developed quickly by tapping into a worldwide network of experts. The organization can continually redefine itself to meet changing product or market opportunities. A final strength is reduced administrative overhead. Large teams of staff specialists and administrators are not needed. Managerial and technical talent can be focused on key activities that provide competitive advantage while other activities are outsourced.

EXHIBIT 2.17
Strengths and
Weaknesses of Virtual
Network Structure

Strengths	Weaknesses
1. Enables even small organizations to obtain talent and resources worldwide	1. Managers do not have hands-on control over many activities and employees
2. Gives a company immediate scale and reach without huge investments in factories, equipment, or distribution facilities	2. Requires a great deal of time to manage relationships and potential conflicts with contract partners
3. Enables the organization to be highly flexible and responsive to changing needs	3. There is a risk of organizational failure if a partner fails to deliver or goes out of business
4. Reduces administrative overhead costs	4. Employee loyalty and corporate culture might be weak because employees feel they can be replaced by contract services

Sources: Based on Linda S. Ackerman, "Transition Management: An In-Depth Look at Managing Complex Change," *Organizational Dynamics* (Summer 1982), 46–66; and Frank Ostroff, *The Horizontal Organization* (New York: Oxford University Press, 1999), Fig 2.1, 34.

The virtual network structure also has a number of weaknesses. The primary weakness is a lack of control. The network structure takes decentralization to the extreme. Managers do not have all operations under their jurisdiction and must rely on contracts, coordination, and negotiation to hold things together. This also means increased time spent managing relationships with partners and resolving conflicts.

A problem of equal importance is the risk of failure if one organizational partner fails to deliver, has a plant burn down, or goes out of business. Managers in the headquarters organization have to act quickly to spot problems and find new arrangements. Finally, from a human resource perspective, employee loyalty can be weak in a network organization because of concerns over job security. Employees may feel that they can be replaced by contract services. In addition, it is more difficult to develop a cohesive corporate culture. Turnover may be higher because emotional commitment between the organization and employees is low. With changing products, markets, and partners, the organization may need to reshuffle employees at any time to get the correct mix of skills and capabilities.

HYBRID STRUCTURE

As a practical matter, many structures in the real world do not exist in the pure forms we have outlined in this chapter. Most large organizations, in particular, often use a **hybrid structure** that combines characteristics of various approaches tailored to specific strategic needs. Most companies combine characteristics of functional, divisional, geographic, horizontal, or network structures to take advantage of the strengths of various structures and avoid some of the weaknesses. Hybrid structures tend to be used in rapidly changing environments because they offer the organization greater flexibility.

One type of hybrid that is often used is to combine characteristics of the functional and divisional structures. When a corporation grows large and has several products or markets, it typically is organized into self-contained divisions of some type. Functions that are important to each product or market are decentralized to the self-contained units. However, some functions that are relatively stable and require economies of scale and in-depth specialization are also centralized at headquarters. Sun Petroleum Products Corporation (SPPC) reorganized to a hybrid structure to be more responsive to changing markets. The hybrid organization structure adopted by SPPC is illustrated in part 1 of Exhibit 2.18. Three major product divisions—fuels, lubricants, and chemicals—were created, each serving a different market and requiring a different strategy and management style. Each product-line vice president is now in charge of all functions for that product, such as marketing, planning, supply and distribution, and manufacturing. However, activities such as human resources, legal, technology, and finance were centralized as functional departments at headquarters in order to achieve economies of scale. Each of these departments provides services for the entire organization.[65]

A second hybrid approach that is increasingly used today is to combine characteristics of functional, divisional, and horizontal structures. Ford Motor Company's Customer Service Division, a global operation made up of 12,000 employees serving nearly 15,000 dealers, provides an example of this type of hybrid. Beginning in 1995, when Ford launched its "Ford 2000" initiative aimed at becoming the world's leading automotive firm in the twenty-first century, top executives grew increasingly concerned about complaints regarding customer service. They decided that the horizontal model offered the best chance to gain a faster, more efficient, integrated approach to customer service. Part 2 of Exhibit 2.18 illustrates a portion of the Customer Service Division's hybrid structure. Several horizontally aligned groups, made up of multiskilled teams, focus on core processes such as parts supply and logistics (acquiring parts and getting them to dealers quickly and efficiently), vehicle service and programs (collecting and disseminating information about repair problems), and technical support (ensuring that every service department receives updated technical information). Each group has a process owner who is responsible for seeing that the teams meet overall objectives. Ford's Customer Service Division retained a functional structure for its finance, strategy and communications, and human resources departments. Each of these departments provides services for the entire division.[66]

In a huge organization such as Ford, managers may use a variety of structural characteristics to meet the needs of the total organization. Like many large organizations, for example, Ford also outsources some of its activities to other firms. A hybrid structure is often preferred over the pure functional, divisional, horizontal, or virtual network structure because it can provide some of the advantages of each and overcome some of the disadvantages.

APPLICATIONS OF STRUCTURAL DESIGN

Each type of structure is applied in different situations and meets different needs. In describing the various structures, we touched briefly on conditions such as environmental stability or change and organizational size that are related to structure. Each form of structure—functional, divisional, matrix, horizontal, network, hybrid—represents a tool that can help managers make an organization more effective, depending on the demands of its situation.

EXHIBIT 2.18
Two Hybrid Structures

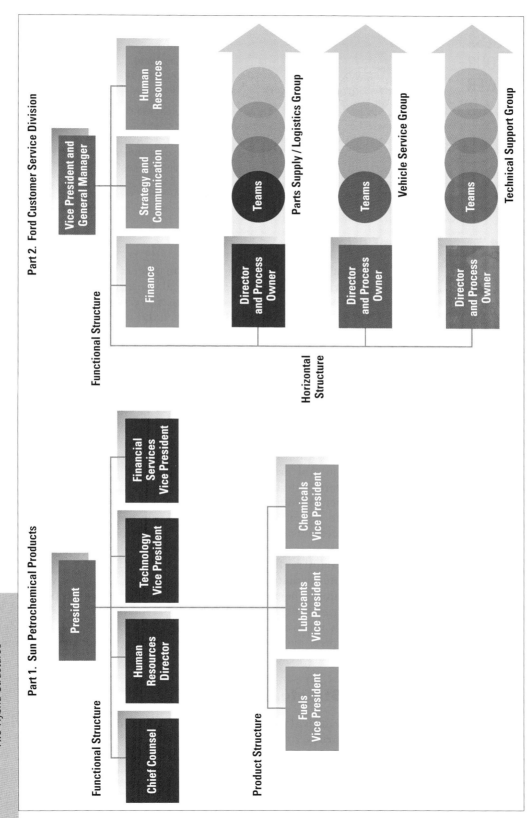

Part 1. Sun Petrochemical Products

Functional Structure

President

Chief Counsel | Human Resources Director | Technology Vice President | Financial Services Vice President

Product Structure

Fuels Vice President | Lubricants Vice President | Chemicals Vice President

Part 2. Ford Customer Service Division

Functional Structure

Vice President and General Manager

Finance | Strategy and Communication | Human Resources

Horizontal Structure

Director and Process Owner — Teams — Parts Supply / Logistics Group

Director and Process Owner — Teams — Vehicle Service Group

Director and Process Owner — Teams — Technical Support Group

ASSESS YOUR ANSWER

3 Top managers are smart to maintain organizational control over the activities of key work units rather than contracting out some work unit tasks to other firms.

ANSWER: *Disagree.* Virtual networks and outsourcing forms of organization design have become popular because they offer increased flexibility and more rapid response in a fast-changing environment. Outsourced departments can be added or dropped as conditions change. Keeping control over all activities in-house might be more comfortable for some managers, but it discourages flexibility.

Structural Alignment

Briefcase

As an organization manager, keep these guidelines in mind:

Find the correct balance between vertical control and horizontal coordination to meet the needs of the organization. Consider a structural reorganization when symptoms of structural deficiency are observed.

Ultimately, the most important decision that managers make about structural design is to find the right balance between vertical control and horizontal coordination, depending on the needs of the organization. Vertical control is associated with goals of efficiency and stability, while horizontal coordination is associated with learning, innovation, and flexibility. Exhibit 2.19 shows a simplified continuum that illustrates how structural approaches are associated with vertical control versus horizontal coordination. The functional structure is appropriate when the organization needs to be coordinated through the vertical hierarchy and when efficiency is important for meeting organizational goals. The functional structure uses task specialization and a strict chain of command to gain efficient use of scarce resources, but it does not enable the organization to be flexible or innovative. At the opposite end of the scale, the horizontal structure is appropriate when the organization has a high need for coordination among functions to achieve innovation and promote learning. The horizontal structure enables organizations to differentiate themselves and respond quickly to changes, but at the expense of efficient resource use. The virtual network structure offers even greater flexibility and potential for rapid response by allowing the organization to add or subtract pieces as needed to adapt and meet changing needs from the environment and marketplace. Exhibit 2.19 also shows how other types of structure defined in this chapter—functional with horizontal linkages, divisional, and matrix—represent intermediate steps on the organization's path to efficiency or innovation and learning. The exhibit does not include all possible structures, but it illustrates how organizations attempt to balance the needs for efficiency and vertical control with innovation and horizontal coordination. In addition, as described in the chapter, many organizations use a hybrid structure to combine characteristics of various structural types.

Symptoms of Structural Deficiency

Top executives periodically evaluate organization structure to determine whether it is appropriate to changing needs. Managers try to achieve the best fit between internal reporting relationships and the needs of the external environment. As a general rule, when organization structure is out of alignment

EXHIBIT 2.19
Relationship of Structure
to Organization's Need
for Efficiency versus
Learning

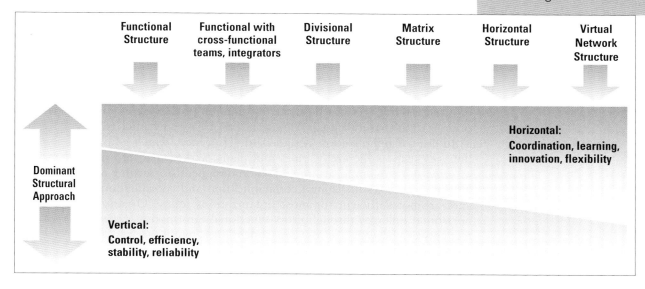

with organization needs, one or more of the following **symptoms of structural deficiency** appear.[67]

- *Decision making is delayed or lacking in quality.* Decision makers may be overloaded because the hierarchy funnels too many problems and decisions to them. Delegation to lower levels may be insufficient. Another cause of poor-quality decisions is that information may not reach the correct people. Information linkages in either the vertical or horizontal direction may be inadequate to ensure decision quality.

- *The organization does not respond innovatively to a changing environment.* One reason for lack of innovation is that departments are not coordinated horizontally. The identification of customer needs by the marketing department and the identification of technological developments in the research department must be coordinated. Organization structure also has to specify departmental responsibilities that include environmental scanning and innovation.

- *Employee performance declines and goals are not being met.* Employee performance may decline because the structure doesn't provide clear goals, responsibilities, and mechanisms for coordination. The structure should reflect the complexity of the market environment yet be straightforward enough for employees to effectively work within.

- *Too much conflict is evident.* Organization structure should allow conflicting departmental goals to combine into a single set of goals for the entire organization. When departments act at cross-purposes or are under pressure to achieve departmental goals at the expense of organizational goals, the structure is often at fault. Horizontal linkage mechanisms are not adequate.

DESIGN ESSENTIALS

- Organization structure must accomplish two things for the organization. It must provide a framework of responsibilities, reporting relationships, and groupings, and it must provide mechanisms for linking and coordinating organizational elements into a coherent whole. The structure is reflected on the organization chart. Linking the organization into a coherent whole requires the use of information systems and linkage devices in addition to the organization chart.

- Organization structure can be designed to provide vertical and horizontal information linkages based on the information processing required to meet the organization's overall goal. Managers can choose whether to orient toward a traditional organization designed for efficiency, which emphasizes vertical linkages such as hierarchy, rules and plans, and formal information systems, or toward a contemporary organization designed for learning and adaptation, which emphasizes horizontal communication and coordination. Vertical linkages are not sufficient for most organizations today. Organizations provide horizontal linkages through cross-functional information systems, direct contact between managers across department lines, temporary task forces, full-time integrators, and teams.

- Alternatives for grouping employees and departments into overall structural design include functional grouping, divisional grouping, multifocused grouping, horizontal grouping, and virtual network grouping. The choice among functional, divisional, and horizontal structures determines where coordination and integration will be greatest. With functional and divisional structures, managers also use horizontal linkage mechanisms to complement the vertical dimension and achieve integration of departments and levels into an organizational whole. With a horizontal structure, activities are organized horizontally around core work processes.

- A virtual network structure extends the concept of horizontal coordination and collaboration beyond the boundaries of the organization. Core activities are performed by a central hub while other functions and activities are outsourced to contract partners.

- The matrix structure attempts to achieve an equal balance between the vertical and horizontal dimensions of structure. Most organizations do not exist in these pure forms, using instead hybrid structures that incorporate characteristics of two or more types of structure.

- Ultimately, managers attempt to find the correct balance between vertical control and horizontal coordination. Signs of structural misalignment include delayed decision making, lack of innovation, poor employee performance, and excessive conflict.

- Finally, an organization chart is only so many lines and boxes on a piece of paper. The purpose of the organization chart is to encourage and direct employees into activities and communications that enable the organization to achieve its goals. The organization chart provides the structure, but employees provide the behavior. The chart is a guideline to encourage people to work together, but management must implement the structure and carry it out.

Key Concepts

centralized
decentralized
departmental grouping
divisional grouping
divisional structure
functional grouping
functional matrix
functional structure
horizontal grouping
horizontal linkage

horizontal structure
hybrid structure
integrator
liaison role
matrix structure
multifocused grouping
organization structure
outsourcing
process
product matrix

reengineering
symptoms of structural deficiency
task force
teams
vertical information system
vertical linkages
virtual network grouping
virtual network structure
virtual team

Discussion Questions

1. What is the difference between a task force and a team? Between liaison role and integrating role? Which of these provides the greatest amount of horizontal coordination?
2. Describe the virtual network structure. What are the advantages and disadvantages of using this structure compared to performing all activities in-house within an organization?
3. What are the primary differences between a traditional organization designed for efficiency and a more contemporary organization designed for learning?
4. What types of organizational activities do you think are most likely to be outsourced? What types are least likely?
5. Large corporations tend to use hybrid structures. Why?

6. Why do companies using a horizontal structure have cultures that emphasize openness, employee empowerment, and responsibility? What do you think a manager's job would be like in a horizontally organized company?
7. When is a functional structure preferable to a divisional structure?
8. The manager of a consumer products firm said, "We use the brand manager position to train future executives." Why do you think the brand manager position is considered a good training ground? Discuss.
9. What is the definition of *organization structure*? Does organization structure appear on the organization chart? Explain.
10. What conditions usually have to be present before an organization should adopt a matrix structure?

Chapter 2 Workbook: You and Organization Structure*

To better understand the importance of organization structure in your life, do the following assignment.

Select one of the following situations to organize:

- A copy and print shop
- A travel agency
- A sports rental (such as Jet Skis or snowmobiles) in a resort area
- A bakery

Background

Organization is a way of gaining some power against an unreliable environment. The environment provides the organization with inputs, which include raw materials, human resources, and financial resources. There is a service or product to produce that involves technology. The output goes to clients, a group that must be nurtured. The complexities of the environment and the technology determine the complexity of the organization.

Planning Your Organization

1. Write down the mission or purpose of the organization in a few sentences.
2. What are the specific tasks to be completed to accomplish the mission?
3. Based on the specifics in question 2, develop an organization chart. Each position in the chart will perform a specific task or is responsible for a certain outcome.

4. You are into your third year of operation, and your business has been very successful. You want to add a second location a few miles away. What issues will you face running the business at two locations? Draw an organization chart that includes the two business locations.

5. Five more years go by and the business has grown to five locations in two cities. How do you keep in touch with it all? What issues of control and coordination have arisen? Draw an up-to-date organization chart and explain your rationale for it.

6. Twenty years later you have seventy-five business locations in five states. What are the issues and problems that have to be dealt with through organizational structure? Draw an organization chart for this organization, indicating such factors as who is responsible for customer satisfaction, how you will know if customer needs are met, and how information will flow within the organization.

*Adapted by Dorothy Marcic from "Organizing," in Donald D. White and H. William Vroman, *Action in Organizations*, 2nd ed. (Boston: Allyn & Bacon, 1982), 154, and Cheryl Harvey and Kim Morouney, "Organization Structure and Design: The Club Ed Exercise," *Journal of Management Education* (June 1985), 425–429.

Case for Analysis: C & C Grocery Stores Inc.*

The first C & C Grocery store was started in 1947 by Doug Cummins and his brother Bob. Both were veterans who wanted to run their own business, so they used their savings to start the small grocery store in Charlotte, North Carolina. The store was immediately successful. The location was good, and Doug Cummins had a winning personality. Store employees adopted Doug's informal style and "serve the customer" attitude. C & C's increasing circle of customers enjoyed an abundance of good meats and produce.

By 1997, C & C had over 200 stores. A standard physical layout was used for new stores. Company headquarters moved from Charlotte to Atlanta in 1985. The organization chart for C & C is shown in Exhibit 2.20. The central offices in Atlanta handled personnel, merchandising, financial, purchasing, real estate, and legal affairs for the entire chain. For management of individual stores, the organization was divided by regions. The southern, southeastern, and northeastern regions each had about seventy stores. Each region was divided into five districts of ten to fifteen stores each. A district director was responsible for supervision and coordination of activities for the ten to fifteen district stores.

Each district was divided into four lines of authority based on functional specialty. Three of these lines reached into the stores. The produce department manager within each store reported directly to the produce specialist for the division, and the same was true for the meat department manager, who reported directly to the district meat specialist. The meat and produce managers were responsible for all activities associated with the acquisition and sale of perishable products. The store manager's responsibility included the grocery line, front-end departments, and store operations. The store manager was responsible for appearance of personnel, cleanliness, adequate checkout service, and price accuracy. A grocery manager reported to the store manager, maintained inventories, and restocked shelves for grocery items. The district merchandising office was responsible for promotional campaigns, advertising circulars, district advertising, and attracting customers into the stores. The grocery merchandisers were expected to coordinate their activities with each store in the district.

Business for the C & C chain has dropped off in all regions in recent years—partly because of a declining economy, but mostly because of increased competition from large discount retailers such as Wal-Mart, Target, and Costco Wholesale. When these large discounters entered the grocery business, they brought a level of competition unlike any C & C had seen before. C & C had managed to hold its own against larger supermarket chains, but now even the big chains were threatened by Wal-Mart, which became no. 1 in grocery sales in 2001. C & C managers knew they couldn't compete on price, but they were considering ways they could use advanced information technology to improve service and customer satisfaction and distinguish the store from the large discounters.

However, the most pressing problem was how to improve business with the resources and stores they now had. A consulting team from a major university was hired to investigate store structure and operations.

The consultants visited several stores in each region, talking to about fifty managers and employees. The consultants wrote a report that pinpointed four problem areas to be addressed by store executives.

1. *The chain was slow to adapt to change.* Store layout and structure were the same as had been designed fifteen years ago. Each store did things the same way, even though some stores were in low-income areas and other stores in suburban areas. A new computerized supply chain management system for ordering and stocking

EXHIBIT 2.20
Organization Structure for
C & C Grocery Stores Inc.

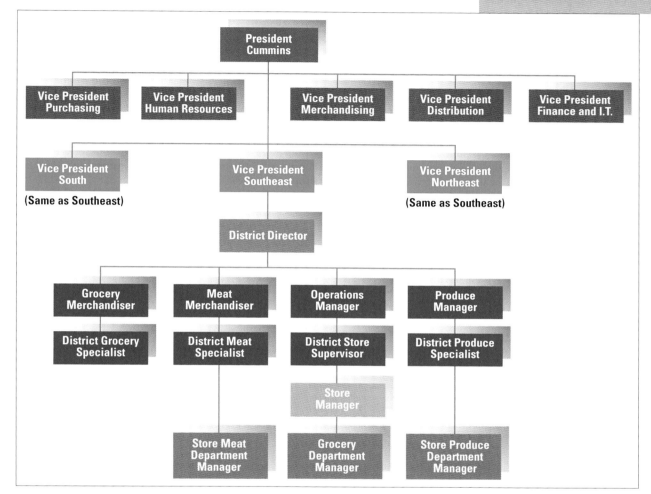

had been developed, but after two years it was only partially implemented in the stores. Other proposed information technology (IT) initiatives were still "on the back burner," not yet even in the development stage.

2. *Roles of the district store supervisor and the store manager were causing dissatisfaction.* The store managers wanted to learn general management skills for potential promotion into district or regional management positions. However, their jobs restricted them to operational activities and they learned little about merchandising, meat, and produce. Moreover, district store supervisors used store visits to inspect for cleanliness and adherence to operating standards rather than to train the store manager and help coordinate operations with perishable departments. Close supervision on the operational details had become the focus of operations management rather than development, training, and coordination.

3. *Cooperation within stores was low and morale was poor. The informal, friendly atmosphere originally created by Doug Cummins was gone.* One example of this problem occurred when the grocery merchandiser and store manager in a Louisiana store decided to promote Coke and Diet Coke as a loss leader. Thousands of cartons of Coke were brought in for the sale, but the stockroom was not prepared and did not have room. The store manager wanted to use floor area in the meat and produce sections to display Coke cartons, but those managers refused. The produce department manager said that Diet Coke did not help his sales and it was okay with him if there was no promotion at all.

4. *Long-term growth and development of the store chain would probably require reevaluation of long-term strategy.* The percent of market share going to traditional grocery stores was declining nationwide due

to competition from large superstores and discount retailers. In the near future, C & C might need to introduce nonfood items into the stores for one-stop shopping, add specialty or gourmet sections within stores, and investigate how new technology could help distinguish the company, such as through targeted marketing and promotion, providing superior service and convenience, and offering their customers the best product assortment and availability.

To solve the first three problems, the consultants recommended reorganizing the district and the store structure as illustrated in Exhibit 2.21. Under this reorganization, the meat, grocery, and produce department managers would all report to the store manager. The store manager would have complete store control and would be responsible for coordination of all store activities. The district supervisor's role would

be changed from supervision to training and development. The district supervisor would head a team that included himself and several meat, produce, and merchandise specialists who would visit area stores as a team to provide advice and help for the store managers and other employees. The team would act in a liaison capacity between district specialists and the stores.

The consultants were enthusiastic about the proposed structure. With the removal of one level of district operational supervision, store managers would have more freedom and responsibility. The district liaison team would establish a cooperative team approach to management that could be adopted within stores. Focusing store responsibility on a single manager would encourage coordination within stores and adaptation to local conditions. It would also provide a focus of responsibility for storewide administrative changes.

EXHIBIT 2.21
Proposed Reorganization
of C & C Grocery
Stores Inc.

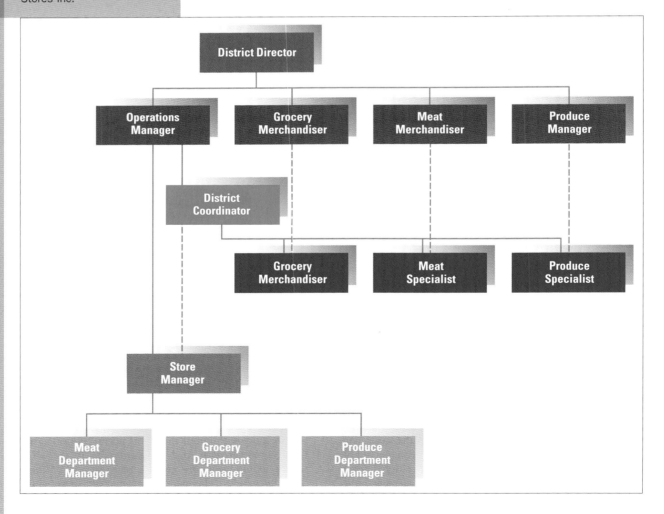

The consultants also believed that the proposed structure could be expanded to accommodate nongrocery lines and gourmet units if these were included in C & C's future plans. Within each store, a new department manager could be added for pharmacy, gourmet/specialty items, or other major departments. The district team could be expanded to include specialists in these lines, as well as an information technology coordinator to act as liaison for stores in the district.

*Prepared by Richard L. Daft, from Richard L. Daft and Richard Steers, *Organizations: A Micro/Macro Approach* (Glenview, Ill.: Scott Foresman, 1986). Reprinted with permission.

Case for Analysis: Aquarius Advertising Agency*

The Aquarius Advertising Agency is a middle-sized firm that offered two basic services to its clients: (1) customized plans for the content of an advertising campaign (for example, slogans and layouts) and (2) complete plans for media (such as radio, TV, newspapers, billboards, and Internet). Additional services included aid in marketing and distribution of products and marketing research to test advertising effectiveness.

Its activities were organized in a traditional manner. The organization chart is shown in Exhibit 2.22. Each department included similar functions.

Each client account was coordinated by an account executive who acted as a liaison between the client and the various specialists on the professional staff of the operations and marketing divisions. The number of direct communications and contacts between clients and Aquarius specialists, clients and account executives, and Aquarius specialists and account executives is indicated in Exhibit 2.23. These sociometric data were gathered by a consultant who conducted a study of the patterns of formal and informal communication. Each intersecting cell of Aquarius personnel and the clients contains an index of the direct contacts between them.

Although an account executive was designated to be the liaison between the client and specialists within the agency, communications frequently occurred directly between clients and specialists and bypassed the account executive. These direct contacts involved a wide range of interactions, such as meetings, telephone calls, e-mail messages, and so on. A large number of direct communications occurred between agency specialists and their counterparts in the client organization. For example, an art specialist working as one member of a team on a particular client account would often be contacted directly by the client's in-house art specialist, and agency research personnel had direct communication with research people of the client firm. Also, some of the unstructured contacts often led to more formal meetings with clients in which agency personnel made presentations, interpreted and defended agency policy, and committed the agency to certain courses of action.

Both hierarchical and professional systems operated within the departments of the operations and marketing divisions. Each department was organized hierarchically with a director, an assistant director, and several levels of authority. Professional communications were widespread and mainly concerned with sharing knowledge and techniques, technical evaluation of work, and development of professional interests. Control in each department was exercised mainly through control of promotions and supervision of work done by subordinates. Many account executives, however, felt the need for more influence, and one commented:

Creativity and art. That's all I hear around here. It is hard as hell to effectively manage six or seven hotshots who claim they have to do their own thing. Each of them tries to sell his or her idea to the client, and most of the time I don't know what has happened until a week later. If I were a despot, I would make all of them check with me first to get approval. Things would sure change around here.

The need for reorganization was made more acute by changes in the environment. Within a short period of time, there was a rapid turnover in the major accounts handled by the agency. It was typical for advertising agencies to gain or lose clients quickly, often with no advance warning as consumer behavior and lifestyle changes emerged and product innovations occurred.

An agency reorganization was one solution proposed by top management to increase flexibility in this unpredictable environment. The reorganization would be aimed at reducing the agency's response time to environmental changes and at increasing cooperation and communication among specialists from different departments. The top managers are not sure what type of reorganization is appropriate. They would like your help analyzing their context and current structure and welcome your advice on proposing a new structure.

*Adapted from John F. Veiga and John N. Yanouzas, "Aquarius Advertising Agency," *The Dynamics of Organization Theory* (St. Paul, Minn.: West, 1984), 212–217, with permission.

EXHIBIT 2.22
Aquarius Advertising
Agency Organization
Chart

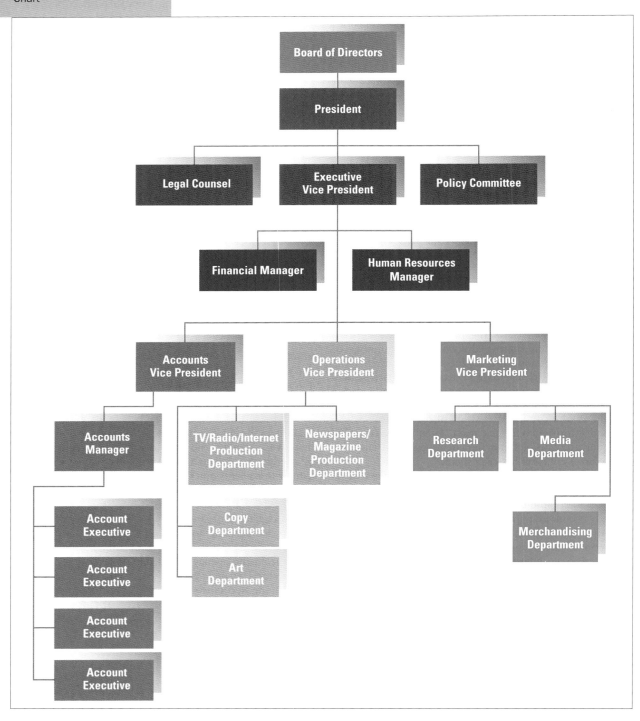

EXHIBIT 2.23
Sociometric Index of Aquarius
Personnel and Clients
F = Frequent—daily
O = Occasional—once or
twice per project
N = None

	Clients	Account Manager	Account Executives	TV/Radio Specialists	Newspaper/Magazine Specialists	Copy Specialists	Art Specialists	Merchandising Specialists	Media Specialists	Research Specialists
Clients	X	F	F	N	N	O	O	O	O	O
Account Manager		X	F	N	N	N	N	N	N	N
Account Executives			X	F	F	F	F	F	F	F
TV/Radio Specialists				X	N	O	O	N	N	O
Newspaper/Magazine Specialists					X	O	O	N	O	O
Copy Specialists						X	N	O	O	O
Art Specialists							X	O	O	O
Merchandising Specialists								X	F	F
Media Specialists									X	F
Research Specialists										X

Chapter 3

Strategy and Effectiveness

Bettina Anzeletti

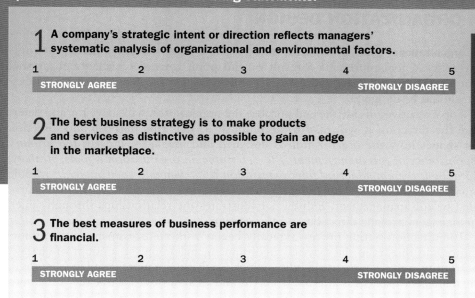

One of the primary responsibilities of managers is to position their organizations for success by establishing goals and strategies that can keep the organization competitive. Consider MySpace. It started as a social networking site, but managers' new goal is to make it a "social portal," of which networking is only a part. MySpace has plenty of users, but revenues haven't been rolling in as quickly as top executives at parent company Fox Interactive Media (owned by News Corporation) would like. To meet tough revenue goals, the company's co-founders, CEO Chris DeWolfe and President Tom Anderson, are expanding MySpace into user-generated videos, global marketing partnerships with big-name brands such as McDonald's, Harley-Davidson, and State Farm Insurance, and a joint venture with major music companies. Other goals include beefing up the company's mobile business and revamping the website to make it both easier to use and more hospitable to advertising. Yet, even as this text is being written, goals and strategic direction might be changing at MySpace. "We are a company that needs to move fast," says Anderson.[1]

Purpose of This Chapter

Top managers give direction to organizations. They set goals and develop the plans for their organization to attain them. The purpose of this chapter is to help you understand the types of goals that organizations pursue and some of the competitive strategies managers use to reach those goals. We will provide an overview of strategic management, examine two significant frameworks for determining strategic action, and look at how strategies affect organization design. The chapter also describes the most popular approaches to measuring the effectiveness of organizational efforts. To manage organizations well, managers need a clear sense of how to measure effectiveness.

THE ROLE OF STRATEGIC DIRECTION IN ORGANIZATION DESIGN

An **organizational goal** is a desired state of affairs that the organization attempts to reach.[2] A goal represents a result or end point toward which organizational efforts are directed. The choice of goals and strategy influences how the organization should be designed.

Top executives decide the end purpose the organization will strive for and determine the direction it will take to accomplish it. It is this purpose and direction that shapes how the organization is designed and managed. Indeed, *the primary responsibility of top management is to determine an organization's goals, strategy, and design, therein adapting the organization to a changing environment.*[3] Middle managers do much the same thing for major departments within the guidelines provided by top management. Exhibit 3.1 illustrates the relationships through which top managers provide direction and then design.

The direction-setting process typically begins with an assessment of the opportunities and threats in the external environment, including the amount of change, uncertainty, and resource availability, which we discuss in more detail in Chapter 6. Top managers also assess internal strengths and weaknesses to define the company's distinctive competence compared with other firms in the industry. This competitive analysis of the internal and external environments is one of the central concepts in strategic management.[4]

ASSESS YOUR ANSWER

1 A company's strategic intent or direction reflects managers' systematic analysis of organizational and environmental factors.

ANSWER: *Agree.* The best strategies come from systematic analysis of organizational strengths and weaknesses combined with analysis of opportunities and threats in the environment. Careful study combined with experience enable top managers to decide on specific goals and strategies.

The next step is to define and articulate the organization's strategic intent. This includes defining an overall mission and official goals based on the correct fit between external opportunities and internal strengths. Leaders then formulate specific operational goals and strategies that define how the organization is to accomplish its overall mission. In Exhibit 3.1, organization design reflects the way goals and strategies are implemented so that the organization's attention and resources are consistently focused toward achieving the mission and goals.

Organization design is the administration and execution of the strategic plan. Organization direction is implemented through decisions about structural form, including whether the organization will be designed for a learning or an efficiency orientation, as discussed in Chapter 1, as well as choices about information and control systems, the type of production technology, human resource policies, culture, and linkages to other organizations. Changes in structure, technology, human resource policies, culture, and interorganizational linkages will be discussed in subsequent chapters. Also note the arrow in Exhibit 3.1 running from organization design back to strategic intent. This means that strategies are often made within the

current structure of the organization, so that current design constrains, or puts limits on, goals and strategy. More often than not, however, the new goals and strategy are selected based on environmental needs, and then top management attempts to redesign the organization to achieve those ends.

Finally, Exhibit 3.1 illustrates how managers evaluate the effectiveness of organizational efforts—that is, the extent to which the organization realizes its goals. This chart reflects the most popular ways of measuring performance, each of which is discussed later in this chapter. It is important to note here that performance measurements feed back into the internal environment, so that past performance of the organization is assessed by top management in setting new goals and strategic direction for the future.

The role of top management is important because managers can interpret the environment differently and develop different goals. For example, a new CEO at Borders Group believed the book retailer was missing an opportunity by emphasizing its bricks and mortar stores while paying little attention to the online world of book retailing. When George Jones took over as CEO, he quickly saw e-commerce as "a necessary component of our business." Borders ended its alliance with Amazon.com and reopened its own branded website. This gave Borders Rewards members the chance to earn benefits online, which they weren't able to do through Amazon. Aiming to become a force in online bookselling, Borders abandoned its strategy of

EXHIBIT 3.1

Top Management Role in Organization Direction, Design, and Effectiveness

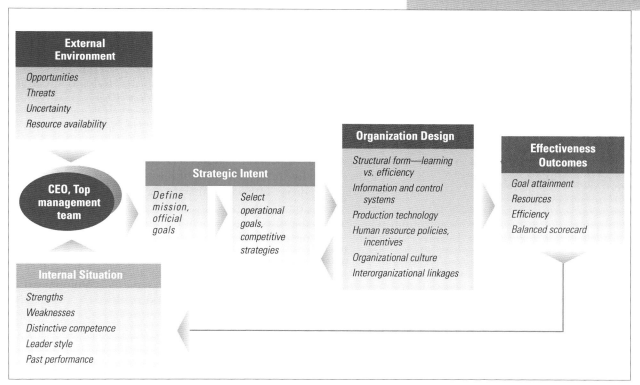

Source: Adapted from Arie Y. Lewin and Carroll U. Stephens, "Individual Properties of the CEO as Determinants of Organization Design," unpublished manuscript, Duke University, 1990; and Arie Y. Lewin and Carroll U. Stephens, "CEO Attributes as Determinants of Organization Design: An Integrated Model," *Organization Studies* 15, no. 2 (1994), 183–212.

expanding the book superstore concept, selling off most of its overseas stores and closing numerous stores in the United States.[5]

The choices top managers make about goals, strategies, and organization design have a tremendous impact on organizational effectiveness. Remember that goals and strategy are not fixed or taken for granted. Top managers and middle managers must select goals for their respective units, and the ability to make good choices largely determines firm success. Organization design is used to implement goals and strategy and also determines organization success.

ORGANIZATIONAL PURPOSE

All organizations, including MySpace, Johnson & Johnson, Google, Harvard University, the Catholic Church, the U.S. Department of Agriculture, the local laundry, and the neighborhood deli, exist for a purpose. This purpose may be referred to as the overall goal, or mission. Different parts of the organization establish their own goals and objectives to help meet the overall goal, mission, or purpose of the organization.

Strategic Intent

Many types of goals exist in organizations, and each type performs a different function. However, to achieve success, organizational goals and strategies are focused with strategic intent. **Strategic intent** means that all the organization's energies and resources are directed toward a focused, unifying, and compelling overall goal.[6] Examples of ambitious goals that demonstrate strategic intent are Komatsu's vision to "Encircle Caterpillar," Canon's to "Beat Xerox," and Coca-Cola's "To put a Coke within 'arm's reach' of every consumer in the world."[7] Strategic intent provides a focus for management action. Three aspects related to strategic intent are the mission, core competence, and competitive advantage.

Mission. The overall goal for an organization is often called the **mission**—the organization's reason for existence. The mission describes the organization's shared values and beliefs and its reason for being. The mission is sometimes called the **official goals,** which refers to the formally stated definition of business scope and outcomes the organization is trying to achieve. Official goal statements typically define business operations and may focus on values, markets, and customers that distinguish the organization. Whether called a mission statement or official goals, the organization's general statement of its purpose and philosophy is often written down in a policy manual or the annual report. The mission statement for State Farm is shown in Exhibit 3.2 Note how the overall mission, values, and vision are all defined.

One of the primary purposes of a mission statement is to serve as a communication tool.[8] The *mission statement* communicates to current and prospective employees, customers, investors, suppliers, and competitors what the organization stands for and what it is trying to achieve. A mission statement communicates legitimacy to internal and external stakeholders, who may join and be committed to the organization because they identify with its stated purpose and vision. Most top leaders want employees, customers, competitors, suppliers, investors, and the local community to look on them in a favorable light, and the concept of legitimacy plays a critical role.[9] In today's corporate world of weakened trust, increasing regulation, and concern for the natural environment, many organizations face the need to redefine their

Briefcase

As an organization manager, keep these guidelines in mind:

Establish and communicate organizational mission and goals. Communicate official goals to provide a statement of the organization's mission to external constituents. Communicate operational goals to provide internal direction, guidelines, and standards of performance for employees.

EXHIBIT 3.2
State Farm's Mission
Statement

STATE FARM INSURANCE
Our Mission, Our Vision, and Our Shared Values

State Farm's mission is to help people manage the risks of everyday life, recover from the unexpected, and realize their dreams.

We are people who make it our business to be like a good neighbor; who built a premier company by selling and keeping promises through our marketing partnerships; who bring diverse talents and experiences to our work of serving the State Farm customer.

Our success is built on a foundation of shared values—quality service and relationships, mutual trust, integrity, and financial strength.

Our vision for the future is to be the customer's first and best choice in the products and services we provide. We will continue to be the leader in the insurance industry and we will become a leader in the financial services arena. Our customers' needs will determine our path. Our values will guide us.

Source: "News and Notes from State Farm," Public Affairs Department, 2500 Memorial Boulevard, Murfreesboro, TN 37131.

mission to emphasize the firm's purpose in more than financial terms.[10] Companies where managers are sincerely guided by mission statements that focus on a larger social purpose, such as Medtronic's "To restore people to full life and health" or Liberty Mutual's "Helping people live safer, more secure lives," typically attract better employees, have better relationships with external parties, and perform better in the marketplace over the long term.[11]

Competitive Advantage. The overall aim of strategic intent is to help the organization achieve a sustainable competitive advantage. **Competitive advantage** refers to what sets the organization apart from others and provides it with a distinctive edge for meeting customer or client needs in the marketplace. Strategy necessarily changes over time to fit environmental conditions, and good managers pay close attention to trends that might require changes in how the company operates. Managers analyze competitors and the internal and external environments to find potential *competitive openings* and learn what new capabilities the organization needs to gain the upper hand against other companies in the industry.[12] Consider how managers at Walgreens are shifting their goals and strategy to maintain a competitive advantage.

For decades, Walgreens has succeeded with strategic goals of opening conveniently located stores faster than competitors and filling more prescriptions than any other drugstore chain. Recently, though, faced with the increased competitiveness of rivals and a weakened U.S. economy, the chain's managers began looking for competitive openings that could keep the company growing.

IN PRACTICE

Walgreens

Rather than just selling prescriptions, Walgreens is redefining its strategic intent to become a broad health care provider. It began by opening pharmacies in hospitals and

(continued)

assisted living facilities and by offering flu shots and other immunizations in its stores. Then, the company established Take Care Health Clinics to provide basic health services inside 136 Walgreens stores. Now, managers are moving aggressively into the health care industry by buying firms that operate health care centers at large corporations. These centers provide everything from treating simple illnesses to counseling employees on managing chronic diseases. Walgreens' managers see a tremendous opportunity. "In the U.S., there are more than 7,600 office sites with 1,000 or more employees that could support a health-care center," CEO Jeffrey Rein said.

Rein envisions Walgreens bringing together its various operations—basic prescription services, in-store clinics, specialty pharmaceuticals, and workplace health care centers—using electronic prescriptions and medical records, so that the company will meet a broad range of customers' health care needs.[13] ∎

Strong customer service and top-notch pharmacist knowledge have always been key strengths for Walgreens. Now these competencies are being applied on a broader scale as the company moves into the larger health care industry. As at Walgreens, managers strive to develop strategies that focus on their core competencies in order to attain a competitive advantage.

Core Competence. A company's **core competence** is something the organization does especially well in comparison to its competitors. A core competence may be in the area of superior research and development, expert technological know-how, process efficiency, or exceptional customer service.[14] At VF, a large apparel company that owns Vanity Fair, Nautica, Wrangler, and The North Face, strategy focuses on the company's core competencies of operational efficiency and merchandising know-how. When VF bought The North Face, for example, its distribution systems were so poor that stores were getting ski apparel at the end of winter and camping gear at the end of summer. The company's operating profit margin was minus 35 percent. Managers at VF revamped The North Face's sourcing, distribution, and financial systems and within five years doubled sales to $500 million and improved profit margins to a healthy 13 percent.[15] Gaylord Hotels, which has large hotel and conference centers in several states as well as the Opryland complex near Nashville, Tennessee, thrives based on a core competence of providing exceptional service for large group meetings.[16] Robinson Helicopter succeeds through superior technological know-how for building small, two-seater helicopters used for everything from police patrols in Los Angeles to herding cattle in Australia.[17] In each case, leaders identified what their company does especially well and built the strategy around it.

Operative Goals

The organization's mission and overall goals provide a basis for developing more specific operative goals. **Operative goals** designate the ends sought through the actual operating procedures of the organization and explain what the organization is actually trying to do.[18] Operative goals describe specific measurable outcomes and are often concerned with the short run. Operative goals typically pertain to the primary tasks an organization must perform.[19] Specific goals for each primary task provide direction for the day-to-day decisions and activities within departments. Typical operative goals include performance goals, resource goals, market goals, employee development goals, productivity goals, and goals for innovation and change.

Overall Performance. Profitability reflects the overall performance of for-profit organizations. Profitability may be expressed in terms of net income, earnings per share, or return on investment. Other overall performance goals are growth and output volume. Growth pertains to increases in sales or profits over time. Volume pertains to total sales or the amount of products or services delivered. For example, Jelly Belly Candy Company, which practically created the market for gourmet jelly beans, has a goal of increasing sales by 25 percent to $200 million by 2010. Related goals include introducing new lines of candies as well as getting Jelly Belly beans into more retail outlets.[20]

Government and nonprofit organizations such as social service agencies or labor unions do not have goals of profitability, but they do have goals that attempt to specify the delivery of services to clients or members within specified expense levels. The Internal Revenue Service has a goal of providing accurate responses to 85 percent of taxpayer questions about new tax laws. Growth and volume goals also may be indicators of overall performance in nonprofit organizations. Expanding their services to new clients is a primary goal for many social service agencies, for example.

Resources. Resource goals pertain to the acquisition of needed material and financial resources from the environment. They may involve obtaining financing for the construction of new plants, finding less expensive sources for raw materials, or hiring top-quality technology graduates. Resource goals for Stanford University include attracting top-notch professors and students. Auto manufacturers such as Honda Motor Company and Toyota Motor Corporation have resource goals of obtaining high-quality auto parts at low cost. For nonprofit organizations, resource goals might include recruiting dedicated volunteers and expanding the organization's funding base.

Market. Market goals relate to the market share or market standing desired by the organization. Market goals are largely the responsibility of marketing, sales, and advertising departments. In the toy industry, Canada's Mega Bloks Inc. achieved its market goal of doubling its share of the toy building block market to 30 percent. The giant of the industry, Denmark's LEGO Group, is reevaluating strategies to try to regain the market share it has lost.[21] Market goals can also apply to nonprofit organizations. Cincinnati Children's Hospital Medical Center, not content with a limited regional role in health care, has gained a growing share of the national market by developing expertise in the niche of treating rare and complex conditions and relentlessly focusing on quality.[22]

Employee Development. Employee development pertains to the training, promotion, safety, and growth of employees. It includes both managers and workers. Strong employee development goals are one of the characteristics common to organizations that regularly show up on *Fortune* magazine's list of "100 Best Companies to Work For." For example, family-owned Wegmans Food Markets, which has appeared on the list every year since its inception and was voted the nation's top supermarket chain by the Food Network in 2007, has a motto of "Employees First, Customers Second," reflecting the company's emphasis on employee development goals.[23]

Productivity. Productivity goals concern the amount of output achieved from available resources. They typically describe the amount of resource inputs required to

reach desired outputs and are thus stated in terms of "cost for a unit of production," "units produced per employee," or "resource cost per employee." Managers at Akamai Technologies, which sells Web content delivery services, keep a close eye on sales per employee to see if the company is meeting productivity goals. Akamai's chief financial officer, Timothy Weller, sees this statistic as "the single easiest measure of employee productivity.[24]

Innovation and Change. Innovation goals pertain to internal flexibility and readiness to adapt to unexpected changes in the environment. Innovation goals are often defined with respect to the development of specific new services, products, or production processes. Procter & Gamble is taking a new approach to innovation that brings in ideas from outside entrepreneurs and researchers. Managers set a goal of getting 50 percent of the company's innovation from outside the organization by 2010, up from about 35 percent in 2004 and only 10 percent in 2000.[25]

Successful organizations use a carefully balanced set of operative goals. Although profitability goals are important, some of today's best companies recognize that a single-minded focus on bottom-line profits may not be the best way to achieve high performance. Innovation and change goals are increasingly important, even though they may initially cause a *decrease* in profits. Employee development goals are critical for helping to maintain a motivated, committed workforce.

The Importance of Goals

Both official goals and operative goals are important for the organization, but they serve very different purposes. Official goals and mission statements describe a value system for the organization and set an overall purpose and vision; operative goals represent the primary tasks of the organization. Official goals legitimize the organization; operative goals are more explicit and well defined.

Operative goals serve several specific purposes, as outlined in Exhibit 3.3. For one thing, goals provide employees with a sense of direction, so that they know what they are working toward. This can help to motivate employees toward specific targets and important outcomes. Numerous studies have shown that specific high goals can significantly increase employee performance.[26] People like having a focus for their activities and efforts. Consider Guitar Center, a fast-growing retailer in the United States. Managers establish specific goals for sales teams at every Guitar Center store each morning, and employees do whatever they need to, short of losing the company money, to meet the targets. Guitar Center's unwritten mantra of "Take the deal" means that salespeople are trained to take any profitable deal, even at razor-thin margins, to meet daily sales goals.[27]

EXHIBIT 3.3
Goal Type and Purpose

Type of Goals	Purpose of Goals
Official goals, mission:	Legitimacy
Operative goals:	Employee direction and motivation
	Decision guidelines
	Standard of performance

Another important purpose of goals is to act as guidelines for employee behavior and decision making. Appropriate goals can act as a set of constraints on individual behavior and actions so that employees behave within boundaries that are acceptable to the organization and larger society.[28] They help to define the appropriate decisions concerning organization structure, innovation, employee welfare, or growth. Finally, goals provide a standard for assessment. The level of organizational performance, whether in terms of profits, units produced, degree of employee satisfaction, level of innovation, or number of customer complaints, needs a basis for evaluation. Operative goals provide this standard for measurement.

A FRAMEWORK FOR SELECTING STRATEGY AND DESIGN

To support and accomplish the organization's strategic intent and keep people focused in the direction determined by organizational mission, vision, and operative goals, managers have to select specific strategy and design options that can help the organization achieve its purpose and goals within its competitive environment. In this section, we examine a couple of practical approaches to selecting strategy and design. The questionnaire in this chapter's "How Do You Fit the Design?" box on page 110 will give you some insight into your own strategic management competencies.

A **strategy** is a plan for interacting with the competitive environment to achieve organizational goals. Some managers think of goals and strategies as interchangeable, but for our purposes, *goals* define where the organization wants to go and *strategies* define how it will get there. For example, a goal might be to achieve 15 percent annual sales growth; strategies to reach that goal might include aggressive advertising to attract new customers, motivating salespeople to increase the average size of customer purchases, and acquiring other businesses that produce similar products. Strategies can include any number of techniques to achieve the goal. The essence of formulating strategies is choosing whether the organization will perform different activities than its competitors or will execute similar activities more efficiently than its competitors do.[29]

Two models for formulating strategies are the Porter model of competitive strategies and Miles and Snow's strategy typology. Each provides a framework for competitive action. After describing the two models, we will discuss how the choice of strategies affects organization design.

Porter's Competitive Forces and Strategies

One popular and effective model for formulating strategy is Porter's competitive forces and strategies. Michael E. Porter studied a number of business organizations and proposed that managers can formulate a strategy that makes the organization more profitable and less vulnerable if they understand five forces in the industry environment.[30] Porter found the following forces determine a company's position vis-à-vis competitors in the industry:

- *The Threat of New Entrants*. The threat of new entrants to an industry can create pressure for established organizations, which might need to hold down prices or increase their level of investment. For example, when managers at Nike

Briefcase

As an organization manager, keep these guidelines in mind:

After goals have been defined, select strategies for achieving those goals. Define specific strategies based on Porter's competitive strategies or Miles and Snow's strategy typology.

learned that fast-growing athletic apparel company Under Armour planned to get into the business of selling athletic footwear, they quickly invested in reviving their company's long-dead cross-training category by designing the new SPARQ trainer.[31]

How Do You Fit the Design?

Your Strategy/Performance Strength

As a potential manager, what are your strengths concerning strategy formulation and implementation? To find out, think about *how you handle challenges and issues* in your school work or job. Then circle *a* or *b* for each of the following items depending on which is more descriptive of your behavior. There are no right or wrong answers. Respond to each item as it best describes how you respond to work situations.

1. When keeping records, I tend to
   a. be very careful about documentation.
   b. be more haphazard about documentation.

2. If I run a group or a project, I
   a. have the general idea and let others figure out how to do the tasks.
   b. try to figure out specific goals, time lines, and expected outcomes.

3. My thinking style could be more accurately described as
   a. linear thinker, going from A to B to C.
   b. thinking like a grasshopper, hopping from one idea to another.

4. In my office or home things are
   a. here and there in various piles.
   b. laid out neatly or at least in reasonable order.

5. I take pride in developing
   a. ways to overcome a barrier to a solution.
   b. new hypotheses about the underlying cause of a problem.

6. I can best help strategy by making sure there is
   a. openness to a wide range of assumptions and ideas.
   b. thoroughness when implementing new ideas.

7. One of my strengths is
   a. commitment to making things work.
   b. commitment to a dream for the future.

8. I am most effective when I emphasize
   a. inventing original solutions.
   b. making practical improvements.

Scoring: For *Strategic Formulator* strength, score one point for each "*a*" answer circled for questions 2, 4, 6, and 8, and for each "*b*" answer circled for questions 1, 3, 5, and 7. For *Strategic Implementer* strength, score one point for each "*b*" answer circled for questions 2, 4, 6, and 8, and for each "*a*" answer circled for questions 1, 3, 5, and 7. Which of your two scores is higher and by how much? The higher score indicates your *Strategy Strength.*

Interpretation: Formulator and Implementer are two important ways managers bring value to strategic management and effectiveness. Managers with implementer strengths tend to work on operative goals and performance to make things more efficient and reliable. Managers with the formulator strength push toward out-of-the-box strategies and like to think about mission, vision, and dramatic breakthroughs. Both styles are essential to strategic management and organizational effectiveness. Strategic formulators often use their skills to create whole new strategies and approaches, and strategic implementers often work with strategic improvements, implementation, and measurement.

If the difference between your two scores is two or less, you have a balanced formulator/implementer style and work well in both arenas. If the difference is 4–5, you have a moderately strong style and probably work best in the area of your strength. And if the difference is 7–8, you have a distinctive strength and almost certainly would want to contribute in the area of your strength rather than in the opposite domain.

Source: Adapted from Dorothy Marcic and Joe Seltzer, *Organizational Behavior: Experiences and Cases* (South-Western, 1998), 284–287, and William Miller, *Innovation Styles* (Global Creativity Corporation, 1997).

The threat of entry in an industry depends largely on the amount and extent of potential barriers, such as cost. It is far more costly to enter the auto manufacturing industry, for instance, than to start a specialty coffee shop.

- *The Power of Suppliers.* Large, powerful suppliers can charge higher prices, limit services or quality, and shift costs to their customers, keeping more of the value for themselves. The concentration of suppliers and the availability of substitute suppliers are significant factors in determining supplier power. The sole supplier of materials or information to a company will have great power, for example. The Nielsen Company has wielded tremendous power with television networks because it has until recently been the sole source of ratings data that network executives use to make advertising and programming decisions. Nielsen's power has recently waned due to quality control problems, as well as the threat presented by TiVo, a provider of digital video recorders, which has begun offering its own detailed audience and ratings data to the networks.[32]
- *The Power of Buyers.* Powerful customers, the flip side of powerful suppliers, can force down prices, demand better quality or service, and drive up costs for the supplying organization. Wal-Mart, for example, is so powerful that it can easily put the screws to manufacturers who supply goods for sale at its stores.
- *The Threat of Substitutes.* The power of alternatives and substitutes for a company's product or service may be affected by changes in cost, new technologies, social trends that will deflect buyer loyalty, and other environmental changes. Large pharmaceutical companies are under intense pressure from generic competition as patents on numerous popular drugs have expired in recent years.[33] Providers of conventional long-distance telephone services have suffered from the introduction of inexpensive Internet-based phone services.
- *Rivalry among Existing Competitors.* Rivalry among competitors is influenced by the preceding four forces, as well as by cost and product differentiation. Porter has referred to the "advertising slugfest" when describing the scrambling and jockeying for position that occurs among fierce rivals within an industry. The rivalry between Coke and Pepsi is a famous example. Recently, Coke scored big with its sponsorship of the Beijing Olympics, but Pepsi's creative marketing had many Chinese consumers thinking it was an official sponsor too.[34]

In finding its competitive edge within these five forces, Porter suggests that a company can adopt one of three strategies: differentiation, low-cost leadership, or focus.[35] The focus strategy, in which the organization concentrates on a specific market or buyer group, is further divided into *focused low cost* and *focused differentiation*. This yields four basic strategies, as illustrated in Exhibit 3.4. To use this model, managers evaluate two factors, competitive advantage and competitive scope. With respect to advantage, managers determine whether to compete through lower costs or through the ability to offer unique or distinctive products and services that can command a premium price. Managers then determine whether the organization will compete on a broad scope (competing in many customer segments) or a narrow scope (competing in a selected customer segment or group of segments). These choices determine the selection of strategies, as illustrated in Exhibit 3.4.

Differentiation. In a **differentiation strategy,** organizations attempt to distinguish their products or services from others in the industry. An organization may use advertising, distinctive product features, exceptional service, or new technology to achieve a product perceived as unique. This strategy usually targets customers who are not particularly concerned with price, so it can be quite profitable.

EXHIBIT 3.4
Porter's Competitive
Strategies

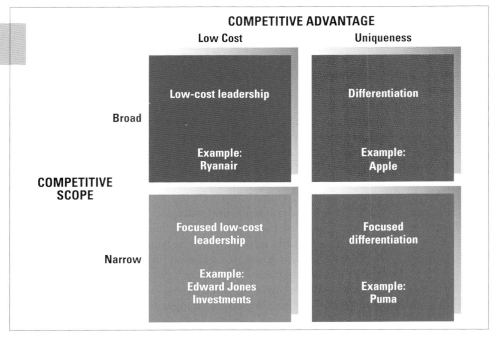

COMPETITIVE ADVANTAGE

	Low Cost	Uniqueness
Broad	Low-cost leadership Example: Ryanair	Differentiation Example: Apple
Narrow	Focused low-cost leadership Example: Edward Jones Investments	Focused differentiation Example: Puma

COMPETITIVE SCOPE

Source: Adapted with the permission of The Free Press, a Division of Simon & Schuster Adult Publishing Group, from *Competitive Advantage: Creating and Sustaining Superior Performance* by Michael E. Porter. Copyright © 1985, 1988 by Michael E. Porter.

A differentiation strategy can reduce rivalry with competitors and fight off the threat of substitute products because customers are loyal to the company's brand. However, companies must remember that successful differentiation strategies require a number of costly activities, such as product research and design and extensive advertising. Companies that pursue a differentiation strategy need strong marketing abilities and creative employees who are given the time and resources to seek innovations. One good illustration of a company that benefits from a differentiation strategy is Apple. Apple has never tried to compete on price and likes being perceived as an "elite" brand. Its personal computers, for example, can command significantly higher prices than other PCs because of their distinctiveness. The company has built a loyal customer base by providing innovative, stylish products and creating a prestigious image. Consider the launch of the iPhone.

IN PRACTICE

Apple

Sure, you can buy a cell phone for next to nothing these days. But when Apple launched the iPhone at a price of more than $599, long lines of shoppers were eager to buy them. Everyone who was anyone had to have an iPhone.

That's a bit of an exaggeration, of course, but demand for the pricey phone was strong even before Apple cut the price to expand sales to a wider group of consumers. Referred to as "perhaps the most-hyped gadget in history," the iPhone quickly became a status symbol. The less-expensive, faster iPhone 3G experienced even stronger demand when it was released in mid-2008. AT&T sold 2.4 million iPhones in the third quarter of that year.

Although Apple is still a small player in the broader cell phone market, the innovative technology of the iPhone, combined with creative marketing and the cachet of Apple, convinced many consumers that they needed a phone that gives them easy access to the Internet, digital music and video, and mobile social networks. So-called "smartphones" have been used for years by business professionals, with Research in Motion's BlackBerry being the leader. But it took Apple to build a strong consumer market for them.

Apple is now aiming directly at the BlackBerry, opening the door to third-party software applications that can make the iPhone more compatible with the needs of business users. The BlackBerry has a huge head start in this market, but as one IT professional said, "The iPhone is the coolest thing you'll touch."[36] ■

Service firms can use a differentiation strategy as well. Umpqua Bank, based in Portland, Oregon, for instance, wants to become a "lifestyle brand," rather than just a financial institution. Many branches have free wi-fi access, spacious seating areas with big-screen televisions, and Umpqua branded coffee. The company recently released its first CD—not a "certificate of deposit," but the kind with music on it. The bank worked with music marketing firm Rumblefish to put together a collection of songs by new or undiscovered artists in the markets where Umpqua operates. Over the past dozen or so years, Umpqua's differentiation strategy has helped it grow from about $150 million in deposits to more than $7 billion.[37]

Low-Cost Leadership. The **low-cost leadership strategy** tries to increase market share by keeping costs low compared to competitors. With a low-cost leadership strategy, the organization aggressively seeks efficient facilities, pursues cost reductions, and uses tight controls to produce products or services more efficiently than its competitors. Low-cost doesn't necessarily mean low-price, but in many cases, low-cost leaders provide goods and services to customers at cheaper prices. For example, the CEO of Irish airline Ryanair said of the company's strategy: "It's the oldest, simplest formula: Pile 'em high and sell 'em cheap... We want to be the Wal-Mart of the airline business. Nobody will beat us on price. EVER." Ryanair can offer low fares because it keeps costs at rock bottom, lower than anyone else in Europe. The company's watchword is cheap tickets, not customer care or unique services.[38]

The low-cost leadership strategy is concerned primarily with stability rather than taking risks or seeking new opportunities for innovation and growth. A low-cost position means a company can achieve higher profits than competitors because of its efficiency and lower operating costs. Low-cost leaders such as Ryanair or Wal-Mart can undercut competitors' prices and still earn a reasonable profit. In addition, if substitute products or potential new competitors enter the picture, the low-cost producer is in a better position to prevent loss of market share.

2 **The best business strategy is to make products and services as distinctive as possible to gain an edge in the marketplace.**

ANSWER: *Disagree.* Differentiation, making the company's products or services distinctive from others in the market, is one effective strategic approach. A low-cost leadership approach can be equally or even more effective depending on the organization's strengths and the nature of competition in the industry.

ASSESS YOUR ANSWER

Focus. With Porter's third strategy, the **focus strategy,** the organization concentrates on a specific regional market or buyer group. The company will try to achieve either a low-cost advantage or a differentiation advantage within a narrowly defined market. One good example of a focused low-cost strategy is Edward Jones, a St. Louis–based brokerage house. The firm has succeeded by building its business in rural and small-town America and providing investors with conservative, long-term investments.[39] An example of a focused differentiation strategy is Puma, the German athletic-wear manufacturer. In the mid-1990s, Puma was on the brink of bankruptcy. CEO Jochen Zeitz, then only 30 years old, revived the brand by targeting selected customer groups, especially armchair athletes, and creating stylish shoes and clothes that are setting design trends. Puma is "going out of its way to be different," says analyst Roland Könen.[40]

Porter found that companies that did not consciously adopt a low-cost, differentiation, or focus strategy achieved below-average profits compared to those that used one of the three strategies. Many Internet companies have failed because managers did not develop competitive strategies that would distinguish them in the marketplace.[41] On the other hand, Google became highly successful with a coherent differentiation strategy that distinguished it from other search engines. The ability of managers to devise and maintain a clear competitive strategy is considered one of the defining factors in an organization's success. However, in today's tumultuous environment, some scholars and consultants emphasize that managers also need to maintain flexibility in their strategic thinking.

Miles and Snow's Strategy Typology

Another strategy typology was developed from the study of business strategies by Raymond Miles and Charles Snow.[42] The Miles and Snow typology is based on the idea that managers seek to formulate strategies that will be congruent with the external environment. Organizations strive for a fit among internal organization characteristics, strategy, and the external environment. The four strategies that can be developed are the prospector, the defender, the analyzer, and the reactor.

Prospector. The **prospector** strategy is to innovate, take risks, seek out new opportunities, and grow. This strategy is suited to a dynamic, growing environment, where creativity is more important than efficiency. Nike, which innovates in both products and internal processes, exemplifies the prospector strategy. Nike's new Air Jordan XX3, for example, is the first in a program of shoes based on designs that can be produced using recycled materials and limited amounts of toxic chemical-based glues. CEO Mark Parker says Nike's growth strategy is based on both outward expansion and inward redesign of operations.[43] Online companies such as Facebook, Google, and MySpace also reflect a prospector strategy.

Defender. The **defender** strategy is almost the opposite of the prospector. Rather than taking risks and seeking out new opportunities, the defender strategy is concerned with stability or even retrenchment. This strategy seeks to hold on to current customers, but it neither innovates nor seeks to grow. The defender is concerned primarily with internal efficiency and control to produce reliable, high-quality products for steady customers. This strategy can be successful when the organization exists in a declining industry or a stable environment. Paramount Pictures has been using a defender strategy for several years.[44] Paramount turns out a steady stream of reliable hits but few blockbusters. Managers shun risk and sometimes turn down potentially

high-profile films to keep a lid on costs. This has enabled the company to remain highly profitable while other studios have low returns or actually lose money.

Analyzer. The **analyzer** tries to maintain a stable business while innovating on the periphery. It seems to lie midway between the prospector and the defender. Some products will be targeted toward stable environments in which an efficiency strategy designed to keep current customers is used. Others will be targeted toward new, more dynamic environments, where growth is possible. The analyzer attempts to balance efficient production for current product or service lines with the creative development of new product lines. Amazon.com provides an example. The company's current strategy is to defend its core business of selling books and other physical goods over the Internet, but also to build a business in digital media, including initiatives such as a digital book service, an online DVD rental business, and a digital music store to compete with Apple's iTunes.[45]

Reactor. The **reactor** strategy is not really a strategy at all. Rather, reactors respond to environmental threats and opportunities in an ad hoc fashion. In a reactor strategy, top management has not defined a long-range plan or given the organization an explicit mission or goal, so the organization takes whatever actions seem to meet immediate needs. Although the reactor strategy can sometimes be successful, it can also lead to failed companies. Some large, once highly successful companies are struggling because managers failed to adopt a strategy consistent with consumer trends. In recent years, managers at Dell, long one of the most successful and profitable makers of personal computers in the world, have been floundering to find the appropriate strategy. Dell had a string of disappointing quarterly profits as the company reached the limits of its "make PCs cheap and build them to order" strategy. Competitors caught up, and Dell had failed to identify new strategic directions that could provide a new edge.[46]

The Miles and Snow typology has been widely used, and researchers have tested its validity in a variety of organizations, including hospitals, colleges, banking institutions, industrial products companies, and life insurance firms. In general, researchers have found strong support for the effectiveness of this typology for organization managers in real-world situations.[47]

How Strategies Affect Organization Design

Choice of strategy affects internal organization characteristics. Organization design characteristics need to support the firm's competitive approach. For example, a company wanting to grow and invent new products looks and "feels" different from a company that is focused on maintaining market share for long-established products in a stable industry. Exhibit 3.5 summarizes organization design characteristics associated with the Porter and Miles and Snow strategies.

With a low-cost leadership strategy, managers take an efficiency approach to organization design, whereas a differentiation strategy calls for a learning approach. Recall from Chapter 1 that organizations designed for efficiency have different characteristics from those designed for learning. A low-cost leadership strategy (efficiency) is associated with strong, centralized authority and tight control, standard operating procedures, and emphasis on efficient procurement and distribution systems. Employees generally perform routine tasks under close supervision and control and are not empowered to make decisions or take action on their own.

Briefcase

As an organization manager, keep these guidelines in mind:

Design the organization to support the firm's competitive strategy. With a low-cost leadership or defender strategy, select design characteristics associated with an efficiency orientation. For a differentiation or prospector strategy, on the other hand, choose characteristics that encourage learning, innovation, and adaptation. Use a balanced mixture of characteristics for an analyzer strategy.

EXHIBIT 3.5
Organization Design
Outcomes of Strategy

Porter's Competitive Strategies	Miles and Snow's Strategy Typology
Strategy: Differentiation **Organization Design:** • Learning orientation; acts in a flexible, loosely knit way, with strong horizontal coordination • Strong capability in research • Values and builds in mechanisms for customer intimacy • Rewards employee creativity, risk taking, and innovation	**Strategy:** Prospector **Organization Design:** • Learning orientation; flexible, fluid, decentralized structure • Strong capability in research
Strategy: Low-Cost Leadership **Organization Design:.** • Efficiency orientation; strong central authority; tight cost control, with frequent, detailed control reports • Standard operating procedures • Highly efficient procurement and distribution systems • Close supervision; routine tasks; limited employee empowerment	**Strategy:** Defender **Organization Des.ign:** • Efficiency orientation; centralized authority and tight cost control • Emphasis on production efficiency; low overhead • Close supervision; little employee empowerment
	Strategy: Analyzer **Organization Design:** • Balances efficiency and learning; tight cost control with flexibility and adaptability • Efficient production for stable product lines; emphasis on creativity, research, risk-taking for innovation
	Strategy: Reactor **Organization Design:** • No clear organizational approach; design characteristics may shift abruptly, depending on current needs

Source: Based on Michael E. Porter, *Competitive Strategy: Techniques for Analyzing Industries and Competitors* (New York: The Free Press, 1980); Michael Treacy and Fred Wiersema, "How Market Leaders Keep Their Edge," *Fortune* (February 6, 1995), 88–98; Michael Hitt, R. Duane Ireland, and Robert E. Hoskisson, *Strategic Management* (St. Paul, Minn.: West, 1995), 100–113; and Raymond E. Miles, Charles C. Snow, Alan D. Meyer, and Henry J. Coleman, Jr., "Organizational Strategy, Structure, and Process," *Academy of Management Review* 3 (1978), 546–562.

A differentiation strategy, on the other hand, requires that employees be constantly experimenting and learning. Structure is fluid and flexible, with strong horizontal coordination. Empowered employees work directly with customers and are rewarded for creativity and risk taking. The organization values research, creativity, and innovativeness over efficiency and standard procedures.

The prospector strategy requires characteristics similar to a differentiation strategy, and the defender strategy takes an efficiency approach similar to low-cost leadership. Because the analyzer strategy attempts to balance efficiency for stable product lines with flexibility and learning for new products, it is associated with a mix of characteristics, as listed in Exhibit 3.5. With a reactor strategy, managers have left the organization with no direction and no clear approach to design.

Other Factors Affecting Organization Design

Strategy is one important factor that affects organization design. Ultimately, however, organization design is a result of numerous contingencies, which will be discussed throughout this book. The emphasis given to efficiency and control versus learning and flexibility is determined by the contingencies of strategy, environment, size and life cycle, technology, and organizational culture. The organization is designed to "fit" the contingency factors, as illustrated in Exhibit 3.6.

For example, in a stable environment, the organization can have a traditional structure that emphasizes vertical control, efficiency, specialization, standard procedures, and centralized decision making. However, a rapidly changing environment may call for a more flexible structure, with strong horizontal coordination and collaboration through teams or other mechanisms. Environment will be discussed in detail in Chapters 4 and 6. In terms of size and life cycle, young, small organizations are generally informal and have little division of labor, few rules and regulations, and ad hoc budgeting and performance systems. Large organizations such as Coca-Cola, Sony, or General Electric, on the other hand, have an extensive division of labor, numerous rules and regulations, and standard procedures and systems for budgeting, control, rewards, and innovation. Size and stages of the life cycle will be discussed in Chapter 12.

Design must also fit the workflow technology of the organization. For example, with mass production technology, such as a traditional automobile assembly line, the organization functions best by emphasizing efficiency, formalization, specialization, centralized decision making, and tight control. An e-business, on the other hand, would need to be more informal and flexible. Technology's impact on design will be discussed in detail in Chapters 11 and 13. A final contingency that affects organization design is corporate culture. An organizational culture that values teamwork, collaboration, creativity, and open communication, for example, would not function well with a tight, vertical structure and strict rules and regulations. The role of culture is discussed in Chapter 9.

One responsibility of managers is to design organizations that fit the contingency factors of strategy, environment, size and life cycle, technology, and culture.

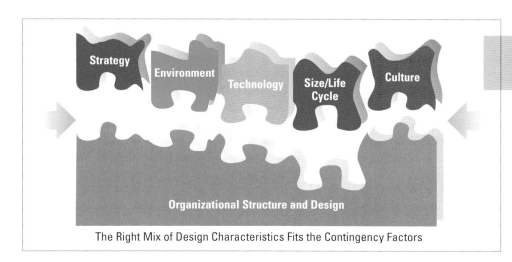

The Right Mix of Design Characteristics Fits the Contingency Factors

EXHIBIT 3.6
Contingency Factors
Affecting Organization
Design

Finding the right fit leads to organizational effectiveness, whereas a poor fit can lead to decline or even the demise of the organization.

ASSESSING ORGANIZATIONAL EFFECTIVENESS

Understanding organizational goals and strategies, as well as the concept of fitting design to various contingencies, is a first step toward understanding organizational effectiveness. Organizational goals represent the reason for an organization's existence and the outcomes it seeks to achieve. The next few sections of the chapter explore the topic of effectiveness and how effectiveness is measured in organizations.

Recall from Chapter 1 that organizational effectiveness is the degree to which an organization realizes its goals.[48] *Effectiveness* is a broad concept. It implicitly takes into consideration a range of variables at both the organizational and departmental levels. Effectiveness evaluates the extent to which multiple goals—whether official or operative—are attained.

Efficiency is a more limited concept that pertains to the internal workings of the organization. Organizational efficiency is the amount of resources used to produce a unit of output.[49] It can be measured as the ratio of inputs to outputs. If one organization can achieve a given production level with fewer resources than another organization, it would be described as more efficient.[50]

Sometimes efficiency leads to effectiveness, but in other organizations, efficiency and effectiveness are not related. An organization may be highly efficient but fail to achieve its goals because it makes a product for which there is no demand. Likewise, an organization may achieve its profit goals but be inefficient. Efforts to increase efficiency, particularly through severe cost cutting, can also sometimes make the organization less effective. One regional fast food chain wanting to cut costs decided to reduce food waste by not cooking any food until it was ordered. The move reduced the chain's costs, but it also led to delayed service, irritated customers, and lower sales.[51]

Overall effectiveness is difficult to measure in organizations. Organizations are large, diverse, and fragmented. They perform many activities simultaneously, pursue multiple goals, and generate many outcomes, some intended and some unintended.[52] Managers determine what indicators to measure in order to gauge the effectiveness of their organizations. Studies and surveys have found that many managers have a difficult time with the concept of evaluating effectiveness based on characteristics that are not subject to hard, quantitative measurement.[53] However, top executives at some of today's leading companies are finding new ways to measure effectiveness, including the use of such "soft" indications as customer loyalty and employee engagement.

First, we will discuss several traditional approaches to measuring effectiveness that focus on which indicators managers consider most important to track. Later, we will examine an approach that integrates concern for various parts of the organization.

TRADITIONAL EFFECTIVENESS APPROACHES

Organizations bring resources in from the environment, and those resources are transformed into outputs delivered back into the environment, as shown in Exhibit 3.7 Traditional approaches to measuring effectiveness look at different

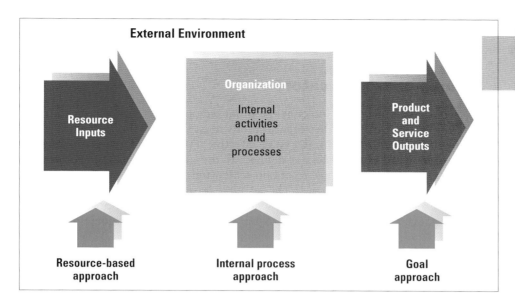

EXHIBIT 3.7
Traditional Approaches to
Measuring Organizational
Effectiveness

parts of the organization and measure indicators connected with outputs, inputs, or internal activities.

Goal Indicators

The **goal approach** to effectiveness consists of identifying an organization's output goals and assessing how well the organization has attained those goals.[54] This is a logical approach because organizations do try to attain certain levels of output, profit, or client satisfaction. The goal approach measures progress toward attainment of those goals. For example, an important measure for the Women's National Basketball Association is number of tickets sold per game. During the league's first season, President Val Ackerman set a goal of 4,000 to 5,000 tickets per game. The organization actually averaged nearly 9,700 tickets per game, indicating that the WNBA was highly effective in meeting its goal for attendance.[55]

The important goals to consider are operative goals, because official goals (mission) tend to be abstract and difficult to measure.[56] Indicators tracked with the goal approach include:

- Profitability—the positive gain from business operations or investments after expenses are subtracted
- Market share—the proportion of the market the firm is able to capture relative to competitors
- Growth—the ability of the organization to increase its sales, profits, or client base over time
- Social responsibility—how well the organization serves the interests of society as well as itself

- Product quality—the ability of the organization to achieve high quality in its products or services

Resource-based Indicators

The **resource-based approach** looks at the input side of the transformation process shown in Exhibit 3.7. It assumes organizations must be successful in obtaining and managing valued resources in order to be effective. From a resource-based perspective, organizational effectiveness is defined as the ability of the organization, in either absolute or relative terms, to obtain scarce and valued resources and successfully integrate and manage them.[57] The resource-based approach is valuable when other indicators of performance are difficult to obtain. In many nonprofit and social welfare organizations, for example, it is hard to measure output goals or internal efficiency.

In a broad sense, resource indicators of effectiveness encompass the following dimensions:

- Bargaining position—the ability of the organization to obtain from its environment scarce and valued resources, including financial resources, raw materials, human resources, knowledge, and technology
- The abilities of the organization's decision makers to perceive and correctly interpret the real properties of the external environment
- The abilities of managers to use tangible (e.g., supplies, people) and intangible (e.g., knowledge, corporate culture) resources in day-to-day organizational activities to achieve superior performance
- The ability of the organization to respond to changes in the environment

Internal Process Indicators

In the **internal process approach,** effectiveness is measured as internal organizational health and efficiency. An effective organization has a smooth, well-oiled internal process. Employees are happy and satisfied. Department activities mesh with one another to ensure high productivity. This approach does not consider the external environment. The important element in effectiveness is what the organization does with the resources it has, as reflected in internal health and efficiency. The best-known proponents of an internal process model are from the human relations approach to organizations. Such writers as Chris Argyris, Warren G. Bennis, Rensis Likert, and Richard Beckhard have all worked extensively with human resources in organizations and emphasize the connection between human resources and effectiveness.[58] Results from a study of nearly 200 secondary schools showed that both human resources and employee-oriented processes were important in explaining and promoting effectiveness in those organizations.[59]

Internal process indicators include:[60]

- A strong, adaptive corporate culture and positive work climate
- Operational efficiency, such as using minimal resources to achieve outcomes
- Undistorted horizontal and vertical communication
- Growth and development of employees

Briefcase

As an organization manager, keep this guideline in mind:

Use the goal approach, internal process approach, and resource-based approach to obtain specific pictures of organizational effectiveness. Assess the four components of the balanced scorecard to obtain a broader, more balanced picture of effectiveness.

THE BALANCED SCORECARD APPROACH TO EFFECTIVENESS

Business organizations have typically focused on financial measures such as profit and return on investment to assess performance. Nonprofit organizations also have to assess budgets, spending, and fund-raising income, and each of these measures is concerned with finances. Traditional approaches based on goal, resource-based, or internal process indicators all have something to offer, but each one, just like sole reliance on financial numbers, tells only part of the story. In recent years, a new approach that balances a concern for various parts of the organization rather than focusing on one aspect has become popular. The **balanced scorecard** combines several indicators of effectiveness into a single framework, balancing traditional financial measures with operational measures relating to a company's critical success factors.[61]

Exhibit 3.8 illustrates the four effectiveness categories considered by the balanced scorecard. Within each area of effectiveness—financial performance, customer service, internal business processes, and the organization's capacity for learning and growth—managers identify key performance indicators the organization will track. The *financial perspective* reflects a concern that the organization's activities contribute to improving short- and long-term financial performance. It includes traditional measures such as net income and return on investment. *Customer service indicators* measure such things as how customers view the organization, as well as customer retention and satisfaction. *Business process indicators* focus on production and operating statistics, such as speed of order fulfillment and cost per order. The final component looks at the organization's *potential for learning and growth,* focusing on how well resources and hu man capital are being managed for the company's future. Measurements include such things as employee satisfaction and retention, amount of training people receive, business process improvements, and the introduction of new products. The components of the scorecard are designed in an integrative manner so that they reinforce one another and link short-term actions with long-term strategic goals, as illustrated in Exhibit 3.8.

3 **The best measures of business performance are financial.**

ANSWER: *Disagree.* If you can have only one type of measure of business performance, it might have to be financial. But diverse views of performance, such as using the balanced scorecard, have proven to be more effective than financials alone, because managers can understand and control the actions that cause business effectiveness. Financial numbers alone provide narrow and limited information.

ASSESS
YOUR
ANSWER

The balanced scorecard helps managers assess the organization from many perspectives so they have a better understanding of total effectiveness. Successful managers keep the organization focused on data in all four components rather than relying on just one, such as finances, which tells only part of the story. Companies such as Best Buy, Wells Fargo, and Hilton Corporation, for instance, are striving

EXHIBIT 3.8
Balanced Scorecard
Effectiveness Criteria

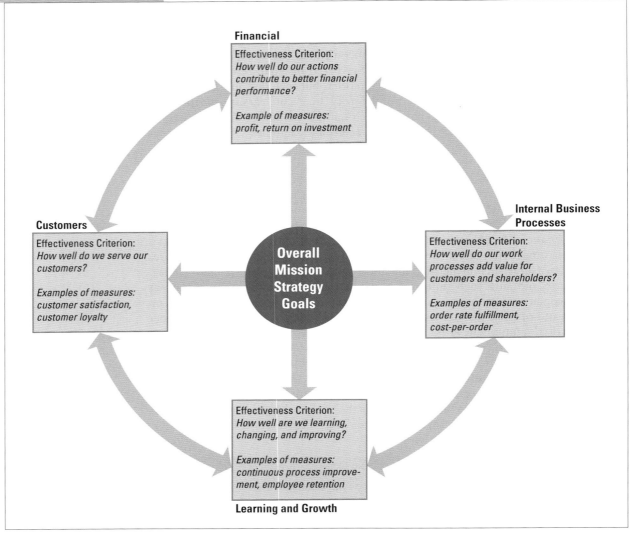

Financial

Effectiveness Criterion:
How well do our actions contribute to better financial performance?

Example of measures: profit, return on investment

Customers

Effectiveness Criterion:
How well do we serve our customers?

Examples of measures: customer satisfaction, customer loyalty

Overall Mission Strategy Goals

Internal Business Processes

Effectiveness Criterion:
How well do our work processes add value for customers and shareholders?

Examples of measures: order rate fulfillment, cost-per-order

Effectiveness Criterion:
How well are we learning, changing, and improving?

Examples of measures: continuous process improvement, employee retention

Learning and Growth

Source: Based on Robert S. Kaplan and David P. Norton, "Using the Balanced Scorecard as a Strategic Management System," *Harvard Business Review* (January–February 1996), 75–85; Chee W. Chow, Kamal M. Haddad, and James E. Williamson, "Applying the Balanced Scorecard to Small Companies," *Management Accounting* 79, no. 2 (August 1997), 21–27; and Cathy Lazere, "All Together Now," *CFO* (February 1998), 28–36.

to understand how they perform on all four components of effectiveness and looking at the relationships among the components. For example, how does internal efficiency relate to customer satisfaction or financial outcomes? How do measures of employee engagement, customer satisfaction, sales performance, and profitability interconnect and contribute to overall effectiveness? Hilton found that a boost in customer retention rates led to an increase in revenues. Best Buy has connected employee engagement to better store performance.[62]

Thus, the balanced scorecard has evolved into a system that helps managers see how organizational effectiveness results from accomplishing outcomes in four consistent and mutually supportive areas. Overall effectiveness is a result of how well

these interdependent elements are aligned, so that individuals, teams, departments, and so forth are working in concert to attain specific goals that ultimately help the organization achieve high performance and fulfill its mission.[63]

DESIGN ESSENTIALS

■ Organizations exist for a purpose. Top managers decide the organization's strategic intent, including a specific mission to be accomplished. The mission statement, or official goals, makes explicit the purpose and direction of an organization. Operative goals designate specific ends sought through actual operating procedures. Official and operative goals are a key element in organizations because they meet these needs—establishing legitimacy with external groups, providing employees with a sense of direction and motivation, and setting standards of performance.

■ Two other aspects related to strategic intent are competitive advantage and core competence. Competitive advantage refers to what sets the organization apart from others and provides it with a distinctive edge. A core competence is something the organization does extremely well compared to competitors. Managers look for competitive openings and develop strategies based on their core competencies.

■ Strategies may include any number of techniques to achieve the stated goals. Two models for formulating strategies are Porter's competitive forces and strategies and the Miles and Snow strategy typology. Organization design needs to fit the firm's competitive approach to contribute to organizational effectiveness.

■ Assessing organizational effectiveness reflects the complexity of organizations as a topic of study. No easy, simple, guaranteed measure will provide an unequivocal assessment of performance. Organizations must perform diverse activities well—from obtaining resource inputs to delivering outputs—to be successful. Traditional approaches use output goals, resource acquisition, or internal health and efficiency as the indicators of effectiveness.

■ No approach is suitable for every organization, but each offers some advantages that the others may lack. In addition, a more recent approach to measuring effectiveness is the balanced scorecard approach, which takes into consideration financial performance, customer service, internal business processes, and the organization's capacity for learning and growth. Managers track and analyze key metrics in these four areas to see how they are interconnected and contribute to overall effectiveness.

Key Concepts

analyzer	goal approach	prospector
balanced scorecard	internal process approach	reactor
competitive advantage	low-cost leadership strategy	resource-based approach
core competence	mission	strategic intent
defender	official goals	strategy
differentiation strategy	operative goals	
focus strategy	organizational goal	

Discussion Questions

1. Discuss the similarities and differences in the strategies described in Porter's competitive strategies and Miles and Snow's typology.
2. A noted organization theorist once said, "Organizational effectiveness can be whatever top management defines it to be." Discuss.
3. What is the difference between a goal and a strategy as defined in the text? Identify both a goal and a strategy for a campus or community organization with which you are involved.
4. What are the similarities and differences between assessing effectiveness on the basis of the balanced scorecard versus the stakeholder approach described in Chapter 1? Explain.
5. What is a goal for the class for which you are reading this text? Who established this goal? Discuss how the goal affects your direction and motivation.
6. What are the advantages and disadvantages of the resource-based approach versus the goal approach for measuring organizational effectiveness?
7. How might a company's goals for employee development be related to its goals for innovation and change? To goals for productivity? Can you discuss ways these types of goals might conflict in an organization?
8. Suppose you have been asked to evaluate the effectiveness of the police department in a medium-sized community. Where would you begin, and how would you proceed? What effectiveness approach would you prefer?
9. Discuss the role of top management in setting organizational direction.
10. Do you believe mission statements and official goal statements provide an organization with genuine legitimacy in the external environment? Discuss.

Chapter 3 Workbook: Identifying Company Strategies and Effectiveness Criteria*

Choose three companies, either in the same industry or in three different industries. Search the Internet for information on the companies, including annual reports. In each company look particularly at descriptions of goals and performance criteria. Refer back to the four effectiveness criteria in Exhibit 3.8 and also to Porter's competitive strategies in Exhibit 3.4.

	Effectiveness Criteria from Exhibit 3.8 Articulated	Strategies from Porter Used (Exhibit 3.4)
Company #1		
Company #2		
Company #3		

Questions

1. Which goals seem most important?
2. Look for differences in the goals and strategies of the three companies and develop an explanation for those differences.
3. Which of the goals or strategies should be changed? Why?

4. *Optional:* Compare your table with those of other students and look for common themes. Which companies seem to articulate and communicate their goals and strategies best?

Case for Analysis: The University Art Museum*

Visitors to the campus were always shown the University Art Museum, of which the large and distinguished university was very proud. A photograph of the handsome neoclassical building that housed the museum had long been used by the university for the cover of its brochures and catalogs.

The building, together with a substantial endowment, was given to the university around 1912 by an alumnus, the son of the university's first president, who had become very wealthy as an investment banker. He also gave the university his own small, but high-quality, collections—one of Etruscan figurines, and one, unique in America, of English pre-Raphaelite paintings. He then served as the museum's unpaid director until his death. During his tenure he brought a few additional collections to the museum, largely from other alumni of the university. Only rarely did the museum purchase anything. As a result, the museum housed several small collections of uneven quality. As long as the founder ran the museum, none of the collections was ever shown to anybody except a few members of the university's art history faculty, who were admitted as the founder's private guests.

After the founder's death, in the late 1920s, the university intended to bring in a professional museum director. Indeed, this had been part of the agreement under which the founder had given the museum. A search committee was to be appointed; but in the meantime a graduate student in art history, who had shown interest in the museum and who had spent a good many hours in it, took over temporarily. At first, Miss Kirkoff did not even have a title, let alone a salary. But she stayed on acting as the museum's director and over the next 30 years was promoted in stages to that title. But from the first day, whatever her title, she was in charge. She immediately set about changing the museum altogether. She cataloged the collections. She pursued new gifts, again primarily small collections from alumni and other friends of the university. She organized fund raising for the museum. But, above all, she began to integrate the museum into the work of the university.

When a space problem arose in the years immediately following World War II, Miss Kirkoff offered the third floor of the museum to the art history faculty, which moved its offices there. She remodeled the building to include classrooms and a modern and well-appointed auditorium. She raised funds to build one of the best research and reference libraries in art history in the country. She also began to organize a series of special exhibitions built around one of the museum's own collections, complemented by loans from outside collections. For each of these exhibitions, she had a distinguished member of the university's art faculty write a catalog. These catalogs speedily became the leading scholarly texts in the fields.

Miss Kirkoff ran the University Art Museum for almost half a century. But at the age of 68, after suffering a severe stroke, she had to retire. In her letter of resignation she proudly pointed to the museum's growth and accomplishment under her stewardship. "Our endowment," she wrote, "now compares favorably with museums several times our size. We never have had to ask the university for any money other than our share of the university's insurance policies. Our collections in the areas of our strength, while small, are of first-rate quality and importance. Above all, we are being used by more people than any museum of our size. Our lecture series, in which members of the university's art history faculty present a major subject to a university audience of students and faculty, attracts regularly three hundred to five hundred people; and if we had the seating capacity, we could easily have a larger audience. Our exhibitions are seen and studied by more visitors, most of them members of the university community, than all but the most highly publicized exhibitions in the very big museums ever draw. Above all, the courses and seminars offered in the museum have become one of the most popular and most rapidly growing educational features of the university. No other museum in this country or anywhere else," concluded Miss Kirkoff, "has so successfully integrated art into the life of a major university and a major university into the work of a museum."

Miss Kirkoff strongly recommended that the university bring in a professional museum director as her successor. "The museum is much too big and much too important to be entrusted to another amateur such as I was forty-five years ago," she wrote. "And it needs careful thinking regarding its direction, its basis of support, and its future relationship with the university."

The university took Miss Kirkoff's advice. A search committee was duly appointed and, after one year's work, it produced a candidate whom everybody approved. The candidate was himself a graduate of the university who had then obtained his Ph.D. in art history and in museum work from the university. Both his teaching and his administrative record were sound, leading to his current museum directorship in a medium-sized city. There he converted an old, well-known, but rather sleepy museum to a lively, community-oriented museum whose exhibitions were well publicized and attracted large crowds.

The new museum director took over with great fanfare in September 1981. Less than three years later he left—with less fanfare, but still with considerable noise. Whether

he resigned or was fired was not quite clear. But that there was bitterness on both sides was only too obvious.

The new director, upon his arrival, had announced that he looked upon the museum as a "major community resource" and intended to "make the tremendous artistic and scholarly resources of the museum fully available to the academic community as well as to the public." When he said these things in an interview with the college newspaper, everybody nodded in approval. It soon became clear that what he meant by "community resource" and what the faculty and students understood by these words were not the same. The museum had always been "open to the public" but, in practice, it was members of the college community who used the museum and attended its lectures, its exhibitions, and its frequent seminars.

The first thing the new director did, however, was to promote visits from the public schools in the area. He soon began to change the exhibition policy. Instead of organizing small shows, focused on a major collection of the museum and built around a scholarly catalog, he began to organize "popular exhibitions" around "topics of general interest" such as "Women Artists through the Ages." He promoted these exhibitions vigorously in the newspapers, in radio and television interviews, and, above all, in the local schools. As a result, what had been a busy but quiet place was soon knee-deep with schoolchildren, taken to the museum in special buses that cluttered the access roads around the museum and throughout the campus. The faculty, which was not particularly happy with the resulting noise and confusion, became thoroughly upset when the scholarly old chairman of the art history department was mobbed by fourth graders who sprayed him with their water pistols as he tried to push his way through the main hall to his office.

Increasingly, the new director did not design his own shows, but brought in traveling exhibitions from major museums, importing their catalog as well rather than have his own faculty produce one.

The students, too, were apparently unenthusiastic after the first six or eight months, during which the new director had been somewhat of a campus hero. Attendance at the classes and seminars held at the art museum fell off sharply, as did attendance at the evening lectures. When the editor of the campus newspaper interviewed students for a story on the museum, he was told again and again that the museum had become too noisy and too "sensational" for students to enjoy the classes and to have a chance to learn.

What brought all this to a head was an Islamic art exhibit in late 1983. Since the museum had little Islamic art, nobody criticized the showing of a traveling exhibit, offered on very advantageous terms with generous financial assistance from some of the Arab governments. But then, instead of inviting one of the university's own faculty members to deliver the customary talk at the opening of the exhibit, the director brought in a cultural attaché of one of the Arab embassies in Washington. The speaker, it was reported, used the occasion to deliver a violent attack on Israel and on the American policy of supporting Israel against the Arabs. A week later, the university senate decided to appoint an advisory committee, drawn mostly from members of the art history faculty, which, in the future, would have to approve all plans for exhibits and lectures. The director thereupon, in an interview with the campus newspaper, sharply attacked the faculty as "elitist" and "snobbish" and as believing that "art belongs to the rich." Six months later, in June 1984, his resignation was announced.

Under the bylaws of the university, the academic senate appoints a search committee. Normally, this is pure formality. The chairperson of the appropriate department submits the department's nominees for the committee who are approved and appointed, usually without debate. But when the academic senate early the following semester was asked to appoint the search committee, things were far from "normal." The dean who presided, sensing the tempers in the room, tried to smooth over things by saying, "Clearly, we picked the wrong person the last time. We will have to try very hard to find the right one this time."

He was immediately interrupted by an economist, known for his populism, who broke in and said, "I admit that the late director was probably not the right personality. But I strongly believe that his personality was not at the root of the problem. He tried to do what needs doing, and this got him in trouble with the faculty. He tried to make our museum a community resource, to bring in the community and to make art accessible to broad masses of people, to the blacks and the Puerto Ricans, to the kids from the ghetto schools and to a lay public. And this is what we really resented. Maybe his methods were not the most tactful ones—I admit I could have done without those interviews he gave. But what he tried to do was right. We had better commit ourselves to the policy he wanted to put into effect, or else we will have deserved his attacks on us as 'elitist' and 'snobbish.'"

"This is nonsense," cut in the usually silent and polite senate member from the art history faculty. "It makes absolutely no sense for our museum to become the kind of community resource our late director and my distinguished colleague want it to be. First, there is no need. The city has one of the world's finest and biggest museums, and it does exactly that and does it very well. Secondly, we have neither the artistic resources nor the financial resources to serve the community at large. We can do something different but equally important and indeed unique. Ours is the only museum in the country, and perhaps in the world, that is fully integrated with an academic community and truly a teaching institution. We are using it, or at least we used to until the last few unfortunate years, as a major educational resource for all

our students. No other museum in the country, and as far as I know in the world, is bringing undergraduates into art the way we do. All of us, in addition to our scholarly and graduate work, teach undergraduate courses for people who are not going to be art majors or art historians. We work with the engineering students and show them what we do in our conservation and restoration work. We work with architecture students and show them the development of architecture through the ages. Above all, we work with liberal arts students, who often have had no exposure to art before they came here and who enjoy our courses all the more because they are scholarly and not just 'art appreciation.' This is unique and this is what our museum can do and should do."

"I doubt that this is really what we should be doing," commented the chairman of the mathematics department. "The museum, as far as I know, is part of the graduate faculty. It should concentrate on training art historians in its Ph.D. program, on its scholarly work, and on its research. I would strongly urge that the museum be considered an adjunct to graduate and especially to Ph.D. education, confine itself to this work, and stay out of all attempts to be 'popular,' both on campus and outside of it. The glory of the museum is the scholarly catalogs produced by our faculty, and our Ph.D. graduates who are sought after by art history faculties throughout the country. This is the museum's mission, which can only be impaired by the attempts to be 'popular,' whether with students or with the public."

"These are very interesting and important comments," said the dean, still trying to pacify. "But I think this can wait until we know who the new director is going to be. Then we should raise these questions with him."

"I beg to differ, Mr. Dean," said one of the elder statesmen of the faculty. "During the summer months, I discussed this question with an old friend and neighbor of mine in the country, the director of one of the nation's great museums. He said to me: 'You do not have a personality problem; you have a management problem. You have not, as a university, taken responsibility for the mission, the direction, and the objectives of your museum. Until you do this, no director can succeed. And this is your decision. In fact, you cannot hope to get a good director until you can tell that person what your basic objectives are. If your late director is to blame—I know him and I know that he is abrasive—it is for being willing to take on a job when you, the university, had not faced up to the basic management decisions. There is no point talking about who should manage until it is clear what it is that has to be managed and for what.'"

At this point the dean realized that he had to adjourn the discussion unless he wanted the meeting to degenerate into a brawl. But he also realized that he had to identify the issues and possible decisions before the next senate meeting a month later.

*Case #3, "The University Art Museum: Defining Purpose and Mission" (pp. 28–35), from *Management Cases* by Peter F. Drucker. Copyright © 1977 by Peter F. Drucker. Reprinted by permission of the author.

Case for Analysis: Airstar Inc.*

Airstar manufactures, repairs, and overhauls pistons and jet engines for smaller, often previously owned aircraft. The company had a solid niche, and most managers had been with the founder for more than twenty years. With the founder's death five years ago, Roy Morgan took over as president at Airstar. Mr. Morgan has called you in as a consultant.

Your research indicates that this industry is changing rapidly. Airstar is feeling encroachment of huge conglomerates like General Electric and Pratt &Whitney, and its backlog of orders is the lowest in several years. The company has always been known for its superior quality, safety, and customer service. However, it has never been under threat before, and senior managers are not sure which strategic direction to take. They have considered potential acquisitions, imports and exports, more research, and additional repair lines. The organization is becoming more chaotic, which is frustrating Morgan and his vice presidents.

Before a meeting with his team, he confides to you, "Organizing is supposed to be easy. For maximum efficiency, work should be divided into simple, logical, routine tasks. These business tasks can be grouped by similar kinds of work characteristics and arranged within an organization under a particularly suited executive. So why are we having so many problems with our executives?"

Morgan met with several of his trusted corporate officers in the executive dining room to discuss what was happening to corporate leadership at Airstar. Morgan went on to explain that he was really becoming concerned with the situation. There had been outright conflicts between the vice president of marketing and the controller over merger and acquisition opportunities. There had been many instances of duplication of work, with corporate officers trying to outmaneuver each other.

"Communications are atrocious," Morgan said to the others. "Why, I didn't even get a copy of the export finance

report until my secretary made an effort to find one for me. My basis for evaluation and appraisal of corporate-executive performance and goal accomplishment is fast becoming obsolete. People have been working up their own job descriptions, and they all include overlapping responsibilities. Changes and decisions are being made on the basis of expediency and are perpetuating too many mistakes. We must take a good look at these organizational realities and correct the situation immediately."

Jim Robinson, vice president of manufacturing, pointed out to Morgan that Airstar was not really following the "principles of good organization." "For instance," explained Robinson, "let's review what we should be practicing as administrators." Some of the principles Robinson believed they should be following were:

1. Determine the goals, policies, programs, plans, and strategies that will best achieve the desired results for the company.
2. Determine the various business tasks to be done.
3. Divide the business tasks into a logical and understandable organizational structure.
4. Determine the suitable personnel to occupy positions within the organizational structure.
5. Define the responsibility and authority of each supervisor clearly in writing.
6. Keep the number and kinds of levels of authority at a minimum.

Robinson proposed that the group study the corporate organizational chart, as well as the various corporate business tasks. After reviewing the corporate organizational chart, Robinson, Morgan, and the others agreed that the number and kinds of formal corporate authority were logical and not much different from other corporations. The group then listed the various corporate business tasks that went on within Airstar.

Robinson continued. "How did we ever decide who should handle mergers or acquisitions?" Morgan answered, "I guess it just occurred over time that the vice president of marketing should have the responsibility." "But," Robinson queried, "where is it written down? How would the controller know it?" "Aha," Morgan exclaimed. "It looks like I'm part of the problem. There isn't anything in writing. Tasks were assigned superficially, as they became problems. This has all been rather informal. I'll establish a group to decide who should have responsibility for what so things can return to our previous level of efficiency."

*Adapted from Bernard A. Deitzer and Karl A. Shilliff, *Contemporary Management Incidents* (Columbus, Ohio: Grid, Inc., 1977), 43–46. Copyright © 1997 by John Wiley & Sons, Inc. This material is used by permission of John Wiley & Sons, Inc.

Chapter 3 Workshop: The Balanced Scorecard and Organizational Effectiveness*

1. Divide into groups of four to six members.
2. Select an organization to study for this exercise. It should be an organization for which one of you has worked, or it could be part of the university.
3. Using the exhibit "The Balanced Scorecard Approach to Effectiveness" (Exhibit 3.8), your group should list eight potential measures that show a balanced view of performance across the four categories. Use the following table.
4. How will achieving these goals help the organization to become more effective? Which goals could be given more weight than others? Why?
5. Present your chart to the rest of the class. Each group should explain why it chose those particular measures and which they think are more important. Be prepared to defend your position to the other groups, which are encouraged to question your choices.

Effectiveness Category	Goal or Subgoal	Performance Gauge	How to Measure	Source of Data	What Do You Consider Effective?
(Example)	Equilibrium	Turnover rates	Compare percentages of workers who left	HRM files	25% reduction in first year
Financial	1.				
	2.				
Customers	3.				
	4.				
Internal Business Processes	5.				
	6.				
Learning and Growth	7.				
	8.				

*Adapted by Dorothy Marcic from general ideas in Jennifer Howard and Larry Miller, *Team Management*, The Miller Consulting Group, 1994, p. 92.

Integrative Case 1.0
Rondell Data Corporation*

"Damn it, he's done it again!" Frank Forbus threw the stack of prints and specifications down on his desk in disgust. *The Model 802 wide-band modulator, released for production the previous Thursday, had just come back to Frank's Engineering Services Department with a caustic note that began, "This one can't be produced either. . . ." It was the fourth time production had kicked the design back.*

Frank Forbus, director of engineering for Rondell Data Corporation, was normally a quiet man. But the Model 802 was stretching his patience; it was beginning to look just like other new products that had hit delays and problems in the transition from design to production during the eight months Frank had worked for Rondell. These problems were nothing new at the sprawling old Rondell factory; Frank's predecessor in the engineering job had run afoul of them, too, and had finally been fired for protesting too vehemently about the other departments. But the Model 802 should have been different. Frank had met two months before (July 3, 1978) with the firm's president, Bill Hunt, and with factory superintendent Dave Schwab to smooth the way for the new modulator design. He thought back to the meeting. . . .

"Now we all know there's a tight deadline on the 802," Bill Hunt said, "and Frank's done well to ask us to talk about its introduction. I'm counting on both of you to find any snags in the system and to work together to get that first production run out by October 2nd. Can you do it?"

"We can do it in production if we get a clean design two weeks from now, as scheduled," answered Dave Schwab, the grizzled factory superintendent. "Frank and I have already talked about that, of course. I'm setting aside time in the card room and the machine shop, and we'll be ready. If the design goes over schedule, though, I'll have to fill in with other runs, and it will cost us a bundle to break in for the 802. How does it look in engineering, Frank?"

"I've just reviewed the design for the second time," Frank replied. "If Ron Porter can keep the salesmen out of our hair and avoid any more last-minute changes, we've got a shot. I've pulled the draftsmen off three other overdue jobs to get this one out. But, Dave, that means we can't spring engineers loose to confer with your production people on manufacturing problems."

"Well, Frank, most of those problems are caused by the engineers, and we need them to resolve the difficulties.

We've all agreed that production bugs come from both of us bowing to sales pressure, and putting equipment into production before the designs are really ready. That's just what we're trying to avoid on the 802. But I can't have 500 people sitting on their hands waiting for an answer from your people. We'll have to have some engineering support."

Bill Hunt broke in. "So long as you two can talk calmly about the problem I'm confident you can resolve it. What a relief it is, Frank, to hear the way you're approaching this. With Kilmann (the previous director of engineering) this conversation would have been a shouting match. Right, Dave?" Dave nodded and smiled.

"Now there's one other thing you should both be aware of," Hunt continued. "Doc Reeves and I talked last night about a new filtering technique, one that might improve the signal-to-noise ratio of the 802 by a factor of two. There's a chance Doc can come up with it before the 802 reaches production, and if it's possible, I'd like to use the new filters. That would give us a real jump on the competition."

Four days after that meeting, Frank found that two of his key people on the 802 design had been called to production for emergency consultation on a bug found in final assembly: two halves of a new data transmission interface wouldn't fit together because recent changes in the front end required a different chassis design for the back end.

Another week later, Doc Reeves walked into Frank's office, proud as a new parent, with the new filter design. "This won't affect the other modules of the 802 much," Doc had said. "Look, it takes three new cards, a few connectors, some changes in the wiring harness, and some new shielding, and that's all."

Frank had tried to resist the last-minute design changes, but Bill Hunt had stood firm. With a lot of overtime by the engineers and draftsmen, engineering services should still be able to finish the prints in time.

Two engineers and three draftsmen went onto 12-hour days to get the 802 ready, but the prints were still five days late reaching Dave Schwab. Two days later, the prints came back to Frank, heavily annotated in red. Schwab had worked all day Saturday to review the job and had found more than a dozen discrepancies in the prints—most of them caused by the new filter design and insufficient checking time before release. Correction of those design faults

*John A. Seeger, Professor of Management, Bentley College. Reprinted with permission.

had brought on a new generation of discrepancies; Schwab's cover note on the second return of the prints indicated he'd had to release the machine capacity he'd been holding for the 802. On the third iteration, Schwab committed his photo and plating capacity to another rush job. The 802 would be at least one month late getting into production. Ron Porter, vice president for sales, was furious. His customer needed 100 units NOW, he said. Rondell was the customer's only late supplier.

"Here we go again," thought Frank Forbus.

Company History

Rondell Data Corporation traced its lineage through several generations of electronics technology. Its original founder, Bob Rondell, had set the firm up in 1920 as "Rondell Equipment Company" to manufacture several electrical testing devices he had invented as an engineering faculty member at a large university. The firm branched into radio broadcasting equipment in 1947 and into data transmission equipment in the early 1960s. A well-established corps of direct salespeople, mostly engineers, called on industrial, scientific, and government accounts, but concentrated heavily on original equipment manufacturers. In this market, Rondell had a long-standing reputation as a source of high-quality, innovative designs. The firm's salespeople fed a continual stream of challenging problems into the Engineering Department, where the creative genius of Ed "Doc" Reeves and several dozen other engineers "converted problems to solutions" (as the sales brochure bragged). Product design formed the spearhead of Rondell's growth.

By 1978, Rondell offered a wide range of products in its two major lines. Broadcast equipment sales had benefitted from the growth of UHFTV and FM radio; it now accounted for 35 percent of company sales. Data transmission had blossomed, and in this field an increasing number of orders called for unique specifications, ranging from specialized display panels to entirely untried designs.

The company had grown from 100 employees in 1947 to over 800 in 1978. (Exhibit 1 shows the 1978 organization chart of key employees.) Bill Hunt, who had been a student of the company's founder, had presided over most of that growth and took great pride in preserving the "family spirit" of the old organization. Informal relationships between Rondell's veteran employees formed the backbone of the firm's day-to-day operations; all the managers relied on personal contact, and Hunt often insisted that the absence of bureaucratic red tape was a key factor in recruiting outstanding engineering talent. The personal management approach extended throughout the factory. All exempt employees were paid on a straight salary plus a share of the profits. Rondell boasted an extremely loyal group of senior employees and very low turnover in nearly all areas of the company.

The highest turnover job in the firm was Frank Forbus's. Frank had joined Rondell in January 1978, replacing Jim Kilmann, who had been director of engineering for only 10 months. Kilmann, in turn, had replaced Tom MacLeod, a talented engineer who had made a promising start but had taken to drink after a year in the job. MacLeod's predecessor had been a genial old-timer who retired at 70 after 30 years in charge of engineering. (Doc Reeves had refused the directorship in each of the recent changes, saying, "Hell, that's no promotion for a bench man like me. I'm no administrator.")

For several years, the firm had experienced a steadily increasing number of disputes between research, engineering, sales, and production people—disputes generally centered on the problem of new product introduction. Quarrels between departments became more numerous under MacLeod, Kilmann, and Forbus. Some managers associated those disputes with the company's recent decline in profitability—a decline that, in spite of higher sales and gross revenues, was beginning to bother people in 1978. President Bill Hunt commented:

Better cooperation, I'm sure, could increase our output by 5–10 percent. I'd hoped Kilmann could solve the problems, but pretty obviously he was too young, too arrogant. People like him—conflict type of personality—bother me. I don't like strife, and with him it seemed I spent all my time smoothing out arguments. Kilmann tried to tell everyone else how to run their departments, without having his own house in order. That approach just wouldn't work here at Rondell. Frank Forbus, now, seems much more in tune with our style of organization. I'm really hopeful now.

Still, we have just as many problems now as we did last year. Maybe even more. I hope Frank can get a handle on engineering services soon. . . .

The Engineering Department: Research

According to the organization chart (see Exhibit 1), Frank Forbus was in charge of both research (really the product development function) and engineering services (which provided engineering support). To Forbus, however, the relationship with research was not so clear-cut:

Doc Reeves is one of the world's unique people, and none of us would have it any other way. He's a creative genius. Sure, the chart says he works for me, but we all know Doc does his own thing. He's not the least bit interested in management routines, and I can't count on him to take any responsibility in scheduling projects, or checking budgets, or what-have-you. But as long as Doc is director of research, you can bet this company will keep on leading the field. He has more ideas per hour than most people have per year, and he keeps the whole engineering staff fired up. Everybody loves Doc—and you can count me in on that, too. In a way, he works for me, sure. But that's not what's important.

EXHIBIT 1
Rondell Data Corporation
1978 Organization Chart

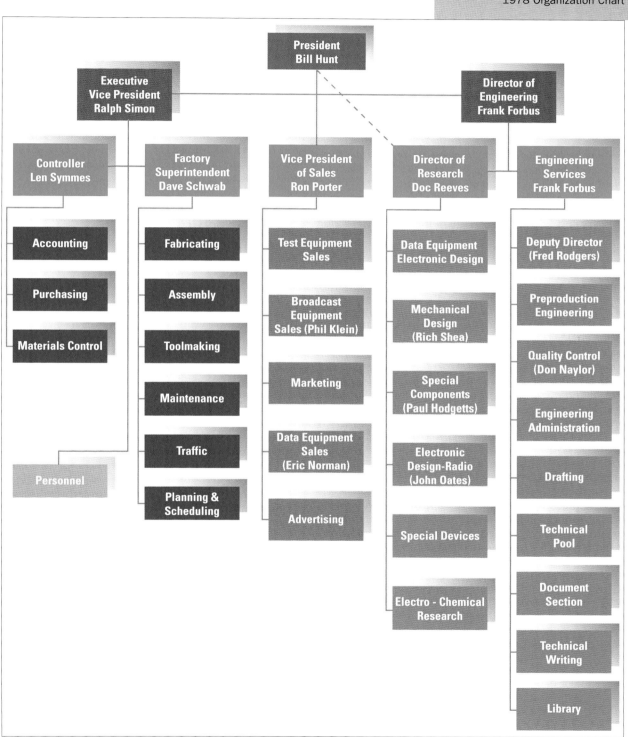

Doc Reeves—unhurried, contemplative, casual, and candid—tipped his stool back against the wall of his research cubicle and talked about what was important:

Development engineering. That's where the company's future rests. Either we have it there, or we don't have it.

There's no kidding ourselves that we're anything but a bunch of Rube Goldbergs here. But that's where the biggest kicks come from—from solving development problems, and dreaming up new ways of doing things. That's why I so look forward to the special contracts we get involved in. We accept them not for the revenue they represent, but because they subsidize the basic development work which goes into all our basic products.

This is a fantastic place to work. I have a great crew and they can really deliver when the chips are down. Why, Bill Hunt and I (he gestured toward the neighboring cubicle, where the president's name hung over the door) are likely to find as many people here at work at 10:00 P.M. as at 3:00 in the afternoon. The important thing here is the relationships between people; they're based on mutual respect, not on policies and procedures. Administrative red tape is a pain. It takes away from development time.

Problems? Sure, there are problems now and then. There are power interests in production, where they sometimes resist change. But I'm not a fighting man, you know. I suppose if I were, I might go in there and push my weight around a little. But I'm an engineer and can do more for Rondell sitting right here or working with my own people. That's what brings results.

Other members of the Research Department echoed Doc's views and added some additional sources of satisfaction with their work. They were proud of the personal contacts they built up with customers' technical staffs—contacts that increasingly involved travel to the customers' factories to serve as expert advisers in the preparation of overall system design specifications. The engineers were also delighted with the department's encouragement of their personal development, continuing education, and independence on the job.

But there were problems, too. Rick Shea, of the mechanical design section, noted:

In the old days I really enjoyed the work—and the people I worked with. But now there's a lot of irritation. I don't like someone breathing down my neck. You can be hurried into jeopardizing the design.

John Oates, head of the radio electronic design section, was another designer with definite views:

Production engineering is almost nonexistent in this company. Very little is done by the preproduction section in engineering services. Frank Forbus has been trying to get preproduction into the picture, but he won't succeed because you can't start from such an ambiguous position. There have been three directors of engineering in three years. Frank can't hold his own against the others in the company, Kilmann was too aggressive. Perhaps no amount of tact would have succeeded.

Paul Hodgetts was head of special components in the R & D department. Like the rest of the department, he valued bench work. But he complained of engineering services:

The services don't do things we want them to do. Instead, they tell us what they're going to do. I should probably go to Frank, but I don't get any decisions there. I know I should go through Frank, but this holds things up, so I often go direct.

The Engineering Department: Engineering Services

The Engineering Services Department provided ancillary services to R & D and served as liaison between engineering and the other Rondell departments. Among its main functions were drafting; management of the central technicians' pool; scheduling and expediting engineering products; documentation and publication of parts lists and engineering orders; preproduction engineering (consisting of the final integration of individual design components into mechanically compatible packages); and quality control (which included inspection of incoming parts and materials, and final inspection of subassemblies and finished equipment). Top management's description of the department included the line, "ESD is responsible for maintaining cooperation with other departments, providing services to the development engineers, and freeing more valuable people in R & D from essential activities that are diversions from and beneath their main competence."

Many of Frank Forbus's 75 employees were located in other departments. Quality control people were scattered through the manufacturing and receiving areas, and technicians worked primarily in the research area or the prototype fabrication room. The remaining ESD personnel were assigned to leftover nooks and crannies near production or engineering sections.

Frank Forbus described his position:

My biggest problem is getting acceptance from the people I work with. I've moved slowly rather than risk antagonism. I saw what happened to Kilmann, and I want to avoid that. But although his precipitate action had won over a few of the younger R & D people, he certainly didn't have the department's backing. Of course, it was the resentment of other departments that eventually caused his discharge. People have been slow accepting me here. There's nothing really overt, but I get a negative reaction to my ideas.

My role in the company has never been well defined really. It's complicated by Doc's unique position, of course, and also by the fact that ESD sort of grew by itself over the years, as the design engineers concentrated more and more on the creative parts of product development. I wish I could be more involved in the technical side. That's been my training, and it's a lot of fun. But in our setup, the technical side is the least necessary for me to be involved in.

Schwab (production head) is hard to get along with. Before I came and after Kilmann left, there were six months intervening when no one was really doing any scheduling. No work loads were figured, and unrealistic promises were made about releases. This puts us in an awkward position. We've been scheduling way beyond our capacity to manufacture or engineer.

Certain people within R & D—for instance, John Oates, head of the radio electronic design section—understand scheduling well and meet project deadlines, but this is not generally true of the rest of the R & D department, especially the mechanical engineers who won't commit themselves. Most of the complaints come from sales and production department heads because items—like the 802—are going to production before they are fully developed, under pressure from sales to get out the unit, and this snags the whole process. Somehow, engineering services should be able to intervene and resolve these complaints, but I haven't made much headway so far. I should be able to go to Hunt for help, but he's too busy most of the time, and his major interest is the design side of engineering, where he got his own start. Sometimes he talks as though he's the engineering director as well as president. I have to put my foot down; there are problems here that the front office just doesn't understand.

Salespeople were often observed taking their problems directly to designers, while production frequently threw designs back at R & D, claiming they could not be produced and demanding the prompt attention of particular design engineers. The latter were frequently observed in conference with production supervisors on the assembly floor. Frank went on:

The designers seem to feel they're losing something when one of us tries to help. They feel it's a reflection on them to have someone take over what they've been doing. They seem to want to carry a project right through to the final stages, particularly the mechanical people. Consequently, engineering services people are used below their capacity to contribute and our department is denied functions it should be performing. There's not as much use made of engineering services as there should be.

Frank Forbus's technician supervisor added his comments:

Production picks out the engineer who'll be the "bum of the month." They pick on every little detail instead of using

their heads and making the minor changes that have to be made. The 15-to-20-year people shouldn't have to prove their ability any more, but they spend four hours defending themselves and four hours getting the job done. I have no one to go to when I need help. Frank Forbus is afraid. I'm trying to help him but he can't help me at this time. I'm responsible for fifty people and I've got to support them.

Fred Rodgers, whom Frank had brought with him to the company as an assistant, gave another view of the situation:

I try to get our people in preproduction to take responsibility, but they're not used to it and people in other departments don't usually see them as best qualified to solve the problem. There's a real barrier for a newcomer here. Gaining people's confidence is hard. More and more, I'm wondering whether there really is a job for me here.

(Rodgers left Rondell a month later.) Another of Forbus's subordinates gave his view:

If Doc gets a new product idea, you can't argue. But he's too optimistic. He judges that others can do what he does—but there's only one Doc Reeves. We've had 900 production change orders this year—they changed 2,500 drawings. If I were in Frank's shoes I'd put my foot down on all this new development. I'd look at the reworking we're doing and get production set up the way I wanted it. Kilmann was fired when he was doing a good job. He was getting some system in the company's operations. Of course, it hurt some people. There is no denying that Doc is the most important person in the company. What gets overlooked is that Hunt is a close second, not just politically but in terms of what he contributes technically and in customer relations.

This subordinate explained that he sometimes went out into the production department but that Schwab, the production head, resented this. Personnel in production said that Kilmann had failed to show respect for old-timers and was always meddling in other departments' business. This was why he had been fired, they contended.

Don Taylor was in charge of quality control. He commented:

I am now much more concerned with administration and less with work. It is one of the evils you get into. There is tremendous detail in this job. I listen to everyone's opinion. Everybody is important. There shouldn't be distinctions—distinctions between people. I'm not sure whether Frank has to be a fireball like Kilmann. I think the real question is whether Frank is getting the job done. I know my job is essential. I want to supply service to the more talented people and give them information so they can do their jobs better.

The Sales Department

Ron Porter was angry. His job was supposed to be selling, he said, but instead it had turned into settling disputes inside the plant and making excuses to waiting customers. He jabbed a finger toward his desk:

You see that telephone? I'm actually afraid nowadays to hear it ring. Three times out of five, it will be a customer who's hurting because we've failed to deliver on schedule. The other two calls will be from production or ESD, telling me some schedule has slipped again.

The Model 802 is typical. Absolutely typical. We padded the delivery date by six weeks, to allow for contingencies. Within two months, the slack had evaporated. Now it looks like we'll be lucky to ship it before Christmas. (It was now November 28.) We're ruining our reputation in the market. Why, just last week one of our best customers—people we've worked with for 15 years—tried to hang a penalty clause on their latest order.

We shouldn't have to be after the engineers all the time. They should be able to see what problems they create without our telling them.

Phil Klein, head of broadcast sales under Porter, noted that many sales decisions were made by top management. Sales was understaffed, he thought, and had never really been able to get on top of the job.

We have grown further and further away from engineering. The director of engineering does not pass on the information that we give him. We need better relationships there. It is very difficult for us to talk to customers about development problems without technical help. We need each other. The whole of engineering is now too isolated from the outside world. The morale of ESD is very low. They're in a bad spot—they're not well organized.

People don't take much to outsiders here. Much of this is because the expectation is built up by top management that jobs will be filled from the bottom. So it's really tough when an outsider like Frank comes in.

Eric Norman, order and pricing coordinator for data equipment, talked about his own relationship with the Production Department:

Actually, I get along with them fairly well. Oh, things could be better of course, if they were more cooperative generally. They always seem to say, "It's my bat and ball, and we're playing by my rules." People are afraid to make production mad; there's a lot of power in there. But you've got to understand that production has its

own set of problems. And nobody in Rondell is working any harder than Dave Schwab to try to straighten things out.

The Production Department

Dave Schwab had joined Rondell just after the Korean War, in which he had seen combat duty (at the Yalu River) and intelligence duty at Pyong Yang. Both experiences had been useful in his first year of civilian employment at Rondell. The wartime factory superintendent and several middle managers had been, apparently, indulging in highly questionable side deals with Rondell's suppliers. Dave Schwab had gathered evidence, revealed the situation to Bill Hunt, and stood by the president in the ensuing unsavory situation. Seven months after joining the company, Dave was named factory superintendent.

His first move had been to replace the fallen managers with a new team from outside. This group did not share the traditional Rondell emphasis on informality and friendly personal relationships and had worked long and hard to install systematic manufacturing methods and procedures. Before the reorganization, production had controlled purchasing, stock control, and final quality control (where final assembly of products in cabinets was accomplished). Because of the wartime events, management decided on a checks-and-balance system of organization and removed these three departments from production jurisdiction. The new production managers felt they had been unjustly penalized by this organization, particularly since they had uncovered the behavior that was detrimental to the company in the first place.

By 1978, the production department had grown to 500 employees, 60 percent of whom worked in the assembly area—an unusually pleasant environment that had been commended by *Factory* magazine for its colorful decoration, cleanliness, and low noise level. An additional 30 percent of the work force, mostly skilled machinists, staffed the finishing and fabrication department. About 60 others performed scheduling, supervisory, and maintenance duties. Production workers were nonunion, hourly-paid, and participated in both the liberal profit-sharing program and the stock purchase plan. Morale in production was traditionally high, and turnover was extremely low.

Dave Schwab commented:

To be efficient, production has to be a self-contained department. We have to control what comes into the department and what goes out. That's why purchasing, inventory control, and quality ought to run out of this office. We'd eliminate a lot of problems with better control there. Why, even Don Taylor in QC would rather work for me than for ESD; he's said so himself. We understand his problems better.

The other departments should be self-contained too. That's why I always avoid the underlings and go straight to the department heads with any questions. I always go down the line.

I have to protect my people from outside disturbances. Look what would happen if I let unfinished, half-baked designs in here—there'd be chaos. The bugs have to be found before the drawings go into the shop, and it seems I'm the one who has to find them. Look at the 802, for example. (Dave had spent most of Thanksgiving red-penciling the latest set of prints.) ESD should have found every one of those discrepancies. They just don't check drawings properly. They change most of the things I flag, but then they fail to trace through the impact of those changes on the rest of the design. I shouldn't have to do that. And those engineers are tolerance crazy. They want everything to a millionth of an inch. I'm the only one in the company who's had any experience with actually machining things to a millionth of an inch. We make sure that the things that engineers say on their drawings actually have to be that way and whether they're obtainable from the kind of raw material we buy.

That shouldn't be production's responsibility, but I have to do it. Accepting bad prints wouldn't let us ship the order any quicker. We'd only make a lot of junk that had to be reworked. And that would take even longer.

This way, I get to be known as the bad guy, but I guess that's just part of the job. (He paused with a wry smile.) Of course, what really gets them is that I don't even have a degree.

Dave had fewer bones to pick with the Sales Department because, he said, they trusted him.

When we give Ron Porter a shipping date, he knows the equipment will be shipped then.

You've got to recognize, though, that all of our new-product problems stem from sales making absurd commitments on equipment that hasn't been fully developed. That always means trouble. Unfortunately, Hunt always backs sales up, even when they're wrong. He always favors them over us.

Ralph Simon, age 65, executive vice president of the company, had direct responsibility for Rondell's production department. He said:

There shouldn't really be a dividing of departments among top management in the company. The president should be czar over all. The production people ask me to do something for them, and I really can't do it. It creates bad feelings between engineering and production, this special attention that they [R & D] get from Bill. But then Hunt likes to dabble in design. Schwab feels that production is treated like a poor relation.

The Executive Committee

At the executive committee meeting on December 6, it was duly recorded that Dave Schwab had accepted the prints and specifications for the Model 802 modulator, and had set

Friday, December 29, as the shipping date for the first 10 pieces. Bill Hunt, in the chairperson's role, shook his head and changed the subject quickly when Frank tried to open the agenda to a discussion of interdepartmental coordination.

The executive committee itself was a brainchild of Rondell's controller, Len Symmes, who was well aware of the disputes that plagued the company. Symmes had convinced Bill Hunt and Ralph Simon to meet every two weeks with their department heads, and the meetings were formalized with Hunt, Simon, Ron Porter, Dave Schwab, Frank Forbus, Doc Reeves, Symmes, and the personnel director attending. Symmes explained his intent and the results:

Doing things collectively and informally just doesn't work as well as it used to. Things have been gradually getting worse for at least two years now. We had to start thinking in terms of formal organization relationships. I did the first organization chart, and the executive committee was my idea too—but neither idea is contributing much help, I'm afraid. It takes top management to make an organization click. The rest of us can't act much differently until the top people see the need for us to change.

I had hoped the committee especially would help get the department managers into a constructive planning process. It hasn't worked out that way because Mr. Hunt really doesn't see the need for it. He uses the meetings as a place to pass on routine information.

Merry Christmas

"Frank, I didn't know whether to tell you now, or after the holiday." It was Friday, December 22, and Frank Forbus was standing awkwardly in front of Bill Hunt's desk.

"But, I figured you'd work right through Christmas Day if we didn't have this talk, and that just wouldn't have been fair to you. I can't understand why we have such poor luck in the engineering director's job lately. And I don't think it's entirely your fault. But . . ."

Frank only heard half of Hunt's words, and said nothing in response. He'd be paid through February 28. . . . He should use the time for searching. . . . Hunt would help all he could. . . . Jim Kilmann was supposed to be doing well at his own new job, and might need more help. . . .

Frank cleaned out his desk and numbly started home. The electronic carillon near his house was playing a Christmas carol. Frank thought again of Hunt's rationale: Conflict still plagued Rondell—and Frank had not made it go away. Maybe somebody else could do it.

"And what did Santa Claus bring you, Frankie?" he asked himself.

"The sack. Only the empty sack."

Integrative Case 2.0
It Isn't So Simple: Infrastructure Change at Royce Consulting*

2.0

The lights of the city glittered outside Ken Vincent's twelfth-floor office. After nine years of late nights and missed holidays, Ken was in the executive suite with the words "Associate Partner" on the door. Things should be easier now, but the proposed changes at Royce Consulting had been more challenging than he had expected. "I don't understand," he thought. "At Royce Consulting our clients, our people, and our reputation are what count, so why do I feel so much tension from the managers about the changes that are going to be made in the office? We've analyzed why we have to make the changes. Heck, we even got an outside person to help us. The administrative support staff are pleased. So why aren't the managers enthusiastic? We all know what the decision at tomorrow's meeting will be—Go! Then it will all be over. Or will it?" Ken thought as he turned out the lights.

Background

Royce Consulting is an international consulting firm whose clients are large corporations, usually with long-term contracts. Royce employees spend weeks, months, and even years working under contract at the client's site. Royce consultants are employed by a wide range of industries, from manufacturing facilities to utilities to service businesses. The firm has over 160 consulting offices located in 65 countries. At this location Royce employees included 85 staff members, 22 site managers, 9 partners and associate partners, 6 administrative support staff, 1 human resource professional, and 1 financial support person.

For the most part, Royce Consulting hired entry-level staff straight out of college and promoted from within. New hires worked on staff for five or six years; if they did well, they were promoted to manager. Managers were responsible for maintaining client contracts and assisting partners in creating proposals for future engagements. Those who were not promoted after six or seven years generally left the company for other jobs.

Newly promoted managers were assigned an office, a major perquisite of their new status. During the previous year, some new managers had been forced to share an office because of space limitations. To minimize the friction of sharing an office, one of the managers was usually assigned to a long-term project out of town. Thus, practically speaking, each manager had a private office.

Infrastructure and Proposed Changes

Royce was thinking about instituting a hoteling office system—also referred to as a "nonterritorial" or "free-address"

office. A hoteling office system made offices available to managers on a reservation or drop-in basis. Managers are not assigned a permanent office; instead, whatever materials and equipment the manager needs are moved into the temporary office. These are some of the features and advantages of a hoteling office system:

- No permanent office assigned
- Offices are scheduled by reservations
- Long-term scheduling of an office is feasible
- Storage space would be located in a separate file room
- Standard manuals and supplies would be maintained in each office
- Hoteling coordinator is responsible for maintaining offices
- A change in "possession of space"
- Eliminates two or more managers assigned to the same office
- Allows managers to keep the same office if desired
- Managers would have to bring in whatever files they needed for their stay
- Information available would be standardized regardless of office
- Managers do not have to worry about "housekeeping issues"

The other innovation under consideration was an upgrade to state-of-the-art electronic office technology. All managers would receive a new notebook computer with updated communications capability to use Royce's integrated and proprietary software. Also, as part of the electronic office technology, an electronic filing system was considered. The electronic filing system meant information regarding proposals, client records, and promotional materials would be electronically available on the Royce Consulting network.

The administrative support staff had limited experience with many of the application packages used by the managers.

*Presented to and accepted by the Society for Case Research. All rights reserved to the authors and SCR.

This case was prepared by Sally Dresdow of the University of Wisconsin at Green Bay and Joy Benson of the University of Illinois at Springfield and is intended to be used as a basis for class discussion. The views represented here are those of the case authors and do not necessarily reflect the views of the Society for Case Research. The authors' views are based on their own professional judgments. The names of the organization, individuals, and location have been disguised to preserve the organization's request for anonymity.

While they used word processing extensively, they had little experience with spreadsheets, communications, or graphics packages. The firm had a graphics department and the managers did most of their own work, so the administrative staff did not have to work with those application software packages.

Work Patterns

Royce Consulting was located in a large city in the Midwest. The office was located in the downtown area, but it was easy to get to. Managers assigned to in-town projects often stopped by for a few hours at various times of the day. Managers who were not currently assigned to client projects were expected to be in the office to assist on current projects or work with a partner to develop proposals for new business.

In a consulting firm, managers spend a significant portion of their time at client sites. As a result, the office occupancy rate at Royce Consulting was about 40 to 60 percent. This meant that the firm paid lease costs for offices that were empty approximately half of the time. With the planned growth over the next ten years, assigning permanent offices to every manager, even in doubled-up arrangements, was judged to be economically unnecessary given the amount of time offices were empty.

The proposed changes would require managers and administrative support staff to adjust their work patterns. Additionally, if a hoteling office system was adopted, managers would need to keep their files in a centralized file room.

Organizational Culture

Royce Consulting had a strong organizational culture, and management personnel were highly effective at communicating it to all employees.

Stability of Culture

The culture at Royce Consulting was stable. The leadership of the corporation had a clear picture of who they were and what type of organization they were. Royce Consulting had positioned itself to be a leader in all areas of large business consulting. Royce Consulting's CEO articulated the firm's commitment to being client-centered. Everything that was done at Royce Consulting was because of the client.

Training

New hires at Royce Consulting received extensive training in the culture of the organization and the methodology employed in consulting projects. They began with a structured program of classroom instruction and computer-aided courses covering technologies used in the various industries in which the firm was involved. Royce Consulting recruited top young people who were aggressive and who

were willing to do whatever was necessary to get the job done and build a common bond. Among new hires, camaraderie was encouraged along with a level of competition. This kind of behavior continued to be cultivated throughout the training and promotion process.

Work Relationships

Royce Consulting employees had a remarkably similar outlook on the organization. Accepting the culture and norms of the organization was important for each employee. The norms of Royce Consulting revolved around high performance expectations and strong job involvement.

By the time people made manager, they were aware of what types of behaviors were acceptable. Managers were formally assigned the role of coach to younger staff people, and they modeled acceptable behavior. Behavioral norms included when they came into the office, how late they stayed at the office, and the type of comments they made about others. Managers spent time checking on staff people and talking with them about how they were doing.

The standard for relationships was that of professionalism. Managers knew they had to do what the partners asked and they were to be available at all times. A norms survey and conversations made it clear that people at Royce Consulting were expected to help each other with on-the-job problems, but personal problems were outside the realm of sanctioned relationships. Personal problems were not to interfere with performance on a job. To illustrate, vacations were put on hold and other kinds of commitments were set aside if something was needed at Royce Consulting.

Organizational Values

Three things were of major importance to the organization: its clients, its people, and its reputation. There was a strong client-centered philosophy communicated and practiced. Organization members sought to meet and exceed customer expectations. Putting clients first was stressed. The management of Royce Consulting listened to its clients and made adjustments to satisfy the client.

The reputation of Royce Consulting was important to those leading the organization. They protected and enhanced it by focusing on quality services delivered by quality people. The emphasis on clients, Royce Consulting personnel, and the firm's reputation was cultivated by developing a highly motivated, cohesive, and committed group of employees.

Management Style and Hierarchical Structure

The company organization was characterized by a directive style of management. The partners had the final word on all issues of importance. It was common to hear statements like "Managers are expected to solve problems, and do whatever it takes to finish the job" and "Whatever the partners want, we do." Partners accepted and asked for managers' feedback on projects, but in the final analysis, the partners made the decisions.

Current Situation

Royce Consulting had an aggressive five-year plan that was predicated on a continued increase in business. Increases in the total number of partners, associate partners, managers, and staff were forecast. Additional office space would be required to accommodate the growth in staff; this would increase rental costs at a time when Royce's fixed and variable costs were going up.

The partners, led by managing partner Donald Gray and associate partner Ken Vincent, believed that something had to be done to improve space utilization and the productivity of the managers and administrative personnel. The partners approved a feasibility study of the innovations and their impact on the company.

The ultimate decision makers were the partner group who had the power to approve the concepts and commit the required financial investment. A planning committee consisted of Ken Vincent; the human resources person; the financial officer; and an outside consultant, Mary Schrean.

The Feasibility Study

Within two working days of the initial meeting, all the partners and managers received a memo announcing the hoteling office feasibility study. The memo included a brief description of the concept and stated that it would include an interview with the staff. By this time, partners and managers had already heard about the possible changes and knew that Gray was leaning toward hoteling offices.

Interviews with the Partners

All the partners were interviewed. One similarity in the comments was that they thought the move to hoteling offices was necessary but they were glad it would not affect them. Three partners expressed concern about managers' acceptance of the change to a hoteling system. The conclusion of each partner was that if Royce Consulting moved to hoteling offices, with or without electronic office technology, the managers would accept the change. The reason given by the partners for such acceptance was that the managers would do what the partners wanted done.

The partners all agreed that productivity could be improved at all levels of the organization: in their own work as well as among the secretaries and the managers. Partners acknowledged that current levels of information technology at Royce Consulting would not support the move to hoteling offices and that advances in electronic office technology needed to be considered.

Partners viewed all filing issues as secondary to both the office layout change and the proposed technology improvement. What eventually emerged, however, was that ownership and control of files was a major concern, and most partners and managers did not want anything centralized.

Interviews with the Managers

Personal interviews were conducted with all ten managers who were in the office. During the interviews, four of the managers asked Schrean whether the change to hoteling offices was her idea. The managers passed the question off as a joke; however, they expected a response from her. She stated that she was there as an adviser, that she had not generated the idea, and that she would not make the final decision regarding the changes.

The length of time that these managers had been in their current positions ranged from six months to five years. None of them expressed positive feelings about the hoteling system, and all of them referred to how hard they had worked to make manager and gain an office of their own. Eight managers spoke of the status that the office gave them and the convenience of having a permanent place to keep their information and files. Two of the managers said they did not care so much about the status but were concerned about the convenience. One manager said he would come in less frequently if he did not have his own office. The managers believed that a change to hoteling offices would decrease their productivity. Two managers stated that they did not care how much money Royce Consulting would save on lease costs; they wanted to keep their offices.

However, for all the negative comments, all the managers said that they would go along with whatever the partners decided to do. One manager stated that if Royce Consulting stays busy with client projects, having a permanently assigned office was not a big issue.

During the interviews, every manager was enthusiastic and supportive of new productivity tools, particularly the improved electronic office technology. They believed that new computers and integrated software and productivity tools would definitely improve their productivity. Half the managers stated that updated technology would make the change to hoteling offices "a little less terrible," and they wanted their secretaries to have the same software as they did.

The managers' responses to the filing issue varied. The volume of files managers had was in direct proportion to their tenure in that position: The longer a person was a manager, the more files he or she had. In all cases, managers took care of their own files, storing them in their offices and in whatever filing drawers were free.

As part of the process of speaking with managers, their administrative assistants were asked about the proposed changes. Each of the six thought that the electronic office upgrade would benefit the managers, although they were somewhat concerned about what would be expected of

2.0

them. Regarding the move to hoteling offices, each said that the managers would hate the change, but that they would agree to it if the partners wanted to move in that direction.

Results of the Survey

A survey developed from the interviews was sent to all partners, associate partners, and managers two weeks after the interviews were conducted. The completed survey was returned by 6 of the 9 partners and associate partners and 16 of the 22 managers. This is what the survey showed.

Work Patterns. It was "common knowledge" that managers were out of the office a significant portion of their time, but there were no figures to substantiate this belief, so the respondents were asked to provide data on where they spent their time. The survey results indicated that partners spent 38 percent of their time in the office; 54 percent at client sites; 5 percent at home; and 3 percent in other places, such as airports. Managers reported spending 32 percent of their time in the office, 63 percent at client sites, 4 percent at home, and 1 percent in other places.

For 15 workdays, the planning team also visually checked each of the 15 managers' offices four times each day: at 9 a.m., 11 a.m., 2 p.m., and 4 p.m. These times were selected because initial observations indicated that these were the peak occupancy times. An average of six offices (40 percent of all manager offices) were empty at any given time; in other words, there was a 60 percent occupancy rate.

Alternative Office Layouts. One of the alternatives outlined by the planning committee was a continuation of and expansion of shared offices. Eleven of the managers responding to the survey preferred shared offices to hoteling offices. Occasions when more than one manager was in the shared office at the same time were infrequent. Eight managers reported 0 to 5 office conflicts per month; three managers reported 6 to 10 office conflicts per month. The type of problems encountered with shared offices included not having enough filing space, problems in directing telephone calls, and lack of privacy.

Managers agreed that having a permanently assigned office was an important perquisite. The survey confirmed the information gathered in the interviews about managers' attitudes: All but two managers preferred shared offices over hoteling, and managers believed their productivity would be negatively impacted. The challenges facing Royce Consulting if they move to hoteling offices centered around tradition and managers' expectations, file accessibility and organization, security and privacy issues, unpredictable work schedules, and high-traffic periods.

Control of Personal Files. Because of the comments made during the face-to-face interviews, survey respondents were asked to rank the importance of having personal control of their files. A 5-point scale was used, with 5 being "strongly agree" and 1 being "strongly disagree." Here are the responses.

Respondents	Sample	Rank
Partners	6	4.3
Managers:		
0–1 year	5	4.6
2–3 years	5	3.6
4+ years	6	4.3

Electronic Technology. Royce Consulting had a basic network system in the office that could not accommodate the current partners and managers working at a remote site. The administrative support staff had a separate network, and the managers and staff could not communicate electronically. Of managers responding to the survey, 95 percent wanted to use the network but only 50 percent could actually do so.

Option Analysis

A financial analysis showed that there were significant cost differences between the options under consideration:

Option 1: Continue private offices with some office sharing
- Lease an additional floor in existing building; annual cost, $360,000
- Build out the additional floor (i.e., construct, furnish, and equip offices and work areas): one-time cost, $600,000

Option 2: Move to hoteling offices with upgraded office technology
- Upgrade office electronic technology: one-time cost, $190,000

Option 1 was expensive because under the terms of the existing lease, Royce had to commit to an entire floor if it wanted additional space. Hoteling offices showed an overall financial advantage of $360,000 per year and a one-time savings of $410,000 over shared or individual offices.

The Challenge

Vincent met with Mary Schrean to discuss the upcoming meeting of partners and managers, where they would present the results of the study and a proposal for action. Included in the report were proposed layouts for both shared and hoteling offices. Vincent and Gray were planning to recommend a hoteling office system, which would include storage areas, state-of-the-art electronic office technology for managers and administrative support staff, and centralized files. The rationale for their decision emphasized the amount of time that managers were out of the office and the high cost of maintaining the status quo and was built around the following points:

1. Royce's business is different: offices are empty from 40 to 60 percent of the time.
2. Real estate costs continue to escalate.
3. Projections indicate there will be increased need for offices and cost-control strategies as the business develops.
4. Royce Consulting plays a leading role in helping organizations implement innovation.

"It's still a go," thought Vincent as he and the others returned from a break. "The cost figures support it and the growth figures support it. It's simple—or is it? The decision is the easy part. What is it about Royce Consulting that will help or hinder its acceptance? In the long run, I hope we strengthen our internal processes and don't hinder our effectiveness by going ahead with these simple changes."

© Ken Kan

Part 3

External Factors and Design

Chapter 4

Relationships Between Organizations

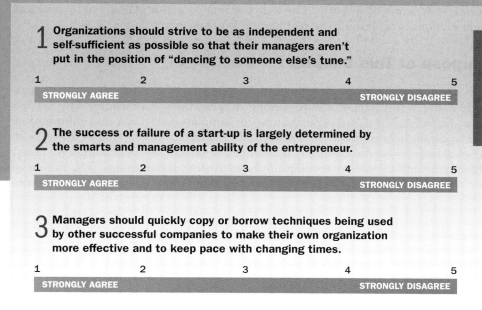

Before reading this chapter, please circle your opinion below for each of the following statements:

Managing by Design Questions

1 Organizations should strive to be as independent and self-sufficient as possible so that their managers aren't put in the position of "dancing to someone else's tune."

1	2	3	4	5
STRONGLY AGREE				STRONGLY DISAGREE

2 The success or failure of a start-up is largely determined by the smarts and management ability of the entrepreneur.

1	2	3	4	5
STRONGLY AGREE				STRONGLY DISAGREE

3 Managers should quickly copy or borrow techniques being used by other successful companies to make their own organization more effective and to keep pace with changing times.

1	2	3	4	5
STRONGLY AGREE				STRONGLY DISAGREE

SAP and Microsoft go at each other tooth-and-nail for customers, but the two called a truce to jointly develop a piece of software that allows a Microsoft spreadsheet to bring in data from an SAP accounting program. Rival Internet companies Google, Yahoo!, and MySpace created an alliance to develop new technologies that will benefit all of the partners.[1] All over corporate America, and particularly in the rapidly changing and uncertain high-tech industry, companies are cheerfully sleeping with the enemy.

A widespread organizational trend today is to reduce boundaries and increase collaboration between companies, sometimes even between competitors. In many industries, the business environment is so complicated that no single company can develop all the expertise and resources needed to stay competitive. Why? Globalization and rapid advances in technology, communications, and transportation have created amazing new opportunities, but they have also raised the cost of doing business and made it increasingly difficult for any company to take advantage of those opportunities on its own. In this new economy, webs of organizations are emerging. Collaboration and partnership is the new way of doing business. Organizations think of themselves as teams that create value jointly rather than as autonomous companies that are in competition with all others.

You can see the results of interorganizational collaboration when a movie like the animated *Star Wars: The Clone Wars* from Lucasfilm Ltd. is launched. More than a month before the movie opened, Toys "R" Us mounted digital clocks in many of its stores, counting down the days until the chain began selling toys and action figures based on the film. Two of the retailer's flagship stores held midnight costume parties and trivia contests in connection with the opening. McDonald's teamed up with Lucasfilm to put together a Star Wars Happy Meal promotion, each meal coming with a specially-designed box and one of eighteen exclusive toys. Kids could continue their Star Wars experience online at the Happy Meal Virtual World, where codes printed on Happy Meal packaging enabled them to unlock top-secret Jedi quests.[2] For some blockbuster movies, coordinated action among companies can yield millions in addition to box-office and DVD profits.

Purpose of This Chapter

This chapter explores the most recent trend in organizing, which is the increasingly dense web of relationships among organizations. Companies have always been dependent on other organizations for supplies, materials, and information. The question is how these relationships are managed. At one time it was a matter of a large, powerful company tightening the screws on small suppliers. Today a company can choose to develop positive, trusting relationships. The notion of horizontal relationships described in Chapter 2 and the understanding of environmental uncertainty in Chapter 6 are leading to the next stage of organizational evolution, which is horizontal relationships *across* organizations. Organizations can choose to build relationships in many ways, such as appointing preferred suppliers, establishing agreements, business partnering, joint ventures, or even mergers and acquisitions.

Interorganizational research has yielded perspectives such as resource dependence, collaborative networks, population ecology, and institutionalism. The sum total of these ideas can be daunting, because it means managers no longer can rest in the safety of managing a single organization. They have to figure out how to manage a whole set of interorganizational relationships, which is a great deal more challenging and complex.

ORGANIZATIONAL ECOSYSTEMS

Interorganizational relationships are the relatively enduring resource transactions, flows, and linkages that occur among two or more organizations.[3] Traditionally, these transactions and relationships have been seen as a necessary evil to obtain what an organization needs. The presumption has been that the world is composed of distinct businesses that thrive on autonomy and compete for supremacy. A company may be forced into interorganizational relationships depending on its needs and the instability and complexity of the environment.

A new view described by James Moore argues that organizations are now evolving into business ecosystems. An **organizational ecosystem** is a system formed by the interaction of a community of organizations and their environment. An ecosystem cuts across traditional industry lines.[4] A company can create its own ecosystem. Apple, for instance, travels in several major industries, including consumer electronics, Internet services, mobile phones, personal computers, and entertainment. Its ecosystem also includes hundreds of suppliers and millions of customers across many markets. Google is getting into the entertainment business as well, rolling out dozens of short cartoons by "Family Guy" creator Seth McFarlane and building a role as "middleman to Hollywood talent coming online."[5] Cable television companies are offering new forms of phone service, and telephone companies are getting into the television business. Today, successful companies develop relationships with numerous other organizations cutting across traditional business boundaries.

Briefcase

As an organization manager, keep these guidelines in mind:

Look for and develop relationships with other organizations. Don't limit your thinking to a single industry or business type. Build an ecosystem of which your organization is a part.

Is Competition Dead?

No company can go it alone under a constant onslaught of international competitors, changing technology, and new regulations. Organizations around the world are embedded in complex networks of confusing relationships—collaborating in some markets, competing fiercely in others. The number of corporate alliances has been increasing at a rate of 25 percent a year, and many of those have been between competitors.[6] These alliances influence organizations' competitive behavior in varied ways.

Traditional competition, which assumes a distinct company competing for survival and supremacy with other stand-alone businesses, no longer exists because each organization both supports and depends on the others for success, and perhaps for survival. However, most managers recognize that the competitive stakes are higher than ever in a world where market share can crumble overnight and no industry is immune from almost instant obsolescence.[7] In today's world, a new form of competition is in fact intensifying.[8]

For one thing, companies now need to coevolve with others in the ecosystem so that everyone gets stronger. Consider the wolf and the caribou. Wolves cull weaker caribou, which strengthens the herd. A strong herd means that wolves must become stronger themselves. With coevolution, the whole system becomes stronger. In the same way, companies coevolve through discussion with each other, shared visions, alliances, and managing complex relationships.

Exhibit 4.1 illustrates the complexity of an ecosystem by showing the myriad overlapping relationships in which high-tech companies were involved in 1999. Since then, many of these companies have merged, been acquired, or gone out of business. Ecosystems constantly change and evolve, with some relationships growing stronger while others weaken or are terminated. The changing pattern of relationships and interactions in an ecosystem contributes to the health and vitality of the system as an integrated whole.[9]

In an organizational ecosystem, conflict and cooperation exist at the same time. Consider the partnership between rivals Sony and Samsung.

Sony and Samsung illustrate the tangled connections that have developed among consumer electronics firms over the past several years. Many electronics companies that long prided themselves on independence have shifted to an ecosystem approach.

Samsung's mission has long been clear: knock off Sony as the world's top electronics maker. Within the past several years, the Korean underdog surpassed giant Sony in market capitalization, revenue, and profits. The two companies continue to battle, along with a few other top electronics makers, for the No. 1 spot in global television sales.

So what possible reason could Samsung have for letting Sony use some of its key technologies for flat-panel televisions before Samsung's own products used them? Sony's televisions using those technologies ended up outselling Samsung's LCD sets by more than three to one in the year they were released. Not such a smart move on Samsung's part, you would think, but you might be wrong. By working closely with Sony, Samsung engineers and managers knew they were getting a crash course in how to make better LCD televisions. Previously the company had used the technology primarily for computer monitors and cellphones. Samsung engineer Jang Insik and his Sony counterpart Hiroshi Murayama talk by phone several times a day. "If we can learn from Sony," says Jang, "it will help us in advancing our technology."

IN PRACTICE

Sony Corporation and Samsung Electronics Company

(continued)

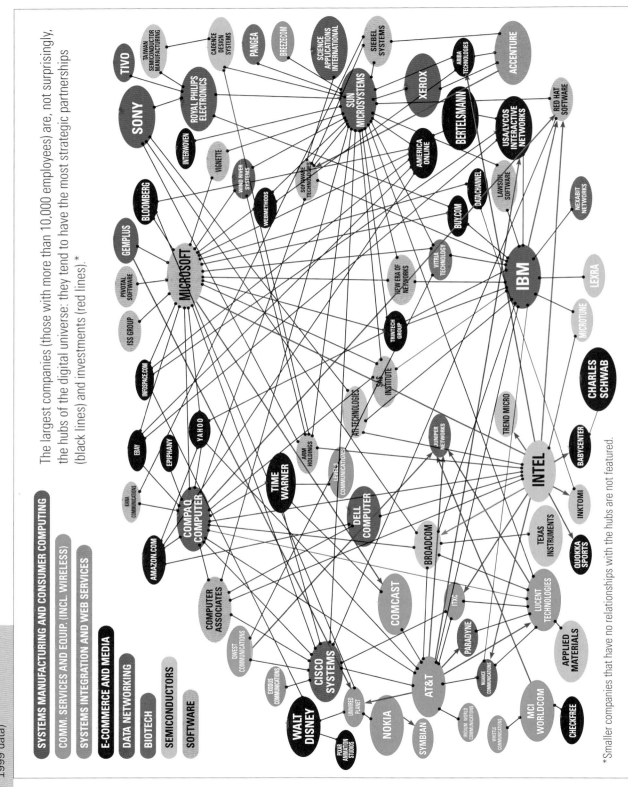

EXHIBIT 4.1
An Organizational Ecosystem (based on 1999 data)

SYSTEMS MANUFACTURING AND CONSUMER COMPUTING

COMM. SERVICES AND EQUIP. (INCL. WIRELESS)

SYSTEMS INTEGRATION AND WEB SERVICES

E-COMMERCE AND MEDIA

DATA NETWORKING

BIOTECH

SEMICONDUCTORS

SOFTWARE

The largest companies (those with more than 10,000 employees) are, not surprisingly, the hubs of the digital universe: they tend to have the most strategic partnerships (black lines) and investments (red lines).*

*Smaller companies that have no relationships with the hubs are not featured.

As competition in electronics has intensified, Sony and Samsung have come to realize that they depend on each other in areas of technology and developing new products. The partnership between the two companies began in 2003, when both first started making LCD panels. Samsung had the better technology, but Sony had a far superior understanding of how to turn that technology into top-selling products. Sony closely guards its know-how, but Samsung was able to get a close-up look because of the partnership. Samsung televisions that came out the following year used some of the same features that made Sony's designs so popular. The two firms continue to try to out-do one another, but they continue to share information too, because managers at both companies know it's the best route to growing stronger.[10] ■

Mutual dependencies and partnerships have become a fact of life. Is competition dead? Companies today may use their strength to achieve victory over competitors, but ultimately cooperation carries the day.

The Changing Role of Management

Within business ecosystems managers learn to move beyond traditional responsibilities of corporate strategy and designing hierarchical structures and control systems. If a top manager looks down to enforce order and uniformity, the company is missing opportunities for new and evolving external relationships.[11] In this new world, managers think about horizontal processes rather than vertical structures. Important initiatives are not just top down; they cut across the boundaries separating organizational units. Moreover, horizontal relationships now include linkages with suppliers and customers, who become part of the team. Business leaders can learn to lead economic coevolution. Managers learn to see and appreciate the rich environment of opportunities that grow from cooperative relationships with other contributors to the ecosystem. Rather than trying to force suppliers into low prices or customers into high prices, managers strive to strengthen the larger system evolving around them, finding ways to understand this big picture and how to contribute.

This is a broader leadership role than ever before. Managers in charge of coordinating with other companies have to learn new executive skills. A study of executive roles by the Hay Group distinguished between *operations roles* and *collaborative roles*. Most traditional managers are skilled in handling operations roles, which have traditional vertical authority and are accountable for business results primarily through direct control over people and resources. Collaborative roles, on the other hand, don't have direct authority over horizontal colleagues or partners, but are nonetheless accountable for specific business results. Managers in collaborative roles have to be highly flexible and proactive. They achieve results through personal communication and assertively seeking out needed information and resources.[12]

The old way of managing relied almost exclusively on operations roles, defending the organization's boundaries and maintaining direct control over resources. Today, though, collaborative roles are becoming more important for success. When alliances fail, it is usually because of an inability of the partners to develop trusting, collaborative relationships rather than due to the lack of a solid business plan or strategy. In successful alliances, people work together almost as if they were members of the same company.[13] Donovan Neale-May, president of advertising firm Neale-May & Partners, provides an example of the new collaborative management style. Neale-May realized that his agency was having trouble winning accounts because of its lack of international experience. He talked with other ad executives and learned that they experienced the same frustrations. "We have companies—our own neighbors here in Colorado—that won't hire us because we don't have offices in sixty-five countries," said John Metzger, CEO of a Boulder firm. Neale-May eventually spearheaded GlobalFluency, an international alliance of forty independent high-tech public relations agencies that share information and jointly market their services. The power of GlobalFluency has enabled small, owner-run agencies to win accounts that once went only to large competitors. Alliance members maintain their independence for small jobs but they work together through GlobalFluency to pitch for regional projects or international campaigns.[14]

Interorganizational Framework

Appreciating the larger organizational ecosystem is one of the most exciting areas of organization theory. The models and perspectives for understanding interorganizational relationships ultimately help managers change their role from top-down management to horizontal management across organizations. Exhibit 4.2 shows a framework for analyzing the different views of interorganizational relationships. Relationships among organizations can be characterized by whether the organizations are dissimilar or similar and whether relationships are competitive or cooperative. By understanding these perspectives, managers can assess their environment and adopt strategies to suit their needs. The first perspective is called resource-dependence theory, which is briefly described in Chapter 6. It describes rational ways organizations deal with each other to reduce dependence on the environment. The second perspective is about collaborative networks, wherein organizations allow themselves to become dependent on other organizations to increase value and productivity for all. The third perspective is population ecology, which examines how new organizations fill niches left open by established organizations and how a rich variety of new organizational forms benefits society. The final approach is called institutionalism and explains why and how organizations legitimate themselves in

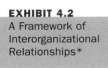

EXHIBIT 4.2
A Framework of
Interorganizational
Relationships*

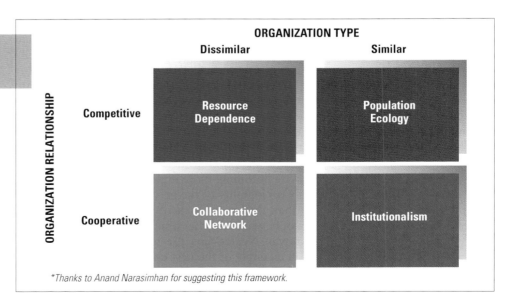

Thanks to Anand Narasimhan for suggesting this framework.

the larger environment and design structures by borrowing ideas from each other. These four approaches to the study of interorganizational relationships are described in the remainder of this chapter.

RESOURCE DEPENDENCE

Resource dependence represents the traditional view of relationships among organizations. As will be described in Chapter 6, **resource-dependence theory** argues that organizations try to minimize their dependence on other organizations for the supply of important resources and try to influence the environment to make resources available.[15] Organizations succeed by striving for independence and autonomy. When threatened by greater dependence, organizations will assert control over external resources to minimize that dependence.

When organizations feel resource or supply constraints, the resource dependence perspective says they maneuver to maintain their autonomy through a variety of strategies, several of which are described in Chapter 6. One strategy is to adapt to or alter the interdependent relationships. This could mean purchasing ownership in suppliers, developing long-term contracts or joint ventures to lock in necessary resources, or building relationships in other ways. Other techniques, as will be described in Chapter 6, include interlocking directorships to include members of supplier companies on the board of directors, joining trade associations to coordinate needs, using lobbying and political activities, or merging with another firm to guarantee resources and material supplies. Organizations operating under the resource-dependence philosophy will do whatever is needed to avoid excessive dependence on the environment and maintain control of resources, thereby reducing uncertainty. Locking in resources through long-term supplier relationships is one of the most common strategies.

Supply Chain Relationships

To operate efficiently and produce high-quality items that meet customers' needs, an organization must have reliable deliveries of high-quality, reasonably priced supplies and materials. Many organizations develop close relationships with key suppliers to gain control over necessary resources. **Supply chain management** refers to managing the sequence of suppliers and purchasers, covering all stages of processing from obtaining raw materials to distributing finished goods to consumers.[16] Exhibit 4.3 illustrates a basic supply chain model. A supply chain is a network of multiple businesses and individuals that are connected through the flow of products or services. Research indicates that formalizing collaborative supply chain relationships can help organizations obtain and use resources more efficiently and improve their performance.[17]

Many organizations manage supply chain relationships using the Internet and other sophisticated technologies, establishing electronic linkages between the organization and these external partners for the sharing and exchange of data.[18] Companies such as Apple, Wal-Mart, Nokia, Toyota, Tesco, and Samsung, for instance, are electronically connected with their partners so that everyone along the supply chain has almost completely transparent information about sales, orders, shipments, and other data. That means suppliers have data about orders, production levels, and needed materials, ensuring that resources are available when needed. In a recent study of supply chains, AMR Research ranked Apple as the best-performing supply

EXHIBIT 4.3
A Basic Supply Chain
Model

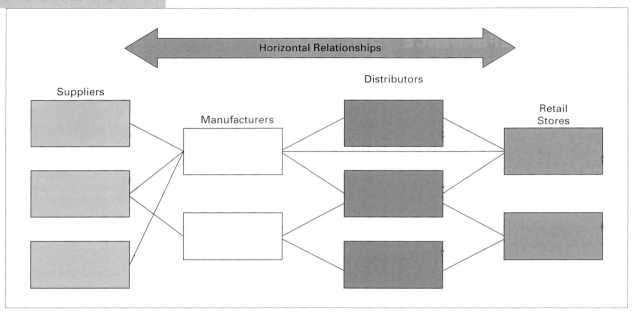

Source: Global Supply Chain Games Project, Delft University and the University of Maryland, R. H. Smith School of Business, *http://www.gscg.org:8080/opencms/export/sites/default/gscg/images/supplychain_simple.gif* (accessed on February 6, 2008).

chain in the world, with Nokia at No. 2, Wal-Mart at No. 6, Samsung Electronics at No. 9, and the British supermarket chain Tesco at No. 12.[19]

Power Implications

In resource-dependence theory, large, independent companies have power over small suppliers.[20] For example, power in consumer products has shifted from vendors such as Rubbermaid and Procter & Gamble to the big discount retail chains, which can demand—and receive—special pricing deals. Wal-Mart has grown so large and powerful that it can dictate the terms with virtually any supplier. When one company has power over another, it can ask suppliers to absorb more costs, ship more efficiently, and provide more services than ever before, often without a price increase. Often the suppliers have no choice but to go along, and those who fail to do so may go out of business.

Power is also shifting in other industries. For decades, technology vendors have been putting out incompatible products and expecting their corporate customers to assume the burden and expense of making everything work together. Those days may be coming to an end. With a shaky economy, big corporations cut back their spending on technology, which led to stiffer competition among technology vendors and gave their corporate customers greater power to make demands. Another area that is seeing a big power shift is the publishing and bookselling industry, as illustrated by the following example.

Amazon calls itself the most customer-centric company on earth, but many small publishers and authors are beginning to call it the biggest bully in the publishing indus-

IN PRACTICE

Amazon.com

try. If you've purchased from Amazon, you might have used the "Buy Now with 1 Click" button, which allows registered users to buy a book from Amazon instantly and get free shipping. But if you're a publisher and you cross the giant online retailer, you're likely to have the "Buy Now" button disabled for your titles. Customers can still buy the books, but they have to navigate to an open marketplace linking them to third-party sellers.

That's what happened to books published by the British unit of Hachette Livre, a subsidiary of French media company Lagardère, after a dispute with Amazon over the division of revenues from online sales. In Britain, as in other markets where Amazon has a commanding position, publishers have tough annual negotiations with Amazon about their cut of sales. Hachette Livre says Amazon has demanded an ever-increasing slice of the revenue pie that is shared between author, publisher, retailer, printer, and so forth.

Amazon has also disabled the "Buy Now" button for some small publishers in the United States that resisted the giant company's demands that they use an Amazon-owned company, BookSurge, for print-on-demand services. "This is a clear indication that once they have the clout they are willing to use it to the full extent that they can," said Paul Aiken, executive director of the Authors Guild, a trade group that uses BackinPrint.com for print-on-demand books. "It's ugly with Amazon and will probably get uglier."[21] ∎

COLLABORATIVE NETWORKS

The **collaborative-network** perspective is an emerging alternative to resource-dependence theory. Companies join together to become more competitive and to share scarce resources. Large aerospace firms partner with one another and with smaller companies and suppliers to design next-generation jets. Large pharmaceutical companies join with small biotechnology firms to share resources and knowledge and spur innovation. Consulting firms, investment companies, and accounting firms may join in an alliance to meet customer demands for expanded services.[22] As companies move into their own uncharted territory, they are also racing into alliances. Sprint, Clearwire, Comcast, Google, Time Warner, Intel, and Bright House formed an alliance to develop new technology for ultrafast wireless Internet access for cell phones and laptops, called WiMax. They believed the collaborative network approach was the best way to get a jump on rivals Verizon and AT&T in developing next-generation wireless services. So far, the companies have jointly invested more than $3 billion to develop a national WiMax network that will have the Internet download speed of a cable connection and the broad reach of a cell phone network.[23] Corporate alliances require managers who are good at building personal networks across boundaries. How effective are you at networking? Complete the questionnaire in the "How Do You Fit the Design?" box to find out.

Why Collaboration?

Why all this interest in interorganizational collaboration? Some key reasons include sharing risks when entering new markets, mounting expensive new programs and reducing costs, and enhancing organizational profile in selected industries or technologies. Cooperation is a prerequisite for greater innovation, problem solving, and performance.[24] In addition, partnerships are a major avenue for entering global markets, with both large and small firms developing partnerships overseas and in North America.

North American companies traditionally have worked alone, competing with each other and believing in the tradition of individualism and self-reliance, but they have learned from their international experience just how effective interorganizational relationships can be. Both Japan and Korea have long traditions of corporate clans or industrial groups that collaborate and assist each other. North Americans typically have considered interdependence a bad thing, believing it would reduce competition. However, the experience of collaboration in other countries has shown that competition among companies can be fierce in some areas even as they collaborate

How Do You Fit the Design?

Personal Networking

Are you a natural at reaching out to others for personal networking? Having multiple sources of information is a building block for partnering with people in other organizations. To learn something about your networking, answer the following questions. Please answer whether each item is Mostly True or Mostly False for you in school or at work.

	Mostly True	Mostly False
1. I learn early on about changes going on in the organization and how they might affect me or my job.	_____	_____
2. I network as much to help other people solve problems as to help myself.	_____	_____
3. I join professional groups and associations to expand my contacts and knowledge.	_____	_____
4. I know and talk with peers in other organizations.	_____	_____
5. I act as a bridge from my work group to other work groups.	_____	_____
6. I frequently use lunches to meet and network with new people.	_____	_____
7. I regularly participate in charitable causes.	_____	_____
8. I maintain a list of friends and colleagues to whom I send Christmas cards.	_____	_____
9. I maintain contact with people from previous organizations and school groups.	_____	_____
10. I actively give information to subordinates, peers, and my boss.	_____	_____

Scoring: Give yourself one point for each item marked as Mostly True. A score of 7 or higher suggests very active networking. If you scored three or less, reaching out to others may not be natural for you and will require extra effort.

Interpretation: In a world of adversarial relationships between organizations, networking across organizational boundaries was not important. However, in a world of interorganizational partnerships, many good things flow from active networking, which will build a web of organizational relationships to get things done. If you are going to manage relationships with other organizations, networking is an essential part of your job. Networking builds social, work, and career relationships that facilitate mutual benefit. People with large, active networks tend to enjoy and contribute to partnerships and have broader impact on interorganizational relationships.

1 Organizations should strive to be as independent and self-sufficient as possible so that their managers aren't put in the position of "dancing to someone else's tune."

ANSWER: *Disagree.* Trying to be separate and independent is the old way of thinking. This view says organizations should minimize their dependence on other firms so that they do not become vulnerable. Today, though, successful companies see collaboration as a better approach to maintaining a balance of power and getting things done.

in others. It is as if the brothers and sisters of a single family went into separate businesses and want to outdo one another, but they will help each other out when push comes to shove.

Interorganizational linkages provide a kind of safety net that encourages long-term investment and risk taking. Organizations can achieve higher levels of innovation and performance as they learn to shift from an adversarial to a partnership mindset.[25] Consider the following examples:

- Nintendo had become an "also-ran" in the video game console market, but it had a clear hit with the Wii. Why? Partly because, for the first time, Nintendo reached out to independent software developers and game makers. Nintendo executives made a special presentation at Namco Bandai Games, for example, listing reasons why the Wii would be profitable for both companies. By being a partner with other game developers rather that a rival, Nintendo dramatically increased the number and diversity of games that can run on the Wii.[26]
- Procter & Gamble (P&G) and Clorox are fierce rivals in cleaning products and water purification, but both companies profited when they collaborated to produce Glad Press 'n Seal. The technology for the innovative plastic wrap was invented in P&G labs, but the company didn't have a plastic-wrap category of products. Managers approached Clorox with the idea of a joint venture to market the new plastic wrap under the well-established Glad brand name. Glad's share of the wrap market shot up 23 percent virtually overnight with the introduction of Glad Press 'n Seal.[27]
- The Disney Channel invites magazines such as *J-14, Twist,* and *Popstar* to visit the sets of shows like "Hannah Montana" and "High School Musical," gives reporters access for interviews and photo shoots, and provides brief videos for the magazines to post on their websites. By working together, these companies continually find new ways to keep preteen interest booming for both the television shows and the magazines.[28]

From Adversaries to Partners

Fresh flowers are blooming on the battle-scarred landscape where once-bitter rivalries once took place. In North America, collaboration among organizations initially occurred in nonprofit social service and mental health organizations, where public interest was involved. Community organizations collaborated to achieve greater effectiveness and better use of scarce resources.[29] With the push from international competitors and international examples, hard-nosed American business managers soon began shifting to a new partnership paradigm on which to base their relationships.

Briefcase

As an organization manager, keep these guidelines in mind:

Seek collaborative partnerships that enable mutual dependence and enhance value and gain for both sides. Get deeply involved in your partner's business, and vice versa, to benefit both.

Exhibit 4.4 provides a summary of this change in mindset. Rather than organizations maintaining independence, the new model is based on interdependence and trust. Performance measures for the partnership are loosely defined, and problems are resolved through discussion and dialogue. Managing strategic relationships with other firms has become a critical management skill. In the new orientation, people try to add value to both sides and believe in high commitment rather than suspicion and competition. Companies work toward equitable profits for both sides rather than just for their own benefit. The new model is characterized by lots of shared information, including electronic linkages and face-to-face discussions to provide feedback and solve problems. Sometimes people from other companies are on site to enable very close coordination. Partners develop equitable solutions to conflicts rather than relying on legal contracts and lawsuits. Contracts may be loosely specified, and it is not unusual for business partners to help each other outside whatever is specified in the contract.[30]

In this new view of partnerships, dependence on another company is seen to reduce rather than increase risks. Greater value can be achieved by both parties. By being entwined in a system of interorganizational relationships, everyone does better because they help one another. This is a far cry from the belief that organizations do best by being autonomous. The partnership mindset can be seen in a number of industries. Chrysler and Nissan formed a partnership whereby

EXHIBIT 4.4

Changing Characteristics of Interorganizational Relationships

Traditional Orientation: Adversarial	New Orientation: Partnership
Low dependence	High dependence
Suspicion, competition, arm's length	Trust, addition of value to both sides, high commitment
Detailed performance measures, closely monitored	Loose performance measures; problems discussed
Price, efficacy, own profits	Equity, fair dealing, both profit
Limited information and feedback	Electronic linkages to share key information, problem feedback, and discussion
Legal resolution of conflict	Mechanisms for close coordination; people on site
Minimal involvement and up-front investment, separate resources	Involvement in partner's product design and production, shared resources
Short-term contracts	Long-term contracts
Contract limiting the relationship	Business assistance beyond the contract

Source: Based on Mick Marchington and Steven Vincent, "Analysing the Influence of Institutional, Organizational, and Interpersonal Forces in Shaping Inter-Organizational Relations," *Journal of Management Studies* 41, no. 6 (September 2004), 1029–1056; Jeffrey H. Dyer, "How Chrysler Created an American *Keiretsu*," *Harvard Business Review* (July–August 1996), 42–56; Myron Magnet, "The New Golden Rule of Business," *Fortune* (February 21, 1994), 60–64; and Peter Grittner, "Four Elements of Successful Sourcing Strategies," *Management Review* (October 1995), 41–45.

Nissan will build a fuel-efficient small car for Chrysler and Chrysler will build a full-size pickup based on the Dodge Ram to be sold by Nissan.[31] Deere & Company joined with several independent Deere dealerships and two technical colleges to develop programs for training technicians to service agricultural and construction machines that now rely heavily on electronics and complex advanced technologies.[32]

Canada's Bombardier and its suppliers were linked together almost like one organization to build the Continental, a "super-midsize" business jet that can comfortably fly eight passengers nonstop from coast to coast. Bombardier relied heavily on suppliers all over the world for design and manufacturing help. At one point, about 250 team members from Bombardier and 250 from outsider suppliers worked together in Montreal to make sure the design was going to be good for everyone. Integrating the partners and managing this multinational, multicompany endeavor was no easy task, but with development costs for a new plane reaching more than $1 billion, the partnership approach just made sense.[33]

By breaking down boundaries and becoming involved in partnerships with an attitude of fair dealing and adding value to both sides, today's companies are changing the concept of what makes an organization. The type of collaborative network illustrated by Bombardier is also being used by a growing number of automotive companies. These companies are pushing the idea of partnership further than ever before, moving somewhat toward a network approach to organization design, as described in Chapter 2.

POPULATION ECOLOGY

This section introduces a different perspective on relationships among organizations. The **population-ecology perspective** differs from the other perspectives because it focuses on organizational diversity and adaptation within a population of organizations.[34] A **population** is a set of organizations engaged in similar activities with similar patterns of resource utilization and outcomes. Organizations within a population compete for similar resources or similar customers, such as financial institutions in the Seattle area or car dealerships in Houston, Texas.

Within a population, the question asked by ecology researchers is about the large number and variation of organizations in society. Why are new organizational forms that create such diversity constantly appearing? The answer is that individual organizational adaptation is severely limited compared to the changes demanded by the environment. Innovation and change in a population of organizations take place through the birth of new types of organizations more so than by the reform and change of existing organizations. Indeed, organizational forms are considered relatively stable, and the good of a whole society is served by the development of new forms of organization through entrepreneurial initiatives. New organizations meet the new needs of society more than established organizations that are slow to change.[35]

What does this theory mean in practical terms? It means that large, established organizations often become dinosaurs. Consider that among the companies that appeared on the first *Fortune* 500 list in 1955, only 71 are still on the list today. The most powerful companies on today's list—companies like Apple, Google, or Intel—hadn't even been thought of then. Large, established firms often have tremendous difficulty adapting to a rapidly changing environment. Hence, new organizational forms that fit the current environment emerge, fill a new niche, and over time take away business from established companies.[36] According to the population-ecology view, when looking at an organizational population as a whole, the changing environment determines which organizations survive or fail. The assumption is that individual organizations suffer from structural inertia and find it difficult to adapt to environmental changes. Thus, when rapid change occurs, old organizations are likely to decline or fail, and new organizations emerge that are better suited to the needs of the environment.

Why do established organizations have such a hard time adapting to a rapidly changing environment? Michael Hannan and John Freeman, originators of the population ecology model of organization, argue that there are many limitations on the ability of organizations to change. The limitations come from heavy investment in plants, equipment, and specialized personnel, limited information, established viewpoints of decision makers, the organization's own successful history that justifies current procedures, and the difficulty of changing corporate culture. True transformation is a rare and unlikely event in the face of all these barriers.[37]

The population–ecology model is developed from theories of natural selection in biology, and the terms *evolution* and *selection* are used to refer to the underlying behavioral processes. Theories of biological evolution try to explain why certain life forms appear and survive whereas others perish. Some theories suggest the forms that survive are typically best fitted to the immediate environment.

The environment of the 1940s and 1950s was suitable to Woolworth, but new organizational forms like Wal-Mart became dominant in the 1980s. Now, the environment is shifting again, indicating that the "Wal-Mart Era" might be coming to a close. Though Wal-Mart is still profitable and powerful, its influence in retail is slipping. Wal-Mart managers find themselves scrambling to keep up with swifter competitors and new types of retailers that offer greater selection or higher quality.[38] No company is immune to the processes of social change. In recent years, technology has brought tremendous environmental change, leading to the decline of many outdated organizations and a proliferation of new companies such as Google, Facebook, TiVo, MySpace, and eBay.

Organizational Form and Niche

The population-ecology model is concerned with organizational forms. **Organizational form** is an organization's specific technology, structure, products, goals, and personnel, which can be selected or rejected by the environment. Each new organization tries to find a **niche** (a domain of unique environmental resources and needs) sufficient to support it. The niche is usually small in the early stages of an organization but may increase in size over time if the organization is successful. If the organization does not find an appropriate niche, it will decline and may perish.

From the viewpoint of a single firm, luck, chance, and randomness play important parts in survival. New products and ideas are continually being proposed by both entrepreneurs and large organizations. Whether these ideas and organizational forms survive or fail is often a matter of chance—whether external circumstances happen to support them. A woman who started a small electrical contracting business in a rapidly growing area such as Austin, Texas, or Atlanta, Georgia, would have an excellent chance of success. If the same woman were to start the same business in a declining community elsewhere in the United States, her chance of success would be far less. Success or failure of a single firm thus is predicted by the characteristics of the environment as much as by the skills or strategies used by the organization's managers.

2 **The success or failure of a start-up is largely determined by the smarts and management ability of the entrepreneur.**

ANSWER: *Disagree.* Luck is often as important as smarts because larger forces in the environment, typically unseen by managers, allow some firms to succeed and others to fail. If a start-up happens to be in the right place at the right time, chances for success are much higher, regardless of management ability.

Process of Ecological Change

The population-ecology model assumes that new organizations are always appearing in the population. Thus, organizational populations are continually undergoing change. The process of change in the population occurs in three stages: variation, selection, and retention, as summarized in Exhibit 4.5.

- *Variation.* **Variation** means the appearance of new, diverse forms in a population of organizations. These new organizational forms are initiated by entrepreneurs, established with venture capital by large corporations, or set up by governments seeking to provide new services. Some forms may be conceived to cope with a perceived need in the external environment. In recent years, a large number of new firms have been initiated to develop computer software, to provide consulting and other services to large corporations, and to develop products and technologies for Internet commerce. Other new organizations produce a traditional product or service, but do it using new technology, new business models, or new management techniques that make the new companies far more able to survive. Organizational variations are analogous to mutations in biology, and they add to the scope and complexity of organizational forms in the environment. Two entrepreneurs in New York started a new type of law firm that experienced immediate success.

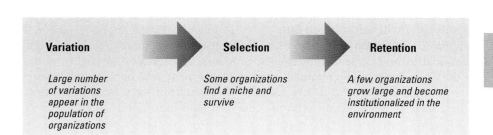

Variation

Large number of variations appear in the population of organizations

Selection

Some organizations find a niche and survive

Retention

A few organizations grow large and become institutionalized in the environment

EXHIBIT 4.5
Elements in the Population–Ecology Model of Organizations

When Mark Harris was a young associate at a prestigious law firm, he happened to glimpse a client's bill for a case he was working on. "It was only February, and already we'd billed an amount equal to my salary for the year," Harris said. He realized that most of the money big law firms bring in goes to defray overhead expenses or into the pockets of the firm's partners. "The model seemed broken to me," Harris explains about his idea for a new kind of law firm.

Along with partner Alec Guettel, Harris founded Axiom Global Inc. Axiom provides legal services to corporations on an as-needed basis, typically charging fees that are far less than traditional law firms. Axiom can charge less because it doesn't have to compensate highly-paid partners, and the company's lawyers often work from home or at a client's offices, helping to keep overhead to a minimum. Axiom has a staff of around 220 lawyers who take temporary assignments with corporate clients. They are employed full-time by Axiom and get benefits but no pay between assignments. Harris and Guettel found there were many highly-trained lawyers who wanted a different kind of life—more time with family, time to try their hand at writing a book, or just a break from the grueling pace. Joe Risco, for example, says he "wanted to chill out and try something different." Risco's first assignment was a nine-month project for Goldman Sachs. Although it took a while for Risco to get used to the prestige disparity between working for a big well-known firm and working for Axiom, he says he loves the broad range of experience he's getting.

Axiom has scored a number of *Fortune* 500 companies as clients, including Cisco Systems, General Electric, Google, and Xerox Corporation. "The model makes a lot of sense," says Don Liu of Xerox. Axiom isn't trying to displace top law firms for high-end work such as a major merger or a make-or-break lawsuit. But for more modest projects, this new type of law firm fits the bill—and cuts it by 25 to 50 percent.[39] ■

Axiom is one of a number of start-ups using this variation on the traditional law firm. Some work primarily with smaller businesses that don't have in-house legal departments, while others aim for projects with large corporate clients. By providing services on an as-needed project basis at a lower cost, these new organizations are challenging the grip big law firms have on corporate business.

- *Selection.* **Selection** refers to whether a new organizational form such as Axiom is suited to the environment and can survive. Only a few variations are "selected in" by the environment and survive over the long term. Some variations will suit the external environment better than others. Some prove beneficial and thus are able to find a niche and acquire the resources from the environment necessary to survive. Other variations fail to meet the needs of the environment and perish. When there is insufficient demand for a firm's product and when insufficient resources are available to the organization, that organization will be "selected out."
- *Retention.* **Retention** is the preservation and institutionalization of selected organizational forms. Certain technologies, products, and services are highly valued by the environment. The retained organizational form may become a dominant part of the environment. Many forms of organization have been institutionalized, such as government, schools, churches, and automobile manufacturers. McDonald's, which owns 43 percent of the fast-food market and provides the first job for many teenagers, has become institutionalized in American life.

Institutionalized organizations like McDonald's seem to be relatively permanent features in the population of organizations, but they are not permanent in the long run. The environment is always shifting, and if the dominant organizational forms do not adapt to external change, they will gradually diminish and be replaced by other organizations. McDonald's has struggled in recent years to adapt to a changing fast-food market. Consumer satisfaction surveys reveal that customers think rivals Burger King and Wendy's provide fresher, higher-quality food at better prices. In addition, chains such as Subway and Quizno's are offering today's health-conscious customer an alternative to burgers and fries.[40]

From the population-ecology perspective, the environment is the important determinant of organizational success or failure. The organization must meet an environmental need, or it will be selected out. The principles of variation, selection, and retention lead to the establishment of new organizational forms in a population of organizations.

Strategies for Survival

Another principle that underlies the population ecology model is the **struggle for existence,** or competition. Organizations and populations of organizations are engaged in a competitive struggle over resources, and each organizational form is fighting to survive. The struggle is most intense among new organizations, and both the birth and survival frequencies of new organizations are related to factors in the larger environment. Factors such as size of urban area, percentage of immigrants, political turbulence, industry growth rate, and environmental variability, for example, have influenced the launching and survival of newspapers, telecommunication firms, railroads, government agencies, labor unions, and even voluntary organizations.[41]

In the population ecology perspective, **generalist** and **specialist** strategies distinguish organizational forms in the struggle for survival. Organizations with a wide niche or domain, that is, those that offer a broad range of products or services or that serve a broad market, are generalists. Organizations that provide a narrower range of goods or services or that serve a narrower market are specialists.

In the natural environment, a specialist form of flora and fauna would evolve in protective isolation in a place like Hawaii, where the nearest body of land is 2,000 miles away. The flora and fauna are heavily protected. In contrast, a place like Costa Rica, which experienced wave after wave of external influences, developed a generalist set of flora and fauna that has better resilience and flexibility for adapting to a broad range of environments. In the business world, Amazon.com started with a specialist strategy, selling books over the Internet, but evolved to a generalist strategy with the addition of music, DVDs, greeting cards, and other products, plus partnering with other organizations as an online shopping mall to sell a wide range of products. A company such as Olmec Corporation, which sells African-American and Hispanic dolls, would be considered a specialist, whereas Mattel is a generalist, marketing a broad range of toys for boys and girls of all ages.[42]

Specialists are generally more competitive than generalists in the narrow area in which their domains overlap. However, the breadth of the generalist's domain serves to protect it somewhat from environmental changes. Though demand may decrease for some of the generalist's products or services, it usually increases for others at the same time. In addition, because of the diversity of products, services, and customers, generalists are able to reallocate resources internally to adapt to a changing environment, whereas specialists are not. However, because specialists are often smaller companies, they can sometimes move faster and be more flexible in adapting to changes.[43]

Managerial impact on company success often comes from selecting a strategy that steers a company into an open niche. Axiom's founders, for example, saw that traditional law firms weren't meeting the needs of many small businesses as well as large corporations wanting lower-cost, as-needed legal services.

INSTITUTIONALISM

The institutional perspective provides yet another view of interorganizational relationships.[44] The **institutional perspective** describes how organizations survive and succeed through congruence between an organization and the expectations from its environment. The **institutional environment** is composed of norms and values from stakeholders (customers, investors, associations, boards, other organizations, government, the community, and so on). Thus the institutional view believes that organizations adopt structures and processes to please outsiders, and these activities come to take on rule-like status in organizations. The institutional environment reflects what the greater society views as correct ways of organizing and behaving.[45]

Legitimacy is defined as the general perception that an organization's actions are desirable, proper, and appropriate within the environment's system of norms, values, and beliefs.[46] Institutional theory thus is concerned with the set of intangible norms and values that shape behavior, as opposed to the tangible elements of technology and structure. Organizations and industries must fit within the cognitive and emotional expectations of their audience. For example, people will not deposit money in a bank unless it sends signals of compliance with norms of wise financial management. Consider also your local government and whether it could raise property taxes for increased school funding if community residents did not approve of the school district's policies and activities.

Most organizations are concerned with legitimacy, as reflected in the annual *Fortune* magazine survey that ranks corporations based on their reputations, and the annual Reputation Quotient study, a survey of public opinion conducted by Harris Interactive and the Reputation Institute.[47] The fact that there is a payoff for having a good reputation is verified by a study of organizations in the airline industry. Having a good reputation was significantly related to higher levels of performance based on measures such as return on assets and net profit margin.[48]

Many corporations actively shape and manage their reputations to increase their competitive advantage. In the wake of the mortgage meltdown and the failure of giants Bear Stearns and Lehman Brothers, for example, many companies in the finance industry began searching for new ways to bolster legitimacy. Citigroup, Merrill Lynch, and Wachovia all ousted their chief executives over mortgage-related issues, partly as a way to signal a commitment to better business practices.

The notion of legitimacy answers an important question for institutional theorists: Why is there so much homogeneity in the forms and practices of established organizations? For example, visit banks, high schools, hospitals, government departments, or business firms in a similar industry, in any part of the country, and they will look strikingly similar. When an organizational field is just getting started, such as in Internet-related businesses, diversity is the norm. New organizations fill emerging niches. However, once an industry becomes established, there is an invisible push toward similarity. *Isomorphism* is the term used to describe this move toward similarity.

The Institutional View and Organization Design

The institutional view also sees organizations as having two essential dimensions—technical and institutional. The technical dimension is the day-to-day work, technology, and operating requirements. The institutional structure is that part of the organization most visible to the outside public. Moreover, the technical dimension is governed by norms of rationality and efficiency, but the institutional dimension is governed by expectations from the external environment. As a result of pressure to do things in a proper and correct way, the formal structures of many organizations reflect the expectations and values of the environment rather than the demand of work activities. This means that an organization may incorporate positions or activities (equal employment officer, e-commerce division, chief ethics officer) perceived as important by the larger society to increase its legitimacy and survival prospects, even though these elements may decrease efficiency. For example, many small companies set up websites, even though the benefits gained from the site are sometimes outweighed by the costs of maintaining it. Having a website is perceived as essential by the larger society today. The formal structure and design of an organization may not be rational with respect to workflow and products or services, but it will ensure survival in the larger environment.

Organizations adapt to the environment by signaling their congruence with the demands and expectations stemming from cultural norms, standards set by professional bodies, funding agencies, and customers. Structure is something of a facade disconnected from technical work through which the organization obtains approval, legitimacy, and continuing support. The adoption of structures thus might not be linked to actual production needs and might occur regardless of whether specific internal problems are solved. Formal structure is separated from technical action in this view.[49]

Institutional Similarity

Organizations have a strong need to appear legitimate. In so doing, many aspects of structure and behavior may be targeted toward environmental acceptance rather than toward internal technical efficiency. Interorganizational relationships thus are characterized by forces that cause organizations in a similar population to look like one another. **Institutional similarity,** called *institutional isomorphism* in the academic literature, is the emergence of a common structure and approach among organizations in the same field. Isomorphism is the process that causes one unit in a population to resemble other units that face the same set of environmental conditions.[50]

Exactly how does increasing similarity occur? How are these forces realized? Exhibit 4.6 provides a summary of three mechanisms for institutional adaptation. These three core mechanisms are *mimetic forces*, which result from responses to uncertainty; *coercive forces*, which stem from political influence; and *normative forces*, which result from common training and professionalism.[51]

Mimetic Forces. Most organizations, especially business organizations, face great uncertainty. It is not clear to senior executives exactly what products, services, technologies, or management practices will achieve desired goals, and sometimes the goals themselves are not clear. In the face of this uncertainty, **mimetic forces,**

Briefcase

As an organization manager, keep these guidelines in mind:

Pursue legitimacy with your organization's major stakeholders in the external environment. Adopt strategies, structures, and management techniques that meet the expectations of significant parties, thereby ensuring their cooperation and access to resources.

EXHIBIT 4.6
Three Mechanisms
for Institutional
Adaptation

	Mimetic	Coercive	Normative
Reason to become similar:	Uncertainty	Dependence	Duty, obligation
Events:	Innovation visibility	Political law, rules, sanctions	Professionalism— certification, accreditation
Social basis:	Culturally supported	Legal	Moral
Example:	Reengineering, benchmarking	Pollution controls, school regulations	Accounting standards, consultant training

Source: Adapted from W. Richard Scott, *Institutions and Organizations* (Thousand Oaks, Calif.: Sage, 1995).

the pressure to copy or model other organizations, occur. Executives observe an innovation in a firm generally regarded as successful, so the practice is quickly copied. One example was the rapid growth of wi-fi hotspots in cafes, hotels, airports, and other public areas. Starbucks was one of the first companies to adopt wi-fi, enabling customers to use laptops and handheld computers at its stores. The practice was quickly copied by both large and small companies, from Holiday Inns to the local deli.

Many times, this modeling is done without any clear proof that performance will be improved. Mimetic processes explain why fads and fashions occur in the business world. Once a new idea starts, many organizations grab onto it, only to learn that the application is difficult and may cause more problems than it solves. This was the case with the recent merger wave that swept many industries. The past few decades have seen the largest merger and acquisition wave in history, but evidence shows that many of these mergers did not produce the expected financial gains and other benefits. The sheer momentum of the trend was so powerful that many companies chose to merge not because of potential increases in efficiency or profitability but simply because it seemed like the right thing to do.[52]

Techniques such as outsourcing, teams, Six Sigma quality programs, brainstorming, and the balanced scorecard have all been adopted without clear evidence that they will improve efficiency or effectiveness. The one certain benefit is that management's feelings of uncertainty will be reduced, and the company's image will be enhanced because the firm is seen as using the latest management techniques. A study of 100 organizations confirmed that those companies associated with using popular management techniques were more admired and rated higher in quality of management, even though these organizations often did not reflect higher economic performance.[53] Perhaps the clearest example of official copying is the technique of benchmarking that occurs as part of the total quality movement. *Benchmarking* means identifying who's best at something in an industry and then duplicating the technique for creating excellence, perhaps even improving it in the process.

The mimetic process works because organizations face high uncertainty, they are aware of innovations occurring in the environment, and the innovations are culturally supported, thereby giving legitimacy to adopters. This is a strong mechanism by which a group of banks, or high schools, or manufacturing firms begin to look and act like one another.

3 **Managers should quickly copy or borrow techniques being used by other successful companies to make their own organization more effective and to keep pace with changing times.**

ANSWER: *Agree.* Managers frequently copy techniques used by other, successful organizations as a way to appear legitimate and up to date. Copying other firms is one reason organizations may begin to look and act similar in their structures, processes, and management systems.

Coercive Forces. All organizations are subject to pressure, both formal and informal, from government, regulatory agencies, and other important organizations in the environment, especially those on which a company is dependent. **Coercive forces** are the external pressures exerted on an organization to adopt structures, techniques, or behaviors similar to other organizations. For example, large corporations have recently been putting pressure on service providers, such as accounting or law firms, to step up their diversity efforts. Managers in these corporations have felt pressure to increase diversity within their own organizations and they want the firms with which they do business to reflect a commitment to hiring and promoting more women and minorities as well.[54]

Some pressures may have the force of law, such as government mandates to adopt new pollution control equipment. Health and safety regulations may demand that a safety officer be appointed. New regulations and government oversight boards have been set up for the accounting industry following widespread accounting scandals.

Coercive pressures may also occur between organizations where there is a power difference, as described in the resource-dependence section earlier in this chapter. Large retailers and manufacturers often insist that certain policies, procedures, and techniques be used by their suppliers. Wal-Mart, for instance, requires many of its suppliers to affix radio-frequency identification (RFID) tags to their products to enable easier tracking of merchandise. The giant retailer has also begun granting preference to suppliers who make their products more environmentally friendly, which acts as a coercive force.

As with other changes, those brought about because of coercive forces may not make the organization more effective, but it will look more effective and will be accepted as legitimate in the environment. Organizational changes that result from coercive forces occur when an organization is dependent on another, when there are political factors such as rules, laws, and sanctions involved, or when some other contractual or legal basis defines the relationship. Organizations operating under those constraints will adopt changes and relate to one another in a way that increases homogeneity and limits diversity.

Normative Forces. The third reason organizations change according to the institutional view is normative forces. **Normative forces** are pressures to change to achieve standards of professionalism and to adopt techniques that are considered by the professional community to be up to date and effective. Changes may be in any area, such as information technology, accounting requirements, marketing techniques, or collaborative relationships with other organizations.

Professionals share a body of formal education based on university degrees and professional networks through which ideas are exchanged by consultants and professional leaders. Universities, consulting firms, trade associations, and professional training institutions develop norms among professional managers. People are exposed to similar training and standards and adopt shared values, which are implemented in organizations with which they work. Business schools teach finance, marketing, and human resource majors that certain techniques are better than others, so using those techniques becomes a standard in the field. In one study, for example, a radio station changed from a functional to a multidivisional structure because a consultant recommended it as a "higher standard" of doing business. There was no proof that this structure was better, but the radio station wanted legitimacy and to be perceived as fully professional and up to date in its management techniques.

Companies accept normative pressures to become like one another through a sense of obligation or duty to high standards of performance based on professional norms shared by managers and specialists in their respective organizations. These norms are conveyed through professional education and certification and have almost a moral or ethical requirement based on the highest standards accepted by the profession at that time. In some cases, though, normative forces that maintain legitimacy break down, as they recently did in the accounting and finance industries, and coercive forces are needed to shift organizations back toward acceptable standards.

An organization may use any or all of the mechanisms of mimetic, coercive, or normative forces to change itself for greater legitimacy in the institutional environment. Firms tend to use these mechanisms when they are acting under conditions of dependence, uncertainty, ambiguous goals, and reliance on professional credentials. The outcome of these processes is that organizations become far more homogeneous than would be expected from the natural diversity among managers and environments.

DESIGN ESSENTIALS

■ This chapter has been about the important evolution in interorganizational relationships. At one time organizations considered themselves autonomous and separate, trying to outdo other companies. Today more organizations see themselves as part of an ecosystem. The organization may span several industries and will be anchored in a dense web of relationships with other companies. In this ecosystem, collaboration is as important as competition. Indeed, organizations may compete and collaborate at the same time, depending on the location and issue. In business ecosystems, the role of management is changing to include the development of horizontal relationships with other organizations.

■ Four perspectives have been developed to explain relationships among organizations. The resource-dependence perspective is the most traditional, arguing that organizations try to avoid excessive dependence on other organizations. In this view, organizations devote considerable effort to controlling the environment to ensure ample resources while maintaining independence. One key approach is to develop close relationships with suppliers through supply chain management.

■ The collaborative-network perspective is an emerging alternative to resource dependence. Organizations welcome collaboration and interdependence with other organizations to enhance value for both. Many executives are changing mindsets away from autonomy toward collaboration, often with former corporate enemies. The new partnership mindset emphasizes trust, fair dealing, and achieving profits for all parties in a relationship.

■ The population-ecology perspective explains why organizational diversity continuously increases with the appearance of new organizations filling niches left open by established companies. This perspective says that large companies usually cannot adapt to meet a changing environment; hence, new companies emerge with the appropriate form and skills to serve new needs. Through the process of variation, selection, and retention, some organizations will survive and grow while others perish. Companies may adopt a generalist or specialist strategy to survive in the population of organizations.

■ The institutional perspective argues that interorganizational relationships are shaped as much by a company's need for legitimacy as by the need for providing products and services. The need for legitimacy means that the organization will adopt structures and activities that are perceived as valid, proper, and up to date by external stakeholders. In this way, established organizations copy techniques from one another and begin to look very similar. The emergence of common structures and approaches in the same field is called institutional similarity or institutional isomorphism. There are three core mechanisms that explain increasing organizational homogeneity: mimetic forces, which result from responses to uncertainty; coercive forces, which stem from power differences and political influences; and normative forces, which result from common training and professionalism.

■ Each of the four perspectives is valid. They each represent different lenses through which the world of interorganizational relationships can be viewed: organizations experience a competitive struggle for autonomy; they can thrive through collaborative relationships with others; the slowness to adapt provides openings for new organizations to flourish; and organizations seek legitimacy as well as profits from the external environment. The important thing is for managers to be aware of interorganizational relationships and to consciously manage them.

Key Concepts

coercive forces	mimetic forces	retention
collaborative network	niche	selection
generalist	normative forces	specialist
institutional environment	organizational ecosystem	struggle for existence
institutional perspective	organizational form	supply chain management
institutional similarity	population	variation
interorganizational relationships	population-ecology perspective	
legitimacy	resource dependence	

Discussion Questions

1. Discuss how the adversarial versus partnership orientations work among students in class. Is there a sense of competition for grades? Is it possible to develop true partnerships in which your work depends on others?
2. How do mimetic forces differ from normative forces? Give an example of each.
3. Many managers today were trained under assumptions of adversarial relationships with other companies. Do you think operating as adversaries is easier or more difficult than operating as partners with other companies? Discuss.
4. How does the desire for legitimacy result in organizations becoming more similar over time?
5. Assume you are the manager of a small firm that is dependent on a large computer manufacturing customer that uses the resource-dependence perspective. Put yourself in the position of the small firm, and describe what actions you would take to survive and succeed. What actions would you take from the perspective of the large firm?
6. Do you believe that legitimacy really motivates a large, powerful organization such as Wal-Mart? Is acceptance by other people a motivation for individuals as well? Explain.
7. How do you feel about the prospect of becoming a manager and having to manage a set of relationships with other companies rather than just managing your own company? Discuss.
8. Explain how the process of variation, selection, and retention might explain innovations that take place within an organization.
9. The concept of business ecosystems implies that organizations are more interdependent than ever before. From personal experience, do you agree? Explain.
10. The population-ecology perspective argues that it is healthy for society to have new organizations emerging and old organizations dying as the environment changes. Do you agree? Why would European countries pass laws to sustain traditional organizations and inhibit the emergence of new ones?

Chapter 4 Workbook: Management Fads*

Look up one or two articles on current trends or fads in management. Then, find one or two articles on a management fad from several years ago. Finally, use an Internet search engine to locate information on both the current and previous fads.

Questions

1. How were these fads used in organizations? Use real examples from your readings.
2. Why do you think the fads were adopted? To what extent were the fads adopted to truly improve productivity and morale versus the company's desire to appear current in its management techniques compared to the competition?
3. Give an example in which a fad did not work as expected. Explain the reason it did not work.

*Copyright 1996 by Dorothy Marcic. All rights reserved.

Case for Analysis: Oxford Plastics Company*

Oxford Plastics manufactures high-quality plastics and resins for use in a variety of products, from lawn ornaments and patio furniture to automobiles. The Oxford plant located near Beatty, a town of about 45,000 in a southeastern state, employs about 3,000 workers. It plays an important role in the local economy and, indeed, that of the entire state, which offers few well-paying factory jobs.

In early 2004, Sam Henderson, plant manager of the Beatty facility, notified Governor Tom Winchell that Oxford was ready to announce plans for a major addition to the factory—a state-of-the-art color lab and paint shop that would enable better and faster matching of colors to customer requirements. The new shop would keep Oxford competitive in the fast-paced global market for plastics, as well as bring the Beatty plant into full compliance with updated U.S. Environmental Protection Agency (EPA) regulations.

Plans for the new facility were largely complete. The biggest remaining task was identifying the specific location. The new color lab and paint shop would cover approximately 25 acres, requiring Oxford to purchase some additional land adjacent to its 75-acre factory campus. Henderson was somewhat concerned with top management's preferred site because it fell outside the current industrial zoning boundary, and, moreover, would necessitate destruction of several 400- to 500-year-old beech trees. The owner of the property, a nonprofit agency, was ready to sell, whereas property located on the other side of the campus might be more difficult to obtain in a timely manner. Oxford was on a tight schedule to get the project completed. If the new facility wasn't up and running in a timely manner, there was a chance the EPA could force Oxford to stop using its old process—in effect, shutting down the factory.

The governor was thrilled with Oxford's decision to build the new shop in Beatty and he urged Henderson to immediately begin working closely with local and state officials to circumvent any potential problems. It was essential, he stressed, that the project not be bogged down or thwarted by conflict among different interest groups, as it was too important to the economic development of the region. Governor Winchell assigned Beth Friedlander, director of the Governor's Office of Economic Development, to work closely with Henderson on the project. However, Winchell was not willing to offer his commitment to help push through the rezoning, as he had been an enthusiastic public supporter of environmental causes.

Following his conversation with Governor Winchell, Henderson sat down to identify the various people and organizations that would have an interest in the new color lab project and that would need to collaborate in order for it to proceed in a smooth and timely manner. They are:

Oxford Plastics

- Mark Thomas, vice president of North American Operations. Thomas would be flying in from Oxford's Michigan headquarters to oversee land purchase and negotiations regarding the expansion.
- Sam Henderson, Beatty plant manager, who has spent his entire career at the Beatty facility, beginning on the factory floor fresh out of high school.
- Wayne Talbert, local union president. The union is strongly in favor of the new shop being located in Beatty because of the potential for more and higher-wage jobs.

State Government

- Governor Tom Winchell, who can exert pressure on local officials to support the project.
- Beth Friedlander, director of the Governor's Office of Economic Development.

- Manu Gottlieb, director of the State Department of Environmental Quality.

City Government

- Mayor Barbara Ott, a political newcomer, who has been in office for less than a year and who campaigned on environmental issues.
- Major J. Washington, the Chamber of Commerce chair of local economic development.

Public

- May Pinelas, chairman of Historic Beatty, who argues vociferously that the future of the region lies in historic and natural preservation and tourism.
- Tommy Tompkins, president of the Save Our Future Foundation, a coalition of private individuals and representatives from the local university who have long been involved in public environmental issues and have successfully thwarted at least one previous expansion project.

Henderson is feeling torn about how to proceed. He thinks to himself, "To move forward, how will I build a coalition among these diverse organizations and groups?" He understands the need for Oxford to move quickly, but he wants Oxford to have a good relationship with the people and organizations that will surely oppose destruction of more of Beatty's natural beauty. Henderson has always liked finding a win-win compromise, but there are so many groups with an interest in this project that he's not sure where to start. Maybe he should begin by working closely with Beth Friedlander from the governor's office—there's no doubt this is an extremely important project for the state's economic development. On the other hand, it's the local people who are going to be most affected and most involved in the final decisions. Oxford's vice president has suggested a press conference to announce the new shop at the end of the week, but Henderson is worried about putting the news out cold. Perhaps he should call a meeting of interested parties now and let everyone get their feelings out into the open? He knows it could get emotional, but he wonders if things won't get much uglier later on if he doesn't.

*Source: Based on "Mammoth Motors' New Paint Shop," a role play originally prepared by Arnold Howitt, executive director of the A. Alfred Taubman Center for State and Local Government at the Kennedy School of Government, Harvard University, and subsequently edited by Gerald Cormick, a principal in the CSE Group and senior lecturer for the Graduate School of Public Affairs at the University of Washington.

Case for Analysis: Hugh Russel, Inc.*

The following story is a personal recollection by David Hurst of the experience of a group of managers in a mature organization undergoing profound change. . . . The precipitating event in this change was a serious business crisis. . . .

When I joined Hugh Russel Inc. in 1979, it was a medium-sized Canadian distributor of steel and industrial products. With sales of CDN $535 million and 3,000 employees, the business was controlled by the chairman, Archie Russel, who owned 16 percent of the common shares. The business consisted of four groups—the core steel distribution activities (called "Russelsteel"), industrial bearings and valves distribution, a chain of wholesalers of hardware and sporting goods, and a small manufacturing business. . . .

The company was structured for performance. . . . The management was professional, with each of the divisional hierarchies headed by a group president reporting to Peter Foster in his capacity as president of the corporation. Jobs were described in job descriptions, and their mode of execution was specified in detailed standard operating procedures. Three volumes of the corporate manual spelled out policy on everything from accounting to vacation pay. Extensive accounting and data processing systems allowed managers to track the progress of individual operations against budgets and plans. Compensation was performance-based, with return on net assets (RONA) as the primary measure and large bonuses (up to 100 percent of base) for managers who made their targets.

At the senior management level, the culture was polite but formal. The board of directors consisted of Archie's friends and associates together with management insiders. Archie and Peter ran the organization as if they were majority owners. Their interaction with management outside of the head office was restricted to the occasional field trip. . . .

Crisis

Nine months after I joined the company as a financial planner, we were put "in play" by a raider and, after a fierce bidding war, were acquired in a hostile takeover. Our acquirer was a private company controlled by the eldest son of an entrepreneur of legendary wealth and ability, so we had no inkling at the time of the roller-coaster ride that lay ahead of us. We were unaware that not only did the son not have the support of his father in this venture but also he had neglected to consult his two brothers, who were joint owners of the acquiring company! As he had taken on $300 million of debt to do the deal, this left each of the brothers on the hook for a personal guarantee of $100 million. They were not amused, and it showed! Within days of the deal, we were inundated by waves of consultants, lawyers, and accountants: each shareholder

seemed to have his or her own panel of advisers. After six weeks of intensive analysis, it was clear that far too much had been paid for us and that the transaction was vastly overleveraged. At the start of the deal, the acquirer had approached our bankers and asked them if they wanted a piece of the "action." Concerned at the possible loss of our banking business and eager to be associated with such a prominent family, our bankers had agreed to provide the initial financing on a handshake. Now, as they saw the detailed numbers for the first time and became aware of the dissent among the shareholders, they withdrew their support and demanded their money back. We needed to refinance $300 million of debt—fast. . . .

Change

The takeover and the subsequent merger of our new owner's moribund steel-fabricating operations into Hugh Russel changed our agenda completely. We had new shareholders (who fought with each other constantly), new bankers, and new businesses in an environment of soaring interest rates and plummeting demand for our products and services. Almost overnight, the corporation went from a growth-oriented, acquisitive, earnings-driven operation to a broken, cash-starved company, desperate to survive. Closures, layoffs, downsizing, delayering, asset sales, and "rationalization" became our new priorities. . . . At the head office, the clarity of jobs vanished. For example, I had been hired to do financial forecasting and raise capital in the equity markets, but with the company a financial mess, this clearly could not be done. For all of us, the future looked dangerous and frightening as bankruptcy, both personal and corporate, loomed ahead.

And so it was in an atmosphere of crisis that Wayne Mang, the new president (Archie Russel and Peter Foster left the organization soon after the deal), gathered the first group of managers together to discuss the situation. Wayne Mang had been in the steel business for many years and was trusted and respected by the Hugh Russel people. An accountant by training, he used to call himself the "personnel manager" to underscore his belief in both the ability of people to make the difference in the organization and the responsibility of line management to make this happen. The hastily called first meeting consisted of people whom Wayne respected and trusted from all over the organization. They had been selected without regard for their position in the old hierarchy.

The content and style of that first meeting were a revelation to many! Few of them had ever been summoned to the head office for anything but a haranguing over their budgets. Now they were being told the complete gory details of the company's situation and, for the first time, being treated as if they had something to contribute. Wayne asked for their help.

During that first meeting, we counted nineteen major issues confronting the corporation. None of them fell under a single functional area. We arranged ourselves into task forces to deal with them. I say "arranged ourselves" because that was the way it seemed to happen. Individuals volunteered without coercion to work on issues in which they were interested or for which their skills were relevant. They also volunteered others who were not at the meeting but, it was thought, could help. There was some guidance—each task force had one person from the head office whose function it was to report what was happening back to the "center"—and some members found themselves on too many task forces, which required that substitutes be found. But that was the extent of the conscious management of the process.

The meeting broke up at 2:00 A.M., when we all went home to tell our incredulous spouses what had happened. . . .

The cross-functional project team rapidly became our preferred method of organizing new initiatives, and at the head office, the old formal structure virtually disappeared. The teams could be formed at a moment's notice to handle a fast-breaking issue and dissolved just as quickly. We found, for example, that even when we weren't having formal meetings, we seemed to spend most of our time talking to each other informally. Two people would start a conversation in someone's office, and almost before you knew it, others had wandered in and a small group session was going. Later on, we called these events "bubbles"; they became our equivalent of campfire meetings. . . .

Later, when I became executive vice president, Wayne and I deliberately shared an office so we could each hear what the other was doing in real time and create an environment in which "bubbles" might form spontaneously. As people wandered past our open door, we would wave them in to talk; others would wander in after them. The content of these sessions always had to do with our predicament, both corporate and personal. It was serious stuff, but the atmosphere was light and open. Our fate was potentially a bad one, but at least it would be shared. All of us who were involved then cannot remember ever having laughed so much. We laughed at ourselves and at the desperate situation. We laughed at the foolishness of the bankers in having financed such a mess, and we laughed at the antics of the feuding shareholders, whose outrageous manners and language we learned to mimic to perfection.

I think it was the atmosphere from these informal sessions that gradually permeated all our interactions—with employees, bankers, suppliers, everyone with whom we came into contact. Certainly, we often had tough meetings, filled with tension and threat, but we were always able to "bootstrap" ourselves back up emotionally at the informal debriefings afterward. . . .

Perhaps the best example of both the change in structure and the blurring of the boundaries of the organization was our changing relationships with our bankers. In the beginning, at least for the brief time that the loan was in good standing, the association was polite and at arm's length. Communication was formal. As the bank realized the full horror of what it had financed (a process that took about 18 months), the relationship steadily grew more hostile. Senior executives of the bank became threatening, spelling out what actions they might take if we did not solve our problem. This hostility culminated in an investigation by the bank for possible fraud (a standard procedure in many banks when faced with a significant loss).

Throughout this period, we had seen a succession of different bankers, each of whom had been assigned to our account for a few months. As a result of our efforts to brief every new face that appeared, we had built a significant network of contacts within the bank with whom we had openly shared a good deal of information and opinion. When no fraud was found, the bank polled its own people on what to do. Our views presented so coherently by our people (because everyone knew what was going on), and shared so widely with so many bankers, had an enormous influence on the outcome of this process. The result was the formation of a joint company-bank team to address a shared problem that together we could solve. The boundary between the corporation and the bank was now blurred: to an outside observer, it would have been unclear where the corporation ended and the bank began. . . .

Our corporation had extensive formal reporting systems to allow the monitoring of operations on a regular basis. After the takeover, these systems required substantial modifications. For example . . . we had to report our results to the public every quarter at a time when we were losing nearly 2 million dollars a week! We knew that unless we got to our suppliers ahead of time, they could easily panic and refuse us credit. Hasty moves on their part could have had fatal consequences for the business.

In addition, our closure plans for plants all over Canada and the United States brought us into contact with unions and governments in an entirely different way. We realized that we had no option but to deal with these audiences in advance of events.

I have already described how our relationship with the bankers changed as a result of our open communication. We found exactly the same effect with these new audiences. Initially, our major suppliers could not understand why we had told them we were in trouble before we had to. We succeeded, however, in framing the situation in a way that enlisted their cooperation in our survival, and by the time the "war story" was news, we had their full support. Similarly, most government and union organizations were so pleased to be involved in the process before announcements were made that they bent over backward to be of assistance. Just as had been the case with the bank, we set up joint task forces with these "outside" agencies to resolve what had become shared problems. A significant contributor to our ability to pull this off was the high quality of our internal communication. Everyone on the teams knew the complete, up-to-date picture of what was happening. An outside agency could talk to anyone on a team and get the same story. In this way, we constructed a formidable network of contacts, many of whom had special skills and experience in areas that would turn out to be of great help to us in the future.

The addition of multiple networks to our information systems enhanced our ability both to gather and to disseminate information. The informality and openness of the networks, together with the high volume of face-to-face dialogues, gave us an early-warning system with which to detect hurt feelings and possible hostile moves on the part of shareholders, suppliers, nervous bankers, and even customers. This information helped us head off trouble before it happened. The networks also acted as a broadcast system through which we could test plans and actions before announcing them formally. In this way, not only did we get excellent suggestions for improvement, but everyone felt that he or she had been consulted before action was taken. . . .

We had a similar experience with a group of people outside the company during the hectic last six months of 1983, when we were trying to finalize a deal for the shareholders and bankers to sell the steel distribution business to new owners. The group of people in question comprised the secretaries of the numerous lawyers and accountants involved in the deal. . . .

We made these secretaries part of the network, briefing them in advance on the situation, explaining why things were needed, and keeping them updated on the progress of the deal. We were astounded at the cooperation we received: our calls were put through, our messages received prompt responses, and drafts and opinions were produced on time. In the final event, a complex deal that should have taken nine months to complete was done in three. All of this was accomplished by ordinary people going far beyond what might have been expected of them. . . .

We had been thrust into crisis without warning, and our initial activities were almost entirely reactions to issues that imposed themselves upon us. But as we muddled along in the task forces, we began to find that we had unexpected sources of influence over what was happening. The changing relationship with the bank illustrates this neatly. Although we had no formal power in that situation, we found that by framing a confusing predicament in a coherent way, we could, via our network, influence the outcomes of the bank's decisions. The same applied to suppliers: by briefing them ahead of time and presenting a reasonable scenario for the recovery of their advances, we could influence the decisions they would make.

Slowly we began to realize that, although we were powerless in a formal sense, our networks, together with our own internal coherence, gave us an ability to get things done invisibly. As we discussed the situation with all the parties involved, a strategy began to emerge. A complicated financial/tax structure would allow the bank to "manage" its loss and give it an incentive not to call on the shareholders' personal guarantees. The core steel distribution business could be refinanced in the process and sold to new owners. The wrangle between the shareholders could be resolved, and each could go his or her own way. All that had to be done was to bring all the parties together, including a buyer for the steel business, and have them agree that this was the best course to follow. Using our newfound skills, we managed to pull it off.

It was not without excitement: at the last minute, the shareholders raised further objections to the deal. Only the bank could make them sell, and they were reluctant to do so, fearful that they might attract a lawsuit. Discreet calls to the major suppliers, several of whose executives were on the board of the bank, did the trick. "This business needs to be sold and recapitalized," the suppliers were told. "If the deal does not go through, you should probably reduce your credit exposure." The deal went through. By the end of 1983, we had new owners, just in time to benefit from the general business recovery. The ordeal was over.

Chapter 4 Workshop: Ugli Orange Case*

1. Form groups of three members. One person will be Dr. Roland, one person will be Dr. Jones, and the third person will be an observer.
2. Roland and Jones will read only their own roles, but the observer will read both.
3. Role play: Instructor announces, "I am Mr./Ms. Cardoza, the owner of the remaining Ugli oranges. My fruit export firm is based in South America. My country does not have diplomatic relations with your country, although we do have strong trade relations."

The groups will spend about 10 minutes meeting with the other firm's representative and will decide on a course of action. Be prepared to answer the following questions:

  a. What do you plan to do?

  b. If you want to buy the oranges, what price will you offer?

  c. To whom and how will the oranges be delivered?

4. The observers will report the solutions reached. The groups will describe the decision-making process used.

5. The instructor will lead a discussion on the exercise addressing the following questions:

  a. Which groups had the most trust? How did that influence behavior?

  b. Which groups shared more information? Why?

  c. How are trust and disclosure important in negotiations?

Role of "Dr. Jones"

You are Dr. John W. Jones, a biological research scientist employed by a pharmaceutical firm. You have recently developed a synthetic chemical useful for curing and preventing Rudosen. Rudosen is a disease contracted by pregnant women. If not caught in the first four weeks of pregnancy, the disease causes serious brain, eye, and ear damage to the unborn child. Recently there has been an outbreak of Rudosen in your state, and several thousand women have contracted the disease. You have found, with volunteer patients, that your recently developed synthetic serum cures Rudosen in its early stages. Unfortunately, the serum is made from the juice of the Ugli orange, which is a very rare fruit. Only a small quantity (approximately 4,000) of these oranges were produced last season. No additional Ugli oranges will be available until next season, which will be too late to cure the present Rudosen victims.

You've demonstrated that your synthetic serum is in no way harmful to pregnant women. Consequently, there are no side effects. The Food and Drug Administration has approved production and distribution of the serum as a cure for Rudosen. Unfortunately, the current outbreak was unexpected, and your firm had not planned on having the compound serum available for 6 months. Your firm holds the patent on the synthetic serum, and it is expected to be a highly profitable product when it is generally available to the public.

You have recently been informed on good evidence that Mr. R. H. Cardoza, a South American fruit exporter, is in possession of 3,000 Ugli oranges in good condition. If you could obtain the juice of all 3,000 you would be able to both cure present victims and provide sufficient inoculation for the remaining pregnant women in the state. No other state currently has a Rudosen threat.

You have recently been informed that Dr. P. W. Roland is also urgently seeking Ugli oranges and is also aware of Mr. Cardoza's possession of the 3,000 available. Dr. Roland is employed by a competing pharmaceutical firm. He has been working on biological warfare research for the past several years. There is a great deal of industrial espionage in the pharmaceutical industry. Over the past several years, Dr. Roland's firm and yours have sued each other for infringement of patent rights and espionage law violations several times.

You've been authorized by your firm to approach Mr. Cardoza to purchase the 3,000 Ugli oranges. You have been told he will sell them to the highest bidder. Your firm has authorized you to bid as high as $250,000 to obtain the juice of the 3,000 available oranges.

Role of "Dr. Roland"

You are Dr. P. W. Roland. You work as a research biologist for a pharmaceutical firm. The firm is under contract with the government to do research on methods to combat enemy uses of biological warfare.

Recently several World War II experimental nerve gas bombs were moved from the United States to a small island just off the U.S. coast in the Pacific. In the process of transporting them, two of the bombs developed a leak. The leak is currently controlled by government scientists, who believe that the gas will permeate the bomb chambers within two weeks. They know of no method of preventing the gas from getting into the atmosphere and spreading to other islands and very likely to the West Coast as well. If this occurs, it is likely that several thousand people will incur serious brain damage or die.

You've developed a synthetic vapor that will neutralize the nerve gas if it is injected into the bomb chamber before the gas leaks out. The vapor is made with a chemical taken from the rind of the Ugli orange, a very rare fruit. Unfortunately, only 4,000 of these oranges were produced this season.

You've been informed on good evidence that a Mr. R. H. Cardoza, a fruit exporter in South America, is in possession of 3,000 Ugli oranges. The chemicals from the rinds of all 3,000 oranges would be sufficient to neutralize the gas if the vapor is developed and injected efficiently. You have been informed that the rinds of these oranges are in good condition.

You have learned that Dr. J. W. Jones is also urgently seeking to purchase Ugli oranges and that he is aware of Mr. Cardoza's possession of the 3,000 available. Dr. Jones works for a firm with which your firm is highly competitive. There is a great deal of industrial espionage in the pharmaceutical industry. Over the years, your firm and Dr. Jones's have sued each other for violations of industrial espionage laws and infringement of patent rights several times. Litigation on two suits is still in process.

The federal government has asked your firm for assistance. You've been authorized by your firm to approach Mr. Cardoza to purchase 3,000 Ugli oranges. You have been told he will sell them to the highest bidder. Your firm has authorized you to bid as high as $250,000 to obtain the rinds of the oranges.

Before approaching Mr. Cardoza, you have decided to talk to Dr. Jones to influence him so that he will not prevent you from purchasing the oranges.

*By Dr. Robert House, University of Toronto. Used with permission.

Chapter 5

Global Organization Design

© Ken Kan

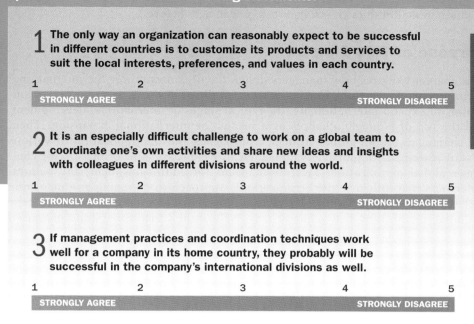

1 **The only way an organization can reasonably expect to be successful in different countries is to customize its products and services to suit the local interests, preferences, and values in each country.**

1	2	3	4	5
STRONGLY AGREE				STRONGLY DISAGREE

2 **It is an especially difficult challenge to work on a global team to coordinate one's own activities and share new ideas and insights with colleagues in different divisions around the world.**

1	2	3	4	5
STRONGLY AGREE				STRONGLY DISAGREE

3 **If management practices and coordination techniques work well for a company in its home country, they probably will be successful in the company's international divisions as well.**

1	2	3	4	5
STRONGLY AGREE				STRONGLY DISAGREE

Saks Incorporated planned to open a store in China in time for the Beijing Olympics, but the games came and went before construction ever got underway. Bertlesmann AG's Gruner + Jahr division, Europe's largest magazine publisher, tried for decades to extend that success into the United States but eventually sold off its U.S. assets in what one reporter called "a billion dollar experiment gone horribly wrong." The entrepreneurial firm First Net Card was established with a goal of providing credit for online transactions to anyone in the world, but managers found the complications of dealing with international credit and banking laws mind-boggling. After two years and a mountain of legal research, First Net was licensed to provide credit only in the United States, Canada, and Britain.[1]

That's the reality of international business. When an organization decides to do business in another country, managers face a whole new set of challenges and roadblocks. They sometimes find that transferring their domestic success internationally requires a totally different approach. Wal-Mart entered South Korea with high hopes in 1996, but ten years later sold all its South Korean stores to a local retailer and withdrew from that country.[2] It is not the only successful organization to have pulled out of one or another foreign market battered and bruised, managers scratching their heads over what went wrong.

Succeeding on a global scale isn't easy. Managers have to make tough decisions about strategic approach, how best to get involved in international markets, and how to design the organization to reap the benefits of international expansion. Despite the challenges, managers in most organizations think the potential rewards outweigh the risks. U.S.-based firms set up foreign operations to produce goods and services needed by consumers in other countries, as well as to obtain lower costs or technical know-how for producing products and services to sell domestically. In return, companies from Japan, Germany, the United Kingdom, and other countries compete with American organizations on their own turf as well as abroad. Interest in international business is stronger today than ever before.

Purpose of This Chapter

This chapter explores how managers design the organization for the international environment. We begin by looking at some of the primary motivations for organizations to expand internationally, the typical stages of international development, and the use of strategic alliances as a means for international expansion. Then, the chapter examines global strategic approaches and the application of various structural designs for global advantage. Next, we discuss some of the specific challenges global organizations face, mechanisms for addressing them, and cultural differences that influence the organization's approach to designing and managing a global firm. Finally, the chapter takes a look at the *transnational model*, a type of global organization that achieves high levels of the varied capabilities needed to succeed in a complex and volatile international environment.

ENTERING THE GLOBAL ARENA

Only a few decades ago, many companies could afford to ignore the international environment. Today, the number of companies doing business on a global scale is increasing and the awareness of national borders decreasing, as reflected in the frequency of foreign participation at the top management level. Fourteen of the *Fortune* 100 companies are now run by foreign-born CEOs. Citigroup picked India-born Vikram S. Pandit as its CEO, Alcoa's top leader was born in Morocco, and Dow Chemical is headed by a native Australian.[3] The trend is seen in other countries as well. Wales-born Howard Stringer was named Sony's first non-Japanese CEO in 2004, and Nancy McKinstry is the first American to head Dutch publisher Wolters Kluwer.[4]

Why has global experience at the top become so important to organizations? Because the world is rapidly developing into a unified global field, and companies need top leaders who have a global outlook. Extraordinary advancements in communications, technology, and transportation have created a new, highly competitive landscape. Products can be made and sold anywhere in the world, communications are instant, and product-development life cycles are growing shorter. No company is isolated from global influence. Some large so-called American companies such as Coca-Cola, IBM, McDonald's, and Procter & Gamble rely on international sales for a substantial portion of their sales and profits. Yum! Brands, which owns Pizza Hut, Taco Bell, KFC, and Long John Silver's, gets 55 percent of its profits from overseas, and managers expect that to grow to 70 percent within a decade.[5] On the other hand, organizations in other countries search for customers in the United States. Vietnam-based Kinh Do Foods Corporation operates fast food restaurants in the Philippines, Singapore, and South Korea, as well as Vietnam, and managers are aiming at both the British and U.S. markets. Russia's Lukoil has hundreds of gas stations in New Jersey and Pennsylvania and plans further expansion. India's top technology-services companies get 60 to 70 percent of their sales from North America, while Armonk, New York-based IBM gets about the same percentage of its revenues from overseas.[6]

Motivations for Global Expansion

Economic, technological, and competitive forces have combined to push many companies from a domestic to a global focus. The importance of the global environment for today's organizations is reflected in the shifting global economy. As one indication, *Fortune* magazine's list of the Global 500, the world's 500 largest companies by revenue, indicates that economic clout is being diffused across a broad global scale. In Exhibit 5.1, each circle represents the total revenues of all Global 500 companies in each country. Although the United States accounts for the majority of the Global 500 revenues, a number of less-developed countries are growing stronger. China, for example, had fifteen companies on the Global 500 in 2003, the year this chart was produced by *Fortune*, compared to only three companies on the list ten years earlier. China has grown even stronger since then, with twenty-nine companies on the 2008 Global 500 list. Japan, on the other hand, has continued to decline in importance, dropping from 149 companies in 1993 to eighty-two in 2003 and down to sixty-four in 2008.[7]

As power continues to shift, organizations are viewing participation in global business as a necessity. Indeed, in some industries, a company can be successful only by succeeding on a global scale. In general, three primary factors motivate companies to expand internationally: economies of scale, economies of scope, and low-cost production factors.[8]

EXHIBIT 5.1

The Global Economy as Reflected in the Fortune Global 500.

Note: Each circle represents the total revenues of all Global 500 companies in that country in 2003. The number in parentheses indicates the number of companies that country had on the Global 500 list in that year.

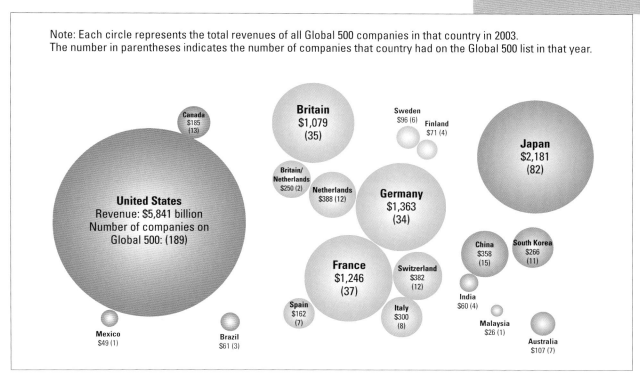

Economies of Scale. Building a global presence expands an organization's scale of operations, enabling it to realize **economies of scale**. The trend toward large organizations was initially sparked by the Industrial Revolution, which created pressure in many industries for larger factories that could seize the benefits of economies of scale offered by new technologies and production methods. Through large-volume production, these industrial giants were able to achieve the lowest possible cost per unit of production. However, for many companies, domestic markets no longer provide the high level of sales needed to maintain enough volume to achieve scale economies. In an industry such as automobile manufacturing, for example, a company would need a tremendous share of the domestic market to achieve scale economies. Thus, an organization such as Ford Motor Company is forced to become international in order to survive. Economies of scale also enable companies to obtain volume discounts from suppliers, lowering the organization's cost of production.

Economies of Scope. A second factor is the enhanced potential for exploiting **economies of scope**. *Scope* refers to the number and variety of products and services a company offers, as well as the number and variety of regions, countries, and markets it serves. Having a presence in multiple countries provides marketing power and synergy compared to the same size firm that has presence in fewer countries. For example, an advertising agency with a presence in several global markets gains a competitive edge serving large companies that span the globe. Or consider the case of McDonald's, which has to obtain nearly identical ketchup and sauce packets for its restaurants around the world. A supplier that has a presence in every country McDonald's serves has an advantage because it provides cost, consistency, and convenience benefits to McDonald's, which does not have to deal with a number of local suppliers in each country. Transmatic Manufacturing Co., based in Holland, Michigan, supplies high-precision metal parts to companies such as Motorola and Delphi Corp. When Transmatic began losing contracts to suppliers in China, where the large U.S. firms had manufacturing facilities, owner P. J. Thompson decided to make the international leap. "My customers are multinational and they want me to be multinational too," says Thompson.[9]

Economies of scope can also increase a company's market power as compared to competitors, because the company develops broad knowledge of the cultural, social, economic, and other factors that affect its customers in varied locations and can provide specialized products and services to meet those needs.

Low-Cost Production Factors. The third major force motivating global expansion relates to **factors of production**. One of the earliest, and still one of the most powerful, motivations for U.S. companies to invest abroad is the opportunity to obtain raw materials, labor, and other resources at the lowest possible cost. Organizations have long turned overseas to secure raw materials that were scarce or unavailable in their home country. In the early twentieth century, for example, tire companies went abroad to develop rubber plantations to supply tires for America's growing automobile industry. Today, U.S. paper manufacturers such as Weyerhaeuser and U.S. Paper Co., forced by environmental concerns to look overseas for new timberlands, are managing millions of acres of tree farms in New Zealand and other areas.[10]

Many companies also turn to other countries as a source of cheap labor. Textile manufacturing in the United States is now practically nonexistent as companies have shifted most production to Asia, Mexico, Latin America, and the Caribbean, where the costs of labor and supplies are much lower. Aerospace-related companies are building factories in Mexico, where they get cheaper labor and favorable government regulations. U.S. makers of toys, consumer electronics, and other goods outsource work to China and other low-wage countries. Manufacturing of non-upholstered furniture is rapidly following the same pattern. Companies are closing plants in the United States and importing high-quality wooden furniture from China, where as many as thirty workers can be hired for the cost of one cabinet-maker in the United States.[11] But the trend isn't limited to manufacturing. A number of growing service firms in India, for example, write software, perform consulting work, integrate back-office solutions, and handle technical support for some of the biggest corporations in the United States—and do the work for 40 percent less than comparable U.S. firms.[12]

Other organizations have gone international in search of lower costs of capital, sources of cheap energy, reduced government restrictions, or other factors that lower the company's total production costs. Companies can locate facilities wherever it makes the most economic sense in terms of needed employee education and skill levels, labor and raw materials costs, and other production factors. Companies such as Yahoo! and Google, for instance, can't find the technological brainpower they need in the United States, so they are building research and development facilities in India to take advantage of highly-skilled workers.[13] Automobile manufacturers such as Toyota, BMW, General Motors, and Ford have built plants in South Africa, Brazil, and Thailand, where they typically get dramatically lower costs for factors such as land, water, and electricity.[14] Foreign companies also come to the United States to obtain favorable circumstances. Kalexsyn, a small chemical research firm in Kalamazoo, Michigan, does about 25 percent of its business with Western European biotechnology firms that need high quality instead of low prices.[15] Japan's Honda and Toyota, South Korea's Samsung Electronics, and the Swiss drug company Novartis have all built plants or research centers in the United States to take advantage of tax breaks, find skilled workers, or be closer to major customers and suppliers.[16]

Stages of International Development

No company can become a global giant overnight. Managers have to consciously adopt a strategy for global development and growth. Organizations enter foreign markets in a variety of ways and follow diverse paths. However, the shift from domestic to global typically occurs through stages of development, as illustrated in Exhibit 5.2.[17] In stage one, the **domestic stage**, the company is domestically oriented, but managers are aware of the global environment and may want to consider initial foreign involvement to expand production volume and realize economies of scale. Market potential is limited and is primarily in the home country. The structure of the company is domestic, typically functional or divisional, and initial foreign sales are handled through an export department. The details of freight forwarding, customs problems, and foreign exchange are handled by outsiders.

In stage two, the **international stage**, the company takes exports seriously and begins to think multidomestically. **Multidomestic** means competitive issues in each country are independent of other countries; the company deals with each country individually. The concern is with international competitive positioning compared with other firms in the industry. At this point, an international division has replaced the export department, and specialists are hired to handle sales, service, and warehousing abroad. Multiple countries are identified as a potential market. For example, Purafil, a small company with headquarters in Doraville, Georgia, sells air filters that remove pollution and cleanse the air in fifty different countries.

EXHIBIT 5.2
Four Stages of
International Evolution

	I. Domestic	II. International	III. Multinational	IV. Global
Strategic Orientation	Domestically oriented	Export-oriented, multidomestic	Multinational	Global
Stage of Development	Initial foreign involvement	Competitive positioning	Explosion	Global
Structure	Domestic structure plus export department	Domestic structure plus international division	Worldwide geographic product	Matrix, transnational
Market Potential	Moderate, mostly domestic	Large, multidomestic	Very large, multinational	Whole world

Source: Based on Nancy J. Adler, *International Dimensions of Organizational Behavior,* 4th ed. (Cincinnati, Ohio: South-Western, 2002), 8–9; and Theodore T. Herbert, "Strategy and Multinational Organization Structure: An Interorganizational Relationships Perspective," *Academy of Management Review* 9 (1984), 259–271.

Although Purafil is small, it maintains contracts with independent sales firms in the various countries who know the local markets and cultures.[18] The company first began exporting in the early 1990s and now gets 60 percent of its revenues from overseas.

In stage three, the **multinational stage**, the company has extensive experience in a number of international markets and has established marketing, manufacturing, or research and development (R&D) facilities in several foreign countries. The organization obtains a large percentage of revenues from sales outside the home country. Explosive growth occurs as international operations take off, and the company has business units scattered around the world along with suppliers, manufacturers, and distributors. Examples of companies in the multinational stage include Siemens of Germany, Sony of Japan, and Coca-Cola of the United States. Wal-Mart, although it is the world's biggest company, is just moving into the multinational stage, with only about 22 percent of sales from international business in fiscal year 2006 (the most recent figures available). However, international sales are the fastest growing part of the retail giant's business.[19]

The fourth and ultimate stage is the **global stage**, which means the company transcends any single country. The business is not merely a collection of domestic industries; rather, subsidiaries are interlinked to the point where competitive position in one country significantly influences activities in other countries.[20] Truly **global companies** no longer think of themselves as having a single home country, and, indeed, have been called *stateless corporations.*[21] This represents a new and dramatic evolution from the multinational company of the 1960s and 1970s. For example, the CEO of digital-media company Thomson SA says he doesn't want people to think of the company as being based any particular place.[22]

Global companies operate in truly global fashion, and the entire world is their marketplace. Global companies such as Nestlé, Royal Dutch/Shell, Unilever, and Matsushita Electric may operate in more than a hundred countries. The structural

problem of holding together this huge complex of subsidiaries scattered thousands of miles apart is immense. Organization structure for global companies can be extremely complex and often evolves into an international matrix or transnational model, which will be discussed later in this chapter.

Global Expansion through International Strategic Alliances

One of the most popular ways companies get involved in international operations is through international strategic alliances. Companies in rapidly changing industries such as media and entertainment, pharmaceuticals, biotechnology, and software might have hundreds of these relationships.[23]

Typical alliances include licensing, joint ventures, and consortia.[24] For example, when entering new markets, particularly in developing areas of the world, retailers such as Saks Fifth Avenue and Barneys New York limit their risks by licensing their names to foreign partners. Saks has licensed stores in Riyadh and Dubai, Saudi Arabia, and in Mexico, for instance, and Barneys has a licensed store in Japan. Both firms, as well as other U.S.-based department stores, are currently making a strong international push in light of weak sales and stiff competition in the United States.[25] A **joint venture** is a separate entity created with two or more active firms as sponsors. This is a popular approach to sharing development and production costs and penetrating new markets. Joint ventures may be with either customers or competitors.[26] Competing firms Sprint, Deutsche Telecom, and Telecom France cooperate with each other and with several smaller firms in a joint venture that serves the telecommunication needs of global corporations in sixty-five countries.[27] Navistar International Corporation, based in Warrenville, Illinois, formed a joint venture with rival Mahindra & Mahindra Ltd., a fast-growing equipment maker in India, to build trucks and buses for export.[28] And Wal-Mart hopes to get a foothold in India's fast-growing but difficult retail market through a joint venture with Bharti Enterprises to establish Bharti Wal-Mart Private Limited.[29]

Companies often seek joint ventures to take advantage of a partner's knowledge of local markets, to achieve production cost savings through economies of scale, to share complementary technological strengths, or to distribute new products and services through another country's distribution channels. Another growing approach is for companies to become involved in **consortia**, groups of independent companies— including suppliers, customers, and even competitors—that join together to share skills, resources, costs, and access to one another's markets.[30] Consortia are often used in other parts of the world, such as the *keiretsu* family of corporations in Japan. In Korea, these interlocking company arrangements are called *chaebol*.

DESIGNING STRUCTURE TO FIT GLOBAL STRATEGY

As we discussed in Chapter 2, an organization's structure must fit its situation by providing sufficient information processing for coordination and control while focusing employees on specific functions, products, or geographic regions. Organization design for international firms follows a similar logic, with special interest in global versus local strategic opportunities.

Model for Global versus Local Opportunities

When organizations venture into the international domain, managers strive to formulate a coherent global strategy that will provide synergy among worldwide operations for the purpose of achieving common organizational goals. One dilemma they face is choosing whether to emphasize global **standardization** versus national responsiveness. Managers must decide whether they want each global affiliate to act autonomously or whether activities should be standardized across countries. These decisions are reflected in the choice between a *globalization* versus a *multidomestic* global strategy.

The **globalization strategy** means that product design, manufacturing, and marketing strategy are standardized throughout the world.[31] For example, the Japanese took business away from Canadian and American companies by developing similar high-quality, low-cost products for all countries. The Canadian and American companies incurred higher costs by tailoring products to specific countries. Black & Decker became much more competitive internationally when it standardized its line of power hand tools. Other products, such as Coca-Cola, are naturals for globalization, because only advertising and marketing need to be tailored for different regions. In general, services are less suitable for globalization because different customs and habits often require a different approach to providing service. This was part of Wal-Mart's trouble in the South Korean market. The retailer continued to use Western-style displays and marketing strategies, whereas successful South Korean retailers build bright, eye-catching displays and hire clerks to promote their goods using megaphones and hand-clapping. Wal-Mart similarly flubbed in Indonesia, where it closed its stores after only a year. Customers didn't like the brightly lit, highly organized stores, and, because no haggling was permitted, they perceived the goods as being overpriced.[32]

Other companies have also begun shifting away from a strict globalization strategy. Economic and social changes, including a backlash against huge global corporations, have prompted consumers to be less interested in global brands and more in favor of products that have a local feel.[33] However, a globalization strategy can help a manufacturing organization reap economy-of-scale efficiencies by standardizing product design and manufacturing, using common suppliers, introducing products around the world faster, coordinating prices, and eliminating overlapping facilities. By sharing technology, design, suppliers, and manufacturing standards worldwide in a coordinated global automotive operation, Ford saved $5 billion during the first three years.[34] Similarly, Gillette Company, which makes grooming products such as the Mach3 shaving system for men and the Venus razor for women, has large production facilities that use common suppliers and processes to manufacture products whose technical specifications are standardized around the world.[35]

ASSESS YOUR ANSWER

1 **The only way an organization can reasonably expect to be successful in different countries is to customize its products and services to suit the local interests, preferences, and values in each country.**

ANSWER: *Disagree.* It is the case that people around the world often want products and services that are tailored to their local needs and interests, and many organizations are quite successful by responding to local market demands. However, other international organizations attain competitive advantages by using the same product design and marketing strategies in many countries throughout the world.

A **multidomestic strategy** means that competition in each country is handled independently of competition in other countries. Thus, a multidomestic strategy would encourage product design, assembly, and marketing tailored to the specific needs of each country. Some companies have found that their products do not thrive in a single global market. For instance, people in different countries have very different expectations for personal-care products such as deodorant or toothpaste. Many people in parts of Mexico use laundry detergent for washing dishes. Food companies such as Kraft have discovered that they must tailor their cookies and crackers to different markets. Kraft's Oreo, the top-selling cookie in the United States, sold poorly in China until the company reformulated it to suit local tastes. Now, it's the top seller in that country too.[36]

Different global organization designs, as well, are better suited to the need for either global standardization or national responsiveness. Recent research on more than 100 international firms based in Spain has provided further support for the connection between international structure and strategic focus.[37] The model in Exhibit 5.3 illustrates how organization design and international strategy fit the needs of the environment.[38]

Companies can be characterized by whether their product and service lines have potential for globalization, which means advantages through worldwide standardization. Companies that sell similar products or services across many countries have a globalization strategy. On the other hand, some companies have products and services appropriate for a multidomestic strategy, which means local-country advantages through differentiation and customization to meet local needs.

As indicated in Exhibit 5.3, when forces for both global standardization and national responsiveness in many countries are low, simply using an international division with the domestic structure is an appropriate way to handle international business. For some industries, however, technological, social, or economic forces

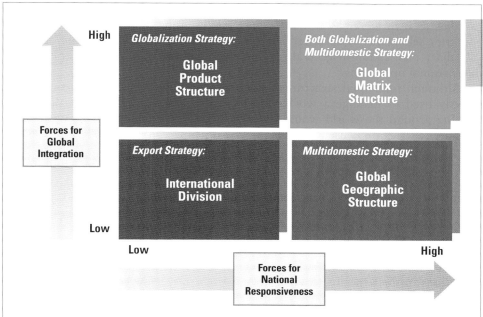

EXHIBIT 5.3
Model to Fit
Organization Structure
to International
Advantages

Source: Roderick E. White and Thomas A. Poynter, "Organizing for Worldwide Advantage," *Business Quarterly* (Summer 1989), 84–89. Adapted by permission of *Business Quarterly*, published by the Western Business School, the University of Western Ontario, London, Ontario, Canada.

may create a situation in which selling standardized products worldwide provides a basis for competitive advantage. In these cases, a global product structure is appropriate. This structure provides product managers with authority to handle their product lines on a global basis and enables the company to take advantage of a unified global marketplace. In other cases, companies can gain competitive advantages through national responsiveness—by responding to unique needs in the various countries in which they do business. For these companies, a worldwide geographic structure is appropriate. Each country or region will have subsidiaries modifying products and services to fit that locale. A good illustration is the advertising firm of Ogilvy & Mather, which divides its operations into four primary geographic regions because advertising approaches need to be modified to fit the tastes, preferences, cultural values, and government regulations in different parts of the world.[39] Children are frequently used to advertise products in the United States, but this approach in France is against the law. The competitive claims of rival products regularly seen on U.S. television would violate government regulations in Germany.[40]

In many instances, companies need to respond to both global and local opportunities simultaneously, in which case the global matrix structure can be used. Part of the product line may need to be standardized globally and other parts tailored to the needs of local countries. Let's discuss each of the structures in Exhibit 5.3 in more detail.

International Division

As companies begin to explore international opportunities, they typically start with an export department that grows into an **international division**. The international division has a status equal to the other major departments or divisions within the company and is illustrated in Exhibit 5.4. Whereas the domestic divisions are typically organized along functional or product lines, the international division is organized according to geographic interests, as illustrated in the exhibit. The international division has its own hierarchy to handle business (licensing, joint ventures) in various countries, selling the products and services created by the domestic divisions, opening subsidiary plants, and in general moving the organization into more sophisticated international operations.

Although functional structures are often used domestically, they are less frequently used to manage a worldwide business.[41] Lines of functional hierarchy running around the world would extend too long, so some form of product or geographic structure is used to subdivide the organization into smaller units. Firms typically start with an international department and, depending on their strategy, later use product or geographic division structures or a matrix. One study found that 48 percent of organizations identified as global leaders use divisional structures, while 28 percent reported using matrix structures.[42]

Global Product Division Structure

In a **global product structure**, the product divisions take responsibility for global operations in their specific product area. This is one of the most commonly used structures through which managers attempt to achieve global goals because it provides a fairly straightforward way to effectively manage a variety of businesses and products around the world. Managers in each product division can focus on organizing for international operations as they see fit and directing employees' energy toward their own division's unique set of global problems or opportunities.[43] In

Briefcase

As an organization manager, keep these guidelines in mind:

Choose a global product structure when the organization can gain competitive advantages through a globalization strategy (global integration). Choose a global geographic structure when the company has advantages with a multidomestic strategy (national responsiveness). Use an international division when the company is primarily domestic and has only a few international operations.

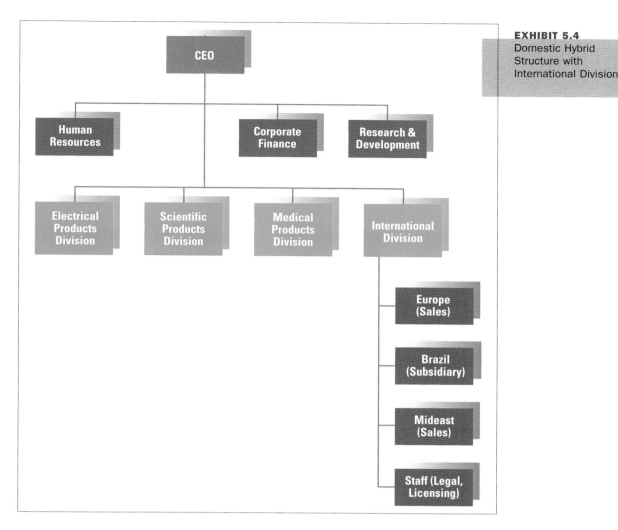

EXHIBIT 5.4
Domestic Hybrid
Structure with
International Division

addition, the structure provides top managers at headquarters with a broad perspective on competition, enabling the entire corporation to respond more rapidly to a changing global environment.[44]

With a global product structure, each division's manager is responsible for planning, organizing, and controlling all functions for the production and distribution of its products for any market around the world. As we saw in Exhibit 5.3, the global product structure works best when the company has opportunities for worldwide production and sale of standard products for all markets, thus providing economies of scale and standardization of production, marketing, and advertising.

Eaton Corporation has used a form of worldwide product structure, as illustrated in Exhibit 5.5. In this structure, the automotive components group, industrial group, and so on are responsible for manufacture and sale of products worldwide. The vice president of the international division is responsible for coordinators in each region, including a coordinator for Japan, Australia, South America, and northern Europe. The coordinators find ways to share facilities and improve production and delivery across all product lines sold in their regions. These coordinators fulfill the same function as integrators described in Chapter 2.

EXHIBIT 5.5
Partial Global Product
Structure Used by Eaton
Corporation

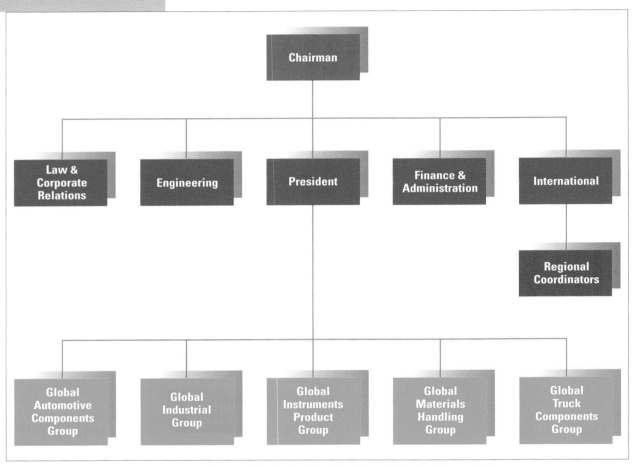

Source: Based on *New Directions in Multinational Corporate Organization* (New York: Business International Corp., 1981).

The product structure is great for standardizing production and sales around the globe, but it also has problems. Often the product divisions do not work well together, competing instead of cooperating in some countries; and some countries may be ignored by product managers. The solution adopted by Eaton Corporation of using country coordinators who have a clearly defined role is a superb way to overcome these problems.

Global Geographic Division Structure

A regionally based organization is well suited to companies that want to emphasize adaptation to regional or local market needs through a multidomestic strategy, as illustrated earlier in Exhibit 5.3. The **global geographic structure** divides the world into

geographic regions, with each geographic division reporting to the CEO. Each division has full control of functional activities within its geographic area. For example, Nestlé, with headquarters in Switzerland, puts great emphasis on the autonomy of regional managers who know the local culture. The largest branded food company in the world, Nestlé rejects the idea of a single global market and uses a geographic structure to focus on the local needs and competition in each country. Local managers have the authority to tinker with a product's flavoring, packaging, portion size, or other elements as they see fit. Many of the company's 8,000 brands are registered in only one country.[45]

Companies that use this type of structure have typically been those with mature product lines and stable technologies. They can find low-cost manufacturing within countries, as well as meet different needs across countries for marketing and sales. However, several business and organizational trends have led to a broadening of the kinds of companies that use the global geographic structure.[46] The growth of service organizations has outpaced manufacturing for several years, and services by their nature must occur on a local level. In addition, to meet new competitive threats, many manufacturing firms are emphasizing the ability to customize their products to meet specific needs, which requires a greater emphasis on local and regional responsiveness. All organizations are compelled by current environmental and competitive challenges to develop closer relationships with customers, which may lead companies to shift from product-based to geographic-based structures. IBM, for example, is creating new regional divisions for developing markets, such as the Middle East, Asia, the Americas, Africa, and Eastern Europe. CEO Sam Palmisano believes developing relationships with governments, utilities, and other organizations in each region is critical to helping IBM tailor software and services to the needs of these emerging and fast-growing information technology markets.[47]

The problems encountered by senior management using a global geographic structure result from the autonomy of each regional division. For example, it is difficult to do planning on a global scale—such as new-product R&D—because each division acts to meet only the needs of its region. New domestic technologies and products can be difficult to transfer to international markets because each division thinks it will develop what it needs. Likewise, it is difficult to rapidly introduce products developed offshore into domestic markets, and there is often duplication of line and staff managers across regions. Because regional divisions act to meet specific needs in their own areas, tracking and maintaining control of costs can be a real problem. The following example illustrates how executives at Colgate-Palmolive overcame some of the problems associated with the geographic structure.

For several years, Colgate-Palmolive Company, which manufactures and markets personal-care, household, and specialty products, used a global geographic structure of the form illustrated in Exhibit 5.6. Colgate has a long, rich history of international involvement and has relied on regional divisions in North America, Europe, Latin America, the Far East, and the South Pacific to stay on the competitive edge. Well over half of the company's total sales are generated outside of the United States.

The regional approach supports Colgate's cultural values, which emphasize individual autonomy, an entrepreneurial spirit, and the ability to act locally. Each regional president reports directly to the chief operating officer, and each division has its own staff functions such

Colgate-Palmolive Company

(continued)

as human resources (HR), finance, manufacturing, and marketing. Colgate handled the problem of coordination across geographic divisions by creating an *international business development group* that has responsibility for long-term company planning and worldwide product coordination and communication. It used several product team leaders, many of whom had been former country managers with extensive experience and knowledge. The product leaders are essentially coordinators and advisors to the geographic divisions; they have no power to direct, but they have the ability and the organizational support needed to exert substantial influence. The addition of this business development group quickly reaped positive results in terms of more rapid introduction of new products across all countries and better, lower-cost marketing.

The success of the international business development group prompted Colgate's top management to add two additional coordinating positions—a *vice president of corporate development* to focus on acquisitions, and a *worldwide sales and marketing group* that coordinates sales and marketing initiatives across all geographic locations. With these worldwide positions added to the structure, Colgate maintains its focus on each region and achieves global coordination for overall planning, faster product introductions, and enhanced sales and marketing efficiency.[48] ∎

EXHIBIT 5.6
Global Geographic
Structure of Colgate-
Palmolive Company

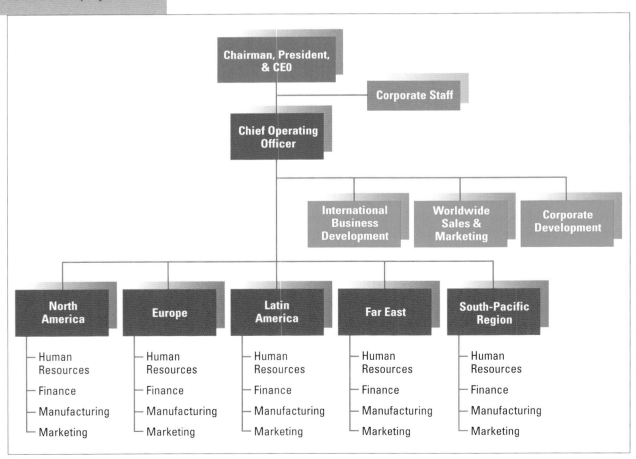

Source: Based on Robert J. Kramer, *Organizing for Global Competitiveness: The Geographic Design* (New York: The Conference Board, 1993), 30.

Global Matrix Structure

We've discussed how Eaton used a global product division structure and found ways to coordinate across worldwide divisions. Colgate-Palmolive used a global geographic division structure and found ways to coordinate across geographic regions. Each of these companies emphasized a single dimension. Recall from Chapter 2 that a matrix structure provides a way to achieve vertical and horizontal coordination simultaneously along two dimensions. A **global matrix structure** is similar to the matrix described in Chapter 2, except that for multinational corporations the geographic distances for communication are greater and coordination is more complex.

The matrix works best when pressure for decision making balances the interests of both product standardization and geographic localization and when coordination to share resources is important. For many years, Asea Brown Boveri (ABB), an electrical equipment corporation headquartered in Zurich, used a global matrix structure that worked extremely well to coordinate a 200,000-employee company operating in more than 140 countries.

ABB has given new meaning to the notion of "being local worldwide." ABB owns 1,300 subsidiary companies, divided into 5,000 profit centers located in 140 countries. ABB's average plant has fewer than 200 workers and most of the company's 5,000 profit centers contain only forty to fifty people, meaning almost everyone stays close to the customer. For many years, ABB used a complex global matrix structure similar to Exhibit 5.7 to achieve worldwide economies of scale combined with local flexibility and responsiveness.

IN PRACTICE

Asea Brown Boveri Ltd. (ABB)

At the top are the chief executive officer and an international committee of eight top managers, who hold frequent meetings around the world. Along one side of the matrix are sixty-five or so business areas located worldwide, into which ABB's products and services are grouped. Each business area leader is responsible for handling business on a global scale, allocating export markets, establishing cost and quality standards, and creating mixed-nationality teams to solve problems. For example, the leader for power transformers is responsible for twenty-five factories in sixteen countries.

Along the other side of the matrix is a country structure; ABB has more than 100 country managers, most of them citizens of the country in which they work. They run national companies and are responsible for local balance sheets, income statements, and career ladders. The German president, for example, is responsible for 36,000 people across several business areas that generate annual revenues in Germany of more than $4 billion.

The matrix structure converges at the level of the 1,300 local companies. The presidents of local companies report to two bosses—the business area leader, who is usually located outside the country, and the country president, who runs the company of which the local organization is a subsidiary.

ABB's philosophy is to decentralize things to the lowest levels. Global managers are generous, patient, and multilingual. They must work with teams made up of different nationalities and be culturally sensitive. They craft strategy and evaluate performance for people and subsidiaries around the world. Country managers, by contrast, are regional line managers responsible for several country subsidiaries. They must cooperate with business area managers to achieve worldwide efficiencies and the introduction of new products. Finally, the presidents of local companies have both a global boss—the business area manager—and a country boss, and they learn to coordinate the needs of both.[49] ■

EXHIBIT 5.7
Global Matrix Structure

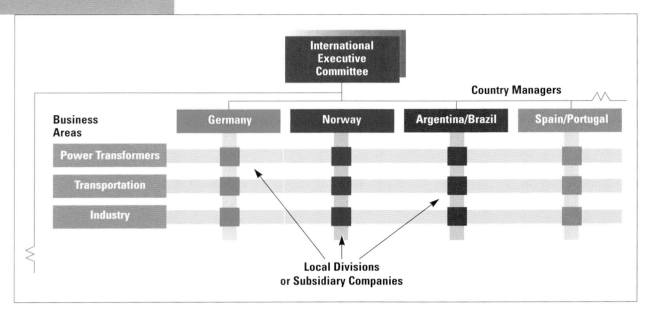

ABB is a large, successful company that achieved the benefits of both product and geographic organizations through this matrix structure. However, over the past several years, as ABB has faced increasingly complex competitive issues, leaders have transformed the company toward a complex structure called the *transnational model*, which will be discussed later in this chapter.

In the real world, as with the domestic hybrid structure, many international firms such as ABB, Colgate, IBM, Nestlé, or Eaton Corp. apply a *global hybrid* or *mixed structure*, in which two or more different structures or elements of different structures are used. Hybrid structures are typical in highly volatile environments. Siemens AG of Germany, for example, combines elements of functional, geographic, and product divisions to respond to dynamic market conditions in the multiple countries where it operates.[50]

Organizations that operate on a global scale frequently have to make adjustments to their structures to overcome the challenges of doing business in a global environment. In the following sections, we will look at some specific challenges organizations face in the global arena and mechanisms for successfully addressing them.

BUILDING GLOBAL CAPABILITIES

There are many instances of well-known companies that have trouble transferring successful ideas, products, and services from their home country to the international domain. We talked earlier about the struggles Wal-Mart is facing internationally, but Wal-Mart is not alone. PepsiCo set a five-year goal to triple its international soft-drink revenues and boldly expanded its presence in international markets. Yet five years later, the company had withdrawn from some of those markets and had to take a nearly $1 billion loss from international beverage operations.[51] Hundreds of American companies that saw Vietnam as a tremendous international opportunity in the mid-1990s are now calling it quits amid heavy losses. Political and cultural differences sidetracked most of the ventures. Only a few companies, such as Citigroup's Citibank unit and Caterpillar's heavy-equipment business, have found success in that country.[52] Managers taking their companies international face a tremendous challenge in how to capitalize on the incredible opportunities that global expansion presents.

The Global Organizational Challenge

Exhibit 5.8 illustrates the three primary segments of the global organizational challenge: greater complexity and differentiation, the need for integration, and the problem of transferring knowledge and innovation across a global firm. Organizations have to accept an extremely high level of environmental complexity in the international domain and address the many differences that occur among countries. Environmental complexity and country variations require greater organizational differentiation, as described in Chapter 6.

At the same time, organizations must find ways to effectively achieve coordination and collaboration among far-flung units and facilitate the development and transfer of organizational knowledge and innovation for global learning.[53] Although many small companies are involved in international business, most international companies grow very large, creating a huge coordination problem. Exhibit 5.9 provides some understanding of the size and impact of international firms by comparing the revenues of several large multinational companies with the gross domestic product (GDP) of selected countries.

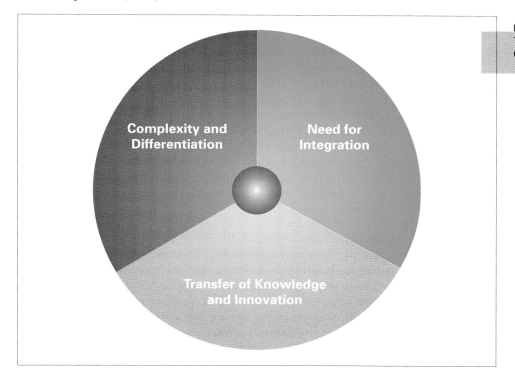

EXHIBIT 5.8
The Global Organizational Challenge

EXHIBIT 5.9
Comparison of Leading
Multinational Companies
and Selected Countries,
2008 (in U.S. dollars)

Company	Revenue*	Country	Annual GDP†
Exxon Mobil	$404.6 billion	Egypt	$403.9 billion
Wal-Mart	$378.8 billion	Greece	$370.2 billion
Royal Dutch Shell	$355.8 billion	Malaysia	$355.2 billion
BP	$291.4 billion	Nigeria	$292.6 billion
Toyota	$262.3 billion	Algeria	$269.2 billion
ING Group	$212.0 billion	Peru	$218.8 billion
General Motors	$181.1 billion	Finland	$182.0 billion
General Electric	$172.7 billion	Kazakhstan	$167.6 billion

*This size comparison is assuming revenues were valued at the equivalent of GDP.
†Gross domestic product.

Source: "Count: *Really* Big Business," *Fast Company* (December 2008–January 2009), 46.

Increased Complexity and Differentiation. When organizations enter the international arena, they encounter a greater level of internal and external complexity than anything experienced on the domestic front. Companies have to create a structure to operate in numerous countries that differ in economic development, language, political systems and government regulations, cultural norms and values, and infrastructure such as transportation and communication facilities. For example, computer maker Lenovo, incorporated in Hong Kong, has nine operational hubs, and its top managers and corporate functions are spread around the world. The CEO is in Singapore, the chairman in Raleigh, North Carolina, and the chief financial officer in Hong Kong. Worldwide marketing is coordinated in India.[54]

One factor increasing the complexity for organizations is the growing consumer demand for products and services that meet local needs and preferences. Even American fast food chains, once considered ultimate examples of standardization for a world market, have felt the need to be more responsive to local and national differences. KFC sells chicken in China, but you can also find congee soup and fried dough there for breakfast. McDonald's sells Rice Burgers in Taiwan, a deep-fried patty of beef ragout called the McKroket in the Netherlands, a Maharaja Mac made with chicken instead of beef in India, and the Bulgogi Burger, a pork patty marinated in soy-sauce, in South Korea. Restaurant design and décor may also vary widely in different countries.[55]

All the complexity in the international environment is mirrored in a greater internal organizational complexity. As you will learn in Chapter 6, as environments become more complex and uncertain, organizations grow more highly differentiated, with many specialized positions and departments to cope with specific sectors in the environment. Top management might need to set up specialized departments to deal with the diverse government, legal, and accounting regulations in various countries, for example. More boundary-spanning departments are needed to sense and respond to the external environment. Companies operating globally frequently disperse operations such as engineering, design, manufacturing, marketing, and sales around the world. In particular, many organizations have set up global product development systems to achieve greater access to international expertise and design products that are better suited to global markets. A Deloitte Research study found that 48 percent of North American and Western European manufacturers surveyed had set up engineering operations in other countries.[56] In addition, organizations might implement a variety of strategies, a broader array of activities, and a much larger number of products and services on an international level.

Need for Integration. As organizations become more differentiated, with multiple products, divisions, departments, and positions scattered across numerous countries, managers face a tremendous integration challenge. *Integration* refers to the quality of collaboration across organizational units. The question is how to achieve the coordination and collaboration that is necessary for a global organization to reap the benefits of economies of scale, economies of scope, and labor and production cost efficiencies that international expansion offers. Even in a domestic firm, high differentiation among departments requires that more time and resources be devoted to achieving coordination because employees' attitudes, goals, and work orientations differ widely. Imagine what it must be like for an international organization, whose operating units are divided not only by goals and work attitudes but by geographic distance, time differences, cultural values, and perhaps even language as well. Recall how Colgate-Palmolive created several specific units to achieve coordination and integration among regional divisions. Other companies, too, must find ways to share information, ideas, new products, and technologies across the organization. Consider how IBM is striving for better integration as it tries to fend off growing competition from Indian technology services companies.

IN PRACTICE

IBM

IBM has more than 200,000 employees around the world, but that doesn't help if the skills needed by a specific client in London or New York or Bangalore can't be rapidly put into action because the experts are located elsewhere.

In its globalization effort, IBM created geographic divisions around the world that each had their own administration, manufacturing, and service operations. Yet, as competition has increased, particularly from companies such as India's Tata Consultancy Services and Infosys Technologies, that approach is too slow and too costly. Thus, IBM has embarked on a massive project to go one step further and organize employees along skill lines rather than just geography. "Our customers need us to put the right skills in the right place at the right time," says Senior Vice President Robert W. Moffatt Jr., the manager in charge of the operation.

The new organization involves bunching employees into "competency centers" spread around the world, so that people with specific skills are grouped together. The approach enables IBM to take advantage of low-cost labor in some places, yet also have highly-skilled employees in close proximity to clients. Instead of each country division having its own complete workforce, some people are drawn from the competency centers long enough to complete a specific client project. IBM has even come up with mathematical formulas to identify who should be pulled from the various centers to work on a particular project. Managers believe their new approach, which they call "globally integrated operations," can help lower costs, provide superior service, and give IBM an edge over fast-growing rivals.[57] ■

All organizations working globally, like IBM, face the challenge of getting all the pieces working together in the right way at the right time and in the right place. Another issue is how to share knowledge and innovations across global divisions.

Transfer of Knowledge and Innovation. The third piece of the international challenge is for organizations to learn from their international experiences by sharing knowledge and innovations across the enterprise. The diversity of the international environment offers extraordinary opportunities for learning and the development of diverse capabilities.

Organizational units in each location acquire the skills and knowledge to meet environmental challenges that arise in that particular locale. Much of that knowledge, which may be related to product improvements, operational efficiencies, technological advancements, or myriad other competencies, is relevant across multiple countries, so organizations need systems that promote the transfer of knowledge and innovation across the global enterprise. One good example comes from Procter & Gamble. Liquid Tide was one of P&G's most successful U.S. product launches in the 1980s, but the product came about from the sharing of innovations developed in diverse parts of the firm. Liquid Tide incorporated a technology for helping to suspend dirt in wash water from P&G headquarters in the United States, the formula for its cleaning agents from P&G technicians in Japan, and special ingredients for fighting mineral salts present in hard water from company scientists in Brussels.[58]

However, getting employees to transfer ideas and knowledge across national boundaries can be exceedingly challenging. Consider what happened in one virtual team made up of members from India, Israel, Canada, the United States, Singapore, Spain, Brussels, Great Britain, and Australia:

"Early on … team members were reluctant to seek advice from teammates who were still strangers, fearing that a request for help might be interpreted as a sign of incompetence. Moreover, when teammates did ask for help, assistance was not always forthcoming. One team member confessed to carefully calculating how much information she was willing to share. Going the extra mile on behalf of a virtual teammate, in her view, came at a high price of time and energy, with no guarantee of reciprocation."[59]

This lack of trust among people scattered at different locations around the world is one primary reason why many organizations tap only a fraction of the potential that is available from the cross-border transfer of knowledge and innovation. Other reasons include:[60]

- Language barriers, cultural dissimilarities, and geographic distances can prevent managers from spotting the knowledge and opportunities that exist across disparate country units.
- Sometimes managers don't appreciate the value of organizational integration and want to protect the interests of their own division rather than cooperate with other divisions.
- Divisions sometimes view knowledge and innovation as power and want to hold onto it as a way to gain an influential position within the global firm.
- The "not-invented-here" syndrome makes some managers reluctant to tap into the know-how and expertise of other units.
- Much of an organization's knowledge is in the minds of employees and cannot easily be written down and shared with other units.

Organizations have to encourage both the development and the sharing of knowledge, implement systems for tapping into knowledge wherever it exists, and share innovations to meet global challenges.

Global Coordination Mechanisms

Managers meet the global challenge of coordination and transferring knowledge and innovation across highly differentiated units in a variety of ways. Some of the most common are the use of global teams, stronger headquarters planning and control, and specific coordination roles.

Global Teams. The popularity and success of teams on the domestic front allowed managers to see firsthand how this mechanism can achieve strong horizontal coordination, as described in Chapter 2, and thus recognize the promise teams held for coordination across a global firm as well. **Global teams**, also called *transnational teams*, are cross-border work groups made up of multiskilled, multinational members whose activities span multiple countries.[61] Typically, teams are of two types: intercultural teams, whose members come from different countries and meet face to face, and virtual global teams, whose members remain in separate locations around the world and conduct their work electronically.[62] Heineken formed the European Production Task Force, a thirteen-member team made up of multinational members, to meet regularly and come up with ideas for optimizing the company's production facilities across Europe.[63] Tandem Services uses virtual global teams of software developers who coordinate their work electronically so that the team is productive around the clock. Team members in London code a project and transmit the code each evening to members in the United States for testing. U.S. team members then forward the code they've tested to Tokyo for debugging. The next morning, the London team members pick up with the code debugged by their Tokyo colleagues, and another cycle begins.[64]

The most advanced and competitive use of global teams involves simultaneous contributions in three strategic areas.[65] First, global teams help companies address the differentiation challenge, enabling them to be more locally responsive by providing knowledge to meet the needs of different regional markets, consumer preferences, and political and legal systems. At the same time, teams provide integration benefits, helping organizations achieve global efficiencies by developing regional or worldwide cost advantages and standardizing designs and operations across countries. Finally, these teams contribute to continuous organizational learning, knowledge transfer, and adaptation on a global level.

However, building effective global teams is not easy. Cultural and language differences can create misunderstandings, and resentments and mistrust can quickly derail the team's efforts. Many times an "us against them" mentality develops, which is just the opposite of what organizations want from global teams.[66] No wonder when the executive council of *CIO* magazine asked global chief information officers to rank their greatest challenges, managing virtual global teams ranked as the most pressing issue.[67]

Managers have to invest the time and energy to enable global teams to communicate and collaborate effectively. For example, managers at Nokia are careful to select people who have a collaborative mindset, and they form many teams with volunteers who are highly committed to the task or project. The company also tries to make sure some members of a team have worked together before, providing a base for trusting relationships. Making the best use of technology is critical. In addition to a virtual

2 **It is an especially difficult challenge to work on a global team to coordinate one's own activities and share new ideas and insights with colleagues in different divisions around the world.**

ANSWER: *Agree.* The problems of different languages, locations, cultural values, and business practices make membership on an international team especially difficult. Global teams can be effective only if members have the patience and skills to surmount the barriers and openly share information and ideas. Global teams made up of people who are culturally astute and genuinely want to coordinate and communicate with their counterparts in other countries perform better.

work space that team members can access twenty-four hours a day, Nokia provides an online resource where virtual workers are encouraged to post photos and share personal information. Given that the inability of members to get to know one another is one of the biggest barriers to effective global teamwork, encouraging and supporting social networking has paid off for Nokia. In a study of fifty-two virtual teams in fifteen leading multinational companies, London Business School researchers found that Nokia's teams were among the most effective, even though they were made up of people working in several different countries, across time zones and cultures.[68]

Headquarters Planning. A second approach to achieving stronger global coordination is for headquarters to take an active role in planning, scheduling, and control to keep the widely distributed pieces of the global organization working together and moving in the same direction. In one survey, 70 percent of global companies reported that the most important function of corporate headquarters was to "provide enterprise leadership."[69] Without strong leadership, highly autonomous divisions can begin to act like independent companies rather than coordinated parts of a global whole. To counteract this, top management may delegate responsibility and decision-making authority in some areas, such as adapting products or services to meet local needs, while maintaining strong control through centralized systems in other areas to provide the coordination and integration needed.[70] Plans, schedules, and formal rules and procedures can help ensure greater communication among divisions and with headquarters, as well as foster cooperation and synergy among far-flung units to achieve the organization's goals in a cost-efficient way. Top managers can provide clear strategic direction, guide far-flung operations, and resolve competing demands from various units.

Expanded Coordination Roles. Organizations may also implement structural solutions to achieve stronger coordination and collaboration.[71] Creating specific organizational roles or positions for coordination is a way to integrate all the pieces of the enterprise to achieve a strong competitive position. In successful international firms, the role of top *functional managers*, for example, is expanded to include responsibility for coordinating across countries, identifying and linking the organization's expertise and resources worldwide. In an international organization, the manufacturing manager has to be aware of and coordinate with manufacturing operations of the company in various other parts of the world so that the company achieves manufacturing efficiency and shares technology and ideas across

Briefcase

As an organization manager, keep this guideline in mind:

Use mechanisms such as global teams, headquarters planning, and specific coordination roles to provide needed coordination and integration among far-flung international units. Emphasize information and knowledge sharing to help the organization learn and improve on a global scale.

units. A new manufacturing technology developed to improve efficiency in Ford's Brazilian operations may be valuable for European and North American plants as well. Manufacturing managers are responsible for being aware of new developments wherever they occur and for using their knowledge to improve the organization. Similarly, marketing managers, HR managers, and other functional managers at an international company are involved not only in activities for their particular location but in coordinating with their sister units in other countries as well.

Whereas functional managers coordinate across countries, *country managers* coordinate across functions. A country manager for an international firm has to coordinate all the various functional activities located within the country to meet the problems, opportunities, needs, and trends in the local market, enabling the organization to achieve multinational flexibility and rapid response. The country manager in Venezuela for a global consumer products firm such as Colgate-Palmolive would coordinate everything that goes on in that country, from manufacturing to HR to marketing, to ensure that activities meet the language, cultural, government, and legal requirements of Venezuela. The country manager in Ireland or Canada would do the same for those countries. Country managers also help with the transfer of ideas, trends, products, and technologies that arise in one country and might have significance on a broader scale. Some organizations also use *business integrators* to provide coordination on a regional basis that might include several countries. These managers reach out to various parts of the organization to resolve problems and coordinate activities across groups, divisions, or countries.

Another coordination role is that of formal *network coordinator* to coordinate information and activities related to key customer accounts. These coordinators would enable a manufacturing organization, for example, to provide knowledge and integrated solutions across multiple businesses, divisions, and countries for a large retail customer such as Tesco, Wal-Mart, or Carrefour.[72] Top managers in successful global firms also encourage and support informal networks and relationships to keep information flowing in all directions. Much of an organization's information exchange occurs not through formal systems or structures but through informal channels and relationships. By supporting these informal networks, giving people across boundaries opportunities to get together and develop relationships and then ways to keep in close touch, executives enhance organizational coordination.

International companies today have a hard time staying competitive without strong interunit coordination and collaboration. Those firms that stimulate and support collaboration are typically better able to leverage dispersed resources and capabilities to reap operational and economic benefits.[73] Benefits that result from interunit collaboration include the following:

- *Cost savings.*   Collaboration can produce real, measurable results in the way of cost savings from the sharing of best practices across global divisions. For example, at BP, a business unit head in the United States improved inventory turns and cut the working capital needed to run U.S. service stations by learning the best practices from BP operations in the United Kingdom and the Netherlands.
- *Better decision making.*   By sharing information and advice across divisions, managers can make better business decisions that support their own unit as well as the organization as a whole.
- *Greater revenues.*   By sharing expertise and products among various divisions, organizations can reap increased revenues. BP again provides an example. More than seventy-five people from various units around the world flew to China to

assist the team developing an acetic acid plant there. As a result, BP finished the project and began realizing revenues sooner than project planners had expected.

- *Increased innovation.* The sharing of ideas and technological innovations across units stimulates creativity and the development of new products and services. McDonald's is taking an approach called "freedom within a framework" that allows regional and national managers to develop practices and products suited to the local area. The company then makes sure international managers have plenty of both formal and informal ways to communicate and share ideas. The Big Tasty, a whopping 5.5 oz. beef patty slathered in barbeque sauce and topped with three slices of cheese, was created in a test kitchen in Germany and launched in Sweden, but as word spread, the sandwich was adopted by restaurants in places like Brazil, Italy, and Portugal, where it became a huge hit.[74]

CULTURAL DIFFERENCES IN COORDINATION AND CONTROL

Just as social and cultural values differ from country to country, the management values and organizational norms of international companies tend to vary depending on the organization's home country. Organizational norms and values are influenced by the values in the larger national culture, and these in turn influence the organization's structural approach and the ways managers coordinate and control an international firm.

National Value Systems

Briefcase

As an organization manager, keep this guideline in mind:

Appreciate cultural value differences and strive to use coordination mechanisms that are in tune with local values. When broader coordination mechanisms are needed, focus on education and corporate culture as ways to gain understanding and acceptance.

Studies have attempted to determine how national value systems influence management and organizations. One of the most influential was conducted by Geert Hofstede, who identified several dimensions of national value systems that vary widely across countries.[75] More recent research by Project GLOBE (Global Leadership and Organizational Behavior Effectiveness) has supported and extended Hofstede's assessment. Project GLOBE used data collected from 18,000 managers in 62 countries to identify 9 dimensions that explain cultural differences, including those identified by Hofstede.[76] These studies provide managers with an understanding of key cultural differences that can enhance their and their organizations' effectiveness on a global scale.[77] Complete the questionnaire in the "How Do You Fit the Design?" box to see how prepared you are to work internationally.

Two dimensions that seem to have a strong impact within organizations are *power distance* and *uncertainty avoidance*. High **power distance** means that people accept inequality in power among institutions, organizations, and people. Low power distance means that people expect equality in power. High **uncertainty avoidance** means that members of a society feel uncomfortable with uncertainty and ambiguity and thus support beliefs that promise certainty and conformity. Low uncertainty avoidance means that people have a high tolerance for the unstructured, the unclear, and the unpredictable.

The value dimensions of *power distance* and *uncertainty avoidance* are reflected within organizations in beliefs regarding the need for hierarchy, centralized decision making and control, formal rules and procedures, and specialized jobs.[78] In countries that value high power distance, for example, organizations tend to be more hierarchical and centralized, with greater control and coordination from the top levels of the organization. On the other hand, organizations in countries that value low power distance are more likely to be decentralized. A low tolerance for uncertainty tends to be reflected in a preference for coordination through rules and procedures. Organizations in countries where people have a high tolerance for uncertainty typically have fewer rules and formal systems, relying more on informal networks and personal communication for coordination.

How Do You Fit the Design?

Are You Ready to Fill an International Role?

Are you ready to negotiate a sales contract with someone from another country? Coordinate a new product for use overseas? Companies large and small deal on a global basis. To what extent do you display the behaviors below? Please answer each item as Mostly True or Mostly False for you.

Are You Typically:	Mostly True	Mostly False
1. Impatient? Do you have a short attention span? Do you want to keep moving to the next topic?	____	____
2. A poor listener? Are you uncomfortable with silence? Does your mind think about what you want to say next?	____	____
3. Argumentative? Do you enjoy arguing for its own sake?	____	____
4. Not familiar with cultural specifics in other countries? Do you have limited experience in other countries?	____	____
5. Placing more emphasis on the short-term than on the long-term in your thinking and planning?	____	____
6. Thinking that it is a waste of time getting to know someone personally before discussing business?	____	____
7. Legalistic to win your point? Holding others to an agreement regardless of changing circumstances?	____	____
8. Thinking "win/lose" when negotiating? Trying to win a negotiation at the other's expense?	____	____

Scoring: Give yourself one point for each Mostly True answer. A score of 3 or lower suggests that you may have international style and awareness. A score of 6 or higher suggests low presence or awareness with respect to other cultures.

Interpretation: A low score on this exercise is a good thing. American managers often display cross-cultural ignorance during business negotiations compared to counterparts from other countries. American habits can be disturbing, such as emphasizing areas of disagreement over agreement, spending little time understanding the views and interests of the other side, and adopting an adversarial attitude. Americans often like to leave a negotiation thinking they won, which can be embarrassing to the other side. For this quiz, a low score shows better international presence. If you answered "Mostly True" to three or fewer questions, then consider yourself ready to assist with an international negotiation. If you scored six or higher "Mostly True" responses, it is time to learn more about how business people behave in other national cultures before participating in international business deals. Try to develop greater focus on other people's needs and an appreciation for different viewpoints. Be open to compromise and develop empathy for people who are different from you.

Source: Adapted from Cynthia Barnum and Natasha Wolniansky, "Why Americans Fail at Overseas Negotiations," *Management Review* (October 1989), 54–57.

Although organizations do not always reflect the dominant cultural values, studies have found rather clear patterns of different management structures when comparing countries in Europe, the United States, and Asia.

Three National Approaches to Coordination and Control

Let's look at three primary approaches to coordination and control as represented by Japanese, American, and European companies.[79] It should be noted that companies in each country use tools and techniques from each of the three coordination methods. However, there are broad, general patterns that illustrate cultural differences.

Centralized Coordination in Japanese Companies. When expanding internationally, Japanese companies have typically developed coordination mechanisms that rely on centralization. Top managers at headquarters actively direct and control overseas operations, whose primary focus is to implement strategies handed down from headquarters. A recent study of R&D activities in high-tech firms in Japan and Germany supports the idea that Japanese organizations tend to be more centralized. Whereas the German firms leaned toward dispersing R&D groups out into different regions, Japanese companies tended to keep these activities centralized in the home country.[80] This centralized approach enables Japanese companies to leverage the knowledge and resources located at the corporate center, attain global efficiencies, and coordinate across units to obtain synergies and avoid turf battles. Top managers use strong structural linkages to ensure that managers at headquarters remain up to date and fully involved in all strategic decisions. However, centralization has its limits. As the organization expands and divisions grow larger, headquarters can become overloaded and decision making slows. The quality of decisions may also suffer as greater diversity and complexity make it difficult for headquarters to understand and respond to local needs in each region.

China is a rapidly growing part of the international business environment, and limited research has been done into management structures of Chinese firms. Many Chinese-based firms are still relatively small and run in a traditional family-like manner. However, similar to Japan, organizations typically reflect a distinct hierarchy of authority and relatively strong centralization. Hierarchy plays an important role in Chinese culture and management, so employees feel obligated to follow orders directed from above.[81] Interestingly, though, one study found that Chinese employees are loyal not just to the boss, but also to company policies.[82] As Chinese organizations grow larger, more insight will be gained into how these firms handle the balance of coordination and control.

European Firms' Decentralized Approach. A different approach has typically been taken by European companies. Rather than relying on strong, centrally directed coordination and control as in the Japanese firms, international units tend to have a high level of independence and decision-making autonomy. Companies rely on a strong mission, shared values, and informal personal relationships for coordination. Thus, great emphasis is placed on careful selection, training, and development of key managers throughout the international organization. Formal management and control systems are used primarily for financial rather than technical or operational control. Many European managers don't appreciate headquarters taking control over operational issues. When SAP AG tried to assert a more centralized control system to speed up development of new software and fend off growing competition, German engineers rebelled at the loss of autonomy. "They said, 'You don't tell us what to do—we tell you what to build,'" one former executive recalls.[83]

With a decentralized approach, each international unit focuses on its local markets, enabling the company to excel in meeting diverse needs. One disadvantage is the cost of ensuring, through training and development programs, that managers throughout a huge, global firm share goals, values, and priorities. Decision making can also be slow and complex, and disagreements and conflicts among divisions are more difficult to resolve.

The United States: Coordination and Control through Formalization. U.S.-based companies that have expanded into the international arena have taken still a third direction. Typically, these organizations have delegated responsibility to international divisions, yet retained overall control of the enterprise through the use of sophisticated management control systems and the development of specialist headquarters staff. Formal systems, policies, standards of performance, and a regular flow of information from divisions to headquarters are the primary means of coordination and control. Decision making is based on objective data, policies, and procedures, which provides for many operating efficiencies and reduces conflict among divisions and between divisions and headquarters. However, the cost of setting up complex systems, policies, and rules for an international organization may be quite high. This approach also requires a larger headquarters staff for reviewing, interpreting, and sharing information, thus increasing overhead costs. Finally, standard routines and procedures don't always fit the needs of new problems and situations. Flexibility is limited if managers pay so much attention to the standard systems that they fail to recognize opportunities and threats in the environment.

Clearly, each of these approaches has advantages. But as international organizations grow larger and more complex, the disadvantages of each tend to become more pronounced. Because traditional approaches have been inadequate to meet the demands of a rapidly changing, complex global environment, many large international companies are moving toward a *transnational model* of organization, which is highly differentiated to address the increased complexity of the global environment, yet offers very high levels of coordination, learning, and transfer of organizational knowledge and innovations.

THE TRANSNATIONAL MODEL OF ORGANIZATION

The **transnational model** represents the most advanced kind of international organization. It reflects the ultimate in both organizational complexity, with many diverse units, and organizational coordination, with mechanisms for integrating the varied parts. The transnational model is useful for large, multinational companies with subsidiaries in many countries that try to exploit both global and local advantages as well as technological advancements, rapid innovation, and global learning and knowledge sharing. Rather than building capabilities primarily in one area, such as global efficiency, national responsiveness, or global learning, the transnational model seeks to achieve all three simultaneously. Dealing with multiple, interrelated, complex issues requires a complex form of organization and structure.

The transnational model represents the most current thinking about the kind of structure needed by highly complex global organizations such as Philips NV, illustrated in Exhibit 5.10. Incorporated in the Netherlands, Philips has hundreds of operating units all over the world and is typical of global companies such as Unilever, Matsushita, or Procter & Gamble.[84] General Electric is shifting toward a transnational structure as it strives to become a truly global organization. CEO Jeff Immelt is dispersing operations around the world and shifting the giant firm's culture and training programs toward a global outlook. As Christopher Bartlett, a Harvard professor who has studied GE, said, the company's executives are learning to manage a worldwide organization "as a network, not a centralized hub with foreign appendages."[85]

The units of a transnational organization network, as illustrated in Exhibit 5.10, are far-flung. Achieving coordination, a sense of participation and involvement by subsidiaries, and a sharing of information, knowledge, new technology, and customers is a tremendous challenge. For example, a global corporation like Philips, Unilever, or GE is so large that size alone is a huge problem in coordinating global operations. In addition, some subsidiaries become so large that they no longer fit a narrow strategic role defined by headquarters. While being part of a larger organization, individual units need some autonomy for themselves and the ability to have an impact on other parts of the organization.

The transnational model addresses these challenges by creating an integrated network of individual operations that are linked together to achieve the multidimensional goals of the overall organization.[86] The management philosophy is based on *interdependence* rather than either full divisional independence or total dependence of these units on headquarters for decision making and control. The transnational model is more than just an organization chart. It is a managerial state of mind, a set of values, a shared desire to make a worldwide learning system work, and an idealized structure for effectively managing such a system. Several characteristics distinguish the transnational organization from other global organization forms such as the matrix, described earlier.

1. *Assets and resources are dispersed worldwide into highly specialized operations that are linked together through interdependent relationships.* Resources and capabilities are widely distributed to help the organization sense and respond to diverse stimuli such as market needs, technological developments, or consumer trends that emerge in different parts of the world. To manage this increased complexity and differentiation, managers forge interdependent relationships among the various product, functional, or geographic units. Mechanisms such

EXHIBIT 5.10
International
Organizational Units
and Interlinkages within
Philips NV

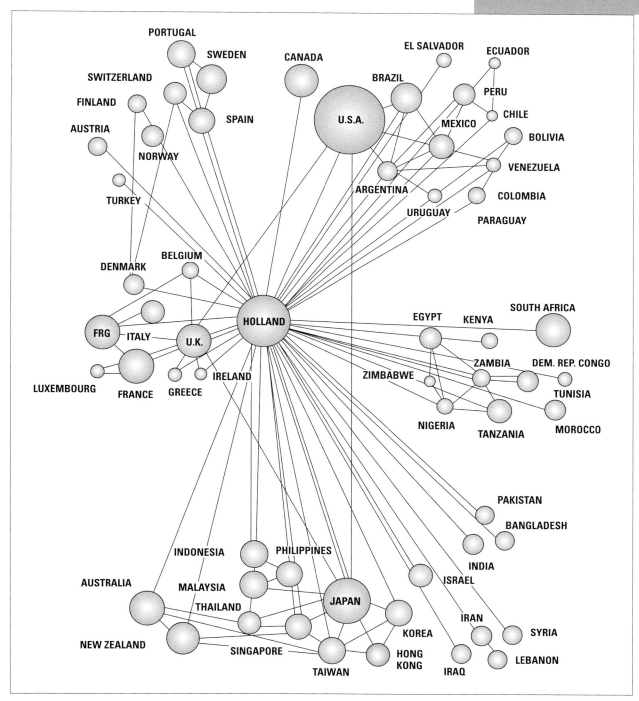

Source: *Academy of Management Review* by Ghoshal and Bartlett. Copyright 1990 by Academy of Management (NY). Reproduced with permission of Academy of Management (NY) in the format Other book via Copyright Clearance Center.

as cross-subsidiary teams, for example, compel units to work together for the good of their own unit as well as the overall organization. Rather than being completely self-sufficient, each group has to cooperate to achieve its own goals. Such interdependencies encourage the collaborative sharing of information and resources, cross-unit problem solving, and collective implementation demanded by today's competitive international environment. Materials, people, products, ideas, resources, and information are continually flowing among the dispersed parts of the integrated network. In addition, managers actively shape, manage, and reinforce informal information networks that cross functions, products, divisions, and countries.

2. *Structures are flexible and ever-changing.* The transnational operates on a principle of *flexible centralization.* It may centralize some functions in one country, some in another, yet decentralize still other functions among its many geographically dispersed operations. An R&D center may be centralized in Holland and a purchasing center may be located in Sweden, while financial accounting responsibilities are decentralized to operations in many countries. A unit in Hong Kong may be responsible for coordinating activities across Asia, while activities for all other countries are coordinated by a large division headquarters in London. The transnational model requires that managers be flexible in determining structural needs based on the benefits to be gained. Some functions, products, and geographic regions by their nature may need more central control and coordination than others. In addition, coordination and control mechanisms will change over time to meet new needs or competitive threats. Some companies have begun setting up multiple headquarters in different countries as the organization gets too large and too complex to manage from one place. Irdeto Holdings BV, for example, now has headquarters in both Amsterdam and Beijing. U.S.-based Halliburton Company is planning to open a second corporate headquarters in Dubai.[87]

3. *Subsidiary managers initiate strategy and innovations that become strategy for the corporation as a whole.* In traditional structures, managers have a strategic role only for their division. In a transnational structure, various centers and subsidiaries can shape the company from the bottom up by developing creative responses and initiating programs in response to local needs, then dispersing those innovations worldwide. Transnational companies recognize each of the worldwide units as a source of capabilities and knowledge that can be used to benefit the entire organization. In addition, environmental demands and opportunities vary from country to country, and exposing the whole organization to this broader range of environmental stimuli triggers greater learning and innovation.

4. *Unification and coordination are achieved primarily through corporate culture, shared vision and values, and management style, rather than through formal structures and systems.* A study by Hay Group found that one of the defining characteristics of companies that succeed on a global scale is that they successfully coordinate worldwide units and subsidiaries around a common strategic vision and values rather than relying on formal coordination systems alone.[88] Achieving unity and coordination in an organization in which employees come from a variety of different national backgrounds, are separated by time and geographic distance, and have different cultural norms is more easily accomplished through shared understanding than through formal systems. Top leaders build a context of shared vision, values, and perspectives among managers who in turn cascade these elements through all parts of the organization. Selection and training of managers emphasizes flexibility and open-mindedness. In addition,

people are often rotated through different jobs, divisions, and countries to gain broad experience and become socialized into the corporate culture. Achieving coordination in a transnational organization is a much more complex process than simple centralization or decentralization of decision making. It requires shaping and adapting beliefs, culture, and values so that everyone participates in information sharing and learning.

Taken together, these characteristics facilitate strong coordination, organizational learning, and knowledge sharing on a broad global scale. The transnational model is truly a complex and messy way to conceptualize organization structure, but it is becoming increasingly relevant for large, global firms that treat the whole world as their playing field and do not have a single country base. The autonomy of organizational parts gives strength to smaller units and allows the firm to be flexible in responding to rapid change and competitive opportunities on a local level, while the emphasis on interdependency enables global efficiencies and organizational learning. Each part of the transnational company is aware of and closely integrated with the organization as a whole so local actions complement and enhance other company parts.

DESIGN ESSENTIALS

- This chapter examined how managers design organizations for a complex international environment. Almost every company today is affected by significant global forces, and many are developing overseas operations to take advantage of global markets. Three primary motivations for global expansion are to realize economies of scale, exploit economies of scope, and achieve scarce or low-cost factors of production such as labor, raw materials, or land. One popular way to become involved in international operations is through strategic alliances with international firms. Alliances include licensing, joint ventures, and consortia.

- Organizations typically evolve through four stages, beginning with a domestic orientation, shifting to an international orientation, then changing to a multinational orientation, and finally moving to a global orientation that sees the whole world as a potential market. Organizations typically use an export department, then use an international department, and eventually develop into a worldwide geographic or product structure.

- Geographic structures are most effective for organizations that can benefit from a multidomestic strategy, meaning that products and services will do best if tailored to local needs and cultures. A product structure supports a globalization strategy, which means that products and services can be standardized and sold worldwide. Huge global firms might use a matrix structure to respond to both local and global forces simultaneously. Many firms use hybrid structures by combining elements of two or more different structures to meet the dynamic conditions of the global environment.

- Succeeding on a global scale is not easy. Three aspects of the global organizational challenge are addressing environmental complexity through greater organizational complexity and differentiation, achieving integration and coordination among the highly differentiated units, and implementing mechanisms

for the transfer of knowledge and innovations. Common ways to address the problem of integration and knowledge transfer are through global teams, stronger headquarters planning and control, and specific coordination roles.

■ Managers also recognize that diverse national and cultural values influence the organization's approach to coordination and control. Three varied national approaches are the centralized coordination and control typically found in many Japanese-based firms, a decentralized approach common among European firms, and the formalization approach often used by U.S.-based international firms. Most companies, however, no matter their home country, use a combination of elements from each of these approaches.

■ Companies operating globally need broad coordination methods, and some are moving toward the transnational model of organization. The transnational model is based on a philosophy of interdependence. It is highly differentiated yet offers very high levels of coordination, learning, and transfer of knowledge across far-flung divisions. The transnational model represents the ultimate global design in terms of both organizational complexity and organizational integration. Each part of the transnational organization is aware of and closely integrated with the organization as a whole so that local actions complement and enhance other company parts.

Key Concepts

consortia	global product structure	multidomestic strategy
domestic stage	global stage	multinational stage
economies of scale	global teams	power distance
economies of scope	globalization strategy	standardization
factors of production	international division	transnational model
global companies	international stage	uncertainty avoidance
global geographic structure	joint venture	
global matrix structure	multidomestic	

Discussion Questions

1. What are some of the primary reasons a company decides to expand internationally? Identify a company in the news that has recently built a new overseas facility. Which of the three motivations for global expansion described in the chapter do you think best explains the company's decision? Discuss.

2. Compare the description of the transnational model in this chapter to the elements of the learning organization described in Chapter 1. Do you think the transnational model seems workable for a huge global firm? Discuss.

3. Do you think it makes sense for a transnational organization to have more than one headquarters? What might be some advantages associated with two headquarters, each responsible for different things? Can you think of any drawbacks?

4. Do you believe it is possible for a global company to simultaneously achieve the goals of global efficiency and integration, national responsiveness and flexibility, and the worldwide transfer of knowledge and innovation? Discuss.

5. Why would a company want to join a strategic alliance rather than go it alone in international operations? What do you see as the potential advantages and disadvantages of international alliances?

6. Traditional values in Mexico support high power distance and a low tolerance for uncertainty. What would you predict about a company that opens a division in Mexico and tries to implement global teams characterized by shared power and authority and the lack of formal guidelines, rules, and structure?

7. Name some companies that you think could succeed today with a globalization strategy and explain why you selected those companies. How does the globalization strategy differ from a multidomestic strategy?

8. Name some of the elements that contribute to greater complexity for international organizations. How do organizations address this complexity? Do you think these elements apply to an online company such as MySpace that wants to grow internationally? Discuss.

9. Under what conditions should a company consider adopting a global geographic structure as opposed to a global product structure?

10. When would an organization consider using a matrix structure? How does the global matrix differ from the domestic matrix structure described in Chapter 2?

Chapter 5 Workbook: Made in the U.S.A.?

Find three different consumer products, such as a shirt, a toy, and a shoe. Try to find out the following information for each product, as shown in the table. To find this information, use websites, articles on the company from various business newspapers and magazines, and the labels on the items. You could also try calling the company and talking with someone there.

Product	What country do materials come from?	Where is it manufactured or assembled?	Which country does the marketing and advertising?	In what different countries is the product sold?
1.				
2.				
3.				

What can you conclude about international products and organizations based on your analysis?

Case for Analysis: TopDog Software*

At the age of 39, after working for nearly fifteen years at a leading software company on the West Coast, Ari Weiner and his soon-to-be-wife, Mary Carpenter, had cashed in their stock options, withdrew all their savings, maxed out their credit cards, and started their own business, naming it TopDog Software after their beloved Alaskan malamute. The two had developed a new software package for customer relationship management (CRM) applications that they were certain was far superior to anything on the market at that time. TopDog's software was particularly effective for use in call centers because it provided a highly efficient way to integrate massive amounts of customer data and make it almost immediately accessible to call center representatives as they worked the phones. The software, which could be used as a stand-alone product or easily integrated with other major CRM software packages, dramatically expedited customer identification and verification, rapidly selected pertinent bits of data, and provided them in an easily interpreted format so that call center or customer service reps could provide fast, friendly, and customized service.

The timing proved to be right on target. CRM was just getting hot, and TopDog was poised to take advantage of the trend as a niche player in a growing market. Weiner and Carpenter brought in two former colleagues as partners and were soon able to catch the attention of a venture capitalist firm to gain additional funding. Within a couple of years, TopDog had twenty-eight employees and sales had reached nearly $4 million.

Now, though, the partners are facing the company's first major problem. TopDog's head of sales, Samantha Jenkins, has learned of a new company based in London that is beta testing a new CRM package that promises to outpace TopDog's—and the London-based company, FastData, has been talking up its global aspirations in the press. "If we stay focused on the United States and they start out as a global player, they'll kill us within months!" Sam moaned. "We've got to come up with an international strategy to deal with this kind of competition."

In a series of group meetings, off-site retreats, and one-on-one conversations, Weiner and Carpenter have gathered opinions and ideas from their partners, employees, advisors, and friends. Now they have to make a decision—should TopDog go global? And if so, what approach would be most effective? There's a growing market for CRM software overseas, and new companies such as FastData will soon be cutting into TopDog's U.S. market share as well. Samantha Jenkins isn't alone in her belief that TopDog has no choice but to enter new international markets or get eaten alive. Others, however, are concerned that TopDog isn't ready for that step. The company's resources are already stretched to the limit, and some advisors have warned that rapid global expansion could spell disaster. TopDog isn't even well established in the United States, they argue, and expanding internationally could strain the company's capabilities and resources. Others have pointed out that none of the managers has any international experience and the company would have to hire someone with significant global exposure to even think about entering new markets.

Although Mary tends to agree that TopDog for the time being should stay focused on building its business in the United States, Ari has come to believe that global expansion of some type is a necessity. But if TopDog does eventually decide on global expansion, he wonders how on earth they should proceed in such a huge, complex environment. Sam, the sales manager, is arguing that the company should set up its own small foreign offices from scratch and staff them primarily with local people. Building a U.K. office and an Asian office, she asserts, would give

TopDog an ideal base for penetrating markets around the world. However, it would be quite expensive, not to mention the complexities of dealing with language and cultural differences, legal and government regulations, and other matters. Another option would be to establish alliances or joint ventures with small European and Asian companies that could benefit from adding CRM applications to their suite of products. The companies could share expenses in setting up foreign production facilities and a global sales and distribution network. This would be a much less costly operation and would give TopDog the benefit of the expertise of the foreign partners. However, it might also require lengthy negotiations and would certainly mean giving up some control to the partner companies.

One of TopDog's partners is urging still a third, even lower-cost approach, that of licensing TopDog's software to foreign distributors as a route to international expansion. By giving foreign software companies rights to produce, market, and distribute its CRM software, TopDog could build brand identity and customer awareness while keeping a tight rein on expenses. Ari likes the low-cost approach, but he wonders if licensing would give TopDog enough participation and control to successfully develop its international presence. As another day winds down, Weiner and Carpenter are no closer to a decision about global expansion than they were when the sun came up.

*Source: Based on Walter Kuemmerle, "Go Global—Or No?" *Harvard Business Review* (June 2001), 37–49.

Case for Analysis: Rhodes Industries

David Javier was reviewing the consulting firm's proposed changes in organization structure for Rhodes Industries (RI). As Javier read the report, he wondered whether the changes recommended by the consultants would do more harm than good for RI. Javier had been president of RI for eighteen months, and he was keenly aware of the organizational and coordination problems that needed to be corrected in order for RI to improve profits and growth in its international businesses.

Company Background
Rhodes Industries was started in the 1950s in Southern Ontario, Canada, by Robert Rhodes, an engineer who was an entrepreneur at heart. He started the business by first making pipe and then glass for industrial uses, but as soon as the initial business was established, he quickly branched into new areas such as industrial sealants, coatings, and cleaners, and even into manufacturing mufflers and parts for the trucking industry. Much of this expansion occurred

by acquiring small firms in Canada and the United States during the 1960s. RI had a conglomerate-type structure with rather diverse subsidiaries scattered around North America, all reporting directly to the Ontario headquarters. Each subsidiary was a complete local business and was allowed to operate independently so long as it contributed profits to RI.

During the 1970s and 1980s, the president at the time, Clifford Michaels, brought a strong international focus to RI. His strategy was to acquire small companies worldwide with the belief they could be formed into a cohesive unit that would bring RI synergies and profits through low cost of manufacturing and by serving businesses in international markets. Some of RI's businesses were acquired simply because they were available at a good price, and RI found itself in new lines of business such as consumer products (paper and envelopes) and electrical equipment (switchboards, lightbulbs, and security systems), in addition to its previous lines of business. Most of these products had local brand names or were manufactured for major international companies such as General Electric or Corning Glass.

During the 1990s, a new president of RI, Sean Rhodes, the grandson of the founder, took over the business and adopted the strategy of focusing RI on three lines of business—Industrial Products, Consumer Products, and Electronics. He led the acquisition of more international businesses that fit these three categories, and divested a few businesses that didn't fit. Each of the three divisions had manufacturing plants as well as marketing and distribution systems in North America, Asia, and Europe. The Industrial Products division included pipe, glass, industrial sealants and coatings, cleaning equipment, and truck parts. The Electronics division included specialty lightbulbs, switchboards, computer chips, and resistors and capacitors for original equipment manufacturers. Consumer Products included dishes and glassware, paper and envelopes, and pencils and pens.

Structure

In 2004 David Javier replaced Sean Rhodes as president. He was very concerned about whether a new organization structure was needed for RI. The current structure was based on three major geographic areas—North America, Asia, and Europe—as illustrated in Exhibit 5.11. The various

autonomous units within those regions reported to the office of the regional vice president. When several units existed in a single country, one of the subsidiary presidents was also responsible for coordinating the various businesses in that country, but most coordination was done through the regional vice president. Businesses were largely independent, which provided flexibility and motivation for the subsidiary managers.

The headquarters functional departments in Ontario were rather small. The three central departments—Corporate Relations and Public Affairs, Finance and Acquisitions, and Legal and Administrative—served the corporate business worldwide. Other functions such as HR management, new product development, marketing, and manufacturing all existed within individual subsidiaries and there was little coordination of these functions across geographic regions. Each business devised its own way to develop, manufacture, and market its products in its own country and region.

Organizational Problems

The problems Javier faced at RI, which were confirmed in the report on his desk, fell into three areas. First, each subsidiary acted as an independent business, using its own reporting systems and acting to maximize its own profits. This autonomy made it increasingly difficult to consolidate

EXHIBIT 5.11
Rhodes Industries
Organization Chart

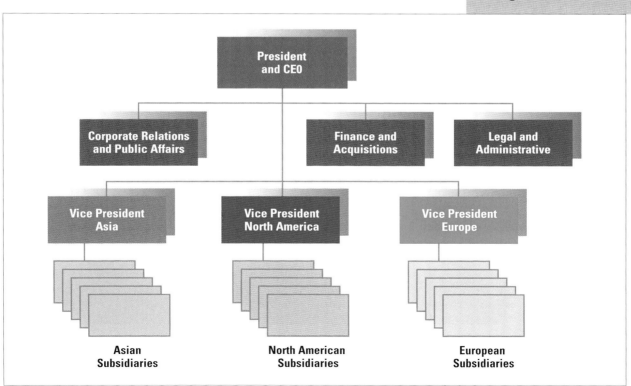

financial reports worldwide and to gain the efficiencies of uniform information and reporting systems.

Second, major strategic decisions were made to benefit individual businesses or for a country's or region's local interests. Local projects and profits received more time and resources than did projects that benefited RI worldwide. For example, an electronics manufacturer in Singapore refused to increase production of chips and capacitors for sale in the United Kingdom because it would hurt the bottom line of the Singapore operation. However, the economies of scale in Singapore would more than offset shipping costs to the United Kingdom and would enable RI to close expensive manufacturing facilities in Europe, increasing RI's efficiency and profits.

Third, there had been no transfer of technology, new product ideas, or other innovations within RI. For example, a cost-saving technology for manufacturing lightbulbs in Canada had been ignored in Asia and Europe. A technical innovation that provided homeowners with cell phone access to home security systems developed in Europe has

been ignored in North America. The report on Javier's desk stressed that RI was failing to disperse important innovations throughout the organization. These ignored innovations could provide significant improvements in both manufacturing and marketing worldwide. The report said, "No one at RI understands all the products and locations in a way that allows RI to capitalize on manufacturing improvements and new product opportunities." The report also said that better worldwide coordination would reduce RI's costs by 7 percent each year and increase market potential by 10 percent. These numbers were too big to ignore.

Recommended Structure

The report from the consultant recommended that RI try one of two options for improving its structure. The first alternative was to create a new international department at headquarters with the responsibility to coordinate technology transfer and product manufacturing and marketing worldwide (Exhibit 5.12). This department would have a

EXHIBIT 5.12
Proposed Product
Director Structure

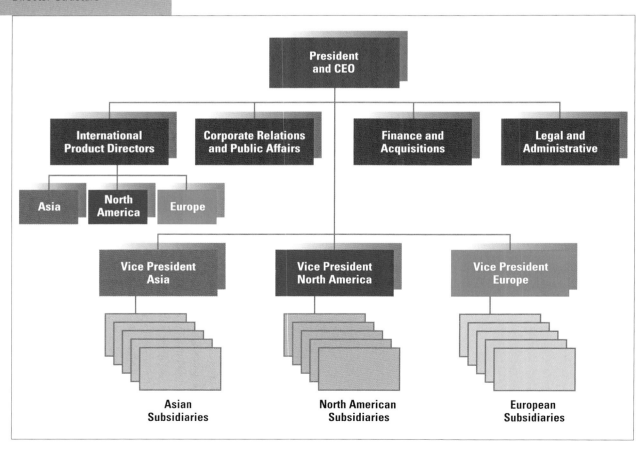

product director for each major product line—Industrial, Consumer, and Electronics—who would have authority to coordinate activities and innovations worldwide. Each product director would have a team that would travel to each region and carry information on innovations and improvements to subsidiaries in other parts of the world.

The second recommendation was to reorganize into a worldwide product structure, as shown in Exhibit 5.13. All subsidiaries worldwide associated with a product line would report to the product line business manager. The business manager and staff would be responsible for developing business strategies and for coordinating all manufacturing efficiencies and product developments worldwide for its product line.

This worldwide product structure would be a huge change for RI. Many questions came to Javier's mind. Would the subsidiaries still be competitive and adaptive in local markets if forced to coordinate with other subsidiaries around the world? Would business managers be able to change the habits of subsidiary managers toward more global behavior? Would it be a better idea to appoint product director coordinators as a first step, or jump to the business manager product structure right away? Javier had a hunch that the move to worldwide product coordination made sense, but he wanted to think through all the potential problems and how RI would implement the changes.

EXHIBIT 5.13
Proposed Worldwide Business Manager Structure

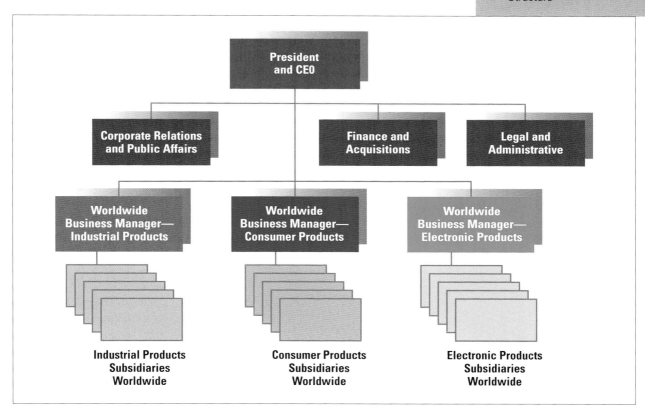

Chapter 5 Workshop: Comparing Cultures*

As a group, rent a video of a foreign movie (or, alternately, go to the cinema when a foreign movie is shown). Take notes as you watch the movie, looking for any differences in cultural norms compared to your own. For example,

identify any differences in the following compared to your own cultural norms:

a. The way people interact with one another
b. The formality or informality of relationships
c. The attitudes toward work
d. The amount of time people spend on work versus family
e. The connection to family
f. How people have fun

Questions

1. What were the key differences you observed in the movie's culture versus your own?
2. What are the advantages and disadvantages of using movies to understand another culture?

Chapter 6

The Impact of Environment

© Ken Kan

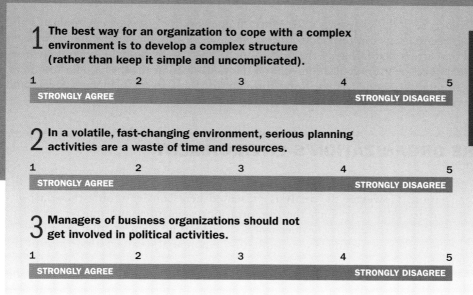

1 The best way for an organization to cope with a complex
environment is to develop a complex structure
(rather than keep it simple and uncomplicated).

1	2	3	4	5
STRONGLY AGREE				STRONGLY DISAGREE

2 In a volatile, fast-changing environment, serious planning
activities are a waste of time and resources.

1	2	3	4	5
STRONGLY AGREE				STRONGLY DISAGREE

3 Managers of business organizations should not
get involved in political activities.

1	2	3	4	5
STRONGLY AGREE				STRONGLY DISAGREE

Managing
by Design
Questions

In the spring and summer of 2008, anyone in the United States with a car felt the
effects of skyrocketing oil prices each time they had to fill the gas tank. It was a
surprise change in the environment that hit consumers on a personal level, causing them to alter their buying habits, travel routes, and vacation plans. That, in
turn, created even bigger headaches for organizations already struggling with higher
costs. Several restaurant chains filed for bankruptcy as people stayed home to save
money and reduce their gasoline use. Amusement parks such as Six Flags and Cedar
Fair saw their attendance slump. Airlines suffered the double whammy of fewer customers and exorbitant fuel costs. Retailers, auto makers, food processors, trucking
companies, school systems, car rental firms, and every other type of organization
felt the pinch.

On the other hand, some companies also benefited from the crisis. "Four-
dollar gas is the best marketing tool I have," said Betsy Kachmar, assistant
general manager of Fort Wayne Public Transportation Corporation, which saw
a dramatic jump in bus ridership. Organic farmers and small companies producing food or other products for a local market became more competitive as prices
of mass-produced goods increased due to transportation costs. Manufacturers
of energy efficient appliances saw a rise in sales with consumers looking for
ways to cut their energy use on everything from washing clothes to heating their
homes.[1] Sales at New York-based Eco Bags, which makes reusable fishnet shopping bags, doubled as grocers and customers turned away from using plastic
bags made with oil.[2]

The rapid rise in oil prices provides a dramatic example of how shifts in the external
environment create both threats and opportunities for organizations. Organizations
face tremendous uncertainty in dealing with events in the external environment and
often have to adapt quickly to new competition, economic turmoil, changes in consumer interests, or innovative technologies.

Purpose of This Chapter

The purpose of this chapter is to develop a framework for assessing environments and how organizations can respond to them. First, we identify the organizational domain and the sectors that influence the organization. Then, we explore two major environmental forces on the organization—the need for information and the need for resources. Organizations respond to these forces through structural design, planning systems, and attempts to adapt to and influence elements in the external environment.

THE ORGANIZATION'S ENVIRONMENT

In a broad sense the environment is infinite and includes everything outside the organization. However, the analysis presented here considers only those aspects of the environment to which the organization is sensitive and must respond to survive. Thus, **organizational environment** is defined as all elements that exist outside the boundary of the organization and have the potential to affect all or part of the organization.

The environment of an organization can be understood by analyzing its domain within external sectors. An organization's **domain** is the chosen environmental field of action. It is the territory an organization stakes out for itself with respect to products, services, and markets served. Domain defines the organization's niche and defines those external sectors with which the organization will interact to accomplish its goals.

The environment comprises several **sectors** or subdivisions that contain similar elements. Ten sectors can be analyzed for each organization: industry, raw materials, human resources, financial resources, market, technology, economic conditions, government, sociocultural, and international. The sectors and a hypothetical organizational domain are illustrated in Exhibit 6.1. For most companies, the sectors in Exhibit 6.1 can be further subdivided into the task environment and general environment.

Briefcase

As an organization manager, keep these guidelines in mind:

Organize elements in the external environment into ten sectors for analysis: industry, raw materials, human resources, financial resources, market, technology, economic conditions, government, sociocultural, and international. Focus on sectors that may experience significant change at any time.

Task Environment

The **task environment** includes sectors with which the organization interacts directly and that have a direct impact on the organization's ability to achieve its goals. The task environment typically includes the industry, raw materials, and market sectors, and perhaps the human resources and international sectors.

The following examples illustrate how each of these sectors can affect organizations:

- In the industry sector, the retail landscape has begun a decided shift, with consumers rejecting huge stores for smaller shops or Internet retailers that offer greater choice, better service, or higher quality. In clothing, for instance, shoppers favor small niche retailers that offer rapid style changes. Regional grocery chains have grown more competitive by offering fresher and organic foods as well as prepared meals.[3]
- An interesting example in the *raw materials sector* concerns the beverage can industry. Steelmakers owned the beverage can market until the mid-1960s, when Reynolds Aluminum Company launched a huge aluminum recycling program to

EXHIBIT 6.1
An Organization's Environment

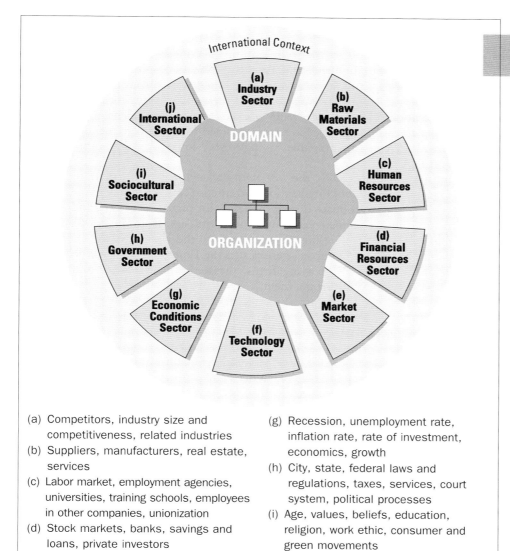

(a) Competitors, industry size and competitiveness, related industries

(b) Suppliers, manufacturers, real estate, services

(c) Labor market, employment agencies, universities, training schools, employees in other companies, unionization

(d) Stock markets, banks, savings and loans, private investors

(e) Customers, clients, potential users of products and services

(f) Techniques of production, science, computers, information technology, e-commerce

(g) Recession, unemployment rate, inflation rate, rate of investment, economics, growth

(h) City, state, federal laws and regulations, taxes, services, court system, political processes

(i) Age, values, beliefs, education, religion, work ethic, consumer and green movements

(j) Competition from and acquisition by foreign firms, entry into overseas markets, foreign customs, regulations, exchange rate

gain a cheaper source of raw materials and make aluminum cans price-competitive with steel.[4]

- In the *market sector*, makers of computer games have benefitted from a shift in consumer interest away from gaming consoles and back to lower-cost options. Today's more powerful PCs and bigger screens are perfect for gamers, and with the tough economy, many people aren't interested in laying out the big bucks for a console and a big screen television. After being overshadowed for several year by consoles, PC games made a big comeback, particularly for role-playing adventure games.[5]

- The *human resources sector* is of significant concern to every business. At a recent CEO roundtable discussion, Steve Creamer, president and CEO of Energy Solutions, said his company's single biggest problem is human capital. Other leaders agreed that factors such as the aging of the workforce, government limitations on visas for foreign workers, and fewer students entering fields such as engineering and science have combined to create a tremendous human resources headache for companies trying to stay competitive in a rapidly changing world.[6]

- For most companies today, the *international sector* is also a part of the task environment because of globalization and intense competition. China is already the world's largest producer of raw materials for pharmaceuticals, and in 2007, for the first time, a Chinese company won permission from the Food and Drug Administration to export finished medicines to the United States. India-based companies have been exporting generics to the United States for a decade, but experts believe China's growing firms, blessed with low costs and brilliant scientists, will quickly overtake them.[7]

General Environment

The **general environment** includes those sectors that might not have a direct impact on the daily operations of a firm but will indirectly influence it. The general environment often includes the government, sociocultural, economic conditions, technology, and financial resources sectors. These sectors affect all organizations eventually. Consider the following examples:

- In the *government sector*, regulations influence every phase of organizational life. One of the most prominent and far-reaching changes in the United States in recent years was the 2002 Sarbannes-Oxley Act, often referred to as SOX. SOX required several types of corporate governance reforms, including better internal monitoring to reduce the risk of fraud, certification of financial results by top executives, improved measures for internal auditing, and enhancing public financial disclosure. Additional regulations of this type are certain to follow the financial meltdown of banks and firms on Wall Street in 2008.

- Shifting demographics is a significant element in the *sociocultural sector*. In the United States, Hispanics have passed African Americans as the nation's largest minority group, and their numbers are growing so fast that Hispanics (or Latinos, as some prefer to be called) are becoming a driving force in U.S. politics, economics, and culture. The growing Hispanic population is forcing gradual changes in organizations from the U.S. Labor Department to the major television networks to the local auto parts store.[8]

- General *economic conditions* often affect the way a company must do business. The already-struggling auto industry had an abysmal year in 2008. Sales of cars and light trucks in the United States dropped about 20 percent and sales of gas-guzzling large trucks and sport utility vehicles slowed to a crawl due to high gas prices, a weakening economy, the credit crunch, and declining consumer confidence. Auto makers had to scale back production, offer incentives to car buyers, and cut back their sales goals.[9]

- The *technology sector* is an area in which massive changes have occurred in recent years, from digital music and advances in mobile technology to cloning and stem-cell research. Chris DeWolfe, CEO of MySpace, believes the world has seen only the beginning of the "mobile revolution." Mobile devices extend the phenomenal power of blogging and social networking, which are breaking down barriers to the exchange of knowledge, information, opinions, and ideas around the world. The exchange of new scientific insights, for example, now happens in hours instead of years. So, too, does the exchange of opinions about a company's products or services.[10]

- All businesses have to be concerned with *financial resources*, and this sector is often first and foremost in the minds of entrepreneurs. Many small business owners have turned to online person-to-person (P-to-P) lending networks for small loans as banks have tightened their lending standards. Jeff Walsh, for example, borrowed around $22,000 through Prosper.com for his coin laundry business. Alex Kalempa needed $15,000 to expand his business of developing racing shift systems for motorcycles, but banks offered him credit lines of only $500 to $1,000. Kalempa went to LendingClub.com, where he got the $15,000 loan at an interest rate several points lower than the banks were offering.[11]

International Environment

The international sector can directly affect many organizations, and it has become extremely important in the last few years. In addition, international events can influence all domestic sectors of the environment as well. For example, adverse weather and a workers' strike in Western Africa, which supplies about two-thirds of the world's cocoa beans, sharply increased raw materials costs for Choco-Logo, a small maker of gourmet chocolates in Buffalo, New York.[12] Farmers, fertilizer companies, food manufacturers, and grocers in the United States faced new competitive issues because of an unexpected grain shortage and rising costs related to international changes. Strong economic growth in developing countries has enabled millions of people to afford richer diets, including grain-fed meat, which directly contributed to the grain shortage in the United States.[13] Countries and organizations around the world are connected as never before, and economic, political, and sociocultural changes in one part of the world eventually affect other areas.

Moreover, the distinctions between foreign and domestic operations have become increasingly irrelevant. Thomas Middelhoff of Germany's Bertelsmann AG, which purchased U.S. publisher Random House, put it this way: "There are no German and American companies. There are only successful and unsuccessful companies."[14] U.S.-based Ford Motor Company owns Sweden's Volvo, while the iconic American beer Miller is owned by a South African company. Toyota is a Japanese corporation, but it has manufactured millions of vehicles in North American factories. The technology behind Intel's Centrino wireless components was born in a lab in Haifa, Israel, and Chinese researchers designed the microprocessors that control the pitch of the blade on General Electric's giant wind turbines.[15] Because of the significance of the international sector and its tremendous impact on organization design, this topic will be covered in detail in Chapter 5.

Every organization faces uncertainty domestically as well as globally. Consider a new challenge facing managers at television network Univision.

Univision

The Latino population in the United States is growing by leaps and bounds, and Univision, the giant of Spanish-language television in the United States, now challenges the major networks CBS, NBC, ABC, and Fox, especially in large cities. Univision won the loyalty of Latino audiences by keeping English out of its programs and commercials. Its prime-time lineup is based on telenovelas from Mexico, sexy soap-opera stories that attract a vast audience. Nielsen ratings indicate that Univision has 90 of the 100 most-watched Spanish-language shows in the United States.

But there's a shift taking place that Univision managers have so far failed to respond to: the interests and tastes of viewers are changing much more rapidly than Univision's shows. Births, not immigration, are now the main source of Latino growth, and American-born Latinos aren't interested in the same type of programs their parents and grandparents were. "I think of [Univision] as a horse-and-buggy company," said David R. Morse, president and CEO of New American Dimensions, which conducted a study of younger Latino viewers. Younger Latinos are more likely to speak English as their primary language, are better educated than their parents, and are more prone to marry outside their ethnic group. They want a broader variety of programs, and many prefer English-language television or bilingual programming.

Second- and third-generation bilingual Latinos are largely underserved by both Spanish and English language networks. Although they are ethnically proud, they don't feel they have to prove themselves. They just want quality programming that addresses their interests. As Jeff Valdez, founder of SiTV, an English language cable start-up that caters to young Latinos says, "They want to see themselves on screen. They want to hear their stories."[16] ■

Can Univision transform its programming to satisfy younger Latino viewers, or is it destined to fade away as new companies like SiTV come on the scene with hip programs that attract the coveted audience of 18-to-34-year-olds? Univision is still a powerhouse, and it can succeed for years using its current formula. However, if the network doesn't keep pace with changing demands from the environment, it could indeed go the way of the horse and buggy.

Television networks are not the only organizations that have to adapt to both subtle and massive shifts in the environment. In the following sections, we will discuss in greater detail how companies can cope with and respond to environmental uncertainty and instability.

THE CHANGING ENVIRONMENT

How does the environment influence an organization? The patterns and events occurring in the environment can be described along several dimensions, such as whether the environment is stable or unstable, homogeneous or heterogeneous, simple or complex; the *munificence*, or amount of resources available to support the organization's growth; whether those resources are concentrated or dispersed; and the degree of consensus in the environment regarding the organization's intended domain.[17] These dimensions boil down to two essential ways the environment influences organizations: (1) the need for information about the environment and (2) the need for resources from the environment. The environmental conditions of complexity and change create a greater need to gather information and to respond based on that information. The organization also is concerned with scarce material and financial resources and with the need to ensure availability of resources.

Environmental uncertainty pertains primarily to those sectors that an organization deals with on a regular, day-to-day basis. Although sectors of the general environment—such as economic conditions, social trends, or technological changes—can create uncertainty for organizations, determining an organization's environmental uncertainty generally means focusing on sectors of the *task environment*, such as how many elements the organization deals with regularly, how rapidly these elements change, and so forth. To assess uncertainty, each sector of the organization's task environment can be analyzed along dimensions such as stability or instability and degree of complexity.[18] The total amount of uncertainty felt by an organization is the uncertainty accumulated across environmental sectors.

Organizations must cope with and manage uncertainty to be effective. **Uncertainty** means that decision makers do not have sufficient information about environmental factors, and they have a difficult time predicting external changes. Uncertainty increases the risk of failure for organizational responses and makes it difficult to compute costs and probabilities associated with decision alternatives.[19] The remainder of this section will focus on the information perspective, which is concerned with uncertainty created by the extent to which the environment is simple or complex and the extent to which events are stable or unstable. Later in the chapter, we discuss how organizations influence the environment to acquire needed resources.

Simple–Complex Dimension

The **simple–complex dimension** concerns environmental complexity, which refers to heterogeneity, or the number and dissimilarity of external elements relevant to an organization's operations. The more external factors that regularly influence the organization and the greater number of other companies in an organization's domain, the greater the complexity. A complex environment is one in which the organization interacts with and is influenced by numerous diverse external elements. In a simple environment, the organization interacts with and is influenced by only a few similar external elements.

Aerospace firms such as Boeing and Airbus operate in a complex environment, as do universities. Universities span a large number of technologies and are continually buffeted by social, cultural, and value changes. Universities also must cope with numerous ever-changing government regulations, competition for quality students and highly educated employees, and scarce financial resources for many programs. They deal with granting agencies, professional and scientific associations, alumni, parents, foundations, legislators, community residents, international agencies, donors, corporations, and athletic teams. This large number of external elements makes up the organization's domain, creating a complex environment. On the other hand, a family-owned hardware store in a suburban community is in a simple environment. The store does not have to deal with complex technologies or extensive government regulations, and cultural and social changes have little impact. Human resources are not a problem because the store is run by family members and part-time help. The only external elements of real importance are a few competitors, suppliers, and customers.

Stable–Unstable Dimension

The **stable–unstable dimension** refers to whether elements in the environment are dynamic. An environmental domain is stable if it remains the same over a period of months or years. Under unstable conditions, environmental elements shift abruptly. Environmental domains seem to be increasingly unstable for most organizations.

Instability may occur when competitors react with aggressive moves and countermoves regarding advertising and new products or services. For example, News Corporation's MySpace held the crown as king of social networking until managers at upstart Facebook began aggressively promoting the college-focused niche site as a place for everyone. The "face" of Facebook—youthful founder and CEO Mark Zuckerberg—was suddenly crowding MySpace off of magazine covers and television talk shows, and the size of Facebook's worldwide user base surpassed MySpace before managers at MySpace even had time to react.[20] Sometimes specific, unpredictable events—such as reports of lead-tainted paint in Mattel toys made in China, the Pakistani government's attempt to block access to certain videos on YouTube, or the discovery of heart problems related to pain drugs such as Vioxx and Celebrex—create unstable conditions for organizations. Today, freewheeling bloggers are a tremendous source of instability for scores of companies, able to destroy a company's reputation virtually overnight. Kryptonite's reputation in bicycle locks plummeted after a blog noted that the locks could be opened with a Bic pen. After 10 days of blogging, Kryptonite announced a free product exchange that would cost the company about $10 million.[21]

Although environments are more unstable for most organizations today, an example of a traditionally stable environment is a public utility.[22] In the rural Midwest, demand and supply factors for a public utility are stable. A gradual increase in demand may occur, which is easily predicted over time. Toy companies, by contrast, have an unstable environment. Hot new toys are difficult to predict, a problem compounded by the fact that children are losing interest in toys at a younger age, their interest captured by video and computer games, electronics, and the Internet. Adding to the instability for toymakers is the shrinking retail market, with big toy retailers going out of business trying to compete with discounters such as Wal-Mart. Toymakers are trying to attract more customers in developing markets such as China, Poland, Brazil, and India to make up for the declining U.S. market, but hitting the target in those countries has proven to be a challenge. Companies such as Fisher-Price, owned by Mattel, can find their biggest products languishing on shelves as shoppers turn to less expensive locally made toys in countries where brand consciousness doesn't come into play. As one toy analyst said, "Chinese kids have been growing for 5,000 years without the benefits of Fisher-Price."[23]

Framework

The simple–complex and stable–unstable dimensions are combined into a framework for assessing environmental uncertainty in Exhibit 6.2. In the *simple, stable* environment, uncertainty is low. There are only a few external elements to contend with, and they tend to remain stable. The *complex, stable* environment represents somewhat greater uncertainty. A large number of elements have to be scanned, analyzed, and acted upon for the organization to perform well. External elements do not change rapidly or unexpectedly in this environment.

Even greater uncertainty is felt in the *simple, unstable* environment.[24] Rapid change creates uncertainty for managers. Even though the organization has few

EXHIBIT 6.2
Framework for
Assessing Environmental
Uncertainty

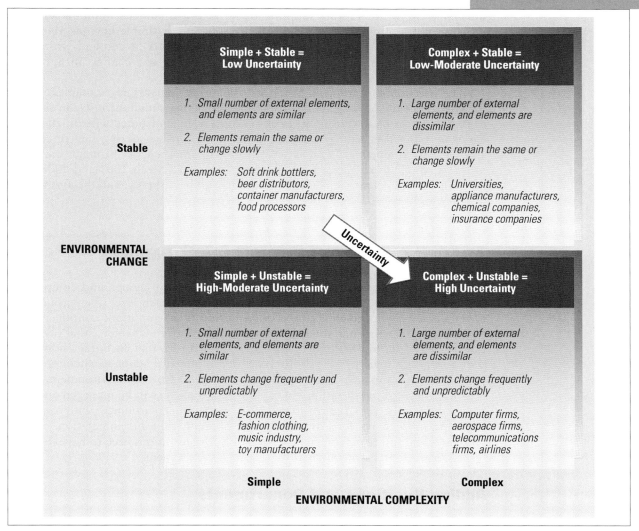

Source: *American Science Quarterly.* Characteristics of Organizational Environments and Perceived Environments Uncertainty by Robert Duncan vol. 17, pp. 313–327, September 1972. Reprinted by permission.

external elements, those elements are hard to predict, and they react unexpectedly to organizational initiatives. The greatest uncertainty for an organization occurs in the *complex, unstable* environment. A large number of elements impinge upon the organization, and they shift frequently or react strongly to organizational initiatives. When several sectors change simultaneously, the environment becomes turbulent.[25]

A soft drink distributor functions in a simple, stable environment. Demand changes only gradually. The distributor has an established delivery route, and supplies of soft drinks arrive on schedule. State universities, appliance manufacturers, and insurance companies are in somewhat stable, complex environments. A large number of external elements are present, but although they change, changes are gradual and predictable.

Toy manufacturers are in simple, unstable environments. Organizations that design, make, and sell toys, as well as those that are involved in the clothing or music industry, face shifting supply and demand. Most Internet companies focus on a specific competitive niche and, hence, operate in simple but unstable environments as well. Although there may be few elements to contend with—e.g., technology, competitors—they are difficult to predict and change abruptly and unexpectedly.

The telecommunications industry and the airline industry face complex, unstable environments. Many external sectors are changing simultaneously. In the case of airlines, in just a few years the major carriers were confronted with an air-traffic controller shortage, aging fleets of planes, labor unrest, soaring fuel prices, the entry of new competitors such as JetBlue and AirTran, a series of major air-traffic disasters, and a drastic decline in customer demand. Between 2001 and 2008, four large airlines and many smaller ones went through bankruptcy, and the airlines collectively laid off 170,000 employees.[26]

ADAPTING TO A CHANGING ENVIRONMENT

Once you see how environments differ with respect to change and complexity, the next question is, "How do organizations adapt to each level of environmental uncertainty?" Environmental uncertainty represents an important contingency for organization structure and internal behaviors. Recall from Chapter 2 that organizations facing uncertainty often use structural mechanisms that encourage horizontal communication and collaboration to help the company adapt to changes in the environment. In this section we discuss in more detail how the environment affects organizations. An organization in a certain environment will be managed and controlled differently from an organization in an uncertain environment with respect to positions and departments, organizational differentiation and integration, control processes, and future planning and forecasting. Organizations need to have the right fit between internal structure and the external environment.

Adding Positions and Departments

As complexity and uncertainty in the external environment increase, so does the number of positions and departments within the organization, leading to increased internal complexity. This relationship is part of being an open system. Each sector in the external environment requires an employee or department to deal with it. The human resource department deals with unemployed people who want to work for the company. The marketing department finds customers. Procurement employees obtain raw materials from hundreds of suppliers. The finance group deals with bankers. The legal department works with the courts and government agencies. E-business departments handle electronic commerce, and information technology departments deal with the increasing complexity of computerized information and knowledge management systems. Adding new positions and departments is a common way for organizations to adapt to growing environmental complexity and uncertainty. Consider this example of how Wal-Mart is trying to mitigate some of the uncertainty in its environment.

Any organization with the size and power of Wal-Mart presents a large target for criticism, and the retailer has come under blistering attack for everything from its low wages and minimal health benefits to its high-pressure tactics with suppliers and its environmental policies. Much of the criticism is organized by two union-backed organizations, Wake Up Wal-Mart and Wal-Mart Watch, which have spearheaded a relentless public relations campaign against the company, including rallies, blogs, letter-writing blitzes, press conferences, and town hall meetings.

Wal-Mart

Wal-Mart managers went on the offensive. The company's tiny public relations department was expanded to dozens of employees, including a "war room" where former political operatives look for ways to dispute the claims of opponents. Additionally, Wal-Mart created two high-level executive positions to act as generals in the PR war. The position of director of media relations, for instance, oversees crisis communications and manages the hundreds of phone calls a day the company receives from reporters. The director is on call 24/7 to assist with "emergency response" related to PR issues. The second new position, senior director of campaign management, includes researching the opposition, managing Wal-Mart's relations with bloggers, and overseeing the war room.

Wal-Mart is profitable and successful, but the intense criticism has had an impact. Surveys reveal that the negative publicity has caused some shoppers to stop buying there. Wal-Mart leaders hope the new executives and expanded PR department can help turn the tide.[27] ■

Building Relationships

The traditional approach to coping with environmental uncertainty was to establish buffer departments. The purpose of **buffering roles** is to absorb uncertainty from the environment.[28] The technical core performs the primary production activity of an organization. Buffer departments surround the technical core and exchange materials, resources, and money between the environment and the organization. They help the technical core function efficiently. The purchasing department buffers the technical core by stockpiling supplies and raw materials. The human resource department buffers the technical core by handling the uncertainty associated with finding, hiring, and training production employees.

A newer approach some organizations are trying is to drop the buffers and expose the technical core to the uncertain environment. These organizations no longer create buffers because they believe being well connected to customers and suppliers is more important than internal efficiency. For example, John Deere has assembly-line workers visiting local farms to determine and respond to customer concerns. LG Electronics pays consumers to test cell phone models, asking them to keep a journal where they jot down their feelings about features they like or don't like and draw pictures that represent their mood when they use the phone.[29] Opening up the organization to the environment by building closer relationships with external parties makes it more fluid and adaptable.

Boundary-spanning roles link and coordinate an organization with key elements in the external environment. Boundary spanning is primarily concerned with the exchange of information to (1) detect and bring into the organization information about changes in the environment and (2) send information into the environment that presents the organization in a favorable light.[30]

Briefcase

As an organization manager, keep these guidelines in mind:

Scan the external environment for threats, changes, and opportunities. Use boundary-spanning roles, such as market research and intelligence teams, to bring into the organization information about changes in the environment. Enhance boundary-spanning capabilities when the environment is uncertain.

Organizations have to keep in touch with what is going on in the environment so that managers can respond to market changes and other developments. A study of high-tech firms found that 97 percent of competitive failures resulted from lack of attention to market changes or the failure to act on vital information.[31] To detect and bring important information into the organization, boundary personnel scan the environment. For example, a market-research department scans and monitors trends in consumer tastes. Boundary spanners in engineering and research and development (R&D) departments scan new technological developments, innovations, and raw materials. Boundary spanners prevent the organization from stagnating by keeping top managers informed about environmental changes. Often, the greater the uncertainty in the environment, the greater the importance of boundary spanners.[32]

One recent approach to boundary spanning is **business intelligence**, which refers to the high-tech analysis of large amounts of internal and external data to spot patterns and relationships that might be significant. For example, Verizon uses business intelligence to actively monitor customer interactions so that it can catch problems and fix them almost immediately.[33] Tools to automate the process are a hot area of software, with companies spending billions on business-intelligence software in recent years.[34]

Business intelligence is related to another important area of boundary spanning, known as *competitive intelligence* (CI). Competitive intelligence gives top executives a systematic way to collect and analyze public information about rivals and use it to make better decisions.[35] Using techniques that range from Internet surfing to digging through trash cans, intelligence professionals dig up information on competitors' new products, manufacturing costs, or training methods and share it with top leaders. Intelligence teams are the newest wave of CI activities. An **intelligence team** is a cross-functional group of managers and employees, usually led by a competitive intelligence professional, who work together to gain a deep understanding of a specific business issue, with the aim of presenting insights, possibilities, and recommendations to top leaders.[36] Intelligence teams can provide insights that enable managers to make more informed decisions about goals, as well as devise contingency plans and scenarios related to major competitive issues.

Many successful companies involve everyone in boundary-spanning activities. People at the grassroots level are often able to see and interpret changes or problems sooner than managers, who are typically more removed from the day-to-day work.[37] At Cognos, which sells planning and budgeting programs to large corporations, any of the company's 3,000 employees can submit scoops about competitors through

ASSESS YOUR ANSWER

1 The best way for an organization to cope with a complex environment is to develop a complex structure (rather than keep it simple and uncomplicated).

ANSWER: *Agree.* As an organization's environment becomes more complex, the organization has to add jobs, departments, and boundary spanning roles to cope with all the elements in the environment. When environmental sectors are complex, there is no way for an organization to stay simple and uncomplicated and continue to be effective.

an internal Web site called Street Fighter. Each day, R&D and sales managers pore over the dozens of entries. Good tips are rewarded with prizes.[38]

The boundary task of sending information into the environment to represent the organization is used to influence other people's perception of the organization. In the marketing department, advertising and sales people represent the organization to customers. Purchasers may call on suppliers and describe purchasing needs. The legal department informs lobbyists and elected officials about the organization's needs or views on political matters. Many companies set up special Web pages and blogs to present the organization in a favorable light.

Differentiation and Integration

Another response to environmental uncertainty is the amount of differentiation and integration among departments. Organizational **differentiation** refers to "the differences in cognitive and emotional orientations among managers in different functional departments, and the difference in formal structure among these departments."[39] When the external environment is complex and rapidly changing, organizational departments become highly specialized to handle the uncertainty in their external sector. Success in each sector requires special expertise and behavior. Employees in an R&D department thus have unique attitudes, values, goals, and education that distinguish them from employees in manufacturing or sales departments.

A study by Paul Lawrence and Jay Lorsch examined three organizational departments—manufacturing, research, and sales—in ten corporations.[40] This study found that each department evolved toward a different orientation and structure to deal with specialized parts of the external environment. Exhibit 6.3 illustrates the

EXHIBIT 6.3
Organizational Departments Differentiate to Meet Needs of Subenvironments

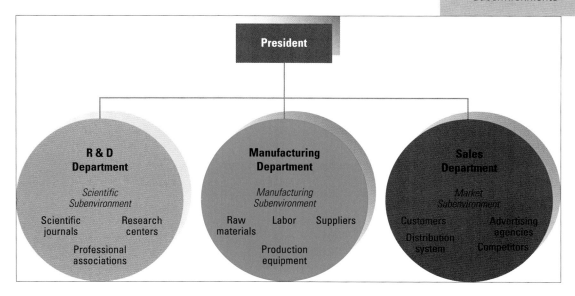

EXHIBIT 6.4
Differences in Goals
and Orientations
among Organizational
Departments

Characteristic	R&D Department	Manufacturing Department	Sales Department
Goals	New developments, quality	Efficient production	Customer satisfaction
Time horizon	Long	Short	Short
Interpersonal orientation	Mostly task	Task	Social
Formality of structure	Low	High	High

Source: Based on Paul R. Lawrence and Jay W. Lorsch, *Organization and Environment* (Homewood, Ill.: Irwin, 1969), 23–29.

market, scientific, and manufacturing subenvironments identified by Lawrence and Lorsch. As shown in the exhibit, each department interacted with different external groups. The differences that evolved among departments within the organizations are shown in Exhibit 6.4. To work effectively with the scientific subenvironment, R&D had a goal of quality work, a long time horizon (up to five years), an informal structure, and task-oriented employees. Sales was at the opposite extreme. It had a goal of customer satisfaction, was oriented toward the short term (two weeks or so), had a very formal structure, and was socially oriented.

One outcome of high differentiation is that coordination among departments becomes difficult. More time and resources must be devoted to achieving coordination when attitudes, goals, and work orientation differ so widely. **Integration** is the quality of collaboration among departments.[41] Formal integrators are often required to coordinate departments. When the environment is highly uncertain, frequent changes require more information processing to achieve horizontal coordination, so integrators become a necessary addition to the organization structure. Sometimes integrators are called liaison personnel, project managers, brand managers, or coordinators. As illustrated in Exhibit 6.5, organizations with highly uncertain environments and a highly differentiated structure assign about 22 percent of management personnel to integration activities, such as serving on committees, on task forces, or in liaison roles.[42] In organizations characterized by very simple, stable environments, almost no managers are assigned to integration roles. Exhibit 6.5 shows that, as environmental uncertainty increases, so does differentiation among departments; hence, the organization must assign a larger percentage of managers to coordinating roles.

EXHIBIT 6.5
Environmental
Uncertainty and
Organizational Integrators

Industry	Plastics	Foods	Container
Environmental uncertainty	High	Moderate	Low
Departmental differentiation	High	Moderate	Low
Percent management in integrating roles	22%	17%	0%

Source: Based on Jay W. Lorsch and Paul R. Lawrence, "Environmental Factors and Organizational Integration," *Organizational Planning: Cases and Concepts* (Homewood, Ill.: Irwin and Dorsey, 1972), 45.

Lawrence and Lorsch's research concluded that organizations perform better when the levels of differentiation and integration match the level of uncertainty in the environment. Organizations that performed well in uncertain environments had high levels of both differentiation and integration, while those performing well in less uncertain environments had lower levels of differentiation and integration.

Organic versus Mechanistic Management Processes

Another response to environmental uncertainty is the amount of formal structure and control imposed on employees. Tom Burns and G. M. Stalker observed twenty industrial firms in England and discovered that internal management structure was related to the external environment.[43] When the external environment was stable, the internal organization was characterized by standard rules, procedures, and a clear hierarchy of authority. Organizations were formalized. They were also centralized, with most decisions made at the top. Burns and Stalker called this a **mechanistic** organization system.

In rapidly changing environments, the internal organization was much looser, free-flowing, and adaptive. Rules and regulations often were not written down or, if written down, were ignored. People had to find their own way through the system to figure out what to do. The hierarchy of authority was not clear. Decision-making authority was decentralized. Burns and Stalker used the term **organic** to characterize this type of management structure.

Exhibit 6.6 summarizes the differences in organic and mechanistic systems. As environmental uncertainty increases, organizations tend to become more organic, which means decentralizing authority and responsibility to lower levels, encouraging employees to take care of problems by working directly with one another, encouraging teamwork, and taking an informal approach to assigning tasks and responsibility. Thus, the organization is more fluid and is able to adapt continually to changes in the external environment.[44] Complete the questionnaire in the "How Do You Fit the Design?" box for some insight into whether you are more suited to working in an organic organization or a mechanistic one.

EXHIBIT 6.6
Mechanistic and Organic Forms

Mechanistic	Organic
1. Tasks are broken down into specialized, separate parts.	1. Employees contribute to the common tasks of the department.
2. Tasks are rigidly defined.	2. Tasks are adjusted and redefined through employee teamwork.
3. There is a strict hierarchy of authority and control, and there are many rules.	3. There is less hierarchy of authority and control, and there are few rules.
4. Knowledge and control of tasks are centralized at the top of the organization.	4. Knowledge and control of tasks are located anywhere in the organization.
5. Communication is vertical.	5. Communication is horizontal.

Source: Adapted from Gerald Zaltman, Robert Duncan, and Jonny Holbek, *Innovations and Organizations* (New York: Wiley, 1973), 131.

The learning organization, described in Chapter 1, and the horizontal and virtual network structures, described in Chapter 2, are organic organizational forms that are used by companies to compete in rapidly changing environments. Guiltless Gourmet, which sells low-fat tortilla chips and other high-quality snack foods, provides an example. When large companies like Frito Lay entered the low-fat snack-food market, Guiltless Gourmet shifted to a flexible network structure to remain competitive. The company redesigned itself to become basically a full-time marketing organization, while production and other activities were outsourced. An 18,000-square-foot plant in Austin was closed and the workforce cut from 125 to about 10 core people who handle marketing and sales promotions. The flexible structure allowed Guiltless Gourmet to adapt quickly to changing market conditions.[45]

How Do You Fit the Design?

Mind and Environment

Does your mind best fit an organization in a certain or an uncertain environment? Think back to how you thought or behaved as a student, employee, or in a formal or informal leader position. Please answer whether each following item was Mostly True or Mostly False for you.

	Mostly True	Mostly False
1. I always offered comments on my interpretation of data or issues.	____	____
2. I welcomed unusual viewpoints of others even if we were working under pressure.	____	____
3. I made it a point to attend industry trade shows and company (school) events.	____	____
4. I explicitly encouraged others to express opposing ideas and arguments.	____	____
5. I asked "dumb" questions.	____	____
6. I enjoyed hearing about new ideas even when working toward a deadline.	____	____
7. I expressed a controversial opinion to bosses and peers.	____	____
8. I suggested ways of improving my and others' ways of doing things.	____	____

Scoring: Give yourself one point for each item you marked as Mostly True. If you scored less than 5, your mindfulness level may be suited to an organization in a stable rather than unstable environment. A score of 5 or above suggests a higher level of mindfulness and a better fit for an organization in an uncertain environment.

Interpretation: In an organization in a highly uncertain environment everything seems to be changing. In that case, an important quality for a professional employee or manager is "mindfulness," which includes the qualities of being open minded and an independent thinker. In a stable environment, an organization will be more "mechanistic," and a manager without mindfulness may perform okay because much work can be done in the traditional way. In an uncertain environment, everyone needs to facilitate new thinking, new ideas, and new ways of working. A high score on this exercise suggests higher mindfulness and a better fit with an "organic" organization in an uncertain environment.

Source: These questions are based on ideas from R. L. Daft and R. M. Lengel, *Fusion Leadership,* Chapter 6 (San Francisco, Calif.: Berrett Koehler, 2000); B. Bass and B. Avolio, *Multifactor Leadership Questionnaire,* 2nd ed. (Menlo Park, Calif.: Mind Garden, Inc); and Karl E. Weick and Kathleen M. Sutcliffe, *Managing the Unexpected: Assuring High Performance in an Age of Complexity* (San Francisco, Calif.: Jossey-Bass, 2001).

Planning, Forecasting, and Responsiveness

The whole point of increasing internal integration and shifting to more organic processes is to enhance the organization's ability to quickly respond to sudden changes in an uncertain environment. It might seem that in an environment where everything is changing all the time, planning is useless. However, in uncertain environments, planning and environmental forecasting actually become *more* important as a way to keep the organization geared for a coordinated, speedy response. When the environment is stable, the organization can concentrate on current operational problems and day-to-day efficiency. Long-range planning and forecasting are not needed because environmental demands in the future will be the same as they are today.

With increasing environmental uncertainty, planning and forecasting become necessary.[46] Indeed, surveys of multinational corporations have found that as environments become more turbulent, managers increase their planning activities, particularly in terms of planning exercises that encourage learning, continual adaptation, and innovation.[47] Following the September 11, 2001, terrorist attacks in the United States, for example, there was a surge in the use of scenario and contingency planning as a way to manage uncertainty.[48]

Planning can soften the adverse impact of external shifts. Organizations that have unstable environments often establish a separate planning department. In an unpredictable environment, planners scan environmental elements and analyze potential moves and countermoves by other organizations. Planning can be extensive and may forecast various scenarios for environmental contingencies. With scenario building, managers mentally rehearse different scenarios based on anticipating various changes that could affect the organization. Scenarios are like stories that offer alternative, vivid pictures of what the future will look like and how managers will respond. Royal Dutch/Shell Oil has long used scenario building and has been a leader in speedy response to massive changes that other organizations failed to perceive until it was too late.[49]

ASSESS YOUR ANSWER

2 **In a volatile, fast-changing environment, serious planning activities are a waste of time and resources.**

ANSWER: *Disagree.* General Colin Powell once said, "No battle plan survives contact with the enemy."[50] Yet no wise general would go into battle without one. Serious planning becomes more important in a turbulent environment, even though a plan will not last long. Planning and environmental forecasting help managers anticipate and be prepared to respond to changes. Lack of planning makes more sense in a stable, easily predictable environment.

Planning, however, cannot substitute for other actions, such as effective boundary spanning and adequate internal integration and coordination. The organizations that are most successful in uncertain environments are those that keep everyone in close touch with the environment so they can spot threats and opportunities, enabling the organization to respond immediately.

FRAMEWORK FOR RESPONSES TO ENVIRONMENTAL CHANGE

Exhibit 6.7 summarizes the ways in which environmental uncertainty influences organizational characteristics. The change and complexity dimensions are combined and illustrate four levels of uncertainty. The low uncertainty environment is simple and stable. Organizations in this environment can have few departments and a mechanistic structure. In a low–moderate uncertainty environment, more

EXHIBIT 6.7

Contingency Framework for Environmental Uncertainty and Organizational Responses

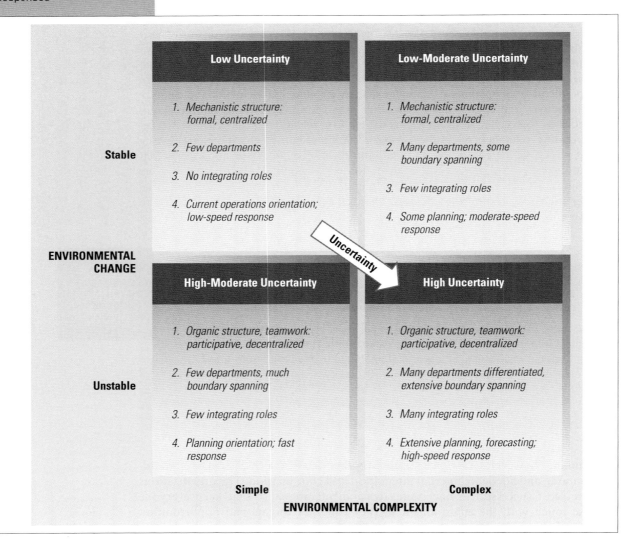

Low Uncertainty

1. Mechanistic structure: formal, centralized
2. Few departments
3. No integrating roles
4. Current operations orientation; low-speed response

Low-Moderate Uncertainty

1. Mechanistic structure: formal, centralized
2. Many departments, some boundary spanning
3. Few integrating roles
4. Some planning; moderate-speed response

High-Moderate Uncertainty

1. Organic structure, teamwork: participative, decentralized
2. Few departments, much boundary spanning
3. Few integrating roles
4. Planning orientation; fast response

High Uncertainty

1. Organic structure, teamwork: participative, decentralized
2. Many departments differentiated, extensive boundary spanning
3. Many integrating roles
4. Extensive planning, forecasting; high-speed response

Stable

Unstable

ENVIRONMENTAL CHANGE

Uncertainty

Simple   Complex

ENVIRONMENTAL COMPLEXITY

departments are needed, along with more integrating roles to coordinate the departments. Some planning may occur. Environments that are high–moderate uncertainty are unstable but simple. Organization structure is organic and decentralized. Planning is emphasized and managers are quick to make internal changes as needed. The high uncertainty environment is both complex and unstable and is the most difficult environment from a management perspective. Organizations are large and have many departments, but they are also organic. A large number of management personnel are assigned to coordination and integration, and the organization uses boundary spanning, planning, and forecasting to enable a high-speed response to environmental changes.

DEPENDENCE ON EXTERNAL RESOURCES

Thus far, this chapter has described several ways in which organizations adapt to the lack of information and to the uncertainty caused by environmental change and complexity. We turn now to the third characteristic of the organization–environment relationship that affects organizations, which is the need for material and financial resources. The environment is the source of scarce and valued resources essential to organizational survival. Research in this area is called the *resource-dependence perspective*. **Resource dependence** means that organizations depend on the environment but strive to acquire control over resources to minimize their dependence.[51] Organizations are vulnerable if vital resources are controlled by other organizations, so they try to be as independent as possible. Organizations do not want to become too vulnerable to other organizations because of negative effects on performance.

Although companies like to minimize their dependence, when costs and risks are high they also team up to share scarce resources and be more competitive on a global basis. Formal relationships with other organizations present a dilemma to managers. Organizations seek to reduce vulnerability with respect to resources by developing links with other organizations, but they also like to maximize their own autonomy and independence. Organizational linkages require coordination,[52] and they reduce the freedom of each organization to make decisions without concern for the needs and goals of other organizations. Interorganizational relationships thus represent a tradeoff between resources and autonomy. To maintain autonomy, organizations that already have abundant resources will tend not to establish new linkages. Organizations that need resources will give up independence to acquire those resources. For example, DHL, the express delivery unit of Germany's Deutsche Post AG, lost billions of dollars trying to take over the U.S. package delivery market. By 2008, the company's boast in an early advertising campaign that "Yellow is the new Brown" (a swipe at package delivery leader UPS and its chocolate-brown trucks) was put on the shelf. DHL joined Big Brown in a strategic partnership that will have UPS handling DHL parcels in the United States. The two companies will continue to compete in overseas markets. In the face of $3 billion in losses, difficulty building a local management team in the United States, and maintenance problems at U.S. package handling facilities, Deutsche Post's CEO Frank Appel called the partnership "a pragmatic and realistic strategy" for his company's U.S. operations.[53] Resource dependence will be discussed in more detail in the next chapter.

INFLUENCING EXTERNAL RESOURCES

In response to the need for resources, organizations try to maintain a balance between linkages with other organizations and their own independence. Organizations maintain this balance through attempts to modify, manipulate, or control other organizations.[54] To survive, the focal organization often tries to reach out and change or control elements in the environment. Two strategies can be adopted to influence resources in the external environment: (1) establish favorable relationships with key elements in the environment and (2) shape the environmental domain by influencing key sectors.[55] Techniques to accomplish each of these strategies are summarized in Exhibit 6.8. As a general rule, when organizations sense that valued resources are scarce, they will use the strategies in Exhibit 6.8 rather than go it alone. Notice how dissimilar these strategies are from the responses to environmental change and complexity described in Exhibit 6.7. The dissimilarity reflects the difference between responding to the need for resources and responding to the need for information.

Establishing Formal Relationships

Building formal relationships includes techniques such as acquiring ownership, establishing joint ventures and partnerships, developing connections with important people in the environment, recruiting key people, and using advertising and public relations.

Acquire an Ownership Stake. Companies use various forms of ownership to reduce uncertainty in an area important to the acquiring company. For example, a firm might buy a part of or a controlling interest in another company, giving it access to technology, products, or other resources it doesn't currently have.

A greater degree of ownership and control is obtained through acquisition or merger. An *acquisition* involves the purchase of one organization by another so that the buyer assumes control, such as when Ford bought Volvo, Hewlett-Packard bought EDS Corporation, and Wal-Mart purchased Britain's ASDA Group. A *merger* is the unification of two or more organizations into a single unit.[56] Sirius Satellite Radio and XM Satellite Radio Holdings merged to become Sirius XM Radio. The merger enabled the companies to combine resources and share risks to

EXHIBIT 6.8

Organizing Strategies for Controlling the External Environment

Establishing Formal Relationships	Influencing Key Sectors
1. Acquire an ownership stake	1. Change where you do business (your domain)
2. Form joint ventures and partnerships	2. Use political activity, regulation
3. Lock in key players	3. Join in trade associations
4. Recruit executives	4. Avoid illegitimate activities
5. Use advertising and public relations	

be more competitive against digital music providers and other emerging types of music distribution. In the past few years, there has been a huge wave of acquisition and merger activity in the telecommunications industry, reflecting how these companies cope with the tremendous uncertainty they face. Consider the emergence of the "new" AT&T.

IN PRACTICE

AT&T

AT&T was once all but dead, but the company has reemerged as a $165 billion giant in the global telecommunications field thanks to mergers and acquisitions. SBC Communications, which was born after the break-up of giant AT&T in 1984, went on an acquisitions spree after the Telecommunications Act of 1996 opened the door to competition, buying Pacific Telesis Group (1997), Southern New England Telecommunications (1998), and Ameritech Corporation (1999). In 2005, SBC acquired AT&T, taking the name of that iconic organization and gaining a foothold in wireless with Cingular Wireless, which was a joint venture between AT&T and BellSouth. A year later, the newly-named AT&T merged with BellSouth, giving AT&T full control of Cingular and creating a telecommunications giant not unlike the "old" AT&T of the 1980s.

However, unlike the old company, AT&T faces a pack of tough rivals, including the No. 2 telecom company, Verizon Communications, which has also been involved in many mergers and acquisitions over the past several years. Other competitors include cable companies such as Comcast and Time Warner Cable, which are bundling together television, broadband, and Internet phone service, stealing customers from AT&T all over the country. The cable providers have also formed a partnership with Sprint, enabling them to provide wireless service as well. For its part, AT&T now sells packages of wireless phone services, Internet access, and pay television, as does Verizon. The two companies have recently taken integration one step further by airing video programming—from Saturday Night Live clips to user-generated video—across all three platforms. That enables them to sell advertising as a new source of revenue as growth in wireless begins to slow. However, the risks are high, and both companies face significant uncertainty and many new rivals as they enter this new area of business.[57] ■

Form Joint Ventures and Partnerships. When there is a high level of complementarity between the business lines, geographical positions, or skills of two companies, the firms often go the route of a strategic alliance rather than ownership through merger or acquisition.[58] Such alliances are formed through contracts and joint ventures.

Contracts and joint ventures reduce uncertainty through a legal and binding relationship with another firm. Contracts come in the form of *license agreements* that involve the purchase of the right to use an asset (such as a new technology) for a specific time and *supplier arrangements* that contract for the sale of one firm's output to another. Contracts can provide long-term security by tying customers and suppliers to specific amounts and prices. For example, the Italian fashion house Versace forged a deal to license its primary asset—its name—for a line of designer eyeglasses. McDonald's contracts for an entire crop of russet potatoes to be certain of its supply of french fries. McDonald's also gains influence over suppliers through these contracts and has changed the way farmers grow potatoes and the profit margins they earn, which is consistent with the resource dependence perspective.[59]

Joint ventures result in the creation of a new organization that is formally independent of the parents, although the parents will have some control.[60] Madrid-based tech startup FON has formed a joint venture with British phone carrier BT that will install FON wi-fi technology in the modems of nearly 2 million BT customers. Office Depot and Reliance Retail Limited, a division of India's largest private-sector employer, entered into a joint venture to provide office products and services to business customers in India. Food and agricultural corporation Cargill Inc. has numerous joint ventures around the world and recently set up a venture with Spanish cooperative Hojiblance to source, trade, and supply customers worldwide with private label and bulk olive oils. As evidenced by these short examples, many joint ventures are undertaken to share risks when companies are doing business in other countries or on a global scale.

Lock in Key Players. Cooptation occurs when leaders from important sectors in the environment are made part of an organization. It takes place, for example, when influential customers or suppliers are appointed to the board of directors, such as when the senior executive of a bank sits on the board of a manufacturing company. As a board member, the banker may become psychologically coopted into the interests of the manufacturing firm. An **interlocking directorate** is a formal linkage that occurs when a member of the board of directors of one company sits on the board of directors of another company. The individual is a communications link between companies and can influence policies and decisions. When one individual is the link between two companies, this is typically referred to as a **direct interlock**. An **indirect interlock** occurs when a director of company A and a director of company B are both directors of company C. They have access to one another but do not have direct influence over their respective companies.[61] Research shows that, as a firm's financial fortunes decline, direct interlocks with financial institutions increase. Financial uncertainty facing an industry also has been associated with greater indirect interlocks between competing companies.[62]

Important business or community leaders also can be appointed to other organizational committees or task forces. By serving on committees or advisory panels, these influential people learn about the needs of the company and are more likely to include the company's interests in their decision making. Today, many companies face uncertainty from environmental pressure groups, so organizations are trying to bring in leaders from this sector, such as when DuPont appointed environmentalists to its biotechnology advisory panel.[63]

Recruit Executives. Transferring or exchanging executives also offers a method of establishing favorable linkages with external organizations. For example, the aerospace industry often hires retired generals and executives from the Department of Defense. These generals have personal friends in the department, so the aerospace companies obtain better information about technical specifications, prices, and dates for new weapons systems. They can learn the needs of the defense department and are able to present their case for defense contracts in a more effective way. Companies without personal contacts find it nearly impossible to get a defense contract. Having channels of influence and communication between organizations serves to reduce financial uncertainty and dependence for an organization.

Get Your Side of the Story Out. A traditional way of establishing favorable relationships is through advertising. Organizations spend large amounts of money to

Briefcase

As an organization manager, keep this guideline in mind:

Reach out and control external sectors that threaten needed resources. Influence the domain by engaging in political activity, joining trade associations, and establishing favorable relationships. Establish relationships through ownership, joint ventures and strategic partnerships, cooptation, interlocking directorates, and executive recruitment. Reduce the amount of change or threat from the external environment so the organization will not have to change internally.

influence the tastes and opinions of consumers. Advertising is especially important in highly competitive industries and in industries that experience variable demand. For example, since the U.S. Food and Drug Administration loosened regulations to permit advertising of prescription drugs in the United States, the major pharmaceutical companies have spent nearly $5 billion annually on advertisements such as a cute cartoon bee pushing Nasonex spray for allergies or heart attack survivors promoting the benefits of cholesterol-fighting Lipitor.[64]

Public relations is similar to advertising, except that stories often are free and aimed at public opinion. Public relations people cast an organization in a favorable light in speeches, on websites, in press reports, and on television. Public relations attempts to shape the company's image in the minds of customers, suppliers, and government officials. Blogging is an important part of public relations activities for many companies today. Randy Baseler, vice president for marketing at Boeing Commercial Airplanes, started a public blog to share the company's view on products and marketing strategies. The open forum exposes Boeing to some stinging criticism, but it also enables the company to tell its side of the story and build better relationships with customers and the public.[65]

Influencing Key Sectors

In addition to establishing favorable linkages, organizations often try to change the environment. There are four techniques for influencing or changing a firm's environment.

Change Where You Do Business. Early in this chapter, we talked about the organization's *domain* and the ten sectors of the task environment. An organization's domain is not fixed. Managers make decisions about which business to be in, the markets to enter, and the suppliers, banks, employees, and location to use, and this domain can be changed if necessary to keep the organization competitive.[66] An organization can seek new environmental relationships and drop old ones. Managers may try to find a domain where there is little competition, no government regulation, abundant suppliers, affluent customers, and barriers to keep competitors out.

Acquisition and divestment are two techniques for altering the domain. For example, Google has acquired a number of companies to expand its domain beyond Internet search, including the $1.65 billion acquisition of YouTube.[67] Divestment occurred when JC Penney sold off its chain of Eckerd drug stores to focus resources on the department store. Time Inc. is altering its domain as more readers and advertisers switch from print to online media. The company is selling off eighteen of its smaller niche magazines, including *Field & Stream* and *Parenting*, as well as cutting hundreds of employees at its other magazines—even such top sellers such as *People* and *Sports Illustrated*. Time managers made a decision to streamline publications in order to bolster the company's presence online.[68]

Get Political. Political activity includes techniques to influence government legislation and regulation. Political strategy can be used to erect regulatory barriers against new competitors or to squash unfavorable legislation. Corporations also try to influence the appointment to agencies of people who are sympathetic to their needs.

As e-commerce continues to evolve, Internet companies such as Yahoo, Amazon, and Google have opened lobbying offices in Washington, D.C., to represent their interests. One example of their political activities is when telecom companies threatened to start charging Internet providers for speedy delivery of the Internet content the phone companies carry on their lines. The Internet firms lobbied Congress to insert language into telecom laws that would prohibit them from doing so.[69] Another Internet company that has become a sophisticated and influential lobbyist is eBay.

IN PRACTICE

eBay

"It is a fast-moving train, and if you get in front of it you'll get flattened," said an official with the state of Louisiana's licensing agency. She was talking about eBay's lobbying machine, which has become so powerful that it can practically make damaging or restrictive regulations disappear.

At any given time, there are approximately 90 million items for sale on eBay, and the company gets a fee for each successful transaction. Managers know that regulations on sellers would slow sales traffic, so lobbying against such regulation is a top priority for the company. In Louisiana, eBay lobbyists worked overtime to promote passage of a bill that would exempt some Internet transactions, such as those on eBay, from the state's licensing requirements for businesses conducting auctions. When Ohio passed a law that would have regulated eBay sellers in that state, the company worked to get it reversed. Auctioning laws in both Maine and Tennessee were also changed to exempt Internet sellers after lobbying efforts from eBay. Managers know that if a law takes hold in one state, other states might follow suit.

In addition to lobbying against unfavorable legislation, eBay also pushes for legislative changes that will benefit the company. For example, eBay's lobbying efforts in Illinois, New York, and Florida influenced those states to revise laws to allow Internet auction sites to compete with licensed ticket brokers and sell tickets for more than their face value, providing another stream of revenue for eBay.[70] ■

Until recently, eBay worked primarily through a corps of local lobbyists in states all across the country. Now, though, like other major Internet firms, eBay has opened its own lobbying office in Washington, D.C. Former CEO Meg Whitman was always heavily involved in lobbying efforts. Many CEOs believe they should participate directly in lobbying. CEOs have easier access than lobbyists and can be especially effective when they do the politicking. Political activity is so important that "informal lobbyist" is an unwritten part of almost any CEO's job description.[71]

ASSESS YOUR ANSWER

3 **Managers of business organizations should not get involved in political activities.**

ANSWER: *Disagree.* Smart business managers get involved in lobbying and other political activities to try to make sure the consequences of new laws and regulations are mostly positive for their own firms. Companies pay huge fees to associations and lobbyists to make sure government actions work out in their favor.

Unite with Others. Much of the work to influence the external environment is accomplished jointly with other organizations that have similar interests. For example, most large pharmaceutical companies belong to Pharmaceutical Research and Manufacturers of America. Manufacturing companies are part of the National Association of Manufacturers, and retailers join the Retail Industry Leaders Association. Many software companies are members of the Initiative for Software Choice (ISC). By pooling resources, these organizations can pay people to carry out activities such as lobbying legislators, influencing new regulations, developing public relations campaigns, and making campaign contributions. The National Tooling and Machining Association (NTMA) conducts lobbying on behalf of its members on issues that affect small business, such as taxes, health insurance, or government mandates. NTMA also gives its members statistics and information that help them become more competitive in the global marketplace.[72]

Don't Fall into Illegitimate Activities. Illegitimate activities represent the final technique companies sometimes use to control their environmental domain, but this technique typically backfires. Conditions such as low profits, pressure from senior managers, or scarce environmental resources may lead managers to adopt behaviors not considered legitimate.[73] One study found that companies in industries with low demand, shortages, and strikes were more likely to be convicted for illegal activities, suggesting that illegal acts are an attempt to cope with resource scarcity. Some nonprofit organizations have been found to use illegitimate or illegal actions to bolster their visibility and reputation as they compete with other organizations for scarce grants and donations, for example.[74]

Types of illegitimate activities include payoffs to foreign governments, illegal political contributions, promotional gifts, and wiretapping. Bribery is one of the most frequent types of illegitimate activity, particularly in companies operating globally. Energy companies face tremendous uncertainty, for example, and need foreign governments to approve giant investments and authorize risky projects. Under pressure to win contracts in Nigeria, Albert "Jack" Stanley, a former executive at KBR (then a division of Halliburton Company), admits he orchestrated a total of about $182 million in bribes to get Nigerian officials to approve the construction of a liquefied natural gas plant in that country. Stanley faces up to seven years in prison and a hefty fine after pleading guilty.[75] In Germany, executives at both Siemens and Volkswagen have been charged with bribing labor representatives on their companies' supervisory boards. German law requires that firms give as many as half of their supervisory board seats to labor representatives. Executives need the board's support to carry out their plans and strategies for the company, and some resort to bribery to get the cooperation they need.[76]

Organization–Environment Integrative Framework

The relationships illustrated in Exhibit 6.9 summarize the two major themes about organization–environment relationships discussed in this chapter. One theme is that the amount of complexity and change in an organization's domain influences the need for information and hence the uncertainty felt within an organization. Greater information uncertainty is resolved through greater structural flexibility and the assignment of additional departments and boundary roles. When uncertainty is low, management structures can be more mechanistic, and the number of departments and boundary roles can be fewer. The second theme pertains to the scarcity of material and financial resources. The more dependent an organization is on other organizations for those resources, the more important it is to either establish favorable linkages with those organizations or control entry into the domain. If

EXHIBIT 6.9
Relationship between
Environmental
Characteristics and
Organizational Actions

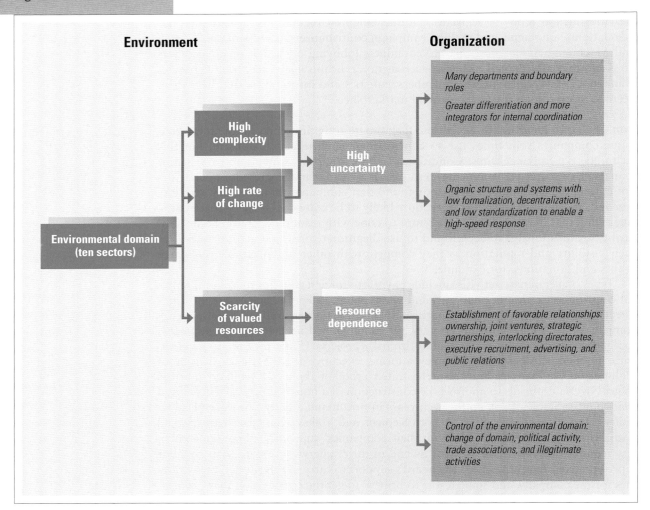

dependence on external resources is low, the organization can maintain autonomy and does not need to establish linkages or control the external domain.

DESIGN ESSENTIALS

■ Change and complexity in the external environment have major implications for organization design and management action. Organizations are open social systems. Most are involved with hundreds of external elements. Important environmental sectors with which organizations deal are the industry, raw materials, human resources, financial resources, market, technology, economic conditions, government, sociocultural, and international.

■ Organizational environments differ in terms of uncertainty and resource dependence. Organizational uncertainty is the result of the stable–unstable and simple–complex dimensions of the environment. Resource dependence is the result of scarcity of the material and financial resources needed by the organization.

■ Organization design takes on a logical perspective when the environment is considered. Organizations try to survive and achieve efficiencies in a world characterized by uncertainty and scarcity. Specific departments and functions are created to deal with uncertainties. The organization can be conceptualized as a technical core and departments that buffer environmental uncertainty. Boundary-spanning roles bring information about the environment into the organization and send information about the organization to the external environment.

■ The concepts in this chapter provide specific frameworks for understanding how the environment influences the structure and functioning of an organization. Environmental complexity and change, for example, have specific impact on internal complexity and adaptability. Under great uncertainty, more resources are allocated to departments that will plan, deal with specific environmental elements, and integrate diverse internal activities. Moreover, organizations in rapidly changing environments typically reflect a loose, organic structure and management processes.

■ When risk is great or resources are scarce, the organization can establish linkages through acquisitions, strategic alliances, interlocking directorates, executive recruitment, or advertising and public relations that will minimize risk and maintain a supply of scarce resources. Other techniques for influencing the environment include a change of the domain in which the organization operates, political activity, participation in trade associations, and perhaps illegitimate activities.

■ Two important themes in this chapter are that organizations can learn and adapt to the environment and that organizations can change and control the environment. These strategies are especially true for large organizations that command many resources. Such organizations can adapt when necessary but can also neutralize or change problematic areas in the environment.

Key Concepts

boundary-spanning roles
buffering roles
business intelligence
cooptation
differentiation
direct interlock
domain

general environment
indirect interlock
integration
intelligence team
interlocking directorate
mechanistic
organic

organizational environment
resource dependence
sectors
simple–complex dimension
stable–unstable dimension
task environment
uncertainty

Discussion Questions

1. Describe differentiation and integration. In what type of environmental uncertainty will differentiation and integration be greatest? Least?
2. Is changing the organization's domain a feasible strategy for coping with a threatening environment? Explain. Can you think of an organization in the recent news that has changed its domain?
3. Discuss the importance of the international sector for today's organizations, compared to domestic sectors. What are some ways in which the international sector affects organizations in your city or community?
4. Assume you have been asked to calculate the ratio of staff employees to production employees in two organizations—one in a simple, stable environment and one in a complex, shifting environment. How would you expect these ratios to differ? Why?
5. Name some factors causing environmental complexity for an organization of your choice. How might this environmental complexity lead to organizational complexity? Explain.

6. Why do organizations become involved in interorganizational relationships? Do these relationships affect an organization's dependency? Performance?
7. What are some forces that influence environmental uncertainty? Which typically has the greatest impact on uncertainty—environmental complexity or environmental change? Why?
8. What is an organic organization? A mechanistic organization? How does the environment influence organic and mechanistic structures?
9. Define organizational environment. Would the task environment of a new Internet-based company be the same as that of a large government agency? Discuss.
10. How do you think planning in today's organizations compares to planning twenty-five years ago? Do you think planning becomes more important or less important in a world where everything is changing fast and crises are a regular part of organizational life? Why?

Chapter 6 Workbook: Organizations You Rely On*

Below, list eight organizations you somehow rely on in your daily life. Examples might be a restaurant, a clothing or CD store, a university, your family, the post office, the telephone company, an airline, a pizzeria that delivers, your place of work, and so on. In the first column, list those eight organizations. Then, in column 2, choose another organization you could use in case the ones in column 1 were not available. In column 3, evaluate your level of dependence on the organizations listed in column 1 as Strong, Medium, or Weak. Finally, in column 4, rate the certainty of that organization being able to meet your needs as High (certainty), Medium, or Low.

Organization	Backup Organization	Level of Dependence	Level of Certainty
1.			
2.			
2.			

4.			
5.			
6.			
7.			
8.			

Questions

1. Do you have adequate backup organizations for those of high dependence? How might you create even more backups?

2. What would you do if an organization you rated high for dependence and high for certainty suddenly became high-dependence and low-certainty? How would your behavior relate to the concept of resource dependence?

3. Have you ever used any behaviors similar to those in Exhibit 6.8 to manage your relationships with the organizations listed in column 1?

*Adapted by Dorothy Marcic from "Organizational Dependencies," in Ricky W. Griffin and Thomas C. Head, *Practicing Management*, 2nd ed. (Dallas: Houghton Mifflin), 2–3.

Case for Analysis: The Paradoxical Twins: Acme and Omega Electronics*

Part I

In 1986, Technological Products of Erie, Pennsylvania, was bought out by a Cleveland manufacturer. The Cleveland firm had no interest in the electronics division of Technological Products and subsequently sold to different investors two plants that manufactured computer chips and printed circuit boards. Integrated circuits, or chips, were the first step into microminiaturization in the electronics industry, and both plants had developed some expertise in the technology, along with their superior capabilities in manufacturing printed circuit boards. One of the plants, located in nearby Waterford, was renamed Acme Electronics; the other plant, within the city limits of Erie, was renamed Omega Electronics, Inc.

Acme retained its original management and upgraded its general manager to president. Omega hired a new president who had been a director of a large electronic research laboratory and upgraded several of the existing personnel within the plant. Acme and Omega often competed for the same contracts. As subcontractors, both firms benefited from the electronics boom and both looked forward to future growth and expansion. The world was going digital, and both companies began producing digital microprocessors along with the production of circuit boards.

Acme had annual sales of $100 million and employed 550 people. Omega had annual sales of $80 million and employed 480 people. Acme regularly achieved greater net profits, much to the chagrin of Omega's management.

Inside Acme

The president of Acme, John Tyler, was confident that, had the demand not been so great, Acme's competitor would not have survived. "In fact," he said, "we have been able to beat Omega regularly for the most profitable contracts, thereby increasing our profit." Tyler credited his firm's greater effectiveness to his managers' abilities to run a "tight ship." He explained that he had retained the basic structure developed by Technological Products because it was most efficient for high-volume manufacturing. Acme had detailed organization charts and job descriptions. Tyler believed everyone should have clear responsibilities and narrowly defined jobs, which would lead to efficient performance and high company profits. People were generally satisfied with their work at Acme; however, some of the managers voiced the desire to have a little more latitude in their jobs.

Inside Omega

Omega's president, Jim Rawls, did not believe in organization charts. He felt his organization had departments similar to Acme's, but he thought Omega's plant was small enough that things such as organization charts just put artificial barriers between specialists who should be working together. Written memos were not allowed since, as Rawls expressed it, "the plant is small enough that if people want to communicate, they can just drop by and talk things over."

The head of the mechanical engineering department said, "Jim spends too much of his time and mine making sure everyone understands what we're doing and listening to suggestions." Rawls was concerned with employee satisfaction and wanted everyone to feel part of the organization. The top management team reflected Rawls's attitudes. They also believed that employees should be familiar with activities throughout the organization so that cooperation between departments would be increased. A newer member of the industrial engineering department said, "When I first got here, I wasn't sure what I was supposed to do. One day I worked with some mechanical engineers and the next day I helped the shipping department design some packing cartons. The first months on the job were hectic, but at least I got a real feel for what makes Omega tick."

Part II

In the 1990s, mixed analog and digital devices began threatening the demand for the complex circuit boards manufactured by Acme and Omega. This "system-on-a-chip" technology combined analog functions, such as sound, graphics, and power management, together with digital circuitry, such as logic and memory, making it highly useful

for new products such as cellular phones and wireless computers. Both Acme and Omega realized the threat to their futures and began aggressively to seek new customers.

In July 1992, a major photocopier manufacturer was looking for a subcontractor to assemble the digital memory units of its new experimental copier. The projected contract for the job was estimated to be $7 million to $9 million in annual sales.

Both Acme and Omega were geographically close to this manufacturer, and both submitted highly competitive bids for the production of 100 prototypes. Acme's bid was slightly lower than Omega's; however, both firms were asked to produce 100 units. The photocopier manufacturer told both firms that speed was critical because its president had boasted to other manufacturers that the firm would have a finished copier available by Christmas. This boast, much to the designer's dismay, required pressure on all subcontractors to begin prototype production before the final design of the copier was complete. This meant Acme and Omega would have at most two weeks to produce the prototypes or would delay the final copier production.

Part III
Inside Acme

As soon as John Tyler was given the blueprints (Monday, July 13, 1992), he sent a memo to the purchasing department asking to move forward on the purchase of all necessary materials. At the same time, he sent the blueprints to the drafting department and asked that it prepare manufacturing prints. The industrial engineering department was told to begin methods design work for use by the production department supervisors. Tyler also sent a memo to all department heads and executives indicating the critical time constraints of this job and how he expected that all employees would perform as efficiently as they had in the past.

The departments had little contact with one another for several days, and each seemed to work at its own speed. Each department also encountered problems. Purchasing could not acquire all the parts on time. Industrial engineering had difficulty arranging an efficient assembly sequence. Mechanical engineering did not take the deadline seriously and parceled its work to vendors so the engineers could work on other jobs scheduled previously. Tyler made it a point to stay in touch with the photocopier manufacturer to let it know things were progressing and to learn of any new developments. He traditionally worked to keep important clients happy. Tyler telephoned someone at the photocopier company at least twice a week and got to know the head designer quite well.

On July 17, Tyler learned that mechanical engineering was far behind in its development work, and he "hit the roof." To make matters worse, purchasing had not obtained all the parts, so the industrial engineers decided to assemble the product without one part, which would be inserted at the last minute. On Thursday, July 23, the final units were being assembled, although the process was delayed several times. On Friday, July 24, the last units were finished while Tyler paced around the plant. Late that afternoon, Tyler received a phone call from the head designer of the photocopier manufacturer, who told Tyler that he had received a call on Wednesday from Jim Rawls of Omega. He explained that Rawls's workers had found an error in the design of the connector cable and taken corrective action on their prototypes. He told Tyler that he had checked out the design error and that Omega was right. Tyler, a bit overwhelmed by this information, told the designer that he had all the memory units ready for shipment and that, as soon as they received the missing component on Monday or Tuesday, they would be able to deliver the final units. The designer explained that the design error would be rectified in a new blueprint he was sending over by messenger and that he would hold Acme to the Tuesday delivery date.

When the blueprint arrived, Tyler called in the production supervisor to assess the damage. The alterations in the design would call for total disassembly and the unsoldering of several connections. Tyler told the supervisor to put extra people on the alterations first thing Monday morning and to try to finish the job by Tuesday. Late Tuesday afternoon, the alterations were finished and the missing components were delivered. Wednesday morning, the production supervisor discovered that the units would have to be torn apart again to install the missing component. When John Tyler was told this, he again "hit the roof." He called industrial engineering and asked if it could help out. The production supervisor and the methods engineer couldn't agree on how to install the component. John Tyler settled the argument by ordering that all units be taken apart again and the missing component installed. He told shipping to prepare cartons for delivery on Friday afternoon.

On Friday, July 31, fifty prototypes were shipped from Acme without final inspection. John Tyler was concerned about his firm's reputation, so he waived the final inspection after he personally tested one unit and found it operational. On Tuesday, August 4, Acme shipped the last fifty units.

Inside Omega

On Friday, July 10, Jim Rawls called a meeting that included department heads to tell them about the potential contract they were to receive. He told them that as soon as he received the blueprints, work could begin. On Monday, July 13, the prints arrived and again the department heads met to discuss the project. At the end of the meeting, drafting had agreed to prepare manufacturing prints, while industrial engineering and production would begin methods design.

Two problems arose within Omega that were similar to those at Acme. Certain ordered parts could not be delivered on time, and the assembly sequence was difficult to engineer. The departments proposed ideas to help one another, however, and department heads and key employees had daily meetings to discuss progress. The head of electrical engineering knew of a Japanese source for the components that could not be purchased from normal suppliers. Most problems were solved by Saturday, July 18.

On Monday, July 20, a methods engineer and the production supervisor formulated the assembly plans, and production was set to begin on Tuesday morning. On Monday afternoon, people from mechanical engineering, electrical engineering, production, and industrial engineering got together to produce a prototype just to ensure that there would be no snags in production. While they were building the unit, they discovered an error in the connector cable design. All the engineers agreed, after checking and rechecking the blueprints, that the cable was erroneously designed. People from mechanical engineering and electrical engineering spent Monday night redesigning the cable, and on Tuesday morning, the drafting department finalized the changes in the manufacturing prints. On Tuesday morning, Rawls was a bit apprehensive about the design changes and decided to get formal approval. Rawls received word on Wednesday from the head designer at the photocopier firm that they could proceed with the design changes as discussed on the phone. On Friday, July 24, the final units were inspected by quality control and were then shipped.

Part IV

Ten of Acme's final memory units were defective, whereas all of Omega's units passed the photocopier firm's tests. The photocopier firm was disappointed with Acme's delivery delay and incurred further delays in repairing the defective Acme units. However, rather than give the entire contract to one firm, the final contract was split between Acme and Omega with two directives added: (1) maintain zero defects and (2) reduce final cost. In 1993, through extensive cost-cutting efforts, Acme reduced its unit cost by 20 percent and was ultimately awarded the total contract.

*Adapted from John F. Veiga, "The Paradoxical Twins: Acme and Omega Electronics," in John F. Veiga and John N. Yanouzas, *The Dynamics of Organizational Theory* (St. Paul: West, 1984), 132–138.

Joanna Reed was walking home through fallen tree blossoms in Guatemala City. Today, however, her mind was more on her work than the natural beauty surrounding her. She unlocked the gate to her colonial home and sat down on the porch, surrounded by riotous toddlers, pets, and plants, to ponder the recommendations she would make to Sam Wilson. The key decisions she needed to make about his Donor Services Department concerned who should run the department and how the work should be structured.

Joanna had worked for a sponsorship agency engaged in international development work with poor people for six years. She and her husband moved from country to country setting up new agencies. In each country, they had to design how the work should be done, given the local labor market and work conditions.

After a year in Guatemala, Joanna, happily pregnant with her third child, had finished setting up the Donor Services Department for the agency and was working only part-time on a research project. A friend who ran a "competing" development agency approached her to do a consulting project for him. Sam Wilson, an American, was the national representative of a U.S.-based agency that had offices all over the world. Sam wanted Joanna to analyze his Donor Services Department, because he'd received complaints from headquarters about its efficiency. Since he'd been told that his office needed to double in size in the coming year, he wanted to get all the bugs worked out beforehand. Joanna agreed to spend a month gathering information and compiling a report on this department.

Sponsorship agencies, with multimillion-dollar budgets, are funded by individuals and groups in developed countries who contribute to development programs in less-developed countries (LDCs). Donors contribute approximately $20.00 per month plus optional special gifts. The agencies use this money to fund education, health, community development, and income-producing projects for poor people affiliated with their agency in various communities. In the eyes of most donors, the specific benefit provided by sponsorship agencies is the personal relationship between a donor and a child and his or her family in the LDC. The donors and children write back and forth, and the agency sends photos of the child and family to the donors. Some donors never write the family they sponsor; others write weekly and visit the family on their vacations. The efficiency of a Donor Services Department and the quality of their translations are key ingredients to keeping donors and attracting new ones.

Good departments also never lose sight of the fact that sponsorship agencies serve a dual constituency—the local people they are trying to help develop and the sponsors who make that help possible through their donations.

What Is a Donor Services Department in a Sponsorship Agency Anyway?

The work of a Donor Services Department consists of more than translating letters, preparing annual progress reports on the families, and answering donor questions directed to the agency. It also handles the extensive, seemingly endless paperwork associated with enrolling new families and assigning them to donors, reassignments when either the donor or the family stops participating, and the special gifts of money sent (and thank you notes for them). Having accurate enrollment figures is crucial because the money the agency receives from headquarters is based upon these figures and affects planning.

The Department Head

Joanna tackled the challenge of analyzing the department by speaking first with the department head (see the organizational chart in Exhibit 1). José Barriga, a charismatic, dynamic man in his forties, was head of both Donor Services and Community Services. In reality, he spent virtually no time in the Donor Services Department and was not bilingual. "My biggest pleasure is working with the community leaders and coming up with programs that will be successful. I much prefer being in the field, driving from village to village talking with people, to supervising paperwork. I'm not sure exactly what goes on in Donor Services, but Elena, the supervisor, is very responsible. I make it a point to walk through the department once a week and say hello to everyone, and I check their daily production figures."

The Cast of Characters in the Department

Like José, Sam was also more interested in working with the communities on projects than in immersing himself in the details of the more administrative departments. In part, Sam had contracted Joanna because he rightfully worried that Donor Services did not receive the attention it deserved from José, who was very articulate and personable but seldom had time to look at anything beyond case histories. José never involved himself in the internal affairs of the department. Even though he was not considered much of a resource to

*Joyce S. Osland, San Jose State University.

them, he was well liked and respected by the staff of Donor Services, and they never complained about him.

The Supervisor

This was not the case with the supervisor José had promoted from within. Elena had the title of departmental supervisor, but she exercised very little authority. A slight, single woman in her thirties, Elena had worked for the organization since its establishment ten years earlier. She was organized, meticulous, dependable, and hard working. But she was a quiet, non-assertive, nervous woman who was anything but proactive. When asked what changes she would make if she were the head of the department, she sidestepped the question by responding, "It is difficult to have an opinion on this subject. I think that the boss can see the necessary changes with greater clarity."

Elena did not enjoy her role as supervisor, which was partly due to the opposition she encountered from a small clique of long-time translators. In the opinion of this subgroup, Elena had three strikes against her. One, unlike her subordinates, she was not bilingual. "How can she be the supervisor when she doesn't even know English well? One of us would make a better supervisor." Bilingual secretaries in status-conscious Guatemala see themselves as a cut above ordinary secretaries. This group looked down on Elena as being less skilled and educated than they were, even though she was an excellent employee. Second, Elena belonged to a different religion than the organization itself and almost all the other employees. This made no difference to Sam and José but seemed important to the clique who could be heard making occasional derogatory comments about Elena's religion.

The third strike against Elena was her lack of authority. No one had ever clarified how much authority she really possessed, and she herself made no effort to assume control of the department. "My instructions are to inform

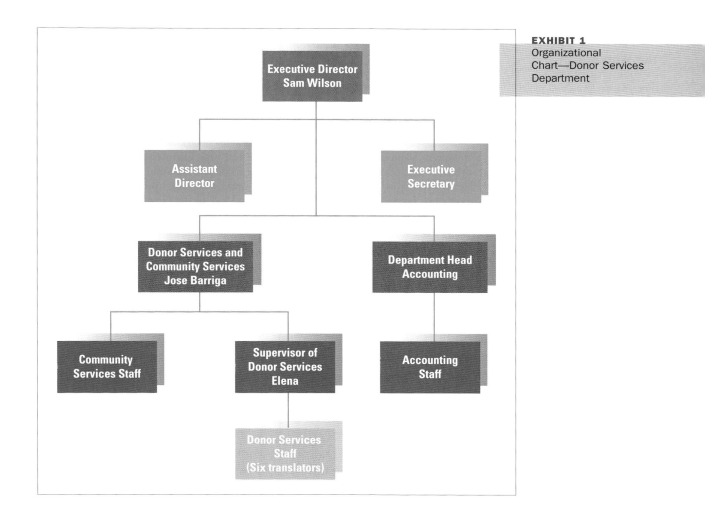

EXHIBIT 1
Organizational Chart—Donor Services Department

Don José Barriga of infractions in my daily production memo. I'm not supposed to confront people directly when infractions occur, although it might be easier to correct things if I did." ("Don" is a Latin American honorific used before the first name to denote respect.)

This subgroup showed their disdain and lack of respect for Elena by treating her with varying degrees of rudeness and ignoring her requests. They saw her as a watchdog, an attitude furthered by José who sometimes announced, "We (senior management) are not going to be here tomorrow, so be good because Elena will be watching you." When Sam and José left the office, the clique often stopped working to socialize. They'd watch Elena smolder out of the corner of their eyes, knowing she would not reprimand them. "I liked my job better before I became supervisor," said Elena. "Ever since, some of the girls have resented me, and I'm not comfortable trying to keep them in line. Why don't they just do their work without needing me to be the policeman? The only thing that keeps me from quitting is the loyalty I feel for the agency and Don José."

The Workers

In addition to the clique already mentioned, there were three other female translators in the department. All the translators but one had the same profile: in their twenties, of working-class backgrounds, and graduates of bilingual secretary schools, possessing average English skills. (As stated earlier, in Latin America, being a bilingual secretary is a fairly prestigious occupation for a woman.) The exception in this group was the best translator, Magdalena, a college-educated recent hire in her late thirties who came from an upper-class family. She worked, not because she needed the money, but because she believed in the mission of the agency. "This job lets me live out my religious beliefs and help people who have less advantages than I do." Magdalena was more professional and mature than the other translators. Although all the employees were proud of the agency and its religious mission, the clique members spent too much time socializing and skirmishing with other employees within and without the department.

The three translators who were not working at full capacity were very close friends. The leader of this group, Juana, was a spunky, bright woman with good oral English skills and a hearty sense of humor. A long-time friend of Barriga's, Juana translated for English-speaking visitors who came to visit the program sites throughout the country. The other translators, tied to their desks, saw this as a huge perk. Juana was the ringleader in the occasional mutinies against Elena and in feuds with people from other departments. Elena was reluctant to complain about Juana to Barriga, given their friendship. Perhaps she feared Juana would make her life even more miserable.

Juana's two buddies (*compañeras*) in the department also had many years with the agency. They'd gotten into the habit of helping each other on the infrequent occasions when they had excessive amounts of work. When they were idle or simply wanted to relieve the boredom of their jobs, they socialized and gossiped. Juana in particular was noted for lethal sarcasm and pointed jokes about people she didn't like. This clique was not very welcoming to the newer members of the department. Magdalena simply smiled at them but kept her distance, and the two younger translators kept a low profile to avoid incurring their disfavor. As one of them remarked, "It doesn't pay to get on Juana's bad side."

Like many small offices in Latin America, the agency was located in a spacious former private home. The Donor Services Department was housed in the 40 × 30-foot living room area. The women's desks were set up in two rows, with Elena's desk in the back corner. Since the offices of both Wilson and Barriga were in former back bedrooms, everyone who visited them walked through the department, greeting and stopping to chat with the long-time employees (Elena, Juana, and her two friends). Elena's numerous visitors also spent a good deal of time working their way through the department to reach her desk, further contributing to the amount of socializing going on in the department.

Elena was the only department member who had "official" visitors since she was the liaison person who dealt with program representatives and kept track of enrollments. The translators each were assigned one work process. For example, Marisol prepared case histories on new children and their families for prospective donors while Juana processed gifts. One of the newer translators prepared files for newly enrolled children and did all the filing for the entire department (a daunting task). Most of the jobs were primarily clerical and required little or no English. The letter translations were outsourced to external translators on a piece-work basis and supervised by Magdalena. Hers was the only job that involved extensive translation; for the most part, however, she translated simple messages (such as greeting cards) that were far below her level of language proficiency. The trickier translations, such as queries from donors in other countries, were still handled by Wilson's executive secretary.

Several translators complained that, "We don't have enough opportunity to use our English skills on the job. Not only are we not getting any better in English, we are probably losing fluency because most of our jobs are just clerical work. We do the same simple, boring tasks over and over, day in and day out. Why did they hire bilingual secretaries for these jobs anyway?"

Another obvious problem was the uneven distribution of work in the office. The desks of Magdalena and the new translators were literally overflowing with several months' backlog of work while Juana and her two friends had time to kill. Nobody, including Elena, made any efforts to even out the work assignments or help out those who were buried. The subject had never been broached.

The agency was growing at a rapid pace, and there were piles of paperwork sitting around waiting to be processed. Joanna spent three weeks having each department member explain her job (in mind-numbing detail), drawing up flow charts of how each type of paperwork was handled, and poking around in their files. She found many unnecessary steps that resulted in slow turnaround times for various processes. There were daily output reports submitted to Barriga, but no statistics kept on the length of time it took to respond to requests for information or process paperwork. No data were shared with the translators, so they had no idea how the department was faring and little sense of urgency about their work. The only goal was to meet the monthly quota of case histories, which only affected Marisol. Trying to keep up with what came across their desks summed up the entire focus of the employees.

Joanna found many instances of errors and poor quality, not so much from carelessness as lack of training and supervision. Both Barriga and Wilson revised the case histories, but Joanna was amazed to discover that no one ever looked at any other work done by the department. Joanna found that the employees were very accommodating when asked to explain their jobs and very conscientious about their work (if not the hours devoted to it). She also found, however, the employees were seldom able to explain why things were done in a certain way, because they had received little training for their jobs and only understood their small part of the department. Morale was obviously low, and all the employees seemed frustrated with the situation in the department. With the exception of Magdalena who had experience in other offices, they had few ideas for Joanna about how the department could be improved.

3.0

A Project to Remember

In June 1991, **Ian Jones** a production manager with **Empire Plastics Northern** (EPN) was pondering the latest project to increase the production rate of oleic acid. This was the third project in 6 years targeting the oleic acid plant for improvement and arose from the policy followed by the group's directors. This was to identify profitable plants and invest in improving their productivity and profitability, thus avoiding the need for investment in new facilities.

The installation of the "wet end" went well and no problems were experienced. However, the "dry end" was a different story. It wasn't working a year after practical completion, except in short bursts. They were still making changes to it. Jones had known all along that the technology on the dry end was relatively new and might prove troublesome, but the procurement department at **Empire Consultants** in their wisdom recommended its use. Granted, they did send a couple of guys over to Italy to see some similar plants first.

Jones constructed an organizational chart and set about examining the key issues raised by this project (Exhibit 1).

Jones had been appointed as commissioning manager at the commencement of the project. He remembered some of the nightmares experienced by colleagues during two earlier oleic acid projects and firmly resolved to make this one different; it was going to be "his" to manage on completion, and he was going to make his presence felt from the outset.

The execution of the project had been overseen by the group's engineering arm, **Empire Consultants** (EC), headed up by **Henry Holdsworth** as site project manager and **John Marshall** as construction engineer. It was a good team. The project was ambitious, but there were several signs of progress in the beginning. What did perplex him, though, was Marshall's apparent lack of enthusiasm.

Holdsworth described the project as a double management contract, and in this respect it was an unusual project. Empire Consultants traditionally assumed the role of management contactor and directly organized the trade contractors and discipline consultants. Times were changing, though, and both Holdsworth and Marshall had commented on the increasing frequency with which projects were now being tendered as complete packages to outside management contractors. This was their first project that involved two management contractors simultaneously, and neither Marshall nor Holdsworth was happy. Their own involvement had not been clearly defined. **Western Construction** had a £3.1 million contract for the "wet end" and **Teknibuild** a £6.0 million contract for the "dry end." These two contractors provided all the design and management effort during the project. EC's role was effectively reduced to acting as construction policemen; checking that design and construction were being carried out in accordance with the original process diagram and that EPN's demanding process control and safety requirements were being maintained.

Selecting the management contractors turned out to be extremely protracted and Holdsworth, encouraged by Jones, went ahead and ordered reactors for the wet end and a fluidized bed dryer for the dry end. Over 50% of the total material requirements were in order before either contractor had been formally appointed. Jones was confident that by doing this they could cut the project duration by several months. Nobody had asked Marshall for his opinion.

Conflict Ahead

The first line breaks were in October 1988. Site operations were supervised by Marshall and the two contractor site managers: **Bob Weald** from Western and **Vic Mason** from Teknibuild.

As a construction engineer, Marshall was familiar with the antics of clients and client representatives, especially regarding their tendency to try to make changes. He commented:

Clients always try and change things! When they see the job in the flesh as it were they go "Oh, we need some extra paving round here, or extra railings there!" But if they didn't ask for that at the start, they won't get it. If they want an extra 100 metres of paving they have to pay for it. In this project we had about £500k set aside for contingency purposes, that is unforeseen eventualities over and above the price fixed with the management contractors. If

*This case was prepared by Dr. Paul D. Gardiner, Department of Business Organisation, Heriot-Watt University, Edinburgh. It is intended to be used as the basis for class discussion rather than to illustrate either effective or ineffective handling of a management situation.

The case was made possible by the cooperation of an organization which wishes to remain anonymous.

that is not used up by the end of the contract, as in this case, then we can give the clients some extras.

Jones recalled that by June 1989 relationships were not going at all well at the dry end. EC had procured a fluidized bed dryer, a cooler, and more than 300 associated parts, and, as the purchasers of this equipment, they were the ones responsible for chasing up design drawings from the supplier, **Sultan Engineering.**

Unfortunately, Teknibuild, who, as management contractors, were supposed to design and build the plant, had problems getting the necessary information from Sultan to design the steelwork and foundations. As Marshall had noted earlier:

They [Teknibuild] *were constantly at our doors and throats looking for more information to get on. They didn't seem to have enough data to design properly, which led to conflict very early on. We got off to a bad start and that feeling carried on right to the end of the job. I think in every discipline we had problems with Teknibuild. Our discipline engineer against their discipline engineer.*

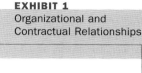

4.0

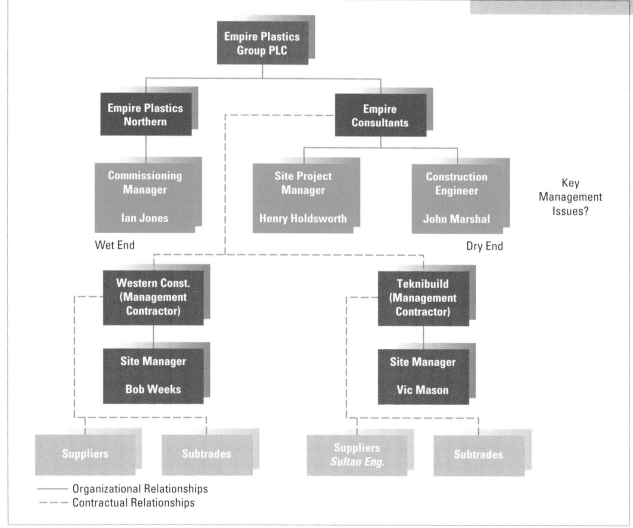

EXHIBIT 1
Organizational and
Contractual Relationships

4.0

The only exception to this was with the electrical and instrumentation (E & I) work. Marshall had put that down to the E & I subcontractor coming in at the end of the log jam of information, giving them more time to get it right.

While this was going on, Jones got more and more frustrated. In his opinion a lot of time was wasted between Teknibuild and EC for no good reason. He was sure that Teknibuild had more than enough design information to do their job.

When confronted by Jones, Marshall remarked that the truth probably lay somewhere in between, but added that he was *"particularly dismayed at Teknibuild's unwillingness to spend man-hours on the design until they had 100% definition from Sultan Engineering,"* almost to the point where they knew where every nut and bolt was. It was a real mess . . . and Marshall was accepting none of the blame.

On the other hand, things went fine with Western Construction. Their approach was much more relaxed; they had a design office on site with low, whereas Teknibuild worked from the head office in a large design office with high.

On one occasion Marshall asked for Teknibuild's planner to come down and take some site measurements. The reply he received was not very constructive: *"I don't know if I can do that, it's at least a couple of hours to get down there."* Holdsworth agreed that Teknibuild were constantly watching their man-hours:

You felt all the time that they were looking for profit rather than trying to get the job done. Even Teknibuild's construction man, Vic Mason, had internal conflict with his own designers. But with Western it was the other way round, you really felt they were seeking to set a good impression.

Jones thought that perhaps communication with Western had been good because their design and construction people operated side by side, communication was just across the corridor; whereas Teknibuild's site men had difficulty getting answers out of their Head Office. Marshall had always maintained that the best-run jobs are the ones in which you get a good design-construction liaison, particularly by having the designers on site with you.

Failing . . . Forward

Jones considered that in the future it might be a good idea to insist that management contractors set up a local design team on site. Current practice was to leave it up to the contractor, but these days EC had few designers of their own to help.

The trouble with management contractors, he surmised, is that you create an extra link in the communications chain—a large link that can easily break down, and, in his experience, did break down.

Relationships had been better at the wet end, he felt, because Marshall and Weald had worked together before. Marshall knew Weald, knew how he worked and where he was coming from. They could trust each other.

At the Teknibuild end, Vic Mason, their site manager, caused no end of conflict. He was a bit belligerent; thought he knew best, had done it all before, and couldn't be told anything. It never really got out of hand . . . just a bit heated at times. At the end of the day, Marshall maintained that Mason's intentions were ultimately to get the job built. But Jones remained unimpressed, even if Mason's main trouble was his own designers and suppliers.

Driving home, Jones wondered what the effect of the company's new policy on managing projects would be on people like Harry Holdsworth and John Marshall. He couldn't help remembering what Marshall had said about Teknibuild and Western independently setting up their own enquiries and going out for bids separately; there did seem to be a lot of repetition—maybe Marshall was right in viewing the new system as *"a very inefficient way of doing projects."*

Part 4

Managing Organizational Processes

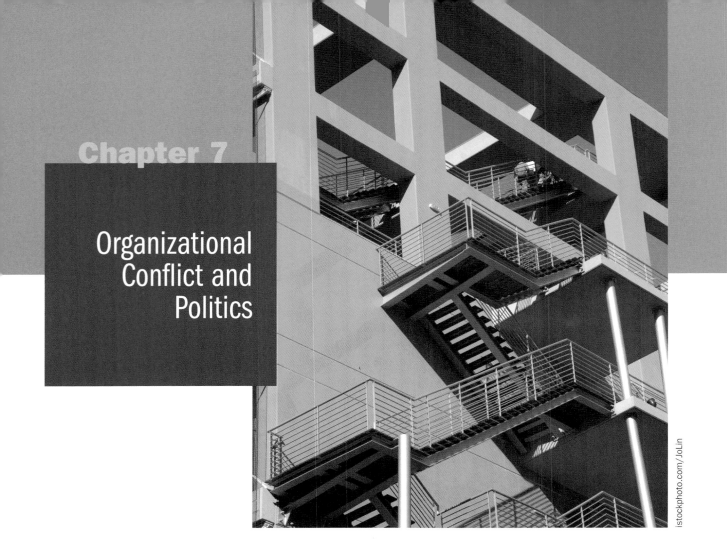

istockphoto.com/JoLin

Chapter 7

Organizational Conflict and Politics

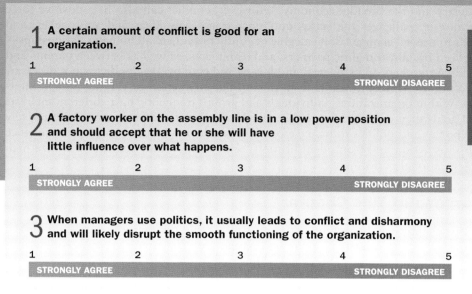

The Los Angeles Times has long been one of the most respected names in journalism. The winner of several Pulitzer Prizes, the *Times* is one of only a handful of newspapers with a claim to national standing. So why can't the newspaper keep an editor? In less than four years, three seasoned editors came and went from the top editorial position. Moreover, the paper has seen the departures of several other high-level editors after short tenures, many of which came as a result of conflict and dissension. All newspapers are facing seriously tough circumstances, but *The Los Angeles Times* has been hit particularly hard, battered by years of flagging circulation even before the housing slump and declining economy cut deeply into ad revenues. Thus, the never-ending battle between the business side (reduce costs, lure advertisers) and the news side (quality news) of the organization became an all-out war at the *Times*. (For more about this age-old conflict at news organizations, read this chapter's Case for Analysis, "The Daily Tribune," on page 291.) Although the internal dissension at the *Times* is complex, most former editors say business-minded executives are cutting out the heart of the storied newspaper by making devastating newsroom cuts, meddling in the affairs of the newsroom by suggesting articles or assessing what is reported, and involving marketing more and more in the business of reporting the news.[1]

All organizations, like *The Los Angeles Times,* are a complex mix of individuals and groups pursuing various goals and interests. Conflict is a natural outcome of the close interaction of people who may have diverse opinions and values, pursue different objectives, and have differential access to information and resources within the organization. Individuals and groups use power and political activity to handle their differences and manage the inevitable conflicts that arise.[2]

Too much conflict can be harmful to an organization, as it has been at *The Los Angeles Times*. The newspaper's parent company, Tribune Company, which owns the *Chicago Tribune* and acquired the Los Angeles paper in 2000, filed for bankruptcy protection in late 2008. The conflicts and tensions that have plagued *The Los Angeles Times* certainly can't be blamed directly for the Tribune Company's woes, but the inability of leaders to effectively manage conflict made it even more difficult for the organization to weather the "perfect storm" of forces roiling the media industry and the broader economy.[3] However, conflict can also be a positive force because it challenges the status quo, encourages new ideas and approaches, and leads to needed change.[4] Some degree of conflict occurs in all human relationships—between friends, romantic partners, and teammates, as well as between parents and children, teachers and students, and bosses and employees. Conflict is not necessarily a negative force; it results from the normal interaction of varying human interests. Within organizations, individuals and groups frequently have different interests and goals they wish to achieve through the organization. Managers can effectively use power and politics to manage conflict, get the most out of employees, enhance job satisfaction and team identification, achieve important goals, and realize high organizational performance.

Purpose of This Chapter

In this chapter we discuss the nature of conflict and the use of power and political tactics to manage and reduce conflict among individuals and groups. The notions of conflict, power, and politics have appeared in previous chapters. In Chapter 2, we talked about horizontal linkages such as task forces and teams that encourage collaboration among functional departments. Chapter 4 touched on conflict and power relationships among organizations. Chapter 6 introduced the concept of differentiation, which means that different departments pursue different goals and may have different attitudes and values. In Chapter 8, coalition building is proposed as one way to resolve disagreements among managers and departments, and Chapter 9 discusses the emergence of subcultures.

The first sections of this chapter explore the nature of intergroup conflict, characteristics of organizations that contribute to conflict, and the use of a political versus a rational model of organization to manage conflicting interests. Subsequent sections examine individual and organizational power, the vertical and horizontal sources of power for managers and other employees, and how power is used to attain organizational goals. We also look at the trend toward empowerment, sharing power with lower-level employees. The latter part of the chapter turns to politics, which is the application of power and influence to achieve desired outcomes. We discuss ways managers increase their power, political tactics for using power, and some ways managers can enhance collaboration among people and departments.

INTERGROUP CONFLICT IN ORGANIZATIONS

Intergroup conflict requires three ingredients: group identification, observable group differences, and frustration. First, employees have to perceive themselves as part of an identifiable group or department.[5] Second, there has to be an observable group difference of some form. Groups may be located on different floors of the building, members may have different social or educational backgrounds, or members may work in different departments. The ability to identify oneself as a part of one group and to observe differences in comparison with other groups is necessary for conflict.[6]

The third ingredient is frustration. Frustration means that if one group achieves its goal, the other will not; it will be blocked. Frustration need not be severe and only needs to be anticipated to set off intergroup conflict. Intergroup conflict will appear when one group tries to advance its position in relation to other groups. **Intergroup conflict** can be defined as the behavior that occurs among organizational groups when participants identify with one group and perceive that other groups may block their group's goal achievement or expectations.[7] Conflict means that groups clash directly, that they are in fundamental opposition. Conflict is similar to competition but more severe. **Competition** is rivalry among groups in the pursuit of a common prize, whereas conflict presumes direct interference with goal achievement.

Intergroup conflict within organizations can occur horizontally across departments or vertically between different levels of the organization.[8] The production department of a manufacturing company may have a dispute with quality control because new quality procedures reduce production efficiency. Teammates may argue about the best way to accomplish tasks and achieve goals. Employees may clash with bosses about new work methods, reward systems, or job assignments. Another typical area of conflict is between groups such as unions and management or franchise owners and headquarters. For example, the United Auto Workers (UAW) has routinely clashed with U.S. automakers over demands from management that union workers accept decreased wages and benefits to alleviate increasing cost pressures. Franchise owners for McDonald's, Taco Bell, Burger King, and KFC have clashed with headquarters because of the increase of company-owned stores in neighborhoods that compete directly with franchisees.[9]

Conflict can also occur between different divisions or business units within an organization, such as between the auditing and consulting units of big firms such as PricewaterhouseCoopers and Deloitte Touche.[10] As we briefly discussed in Chapter 4, with so many companies involved in interorganizational collaboration, conflicts and shifting power relationships are inevitable. Similar problems occur between distinct organizations. In global organizations, conflicts between regional managers and business division managers, among different divisions, or between divisions and headquarters are common because of the complexities of international business, as described in Chapter 5.

Sources of Conflict

Some specific organizational characteristics can generate conflict. These **sources of intergroup conflict** are goal incompatibility, differentiation, task interdependence, and limited resources. These characteristics of organizational relationships are determined by the contextual factors of environment, size, technology, strategy and goals, and organizational structure, which have been discussed in previous chapters. These characteristics, in turn, help shape the extent to which a rational model of behavior versus a political model of behavior is used to accomplish objectives.

1 A certain amount of conflict is good for an organization.

ANSWER: *Agree.* Conflict is inevitable in all human relationships, including those in organizations, and is often a good thing. Some conflict can be healthy because it contributes to diverse thinking and leads to change. If there is no conflict whatsoever, there is likely no growth and development either.

ASSESS YOUR ANSWER

Goal Incompatibility. The goals of each department reflect the specific objectives members are trying to achieve. The achievement of one department's goals often interferes with another department's goals, leading to conflict. University police, for example, have a goal of providing a safe and secure campus. They can achieve their goal by locking all buildings on evenings and weekends and not distributing keys. Without easy access to buildings, however, progress toward the science department's research goals will proceed slowly. On the other hand, if scientists come and go at all hours and security is ignored, police goals for security will not be met. Goal incompatibility throws the departments into conflict with each other.

The potential for conflict is perhaps greater between marketing and manufacturing than between other departments because the goals of these two departments are frequently at odds. Exhibit 7.1 shows examples of goal conflict between typical marketing and manufacturing departments. Marketing strives to increase the breadth of the product line to meet customer tastes for variety. A broad product line means short production runs, so manufacturing has to bear higher costs.[11] Typical areas of goal conflict are quality, cost control, and new products or services. For example, at Rockford Health Systems, the human resources (HR) department wanted to implement a new self-service benefits system that would let employees manage their benefits from their home computers, but the high price of the software licenses conflicted with the finance department's goal of controlling costs.[12] Another example is the goal conflict between business managers and editorial managers at

EXHIBIT 7.1
Marketing-Manufacturing Areas of Potential Goal Conflict

Goal Conflict	MARKETING versus Operative Goal Is Customer Satisfaction	MANUFACTURING Operative Goal Is Production Efficiency
Conflict Area	Typical Comment	Typical Comment
1. Breadth of product line	"Our customers demand variety."	"The product line is too broad—all we get are short, uneconomical runs."
2. New product introduction	"New products are our lifeblood."	"Unnecessary design changes are prohibitively expensive."
3. Product scheduling	"We need faster response. Our customer lead times are too long."	"We need realistic commitments that don't change like wind direction."
4. Physical distribution	"Why don't we ever have the right merchandise in inventory?"	"We can't afford to keep huge inventories."
5. Quality	"Why can't we have reasonable quality at lower cost?"	"Why must we always offer options that are too expensive and offer little customer utility?"

Source: Based on Benson S. Shapiro, "Can Marketing and Manufacturing Coexist?" *Harvard Business Review* 55 (September–October 1977), 104–114; and Victoria L. Crittenden, Lorraine R. Gardiner, and Antonie Stam, "Reducing Conflict between Marketing and Manufacturing," *Industrial Marketing Management* 22 (1993), 299–309.

The Los Angeles Times, described earlier. Goal incompatibility is probably the greatest cause of intergroup conflict in organizations.[13] Goal conflict also occurs within churches and religious groups.

IN PRACTICE

The Purpose-Driven Church

Church schisms are almost as numerous as churches—and they are frequently linked to differences in goals. Recent years have seen splits in some church congregations related to the "purpose-driven" movement espoused by Reverend Rick Warren, pastor of Saddleback Church in Lake Forest, California, and author of *The Purpose Driven Life.* Warren advocates that churches be *purpose driven* and attract nonbelievers by using modern growth techniques, such as marketing research, lively services incorporating rock music, volunteer programs, and more focus on everyday personal problems rather than fighting sin.

At the Valley View Christian Church in Dallas, some leaders who had a goal of increasing membership, particularly in the 20-to-30-year-old age group, believed adopting modern techniques based on Warren's principles was the way to grow. Other leaders, however, preferred a goal of strengthening the church's traditions and continuing an emphasis on atonement and redemption rather than solving marital problems or dealing with personal angst. Eventually, Valley View split, with the traditionalists setting up a new congregation.

The purpose-driven movement is only one aspect of an ongoing conflict within Christian churches over whether they should adapt and modernize their religion or strengthen and honor tradition. Similar conflicts have roiled the Episcopal Church, where some groups have left over issues such as the ordination of women and gays, revisions to the Book of Common Prayer, or changes in liturgical practices. In late 2008, conservatives announced the founding of a rival denomination, to be called the Anglican Church in North America, reflecting a major conflict within Anglican Christianity that will affect the church for years to come.[14] ∎

Differentiation. *Differentiation* was defined in Chapter 6 as "the differences in cognitive and emotional orientations among managers in different functional departments." Functional specialization requires people with specific education, skills, attitudes, and time horizons. For example, people may join a sales department because they have ability and aptitude consistent with sales work. After becoming members of the sales department, they are influenced by departmental norms and values.

Departments or divisions within an organization often differ in values, attitudes, and standards of behavior, and these subcultural differences lead to conflicts.[15] Consider an encounter between a sales manager and a research and development (R&D) scientist about a new product:

The sales manager may be outgoing and concerned with maintaining a warm, friendly relationship with the scientist. He may be put off because the scientist seems withdrawn and disinclined to talk about anything other than the problems in which he is interested. He may also be annoyed that the scientist seems to have such freedom in choosing what he will work on. Furthermore, the scientist is probably often late for appointments, which, from the salesman's point of view, is no way to run a business. Our scientist, for his part, may feel uncomfortable because the salesman seems to be pressing for immediate answers to technical questions that will take a long time to investigate. All the discomforts are concrete manifestations of the relatively wide differences between these two men in respect to their working and thinking styles.[16]

Task Interdependence. Task interdependence refers to the dependence of one unit on another for materials, resources, or information. As described in Chapter 13, *pooled interdependence* means there is little interaction; *sequential interdependence* means the output of one department goes to the next department; and *reciprocal interdependence* means that departments mutually exchange materials and information.[17]

Generally, as interdependence increases, the potential for conflict increases.[18] In the case of pooled interdependence, units have little need to interact. Conflict is at a minimum. Sequential and reciprocal interdependence require employees to spend time coordinating and sharing information. Employees must communicate frequently, and differences in goals or attitudes will surface. Conflict is especially likely to occur when agreement is not reached about the coordination of services to each other. Greater interdependence means departments often exert pressure for a fast response because departmental work has to wait on other departments.[19]

Limited Resources. Another major source of conflict involves competition between groups for what members perceive as limited resources.[20] Organizations have limited money, physical facilities, staff resources, and human resources to share among departments. In their desire to achieve goals, groups want to increase their resources. This throws them into conflict. Managers may develop strategies, such as inflating budget requirements or working behind the scenes, to obtain a desired level of resources.

Resources also symbolize power and influence within an organization. The ability to obtain resources enhances prestige. Departments typically believe they have a legitimate claim on additional resources. However, exercising that claim results in conflict. For example, in almost every organization, conflict occurs during the annual budget exercise, often creating political activity.

Rational versus Political Model

The sources of intergroup conflict are listed in Exhibit 7.2. The degree of goal incompatibility, differentiation, interdependence, and competition for limited resources determines whether a rational or political model of behavior is used within the organization to accomplish goals.

When goals are in alignment, there is little differentiation, departments are characterized by pooled interdependence, and resources seem abundant, managers can use a **rational model** of organization, as outlined in Exhibit 7.2. As with the rational approach to decision making we will describe in Chapter 8, the rational model of organization is an ideal that is not fully achievable in the real world, though managers strive to use rational processes whenever possible. In the rational organization, behavior is not random or accidental. Goals are clear and choices are made in a logical way. When a decision is needed, the goal is defined, alternatives are identified, and the choice with the highest probability of success is selected. The rational model is also characterized by centralized power and control, extensive information systems, and an efficiency orientation.[21]

EXHIBIT 7.2
Sources of Conflict and
Use of Rational versus
Political Model

Sources of Potential Intergroup Conflict	When Conflict Is Low, Rational Model Describes Organization		When Conflict Is High, Political Model Describes Organization
• Goal incompatibility • Differentiation • Task interdependence • Limited resources	Consistent across participants	Goals	Inconsistent, pluralistic within the organization
	Centralized	Power and control	Decentralized, shifting coalitions and interest groups
	Orderly, logical, rational	Decision process	Disorderly, result of bargaining and interplay among interests
	Norm of efficiency	Rules and norms	Free play of market forces; conflict is legitimate and expected
	Extensive, systematic, accurate	Information	Ambiguous; information used and withheld strategically

The opposite view of organizational processes is the **political model**, also described in Exhibit 7.2. When differences are great, organization groups have separate interests, goals, and values. Disagreement and conflict are normal, so power and influence are needed to reach decisions. Groups will engage in the push and pull of debate to decide goals and reach decisions. Information is ambiguous and incomplete. The political model describes the way organizations operate much of the time. Although managers strive to use a rational approach, the political model prevails because each department has different interests it wants met and different goals it wants to achieve. Purely rational procedures do not work for many circumstances.

Typically, both rational and political processes are used in organizations. Neither the rational model nor the political model characterizes things fully, but each will be used some of the time. For example, at Amazon.com, founder and CEO Jeff Bezos says he emphasizes a rational approach to planning and decision making whenever possible. "The great thing about fact-based decisions," he says, "is that they overrule the hierarchy. The most junior person in the company can win an argument with the most senior person with a fact-based decision." For decisions and situations that are complex, ill-defined, and controversial, however, Bezos uses a political model, discussing the issues with people and building agreement among senior executives.[22]

Managers may strive to adopt rational procedures but will find that politics is needed to accomplish objectives. The political model means managers learn to acquire, develop, and use power to achieve important outcomes.

Briefcase

As an organization manager, keep these guidelines in mind:

Use the rational model of organization when alternatives are clear, when goals are defined, and when managers can estimate the outcomes accurately. In these circumstances, coalition building, cooptation, or other political tactics are not needed and will not lead to effective decisions.

POWER AND ORGANIZATIONS

Power is an intangible force in organizations. It cannot be seen, but its effect can be felt. *Power* is often defined as the potential ability of one person (or department) to influence other people (or departments) to carry out orders[23] or to do something they would not otherwise have done.[24] Other definitions stress that power is the ability to achieve goals or outcomes that power holders desire.[25] The achievement of desired outcomes is the basis of the definition used here: **Power** is the ability of one person or department in an organization to influence other people to bring about desired outcomes. It is the potential to influence others within the organization with the goal of attaining desired outcomes for power holders. Powerful managers, for instance, are often able to get bigger budgets for their departments, more favorable production schedules, and more control over the organization's agenda.[26]

Power exists only in a relationship between two or more people, and it can be exercised in either vertical or horizontal directions. The source of power often derives from an exchange relationship in which one position, department, or organization provides scarce or valued resources to other people, departments, or organizations. When one is dependent on another, a power relationship emerges in which the side with the resources has greater power.[27] Power holders can achieve compliance with their requests.

As an illustration, consider how power is shifting in the Hollywood comedy industry. At one time, United Talent Agency (UTA) had control of most of the big names in comedy, including Jim Carrey, Owen Wilson, Ben Stiller, Will Ferrell, and Jack Black. That gave UTA tremendous power in the industry, enabling the agency to virtually dictate the terms it wanted for any star's project. With growing cost pressures, however, studios began to crack down on the prices they were willing to pay, the percentage of revenues they were willing to share, and the extent to which they were willing to meet demands for script changes or other conditions. At the same time, conflicts within UTA led to the departure of several important stars. Power shifted toward the studios, because no single agency had control over a large stable of comedians.[28]

Individual versus Organizational Power

In popular literature, power is often described as a personal characteristic, and a frequent topic is how one person can influence or dominate another person.[29] You probably recall from an earlier management or organizational behavior course that managers have five sources of personal power.[30] *Legitimate power* is the authority granted by the organization to the formal management position a manager holds. *Reward power* stems from the ability to bestow rewards—a promotion, raise, or pat on the back—to other people. The authority to punish or recommend punishment is called *coercive power*. *Expert power* derives from a person's greater skill or knowledge about the tasks being performed. The last, *referent power*, is derived from personal characteristics: people admire the manager and want to be like or identify with the manager out of respect and admiration. Each of these sources may be used by individuals within organizations.

Power in organizations, however, is often the result of structural characteristics.[31] Organizations are large, complex systems that may contain hundreds, even thousands, of people. These systems have a formal hierarchy in which some tasks are more important regardless of who performs them. In addition, some positions have access to more information and greater resources, or their contribution to the organization is more critical. Thus, the important power processes in organizations reflect larger organizational relationships, both horizontal and vertical.

Power versus Authority

Anyone in an organization can exercise power to achieve desired outcomes. For example, when the Discovery Channel wanted to extend its brand beyond cable television, Tom Hicks began pushing for a focus on the Internet. Even though Discovery's CEO favored exploring interactive television instead, Hicks organized a grassroots campaign that eventually persuaded the CEO to focus on Web publishing, indicating that Hicks had power within the organization. Eventually, Hicks was put in charge of running Discovery Channel Online.[32]

The concept of formal authority is related to power but is narrower in scope. **Authority** is also a force for achieving desired outcomes, but only as prescribed by the formal hierarchy and reporting relationships. Three properties identify authority:

1. *Authority is vested in organizational positions.* People have authority because of the positions they hold, not because of personal characteristics or resources.
2. *Authority is accepted by subordinates.* Subordinates comply because they believe position holders have a legitimate right to exercise authority.[33] In most North American organizations, employees accept that supervisors can legitimately tell them what time to arrive at work, the tasks to perform while they're there, and what time they can go home.
3. *Authority flows down the vertical hierarchy.*[34] Authority exists along the formal chain of command, and positions at the top of the hierarchy are vested with more formal authority than are positions at the bottom.

Formal authority is exercised downward along the hierarchy. Organizational power, on the other hand, can be exercised upward, downward, and horizontally in organizations. In addition, managers can have formal authority but little real power. Consider what happened when Bill Gates turned the CEO job at Microsoft over to Steven Ballmer. Although Ballmer got the title and the formal authority, Gates retained the power. He continued to hold sway over many day-to-day business decisions, and sometimes his personal power would undermine Ballmer in front of other executives. Though Gates has now fully stepped aside from management of the company and publicly supports Ballmer's decisions, insiders say the power struggle left the company in a weakened position, without a clear strategic direction.[35] In the following sections, we will examine how employees throughout the organization can tap into both vertical and horizontal sources of power.

Briefcase

As an organization manager, keep this guideline in mind:

Understand and use the vertical sources of power in organizations, including formal position, resources, control of decision premises and information, and network centrality.

Vertical Sources of Power

All employees along the vertical hierarchy have access to some sources of power. Although a large amount of power is typically allocated to top managers by the organization structure, people throughout the organization often obtain power disproportionate to their formal positions and can exert influence in an upward direction, as Tom Hicks did at the Discovery Channel. There are four major sources of vertical power: formal position, resources, control of decision premises and information, and network centrality.[36]

Formal Position. Certain rights, responsibilities, and prerogatives accrue to top positions. People throughout the organization accept the legitimate right of top managers to set goals, make decisions, and direct activities. This is *legitimate power*, as defined earlier. Senior managers often use symbols and language to perpetuate their legitimate power. For example, the new administrator at a large hospital in the San Francisco area symbolized his legitimate position power by issuing a newsletter with his photo on the cover and airing a 24-hour-a-day video to personally welcome patients.[37]

The amount of power provided to middle managers and lower-level participants can be built into the organization's structural design. The allocation of power to middle managers and staff is important because power enables employees to be productive. When job tasks are nonroutine, and when employees participate in self-directed teams and problem-solving task forces, this encourages them to be flexible and creative and to use their own discretion. Allowing people to make their own decisions increases their power.

Power is also increased when a position encourages contact with high-level people. Access to powerful people and the development of a relationship with them provide a strong base of influence.[38] For example, in some organizations an administrative assistant to the president might have more power than a department head because the assistant has access to the senior executive on a daily basis.

The logic of designing positions for more power assumes that an organization does not have a limited amount of power to be allocated among high-level and low-level employees. The total amount of power in an organization can be increased by designing tasks and interactions along the hierarchy so everyone can exert more influence. If the distribution of power is skewed too heavily toward the top, research suggests that the organization will be less effective.[39]

Resources. Organizations allocate huge amounts of resources. Buildings are constructed, salaries are paid, and equipment and supplies are purchased. Each year, new resources are allocated in the form of budgets. These resources are allocated downward from top managers. Top managers often own stock, which gives them property rights over resource allocation. However, in many of today's organizations, employees throughout the organization also share in ownership, which increases their power.

In most cases, top managers control the resources and, hence, can determine their distribution. Resources can be used as rewards and punishments, which are additional sources of power. Resource allocation also creates a dependency relationship. Lower-level participants depend on top managers for the financial and physical resources needed to perform their tasks. Top management can exchange resources in the form of salaries and bonuses, personnel, promotions, and physical facilities for compliance with the outcomes they desire.

Control of Decision Premises and Information. Control of **decision premises** means that top managers place constraints on decisions made at lower levels by specifying a decision frame of reference and guidelines. In one sense, top managers make big decisions, whereas lower-level participants make small decisions. Top management decides which goal an organization will try to achieve, such as increased market share. Lower-level participants then decide how the goal is to be reached. In one company, top management appointed a committee to select a new marketing vice president. The CEO provided the committee with detailed qualifications that the new vice president should have. He also selected people to serve on the committee. In this way, the CEO shaped the decision premises within which the marketing vice president would be chosen. Top manager actions and decisions such as these place limits on the decisions of lower-level managers and thereby influence the outcome of their decisions.[40]

The control of information can also be a source of power. Managers recognize that information is a primary business resource and that by controlling what information is collected, how it is interpreted, and how it is shared, they can influence how decisions are made.[41] In many of today's companies, information is openly and broadly shared, which increases the power of people throughout the organization.

However, top managers generally have access to more information than do other employees. This information can be released as needed to shape the decision outcomes of other people. In one organization, Clark Ltd., the senior information technology (IT) manager controlled information given to the board of directors and thereby influenced the board's decision to purchase a sophisticated computer system.[42] The board of directors had formal authority to decide from which company the system would be purchased. The management services group was asked to recommend which of six computer manufacturers should receive the order. Jim Kenny was in charge of the management services group, and Kenny disagreed with other managers about which system to purchase. As shown in Exhibit 7.3, other managers had to go through Kenny to have their viewpoints heard by the board. Kenny shaped the board's thinking toward selecting the system he preferred by controlling information given to them.

Middle managers and lower-level employees may also have access to information that can increase their power. An assistant to a senior executive can often control information that other people want and will thus be able to influence those

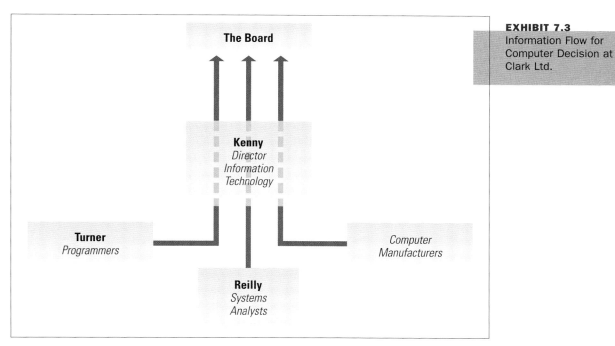

EXHIBIT 7.3
Information Flow for Computer Decision at Clark Ltd.

Source: Andrew M. Pettigrew, *The Politics of Organizational Decision-Making* (London: Tavistock, 1973), 235, reproduced by permission of Taylor & Francis.

people. Top executives depend on people throughout the organization for information about problems or opportunities. Middle managers or lower-level employees may manipulate the information they provide to top managers in order to influence decision outcomes.

Network Centrality. Network centrality means being centrally located in the organization and having access to information and people that are critical to the company's success. Managers as well as lower-level employees are more effective and more influential when they put themselves at the center of a communication network, building connections with people throughout the company. For example, in Exhibit 7.4, Radha has a well-developed communication network, sharing information and assistance with many people across the marketing, manufacturing, and engineering departments. Contrast Radha's contacts with those of Jasmine or Kirill. Who do you think is likely to have greater access to resources and more influence in the organization?

People at all levels of the hierarchy can use the idea of network centrality to accomplish goals and be more successful. A real-life example comes from Xerox Corporation. Several years ago, Cindy Casselman, who had little formal power and authority, began selling her idea for an intranet site to managers all over the company. Casselman had a well-developed network, and she worked behind the scenes, gradually gaining the power she needed to make her vision a reality—and win a promotion in the process.[43]

People can increase their network centrality by becoming knowledgeable and expert about certain activities or by taking on difficult tasks and acquiring specialized knowledge that makes them indispensable to managers above them. People who show initiative, work beyond what is expected, take on undesirable but important projects, and show interest in learning about the company and industry often

EXHIBIT 7.4
An Illustration of Network Centrality

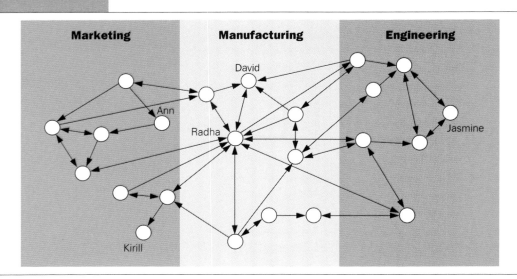

find themselves with influence. Physical location also helps because some locations are in the center of things. Central location lets a person be visible to key people and become part of important interaction networks.

ASSESS YOUR ANSWER

2 **A factory worker on the assembly line is in a low power position and should accept that he or she will have little influence over what happens.**

ANSWER: *Disagree.* Although an assembly line worker typically has little formal power and authority, all employees have access to some sources of power. It is up to the individual to network or gather information to expand his or her power in the organization. In addition, when employees band together, they can have a tremendous amount of power. Managers can't get anything done unless employees cooperate and do the work they're supposed to do.

People. Top leaders often increase their power by surrounding themselves with a group of loyal executives.[44] Loyal managers keep the leader informed and in touch with events and report possible disobedience or troublemaking in the organization. Top executives can use their central positions to build alliances and exercise substantial power when they have a management team that is fully in support of their decisions and actions.

Many top executives strive to build a cadre of loyal and supportive executives to help them achieve their goals for the organization. For example, former New York Stock Exchange Chairman Dick Grasso placed his friends and allies in critical positions and pushed favored candidates for board posts. As another example, the U.S. government handpicked the advisers and committee members who would influence decisions made by the interim Iraqi government.[45]

This idea works in the opposite direction too. Lower-level people have greater power when they have positive relationships and connections with higher-ups. By being loyal and supportive of their bosses, employees sometimes gain favorable status and exert greater influence.

Briefcase

As an organization manager, keep these guidelines in mind:

Do not leave lower organization levels powerless. If vertical power is too heavy in favor of top management, empower lower levels by giving people the tools they need to perform better: information, knowledge and skills, and the power to make substantive decisions.

The Power of Empowerment

In forward-thinking organizations, top managers want lower-level employees to have greater power so they can do their jobs more effectively. These managers intentionally push power down the hierarchy and share it with employees to enable them to achieve goals. **Empowerment** is power sharing, the delegation of power or authority to subordinates in an organization.[46] Increasing employee power heightens motivation for task accomplishment because people improve their own effectiveness, choosing how to do a task and using their creativity.[47]

Empowering employees involves giving them three elements that enable them to act more freely to accomplish their jobs: information, knowledge, and power.[48]

1. *Employees receive information about company performance.* In companies where employees are fully empowered, all employees have access to all financial and operational information.

2. *Employees have knowledge and skills to contribute to company goals.* Companies use training programs and other development tools to help people acquire the knowledge and skills they need to contribute to organizational performance.
3. *Employees have the power to make substantive decisions.* Empowered employees have the authority to directly influence work procedures and organizational performance, such as through quality circles or self-directed work teams.

Many of today's organizations are implementing empowerment programs, but they are empowering workers to varying degrees. At some companies, empowerment means encouraging workers' ideas while managers retain final authority for decisions; at others it means giving employees almost complete freedom and power to make decisions and exercise initiative and imagination.[49] The continuum of empowerment can run from a situation in which front-line workers have almost no discretion, such as on a traditional assembly line, to full empowerment, where workers even participate in formulating organizational strategy. One organization that pushes empowerment to the maximum is Semco.

Semco

The Brazil-based company Semco's fundamental operating principle is to harness the wisdom of all its employees. It does so by letting people control their work hours, location, and even pay plans. Employees also participate in all organizational decisions, including what businesses Semco should pursue.

Semco leaders believe economic success requires creating an atmosphere that puts power and control directly in the hands of employees. People can veto any new product idea or business venture. They choose their own leaders and manage themselves to accomplish goals. Information is openly and broadly shared so that everyone knows where they and the company stand. Instead of dictating Semco's identity and strategy, leaders allow it to be shaped by individual interests and efforts. People are encouraged to seek challenge, explore new ideas and business opportunities, and question the ideas of anyone in the company.

This high level of employee empowerment has helped Semco achieve decades of high profitability and growth despite fluctuations in the economy and shifting markets. "At Semco, we don't play by the rules," says Ricardo Semler. Semler, whose father started the company in the 1950s, says it doesn't unnerve him to "step back and see nothing on the company's horizon." He is happy to watch the company and its employees "ramble through their days, running on instinct and opportunity. . . ."[50] ∎

Horizontal Sources of Power

Horizontal power pertains to relationships across departments, divisions, or other units. All vice presidents are usually at the same level on the organization chart. Does this mean each department has the same amount of power? No. Horizontal power is not defined by the formal hierarchy or the organization chart. Each department makes a unique contribution to organizational success. Some departments will have greater say and will achieve their desired outcomes, whereas others will not. For example, Charles Perrow surveyed managers in several industrial firms.[51] He bluntly asked, "Which department has the most power?" among four major

EXHIBIT 7.5
Ratings of Power among
Departments in Industrial
Firms

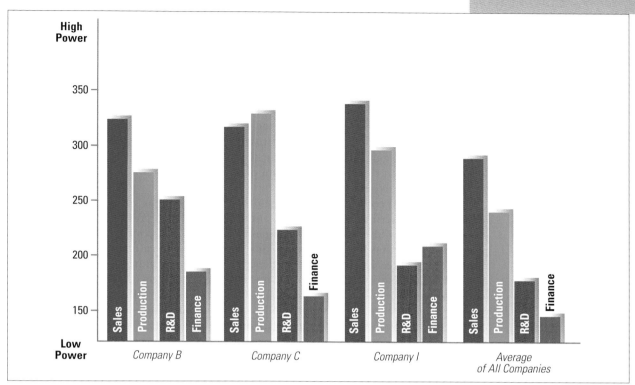

Source: Charles Perrow, "Departmental Power and Perspective in Industrial Firms," in Mayer N. Zald, ed., *Power in Organizations* (Nashville, Tenn.: Vanderbilt University Press, 1970), 64.

departments: production, sales and marketing, R&D, and finance and accounting. Partial survey results are given in Exhibit 7.5.

In most firms, sales had the greatest power. In a few firms, production was also quite powerful. On average, the sales and production departments were more powerful than R&D and finance, although substantial variation existed. Differences in the amount of horizontal power clearly occurred in those firms. Power shifts among departments depending on circumstances. Today, IT departments have growing power in many organizations. In the federal government, watchdog and regulatory agencies for Wall Street are increasing in power because of the 2008 financial meltdown.

Power differences also apply to organizations that join together in alliances or other partnerships, where one company may gain more power because of changing circumstances. For example, when SBC Communications (AT&T's predecessor) and Yahoo! first entered a strategic partnership in 2001, SBC desperately needed Yahoo! to help convince people to sign up for high-speed Internet service. By 2008, though, broadband was in high demand, and AT&T was in a much stronger position overall than Yahoo!, leading to a shift in the power relationship between the two companies. AT&T is negotiating to reduce the fees it pays to Yahoo!, which could kick the Internet company where it hurts even as it tries to become more competitive against Google.[52]

Horizontal power is difficult to measure because power differences are not defined on the organization chart. However, some initial explanations for power differences, such as those shown in Exhibit 7.5, have been found. The theoretical concept that explains relative power is called strategic contingencies.[53]

Strategic Contingencies. Strategic contingencies are events and activities both inside and outside an organization that are essential for attaining organizational goals. Departments involved with strategic contingencies for the organization tend to have greater power. Departmental activities are important when they provide strategic value by solving problems or crises for the organization. For example, if an organization faces an intense threat from lawsuits and regulations, the legal department will gain power and influence over organizational decisions because it copes with such a threat. If product innovation is the key strategic issue, the power of R&D can be expected to be high.

The strategic contingency approach to power is similar to the resource dependence model described in Chapters 4 and 6. Recall that organizations try to reduce dependency on the external environment. The strategic contingency approach to power suggests that the departments or organizations most responsible for dealing with key resource issues and dependencies in the environment will become most powerful. The National Football League, for instance, bowed to the power of the cable companies and arranged for its television partners, CBS and NBC, to simultaneously broadcast along with the NFL Network the highly-anticipated December 2007 game between the undefeated Patriots and the Giants. The NFL tried for years to get the cable companies to add its network to their basic packages along with ESPN and ESPN2, but the cable companies refused because the price was too high. The NFL has a popular product, but with limited distribution options, it is in a low power position compared to the cable operators.[54]

Power Sources. Jeffrey Pfeffer and Gerald Salancik, among others, have been instrumental in conducting research on the strategic contingency theory.[55] Their findings indicate that a department rated as powerful may possess one or more of the characteristics illustrated in Exhibit 7.6.[56] In some organizations these five **power sources** overlap, but each provides a useful way to evaluate sources of horizontal power.

1. *Dependency.* Interdepartmental **dependency** is a key element underlying relative power. Power is derived from having something someone else wants. The power of department A over department B is greater when department B depends on department A.[57] Materials, information, and resources may flow between departments in one direction, such as in the case of sequential task interdependence (see Chapter 13). In such cases, the department receiving resources is in a lower power position than the department providing them. The number and strength of dependencies are also important. When seven or eight departments must come for help to the engineering department, for example, engineering is in a strong power position. In contrast, a department that depends on many other departments is in a low power position. Likewise, a department in an otherwise low power position might gain power through dependencies. If a factory cannot produce without the expertise of maintenance workers to keep the machines

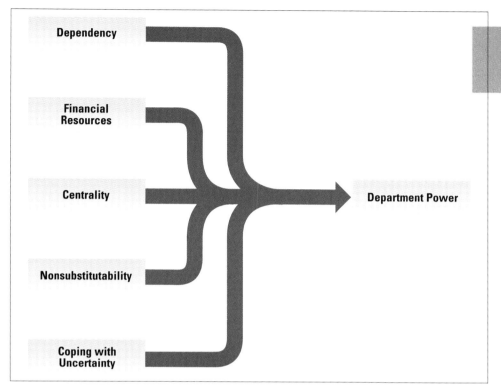

working, the maintenance department is in a strong power position because it has control over a strategic contingency.

2. *Financial resources.*   Control over resources is an important source of power in organizations. Money can be converted into other kinds of resources that are needed by other departments. Money generates dependency; departments that provide financial resources have something other departments want. Departments that generate income for an organization have greater power. Exhibit 7.5 showed sales as the most powerful unit in most industrial firms. This is because salespeople find customers and bring in money, thereby removing an important problem for the organization. An ability to provide financial resources also explains why certain departments are powerful in other organizations, such as universities.

You might expect budget allocation in a state university to be a straightforward process. The need for financial resources can be determined by such things as the number of undergraduate students, the number of graduate students, and the number of faculty in each department.

IN PRACTICE

University
of Illinois

In fact, resource allocation at the University of Illinois is not clear-cut. The University of Illinois has a relatively fixed resource inflow from state government. Beyond that, important resources come from research grants and the quality of students and faculty. University departments that provide the most resources to the university are rated as

(continued)

having the most power. Some departments have more power because of their resource contribution to the university. Departments that generate large research grants are more powerful, for instance, because research grants contain a sizable overhead payment to university administration. This overhead money pays for a large share of the university's personnel and facilities. The size of a department's graduate student body and the national prestige of the department also add to power. Graduate students and national prestige are nonfinancial resources that add to the reputation and effectiveness of the university.

How do university departments use their power? Generally, they use it to obtain even more resources from the rest of the university. Very powerful departments receive university resources, such as graduate-student fellowships, internal research support, and summer faculty salaries, far in excess of their needs based on the number of students and faculty.[58] ■

Briefcase

As an organization manager, keep these guidelines in mind:

Be aware of the important horizontal power relationships that come from the ability of a department to deal with strategic contingencies that confront the organization. Increase the horizontal power of a department by increasing involvement in strategic contingencies.

As shown in the example of the University of Illinois, power accrues to departments that bring in or provide resources that are highly valued by an organization. Power enables those departments to obtain more of the scarce resources allocated within the organization. "Power derived from acquiring resources is used to obtain more resources, which in turn can be employed to produce more power—the rich get richer."[59]

3. *Centrality.* **Centrality** reflects a department's role in the primary activity of an organization.[60] One measure of centrality is the extent to which the work of the department affects the final output of the organization. For example, the production department is more central and usually has more power than staff groups (assuming no other critical contingencies). Centrality is associated with power because it reflects the contribution made to the organization. The corporate finance department of an investment bank generally has more power than the stock research department. By contrast, in the manufacturing firms described in Exhibit 7.5, finance tends to be low in power. When the finance department has the limited task of recording money and expenditures, it is not responsible for obtaining critical resources or for producing the products of the organization. Today, however, finance departments have greater power in many organizations because of the greater need for controlling costs.

4. *Nonsubstitutability.* Power is also determined by **nonsubstitutability,** which means that a department's function cannot be performed by other readily available resources. Similarly, if an employee cannot be easily replaced, his or her power is greater. If an organization has no alternative sources of skill and information, a department's power will be greater. This can be one reason top managers use outside consultants. Consultants might be used as substitutes for staff people to reduce the power of staff groups.

The impact of substitutability on power was studied for programmers in computer departments.[61] When computers were first introduced, programming was a rare and specialized occupation. Programmers controlled the use of organizational computers because they alone possessed the knowledge to program them. Over a period of about 10 years, computer programming became a more common activity. People could be substituted easily, and the power of programming departments dropped. Substitutability affects the power of organizations as well. Major record labels once had tremendous power over artists in the music industry because they had almost total control over which artists got their music recorded and in front of consumers. Today, though, bands like Nine Inch Nails and Radiohead can release albums directly on the Internet without going through a label. In addition, Wal-Mart, the largest music retailer in the United States, has entered the music making and marketing business, buying albums directly from artists like the Eagles and Journey. Intense marketing helped the Eagles' "Long Road Out of Eden" sell 711,000 copies through Wal-Mart in its first week, without a traditional record company ever being involved.[62]

5. *Coping with Uncertainty.*   Elements in the environment can change swiftly and can be unpredictable and complex. In the face of uncertainty, little information is available to managers on appropriate courses of action. Departments that reduce this uncertainty for the organization will increase their power.[63] When market research personnel accurately predict changes in demand for new products, they gain power and prestige because they have reduced a critical uncertainty. But forecasting is only one technique. Sometimes uncertainty can be reduced by taking quick and appropriate action after an unpredictable event occurs.

Departments can cope with critical uncertainties by (1) obtaining prior information, (2) prevention, and (3) absorption.[64] *Obtaining prior information* means a department can reduce an organization's uncertainty by forecasting an event. Departments increase their power through *prevention* by predicting and forestalling negative events. *Absorption* occurs when a department takes action after an event to reduce its negative consequences. Consider the following case from the health care industry.

Because hospitals and other health care providers have to deal with so many complex legal and regulatory matters, the legal department is usually in a high power position. That is certainly the case at Carilion Health System, based in Roanoke, Virginia. Some years ago, the legal department successfully fought off a U.S. Department of Justice antitrust lawsuit and played a crucial role in negotiating a merger between Carilion and Roanoke's only other hospital.

Carilion Health System

Since then, the legal department has been kept busy not only with regulatory issues but also with trying to get payment from patients who say they can't pay their high medical bills. Because Roanoke is now a "one-market town" in terms of health care, critics say Carilion is getting away with charging excessive fees, thereby hurting patients, businesses, insurers, and the entire community. The Roanoke City District Court devotes one morning a week to cases filed by Carilion, which during one recent fiscal year sued nearly 10,000 patients, garnished the wages of more than 5,000 people, and placed liens on nearly 4,000 homes.

The negative press resulting from this, along with a backlash from independent doctors who say Carilion is intentionally stifling competition, means the public relations department has a chance to increase its power as well. The department is actively involved in efforts to bolster Carilion's image as a good corporate citizen, emphasizing that it only sues patients it believes have the ability to pay and pointing out the millions of dollars Carilion dispenses to charity care each year.[65] ∎

At Carilion, the legal department absorbed a critical uncertainty by fighting off the antitrust lawsuit and helping Carilion grow in size and power. It continues to take action after uncertainties appear (such as patients who don't pay).

Horizontal power relationships in organizations change as strategic contingencies change. Whereas the legal department will likely continue in a high power position at Carilion, the need of the hospital to improve its reputation and fend off growing criticism could lead to an increase in the power of the public relations department. The public relations department can gain power by being involved in activities targeted toward both prevention and absorption. Departments that help organizations cope with new strategic issues will increase their power.

POLITICAL PROCESSES IN ORGANIZATIONS

Politics, like power, is intangible and difficult to measure. It is hidden from view and is hard to observe in a systematic way. Two surveys uncovered the following reactions of managers toward political behavior.[66]

1. Most managers have a negative view toward politics and believe that politics will more often hurt than help an organization in achieving its goals.
2. Managers believe that political behavior is common in practically all organizations.
3. Most managers think that political behavior occurs more often at upper rather than lower levels in organizations.
4. Managers believe political behavior arises in certain decision domains, such as structural change, but is absent from other decisions, such as handling employee grievances.

Based on these surveys, politics seems more likely to occur at the top levels of an organization and around certain issues and decisions. Moreover, managers do not approve of political behavior. The remainder of this chapter explores more fully what political behavior is, when it should be used, the type of issues and decisions most likely to be associated with politics, and some political tactics that may be effective.

Definition

Power has been described as the available force or potential for achieving desired outcomes. *Politics* is the use of power to influence decisions in order to achieve those outcomes. The exercise of power and influence has led to two ways to define politics—as self-serving behavior or as a natural organizational decision process. The first definition emphasizes that politics is self-serving and involves activities that are not sanctioned by the organization.[67]

In this view, politics involves deception and dishonesty for purposes of individual self-interest and leads to conflict and disharmony within the work environment. This dark view of politics is widely held by laypeople, and political activity certainly can be used in this way. Recent studies have shown that workers who perceive this kind of political activity within their companies often have related feelings of anxiety and job dissatisfaction. Studies also support the belief that inappropriate use of politics is related to low employee morale, inferior organizational performance, and poor decision making.[68] This view of politics explains why managers in the aforementioned surveys did not approve of political behavior.

Although politics can be used in a negative, self-serving way, the appropriate use of political behavior can serve organizational goals.[69] The second view sees politics as a natural organizational process for resolving differences among organizational interest groups.[70] Politics is the process of bargaining and negotiation that is used to overcome conflicts and differences of opinion. In this view, politics is similar to the coalition-building decision processes we will discuss in Chapter 8.

The organization theory perspective views politics as described in the second definition. Politics is simply the activity through which power is exercised in the resolution of conflicts and uncertainty. Consider that Jeffrey Immelt, CEO of General Electric, considers himself a failure if he exercises his formal authority more than seven or eight times a year. The rest of the time, Immelt is using political activity to persuade and influence others and to resolve conflicting ideas and opinions.[71] Politics is neutral and is not necessarily harmful to the organization. The formal definition of organizational politics is as follows: **Organizational politics** involves activities to acquire, develop, and use power and other resources to influence others and obtain the preferred outcome when there is uncertainty or disagreement about choices.[72]

Political behavior can be either a positive or a negative force. Politics is the use of power to get things accomplished—good things as well as bad. Uncertainty and conflict are natural and inevitable, and politics is the mechanism for reaching agreement. Politics includes informal discussions that enable people to arrive at consensus and make decisions that otherwise might be stalemated or unsolvable.

3 **When managers use politics, it usually leads to conflict and disharmony and will likely disrupt the smooth functioning of the organization.**

ANSWER: *Disagree.* Politics is a natural organizational process for resolving differences and getting things done. Although politics can be used for negative and self-serving purposes, political activity is also the primary way managers are brought together to accomplish good things. Being political is part of the job of a manager, but managers should take care to use politics to serve the interests of the organization rather than themselves.

When Is Political Activity Used?

Politics is a mechanism for arriving at consensus when uncertainty is high and there is disagreement over goals or problem priorities. Recall the rational versus political models described in Exhibit 7.2. The political model is associated with conflict over goals, shifting coalitions and interest groups, ambiguous information, and uncertainty. Thus, political activity tends to be most visible when managers confront nonprogrammed decisions, as will be discussed in Chapter 8, and is related to the Carnegie model of decision making. Because managers at the top of an organization generally deal with more nonprogrammed decisions than do managers at lower levels, more political activity will appear at higher levels. Moreover, some issues are associated with inherent disagreement. Resources, for example, are critical for the survival and effectiveness of departments, so resource allocation often becomes a political issue. Rational methods of allocation do not satisfy participants. Three **domains of political activity** (areas in which politics plays a role) in most organizations are structural change, management succession, and resource allocation.

Structural reorganizations strike at the heart of power and authority relationships. Reorganizations such as those discussed in Chapter 2 change responsibilities and tasks, which also affects the underlying power base from strategic contingencies. For these reasons, a major reorganization can lead to an explosion of political activity.[73] Managers may actively bargain and negotiate to maintain the responsibilities and power bases they have. Mergers and acquisitions also frequently create tremendous political activity.

Organizational changes such as hiring new executives, promotions, and transfers have great political significance, particularly at top organizational levels where uncertainty is high and networks of trust, cooperation, and communication among executives are important.[74] Hiring decisions can generate uncertainty, discussion, and disagreement. Managers can use hiring and promotion to strengthen network alliances and coalitions by putting their own people in prominent positions.

The third area of political activity is resource allocation. Resource allocation decisions encompass all resources required for organizational performance, including salaries, operating budgets, employees, office facilities, equipment, use of the company airplane, and so forth. Resources are so vital that disagreement about priorities exists, and political processes help resolve the dilemmas.

USING POWER, POLITICS, AND COLLABORATION

One theme in this chapter has been that power in organizations is not primarily a phenomenon of the individual. It is related to the resources departments command, the role departments play in an organization, and the environmental contingencies with which departments cope. Position and responsibility, more than personality and style, may determine a manager's ability to influence outcomes in the organization.

Power is used through individual political behavior, however. To fully understand the use of power within organizations, it is important to look at both structural components and individual behavior.[75] Although power often comes from larger organizational forms and processes, the political use of power involves individual-level activities and skills. To learn about your political skills, complete the questionnaire in the "How Do You Fit the Design?" box. Managers with political skill are more effective at influencing others and thus getting what they want. These managers have honed their abilities to observe and understand patterns of interaction and influence in the organization. They are skilled at developing relationships with a broad network of people and can adapt their behavior and approach to

How Do You Fit the Design?

Political Skills

How good are you at influencing people across an organization? To learn something about your political skills, answer the questions that follow. Please answer whether each item is Mostly True or Mostly False for you.

	Mostly True	Mostly False
1. I am able to communicate easily and effectively with others.	_____	_____
2. I spend a lot of time at work developing connections with people outside my area.	_____	_____
3. I instinctively know the right thing to say or do to influence others.	_____	_____
4. I am good at using my connections outside my area to get things done at work.	_____	_____
5. When communicating with others I am absolutely genuine in what I say and do.	_____	_____
6. It is easy for me to reach out to new people.	_____	_____
7. I make strangers feel comfortable and at ease around me.	_____	_____
8. I am good at sensing the motivations and hidden agendas of others.	_____	_____

Scoring: Give yourself one point for each item marked as Mostly True.

Interpretation: Having some basic political skill helps a manager gain broad support and influence. Political skills help a manager build personal and organizational relationships that enhance your team's outcomes. A score of 6 or higher suggests active political skills and a good start for your career, especially in an organization in which things get done politically. If you scored three or less, you may want to focus more on building collegial and supportive relationships as you progress in your career. If not, perhaps join an organization in which decisions and actions are undertaken by rational procedures rather than by support of key coalitions.

Source: Adapted from Gerald R. Ferris, Darren C. Treadway, Robert W. Kolodinsky, Wayne A. Hochwarter, Charles J. Kacmer, Ceasar Douglas, and Dwight D. Frink, "Development and Validation of the Political Skill Inventory," *Journal of Management* 31 (February 2005), 126–152.

diverse people and situations. Politically effective managers understand that influence is about relationships.[76]

Managers can develop political competence, and they can learn to use a wide variety of influence tactics depending on their own position as well as the specific situation. For instance, research indicates that managers in HR departments may use softer, more subtle approaches than do managers in more powerful finance departments. In one study, HR executives, who were not seen as having centrality to the firm's mission, took a low-key approach to try to influence others, whereas finance executives, who had a more central and powerful position, used harder, more direct influence tactics.[77]

EXHIBIT 7.7
Power and Political
Tactics in Organizations

Tactics for Increasing the Power Base	Political Tactics for Using Power	Tactics for Enhancing Collaboration
1. Enter areas of high uncertainty.	1. Build coalitions and expand networks.	1. Create integration devices.
2. Create dependencies.	2. Assign loyal people to key positions.	2. Use confrontation and negotiation.
3. Provide scarce resources.	3. Control decision premises.	3. Schedule intergroup consultation.
4. Satisfy strategic contingencies.	4. Enhance legitimacy and expertise.	4. Practice member rotation.
5. Make a direct appeal.	5. Create superordinate goals.	

The following sections summarize various tactics that managers can use to increase their own or their department's power base, political tactics they can use to achieve desired outcomes, and tactics for increasing cooperation and collaboration, thus reducing damaging conflict. These tactics are summarized in Exhibit 7.7.

Tactics for Increasing Power

Four **tactics for increasing power** are as follows:

1. *Enter areas of high uncertainty.* One source of individual or departmental power is to identify key uncertainties and take steps to remove those uncertainties.[78] Uncertainties could arise from stoppages on an assembly line, from the quality demanded of a new product, or from the inability to predict a demand for new services. Once an uncertainty is identified, the department can take action to cope with it. By their very nature, uncertain tasks will not be solved immediately. Trial and error will be needed, which is to the advantage of the department. The trial-and-error process provides experience and expertise that cannot easily be duplicated by other departments.

2. *Create dependencies.* Dependencies are another source of power.[79] When the organization depends on a department for information, materials, knowledge, or skills, that department will hold power over others. This power can be increased by incurring obligations. There is much research indicating that most people feel a sense of obligation to give something back in return for favors others do for them.[80] This principle of *reciprocity* is one of the key factors affecting influence relationships in organizations. When a manager does a favor for a colleague, the colleague feels obliged to return the favor in the future. Doing additional work that helps out other departments obligates the other departments to respond at a future date.

   An equally effective and related strategy is to reduce dependency on other departments by acquiring necessary information or skills. IT departments have created dependencies in many organizations because of the rapid changes in this area. Employees in other departments depend on the IT unit to master complex software programs, changing use of the Internet, and other advances so that they will have the information they need to perform effectively.

3. *Provide scarce resources.* Resources are always important to organizational survival. Departments that accumulate resources and provide them to an organization in the form of money, information, or facilities will be powerful. An earlier "In Practice" example described how university departments with the greatest power are those that obtain external research funds for contributions to university overhead. Likewise, sales departments are powerful in industrial firms because they bring in financial resources.

4. *Satisfy strategic contingencies.* The theory of strategic contingencies says that some elements in the external environment and within the organization are especially important for organizational success. A contingency could be a critical event, a task for which there are no substitutes, or a central task that is interdependent with many others in the organization. An analysis of the organization and its changing environment will reveal strategic contingencies. To the extent that contingencies are new or are not being satisfied, there is room for a department to move into those critical areas and increase its importance and power.

In summary, the allocation of power in an organization is not random. Power is the result of organizational processes that can be understood and predicted. The abilities to reduce uncertainty, increase dependency on one's own department, obtain resources, and cope with strategic contingencies all enhance a department's power. Once power is available, the next challenge is to use it to attain desired outcomes.

Political Tactics for Using Power

The use of power in organizations requires both skill and willingness. Many decisions are made through political processes because rational decision processes do not fit. Uncertainty or disagreement is too high. **Political tactics for using power** to influence decision outcomes include the following:

1. *Build coalitions and expand networks.* Effective managers develop positive relationships throughout the organization, and they spend time talking with others to learn about their views and build mutually beneficial alliances and coalitions.[81] Most important decisions are made outside of formal meetings. Managers discuss issues with each other and reach agreement. Effective managers are those who huddle, meeting in groups of twos and threes to resolve key issues.[82] They also make sure their networks cross hierarchical, functional, and even organizational boundaries. One research project found that the ability to build networks has a positive impact on both employees' perception of a manager's effectiveness and the ability of the manager to influence performance.[83] Networks can be expanded by (1) reaching out to establish contact with additional managers and (2) coopting dissenters. Establishing contact with additional managers means building good interpersonal relationships based on liking, trust, and respect. Reliability and the motivation to work with rather than exploit others are part of both networking and coalition building.[84] The second approach to expanding networks, cooptation, is the act of bringing a dissenter into one's network. One example of cooptation involved a university committee whose membership was based on promotion and tenure. Several professors who were critical of the tenure and promotion process were appointed to the committee. Once a part of the administrative process, they could see

the administrative point of view. Cooptation effectively brought them into the administrative network.[85]

2. *Assign loyal people to key positions.*   Another political tactic is to assign trusted and loyal people to key positions in the organization or department. Top managers as well as department heads often use the hiring, transfer, and promotion processes to place in key positions people who are sympathetic to the outcomes of the department, thus helping to achieve departmental goals.[86] Top leaders frequently use this tactic, as we discussed earlier. When an outside police chief was hired to take over a major metropolitan police department, he brought three assistant chiefs with him because their thinking and management skills were compatible with his goals to transform the department.

3. *Control decision premises.*   To control decision premises means to constrain the boundaries of a decision. One technique is to choose or limit information provided to other managers. A common method is simply to put your department's best foot forward, such as selectively presenting favorable criteria. A variety of statistics can be assembled to support the departmental point of view. A university department that is growing rapidly and has a large number of students can make claims for additional resources by emphasizing its growth and large size. Such objective criteria do not always work, but they are a valuable step.

   Decision premises can be further influenced by limiting the decision process. Decisions can be influenced by the items put on an agenda for an important meeting or even by the sequence in which items are discussed.[87] Items discussed last, when time is short and people want to leave, will receive less attention than those discussed earlier. Calling attention to specific problems and suggesting alternatives also will affect outcomes. Stressing a specific problem to get it—rather than problems not relevant to your department—on the agenda is an example of agenda setting.

4. *Enhance legitimacy and expertise.*   Managers can exert the greatest influence in areas in which they have recognized legitimacy and expertise. If a request is within the task domain of a department and is consistent with the department's vested interest, other departments will tend to comply. Members can also identify external consultants or other experts within the organization to support their cause.[88] For example, a financial vice president in a large retail firm wanted to fire the director of HR management. She hired a consultant to evaluate the HR projects undertaken to date. A negative report from the consultant provided sufficient legitimacy to fire the director, who was replaced with a director loyal to the financial vice president.

5. *Make a direct appeal.*   If managers do not ask, they seldom receive. An example of direct appeal comes from Drugstore.com, where Jessica Morrison used direct appeal to get a new title and a salary increase. Morrison researched pay scales on PayScale.com and approached her boss armed with that and other pertinent information. Her direct appeal, backed up with research, won her the promotion.[89] Political activity is effective only when goals and needs are made explicit so the organization can respond. An assertive proposal may be accepted because other managers have no better alternatives. Moreover, an explicit proposal will often receive favorable treatment because other alternatives are ambiguous and less well defined. Effective political behavior requires sufficient forcefulness and risk taking to at least ask for what you need to achieve desired outcomes.

Briefcase

As an organization manager, keep these guidelines in mind:

Expect and allow for political behavior in organizations. Politics provides the discussion and clash of interests needed to crystallize points of view and to reach a decision. Build coalitions, expand networks, control decision premises, enhance legitimacy, and make a direct appeal to attain desired outcomes.

Managers can use an understanding of these tactics to assert influence and get things done within the organization. When managers ignore political tactics, they may find themselves failing without understanding why. For example, at the World Bank, Paul Wolfowitz tried to wield power without building the necessary relationships he needed to assert influence.

After former Deputy Secretary of Defense Paul Wolfowitz lost his bids to become defense secretary or national security advisor in the Bush administration, he jumped at the chance to be the new president of World Bank. But Wolfowitz doomed his career at World Bank from the start by failing to develop relationships and build alliances.

World Bank

Most World Bank leaders had been in their positions for many years when Wolfowitz arrived, and they were accustomed to "promoting each other's interests and scratching each other's backs," as one board member put it. Wolfowitz came in and tried to assert his own ideas, goals, and formal authority without considering the interests, ideas, and goals of others. He quickly alienated much of the World Bank leadership team and board by adopting a single-minded position on key issues and refusing to consider alternative views. Rather than attempting to persuade others to his way of thinking, Wolfowitz issued directives to senior bank officers, either personally or through his handpicked managers. Several high-level officers resigned following disputes with the new president.

Eventually, the board asked for Wolfowitz's resignation. "What Paul didn't understand is that the World Bank presidency is not inherently a powerful job," said one former colleague. "A bank president is successful only if he can form alliances with the bank's many fiefdoms. Wolfowitz didn't ally with those fiefdoms. He alienated them."[90] ■

Wolfowitz realized too late that he needed to use a political approach rather than trying to force his own agenda. Even when a manager has a great deal of power, the use of power should not be obvious.[91] If a manager formally draws on her power base in a meeting by saying, "My department has more power, so the rest of you have to do it my way," her power will be diminished. Power works best when it is used quietly. To call attention to power is to lose it. People know who has power. Explicit claims to power are not necessary and can even harm the manager's or department's cause.

Also, when using any of the preceding tactics, recall that most people think self-serving behavior hurts rather than helps an organization. If managers are perceived to be throwing their weight around or pursuing goals that are self-serving rather than beneficial to the organization, they will lose respect. On the other hand, managers must recognize the relational and political aspect of their work. It is not sufficient to be rational and technically competent. Developing and using political skill is an important part of being a good manager.

Tactics for Enhancing Collaboration

Most organizations have at least moderate interunit conflict, and an additional approach in many organizations is to overcome conflict by stimulating cooperation

and collaboration among departments to support the attainment of organizational goals. **Tactics for enhancing collaboration** include the following:

1. *Create integration devices.* As described in Chapter 2, teams, task forces, and project managers who span the boundaries between departments can be used as integration devices. Bringing together representatives from conflicting departments in joint problem-solving teams is an effective way to enhance collaboration because representatives learn to understand each other's point of view.[92] Sometimes a full-time integrator is assigned to achieve cooperation and collaboration by meeting with members of the respective departments and exchanging information. The integrator has to understand each group's problems and must be able to move both groups toward a solution that is mutually acceptable.[93]

Teams and task forces reduce conflict and enhance cooperation because they integrate people from different departments. Integration devices can also be used to enhance cooperation between labor and management. At Magee Rieter Automotive Systems in Bloomsburg, Pennsylvania, for example, empowered cross-functional teams work closely with managers to run the business. Conflicts between labor and management arise, but they are worked out before they ever reach the grievance stage.[94]

   Labor–management teams, which are designed to increase worker participation and provide a cooperative model for solving union–management problems, are increasingly being used at companies such as Goodyear, Ford Motor Company, and Xerox. In the steel industry, companies such as USX and Wheeling-Pittsburgh Steel have signed pacts that give union representatives seats on the board.[95] Although unions continue to battle over traditional issues such as wages, these integration devices are creating a level of cooperation that many managers would not have believed possible just a few years ago.

2. *Use confrontation and negotiation.* **Confrontation** occurs when parties in conflict directly engage one another and try to work out their differences. **Negotiation** is the bargaining process that often occurs during confrontation and that enables the parties to systematically reach a solution. These techniques bring appointed representatives from the departments together to work out a serious dispute.

   Confrontation and negotiation involve some risk. There is no guarantee that discussions will focus on a conflict or that emotions will not get out of hand. However, if members are able to resolve the conflict on the basis of face-to-face discussions, they will find new respect for each other, and future collaboration becomes easier. The beginnings of relatively permanent attitude change are possible through direct negotiation.

   Confrontation and negotiation are successful when managers engage in a *win–win strategy.* Win–win means both sides adopt a positive attitude and strive to resolve the conflict in a way that will benefit each other.[96] If the negotiations deteriorate into a strictly win–lose strategy (each group wants to defeat the other), the confrontation will be ineffective. The differences between win–win and win–lose strategies of negotiation are shown in Exhibit 7.8. With a win–win strategy—which includes defining the problem as mutual, communicating openly, and avoiding threats—understanding can be changed while the dispute is resolved.

   One type of negotiation, used to resolve a disagreement between workers and management, is referred to as **collective bargaining**. The bargaining process is usually accomplished through a union and results in an agreement that specifies each party's responsibilities for the next two to three years.

EXHIBIT 7.8
Negotiating Strategies

Win–Lose Strategy	Win–Win Strategy
1. Define the problem as a win–lose situation.	1. Define the conflict as a mutual problem.
2. Pursue own group's outcomes.	2. Pursue joint outcomes.
3. Force the other group into submission.	3. Find creative agreements that satisfy both groups.
4. Be deceitful, inaccurate, and misleading in communicating the group's needs, goals, and proposals.	4. Be open, honest, and accurate in communicating the group's needs, goals, and proposals.
5. Use threats (to force submission).	5. Avoid threats (to reduce the other's defensiveness).
6. Communicate strong commitment (rigidity) regarding one's position.	6. Communicate flexibility of position.

Source: Adapted from David W. Johnson and Frank P. Johnson, *Joining Together: Group Theory and Group Skills* (Englewood Cliffs, N.J.: Prentice-Hall, 1975), 182–183.

3. *Schedule intergroup consultation.* When conflict is intense and enduring, and department members are suspicious and uncooperative, top managers may intervene as third parties to help resolve the conflict or bring in third-party consultants from outside the organization.[97] This process, sometimes called *workplace mediation*, is a strong intervention to reduce conflict because it involves bringing the disputing parties together and allowing each side to present its version of the situation. The technique has been developed by such psychologists as Robert Blake, Jane Mouton, and Richard Walton.[98]

   Department members attend a workshop, which may last for several days, away from day-to-day work problems. This approach is similar to the organization development (OD) approach described in Chapter 10. The conflicting groups are separated, and each group is invited to discuss and make a list of its perceptions of itself and the other group. Group representatives publicly share these perceptions, and together the groups discuss the results. Intergroup consultation can be quite demanding for everyone involved, but if handled correctly, these sessions can help department employees understand each other much better and lead to improved attitudes and better working relationships for years to come.

4. *Practice member rotation.* Rotation means that individuals from one department can be asked to work in another department on a temporary or permanent basis. The advantage is that individuals become submerged in the values, attitudes, problems, and goals of the other department. In addition, individuals can explain the problems and goals of their original departments to their new colleagues. This enables a frank, accurate exchange of views and information. Rotation works slowly to reduce conflict but is very effective for changing the underlying attitudes and perceptions that promote conflict.[99]

5. *Create shared mission and superordinate goals.* Another strategy is for top management to create a shared mission and establish superordinate goals that

require cooperation among departments.[100] As discussed in Chapter 9, organizations with strong, adaptive cultures, where employees share a larger vision for their company, are more likely to have a united, cooperative workforce. Studies have shown that when employees from different departments see that their goals are linked, they will openly share resources and information.[101] To be effective, superordinate goals must be substantial, and employees must be granted the time and incentives to work cooperatively in pursuit of the superordinate goals rather than departmental subgoals.

DESIGN ESSENTIALS

- The central message of this chapter is that conflict, power, and politics are natural outcomes of organizing. Differences in goals, backgrounds, and tasks are necessary for organizational excellence, but these differences can throw groups into conflict. Managers use power and politics to manage and resolve conflict.

- Two views of organization were presented. The rational model of organization assumes that organizations have specific goals and that problems can be logically solved. The other view, the political model of organization, is the basis for much of the chapter. This view assumes that the goals of an organization are not specific or agreed upon. Departments have different values and interests, so managers come into conflict. Decisions are made on the basis of power and political influence. Bargaining, negotiation, persuasion, and coalition building decide outcomes.

- The chapter also discussed the vertical and horizontal sources of power. Vertical sources of power include formal position, resources, control of decision premises, and network centrality. In general, managers at the top of the organizational hierarchy have more power than people at lower levels. However, positions all along the hierarchy can be designed to increase the power of employees. As organizations face increased competition and environmental uncertainty, top executives are finding that increasing the power of middle managers and lower-level employees can help the organization be more competitive. Empowerment is a popular trend in today's organizations. Empowering employees means giving them three key elements: information and resources, necessary knowledge and skills, and the power to make substantive decisions.

- Research into horizontal power processes has revealed that certain characteristics make some departments more powerful than others. Differences in power can be understood using the concept of strategic contingencies. Departments responsible for dealing with key resource issues and dependencies are more powerful. Such factors as dependency, resources, nonsubstitutability, and dealing with uncertainty determine the influence of departments.

- Managers need political skills. Many people distrust political behavior, fearing that it will be used for selfish ends that benefit the individual but not the organization. However, politics is often needed to achieve the legitimate goals of a department or organization. Three areas in which political behavior often plays a role are structural change, management succession, and resource allocation because these are areas of high uncertainty. Managers use political tactics, including building coalitions, expanding networks, controlling decision premises, enhancing legitimacy, and making a direct appeal, to help their departments achieve desired outcomes.

Although conflict and political behavior are natural and can be used for beneficial purposes, managers also strive to enhance collaboration so that conflict between groups does not become too strong. Tactics for enhancing collaboration include integration devices, confrontation and negotiation, intergroup consultation, member rotation, and shared mission and superordinate goals.

Key Concepts

authority	empowerment	political tactics for using power
centrality	intergroup conflict	power
collective bargaining	labor–management teams	power sources
competition	negotiation	rational model
confrontation	network centrality	sources of intergroup conflict
decision premises	nonsubstitutability	strategic contingencies
dependency	organizational politics	tactics for enhancing collaboration
domains of political activity	political model	tactics for increasing power

Discussion Questions

1. Discuss ways in which a department at a health insurance company might help the organization cope with the increased power of large hospital systems such as Carilion by obtaining prior information, prevention, or absorption.

2. Some researchers argue that the concept of exchange underlying the principle of reciprocity (trading something of value to another for what you want) is the basis of *all* influence. Do you agree? Discuss. To what extent do you feel obligated to return a favor that is done for you?

3. What is the difference between power and authority? Is it possible for a person to have formal authority but no real power? Discuss.

4. The engineering college at a major university brings in three times as many government research dollars as does the rest of the university combined. Engineering appears wealthy and has many professors on full-time research status. Yet, when internal research funds are allocated, engineering gets a larger share of the money, even though it already has substantial external research funds. Why would this happen?

5. In a rapidly changing organization, are decisions more likely to be made using the rational or political model of organization? Discuss.

6. A financial analyst at Merrill Lynch tried for several months to expose the risks of investments in subprime mortgages, but he couldn't get anyone to pay attention to his claims. How would you evaluate this employee's power? What might he have done to increase his power and call notice to the impending problems at the firm?

7. As will be discussed in Chapter 10, consumer products giant Procter & Gamble and Internet leader Google have entered into a marketing partnership. What organizational and environmental factors might determine which organization will have more power in the relationship?

8. State University X receives 90 percent of its financial resources from the state and is overcrowded with students. It is trying to pass regulations to limit student enrollment. Private University Y receives 90 percent of its income from student tuition and has barely enough

students to make ends meet. It is actively recruiting students for next year. In which university will students have greater power? What implications will this have for professors and administrators? Discuss.

9. Give an example from your personal experience of how differences in tasks, personal background, and training lead to conflict among groups. How might task interdependence have influenced that conflict?

10. In Exhibit 7.5, R&D has greater power in company B than in the other firms. Discuss possible strategic contingencies that might give R&D greater power in this firm.

Chapter 7 Workbook: How Do You Handle Conflict?*

Think of some disagreements you have had with a friend, relative, manager, or co-worker. Then indicate how frequently you engage in each of the following behaviors.

There are no right or wrong answers. Respond to all items using the following scale from 1 to 7:

Scale

Always	Very often	Often	Sometimes	Seldom	Very seldom	Never
1	2	3	4	5	6	7

_____ 1. I blend my ideas to create new alternatives for resolving a disagreement.
_____ 2. I shy away from topics that are sources of disputes.
_____ 3. I make my opinion known in a disagreement.
_____ 4. I suggest solutions that combine a variety of viewpoints.
_____ 5. I steer clear of disagreeable situations.
_____ 6. I give in a little on my ideas when the other person also gives in.
_____ 7. I avoid the other person when I suspect that he or she wants to discuss a disagreement.
_____ 8. I integrate arguments into a new solution from the issues raised in a dispute.
_____ 9. I will go 50–50 to reach a settlement.
_____ 10. I raise my voice when I'm trying to get the other person to accept my position.
_____ 11. I offer creative solutions in discussions of disagreements.
_____ 12. I keep quiet about my views in order to avoid disagreements.
_____ 13. I give in if the other person will meet me halfway.
_____ 14. I downplay the importance of a disagreement.
_____ 15. I reduce disagreements by making them seem insignificant.
_____ 16. I meet the other person at a midpoint in our differences.
_____ 17. I assert my opinion forcefully.
_____ 18. I dominate arguments until the other person understands my position.
_____ 19. I suggest we work together to create solutions to disagreements.
_____ 20. I try to use the other person's ideas to generate solutions to problems.
_____ 21. I offer tradeoffs to reach solutions in disagreements.
_____ 22. I argue insistently for my stance.
_____ 23. I withdraw when the other person confronts me about a controversial issue.
_____ 24. I sidestep disagreements when they arise.
_____ 25. I try to smooth over disagreements by making them appear unimportant.
_____ 26. I insist my position be accepted during a disagreement with the other person.
_____ 27. I make our differences seem less serious.
_____ 28. I hold my tongue rather than argue with the other person.
_____ 29. I ease conflict by claiming our differences are trivial.
_____ 30. I stand firm in expressing my viewpoints during a disagreement.

Scoring and Interpretation: Three categories of conflict-handling strategies are measured in this instrument: solution oriented, nonconfrontational, and control. By comparing your scores on the following three scales, you can see which of the three is your preferred conflict-handling strategy.

To calculate your three scores, add the individual scores for the items and divide by the number of items measuring the strategy. Then subtract each of the three mean scores from seven.

Solution oriented: Items 1, 4, 6, 8, 9, 11, 13, 16, 19, 20, 21 (total = 11)

Nonconfrontational: Items 2, 5, 7, 12, 14, 15, 23, 24, 25, 27, 28, 29 (total = 12)

Control: Items 3, 10, 17, 18, 22, 26, 30 (total = 7)

Solution-oriented strategies tend to focus on the problem rather than on the individuals involved. Solutions reached are often mutually beneficial, with neither party defining himself or herself as the winner and the other party as the loser.

Nonconfrontational strategies tend to focus on avoiding the conflict by either avoiding the other party or by simply allowing the other party to have his or her way.

These strategies are used when there is more concern with avoiding a confrontation than with the actual outcome of the problem situation.

Control strategies tend to focus on winning or achieving one's goals without regard for the other party's needs or desires. Individuals using these strategies often rely on rules and regulations in order to win the battle.

Questions

1. Which strategy do you find easiest to use? Most difficult? Which do you use more often?
2. How would your answers have differed if the other person was a friend, family member, or co-worker?
3. What is it about the conflict situation or strategy that tells you which strategy to use in dealing with a conflict situation?

*"How Do You Handle Conflict?" in Robert E. Quinn et al., *Becoming a Master Manager* (New York: Wiley, 1990), 221–223. Copyright 1990 by John Wiley & Sons, Inc. Reproduced with permission of John Wiley & Sons, Inc.

Case for Analysis: The Daily Tribune*

The *Daily Tribune* is the only daily newspaper serving a six-county region of eastern Tennessee. Even though its staff is small and it serves a region of mostly small towns and rural areas, the *Tribune* has won numerous awards for news coverage and photojournalism from the Tennessee Press Association and other organizations.

Rick Arnold became news editor almost fifteen years ago. He has spent his entire career with the *Tribune* and feels a great sense of pride that it has been recognized for its journalistic integrity and balanced coverage of issues and events. The paper has been able to attract bright, talented young writers and photographers thanks largely to Rick's commitment and his support of the news staff. In his early years, the newsroom was a dynamic, exciting place to work—reporters thrived on the fast pace and the chance to occasionally scoop the major daily paper in Knoxville.

But times have changed at the *Daily Tribune*. Over the past five years or so, the advertising department has continued to grow, in terms of both staff and budget, while the news department has begun to shrink. "Advertising pays the bills," publisher John Freeman reminded everyone at this month's managers' meeting. "Today, advertisers can go to direct mail, cable television, even the Internet, if they don't like what we're doing for them."

Rick has regularly clashed with the advertising department regarding news stories that are critical of major advertisers, but the conflicts have increased dramatically over the past few years. Now, Freeman is encouraging greater "horizontal collaboration," as he calls it, asking that managers in the news department and the ad department consult with one another regarding issues or stories that involve the paper's major advertisers. The move was prompted in part by a growing number of complaints from advertisers about stories they deemed unfair. "We print the news," Freeman said, "and I understand that sometimes we've got to print things that some people won't like. But we've got to find ways to be more advertiser-friendly. If we work together, we can develop strategies that both present good news coverage and serve to attract more advertisers."

Rick left the meeting fuming, and he didn't fail to make his contempt for the new "advertiser-friendly" approach known to all, including the advertising manager, Fred Thomas, as he headed down the hallway back to the newsroom. Lisa Lawrence, his managing editor, quietly agreed but pointed out that advertisers were readers too, and the newspaper had to listen to all its constituencies. "If we don't handle this carefully, we'll have Freeman and Thomas in here dictating to us what we can write and what we can't."

Lawrence has worked with Rick since he first came to the paper, and even though the two have had their share of conflicts, the relationship is primarily one of mutual respect and trust. "Let's just be careful," she emphasized. "Read the stories about big advertisers a little more carefully, make sure we can defend whatever we print, and it will all work out. I know this blurring of the line between advertising and editorial rubs you the wrong way, but Thomas is a reasonable man. We just need to keep him in the loop."

Late that afternoon, Rick received a story from one of his corresponding reporters that had been in the works for a couple of days. East Tennessee Healthcorp (ETH), which operated a string of health clinics throughout the region, was closing three of its rural clinics because of mounting financial woes. The reporter, Elisabeth Fraley, who lived in one of the communities, had learned about the closings from her neighbor, who worked as an accountant for ETH, before the announcement had been made just this afternoon. Fraley had written a compelling human-interest story about how the closings would leave people in two counties with essentially no access to health care, while clinics in larger towns that didn't really need them were being kept open. She had carefully interviewed both former patients of the clinics and ETH employees, including the director of one of the clinics and two high-level managers at the corporate office, and she had carefully documented her sources. After this morning's meeting, Rick knew he should run the story by Lisa Lawrence, since East Tennessee Healthcorp was one of the *Tribune's* biggest advertisers, but Lawrence had left for the day. And he simply couldn't bring himself to consult with the advertising department—that political nonsense was for Lawrence to handle. If he held the story for Lawrence's approval, it wouldn't make the Sunday edition. His only other option was to write a brief story simply reporting the closings and leaving out the human-interest aspect.

Rick was sure the major papers from Knoxville and other nearby cities would have the report in their Sunday papers, but none of them would have the time to develop as comprehensive and interesting an account as Fraley had presented. With a few quick strokes of the pen to make some minor editorial changes, Rick sent the story to production.

When he arrived at work the next day, Rick was called immediately to the publisher's office. He knew it was bad news for Freeman to be in on a Sunday. After some general yelling and screaming, Rick learned that tens of thousands of copies of the Sunday paper had been destroyed and a new edition printed. The advertising manager had called Freeman at home in the wee hours of Sunday morning and informed him of the ETH story, which was appearing the same day the corporation was running a full-page ad touting its service to the small towns and rural communities of East Tennessee.

"The story's accurate, and I assumed you'd want to take advantage of a chance to scoop the big papers," Rick began, but Freeman cut his argument short. "You could have just reported the basic facts without implying that the company doesn't care about the people of this region. The next time something like this happens, you'll find yourself and your reporters standing in the unemployment line!"

Rick had heard it before, but somehow this time he almost believed it. "What happened to the days when the primary purpose of a newspaper was to present the news?" Rick mumbled. "Now, it seems we have to dance to the tune played by the ad department."

*This case was inspired by G. Pascal Zachary, "Many Journalists See a Growing Reluctance to Criticize Advertisers," *The Wall Street Journal* (February 6, 1992), A1, A9; and G. Bruce Knecht, "Retail Chains Emerge as Advance Arbiters of Magazine Content," *The Wall Street Journal* (October 22, 1997), A1, A13.

Case for Analysis: Pierre Dux*

Pierre Dux sat quietly in his office considering the news. A third appointment to regional management had been announced and, once again, the promotion he had expected had been given to someone else. The explanations seemed insufficient this time. Clearly, this signaled the end to his career at INCO. Only one year ago, the company president had arrived at Dux's facility with national press coverage to publicize the success of his innovations in the management of manufacturing operations. The intervening year had brought improved operating results and further positive

publicity for the corporation but a string of personal disappointments for Pierre Dux.

Four years earlier, the INCO manufacturing plant had been one of the least productive of the thirteen facilities operating in Europe. Absenteeism and high employee turnover were symptoms of the low morale among the work group. These factors were reflected in mediocre production levels and the worst quality record in INCO. Pierre Dux had been in his current position one year and had derived his only satisfaction from the fact that these poor results might have been worse had he not instituted minor reforms in organizational communication. These allowed workers and supervisors to vent their concerns and frustrations. Although nothing substantial had changed during that first year, operating results had stabilized, ending a period of rapid decline. But this honeymoon was ending. The expectation of significant change was growing, particularly among workers who had been vocal in expressing their dissatisfaction and suggesting concrete proposals for change.

The change process, which had begun three years before, had centered on a redesign of production operations from a single machine-paced assembly line to a number of semi-autonomous assembly teams. Although the change had been referred to as the INCO "Volvo project" or "INCO's effort at Japanese-style management," it had really been neither of these. Rather, it had been the brainchild of a group of managers, led by Dux, who believed that both productivity and working conditions in the plant could be improved through a single effort. Of course, members of the group had visited other so-called innovative production facilities, but the new work groups and job classifications had been designed with the particular products and technology at INCO in mind.

After lengthy discussions among the management group, largely dedicated to reaching agreement on the general direction that the new project would take, the actual design began to emerge. Equally lengthy discussions (often referred to as negotiations) with members of the workforce, supervisors, and representatives of the local unions were part of the design process. The first restructuring into smaller work groups was tried in an experimental project that received tentative approval from top management in INCO headquarters and a "wait and see" response from the union. The strongest initial resistance had come from the plant engineers. They were sold neither on the new structure nor on the process of involving the workforce in the design of operating equipment and production methods. Previously, the engineering group had itself fulfilled these functions, and it felt the present problems were a result of a lack of skill among employees or managerial unwillingness to make the system work.

The experiment was staffed by volunteers supported by a few of the better-trained workers in the plant. The latter were necessary to ensure a start-up of the new equipment, which had been modified from the existing technology on the assembly line.

The initial experiment met with limited success. Although the group was able to meet the productivity levels of the existing line within a few weeks, critics of the new plan attributed the low level of success to the unrepresentative nature of the experimental group or the newness of the equipment on which they were working. However,

even this limited success attracted the attention of numerous people at INCO headquarters and in other plants. All were interested in seeing the new experiment. Visits soon became a major distraction, and Dux declared a temporary halt to permit the project to proceed, although this produced some muttering at headquarters about his "secretive" and "uncooperative" behavior.

Because of the experiment's success, Dux and his staff prepared to convert the entire production operation to the new system. The enthusiasm of workers in the plant grew as training for the changeover proceeded. In fact, a group of production workers asked to help with the installation of the new equipment as a means of learning more about its operation.

Dux and his staff were surprised at the difficulties encountered at this phase. Headquarters seemed to drag its feet in approving the necessary funding for the changeover. Even after the funding was approved, there was a stream of challenges to minor parts of the plan. "Can't you lay the workers off during the changeover?" "Why use workers on overtime to do the changeover when you could hire temporary workers more cheaply?" These criticisms reflected a lack of understanding of the basic operating principles of the new system, and Dux rejected them.

The conversion of the entire assembly line to work groups was finally achieved, with the local management group making few concessions from their stated plans. The initial change and the first days of operation were filled with crises. The design process had not anticipated many of the problems that arose with full-scale operations. However, Dux was pleased to see managers, staff, and workers clustered together at the trouble areas, fine-tuning the design when problems arose. Just as the start-up finally appeared to be moving forward, a change in product specifications from a headquarters group dictated additional changes in the design of the assembly process. The new changes were handled quickly and with enthusiasm by the workforce. While the period was exhausting and seemingly endless to those who felt responsible for the change, the new design took only six months to reach normal operating levels (one year had been forecast as the time needed to reach that level—without the added requirement for a change in product specifications).

Within a year, Dux was certain that he had a major success on his hands. Productivity and product quality measures for the plant had greatly improved. In this relatively short period his plant had moved from the worst, according to these indicators, to the third most productive in the INCO system. Absenteeism had dropped only slightly, but turnover had been reduced substantially. Morale was not measured formally but was considered by all members of the management team to be greatly improved. Now, after three years of full operations, the plant was considered the most productive in the entire INCO system.

Dux was a bit surprised when no other facility in INCO initiated a similar effort or called upon him for help. Increases of the early years had leveled off, with the peak being achieved in the early part of year three. Now the facility seemed to have found a new equilibrium. The calm of smoother operations had been a welcome relief to many who had worked so hard to launch the new design. For Dux it provided the time to reflect on his accomplishment and think about his future career.

It was in this context that he considered the news that he had once again been bypassed for promotion to the next level in the INCO hierarchy.

*This case was prepared by Michael Brimm, Associate Professor of INSEAD. It is intended to be used as a basis for class discussion rather than to illustrate either effective or ineffective handling of an administrative situation. Copyright © 1983 INSEAD Foundation, Fontainebleau, France. Revised 1987.

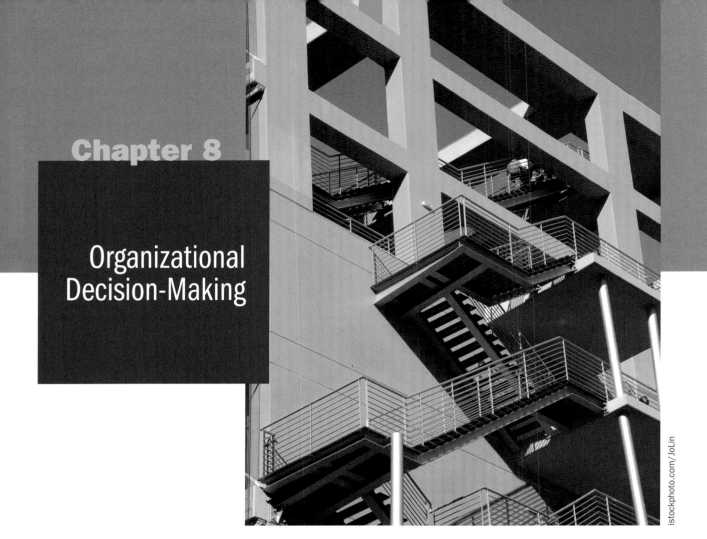

istockphoto.com/JoLin

Chapter 8

Organizational Decision-Making

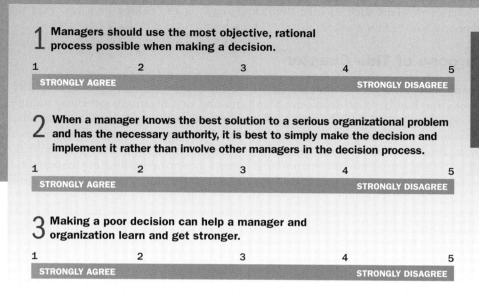

Before reading this chapter, please circle your opinion below for each of the following statements:

Managing by Design Questions

1 **Managers should use the most objective, rational process possible when making a decision.**

1	2	3	4	5
STRONGLY AGREE				STRONGLY DISAGREE

2 **When a manager knows the best solution to a serious organizational problem and has the necessary authority, it is best to simply make the decision and implement it rather than involve other managers in the decision process.**

1	2	3	4	5
STRONGLY AGREE				STRONGLY DISAGREE

3 **Making a poor decision can help a manager and organization learn and get stronger.**

1	2	3	4	5
STRONGLY AGREE				STRONGLY DISAGREE

What is one activity every manager—no matter what level of the hierarchy, what industry, or what size or type of organization—engages in every day? Decision making. Managers are often referred to as *decision makers*, and every organization grows, prospers, or fails as a result of the choices managers make. However, many decisions can be risky and uncertain, without any guarantee of success. Consider what happened at Merrill Lynch. The decision of top managers to invest heavily in the mortgage industry was paying off so well by the end of 2006 that they plunked down $1.3 billion to buy First Franklin, a lender that specialized in making risky mortgages. Pushing further, managers significantly increased Merrill's involvement with exotic and complex derivatives tied to mortgages. The profit potential was huge, so Merrill jumped in even without a clear strategy or well-considered plans for managing this aspect of the business. When the mortgage meltdown began, Merrill was caught in the crossfire. In the first nine months of 2008, the firm recorded net losses of $14.7 billion on its mortgage-related derivatives and the once-venerable firm was taken over by Bank of America.[1]

Merrill Lynch is by no means the only firm that was devastated due to faulty decisions related to the mortgage industry, but it provides an illustration of the uncertainty that characterizes many manager decisions, especially at higher organizational levels. Decision making is done amid constantly changing factors, unclear information, and conflicting points of view, and even the best managers in the most successful companies sometimes make big blunders. Look at Starbucks. A few years ago, it seemed the company could do no wrong. But in an effort to meet dramatic growth goals, managers relaxed their rigorous standards for selecting new store locations and ended up opening many stores in locations that couldn't support them. In 2008, Starbucks began closing hundreds of underperforming stores, many of them opened less than two years earlier.[2]

Yet managers also make many successful decisions every day. Apple, which seemed all but dead in the mid-1990s, topped *Fortune* magazine's list of the world's most admired companies in 2008 thanks to decisions made by CEO Steve Jobs and other top managers.[3] Managers at General Mills are known for making hundreds

of small decisions that add up big. For example, the decision to consolidate the purchases of items such as oils, flour, and sugar in the baking division saves the company $12 billion a year.[4]

Purpose of This Chapter

At any time, an organization may be identifying problems and implementing alternatives for hundreds of decisions. Managers and organizations somehow muddle through these processes.[5] The purpose here is to analyze these processes to learn what decision making is actually like in organizational settings. Decision-making processes can be thought of as the brain and nervous system of an organization. Decision making is the end use of the information and control systems described in Chapter 11.

First, the chapter defines decision making and the different types of decisions managers make. The next section describes an ideal model of decision making and then examines how individual managers actually make decisions. The chapter also explores several models of organizational decision making, each of which is appropriate in a different organizational situation. The next section combines the models into a single framework that describes when and how the various approaches should be used. Finally, the chapter discusses special issues related to decision making, such as high-velocity environments, decision mistakes and learning, and ways to overcome cognitive biases that hinder effective decision making.

DEFINITIONS

Organizational decision making is formally defined as the process of identifying and solving problems. The process has two major stages. In the **problem identification** stage, information about environmental and organizational conditions is monitored to determine if performance is satisfactory and to diagnose the cause of shortcomings. The **problem solution** stage is when alternative courses of action are considered and one alternative is selected and implemented.

Organizational decisions vary in complexity and can be categorized as programmed or nonprogrammed.[6] **Programmed decisions** are repetitive and well defined, and procedures exist for resolving the problem. They are well structured because criteria of performance are normally clear, good information is available about current performance, alternatives are easily specified, and there is relative certainty that the chosen alternative will be successful. Examples of programmed decisions include decision rules, such as when to replace an office copy machine, when to reimburse managers for travel expenses, or whether an applicant has sufficient qualifications for an assembly-line job. Many companies adopt rules based on experience with programmed decisions. For example, a rule for large hotels staffing banquets is to allow one server per thirty guests for a sit-down function and one server per forty guests for a buffet.[7]

Nonprogrammed decisions are novel and poorly defined, and no procedure exists for solving the problem. They are used when an organization has not seen a problem before and may not know how to respond. Clear-cut decision criteria do not exist. Alternatives are fuzzy. There is uncertainty about whether a proposed solution will solve the problem. Typically, few alternatives can be developed for a nonprogrammed decision, so a single solution is custom-tailored to the problem.

Many nonprogrammed decisions involve strategic planning, because uncertainty is great and decisions are complex. One example comes from Dell Inc., where founder Michael Dell has returned as CEO to try to revive the ailing company. Dell's low-cost

Briefcase

As an organization manager, keep these guidelines in mind:

Adapt decision processes to fit the organizational situation. Understand how processes differ for programmed and nonprogrammed decisions.

business model of selling PCs directly to consumers is no longer successful, but managers are having a hard time coming up with the right strategy to help the company move into a new era. Dell's recent decisions involve cost-cutting measures such as layoffs and selling off factories; investing in new products such as a portable music player and a mobile phone; and adding services such as running corporate in-house networks. However, these types of decisions are very complex, and there's no guarantee that a particular choice will succeed. The decision to enter the phone market, for instance, has been put on hold because of the high cost of development and the uncertain market.[8]

Particularly complex nonprogrammed decisions have been referred to as "wicked" decisions, because simply defining the problem can turn into a major task. Wicked problems are associated with manager conflicts over objectives and alternatives, rapidly changing circumstances, and unclear linkages among decision elements. Managers dealing with a wicked decision may hit on a solution that merely proves they failed to correctly define the problem to begin with.[9] Under conditions of such extreme uncertainty, even a good choice can produce a bad outcome.[10] Making the decision about how to turn around a company like Dell could be considered a wicked decision, as could decisions about how to revive the U.S. automakers.

Managers and organizations are dealing with a higher percentage of nonprogrammed decisions because of the rapidly changing business environment. As outlined in Exhibit 8.1, today's environment has increased both the number and complexity of decisions that have to be made and has created a need for new decision-making

EXHIBIT 8.1
Decision Making in Today's Environment

Today's Business Environment

- *Demands more large-scale change via new strategies, reengineering, restructuring, mergers, acquisitions, downsizing, new product or market development, and so on*

Decisions Made Inside the Organization

- *Are based on bigger, more complex, more emotionally charged issues*
- *Are made more quickly*
- *Are made in a less certain environment, with less clarity about means and outcomes*
- *Require more cooperation from more people involved in making and implementing decisions*

A New Decision-Making Process

- *Is required because no one individual has the information needed to make all major decisions*
- *Is required because no one individual has the time and credibility needed to convince lots of people to implement the decision*
- *Relies less on hard data as a basis for good decisions*
- *Is guided by a powerful coalition that can act as a team*
- *Permits decisions to evolve through trial and error and incremental steps as needed*

Source: Reprinted by permission of Harvard Business School Press. From *Leading Change* by John P. Kotter. Boston, MA, 1996, p. 56. Copyright © 1996 by the Harvard Business School Publishing Corporation, all rights reserved.

processes. Managers in rapidly changing e-business departments, for example, often have to make quick decisions based on very limited information. Another example is globalization. The trend toward moving production to low-wage countries has managers all over corporate America struggling with ethical decisions concerning working conditions in the Third World and the loss of jobs in small U.S. communities where there are few employment opportunities.[11]

INDIVIDUAL DECISION MAKING

Individual decision making by managers can be described in two ways. First is the **rational approach**, which suggests an ideal method for how managers should try to make decisions. Second is the **bounded rationality perspective**, which describes how decisions actually have to be made under severe time and resource constraints. The rational approach is an ideal that managers may work toward but never reach.

Rational Approach

The rational approach to individual decision making stresses the need for systematic analysis of a problem followed by choice and implementation in a logical, step-by-step sequence. The rational approach was developed to guide individual decision making because many managers were observed to be unsystematic and arbitrary in their approach to organizational decisions.

Although the rational model is an ideal not fully achievable in the real world of uncertainty, complexity, and rapid change highlighted in Exhibit 8.1, the model does help managers think about decisions more clearly and rationally. Managers should use systematic procedures to make decisions whenever possible. When managers have a deep understanding of the rational decision-making process, it can help them make better decisions even when there is a lack of clear information. The authors of a popular book on decision making use the example of the U.S. Marines, who have a reputation for handling complex problems quickly and decisively. The Marines are trained to quickly go through a series of mental routines that help them analyze the situation and take action.[12]

According to the rational approach, decision making can be broken down into eight steps, as illustrated in Exhibit 8.2 and demonstrated by the department store Marshall Field's in the following discussion.[13]

1. *Monitor the decision environment.*   In the first step, a manager monitors internal and external information that will indicate deviations from planned or acceptable behavior. He or she talks to colleagues and reviews financial statements, performance evaluations, industry indices, competitors' activities, and so forth. For example, during the pressure-packed five-week Christmas season, Linda Koslow, general manager of Marshall Field's Oakbrook, Illinois, store, checks out competitors around the mall, eyeing whether they are marking down merchandise. She also scans printouts of her store's previous day's sales to learn what is or is not moving.[14]
2. *Define the decision problem.*   The manager responds to deviations by identifying essential details of the problem: where, when, who was involved, who was affected, and how current activities are influenced. For Koslow, this means defining whether store profits are low because overall sales are less than expected or because certain lines of merchandise are not moving as expected.
3. *Specify decision objectives.*   The manager determines what performance outcomes should be achieved by a decision.

EXHIBIT 8.2
Steps in the Rational
Approach to Decision
Making

4. *Diagnose the problem.*   In this step, the manager digs below the surface to analyze the cause of the problem. Additional data might be gathered to facilitate this diagnosis. Understanding the cause enables appropriate treatment. For Koslow at Marshall Field's, the cause of slow sales might be competitors' marking down of merchandise or Marshall Field's failure to display hot-selling items in a visible location.

5. *Develop alternative solutions.*   Before a manager can move ahead with a decisive action plan, he or she must have a clear understanding of the various options available to achieve desired objectives. The manager may seek ideas and suggestions from other people. Koslow's alternatives for increasing profits could include buying fresh merchandise, running a sale, or reducing the number of employees.

6. *Evaluate alternatives.*   This step may involve the use of statistical techniques or personal experience to gauge the probability of success. The merits of each alternative are assessed, as well as the probability that it will achieve the desired objectives.

7. *Choose the best alternative.*   This step is when the manager uses his or her analysis of the problem, objectives, and alternatives to select a single alternative that has the best chance for success. At Marshall Field's, Koslow may choose to reduce the number of staff as a way to meet the profit goals rather than increase advertising or markdowns.

8. *Implement the chosen alternative.* Finally, the manager uses managerial, administrative, and persuasive abilities and gives directions to ensure that the decision is carried out, sometimes called *execution* of the decision. This might be considered the core of the decision process because any decision that isn't successfully implemented is a failed decision, no matter how good the chosen alternative might be.[15] Managers have to mobilize the people and resources to put the decision into action. Execution may be the hardest step of decision making. The monitoring activity (step 1) begins again as soon as the solution is implemented. For Linda Koslow, the decision cycle is a continuous process, with new decisions made daily based on monitoring her environment for problems and opportunities.

The first four steps in this sequence are the problem identification stage, and the next four steps are the problem solution stage of decision making, as indicated in Exhibit 8.2. A manager normally goes through all eight steps in making a decision, although each step may not be a distinct element. Managers may know from experience exactly what to do in a situation, so one or more steps will be minimized. The following "In Practice" illustrates how the rational approach is used to make a decision about a personnel problem.

IN PRACTICE

Saskatchewan Consulting

1. *Monitor the decision environment.* It is Monday morning, and Joe DeFoe, Saskatchewan Consulting's accounts receivable supervisor, is absent again.

2. *Define the decision problem.* This is the fourth consecutive Monday DeFoe has been absent. Company policy forbids unexcused absenteeism, and DeFoe has been warned about his excessive absenteeism on the last two occasions. A final warning is in order but can be delayed, if warranted.

3. *Specify decision objectives.* DeFoe should attend work regularly and establish the invoice collection levels of which he is capable. The time period for solving the problem is two weeks.

4. *Diagnose the problem.* Discreet discussions with DeFoe's co-workers and information gleaned from DeFoe indicate that DeFoe has a drinking problem. He apparently uses Mondays to dry out from weekend benders. Discussion with other company sources confirms that DeFoe is a problem drinker.

5. *Develop alternative solutions.* (1) Fire DeFoe. (2) Issue a final warning without comment. (3) Issue a warning and accuse DeFoe of being an alcoholic to let him know you are aware of his problem. (4) Talk with DeFoe to see if he will discuss his drinking. If he admits he has a drinking problem, delay the final warning and suggest that he enroll in the company's new employee assistance program for help with personal problems, including alcoholism. (5) Talk with DeFoe to see if he will discuss his drinking. If he does not admit he has a drinking problem, let him know that the next absence will cost him his job.

6. *Evaluate alternatives.* The cost of training a replacement is the same for each alternative. Alternative 1 ignores cost and other criteria. Alternatives 2 and 3 do not adhere to company policy, which advocates counseling where appropriate. Alternative 4 is designed for the benefit of both DeFoe and the company. It might save a good employee if DeFoe is willing to seek assistance. Alternative 5 is primarily for the benefit of the company. A final warning might provide some incentive for DeFoe to admit he has a drinking problem. If so, dismissal might be avoided, but further absences will no longer be tolerated.

7. *Choose the best alternative.* DeFoe does not admit that he has a drinking problem. Choose alternative 5.

8. *Implement the chosen alternative.* Write up the case and issue the final warning.[16] ■

In the preceding example, issuing the final warning to Joe DeFoe was a programmed decision. The standard of expected behavior was clearly defined, information on the frequency and cause of DeFoe's absence was readily available, and acceptable alternatives and procedures were described. The rational procedure works best in such cases, when the decision maker has sufficient time for an orderly, thoughtful process. Moreover, Saskatchewan Consulting had mechanisms in place to successfully implement the decision once it was made.

When decisions are nonprogrammed, ill-defined, and piling on top of one another, the individual manager should still try to use the steps in the rational approach, but he or she often will have to take shortcuts by relying on intuition and experience. Deviations from the rational approach are explained by the bounded rationality perspective.

Bounded Rationality Perspective

The point of the rational approach is that managers should try to use systematic procedures to arrive at good decisions. When managers are dealing with well-understood issues, they generally use rational procedures to make decisions.[17] Yet research into managerial decision making shows that managers often are unable to follow an ideal procedure. Many decisions must be made very quickly. Time pressure, a large number of internal and external factors affecting a decision, and the ill-defined nature of many problems make systematic analysis virtually impossible. Managers have only so much time and mental capacity and, hence, cannot evaluate every goal, problem, and alternative. The attempt to be rational is bounded (limited) by the enormous complexity of many problems. There is a limit to how rational managers can be.

To understand the bounded rationality approach, think about how most new managers select a job upon graduation from college. Even this seemingly simple decision can quickly become so complex that a bounded rationality approach is used. Graduating students typically will search for a job until they have two or three acceptable job offers, at which point their search activity rapidly diminishes. Hundreds of firms may be available for interviews, and two or three job offers are far short of the maximum number that would be possible if students made the decision based on perfect rationality.

Constraints and Tradeoffs. Not only are large organizational decisions too complex to fully comprehend, but several other constraints impinge on the decision maker, as illustrated in Exhibit 8.3. For many decisions, the organizational circumstances are ambiguous, requiring social support, a shared perspective on what happens, and acceptance and agreement. For example, consider the early U.S. decision to disband the Iraqi army and rebuild security forces from the ground up. Critics say the decision was pushed through by the senior civilian officer in Iraq without consulting military commanders and other U.S. officials who had different views of how to build the new Iraqi military. Disagreements over the momentous decision and ongoing recriminations made it much more difficult for the U.S. military to deal with the vast array of security problems that followed. Without any sizeable Iraqi force to subdue the growing violence, American troops became targets of attack and criticism. In addition, U.S. leaders' lack of agreement to use military force to stop the looting that occurred when troops first entered Iraq alienated many Iraqi citizens, allowed insurgents to gain strength, and made it more difficult to implement

EXHIBIT 8.3
Constraints and
Tradeoffs during
Nonprogrammed Decision
Making

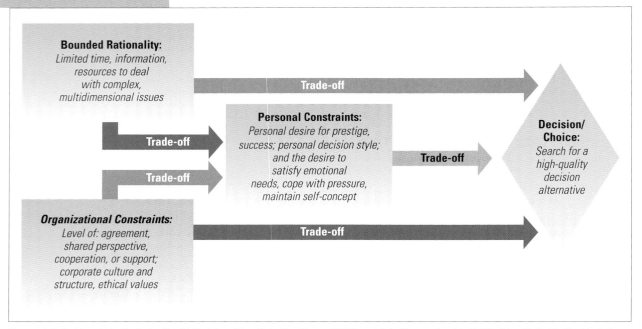

Source: Adapted from Irving L. Janis, *Crucial Decisions* (New York: Free Press, 1989); and A. L. George, *Presidential Decision Making in Foreign Policy: The Effective Use of Information and Advice* (Boulder, Colo.: Westview Press, 1980).

later police and military decisions.[18] Other organizational constraints on decision making outlined in Exhibit 8.3 include corporate culture and ethical values, as will be discussed in Chapter 9, and the organization's structure and design.

At the personal level, managers often make decisions within a context of trying to please upper managers, people who are perceived to have power within the organization, or others they respect and want to emulate.[19] Personal constraints—such as decision style, work pressure, desire for prestige, or simple feelings of insecurity—may constrain either the search for alternatives or the acceptability of an alternative. All of these factors constrain a perfectly rational approach that should lead to an obviously ideal choice.[20]

The Role of Intuition. The bounded rationality perspective is often associated with intuitive decision processes. In **intuitive decision making**, experience and judgment rather than sequential logic or explicit reasoning are used to make decisions.[21] Go to the "How Do You Fit the Design?" box for some insight into your use of rationality versus intuition in making decisions. Intuition is not arbitrary or irrational because it is based on years of practice and hands-on experience, often stored in the subconscious. When managers use their intuition based on long experience with organizational issues, they more rapidly perceive and understand problems, and they develop a gut feeling or hunch about which alternative will solve a

How Do You Fit the Design?

Making Important Decisions

How do you make important decisions? To find out, think about a time when you made an important career decision or made a major purchase or investment. To what extent does each of the following words describe how you reached the final decision? Please check five words that best describe how you made your final choice.

1. Logic_____
2. Inner knowing_____
3. Data_____
4. Felt sense_____
5. Facts_____
6. Instincts_____
7. Concepts_____
8. Hunch_____
9. Reason_____
10. Feelings_____

Scoring: Give yourself one point for each odd-numbered item you checked, and subtract one point for each even-numbered item you checked. The highest possible score is +5 and the lowest possible score is −5.

Interpretation: The odd-numbered items pertain to a linear decision style and the even-numbered items pertain to a nonlinear decision approach. Linear means using logical *rationality* to make decisions, which would be similar to the decision process in Exhibit 8.2. Nonlinear means to use primarily *intuition* to make decisions, as described in the text. If you scored from −3 to −5, then intuition and a satisficing model is your dominant approach to major decisions. If you score +3 to +5, then the rational model of decision making as described in the text is your dominant approach. The rational approach is taught in business schools, but many managers use intuition based on experience, especially at senior management levels when there is little tangible data to evaluate.

Source: Adapted from Charles M. Vance, Kevin S. Groves, Yongsun Paik, and Herb Kindler, "Understanding and Measuring Linear–Nonlinear Thinking Style for Enhanced Management Education and Professional Practice, *Academy of Management Learning & Education,* 6, no. 2 (2007), 167– 185.

problem, speeding the decision-making process.[22] The value of intuition for effective decision making is supported by a growing body of research from psychology, organizational science, and other disciplines.[23] Indeed, many universities are offering courses in creativity and intuition so business students can learn to use these processes effectively.

In a situation of great complexity or ambiguity, previous experience and judgment are needed to incorporate intangible elements at both the problem identification and problem solution stages.[24] A study of manager problem finding showed that thirty of thirty-three problems were ambiguous and ill-defined.[25] Bits and scraps of unrelated information from informal sources resulted in a pattern in the manager's mind. The manager could not prove a problem existed but knew intuitively that a certain area needed attention. A too-simple view of a complex problem is often associated with decision failure,[26] so managers learn to listen to their intuition rather than accepting that things are going okay.

Intuitive processes are also used in the problem solution stage. Executives frequently make decisions without explicit reference to the impact on profits or to other measurable outcomes.[27] As we saw in Exhibit 8.3, many intangible factors—such as a person's concern about the support of other executives, fear of failure, and social attitudes—influence selection of the best alternative. These factors cannot be quantified in a systematic way, so intuition guides the choice of a solution. Managers may make a decision based on what they sense to be right rather than on what they can document with hard data. A survey of managers conducted by executive search firm Christian & Timbers found that 45 percent of corporate executives say they rely more on instinct than on facts and figures to make business decisions.[28]

ASSESS YOUR ANSWER

1 **Managers should use the most objective, rational process possible when making a decision.**

ANSWER: *Disagree.* Striving for perfect rationality in decisions is ideal, but not realistic. Many complex decisions do not lend themselves to a step-by-step analytical process. There are also numerous constraints on decision makers. When making nonprogrammed decisions, managers may try to follow the steps in the rational decision making process, but they also have to rely on experience and intuition.

Stefan Pierer, CEO of KTM Fahrrad GmbH, a large manufacturer of motorcycles with headquarters in Austria, considers intuition critical to good decision making. Two years after Pierer became CEO, he made a decision many thought was foolish: he moved KTM, a leader in the manufacture of off-road motorcycles, into the market for street bikes. Even though the company lacked technical know-how to make street bikes and had little access to this new market, Pierer's intuition told him it was the right move. It paid off. KTM quickly became Europe's second largest sport-motorcycle manufacturer, and by 2006, nearly 30 percent of revenues came from the street bike segment.[29] However, there are also many examples of intuitive decisions that turned out to be complete failures.[30]

Managers may walk a fine line between two extremes: on the one hand, making arbitrary decisions without careful study, and on the other, relying obsessively on numbers and rational analysis.[31] Remember that the bounded rationality perspective and the use of intuition apply mostly to nonprogrammed decisions. The novel, unclear, complex aspects of nonprogrammed decisions mean hard data and logical procedures are not available. Studies of executive decision making find that managers simply cannot use the rational approach for nonprogrammed strategic decisions, such as whether to market a controversial new prescription drug, whether to invest in a complex new project, or whether a city has a need for and can reasonably adopt an enterprise resource planning system.[32] For decisions such as these, managers have limited time and resources, and some factors simply cannot be measured and analyzed. Trying to quantify such information could cause mistakes because it may oversimplify decision criteria. Intuition can also balance and supplement rational analysis to help managers make better decisions.

ORGANIZATIONAL DECISION MAKING

Organizations are composed of managers who make decisions using both rational and intuitive processes; but organization-level decisions are not usually made by a single manager. Many organizational decisions involve several managers. Problem identification and problem solution involve many departments, multiple viewpoints, and even other organizations, which are beyond the scope of an individual manager.

The processes by which decisions are made in organizations are influenced by a number of factors, particularly the organization's own internal structures and the degree of stability or instability of the external environment.[33] Research into organization-level decision making has identified four primary types of organizational decision-making processes: the management science approach, the Carnegie model, the incremental decision model, and the garbage can model.

Management Science Approach

The **management science approach** to organizational decision making is the analog to the rational approach by individual managers. Management science came into being during World War II.[34] At that time, mathematical and statistical techniques were applied to urgent, large-scale military problems that were beyond the ability of individual decision makers.

Mathematicians, physicists, and operations researchers used systems analysis to develop artillery trajectories, antisubmarine strategies, and bombing strategies such as salvoing (discharging multiple shells simultaneously). Consider the problem of a battleship trying to sink an enemy ship several miles away. The calculation for aiming the battleship's guns should consider distance, wind speed, shell size, speed and direction of both ships, pitch and roll of the firing ship, and curvature of the earth. Methods for performing such calculations using trial and error and intuition are not accurate, take far too long, and may never achieve success.

This is where management science came in. Analysts were able to identify the relevant variables involved in aiming a ship's guns and could model them with the use of mathematical equations. Distance, speed, pitch, roll, shell size, and so on could be calculated and entered into the equations. The answer was immediate, and the guns could begin firing. Factors such as pitch and roll were soon measured mechanically and fed directly into the targeting mechanism. Today, the human element is completely removed from the targeting process. Radar picks up the target, and the entire sequence is computed automatically.

Management science yielded astonishing success for many military problems. This approach to decision making diffused into corporations and business schools, where techniques were studied and elaborated. Operations research departments use mathematical models to quantify relevant variables and develop a quantitative representation of alternative solutions and the probability of each one solving the problem. These departments also use such devices as linear programming, Bayesian statistics, PERT charts, and computer simulations.

Management science is an excellent device for organizational decision making when problems are analyzable and when the variables can be identified and measured. Mathematical models can contain a thousand or more variables, each

Briefcase

As an organization manager, keep these guidelines in mind:

Use a rational decision approach—computation, management science—when a problem situation is well understood and can be broken down into variables that can be measured and analyzed.

one relevant in some way to the ultimate outcome. Management science techniques have been used to correctly solve problems as diverse as finding the right spot for a church camp, test-marketing the first of a new family of products, drilling for oil, and radically altering the distribution of telecommunications services.[35] Other problems amenable to management science techniques are the scheduling of ambulance technicians, turnpike toll collectors, and airline crew members.[36] United Airlines is also applying management science techniques to decide how to route planes most efficiently.

United Airlines

In the past, a United Airlines plane bound for Frankfurt from San Francisco would follow a standard path, flying over Montana, then northeast over Canada and Iceland. But thanks to new route-mapping software, the plane can now stay in U.S. airspace until around Cleveland or Detroit. That cuts both United's fuel usage and its Canadian "overfly" fee (most countries charge a fee for using their airspace). Total savings: about $1,400 per plane one way.

Airlines are desperate to cut expenses any way they can, and route-mapping software that helps pilots and dispatchers find the best balance of fuel usage, flight speed, and flight path is one of the newest approaches. United's computers track a massive amount of data, including overflight fees charged by various countries, up-to-the-minute wind and weather conditions, fuel costs, airport locations and available runways, weight and performance of each plane, temporarily blocked airspace, and the location of fixed air routes. The system evaluates multiple scenarios to determine the best solution for the maximum payload.

Before these sophisticated computer systems, dispatchers constructed flight paths manually, poring over manuals from the aircraft manufacturer, analyzing weather patterns and wind data, and so forth, to calculate fuel needs and plan routes. United estimates that the new computerized system will save more than $20 million a year. Most of the major airlines, including Southwest, Lufthansa AG, Delta, Continental, Air Canada, American Airlines, British Airways, Singapore Airlines, and Northwest Airlines, use similar types of routing software. "In the operating world of an airline," said Captain Richard Sowden of Air Canada, "the flight-planning system is absolutely critical to cost control."[37] ■

The airlines have long been big users of management science techniques because many of the problems they encounter are analyzable and measurable and can be structured in a logical way. Management science, especially with increasingly sophisticated computer technology and software, can accurately and quickly solve problems that have too many explicit variables for adequate human processing. Management science is covering a broader range of problems than ever before. For example, rather than relying on hunches, advertising firms like Efficient Frontier, a Silicon Valley startup, use software to optimize online ad campaigns. The software can easily calculate response rates and return on investment for every advertisement. Many retailers, including Home Depot, Bloomingdale's, and Gap, use software to analyze current and historical sales data and determine when, where, and how much to mark down prices. Food and beverage companies are using mathematical formulas to precisely study customer data and make decisions about which new products to develop and how to market them. Even doctors' offices are turning to management science to manage their practices more efficiently, such as by predicting demand for appointments based on the number of patients in their practice, the average no-show rate, and other factors.[38]

One problem with the management science approach is that quantitative data are not rich and do not convey tacit knowledge. Informal cues that indicate the existence of problems have to be sensed on a more personal basis by managers.[39] The most sophisticated mathematical analyses are of no value if the important factors cannot be quantified and included in the model. Such things as competitor reactions, consumer tastes, and product warmth are qualitative dimensions. In these situations, the role of management science is to supplement manager decision making. Quantitative results can be given to managers for discussion and interpretation along with their informal opinions, judgment, and intuition. The final decision can include both qualitative factors and quantitative calculations.

Carnegie Model

The **Carnegie model** of organizational decision making is based on the work of Richard Cyert, James March, and Herbert Simon, who were all associated with Carnegie-Mellon University.[40] Their research helped formulate the bounded rationality approach to individual decision making, as well as provide new insights about organizational decisions.

Until their work, research in economics assumed that business firms made decisions as a single entity, as if all relevant information were funneled to the top decision maker for a choice. Research by the Carnegie group indicated that organization-level decisions involved many managers and that a final choice was based on a coalition among those managers. A **coalition** is an alliance among several managers who agree about organizational goals and problem priorities.[41] It could include managers from line departments, staff specialists, and even external groups, such as powerful customers, bankers, or union representatives.

Management coalitions are needed during decision making for two reasons. First, organizational goals are often ambiguous, and operative goals of departments are often inconsistent. When goals are ambiguous and inconsistent, managers disagree about problem priorities. They must bargain about problems and build a coalition around the question of which problems to address.

The second reason for coalitions is that individual managers intend to be rational but function with human cognitive limitations and other constraints, as described earlier. Managers do not have the time, resources, or mental capacity to identify all dimensions and to process all information relevant to a decision. These limitations lead to coalition-building behavior. Managers talk to each other and exchange points of view to gather information and reduce ambiguity. People who have relevant information or a stake in a decision outcome are consulted. Building a coalition will lead to a decision that is supported by interested parties.

The process of coalition formation has several implications for organizational decision behavior. First, decisions are made to *satisfice* rather than to optimize problem solutions. **Satisficing** means organizations accept a satisfactory rather than a maximum level of performance, enabling them to achieve several goals simultaneously. In decision making, the coalition will accept a solution that is perceived as satisfactory to all coalition members. Second, managers are concerned with immediate problems and short-run solutions. They engage in what Cyert and March called *problemistic search*.[42]

Problemistic search means managers look around in the immediate environment for a solution to quickly resolve a problem. Managers don't expect a perfect solution when the situation is ill-defined and conflict-laden. This contrasts with the management science approach, which assumes that analysis can uncover every reasonable alternative. The Carnegie model says that search behavior is just sufficient to produce a satisfactory solution and that managers typically adopt the first satisfactory solution that emerges. Third, discussion and bargaining are especially important in the problem identification stage of decision making. Unless coalition members perceive a problem, action will not be taken.

The decision process described in the Carnegie model is summarized in Exhibit 8.4. The Carnegie model points out that building agreement through a managerial coalition is a major part of organizational decision making. This is especially true at upper management levels. Discussion and bargaining are time consuming, so search procedures are usually simple and the selected alternative satisfices rather than optimizes problem solution. When problems are programmed—are clear and have been seen before—the organization will rely on previous procedures and routines. Rules and procedures prevent the need for renewed coalition formation and political bargaining. Nonprogrammed decisions, however, require bargaining and conflict resolution.

Organizations suffer when managers are unable to build a coalition around goals and problem priorities. The U.S.-led war and reconstruction in Iraq have been plagued by disagreements and goal conflicts from the beginning, harming both security and reconstruction efforts and the Bush administration. For example, the 2007 decision to send 20,000 additional troops to carry out a new counterinsurgency strategy was successful in reversing the spiral of sectarian killings in Iraq. However, critics argue that the decision took too long because of disagreements among leaders

Briefcase

As an organization manager, keep these guidelines in mind:

Use a coalition-building approach when organizational goals and problem priorities are in conflict. When managers disagree about priorities or the true nature of the problem, they should discuss and seek agreement about priorities.

EXHIBIT 8.4
Choice Processes in the Carnegie Model

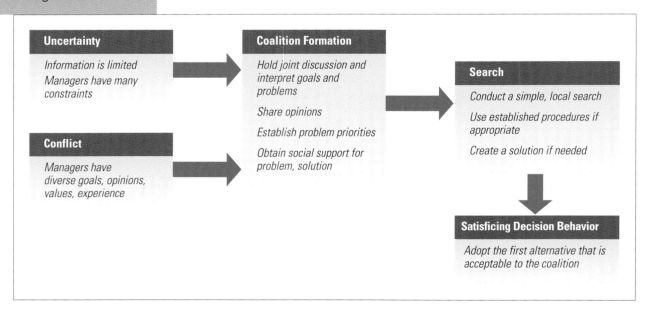

and Bush's difficulty in building a coalition to support his decision. One analysis said the conflicts and disagreements delayed the decision until conditions in Iraq resembled anarchy and civil war.[43]

The Carnegie model is particularly useful at the problem identification stage. However, a coalition of key department managers is also important for smooth implementation of a decision. When top managers perceive a problem or want to make a major decision, they need to reach agreement with other managers to support the decision.[44]

2 When a manager knows the best solution to a serious organizational problem and has the necessary authority, it is best to simply make the decision and implement it rather than involve other managers in the decision process.

ANSWER: *Disagree.* Few organizational decisions are made by a single manager. Organizational decision making is a social process that combines multiple perspectives. Managers have to talk to one another about problem priorities and exchange opinions and viewpoints to reach agreement. When managers don't build coalitions, important problems may go unsolved and good decisions may fail because other managers don't buy into the decisions and effectively implement them.

Incremental Decision Model

Henry Mintzberg and his associates at McGill University in Montreal approached organizational decision making from a different perspective. They identified twenty-five decisions made in organizations and traced the events associated with these decisions from beginning to end.[45] Their research identified each step in the decision sequence. This approach to decision making, called the **incremental decision model**, places less emphasis on the political and social factors described in the Carnegie model, but tells more about the structured sequence of activities undertaken from the discovery of a problem to its solution.[46]

Sample decisions in Mintzberg's research included choosing which jet aircraft to acquire for a regional airline, developing a new supper club, designing a new container terminal in a harbor, identifying a new market for a deodorant, installing a controversial new medical treatment in a hospital, and firing a star radio announcer.[47] The scope and importance of these decisions are revealed in the length of time taken to complete them. Most of these decisions took more than a year, and one-third of them took more than two years. Most of these decisions were nonprogrammed and required custom-designed solutions.

One discovery from this research is that major organizational choices are usually a series of small choices that combine to produce the major decision. Thus, many organizational decisions are a series of nibbles rather than a big bite. Organizations move through several decision points and may hit barriers along the way. Mintzberg called these barriers *decision interrupts*. An interrupt may mean an organization has to cycle back through a previous decision and try something new. Decision loops or cycles are one way the organization learns which alternatives will work. The ultimate solution may be very different from what was initially anticipated.

Briefcase

As an organization manager, keep these guidelines in mind:

Take risks and move the company ahead by increments when a problem is defined but solutions are uncertain. Try solutions step by step to learn whether they work.

The pattern of decision stages discovered by Mintzberg and his associates is shown in Exhibit 8.5. Each box indicates a possible step in the decision sequence. The steps take place in three major decision phases: identification, development, and selection.

Identification Phase. The identification phase begins with *recognition*. Recognition means one or more managers become aware of a problem and the need to make a decision. Recognition is usually stimulated by a problem or an opportunity. A problem exists when elements in the external environment change or when internal performance is perceived to be below standard. In the case of firing a radio announcer, comments about the announcer came from listeners, other announcers, and advertisers. Managers interpreted these cues until a pattern emerged that indicated a problem had to be dealt with.

The second step is *diagnosis*, in which more information is gathered if needed to define the problem situation. Diagnosis may be systematic or informal, depending upon the severity of the problem. Severe problems do not allow time for extensive diagnosis; the response must be immediate. Mild problems are usually diagnosed in a more systematic manner.

Development Phase. In the development phase, a solution is shaped to solve the problem defined in the identification phase. The development of a solution takes one of two directions. First, *search* procedures may be used to seek out alternatives within the organization's repertoire of solutions. For example, in the case of firing a star announcer, managers asked what the radio station had done the last time an announcer had to be let go. To conduct the search, organization participants may look into their own memories, talk to other managers, or examine the formal procedures of the organization.

The second direction of development is to *design* a custom solution. This happens when the problem is novel so that previous experience has no value. Mintzberg found that in these cases, key decision makers have only a vague idea of the ideal solution. Gradually, through a trial-and-error process, a custom-designed alternative will emerge. Development of the solution is a groping, incremental procedure, building a solution brick by brick.

Selection Phase. The selection phase is when the solution is chosen. This phase is not always a matter of making a clear choice among alternatives. In the case of custom-made solutions, selection is more an evaluation of the single alternative that seems feasible.

Evaluation and choice may be accomplished in three ways. The *judgment* form of selection is used when a final choice falls upon a single decision maker, and the choice involves judgment based upon experience. In *analysis*, alternatives are evaluated on a more systematic basis, such as with management science techniques. Mintzberg found that most decisions did not involve systematic analysis and evaluation of alternatives. *Bargaining* occurs when selection involves a group of decision makers. Each decision maker may have a different stake in the outcome, so conflict emerges. Discussion and bargaining occur until a coalition is formed, as in the Carnegie model described earlier.

When a decision is formally accepted by the organization, *authorization* takes place. The decision may be passed up the hierarchy to the responsible hierarchical level. Authorization is often routine because the expertise and knowledge rest with the lower-level decision makers who identified the problem and developed the

EXHIBIT 8.5
The Incremental Decision Model

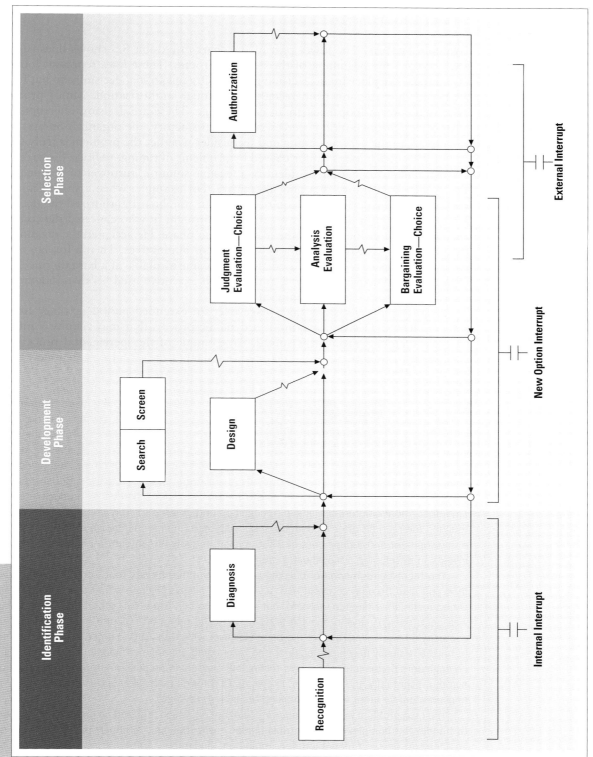

Source: *American Science Quarterly.* "Structure of Unstructured Decision Processes" by Henry Mintzberg, Duru Raisinghani, and André Théorêt vol. 21, pp. 246–275, June 1976. Reprinted by permission.

solution. A few decisions may be rejected because of implications not anticipated by lower-level managers.

Dynamic Factors. The lower part of the chart in Exhibit 8.5 shows lines running back toward the beginning of the decision process. These lines represent loops or cycles that take place in the decision process. Organizational decisions do not follow an orderly progression from recognition through authorization. Minor problems arise that force a loop back to an earlier stage. These are decision interrupts. If a custom-designed solution is perceived as unsatisfactory, the organization may have to go back to the very beginning and reconsider whether the problem is truly worth solving. Feedback loops can be caused by problems of timing, politics, disagreement among managers, inability to identify a feasible solution, turnover of managers, or the sudden appearance of a new alternative. For example, when a small Canadian airline made the decision to acquire jet aircraft, the board authorized the decision, but shortly after, a new chief executive was brought in who canceled the contract, recycling the decision back to the identification phase. He accepted the diagnosis of the problem but insisted upon a new search for alternatives. Then a foreign airline went out of business and two used aircraft became available at a bargain price. This presented an unexpected option, and the chief executive used his own judgment to authorize the purchase of the aircraft.[48]

Because most decisions take place over an extended period of time, circumstances change. Decision making is a dynamic process that may require a number of cycles before a problem is solved. An example of the incremental process and cycling that can take place is illustrated in Gillette's decision to create a new razor.

Gillette Company

The Gillette Company uses incremental decision making to perfect the design of razors such as the Mach3 Turbo, the vibrating M3Power, or the Fusion shaving system. Consider the development of the original Mach3. While searching for a new idea to increase sales in Gillette's mature shaving market, researchers at the company's British research lab came up with a bright idea to create a razor with three blades to produce a closer, smoother, more comfortable shave (recognition and diagnosis). Ten years later, the Mach3 reached the market, after thousands of shaving tests, numerous design modifications, and a development and tooling cost of $750 million, roughly the amount a pharmaceutical firm invests in developing a blockbuster drug.

The technical demands of building a razor with three blades that would follow a man's face and also be easy to clean had several blind alleys. Engineers first tried to find established techniques (search, screen), but none fit the bill. Eventually a prototype called Manx was built (design), and in shaving tests it "beat the pants off" Gillette's Sensor Excel, the company's best-selling razor at the time. However, Gillette's CEO insisted that the razor had to have a radically new blade edge so the razor could use thinner blades (internal interrupt), so engineers began looking for new technology that could produce a stronger blade (search, screen). Eventually, the new edge, known as DLC for diamond-like carbon coating, would be applied atom by atom with chip-making technology (design).

The next problem was manufacturing (diagnosis), which required an entirely new process to handle the complexity of the triple-bladed razor (design). Although the board gave the go-ahead to develop manufacturing equipment (judgment, authorization), some members became concerned because the new blades, which are three times stronger than stainless steel, would last longer and cause Gillette to sell fewer cartridges (internal interrupt). The board eventually made the decision to continue with the new blades, which have a blue indicator strip that fades to white and signals when it's time for a new cartridge.

The board gave final approval for production of the Mach3 to begin in the fall of 1997. The new razor was introduced in the summer of 1998 and began smoothly sliding off shelves. Gillette recovered its huge investment in record time. Gillette then started the process of searching for the next shaving breakthrough all over again, using new technology that can examine a razor blade at the atomic level and high-speed video that can capture the act of cutting a single whisker. The company moved ahead in increments and rolled out its next major shaving product, the five-bladed Fusion, in 2006.[49] ∎

At Gillette, the identification phase occurred because executives were aware of the need for a new razor and became alert to the idea of using three blades to produce a closer shave. The development phase was characterized by the trial-and-error custom design leading to the Mach3. During the selection phase, certain approaches were found to be unacceptable, causing Gillette to cycle back and redesign the razor, including using thinner, stronger blades. Advancing once again to the selection phase, the Mach3 passed the judgment of top executives and board members, and manufacturing and marketing budgets were quickly authorized. This decision took more than a decade, finally reaching completion in the summer of 1998.

ORGANIZATIONAL DECISIONS AND CHANGE

At the beginning of this chapter, we discussed how the rapidly changing business environment is creating greater uncertainty for decision makers. Many organizations are marked by a tremendous amount of uncertainty at both the problem identification and problem solution stages. Two approaches to decision making have evolved to help managers cope with this uncertainty and complexity. One approach is to combine the Carnegie and incremental models just described. The second is a unique approach called the garbage can model.

Combining the Incremental and Carnegie Models

The Carnegie description of coalition building is especially relevant for the problem identification stage. When issues are ambiguous, or if managers disagree about problem severity, discussion, negotiation, and coalition building are needed. The incremental model tends to emphasize the steps used to reach a solution. After managers agree on a problem, the step-by-step process is a way of trying various solutions to see what will work. When problem solution is unclear, a trial-and-error solution may be designed.

The application of the Carnegie and incremental models to the stages in the decision process is illustrated in Exhibit 8.6. The two models do not disagree with one another. They describe different approaches for how organizations make decisions when either problem identification or problem solution is uncertain. When both parts of the decision process are simultaneously highly uncertain, the organization

Briefcase

As an organization manager, keep these guidelines in mind:

Apply both the Carnegie model and the incremental process model in a situation with high uncertainty about both problems and solutions. Decision making may also employ garbage can procedures. Move the organization toward better performance by proposing new ideas, spending time working in important areas, and persisting with potential solutions.

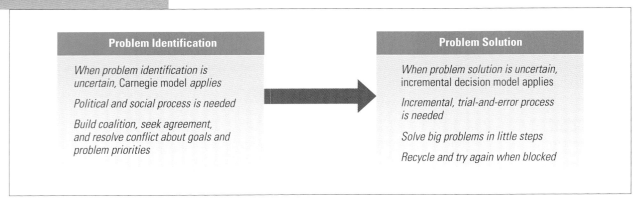

is in an extremely difficult position. Decision processes in that situation may be a combination of the Carnegie and incremental models, and this combination may evolve into a situation described in the garbage can model.

Garbage Can Model

The **garbage can model** is one of the most recent and interesting descriptions of organizational decision processes. It is not directly comparable to the earlier models, because the garbage can model deals with the pattern or flow of multiple decisions within organizations, whereas the incremental and Carnegie models focus on how a single decision is made. The garbage can model helps you think of the whole organization and the frequent decisions being made by managers throughout.

Organized Anarchy. The garbage can model was developed to explain the pattern of decision making in organizations that experience extremely high uncertainty. Michael Cohen, James March, and Johan Olsen, the originators of the model, called the highly uncertain conditions an **organized anarchy**, which is an extremely organic organization.[50] Organized anarchies do not rely on the normal vertical hierarchy of authority and bureaucratic decision rules. They result from three characteristics:

1. *Problematic preferences.* Goals, problems, alternatives, and solutions are ill-defined. Ambiguity characterizes each step of a decision process.
2. *Unclear, poorly understood technology.* Cause-and-effect relationships within the organization are difficult to identify. An explicit database that applies to decisions is not available.
3. *Turnover.* Organizational positions experience turnover of participants. In addition, employees are busy and have only limited time to allocate to any one problem or decision. Participation in any given decision will be fluid and limited.

An organized anarchy is characterized by rapid change and a collegial, nonbureaucratic environment. No organization fits this extremely organic circumstance all the time, although today's Internet-based companies, as well as organizations in rapidly changing industries, may experience it much of the time. Many organizations will occasionally find themselves in positions of making decisions under unclear, problematic circumstances. The garbage can model is useful for understanding the pattern of these decisions.

Streams of Events. The unique characteristic of the garbage can model is that the decision process is not seen as a sequence of steps that begins with a problem and ends with a solution. Indeed, problem identification and problem solution may not be connected to each other. An idea may be proposed as a solution when no problem is specified. A problem may exist and never generate a solution. Decisions are the outcome of independent streams of events within the organization. The four streams relevant to organizational decision making are as follows:

1. *Problems.* Problems are points of dissatisfaction with current activities and performance. They represent a gap between desired performance and current activities. Problems are perceived to require attention. However, they are distinct from solutions and choices. A problem may lead to a proposed solution or it may not. Problems may not be solved when solutions are adopted.

2. *Potential solutions.* A solution is an idea somebody proposes for adoption. Such ideas form a flow of alternative solutions through the organization. Ideas may be brought into the organization by new personnel or may be invented by existing personnel. Participants may simply be attracted to certain ideas and push them as logical choices regardless of problems. Attraction to an idea may cause an employee to look for a problem to which the idea can be attached and, hence, justified. The point is that solutions exist independent of problems.

3. *Participants.* Organization participants are employees who come and go throughout the organization. People are hired, reassigned, and fired. Participants vary widely in their ideas, perception of problems, experience, values, and training. The problems and solutions recognized by one manager will differ from those recognized by another manager.

4. *Choice opportunities.* Choice opportunities are occasions when an organization usually makes a decision. They occur when contracts are signed, people are hired, or a new product is authorized. They also occur when the right mix of participants, solutions, and problems exists. Thus, a manager who happened to learn of a good idea may suddenly become aware of a problem to which it applies and, hence, can provide the organization with a choice opportunity. Match-ups of problems and solutions often result in decisions.

With the concept of four streams, the overall pattern of organizational decision making takes on a random quality. Problems, solutions, participants, and choices all flow through the organization. In one sense, the organization is a large garbage can in which these streams are being stirred, as illustrated in Exhibit 8.7. When a problem, solution, and participant happen to connect at one point, a decision may be made and the problem may be solved; but if the solution does not fit the problem, the problem may not be solved.

Thus, when viewing the organization as a whole and considering its high level of uncertainty, one sees problems arise that are not solved and solutions tried that do not work. Organizational decisions are disorderly and not the result of a

EXHIBIT 8.7
Illustration of
Independent Streams of
Events in the Garbage
Can Model of Decision
Making

logical, step-by-step sequence. Events may be so ill-defined and complex that decisions, problems, and solutions act as independent events. When they connect, some problems are solved, but many are not.[51]

Consequences. There are four specific consequences of the garbage can decision process for organizational decision making:

1. *Solutions may be proposed even when problems do not exist.* An employee might be sold on an idea and might try to sell it to the rest of the organization. An example was the adoption of computers by many organizations during the 1970s. The computer was an exciting solution and was pushed by both computer manufacturers and systems analysts within organizations. The computer did not solve any problems in those initial applications. Indeed, some computers caused more problems than they solved.

2. *Choices are made without solving problems.* A choice—for example, creating a new department or revising work procedures—may be made with the intention of solving a problem; but, under conditions of high uncertainty, the choice may be incorrect. Moreover, many choices just seem to happen. People decide to quit, the organization's budget is cut, or a new policy bulletin is issued. These choices may be oriented toward problems but do not necessarily solve them.

3. *Problems may persist without being solved.* Organization participants get used to certain problems and give up trying to solve them; or participants may not know how to solve certain problems because the technology is unclear. A university in Canada was placed on probation by the American Association of University Professors because a professor had been denied tenure without due process. The probation was a nagging annoyance that the administrators wanted to remove. Fifteen years later, the nontenured professor died. The probation continues because the university did not acquiesce to the demands of the heirs of the association to reevaluate the case. The university would like to solve the problem, but administrators are not sure how, and they do not have the resources to allocate to it. The probation problem persists without a solution.

4. *A few problems are solved.* The decision process does work in the aggregate. In computer simulation models of the garbage can model, important problems were often resolved. Solutions do connect with appropriate problems and participants so that a good choice is made. Of course, not all problems are resolved when choices are made, but the organization does move in the direction of problem reduction.

The effects of independent streams and the rather chaotic decision processes of the garbage can model can be seen in the production of David O. Russell's movie *I ♥ Huckabees*, which has been called an "existential comedy."

IN PRACTICE

I ♥ Huckabees

Screenwriter and director David O. Russell is known for creating intelligent, original movies such as *Spanking the Monkey*, *Flirting with Disaster* and *Three Kings*. His 2004 film *I ♥ Huckabees* might be the most original—or some would say just plain weird—so far. *The New York Times* referred to the movie as "a jumbled, antic exploration of existential and Buddhist philosophy that also involves tree-hugging, African immigrants, and Shania Twain." Yet the movie got decent critical reviews and was picked by the *Village Voice* as one of the best films of 2004.

Russell had a vision of what he wanted the movie to be from the beginning, but few others could grasp what that was. Most of the actors who signed on to star in *I ♥ Huckabees* admit that they didn't really understand the script, but they trusted Russell's vision and imagination. Two of the biggest actors in Hollywood, Jude Law and Gwyneth Paltrow, signed on to play employees at a department store chain called Huckabees. But Paltrow backed out before filming ever started. Nicole Kidman was interested but had a conflict. Jennifer Aniston became—and as quickly unbecame—a possibility. Finally, Naomi Watts, who had been Russell's original choice for the role, was able to free herself from scheduling conflicts to take the part. The casting wasn't quite set though. Jude Law dropped out for unknown reasons—but just as quickly dropped back in.

Filming was chaotic. As the actors were on camera saying the lines they had memorized, Russell was a few feet away continually calling out new lines to them. In one scene, Law became so exhausted and frustrated that he started pounding his fists on the ground and shouting expletives. Russell loved the improvisation and kept the cameras rolling. Actors were unsure of how to develop their characterizations, so they just did whatever seemed right at the time, often based on Russell's efforts to keep them off balance. Scenes were often filmed blindly with no idea of how they were supposed to fit in the overall story.

After Russell's hours in the editing room, the final film turned out to be quite different from what the actors thought they'd shot. Some major scenes, including one that was supposed to articulate the film's theme that "everything is connected," were cut entirely.

(continued)

> Amazingly, considering the chaos on the set, the film was completed on schedule and on budget. Although *I ♥ Huckabees* is emotionally and intellectually dense, and not the kind of movie that reaps big bucks, the haphazard process worked to create the movie David O. Russell wanted to make.[52] ■

The production of *I ♥ Huckabees* was not a rational process that started with a clear problem and ended with a logical solution. Many events occurred by chance and were intertwined, which characterizes the garbage can model. Everyone from the director to the actors continuously added to the stream of new ideas for the story. Some solutions were connected to emerging problems: Naomi Watts cleared her schedule just in time to take the role after Gwyneth Paltrow dropped out, for example. The actors (participants) daily made personal choices regarding characterization that proved to be right for the story line. The garbage can model, however, doesn't always work—in the movies or in organizations. A similar haphazard process during the filming of *Waterworld* led to the most expensive film in Hollywood history and a decided box-office flop for Universal Pictures.[53]

CONTINGENCY DECISION-MAKING FRAMEWORK

This chapter has covered several approaches to organizational decision making, including management science, the Carnegie model, the incremental decision model, and the garbage can model. It has also discussed rational and intuitive decision processes used by individual managers. Each decision approach is a relatively accurate description of the actual decision process, yet all differ from each other. Management science, for example, reflects a different set of decision assumptions and procedures than does the garbage can model.

One reason for having different approaches is that they appear in different organizational situations. The use of an approach is contingent on the organization setting. Two characteristics of organizations that determine the use of decision approaches are (1) problem consensus and (2) technical knowledge about the means to solve those problems.[54] Analyzing organizations along these two dimensions suggests which approach is most appropriate for making decisions.

Problem Consensus

Problem consensus refers to the agreement among managers about the nature of a problem or opportunity and about which goals and outcomes to pursue. This variable ranges from complete agreement to complete disagreement. When managers agree, there is little uncertainty—the problems and goals of the organization are clear, and so are standards of performance. When managers disagree, organization direction and performance expectations are in dispute, creating a situation of high uncertainty. One example of problem uncertainty occurred at Wal-Mart stores regarding the use of parking lot patrols. Some managers believed the stores needed to do more to control parking lot crime, presenting evidence that parking lot patrols increased business because they encouraged more nighttime shopping. Other managers, however, insisted that parking lot crime was a society problem rather than a store problem, and they argued that trying to control parking lot crime would be too expensive.[55]

Problem consensus tends to be low when organizations are differentiated, as described in Chapter 6. Recall that uncertain environments cause organizational departments to differentiate from one another in goals and attitudes to specialize in specific environmental sectors. This differentiation leads to disagreement and conflict, so managers must make a special effort to build coalitions during decision making. For example, NASA has been criticized for failing to identify problems with the *Columbia* space shuttle that might have prevented the February 2003 disaster. Part of the reason was high differentiation and conflicting opinions between safety managers and scheduling managers, in which pressure to launch on time overrode safety concerns. In addition, after the launch, engineers three times requested—and were denied—better photos to assess the damage from a piece of foam debris that struck the shuttle's left wing just seconds after launch. Investigations now indicate that the damage caused by the debris may have been the primary physical cause of the explosion. Mechanisms for hearing dissenting opinions and building coalitions can improve decision making at NASA and other organizations dealing with complex problems.[56]

Problem consensus is especially important for the problem identification stage of decision making. When problems are clear and agreed on, they provide clear standards and expectations for performance. When problems are not agreed on, problem identification is uncertain and management attention must be focused on gaining agreement about goals and priorities.

Technical Knowledge about Solutions

Technical knowledge refers to understanding and agreement about how to solve problems and reach organizational goals. This variable can range from complete agreement and certainty to complete disagreement and uncertainty about cause–effect relationships leading to problem solution. One example of low technical knowledge occurred at PepsiCo's 7-Up division. Managers agreed on the problem to be solved—they wanted to increase market share from 6 percent to 7 percent. However, the means for achieving this increase in market share were not known or agreed on. A few managers wanted to use discount pricing in supermarkets. Other managers believed they should increase the number of soda fountain outlets in restaurants and fast-food chains. A few other managers insisted that the best approach was to increase advertising. Managers did not know what would cause an increase in market share. Eventually, the advertising judgment prevailed at 7-Up, but it did not work very well. The failure of its decision reflected 7-Up's low technical knowledge about how to solve the problem.

When means are well understood, the appropriate alternatives can be identified and calculated with some degree of certainty. When means are poorly understood, potential solutions are ill-defined and uncertain. Intuition, judgment, and trial and error become the basis for decisions.

Contingency Framework

Exhibit 8.8 describes the **contingency decision-making framework**, which brings together the two dimensions of problem consensus and technical knowledge about solutions. Each cell represents an organizational situation that is appropriate for the decision-making approaches described in this chapter.

Cell 1. In cell 1 of Exhibit 8.8, rational decision procedures are used because problems are agreed on and cause–effect relationships are well understood, so there is little uncertainty. Decisions can be made in a computational manner. Alternatives can be identified and the best solution adopted through analysis and calculations. The rational models described earlier in this chapter, both for individuals and for the organization, are appropriate when problems and the means for solving them are well defined.

Cell 2. In cell 2, there is high uncertainty about problems and priorities, so bargaining and compromise are used to reach consensus. Tackling one problem might mean the organization must postpone action on other issues. The priorities given to respective problems are decided through discussion, debate, and coalition building.

   Managers in this situation should use broad participation to achieve consensus in the decision process. Opinions should be surfaced and discussed until compromise is reached. The organization will not otherwise move forward as an integrated unit. The Carnegie model applies when there is dissension about organizational problems. When groups within the organization disagree, or when the organization

EXHIBIT 8.8
Contingency Framework
for Using Decision
Models

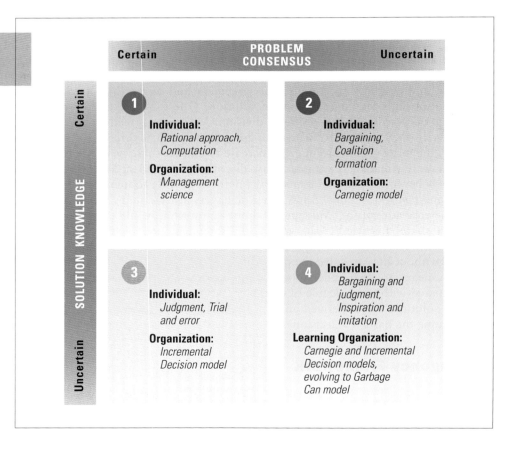

is in conflict with constituencies (government regulators, suppliers, unions), bargaining and negotiation are required. The bargaining strategy is especially relevant to the problem identification stage of the decision process. Once bargaining and negotiation are completed, the organization will have support for one direction.

Cell 3. In a cell 3 situation, problems and standards of performance are certain, but alternative technical solutions are vague and uncertain. Techniques to solve a problem are ill defined and poorly understood. When an individual manager faces this situation, intuition will be the decision guideline. The manager will rely on past experience and judgment to make a decision. Rational, analytical approaches are not effective because the alternatives cannot be identified and calculated. Hard facts and accurate information are not available.

The incremental decision model reflects trial and error on the part of the organization. Once a problem is identified, a sequence of small steps enables the organization to learn a solution. As new problems arise, the organization may recycle back to an earlier point and start over. Eventually, over a period of months or years, the organization will acquire sufficient experience to solve the problem in a satisfactory way.

The situation in cell 3, of senior managers agreeing about problems but not knowing how to solve them, occurs frequently in business organizations. If managers use incremental decisions in such situations, they will eventually acquire the technical knowledge to accomplish goals and solve problems.

Cell 4. The situation in cell 4, characterized by high uncertainty about both problems and solutions, is difficult for decision making. An individual manager making a decision under this high level of uncertainty can employ techniques from both cell 2 and cell 3. The manager can attempt to build a coalition to establish goals and priorities and use judgment, intuition, or trial and error to solve problems. Additional techniques, such as inspiration and imitation, also may be required. **Inspiration** refers to an innovative, creative solution that is not reached by logical means. Inspiration sometimes comes like a flash of insight, but—similar to intuition—it is often based on deep knowledge and understanding of a problem that the unconscious mind has had time to mull over.[57] **Imitation** means adopting a decision tried elsewhere in the hope that it will work in this situation.

For example, in one university, accounting department faculty were unhappy with their current circumstances but could not decide on the direction the department should take. Some faculty members wanted a greater research orientation, whereas others wanted greater orientation toward business firms and accounting applications. The disagreement about goals was compounded because neither group was sure about the best technique for achieving its goals. The ultimate solution was inspirational on the part of the dean. An accounting research center was established with funding from major accounting firms. The funding was used to finance research activities for faculty interested in basic research and to provide contact with business firms for other faculty. The solution provided a common goal and unified people within the department to work toward that goal.

When an entire organization is characterized by high uncertainty regarding both problems and solutions, elements of the garbage can model will appear. Managers may first try techniques from both cells 2 and 3, but logical decision sequences starting with problem identification and ending with problem solution will not occur. Potential solutions will precede problems as often as problems precede solutions.

In this situation, managers should encourage widespread discussion of problems and idea proposals to facilitate the opportunity to make choices. Eventually, through trial and error, the organization will solve some problems.

Research has found that decisions made following the prescriptions of the contingency decision-making framework tend to be more successful. However, the study noted that nearly six of ten strategic management decisions failed to follow the framework, leading to a situation in which misleading or missing information decreased the chance of an effective decision choice.[58] Managers can use the contingency framework in Exhibit 8.8 to improve the likelihood of successful organizational decisions.

SPECIAL DECISION CIRCUMSTANCES

In a highly competitive world beset by global competition and rapid change, decision making seldom fits the traditional rational, analytical model. Today's managers have to make high-stakes decisions more often and more quickly than ever before in an environment that is increasingly less predictable. For example, interviews with CEOs in high-tech industries found that they strive to use some type of rational process, but the uncertainty and change in the industry often make that approach unsuccessful. The way these managers actually reach decisions is through a complex interaction with other managers, subordinates, environmental factors, and organizational events.[59]

Issues of particular concern for today's decision makers are coping with high-velocity environments, learning from decision mistakes, and understanding and overcoming cognitive biases in decision making.

High-Velocity Environments

In some industries, the rate of competitive and technological change is so extreme that market data are either unavailable or obsolete, strategic windows open and shut quickly, perhaps within a few months, and the cost of poor decisions may be company failure. Research has examined how successful companies make decisions in these **high-velocity environments**, especially to understand whether organizations abandon rational approaches or have time for incremental implementation.[60]

A comparison of successful with unsuccessful decisions in high-velocity environments found the following patterns:

Briefcase

As an organization manager, keep these guidelines in mind:

Track real-time information, build multiple alternatives simultaneously, and try to involve everyone—but move ahead anyway when making decisions in a high-velocity environment.

- Successful decision makers tracked information in real time to develop a deep and intuitive grasp of the business. Two to three intense meetings per week with all key players were usual. Decision makers closely tracked operating statistics to constantly feel the pulse of what was happening. Unsuccessful firms were more concerned with future planning and forward-looking information, with only a loose grip on immediate happenings.
- During a major decision, successful companies began immediately to build multiple alternatives. Implementation of alternatives sometimes ran in parallel before managers finally settled on a final choice. Companies that made decisions slowly developed just one alternative, moving to another only after the first one failed.

- Fast, successful decision makers sought advice from everyone and depended heavily on one or two savvy, trusted colleagues as counselors. Slow companies were unable to build trust and agreement among the best people.
- Fast companies involved everyone in the decision and tried for consensus; but if consensus did not emerge, the top manager made the choice and moved ahead. Waiting for everyone to be on board created more delays than was warranted. Slow companies delayed decisions to achieve a uniform consensus.
- Fast, successful choices were well integrated with other decisions and the overall strategic direction of the company. Less successful choices considered the decision in isolation from other decisions; the decision was made in the abstract.[61]

When speed matters, a slow decision can be as ineffective as the wrong decision. Managers can learn to make decisions quickly. To improve the chances of a good decision under high-velocity conditions, some organizations stimulate constructive conflict through a technique called **point–counterpoint**, which divides decision makers into two groups and assigns them different, often competing responsibilities.[62] The groups develop and exchange proposals and debate options until they arrive at a common set of understandings and recommendations. Groups can often make better decisions because multiple and diverse opinions are considered. In the face of complexity and uncertainty, the more people who have a say in the decision making, the better.

In group decision making, a consensus may not always be reached, but the exercise gives everyone a chance to consider options and state their opinions, and it gives top managers a broader understanding. Typically, those involved support the final choice. However, if a very speedy decision is required, top managers are willing to make the decision and move forward.

Decision Mistakes and Learning

Organizational decisions result in many errors, especially when made in conditions of great uncertainty. Managers simply cannot determine or predict which alternative will solve a problem. In these cases, the organization must make the decision—and take the risk—often in the spirit of trial and error. If an alternative fails, the organization can learn from it and try another alternative that better fits the situation. Each failure provides new information and insight. The point for managers is to move ahead with the decision process despite the potential for mistakes. "Chaotic action is preferable to orderly inaction."[63]

In some organizations, managers are encouraged to instill a climate of experimentation to facilitate creative decision making. If one idea fails, another idea should be tried. Failure often lays the groundwork for success, such as when technicians at 3M developed Post-it Notes based on a failed product—a not-very-sticky glue. Managers in the most innovative companies believe that if all their new products succeed, they're doing something wrong, not taking the necessary risks to develop new markets. In other words, they recognize that when failure teaches the company something new, it lays the groundwork for success. The CEO of Coca-Cola, for example, is emphasizing the importance of accepting failure as he tries to change Coke's traditionally risk-averse culture into a more innovative, adaptive one.[64]

Only by making mistakes can managers and organizations go through the process of **decision learning** and acquire sufficient experience and knowledge to perform more effectively in the future. Some companies, such as Intuit, even give awards for failures that lead to learning. One recent winner at Intuit was the team that developed an aggressive marketing campaign to target young tax filers. Through a Website called RockYourRefund.com, Intuit offered discounts to Best Buy and other companies and the ability to deposit tax refunds directly into prepaid Visa cards issued by hip-hop star and entrepreneur Russell Simmons. The campaign was a bust, with Intuit doing "very few returns" through the site. A postmortem of the project gave the team lessons they applied to future projects, such as the fact that young people shun Websites that feel too much like advertising. "It's only a failure if we fail to get the learning," said Intuit Chairman Scott Cook.[65]

Based on what has been said about decision making in this chapter, one can expect companies to be ultimately successful in their decision making by adopting a learning approach toward solutions. They will make mistakes along the way, but they will resolve uncertainty through the trial-and-error process.

ASSESS YOUR ANSWER

3 **Making a poor decision can help a manager and organization learn and get stronger.**

ANSWER: *Agree.* Managers don't want people to intentionally make poor decisions, of course, but smart managers encourage people to take risks and experiment, which can lead to failed decisions. Learning from the failures is the key to growing and improving. In addition, although managers strive to make good decisions, they understand that decisions sometimes must be made quickly based on limited information, and that trial and error is an important way the organization learns and grows stronger.

Cognitive Biases

While encouraging risk-taking and accepting mistakes can lead to learning, one error smart managers strive to avoid is allowing cognitive biases to cloud their decision making. **Cognitive biases** are severe errors in judgment that all humans are prone to and that typically lead to bad choices.[66] Three common biases are escalating commitment, loss aversion, and groupthink.

Escalating Commitment. One well-known cognitive bias is referred to as **escalating commitment**. Research suggests that organizations often continue to invest time and money in a solution despite strong evidence that it is not working. Several explanations are given for why managers escalate commitment to a failing decision.[67] Many times managers simply keep hoping they can recoup their losses. In addition, managers block or distort negative information when they are personally responsible for a bad decision. Another explanation is that consistency and persistence are valued in contemporary society. Consistent managers are considered better leaders than those

who switch around from one course of action to another, so managers have a hard time pulling the plug despite evidence that a decision was wrong.

Prospect Theory. Most people are naturally *loss averse*. The pain one feels from losing a ten-dollar bill is typically much more powerful than the happiness one gets from finding a twenty-dollar one. **Prospect theory**, developed by psychologists Daniel Kahneman and Amos Tversky, suggests that the threat of a loss has a greater impact on a decision than the possibility of an equivalent gain.[68] Therefore, most managers have a tendency to analyze problems in terms of what they fear losing rather than what they might gain. When faced with a specific decision, they over-weight the value of potential losses and underweight the value of potential gains. In addition, research indicates that the regret associated with a decision that results in a loss is stronger than the regret of a missed opportunity. Thus, managers might avoid potentially wonderful opportunities that also have potentially negative outcomes. Prospect theory also helps to explain the phenomenon of escalating commitment, discussed in the previous section. Managers don't want to lose, so they keep throwing good money after bad.

Groupthink. Many decisions in organizations are made by groups, so the desire to go along with the group also can bias decisions. Subtle pressures for conformity exist in almost any group, and particularly when people like one another they tend to avoid anything that might create disharmony. **Groupthink** refers to the tendency of people in groups to suppress contrary opinions.[69] When people slip into group-think, the desire for harmony outweighs concerns over decision quality. Group members emphasize maintaining unity rather than realistically challenging problems and alternatives. People censor their personal opinions and are reluctant to criticize the opinions of others.

Overcoming Personal Biases

How can managers avoid the problems of groupthink, escalating commitment, and being influenced by loss aversion? Several ideas have been proposed that help managers be more realistic and objective when making decisions. Two of the most effective are to use evidence-based management and to encourage dissent and diversity.

Evidence-Based Management. **Evidence-based management** means a commitment to make more informed and intelligent decisions based on the best available facts and evidence.[70] It means being aware of one's biases, seeking and examining evidence with rigor. Managers practice evidence-based decision making by being careful and thoughtful rather than carelessly relying on assumptions, past experience, rules of thumb, or intuition. Evidence-based management can be particularly useful for overcoming fear of loss and the problem of escalating commitment. To practice evidence-based management, managers use data and facts to the extent possible to inform their decisions. Many manager problems are uncertain, and hard facts and data aren't available, but by always seeking evidence, managers can avoid relying on faulty assumptions. Decision makers can also do a post-mortem of decisions to evaluate what worked, what didn't, and how to do things better. The best decision makers have a healthy appreciation

Briefcase

As an organization manager, keep these guidelines in mind:

Don't let cognitive biases cloud your decision making. To avoid the problems of groupthink, escalating commitment, and being influenced by loss aversion, apply evidence-based management and use techniques to encourage diversity and dissent.

for what they don't know. They are always questioning and encouraging others to question their knowledge and assumptions. They foster a culture of inquiry, observation, and experimentation.

Encourage Dissent and Diversity. Dissent and diversity can be particularly useful in complex circumstances because they open the decision process to a wide variety of ideas and opinions rather than being constrained by personal biases or groupthink.[71] Chuck Knight, the former CEO of Emerson Electric, always sparked heated debates during strategic planning meetings. Knight believed rigorous debate gave people a clearer picture of the competitive landscape and forced managers to look at all sides of an issue, helping them reach better decisions.[72] One way to encourage dissent is to ensure that the group is diverse in terms of age and gender, functional area of expertise, hierarchical level, and experience with the business. Some groups assign a **devil's advocate**, who has the role of challenging the assumptions and assertions made by the group.[73] The devil's advocate may force the group to rethink its approach to the problem and avoid reaching premature decisions. Another approach, referred to as *ritual dissent*, puts parallel teams to work on the same problem in a large group meeting. Each team appoints a spokesperson who presents the team's finding and ideas to another team, which is required to listen quietly. Then, the spokesperson turns to face away from the team, which rips into the presentation no-holds-barred while the spokesperson is required to listen quietly. Each team's spokesperson does this with every other team in turn, so that by the end of the session all ideas have been well-dissected and discussed.[74] The point–counterpoint method described earlier is also effective for encouraging dissent. Whatever techniques they use, good managers find ways to get a diversity of ideas and opinions on the table when making complex decisions.

DESIGN ESSENTIALS

■ Most organizational decisions are not made in a logical, rational manner. Most decisions do not begin with the careful analysis of a problem, followed by systematic analysis of alternatives, and finally implementation of a solution. On the contrary, decision processes are characterized by conflict, coalition building, trial and error, speed, and mistakes. Managers operate under many constraints that limit rationality; hence, they use satisficing and intuition as well as rational analysis in their decision making.

■ Another important idea is that individuals make decisions, but organizational decisions are not made by a single individual. Organizational decision-making approaches include the management science approach, the Carnegie model, the incremental decision model, and the garbage can model.

■ Only in rare circumstances do managers analyze problems and find solutions by themselves. Many problems are not clear, so widespread discussion and coalition building take place. Once goals and priorities are set, alternatives to achieve those goals can be tried. When a manager does make an individual decision, it is often a small part of a larger decision process. Organizations solve big problems through a series of small steps. A single manager may initiate one step but should be aware of the larger decision process to which it belongs.

■ The greatest amount of conflict and coalition building occurs when problems are not agreed on. Priorities must be established to indicate which goals are important and what problems should be solved first. If a manager attacks a problem other people do not agree with, the manager will lose support for the solution to be implemented. Thus, time and activity should be spent building a coalition in the problem identification stage of decision making. Then the organization can move toward solutions. Under conditions of low technical knowledge, the solution unfolds as a series of incremental trials that will gradually lead to an overall solution.

■ The most novel description of decision making is the garbage can model. This model describes how decision processes can seem almost random in highly organic organizations. Decisions, problems, ideas, and people flow through organizations and mix together in various combinations. Through this process, the organization gradually learns. Some problems may never be solved, but many are, and the organization will move toward maintaining and improving its level of performance.

■ Many organizations operating in high-velocity environments must make decisions with speed, which means staying in immediate touch with operations and the environment. Moreover, in an uncertain world, organizations will make mistakes, and mistakes made through trial and error should be appreciated. Encouraging trial-and-error increments facilitates organizational learning.

■ On the other hand, allowing cognitive biases to cloud decision making can have serious negative consequences for an organization. Managers can avoid the biases of escalating commitment, loss aversion, and groupthink by using evidence-based management and by encouraging diversity and dissent in the decision-making process.

Key Concepts

bounded rationality perspective
Carnegie model
coalition
cognitive biases
contingency decision-making
    framework
decision learning
devil's advocate
escalating commitment
evidence-based management
garbage can model

groupthink
high-velocity environments
imitation
incremental decision model
inspiration
intuitive decision making
management science approach
nonprogrammed decisions
organizational decision making
organized anarchy
point–counterpoint

problem consensus
problem identification
problem solution
problemistic search
programmed decisions
prospect theory
rational approach
satisficing
technical knowledge

Discussion Questions

1. What are the three major phases in Mintzberg's incremental decision model? Why might an organization recycle through one or more phases of the model?

2. Why are decision mistakes usually accepted in organizations but penalized in college courses and exams that are designed to train managers?

3. The Carnegie model emphasizes the need for a political coalition in the decision-making process. When and why are coalitions necessary?

4. Can you think of a decision you have made in your personal, school, or work life that reflects a stronger desire to avoid a loss than to make a gain? How about a time when you stayed with an idea or project for too long, perhaps even escalating your commitment, to avoid a failure? Discuss.

5. If managers frequently use experience and intuition to make complex, nonprogrammed decisions, how do they apply evidence-based management, which seems to suggest that managers should rely on facts and data?

6. Why would managers in high-velocity environments worry more about the present than the future? Would an individual manager working in this type of environment be more likely to succeed with a rational approach or an intuitive approach? Discuss.

7. A professional economist once told his class, "An individual decision maker should process all relevant information and select the economically rational alternative." Do you agree? Why or why not?

8. How would you make a decision to select a building site for a new waste-treatment plant in the Philippines? Where would you start with this complex decision, and what steps would you take? Explain which decision model in the chapter best describes your approach.

9. When you are faced with choosing between several valid options, how do you typically make your decision? How do you think managers typically choose between several options? What are the similarities between your decision process and what you think managers do?

10. An organization theorist once told her class, "Organizations never make big decisions. They make small decisions that eventually add up to a big decision." Explain the logic behind this statement.

Chapter 8 Workbook: Decision Styles*

Think of some recent decisions that have influenced your life. Choose two significant decisions that you made and two decisions that other people made. Fill out the following table, using Exhibit 12.8 to determine decision styles.

Your decisions	Approach used	Advantages and disadvantages	Your recommended decision style
1.			
2.			
Decisions by others			
1.			
2.			

Questions

1. How can a decision approach influence the outcome of the decision? What happens when the approach fits the decision? When it doesn't fit?

2. How can you know which approach is best?

*Adapted by Dorothy Marcic from "Action Assignment" in Jennifer M. Howard and Lawrence M. Miller, *Team Management* (Miller Consulting Group, 1994), 205.

Case for Analysis: Cracking the Whip*

Harmon Davidson stared dejectedly at the departing figure of his management survey team leader. Their meeting had not gone well. Davidson had relayed to Al Pitcher complaints about his handling of the survey. Pitcher had responded with adamant denial and unveiled scorn.

Davidson, director of headquarters management, was prepared to discount some of the criticism as resentment of outsiders meddling with "the way we've always done business," exacerbated by the turbulence of continual reorganization. But Davidson could hardly ignore the sheer volume of complaints or his high regard for some of their sources. "Was I missing danger signals about Pitcher from the start?" Davidson asked himself. "Or was I just giving a guy I didn't know a fair chance with an inherently controversial assignment?"

With his division decimated in the latest round of downsizing at the Department of Technical Services (DTS) earlier that year, Davidson had been asked to return to the headquarters management office after a five-year hiatus. The director, Walton Drummond, had abruptly taken early retirement.

One of the first things Davidson had learned about his new job was that he would be responsible for a comprehensive six-month survey of the headquarters management structure and processes. The DTS secretary had promised the survey to the White House as a prelude to the agency's next phase of management reform. Drummond had already picked the five-person survey team consisting of two experienced management analysts, a promising younger staff member, an intern, and Pitcher, the team leader. Pitcher was fresh from the Treasury Department, where he had participated in a similar survey. But having gone off after retirement for an extended mountain-climbing expedition in Asia, Drummond was unavailable to explain his survey plans or any understandings he had reached with Pitcher.

Davidson had been impressed with Pitcher's energy and motivation. He worked long hours, wrote voluminously if awkwardly, and was brimming with the latest organizational theory. Pitcher had other characteristics, however, that were disquieting. He seemed uninterested in DTS's history and culture and was paternalistic toward top managers, assuming they were unsophisticated and unconcerned about modern management.

A series of presurvey informational briefings for headquarters office heads conducted by Davidson and Pitcher seemed to go swimmingly. Pitcher deferred to his chief on matters of philosophy and confined his remarks to schedule and procedures. He closed his segment on a friendly note, saying, "If we do find opportunities for improvement, we'll try to have recommendations for you."

But the survey was barely a week old when the director of management received his first call from an outraged customer. It was the assistant secretary for public affairs, Erin Dove, and she was not speaking in her usual upbeat tones. "Your folks have managed to upset my whole supervisory staff with their comments about how we'll have to change our organization and methods," she said. "I thought you were going through a fact-finding study. This guy Pitcher sounds like he wants to remake DTS headquarters overnight. Who does he think he is?"

When Davidson asked him about the encounter with public affairs, Pitcher expressed puzzlement that a few summary observations shared with supervisors in the interest of "prompt informal feedback" had been interpreted as such disturbing conclusions. "I told them we'll tell them how to fix it," he reassured his supervisor.

"Listen, Al," Davidson remonstrated gently. "These are very accomplished managers who aren't used to being told they have to fix anything. This agency's been on a roll for years, and the need for reinvention isn't resonating all that well yet. We've got to collect and analyze the information and assemble a convincing case for change, or we'll be spinning our wheels. Let's hold off on the feedback until you and I have reviewed it together."

But two weeks later, Technology Development Director Phil Canseco, an old and treasured colleague, was on Davidson's doorstep looking as unhappy as Erin Dove had sounded on the phone. "Harmon, buddy, I think you have to rein in this survey team a bit," he said. "Several managers who were scheduled for survey interviews were working on a 24-hour turnaround to give a revised project budget to the Appropriations subcommittee that day. My deputy says Pitcher was put out about postponing interviews and grumbled about whether we understood the new priorities. Is he living in the real world?"

Canseco's comments prompted Davidson to call a few of his respected peers who had dealt with the survey team. With varying degrees of reluctance, they all criticized the team leader and, in some cases, team members, as abrasive and uninterested in the rationales offered for existing structure and processes.

And so Davidson marshaled all of his tact for a review with the survey team leader. But Pitcher was in no mood for either introspection or reconsideration. He took the view that he had been brought in to spearhead a White House–inspired management improvement initiative in a glamour agency that had never had to think much about efficiency. He reminded Davidson that even he had conceded that managers were due some hard lessons on this score. Pitcher didn't see any way to meet his deadline except

Part 4: Managing Organizational Processes

by adhering to a rigorous schedule, since he was working with managers disinclined to cooperate with an outsider pushing an unpopular exercise. He felt Davidson's role was to hold the line against unwarranted criticisms from prima donnas trying to discredit the survey.

Many questions arose in Davidson's mind about the survey plan and his division's capacity to carry it out. Had they taken on too much with too little? Had the right people been picked for the survey team? Had managers and executives, and even the team, been properly prepared for the survey?

But the most immediate question was whether Al Pitcher could help him with these problems.

*This case was prepared by David Hornestay and appeared in *Government Executive*, vol. 30, No. 8, August 1998, 45–46, as part of a series of case studies examining workplace dilemmas confronting federal managers. Reprinted by permission of *Government Executive*.

Case for Analysis: The Dilemma of Aliesha State College: Competence versus Need*

Until the 1980s, Aliesha was a well-reputed, somewhat sleepy state teachers college located on the outer fringes of a major metropolitan area. Then with the rapid expansion of college enrollments, the state converted Aliesha to a four-year state college (and the plans called for it to become a state university with graduate work and perhaps even with a medical school in the late 1990s). Within 10 years, Aliesha grew from 1,500 to 9,000 students. Its budget expanded even faster than the enrollment, increasing twentyfold during that period.

The only part of Aliesha that did not grow was the original part, the teachers' college; there enrollment actually went down. Everything else seemed to flourish. In addition to building new four-year schools of liberal arts, business, veterinary medicine, and dentistry, Aliesha developed many community service programs. Among them were a rapidly growing evening program, a mental health clinic, and a speech-therapy center for children with speech defects—the only one in the area. Even within education, one area grew—the demonstration high school attached to the old teachers college. Even though the high school enrolled only 300 students, its teachers were the leading experts in teacher education, and it was considered the best high school in the area.

Then, in 1992, the budget was suddenly cut quite sharply by the state legislature. At the same time the faculty demanded and got a fairly hefty raise in salary. It was clear that something had to give—the budget deficit was much too great to be covered by ordinary cost reductions. When the faculty committee sat down with the president

and the board of trustees, two candidates for abandonment emerged after long and heated wrangling: the speech-therapy program and the demonstration high school. Both cost about the same—and both were extremely expensive. The speech-therapy clinic, everyone agreed, addressed itself to a real need and one of high priority. But—and everyone had to agree because the evidence was overwhelming—it did not do the job. Indeed, it did such a poor, sloppy, disorganized job that pediatricians, psychiatrists, and psychologists hesitated to refer their patients to the clinic. The reason was that the clinic was a college program run to teach psychology students rather than to help children with serious speech impediments.

The opposite criticism applied to the high school. No one questioned its excellence and the impact it made on the education students who listened in on its classes and on many young teachers in the area who came in as auditors. But what need did it fill? There were plenty of perfectly adequate high schools in the area.

"How can we justify," asked one of the psychologists connected with the speech clinic, "running an unnecessary high school in which each child costs as much as a graduate student at Harvard?"

"But how can we justify," asked the dean of the school of education, himself one of the outstanding teachers in the demonstration high school, "a speech clinic that has no results even though each of its patients costs the state as much as one of our demonstration high school students, or more?"

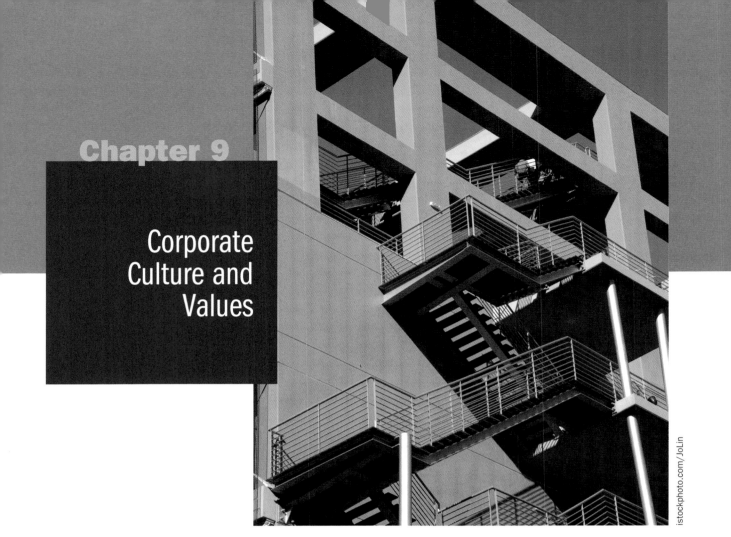

istockphoto.com/JoLin

Chapter 9

Corporate Culture and Values

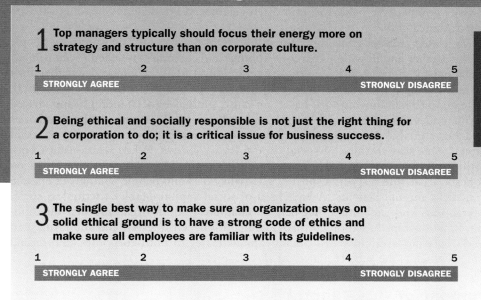

1 Top managers typically should focus their energy more on strategy and structure than on corporate culture.

1	2	3	4	5
STRONGLY AGREE				STRONGLY DISAGREE

2 Being ethical and socially responsible is not just the right thing for a corporation to do; it is a critical issue for business success.

1	2	3	4	5
STRONGLY AGREE				STRONGLY DISAGREE

3 The single best way to make sure an organization stays on solid ethical ground is to have a strong code of ethics and make sure all employees are familiar with its guidelines.

1	2	3	4	5
STRONGLY AGREE				STRONGLY DISAGREE

Walk into the headquarters of Patagonia, and you will likely see people wearing flip flops and shorts. Why not? They might be going surfing later. The successful seller of outdoor clothing and equipment is guided by values of creativity, collaboration, and caring for the environment. Employees who are eligible can take off two months at full pay to work for environmental groups. The feeling inside headquarters is relaxed, yet vibrant; people work hard but they also have fun. Compare that to the headquarters at Exxon Mobil, where most employees are in conventional business attire and the atmosphere is tinged with competitiveness and a rigorous, analytical approach to taking care of business. "They're not in the fun business," said one oil industry analyst. "They're in the profit business." No surfing for these guys (or girls). As one investor said with admiration: "They never take a day off."[1]

Patagonia and Exxon represent two very different corporate cultures. Yet both companies are successful, and both have employees who enjoy their jobs and generally like the way things are done at their company. Every organization, like Patagonia and Exxon, has a set of values that characterize how people behave and how the organization carries out everyday business. One of the most important jobs organizational leaders do is instill and support the kind of values needed for the company to thrive.

Strong cultures can have a profound impact on a company, which can be either positive or negative for the organization. At J. M. Smucker & Company, the first manufacturer ever to earn the top spot on *Fortune* magazine's list of "The 100 Best Companies to Work For," strong values of cooperation, caring for employees and customers, and an "all for one, one for all" attitude enable the company to consistently meet productivity, quality, and customer-service goals in the challenging environment of the food industry.[2] Negative cultural norms, however, can damage a company just as powerfully as positive ones can strengthen it. Consider the case of Enron Corporation, where the corporate culture supported pushing everything to the limits: business practices, rules, personal behavior, and laws. Executives drove expensive cars, challenged employees to participate in risky competitive behavior, and often celebrated big deals by heading off to a bar or dance club.[3]

A related concept concerning the influence of norms and values on how people work together and how they treat one another and customers is called *social capital*. **Social capital** refers to the quality of interactions among people and whether they share a common perspective. In organizations with a high degree of social capital, for example, relationships are based on trust, mutual understandings, and shared norms and values that enable people to cooperate and coordinate their activities to achieve goals.[4] An organization can have either a high or a low level of social capital. One way to think of social capital is as *goodwill*. When relationships both within the organization and with customers, suppliers, and partners are based on honesty, trust, and respect, a spirit of goodwill exists and people willingly cooperate to achieve mutual benefits. A high level of social capital enables frictionless social interactions and exchanges that help to facilitate smooth organizational functioning. Relationships based on cutthroat competition, self-interest, and subterfuge can be devastating to a company. Social capital relates to both corporate culture and ethics, which is the subject matter of this chapter.

Purpose of This Chapter

This chapter explores ideas about corporate culture and associated ethical values and how these are influenced by organizations. The first section describes the nature of corporate culture, its origins and purpose, and how to identify and interpret culture by looking at the organization's rites and ceremonies, stories and myths, symbols, organization structures, power relationships, and control systems. We then examine how culture reinforces the strategy and structural design the organization needs to be effective in its environment and discuss the important role of culture in organizational learning and high performance. Next, the chapter turns to ethical values and corporate social responsibility. We consider how managers implement the structures and systems that influence ethical and socially responsible behavior. The chapter also discusses how leaders shape culture and ethical values in a direction suitable for strategy and performance outcomes. The chapter closes with a brief overview of the complex cultural and ethical issues that managers face in an international environment.

ORGANIZATIONAL CULTURE

The popularity of the corporate culture topic raises a number of questions. Can we identify cultures? Can culture be aligned with strategy? How can cultures be managed or changed? The best place to start is by defining culture and explaining how it is reflected in organizations.

What Is Culture?

Culture is the set of values, norms, guiding beliefs, and understandings that is shared by members of an organization and taught to new members as the correct way to think, feel, and behave.[5] It represents the unwritten, feeling part of the organization. Everyone participates in culture, but culture generally goes unnoticed. It is only when managers try to implement new strategies or programs that go against basic cultural norms and values that they come face to face with the power of culture.

Organizational culture exists at two levels, as illustrated in Exhibit 9.1. On the surface are visible artifacts and observable behaviors—the ways people dress and act, the type of control systems and power structures used by the company, and the symbols, stories, and ceremonies organization members share. The visible elements of culture, however, reflect deeper values in the minds of organization members. These underlying values, assumptions, beliefs, and thought processes operate unconsciously to define the true culture.[6] For example, Steelcase built a new pyramid-shaped corporate development center that has scattered, open "thought stations" with white boards and other idea-inspiring features. There is an open atrium from ground floor to top, with a giant ticking pendulum. The new building is a visible symbol; the underlying values are an emphasis on openness, collaboration, teamwork, innovation, and constant change.[7] The attributes of culture display themselves in many ways but typically evolve into a patterned set of activities carried out through social interactions.[8] Those patterns can be used to interpret culture.

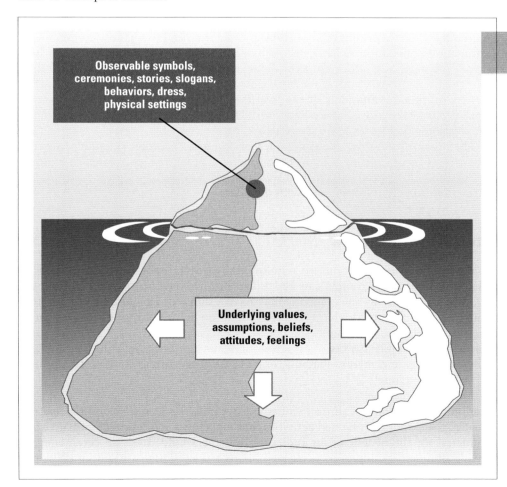

EXHIBIT 9.1
Levels of Corporate Culture

Emergence and Purpose of Culture

Culture provides people with a sense of organizational identity and generates in them a commitment to beliefs and values that are larger than themselves. Though ideas that become part of the culture can come from anywhere within the organization, an organization's culture generally begins with a founder or early leader who articulates and implements particular ideas and values as a vision, philosophy, or business strategy.

When these ideas and values lead to success, they become institutionalized, and an organizational culture emerges that reflects the vision and strategy of the founder or leader.[9] For example, the culture at Whole Foods is based on the values and philosophy of founder and CEO John Mackey—a blend of libertarian politics, a commitment to selling healthy foods and ensuring compassionate treatment of animals, openness and trust among organization members, and a desire for growth. The culture is encapsulated in the firm's "Declaration of Independence," which concludes with the statement, "Whole Foods . . . spurs people toward creating a better person, company, and world."[10]

Cultures serve two critical functions in organizations: (1) to integrate members so that they know how to relate to one another, and (2) to help the organization adapt to the external environment. **Internal integration** means that members develop a collective identity and know how to work together effectively. It is culture that guides day-to-day working relationships and determines how people communicate within the organization, what behavior is acceptable or not acceptable, and how power and status are allocated. **External adaptation** refers to how the organization meets goals and deals with outsiders. Culture helps guide the daily activities of workers to meet certain goals. It can help the organization respond rapidly to customer needs or the moves of a competitor. The right culture can help transform an organization's performance from average to truly great.

The organization's culture also guides employee decision making in the absence of written rules or policies.[11] Thus, both functions of culture are related to building the organization's social capital, by forging either positive or negative relationships both within the organization and with outsiders.

Interpreting Culture

To identify and interpret culture requires that people make inferences based on observable artifacts. Artifacts can be studied but are hard to decipher accurately. An award ceremony in one company may have a different meaning than in another company. To understand what is really going on in an organization requires detective work and probably some experience as an insider. Exhibit 9.2 shows some important observable aspects of organizational culture. These include rites and ceremonies, stories and myths, symbols, organization structures, power relationships, and control systems.[12]

Rites and Ceremonies. Cultural values can typically be identified in **rites and ceremonies**, the elaborate, planned activities that make up a special event and are often conducted for the benefit of an audience. Managers hold rites and ceremonies to provide dramatic examples of what a company values. These are special occasions that reinforce specific values, create a bond among people for sharing an important

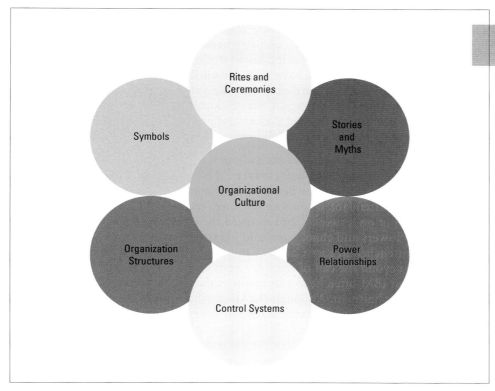

Source: *Long Range Planning. Online* by Johnson. Copyright 1992 by Elsevier Science & Technology Journals. Reproduced with permission of Elsevier Science & Technology Journals in the format Other book via Copyright Clearance Center.

EXHIBIT 9.2
Observable Aspects of
Organizational Culture

understanding, and anoint and celebrate heroes and heroines who symbolize important beliefs and activities.[13]

For example, one type of rite that appears in organizations is a *rite of passage,* which facilitates the transition of employees into new social roles. Another type often used is a *rite of integration,* which creates common bonds and good feelings among employees and increases commitment to the organization. Consider the following examples:

- One major energy company hired new college graduates and enrolled them in a "cadet" training program. Each cadet was rotated on assignments through each of the company's major departments, such as marketing, human resources, etc. At the successful conclusion of each rotation, the cadets were invited to have lunch with senior executives at the "BUG" club, an invitation-only club where senior managers frequently ate lunch.[14] This is a rite of passage.
- Whenever a Wal-Mart executive visits one of the stores, he or she leads employees in the Wal-Mart cheer: "Give me a W! Give me an A! Give me an L! Give me a squiggly! (All do a version of the twist.) Give me an M! Give me an A! Give me an R! Give me a T! What's that spell? Wal-Mart! What's that spell? Wal-Mart! Who's No. 1? THE CUSTOMER!" The cheer strengthens bonds among employees and reinforces their commitment to common goals.[15] This is a rite of integration.

Stories and Myths. Stories are narratives based on true events that are frequently shared among employees and told to new employees to inform them about an organization. Many stories are about company **heroes** who serve as models or ideals for serving cultural norms and values. Some stories are considered **legends** because the events are historic and may have been embellished with fictional details. Other stories are **myths**, which are consistent with the values and beliefs of the organization but are not supported by facts.[16] Stories keep alive the primary values of the organization and provide a shared understanding among all employees. Examples of how stories shape culture are as follows:

- A story is told at Ritz-Carlton hotels about a beach attendant who was stacking chairs for the evening when a guest asked if he would leave out two chairs. The guest wanted to return to the beach in the evening and propose to his girlfriend. Although the attendant was going off duty, he not only left out the chairs, he stayed late, put on a tuxedo, and escorted the couple to their chairs, presenting them with flowers and champagne and lighting candles at their table. The story is firmly entrenched in Ritz-Carlton's folklore and symbolizes the value of going above and beyond the call of duty to satisfy guests.[17]
- Employees at IBM often hear a story about the female security guard who challenged IBM's chairman. Although she knew who he was, the guard insisted that the chairman could not enter a particular area because he wasn't carrying the appropriate security clearance. Rather than getting reprimanded or fired, the guard was praised for her diligence and commitment to maintaining the security of IBM's buildings.[18] By telling this story, employees emphasize both the importance of following the rules and the critical contributions of every employee from the bottom to the top of the organization.

Symbols. Another tool for interpreting culture is the **symbol**. A symbol is something that represents another thing. In one sense, ceremonies, stories, and rites are all symbols because they symbolize deeper values. Another symbol is a physical artifact of the organization. Physical symbols are powerful because they focus attention on a specific item. Examples of physical symbols are as follows:

- At the headquarters of Mother, a small London-based advertising agency known for its strong culture and offbeat ads, there are no private offices. In fact, except for the restrooms, there are no doors in the whole place. This headquarters design symbolizes and reinforces the cultural values of open communication, collaboration, creativity, and equality.[19]
- Symbols can also represent negative elements of corporate culture. At Enron, premium parking spots were symbols of power, wealth, and winning at any cost. At the company's London office, executives submitted blind e-mail bids for the limited spaces. One top manager paid more than $6,000 to use a well-placed company spot for a year.[20]

Organization Structures. A strong reflection of the culture is how the organization is designed. Does it have a rigid *mechanistic* structure or a flexible *organic* structure, as described in Chapter 6? Is there a tall or a flat hierarchy, as discussed in Chapter 2? The way in which people and departments are arranged into a whole, and the degree of flexibility and autonomy people have, tells a lot about which cultural values are emphasized in the organization. Here are a couple of examples:

- Nordstrom's structure reflects the emphasis the department store chain puts on empowering and supporting lower-level employees. Nordstrom is known for its

Briefcase

As an organization manager, keep these guidelines in mind:

Pay attention to corporate culture. Understand the underlying values, assumptions, and beliefs on which culture is based as well as its observable manifestations. Evaluate corporate culture based on rites and ceremonies, stories and myths, symbols, and the structures, control systems and power relationships you can observe in the organization.

extraordinary customer service. Its organization chart, shown in Exhibit 9.3, symbolizes that managers are to support the employees who give the service rather than exercise tight control over them.[21]

- Steelmaker Nucor pushes work that is typically done by supervisors down to line workers and work that is typically done by plant managers down to the supervisors, thus keeping levels of the hierarchy to a minimum. This flat organization structure symbolizes Nucor's emphasis on a team-oriented, egalitarian culture.[22]

Power Relationships. Looking at power relationships means deciphering who influences or manipulates or has the ability to do so. Which people and departments are the key power holders in the organization? In some companies, finance people are quite powerful, whereas in others engineers and designers have the most power. Another aspect is considering whether power relationships are formal or informal, such as whether people have power based primarily on their position in the hierarchy or based on other factors, such as their expertise or admirable character. Consider these examples:

- An investment firm in Atlanta, Georgia, has an "inner sanctum" with special offices, restrooms, and a dining room for senior executives. The entry door has an electronic lock which only members can access. Mid-level managers hold the title of "director" and eat in a separate dining room. First-level supervisors and

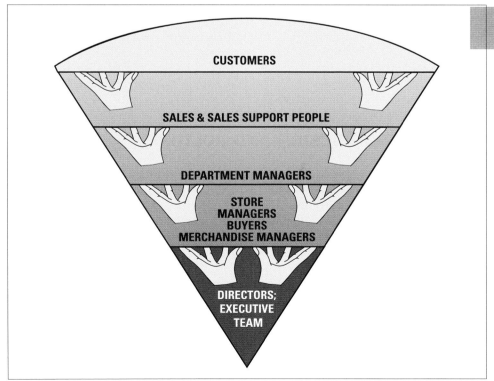

EXHIBIT 9.3
Organization Chart for
Nordstrom Inc.

Source: Used with permission of Nordstrom, Inc.

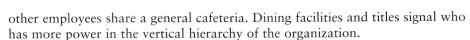

other employees share a general cafeteria. Dining facilities and titles signal who has more power in the vertical hierarchy of the organization.

- At W. L. Gore, few people have titles, and no one has a boss. Rather than people having power based on their position, leaders emerge based on who has a good idea and can recruit people to work on it.[23]

Control Systems. The final element shown in Exhibit 9.2 relates to control systems, or the inner workings of how the organization controls people and operations. This includes looking at such things as how information is managed, whether managers apply behavior or outcome control related to employee activities, quality control systems, methods of financial control, reward systems, and how decisions are made. Two examples of how control systems reflect culture are:

- At InBev NV, the Belgian-Brazilian brewing giant that recently purchased U.S.-based Anheuser-Busch, distribution center managers frequently start the day with a sort of pep rally reviewing the day's sales targets and motivating people to get out and sell more beer. The company's incentive-based compensation system and its focus on increasing sales while relentlessly cutting costs are key elements of a highly competitive corporate culture.[24]
- Netflix lets employees make most of their own choices—even in how to compensate themselves and how much vacation to take. This freedom combined with responsibility reflects what marketing manager Heather McIlhany refers to as a tough, fulfilling, "fully-formed adult" culture.[25]

Recall that culture exists at two levels—the underlying values and assumptions and the visible artifacts and observable behaviors. The rites and ceremonies, stories, symbols, organization structures, power relationships, and control systems just described are visible manifestations of underlying company values. These visible artifacts and behaviors can be used to interpret culture, but they are also used by managers to shape company values and to strengthen the desired corporate culture. Thus, the summary of cultural artifacts shown in Exhibit 9.2 can serve as both a mechanism for interpretation and a guideline for action when managers need to change or strengthen cultural values.[26]

ORGANIZATION DESIGN AND CULTURE

Managers want a corporate culture that reinforces the strategy and structural design that the organization needs to be effective within its environment. For example, if the external environment requires flexibility and responsiveness, such as the environment for Internet-based companies like Twitter, Netflix, Facebook, or Flickr, the culture should encourage adaptability. The correct relationship among cultural values, organizational strategy and structure, and the environment can enhance organizational performance.[27]

Cultures can be assessed along many dimensions, such as the extent of collaboration versus isolation among people and departments, the importance of control and where control is concentrated, or whether the organization's time orientation is short range or long range.[28] Here, we will focus on two specific dimensions: (1) the extent to which the competitive environment requires flexibility or stability; and (2) the extent to which the organization's strategic focus and strength are internal or external. Four categories of culture associated with these differences, as illustrated

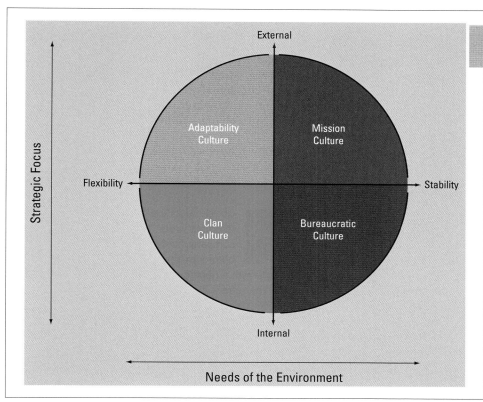

EXHIBIT 9.4
Four Types of
Organizational Culture

Source: Based on Daniel R. Denison and Aneil K. Mishra, "Toward a Theory of Organizational Culture and Effectiveness," *Organization Science* 6, no. 2 (March–April 1995), 204–223; R. Hooijberg and F. Petrock, "On Cultural Change: Using the Competing Values Framework to Help Leaders Execute a Transformational Strategy," *Human Resource Management* 32 (1993), 29–50; and R. E. Quinn, *Beyond Rational Management: Mastering the Paradoxes and Competing Demands of High Performance* (San Francisco: Jossey-Bass, 1988).

in Exhibit 9.4, are adaptability, mission, clan, and bureaucratic.[29] These four categories relate to the fit among cultural values, strategy, structure, and the environment. Each can be successful, depending on the needs of the external environment and the organization's strategic focus.

ASSESS
YOUR
ANSWER

1 Top managers typically should focus their energy more on strategy and structure than on corporate culture.

ANSWER: *Disagree.* Smart top managers know that for the organization to be successful, the right culture has to support and reinforce the strategy and structure to be effective in its environment. Someone once said, "Culture eats strategy for lunch." Managers can invest all the time and resources they have in defining a killer strategy, but if the cultural values are out of line, implementing it will be impossible.

The Adaptability Culture

The **adaptability culture** is characterized by strategic focus on the external environment through flexibility and change to meet customer needs. The culture encourages entrepreneurial values, norms, and beliefs that support the capacity of the organization to detect, interpret, and translate signals from the environment into new behavior responses. This type of company, however, doesn't just react quickly to environmental changes—it actively creates change. Innovation, creativity, and risk taking are valued and rewarded.

A good illustration of the adaptability culture is Google, a company whose values promote individual initiative, experimentation, risk-taking, and entrepreneurship.

Google

Google founders Sergey Brin and Larry Page famously wrote, "Google is not a conventional company." Indeed it isn't. For example, every bathroom stall at Google's corporate headquarters has a Japanese high-tech commode with a heated seat. Then there's the flier posted on the door, titled "Testing on the Toilet," that offers a quiz designed to challenge the brains of software engineers (the quiz changes every few weeks).

It is just another way Google keeps people thinking in unconventional ways to help the company keep innovating. Another way is by putting a premium on success but seeming to shrug off mistakes and failure. Consider what happened when vice president Sheryl Sandberg committed a mistake that cost the company several million dollars. After Page accepted her apology, he said, "I'm so glad you made this mistake. . . . If we don't have any of these mistakes, we're just not taking enough risk." *Fortune* magazine called it "chaos by design." *The Washington Post* referred to it as a "culture of fearlessness." Whatever you call it, Google's culture works.

The atmosphere inside Google feels like a university, where brainy graduate students have fun, work long and hard, and engage in academic debates about ideas that are treated like matters of global importance. They can bring their dogs to work, do their laundry on site, work out in the gym, study Mandarin, Japanese, Spanish, or French, and eat at any of eleven free gourmet cafeterias. Engineers, the "big men" (and women) on campus, spend 20 percent of their time working on their own ideas. Everyone is encouraged to propose outrageously ambitious ideas often, and teams are assigned to explore whether they will work. A lot of them don't, but some take off spectacularly. The innovative culture is visible throughout the campus. Glass-walled workrooms are jammed with groups of people, and whiteboards line the hallways so employees can scribble random thoughts.

The hiring process is designed to find out if the candidate is "Googley." "It's an ill-defined term," says chief culture officer Stacy Sullivan, but it basically means "not someone too traditional or stuck in ways done traditionally by other companies."[30] ■

With rapid growth, Google's culture is beginning to show signs of strain. The company zoomed from a few hundred people at headquarters to more than 20,000 in locations scattered around the world, and the processes needed to manage a large corporation hinder some of its creativity and flexibility. In addition, a global economic downturn has led to stronger top-down management and more control of risks and costs. Leaders are scaling back the anything-goes culture as they look for ways to ensure the company continues to thrive during hard times. Nevertheless, they are also consciously trying to keep the heart of the culture intact. As one said, "Our unique culture is part of what makes Google Google."[31] Most Internet-based companies, like Google, use the adaptability type of culture, as do many companies in the marketing, electronics, and cosmetics industries, because they must move quickly to satisfy customers.

The Mission Culture

An organization concerned with serving specific customers in the external environment, but without the need for rapid change, is suited to the mission culture. The **mission culture** is characterized by emphasis on a clear vision of the organization's purpose and on the achievement of goals, such as sales growth, profitability, or market share, to help achieve the purpose. Individual employees may be responsible for a specified level of performance, and the organization promises specified rewards in return. Managers shape behavior by envisioning and communicating a desired future state for the organization. Because the environment is stable, they can translate the vision into measurable goals and evaluate employee performance for meeting them. In some cases, mission cultures reflect a high level of competitiveness and a profit-making orientation.

InBev, mentioned earlier in the chapter, reflects a mission culture. Professionalism, ambition, and aggressiveness are key values. Managers keep employees focused on achieving high sales and profit levels, and those who meet the demanding goals are handsomely rewarded. Bonuses and promotions are based on performance, not seniority, and top executives are unapologetic about giving special treatment to high achievers.[32]

The Clan Culture

The **clan culture** has a primary focus on the involvement and participation of the organization's members and on rapidly changing expectations from the external environment. This culture is similar to the clan form of control we will discuss in Chapter 12. More than any other, this culture focuses on meeting the needs of employees as the route to high performance. Involvement and participation create a sense of responsibility and ownership and, hence, greater commitment to the organization.

In a clan culture, an important value is taking care of employees and making sure they have whatever they need to help them be satisfied as well as productive. Companies in the fashion and retail industries often adopt this culture because it releases the creativity of employees to respond to rapidly changing tastes. Wegmans, a family-run chain of seventy-one supermarkets, has succeeded with a clan culture. Employee commitment and satisfaction is considered key to success, and Wegmans invests heavily in employee development and support programs. The company pays good wages, sends employees on learning trips, and offers college scholarships for both full- and part-time employees. Employees are empowered to use their own initiative and creativity in serving customers.[33]

The Bureaucratic Culture

The **bureaucratic culture** has an internal focus and a consistency orientation for a stable environment. This type of culture supports a methodical approach to doing business. Symbols, heroes, and ceremonies reinforce the values of cooperation, tradition, and following established policies and practices as ways to achieve goals. Personal involvement is somewhat lower here, but that is outweighed by a high level of consistency, conformity, and collaboration among members. This organization succeeds by being highly integrated and efficient.

Briefcase

As an organization manager, keep these guidelines in mind:

Make sure corporate culture is consistent with strategy and the environment. Culture can be shaped to fit the needs of both. Four types of culture are adaptability culture, mission culture, clan culture, and bureaucratic culture.

Today, most managers are shifting away from bureaucratic cultures because of a need for greater flexibility. However, Pacific Edge Software (now part of Serena Software) successfully implemented elements of a bureaucratic culture to ensure that all its projects stayed on time and on budget. The husband-and-wife co-founders, Lisa Hjorten and Scott Fuller, intentionally implanted a culture of order, discipline, and control. This emphasis on order and focus meant employees generally went home by 6:00 P.M. rather than working all night to finish an important project. Although sometimes being careful means being slow, Pacific Edge managed to keep pace with the demands of the external environment.[34]

Some people like the order and predictability of a bureaucratic culture, whereas other people would feel stifled and constrained by too much discipline and would be happier working in some other type of culture. Complete the question-naire in the "How Do You Fit the Design?" box to get an idea of which type of

How Do You Fit the Design?

Corporate Culture Preference

The fit between a manager or employee and corporate culture can determine both personal success and satisfaction. To understand your culture preference, rank the following items from 1 to 8 based on the strength of your preference (1 = highest preference; 8 = lowest preference).

1. The organization is very personal, much like an extended family. ____

2. The organization is dynamic and changing, where people take risks. ____

3. The organization is achievement oriented, with the focus on competition and getting jobs done.

4. The organization is stable and structured, with clarity and established procedures.

5. Management style is characterized by teamwork and participation.

6. Management style is characterized by innovation and risk-taking.

7. Management style is characterized by high performance demands and achievement.

8. Management style is characterized by security and predictability.

Scoring: To compute your preference for each type of culture, add together the scores for each set of two questions as follows:

Clan culture—total for questions 1, 5:_____
Adaptability culture—total for questions 2, 6:_____
Mission culture—total for questions 3, 7_____
Bureaucratic culture—total for questions 4, 8:_____

Interpretation: Each of the preceding questions pertains to one of the four types of culture in Exhibit 9.4. A lower score means a stronger preference for that specific culture. You will likely be more comfortable and more effective as a manager in a corporate culture that is compatible with your personal preferences. A higher score means the culture would not fit your expectations, and you would have to change your style to be effective. Review the text discussion of the four culture types. Do your cultural preference scores seem correct to you? Can you think of companies that would fit your culture preference?

Source: Adapted from Kim S. Cameron and Robert E. Quinn, *Diagnosing and Changing Organizational Culture* (Reading, Massachusetts: Addison-Wesley, 1999).

culture—adaptability, mission, clan, or bureaucratic—you would be most comfortable and successful working in.

Culture Strength and Organizational Subcultures

Culture strength refers to the degree of agreement among members of an organization about the importance of specific values. If widespread consensus exists about the importance of those values, the culture is cohesive and strong; if little agreement exists, the culture is weak.[35]

A strong culture is typically associated with the frequent use of ceremonies, symbols, and stories, as described earlier, and managers align structures and processes to support the cultural values. These elements increase employee commitment to the values and strategy of a company. However, culture is not always uniform throughout the organization, particularly in large companies. Even in organizations that have strong cultures, there may be several sets of subcultures. **Subcultures** develop to reflect the common problems, goals, and experiences that members of a team, department, or other unit share. An office, branch, or unit of a company that is physically separated from the company's main operations may also take on a distinctive subculture.

For example, although the dominant culture of an organization may be a mission culture, various departments may also reflect characteristics of adaptability, clan, or bureaucratic cultures. The manufacturing department of a large organization may thrive in an environment that emphasizes order, efficiency, and obedience to rules, whereas the research and development (R&D) department may be characterized by employee empowerment, flexibility, and customer focus. This is similar to the concept of differentiation described in Chapter 6, where employees in manufacturing, sales, and research departments studied by Paul Lawrence and Jay Lorsch[36] developed different values with respect to time horizon, interpersonal relationships, and formality in order to perform the job of each particular department most effectively. Consider how the credit division of Pitney Bowes, a huge corporation that manufactures postage meters, copiers, and other office equipment, developed a distinctive subculture to encourage innovation and risk taking.

Pitney Bowes Credit Corporation

Pitney Bowes, a maker of postage meters and other office equipment, has long thrived in an environment of order and predictability. Its headquarters reflects a typical corporate environment and an orderly culture with its blank walls and bland carpeting. But step onto the third floor of the Pitney Bowes building in Shelton, Connecticut, and you might think you're at a different company. The domain of Pitney Bowes Credit Corporation (PBCC) looks more like an indoor theme park, featuring cobblestone-patterned carpets, faux gas lamps, and an ornate town square-style clock. It also has a French-style café, a 1950s-style diner, and the "Cranial Kitchen," where employees sit in cozy booths to surf the Internet or watch training videos. The friendly hallways encourage impromptu conversations, where people can exchange information and share ideas they wouldn't otherwise share.

PBCC traditionally helped customers finance their business with the parent company. However, Matthew Kisner, PBCC's president and CEO, has worked with other managers to redefine the division as a *creator* of services rather than just a provider of services. Rather than just financing sales and leasing of existing products, PBCC now creates new services

(continued)

for customers to buy. For example, Purchase Power is a revolving line of credit that helps companies finance their postage costs. It was profitable within nine months and now has more than 400,000 customers. When PBCC redefined its job, it began redefining its subculture to match, by emphasizing values of teamwork, risk taking, and creativity. "We wanted a fun space that would embody our culture," Kisner says. "No straight lines, no linear thinking. Because we're a financial services company, our biggest advantage is the quality of our ideas." So far, PBCC's new approach is working. In one year, the division, whose 600 employees make up less than 2 percent of Pitney Bowes' total workforce, generated 36 percent of the company's net profits.[37] ■

Subcultures typically include the basic values of the dominant organizational culture plus additional values unique to members of the subculture. However, subcultural differences can sometimes lead to conflicts between departments, especially in organizations that do not have strong overall corporate cultures. When subcultural values become too strong and outweigh the corporate cultural values, conflicts may emerge and hurt organizational performance. Conflict was discussed in detail in Chapter 7.

ORGANIZATIONAL CULTURE, LEARNING, AND PERFORMANCE

Briefcase

As an organization manager, keep this guidelines in mind:

Consciously manage culture to shift values toward high performance and goal accomplishment.

Culture can play an important role in creating an organizational climate that enables learning and innovative response to challenges, competitive threats, or new opportunities. A strong culture that encourages adaptation and change enhances organizational performance by energizing and motivating employees, unifying people around shared goals and a higher mission, and shaping and guiding behavior so that everyone's actions are aligned with strategic priorities. Thus, creating and influencing an adaptive culture is one of a manager's most important jobs. The right culture can drive high performance.[38]

A number of studies have found a positive relationship between culture and performance.[39] In *Corporate Culture and Performance,* Kotter and Heskett provided evidence that companies that intentionally managed cultural values outperformed similar companies that did not. Some companies have developed systematic ways to measure and manage the impact of culture on organizational performance. At Caterpillar, leaders used a tool called the Cultural Assessment Process (CAP), which gave top executives hard data documenting millions of dollars in savings they could attribute directly to cultural factors.[40] Even the U.S. federal government is recognizing the link between culture and effectiveness. The U.S. Office of Personnel Management created its Organizational Assessment Survey as a way for federal agencies to measure culture factors and shift values toward high performance.[41]

Strong cultures that don't encourage adaptation, however, can hurt the organization. A danger for many successful organizations is that the culture becomes set and the company fails to adapt as the environment changes. When organizations are successful, the values, ideas, and practices that helped attain success become institutionalized. As the environment changes, these values may become detrimental to future performance. Many organizations become victims of their own success, clinging to outmoded and even destructive values and behaviors. Thus, the impact of a strong culture is not always positive. Typically, healthy cultures not only provide for smooth internal integration but also encourage adaptation to the external

environment. Nonadaptive cultures encourage rigidity and stability. Strong adaptive cultures often incorporate the following values:

1. *The whole is more important than the parts, and boundaries between parts are minimized.* People are aware of the whole system, how everything fits together, and the relationships among various organizational parts. All members consider how their actions affect other parts and the total organization. This emphasis on the whole reduces boundaries both within the organization and with other companies. Although subcultures may form, everyone's primary attitudes and behaviors reflect the organization's dominant culture. The free flow of people, ideas, and information allows coordinated action and continuous learning.
2. *Equality and trust are primary values.* The culture creates a sense of community and caring for one another. The organization is a place for creating a web of relationships that allows people to take risks and develop to their full potential. The emphasis on treating everyone with care and respect creates a climate of safety and trust that allows experimentation, frequent mistakes, and learning. Managers emphasize honest and open communications as a way to build trust.
3. *The culture encourages risk taking, change, and improvement.* A basic value is to question the status quo. Constant questioning of assumptions opens the gates to creativity and improvement. The culture rewards and celebrates the creators of new ideas, products, and work processes. To symbolize the importance of taking risks, an adaptive culture may also reward those who fail in order to learn and grow.

Briefcase

As an organization manager, keep these guidelines in mind:

To support a learning orientation, emphasize cultural values of openness and collaboration, equality and trust, continuous improvement, and risk taking. Build a strong internal culture that encourages adaptation to changing environmental conditions.

As illustrated in Exhibit 9.5, adaptive corporate cultures have different values and behavior patterns than nonadaptive cultures.[42] In adaptive cultures, managers are concerned with customers and employees as well as with the internal processes and procedures that bring about useful change. Behavior is flexible, and managers initiate change when needed, even if it involves risk. In unadaptive cultures, managers are more concerned about themselves or their own special projects, and

EXHIBIT 9.5
Adaptive versus Nonadaptive Corporate Cultures

	Adaptive Corporate Cultures	Nonadaptive Corporate Cultures
Core Values	Managers care deeply about customers, stockholders, and employees. They also strongly value people and processes that can create useful change (for example, leadership initiatives up and down the management hierarchy).	Managers care mainly about themselves, their immediate work group, or some product (or technology) associated with that work group. They value the orderly and risk-reducing management process much more highly than leadership initiatives.
Common Behavior	Managers pay close attention to all their constituencies, especially customers, and initiate change when needed to serve their legitimate interests, even if it entails taking some risks.	Managers tend to be somewhat isolated, political, and bureaucratic. As a result, they do not change their strategies quickly to adjust to or take advantage of changes in their business environments.

Source: Adapted and reprinted with the permission of The Free Press, a division of Simon & Schuster Adult Publishing Group, from *Corporate Culture and Performance* by John P. Kotter and James L. Heskett. Copyright © 1992 by Kotter Associates, Inc. and James L. Heskett.

their values discourage risk taking and change. Thus, strong, healthy cultures help organizations adapt to the external environment, whereas strong, unhealthy cultures can encourage organizations to march resolutely in the wrong direction. A strong, adaptive culture has been a competitive weapon for biotechnology firm Genentech since it was founded in the mid-1970s.

IN PRACTICE

Genentech

Genentech, the world's first biotechnology company, seemed to come out of nowhere to become a major force in the pharmaceuticals industry. Founded in 1976, Genentech became profitable three years later and has remained so ever since. The secret ingredient, most people agree, is the corporate culture. When Art Levinson became CEO, he set about strengthening Genentech's adaptive culture through a series of moves, such as persuading the board to invest 50 percent of revenues back into research, focusing the company on "meeting significant unmet needs," and breaking down boundaries by insisting that fiefdoms like product development and basic research work closely together. He also did away with projects and people that didn't fit the strategy and values.

People at Genentech feel less like employees and more like partners in a great cause. Employees don't get work assignments, they get "appointments." Every milestone is celebrated with a party, and people are encouraged to goof off and have fun. However, scientists and researchers also go through a rigorous process of defending their work before a review board in order to uncover flaws, avoid dead ends, sift out politics and favoritism, and hold people accountable.

Genentech is characterized by values of collaboration, accountability, creativity, and egalitarianism. There are no special dining rooms or assigned parking spaces. Everyone in the company is considered vital to success. Job candidates often go through as many as twenty interviews because Genentech wants to be sure it gets people with the right values. "We're extremely non-hierarchical," says Levinson. "We're not wearing ties. People don't call us doctor." Candidates who ask too many questions about salary, title, and personal advancement are quickly weeded out. Genentech wants people who care about the science and about the company's mission to find drugs for curing big diseases like cancer. Status is conveyed not by fancy offices or titles, but rather by taking big chances in the name of "making drugs that matter."[43] ∎

ETHICAL VALUES AND SOCIAL RESPONSIBILITY

Of the values that make up an organization's culture, ethical values are now considered among the most important. Widespread corporate accounting scandals and ethical lapses among leaders in business and government have filled the news in recent years. A study of business news related to the 100 largest U.S. corporations found that a whopping 40 percent of them have recently been involved in activities that can be considered unethical.[44] And the problem isn't limited to the United States. Business leaders in countries such as Germany and Japan have also been reeling in recent years from one headline-grabbing scandal after another.[45] Top corporate managers are under scrutiny from the public as never before, and even small companies are finding a need to put more emphasis on ethics to restore trust among their customers and the community.

Sources of Individual Ethical Principles

Ethics refers to the code of moral principles and values that governs the behaviors of a person or group with respect to what is right or wrong. Ethical values set standards as to what is good or bad in conduct and decision making.[46] Ethics are personal and unique to each individual, although in any given group, organization, or society there are many areas of consensus about what constitutes ethical behavior. Exhibit 9.6 illustrates the varied sources of individual ethical principles.[47] Each person is a creation of his or her time and place in history. National culture, religious heritage, historical background, and so forth lead to the development of societal morality, or society's view of what is right and wrong. Societal morality is often reflected in norms of behavior and values about what makes sense for an orderly society. Some principles are codified into laws and regulations, such as laws against drunk driving, robbery, or murder.

These laws, as well as unwritten societal norms and values, shape the local environment within which each individual acts, such as a person's community, family, and place of work. Individuals absorb the beliefs and values of their family, community, culture, society, religious community, and geographic environment, typically discarding some and incorporating others into their own personal ethical standards. Each person's ethical stance is thus a blending of his or her historical, cultural, societal, and family backgrounds and influences, as illustrated in Exhibit 9.6.

EXHIBIT 9.6
Sources of Individual Ethical Principles and Actions

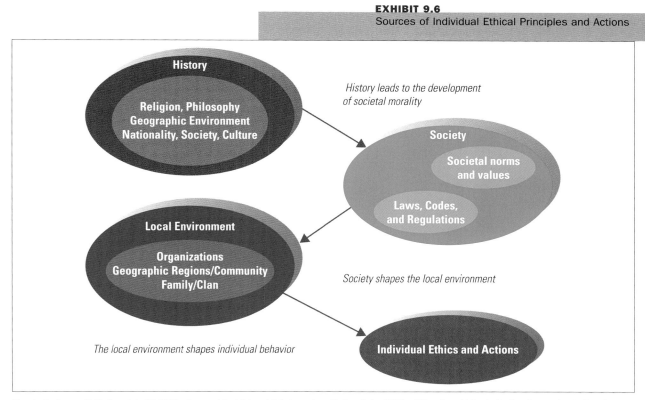

Thanks to Susan H. Taft and Judith White for providing this exhibit, based on their article, "Ethics Education: Using Inductive Reasoning to Develop Individual, Group, Organizational, and Global Perspectives," *Journal of Management Education* 31, no. 5 (October 2007): 614–646.

It is important to look at individual ethics because ethics always involve an individual action, whether it be a decision to act or the failure to take action against wrongdoing by others. In organizations, an individual's ethical stance may be affected by peers, subordinates, and supervisors, as well as by the organizational culture. Organizational culture often has a profound influence on individual choices and can support and encourage ethical actions or promote unethical and socially irresponsible behavior.

Managerial Ethics

Many of the recent scandals in the news have dealt with people and corporations that broke the law. But it is important to remember that ethical decisions go far beyond behaviors governed by law.[48] The **rule of law** arises from a set of codified principles and regulations that describe how people are required to act, that are generally accepted in society, and that are enforceable in the courts.[49]

The relationship between ethical standards and legal requirements is illustrated in Exhibit 9.7. Ethical standards for the most part apply to behavior not covered by the law, and the rule of law applies to behaviors not necessarily covered by ethical standards. Current laws often reflect combined moral judgments, but not all moral judgments are codified into law. The morality of aiding a drowning person, for example, is not specified by law, and driving on the right-hand side of the road has no moral basis; but in acts such as robbery or murder, rules and moral standards overlap. Many people believe that if you are not breaking the law, then you are behaving in an ethical manner, but this is not always true. Many behaviors have not been codified, and managers must be sensitive to emerging norms and values about those issues.

Managerial ethics are principles that guide the decisions and behaviors of managers with regard to whether they are right or wrong. Examples of the need for managerial ethics are as follows:[50]

• Top executives are considering promoting a rising sales manager who consistently brings in $70 million a year and has cracked open new markets in places

EXHIBIT 9.7
Relationship between the
Rule of Law and Ethical
Standards

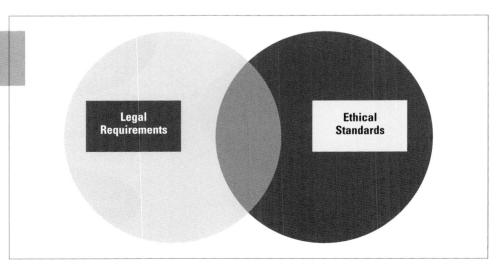

Source: LaRue Tone Hosmer, *The Ethics of Management,* 2nd ed. (Homewood, Ill.: Irwin, 1991).

like Brazil and Turkey that are important for international growth. However, female employees have been complaining for years that the manager is verbally abusive to them, tells offensive jokes, and throws temper tantrums if female employees don't do exactly as he says.

- The manager of a beauty supply store is told that she and her salespeople can receive large bonuses for selling a specified number of boxes of a new product, a permanent-wave solution that costs nearly twice as much as what most of her salon customers typically use. She orders her salespeople to store the old product in the back and tell customers there's been a delay in delivery.
- A North American manufacturer operating abroad was asked to make cash payments (a bribe) to government officials and was told it was consistent with local customs, despite being illegal in North America.

As these examples illustrate, ethics is about making decisions. Managers make choices every day about whether to be honest or deceitful with customers and suppliers, treat employees with respect or disdain, and be a good or a harmful corporate citizen. Some issues are exceedingly difficult to resolve and often represent ethical dilemmas. An **ethical dilemma** arises in a situation concerning right and wrong in which values are in conflict.[51] Right or wrong cannot be clearly identified in such situations. For example, for a salesperson at the beauty supply store, the value conflict is between being honest with customers and adhering to the boss's expectations. The manufacturing manager may feel torn between respecting and following local customs in a foreign country or adhering to U.S. laws concerning bribes. Sometimes, each alternative choice or behavior seems undesirable. Ethical dilemmas are not easy to resolve, but top executives can aid the process by establishing organizational values that provide people with guidelines for making the best decision from a moral standpoint.

Corporate Social Responsibility

The notion of **corporate social responsibility (CSR)** is an extension of the idea of managerial ethics and refers to management's obligation to make choices and take action so that the organization contributes to the welfare and interest of all organizational stakeholders, such as employees, customers, shareholders, the community, and the broader society.[52] Ninety percent of companies surveyed by McKinsey & Company in 2008 said they were doing more than they were five years earlier to incorporate social responsibility issues into their core strategies.[53]

CSR was once seen as the purview of small, offbeat companies like Patagonia or The Body Shop, but it has moved firmly into the mainstream of organizational thinking and behavior. Ernst & Young lends out employees to provide free accounting services to nonprofit organizations or struggling small businesses around the world, paying their salaries and travel expenses. Burger King has made a commitment to begin buying eggs, pork, and poultry from companies that use humane methods of raising and slaughtering animals. Giant corporations from Wal-Mart to General Electric have announced ambitious environmental responsibility goals. More than 1,000 companies around the world have published reports proclaiming their concern for employees, the environment, and their local communities.[54]

ASSESS YOUR ANSWER

2 Being ethical and socially responsible is not just the right thing for a corporation to do; it is a critical issue for business success.

ANSWER: *Agree.* Following years of scandal, employees and the public are demanding a more ethical and socially responsible approach to business. Businesses as well as nonprofits and governmental organizations are looking for ways to restore trust. A new generation of job seekers takes a company's social responsibility into account when considering job offers, so companies that want to hire the best are paying attention.

Does It Pay to Be Good?

Why are so many companies embracing CSR? For one thing, customers and the public are paying closer attention than ever before to what organizations do, and managers recognize that being a good corporate citizen can enhance their firm's reputation and even its profitability.[55] The relationship of an organization's ethics and social responsibility to its performance concerns both managers and organization scholars. Studies have provided varying results but generally have found that there is a positive relationship between ethical and socially responsible behavior and financial results.[56] For example, one study of the financial performance of large U.S. corporations that are considered "best corporate citizens" found that they have both superior reputations and superior financial performance.[57] Similarly, Governance Metrics International, an independent corporate governance ratings agency, found that the stocks of companies run on more selfless principles perform better than those run in a self-serving manner. Top-ranked companies such as Pfizer, Johnson Controls, and Sunoco also outperformed lower-ranking firms on measures like return on assets, return on investment, and return on capital.[58]

As discussed earlier in the chapter, long-term organizational success relies largely on social capital, which means companies need to build a reputation for honesty, fairness, and doing the right thing. There is evidence that people prefer to work for companies that demonstrate a high level of ethics and corporate social responsibility, so these companies can attract and retain high-quality employees.[59] Sarah Antonette says she joined PNC Financial Services rather than two others companies that offered her a job because of PNC's strong employee volunteer program.[60] One vice president at Timberland says she has turned down lucrative offers from other companies because she prefers to work at a company that puts ethics and social responsibility ahead of just making a profit.[61] And a survey of 13-to-25-year-olds found that 79 percent say they want to work for a company that cares about how it affects or contributes to society.[62]

Customers pay attention to a company's ethics and social responsibility too. A study by Walker Research indicates that, price and quality being equal, two-thirds of people say they would switch brands to do business with a company that makes a high commitment to ethics.[63] Another series of experiments by Remi Trudel and June Cotte of the University of Western Ontario's Ivey School of Business found that consumers were willing to pay slightly more for products they were told had been made using high ethical standards.[64]

Companies that put ethics on the back burner in favor of fast growth and short-term profits ultimately suffer. To gain and keep the trust of employees, customers, investors, and the general public, organizations must put ethics and social responsibility first.

HOW LEADERS SHAPE CULTURE AND ETHICS

In a study of ethics policy and practice in successful, ethical companies such as Johnson & Johnson and General Mills, no point emerged more clearly than the role of top management in providing commitment, leadership, and examples for ethical behavior.[65] The CEO and other top managers must be committed to specific ethical values and provide constant leadership in tending and renewing the values. Values can be communicated in a number of ways—speeches, company publications, policy statements, and, especially, personal actions. Top leaders are responsible for creating and sustaining a culture that emphasizes the importance of ethical behavior for every employee. When Vic Sarni was CEO of PPG Industries, he often called himself the chief ethics officer. Sarni didn't believe in using special staff departments to investigate ethical complaints; instead, he personally headed the firm's ethics committee. This sent a powerful symbolic message that ethics was important in the organization.[66] However, it is important to remember that employees are often influenced most by the managers and supervisors they work with closely, rather than by distant top leaders. Managers throughout the organizations need to espouse and model ethical values. Formal ethics programs are worthless if leaders do not live up to high standards of ethical conduct.[67]

The following sections examine how managers signal and implement values through leadership as well as through the formal systems of the organization.

Values-Based Leadership

The underlying value system of an organization cannot be managed in the traditional way. Issuing an authoritative directive, for example, has little or no impact on an organization's value system. Organizational values are developed and strengthened primarily through **values-based leadership**, a relationship between a leader and followers that is based on shared, strongly internalized values that are advocated and acted upon by the leader.[68]

Every act and statement of managers has an impact on culture and values. For example, a survey of readers of the magazine *The Secretary* found that employees are acutely aware of their bosses' ethical lapses. Something as simple as having a secretary notarize a document without witnessing the signature may seem insignificant, but it communicates that the manager doesn't value honesty.[69] Employees learn about values, beliefs, and goals from watching managers, just as students learn which topics are important for an exam, what professors like, and how to get a good grade from watching professors. Actions speak louder than words, so values-based leaders "walk their talk."[70] "Just saying you're ethical isn't very useful," says Charles O. Holliday Jr., chairman and CEO of DuPont. "You have to earn trust by what you do every day."[71]

John Tu and David Sun, co-founders of Kingston Technology Company, illustrate values-based leadership in action. For them, business is not about money, it's

Briefcase

As an organization manager, keep these guidelines in mind:

Act as a leader for the internal culture and ethical values that are important to the organization. Treat people fairly, hold yourself and others to high ethical standards, and communicate a vision for putting ethics before short-term interests. Remember that actions speak louder than words.

about relationships. When the two sold 80 percent of Kingston to Softbank Corp. of Japan for $1.5 billion, they set aside $100 million of the proceeds for employee bonuses. Despite this amazing generosity, when employees talk about why they like working for Kingston, they rarely mention money and benefits. Instead, they talk about personal acts of gentleness or kindness performed by the two top leaders. There are many stories of these leaders quietly offering money, time, other resources—or just genuine concern—to employees who were dealing with family or personal troubles. This approach to leadership creates an emotional bond with employees that builds mutual trust and respect.[72]

Employees learn from and model the behaviors of people they admire. In many cases, employees look up to their managers, so values-based leaders serve as ethical role models. For example, Kathryn Reimann, senior vice president of global compliance at American Express Company, says she learned how to be a values-based leader by watching the actions of a highly respected senior executive she worked with early in her career. When this executive learned that another senior manager was mistreating employees, he publicly fired him—even though the manager was a very strong performer and the company was facing a tough competitive situation. Reimann remembered his courage in firing such a high performer, even in bad times, and his behavior shaped her own ability to stand up and do the right thing.[73]

Exhibit 9.8 outlines some of the characteristics that define values-based leaders.[74] Values-based leaders treat others with care, are helpful and supportive of others, and

EXHIBIT 9.8
Characteristics of Values-Based Leaders

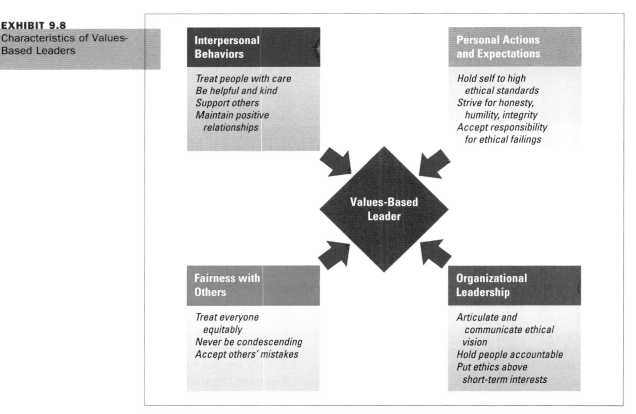

Source: Based on Gary Weaver, Linda Klebe Treviño, and Bradley Agle, "'Somebody I Look Up To': Ethical Role Models in Organizations," *Organizational Dynamics* 34, no. 4 (2005), 313–330.

put effort into maintaining positive interpersonal relationships. They treat everyone fairly and with respect. Values-based leaders accept others' mistakes and failures and are never condescending. They hold themselves to high ethical standards, continuously strive to be honest, humble, and trustworthy and to be consistently ethical in both their public and private lives. However, they are open about and accept responsibility for their own ethical failings.

Values-based leaders also clearly articulate and communicate an uncompromising vision for high ethical standards in the organization, and they institutionalize the vision by holding themselves and others accountable and by putting ethics above short-term personal or company interests. They continuously strengthen ethical values through everyday behaviors, rituals, ceremonies, and symbols, as well as through organizational systems and policies.

Formal Structure and Systems

Another set of tools leaders can use to shape cultural and ethical values is the formal structure and systems of the organization. These systems can be especially effective for influencing managerial ethics.

Structure. Top executives can assign responsibility for ethical values to a specific position. This not only allocates organization time and energy to the problem but symbolizes to everyone the importance of ethics. One example is an **ethics committee**, which is a cross-functional group of executives who oversee company ethics. The committee provides rulings on questionable ethical issues and assumes responsibility for disciplining wrongdoers. By appointing top-level executives to serve on the committee, the organization signals the importance of ethics.

Today, many organizations are setting up ethics departments that manage and coordinate all corporate ethics activities. These departments are headed by a **chief ethics officer**, a high-level company executive who oversees all aspects of ethics, including establishing and broadly communicating ethical standards, setting up ethics training programs, supervising the investigation of ethical problems, and advising managers on the ethical aspects of corporate decisions.[75] The title of chief ethics officer was almost unheard of a decade ago, but recent ethical and legal problems have created a growing demand for these specialists. In the five years after the collapse of Enron, membership in the Ethics and Compliance Officers Association, a trade group based in Waltham, Massachusetts, soared 70 percent to 1,260 members.[76]

Ethics offices sometimes also work as counseling centers to help employees resolve tricky ethical dilemmas. The focus is as much on helping employees make the right decisions as on disciplining wrongdoers. Most ethics offices have confidential **ethics hotlines** that employees can use to seek guidance as well as report questionable behavior. One organization calls its hotline a "Guide Line" to emphasize its use as a tool for making ethical decisions as well as reporting lapses.[77] According to Gary Edwards, president of the Ethics Resource Center, between 65 and 85 percent of calls to hotlines in the organizations he advises are calls for counsel on ethical issues. Northrup Grumman's "Openline" fields about 1,400 calls a year, of which only one-fourth are reports of misdeeds.[78]

Disclosure Mechanisms. A confidential hotline is also an important mechanism for employees to voice concerns about ethical practices. Holding organizations accountable depends to some degree on individuals who are willing to speak up if they

Briefcase

As an organization manager, keep these guidelines in mind:

Use the formal systems of the organization to implement desired cultural and ethical values. These systems include an ethics committee, a chief ethics officer, disclosure mechanisms, a code of ethics, and ethics training programs.

suspect illegal, dangerous, or unethical activities. **Whistle-blowing** is employee disclosure of illegal, immoral, or illegitimate practices on the part of the organization.[79] As ethical problems in the corporate world increase, many companies are looking for ways to protect whistle-blowers. In addition, calls are increasing for stronger legal protection for those who report illegal or unethical business activities.[80] When there are no protective measures, whistle-blowers suffer, and the company may continue its unethical or illegal practices.

Many whistle-blowers suffer financial and personal loss to maintain their personal ethical standards. For example, in Japan, where there has been a rash of whistle-blowing disclosures in recent years, employees who speak out are frequently ostracized both at work and in their communities. Consider what happened to Masakatsu Yamada, a used car salesman who reported falsified sales records at his Toyota dealership. Yamada says he became a pariah among his colleagues and eventually felt that he had to leave his job. Unable to make mortgage payments, Yamada lost his house. The family is struggling to survive on his wife's salary as a part-time postal worker. "My life is all messed up," he says. "But society won't change unless average people like me stand up."[81]

Many governments, including the United States and Japan, have passed laws aimed at protecting whistle-blowers. But that isn't enough. Enlightened companies strive to create a climate and a culture in which employees feel free to point out problems and managers take swift action to address concerns about unethical or illegal activities. Organizations can view whistle-blowing as a benefit to the company, helping to prevent the kind of disasters that hit companies such as Enron, Arthur Andersen, and WorldCom.

Code of Ethics. A **code of ethics** is a formal statement of the company's values concerning ethics and social responsibility; it clarifies to employees what the company stands for and its expectations for employee conduct. The code of ethics at Lockheed Martin, for example, states that the organization "aims to set the standard for ethical conduct" through adhering to the values of honesty, integrity, respect, trust, responsibility, and citizenship. The code specifies the types of behaviors expected to honor these values and encourages employees to use available company resources to help make ethical choices and decisions.[82] Codes of ethics may cover a broad range of issues, including statements of the company's guiding values; guidelines related to issues such as workplace safety, the security of proprietary information, or employee privacy; and commitments to environmental responsibility, product safety, and other matters of concern to stakeholders.

Some companies use broader values statements within which ethics is a part. These statements define ethical values as well as corporate culture and contain language about company responsibility, quality of product, and treatment of employees. A formal statement of values can serve as a fundamental organizational document that defines what the organization stands for and clarifies the expected ethical behaviors and choices.[83]

Although written codes of ethics and value statements are important, it is essential that top managers support and reinforce the codes through their actions, including rewards for compliance and discipline for violations. Otherwise, a code of ethics is nothing more than a piece of paper. Indeed, one study found that companies with a written code of ethics are just as likely as those without a code to be found guilty of illegal activities.[84] Enron is the perfect example of how a company can have a well-developed code of ethics, yet fail to embrace and live up to the stated values.[85]

3 **The single best way to make sure an organization stays on solid ethical ground is to have a strong code of ethics and make sure all employees are familiar with its guidelines.**

ANSWER: *Disagree.* Having a strong code of ethics can be an important part of creating an ethical organization, but leaders' actions are more powerful in determining whether people live up to high ethical standards. If leaders are dishonest, unprincipled, or ruthless and create a culture that supports or ignores these behaviors in others, employees will put little stock in the formal ethics code.

Training Programs. To ensure that ethical issues are considered in daily decision making, many companies supplement a written code of ethics with employee training programs.[86] At Citigroup, an online ethics training program is mandatory for all 300,000 employees worldwide.[87] All Texas Instruments (TI) employees go through an eight-hour ethics training course that includes case examples giving people a chance to wrestle with ethical dilemmas. In addition, TI incorporates an ethics component into every training course it offers.[88]

In an important step, some training programs also include frameworks for ethical decision making. Learning these frameworks helps employees act autonomously and still think their way through a difficult decision. In a few companies, managers are also taught about the stages of moral development, which helps to bring them to a high level of ethical decision making. This training has been an important catalyst for establishing ethical behavior and integrity as critical components of strategic competitiveness.[89]

These formal systems and structures can be highly effective. However, they alone are not sufficient to build and sustain an ethical company. Leaders should integrate ethics into the organizational culture, as well as support and renew ethical values through their words and actions. Only when employees are convinced that ethical values play a key role in all management decisions and actions can they become committed to making them a part of their everyday behavior.

CORPORATE CULTURE AND ETHICS IN A GLOBAL ENVIRONMENT

Organizations operating on a global basis often face particularly tough ethical challenges because of the various cultural and market factors they must deal with. The greater complexity of the environment and organizational domain create a greater potential for ethical problems or misunderstandings.[90] Consider that in Europe, privacy has been defined as a basic human right and there are laws limiting the amount and kind of information companies can collect and governing how they may use it. In U.S. organizations, on the other hand, collecting data, trading it with partners, using it for marketing, and even selling it are all common practice.[91]

Employees from different countries may have varied attitudes and beliefs that make it difficult to establish a sense of community and cohesiveness based on the corporate culture. In fact, research has indicated that national culture has a greater impact on employees than does corporate culture, and differences in national culture also create tremendous variance in ethical attitudes.[92] So, how do managers translate the ideas for developing strong, ethical corporate cultures to a complex global environment?

Vijay Govindarajan, a professor of international business and director of the "Global Leadership 2020" management program at Dartmouth College, offers some guidance. His research indicates that, even though organizational cultures may vary widely, there are specific components that characterize a global culture. These include an emphasis on multicultural rather than national values, basing status on merit rather than nationality, being open to new ideas from other cultures, showing excitement rather than trepidation when entering new cultural environments, and being sensitive to cultural differences without being limited by them.[93]

Managers must also think more broadly in terms of ethical issues. Companies are using a wide variety of mechanisms to support and reinforce their ethics initiatives on a global scale. One of the most useful mechanisms for building global ethics is the **social audit**, which measures and reports the ethical, social, and environmental impact of a company's operations.[94] Concerns about the labor practices and working conditions of many major U.S. corporations' overseas suppliers originally spurred the Council on Economic Priorities Accreditation Agency to propose a set of global social standards to deal with issues such as child labor, low wages, and unsafe working conditions. Today, the Social Accountability 8000, or SA 8000, is the only auditable social standard in the world. The system is designed to work like the ISO 9000 quality-auditing system. Many companies, such as Avon, Eileen Fisher, and Toys "R" Us, are taking steps to ensure that their factories and suppliers meet SA 8000 standards.[95]

In the coming years, organizations will continue to evolve in their ability to work with varied cultures, combine them into a cohesive whole, live up to high social and ethical standards worldwide, and cope with the conflicts that may arise when working in a multicultural environment.

DESIGN ESSENTIALS

■ This chapter covered a range of material on corporate culture, the importance of cultural and ethical values, and techniques managers can use to influence these values. Cultural and ethical values help determine the organization's social capital, and the right values can contribute to organizational success.

■ Culture is the set of key values, beliefs, and norms shared by members of an organization. Organizational cultures serve two critically important functions—to integrate members so that they know how to relate to one another and to help the organization adapt to the external environment. Culture can be interpreted by looking at the organization's rites and ceremonies, stories, symbols, structures, control systems, and power relationships. Managers can also use these elements to influence culture.

■ Organizational culture should reinforce the strategy and structure that the organization needs to be successful in its environment. Four types of culture that may exist in organizations are adaptability culture, mission culture, clan culture, and bureaucratic culture. When widespread consensus exists about the importance of specific values, the organizational culture is strong and cohesive. However, even in organizations with strong cultures, several sets of subcultures may emerge, particularly in large organizations.

- Strong cultures can be either adaptive or nonadaptive. Adaptive cultures have different values and different behavior patterns than nonadaptive cultures. Strong but unhealthy cultures can be detrimental to a company's chances for success. On the other hand, strong adaptive cultures can play an important role in creating high performance and innovative responses to challenges, competitive threats, or new opportunities.

- An important aspect of organizational values is managerial ethics, which is the set of values governing behavior with respect to what is right or wrong. Corporate social responsibility (CSR) is an extension of managerial ethics and refers to management responsibility to make choices that contribute to the welfare of society as well as the organization. CSR has become a critical business issue for organizations.

- The chapter also discussed how leaders shape culture and ethics. One important idea is values-based leadership, which means leaders define a vision of proper values, communicate it throughout the organization, and institutionalize it through everyday behavior, rituals, ceremonies, and symbols. We also discussed formal systems that are important for shaping ethical values. Formal systems include an ethics committee, an ethics department, disclosure mechanisms for whistle-blowing, ethics training programs, and a code of ethics or values statement that specifies desired ethical values and behaviors.

- As business increasingly crosses geographical and cultural boundaries, leaders face difficult challenges in establishing strong cultural and ethical values with which all employees can identify and agree. Companies that develop global cultures emphasize multicultural values, base status on merit rather than nationality, are excited about new cultural environments, remain open to ideas from other cultures, and are sensitive to different cultural values without being limited by them. Social audits are important tools for companies trying to maintain high ethical standards on a global basis.

Key Concepts

adaptability culture	ethics committee	rule of law
bureaucratic culture	ethics hotlines	social audit
chief ethics officer	external adaptation	social capital
clan culture	heroes	stories
code of ethics	internal integration	subcultures
corporate social responsibility (CSR)	legends	symbol
culture	managerial ethics	values-based leadership
culture strength	mission culture	whistle-blowing
ethical dilemma	myths	
ethics	rites and ceremonies	

Discussion Questions

1. Can you recall a situation in which either you or someone you know was confronted by an ethical dilemma, such as being encouraged to inflate an expense account or trade answers on a test? Do you think the decision was affected more by individual moral values or by the accepted values within the team or company? Explain.

2. Codes of ethics have been criticized for transferring responsibility for ethical behavior from the organization to the individual employee. Do you agree? Do you think a code of ethics is valuable for an organization?

3. Why is values-based leadership so important to the influence of culture? Does a symbolic act communicate more about company values than an explicit statement? Discuss.

4. Why has globalization contributed to more complex ethical issues? Do you think it's possible for a company operating in many different countries to have a cohesive corporate culture? To have uniform ethical values?

5. Can a strong bureaucratic culture also be an adaptive culture, as defined in the text and in Exhibit 9.5? Discuss.

6. What importance would you attribute to leadership statements and actions for influencing ethical values and decision making in an organization?

7. Many of the companies on *Fortune* magazine's list of most admired companies are also on its list of most profitable ones. Some people say this proves that high social capital translates into profits. Other people suggest that high profitability is the primary reason the companies have a good culture and are admired in the first place. Discuss your thinking about these two differing interpretations.

8. In a survey of 20,000 people in sixteen European countries plus Russia, Turkey, and the United States, 55 percent of respondents said cheating in business is more common than it was ten years ago. Do you believe this is truly the case, or have new forms of media simply made cheating more visible? Discuss.

9. How much do you think it is possible for an outsider to discern about the underlying cultural values of an organization by analyzing symbols, ceremonies, dress, or other observable aspects of culture, compared to an insider with several years of work experience? Specify a percentage (e.g., 10%, 70%) and discuss your reasoning.

Chapter 9 Workbook: Shop 'til You Drop: Corporate Culture in the Retail World*

To understand more about corporate culture, visit two retail stores and compare them according to various factors. Go to one discount or low-end store, such as Kmart or Wal-Mart, and to one high-end store, such as Saks Fifth Avenue or Macy's. Do not interview any employees, but instead be an observer or a shopper. After your visits, fill out the following table for each store. Spend at least two hours in each store on a busy day and be very observant.

Culture Item	Discount Store	High-End Department Store
1. Mission of store: What is it, and is it clear to employees?		
2. Individual initiative: Is it encouraged?		
3. Reward system: What are employees rewarded for?		

Culture Item	Discount Store	High-End Department Store
4. Teamwork: Do people within one department or across departments work together or talk with each other?		
5. Company loyalty: Is there evidence of loyalty or of enthusiasm to be working there?		
6. Dress: Are there uniforms? Is there a dress code? How strong is it? How do you rate employees' personal appearance in general?		
7. Diversity or commonality of employees: Is there diversity or commonality in age, education, race, personality, and so on?		
8. Service orientation: Is the customer valued or tolerated?		
9. Human resource development: Is there opportunity for growth and advancement?		

Questions

1. How does the culture seem to influence employee behavior in each store?
2. What effect does employees' behavior have on customers?
3. Which store was more pleasant to be in? How does that relate to the mission of the store?

*Copyright 1996 by Dorothy Marcic. All rights reserved.

Case for Analysis: Implementing Change at National Industrial Products*

Curtis Simpson sat staring out the window of his office. What would he say to Tom Lawrence when they met this afternoon? Tom had clearly met the challenge Simpson set for him when he hired him as president of National Industrial Products (National) a little more than a year ago, but the company seemed to be coming apart at the seams. As chairman and CEO of Simpson Industries, which had bought National several years ago, Simpson was faced with the task of understanding the problem and clearly communicating his ideas and beliefs to Lawrence.

National Industrial Products is a medium-sized producer of mechanical seals, pumps, and other flow-control products.

When Simpson Industries acquired the company, it was under the leadership of Jim Carpenter, who had been CEO for almost three decades and was very well liked by employees. Carpenter had always treated his employees like family. He knew most of them by name, often visited them in their homes if they were ill, and spent part of each day just chatting with workers on the factory floor. National sponsored an annual holiday party for its workers, as well as company picnics and other social events several times a year, and Carpenter was always in attendance. He considered these activities to be just as important as his visits with customers or negotiations with suppliers. Carpenter believed it was important to treat people right so they would have a sense of loyalty to the company. If business was slow, he would find something else for workers to do, even if it was just sweeping the parking lot, rather than lay people off. He figured the company couldn't afford to lose skilled workers who were so difficult to replace. "If you treat people right," he said, "they'll do a good job for you without your having to push them."

Carpenter had never set performance objectives and standards for the various departments, and he trusted his managers to run their departments as they saw fit. He offered training programs in communications and HR for managers and team leaders several times each year. Carpenter's approach had seemed to work quite well for much of National's history. Employees were very loyal to Carpenter and the company, and there were many instances in which workers had gone above and beyond the call of duty. For example, when two National pumps that supplied water to a U.S. Navy ship failed on a Saturday night just before the ship's scheduled departure, two employees worked throughout the night to make new seals and deliver them for installation before the ship left port. Most managers and employees had been with the company for many years, and National boasted the lowest turnover rate in the industry.

However, as the industry began to change in recent years, National's competitiveness began to decline. Four of National's major rivals had recently merged into two large companies that were better able to meet customer needs, which was one factor that led to National being acquired by Simpson Industries. Following the acquisition, National's sales and profits had continued to decline, while costs kept going up. In addition, Simpson Industries' top executives were concerned about low productivity at National. Although they had been happy to have Carpenter stay on through the transition, within a year they had gently pressured him into early retirement. Some of the top managers believed Carpenter tolerated poor performance and low productivity in order to maintain a friendly atmosphere. "In today's world, you just can't do that," one had said. "We've got to bring in someone who can implement change and turn this company around in a hurry, or National's going to go bankrupt." That's when Tom Lawrence was brought on board, with a mandate to cut costs and improve productivity and profits.

Lawrence had a growing reputation as a young, dynamic manager who could get things done fast. He quickly began making changes at National. First, he cut costs by discontinuing the company-sponsored social activities, and he even refused to allow the impromptu birthday celebrations that had once been a regular part of life at National. He cut the training programs in communications and HR, arguing that they were a waste of time and money. "We're not here to make people feel good," he told his managers. "If people don't want to work, get rid of them and find someone else who does." He often referred to workers who complained about the changes at National as "crybabies."

Lawrence established strict performance standards for his vice presidents and department managers and ordered them to do the same for their employees. He held weekly meetings with each manager to review department performance and discuss problems. All employees were now subject to regular performance reviews. Any worker who had substandard performance was to be given one warning and then fired if performance did not improve within two weeks. And, whereas managers and sales representatives had once been paid on a straight salary basis, with seniority being the sole criterion for advancement, Lawrence implemented a revised system that rewarded them for meeting productivity, sales, and profit goals. For those who met the standards, rewards were generous, including large bonuses and perks such as company cars and first-class air travel to industry meetings. Those who fell behind were often chided in front of their colleagues to set an example, and if they didn't shape up soon, Lawrence didn't hesitate to fire them.

By the end of Lawrence's first year as president of National, production costs had been reduced by nearly 20 percent, while output was up 10 percent and sales increased by nearly 10 percent as well. However, three experienced and well-respected National managers had left the company for jobs with competitors, and turnover among production workers had increased alarmingly. In the tight labor market, replacements were not easily found. Most disturbing to Simpson were the results of a survey he had commissioned by an outside consultant. The survey indicated that morale at National was in the pits. Workers viewed their supervisors with antagonism and a touch of fear. They expressed the belief that managers were obsessed with profits and quotas and cared nothing about workers' needs and feelings. They also noted that the collegial, friendly atmosphere that had made National a great place to work had been replaced by an environment of aggressive internal competition and distrust.

Simpson was pleased that Lawrence has brought National's profits and productivity up to the standards Simpson Industries expects. However, he was concerned that the low morale and high turnover would seriously damage the company in the long run. Was Lawrence correct that many of the employees at National are just being "crybabies?" Were they so accustomed to being coddled by Carpenter that they weren't willing to make the changes necessary to keep the company competitive? Finally, Simpson wondered if a spirit of competition can exist in an atmosphere of collegiality and cooperativeness such as that fostered by Carpenter.

*Based on Gary Yukl, "Consolidated Products," in Leadership in Organizations, 4th ed. (Englewood Cliffs, N.J.: Prentice-Hall, 1998), 66–67; John M. Champion and John H. James, "Implementing Strategic Change," in Critical Incidents in Management: Decision and Policy Issues, 6th ed. (Homewood, Ill.: Irwin, 1989), 138–140; and William C. Symonds, "Where Paternalism Equals Good Business," BusinessWeek (July 20, 1998), 16E4, 16E6.

George Stein, a college student working for Eastern Dairy during the summer, was suddenly faced with an ethical dilemma. George had very little time to think about his choices, less than a minute. On the one hand, he could do what Paul told him to do, and his shift could go home on time. However, he found it tough to shake the gross mental image of all those innocent kids drinking milkshakes contaminated with pulverized maggots. If he chose instead to go against Paul, what would the guys say? He could almost hear their derisive comments already: "wimp . . . college kid . . ."

Background

George Stein had lived his entire life in various suburbs of a major city on the East Coast. His father's salary as a manager provided the family with a solid middle-class lifestyle. His mother was a homemaker. George's major interests in life were the local teenage gathering place—a drive-in restaurant—hot rod cars, and his girlfriend, Cathy. He had not really wanted to attend college, but relentless pressure by his parents convinced him to try it for a year. He chose mechanical engineering as his major, hoping there might be some similarity between being a mechanical engineer and being a mechanic. After one year of engineering school, however, he has not seen any similarity yet. Once again this summer, his parents had to prod and cajole him to agree to return to school in the fall. They only succeeded by promising to give their blessing to his marriage to Cathy following his sophomore year.

George had worked at menial jobs each of the last four summers to satisfy his immediate need for dating and car money. He did manage to put away a bit to be used for spending money during the school year. He had saved very little for the day that he and Cathy would start their life together, but they planned for Cathy to support them with her earnings as a customer service representative until George either finished or quit school.

The day after George returned home this summer, he heard that Eastern Dairy might hire summer help. He applied at the local plant the next day. Eastern Dairy was unionized, and the wages paid were more than twice the minimum wage George had been paid on previous jobs, so he was quite interested in a position.

Eastern Dairy manufactured milkshake and ice cream mix for a number of customers in the metropolitan area. It sold the ice cream mix in 5- and 10-gallon containers to other firms, which then added the flavoring ingredients (e.g., strawberries or blueberries), packaged and froze the mix, and sold the ice cream under their own brand names. Eastern Dairy sold the milkshake mix in 5-gallon cardboard cartons, which contained a plastic liner. These packages were delivered to many restaurants in the area. The packaging was designed to fit into automatic milkshake machines used in many types of restaurants, including most fast-food restaurants and drive-ins.

George was elated when he received the call asking him to come to the plant on June 8. After a brief visit with the HR director, at which time George filled out the necessary employment forms, he was instructed to report for work at 11:00 P.M. that night. He was assigned to the night shift, working from 11:00 P.M. until 7:00 A.M. six nights per week—Sunday through Friday. With the regular wages paid at Eastern Dairy, supplemented by time-and-a-half pay for 8 hours of guaranteed overtime each week, George thought he could save a tidy sum before he had to return to school at the end of the first week in September.

When George reported to work, he discovered that there were no managers assigned to the night shift. The entire plant was run by a six-person crew of operators. One member of this crew, a young man named Paul Burnham, received each night's production orders from the day shift superintendent as the superintendent left for the day. Although Paul's status was no different from that of his five colleagues, the other crew members looked to him for direction. Paul passed the production orders to the mixer (who was the first stage of the production process) and kept the production records for the shift.

The production process was really quite simple. Mixes moved between various pieces of equipment (including mixing vats, pasteurizers, coolers, homogenizers, and filling machines) through stainless steel pipes suspended from the ceiling. All of the pipes had to be disassembled, thoroughly cleaned, and reinstalled by the conclusion of the night shift. This process took approximately one hour, so all the mix had to be run by 6:00 A.M. in order to complete the cleanup by the 7:00 A.M. quitting time. Paul and one other worker, Fred (the mixer), cleaned the giant mixing vats while the other four on the shift, including George, cleaned and reinstalled the pipes and filters.

George soon learned that Paul felt a sense of responsibility for completing all of the assigned work before the end of the shift. However, as long as that objective was achieved, he did not seem to care about what else went on during the shift. A great deal of story-telling and horseplay was the norm, but the work was always completed by quitting time. George was soon enjoying the easy camaraderie of the work group, the outrageous pranks they pulled on one another, and even the work itself.

George's position required that he station himself beside the conveyor in a large freezer room. He removed containers of mix as they came down the line and stacked them in the appropriate places. Periodically, Paul would decide that they had all worked hard enough and would shut down the line for a while so that they could engage in some nonwork activity like joke telling, hiding each other's lunch boxes, or "balloon" fights. The balloons were actually the 5-gallon, flexible liners for the cardboard boxes in which the mix was sold.

While George did not relish being hit by an exploding bag containing 5 gallons of heavy mix, he found it great fun to lob one at one of his co-workers. The loss of 10 to 40 gallons of mix on a shift did not seem to concern anyone, and these fights were never curtailed. George quickly learned that management had only two expectations of the night shift. First, the shift was expected to complete the production orders each night. Second, management expected the equipment, including the pipes, to be spotlessly clean at the conclusion of the shift. Paul told George that inspectors from the county health department would occasionally drop by unannounced at the end of the shift to inspect the vats and pipes after they had been disassembled and scrubbed. Paul also told George that management would be very upset if the inspectors registered any complaints about cleanliness.

George did join the union but saw very little evidence of its involvement in the day-to-day operations of the plant. Labor relations seemed quite amicable, and George thought of the union only when he looked at a pay stub and noticed that union dues had been deducted from his gross pay. The difference George noticed in working for Eastern Dairy compared to his previous employers was not the presence of the union but the absence of management.

The Current Situation

Things seemed to be going quite well for George on the job—until a few minutes ago. The problem first surfaced when the milkshake mix that was being run started spewing out of one of the joints in the overhead pipe network. The pumps were shut down while George disassembled the joint to see what the problem was. George removed the filter screen from the pipe at the leaking joint and saw that it was completely packed with solid matter. Closer inspection revealed that maggots were the culprits. George hurriedly took the filter to Paul to show him the blockage. Paul did not seem too concerned and told George to clean the filter and reassemble the joint. When George asked how this could have happened, Paul said maggots occasionally got into the bags of certain ingredients that were stored in a warehouse at the back of the lot. "But you don't have to worry," said Paul. "The filters will catch any solid matter."

Feeling somewhat reassured, George cleaned the filter and reassembled the pipe. But still, the image of maggots floating in a milkshake was hard to shake. And, unfortunately for George, that was not the end of it.

Shortly after the pumps were restarted, the mix began to flow out of another joint. Once again, a filter plugged with maggots was found to be the cause.

For the second time, George cleaned the filter and reassembled the connection. This time Paul had seemed a bit more concerned as he noted that they barely had enough time to run the last 500 gallons remaining in the vats before they needed to clean up in preparation for the end of the shift.

Moments after the equipment was again restarted, another joint started to spew. When maggots were found to be clogging this filter, too, Paul called George over and told him to remove all five filters from the line so the last 500 gallons could be run without any filters. Paul laughed when he saw the shocked look on George's face.

"George," he said, "don't forget that all of this stuff goes through the homogenizer, so any solid matter will be completely pulverized. And when it's heated in the pasteurization process, any bacteria will be killed. No one will ever know about this, the company can save a lot of mix—that's money—and, most important, we can run this through and go home on time."

George knew that they would never get this lot packaged if they had to shut down every minute to clean filters, and there was no reason to believe it would not be this way for the rest of the run. The product had been thoroughly mixed in the mixing vats at the beginning of the process, which meant that contaminants would be distributed uniformly throughout the 500 gallons. George also knew that the 500 gallons of milkshake was very expensive. He did not think management would just want it dumped down the drain.

Finally, Paul was definitely right about one thing—removing all of the filters, a 10-minute job at most, would ensure that they could get everything cleaned up and be out on time.

As George walked to the first filter joint, he felt a knot forming in his stomach as he thought of kids drinking all of the milkshakes they were about to produce. He had already decided he would not have another milkshake for at least a month, in order to be absolutely sure that this batch was no longer being served at restaurants. After all, he did not know exactly which restaurants would receive this mix. As he picked up his wrench and approached the first pipe joint that contained a filter, he still could not help wondering if he should do or say something more.

NOTE: This case appeared in Paul F. Buller and Randall S. Schuler, *Managing Organizations and People,* South-Western © 2000.

*This case was prepared by Roland B. Cousins, LaGrange College, and Linda E. Benitz, InterCel, Inc., as a basis for class discussion and not to illustrate either effective or ineffective handling of an administrative situation. The names of the firm and individuals and the location involved have been disguised to preserve anonymity. The situation reported is factual. The authors thank Anne T. Lawrence for her assistance in the development of this case.

Chapter 9 Workshop: The Power of Ethics*

This exercise will help you to better understand the concept of ethics and what it means to you.

1. Spend about 5 minutes individually answering the questions below.
2. Divide into groups of four to six members.
3. Have each group try to achieve consensus with answers to each of the four questions. For question 3, choose one scenario to highlight. You will have 20 to 40 minutes for this exercise, depending on the instructor.
4. Have groups share their answers with the whole class, after which the instructor will lead a discussion on ethics and its power in business.

Questions

1. In your own words, define the concept of ethics in one or two sentences.
2. If you were a manager, how would you motivate your employees to follow ethical behavior? Use no more than two sentences.
3. Describe a situation in which you were faced with an ethical dilemma. What was your decision and behavior? How did you decide to do that? Can you relate your decision to any concept in the chapter?
4. What do you think is a powerful ethical message for others? Where did you get it from? How will it influence your behavior in the future?

*Adapted by Dorothy Marcic from Allayne Barrilleaux Pizzolatto's "Ethical Management: An Exercise in Understanding Its Power," *Journal of Management Education* 17, no. 1 (February 1993), 107–109.

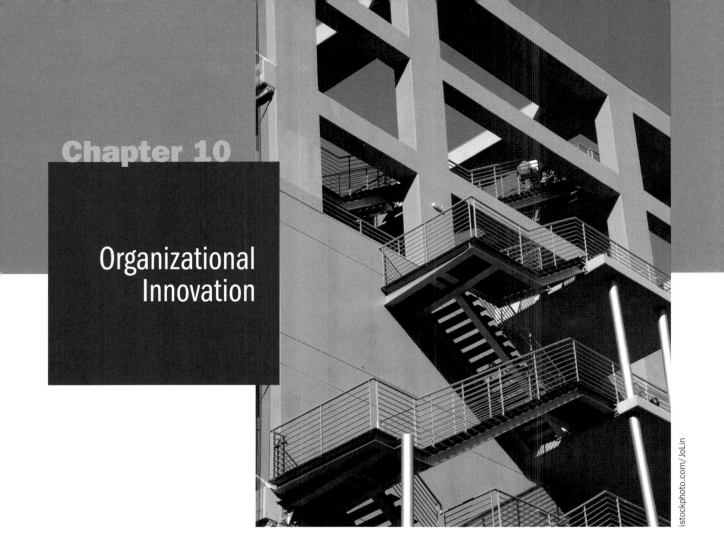

Chapter 10

Organizational Innovation

The Strategic Role of Change
Innovate or Perish · Strategic Types of Change

Elements for Successful Change

Technology Change
The Ambidextrous Approach · Techniques for Encouraging Technology Change

New Products and Services
New Product Success Rate · Reasons for New Product Success · Horizontal Coordination Model · Achieving Competitive Advantage: The Need for Speed

Strategy and Structure Change
The Dual-Core Approach · Organization Design for Implementing Management Change

Culture Change
Forces for Culture Change · Organization Development Culture Change Interventions

Strategies for Implementing Change
Leadership for Change · Barriers to Change · Techniques for Implementation

Design Essentials

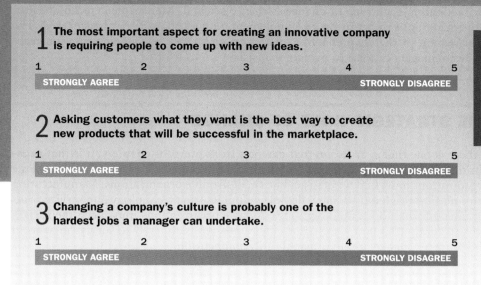

Before reading this chapter, please circle your opinion below for each of the following statements:

Managing by Design Questions

1 **The most important aspect for creating an innovative company is requiring people to come up with new ideas.**

1	2	3	4	5
STRONGLY AGREE				STRONGLY DISAGREE

2 **Asking customers what they want is the best way to create new products that will be successful in the marketplace.**

1	2	3	4	5
STRONGLY AGREE				STRONGLY DISAGREE

3 **Changing a company's culture is probably one of the hardest jobs a manager can undertake.**

1	2	3	4	5
STRONGLY AGREE				STRONGLY DISAGREE

Denise Chudy is a sales team leader at Google, and Aaron Lichtig is a brand manager at Procter & Gamble (P&G), but recently the two have been spending a lot of time together. They are among the two dozen or so Google and P&G employees who are involved in a job swapping program whereby they sit in on each other's staff training programs and participate in high-level business meetings. What's the point? The job swapping strategy is all in the name of spurring innovation. P&G, one of the most successful companies in the world at traditional marketing, knows it needs new approaches to reach a new generation of consumers, while Google knows it needs to find better ways of tapping into the advertising dollars of large, traditional companies like P&G.[1]

Every company faces a challenge in keeping up with changes in the external environment. New discoveries, new inventions, and new approaches quickly replace standard ways of doing things. Organizations like Procter & Gamble, Google, Wal-Mart, UPS, Nokia, and MySpace are searching for any innovation edge they can find. The pace of change is revealed in the fact that the parents of today's college-age students grew up without iPods, video on demand, laser checkout systems, smartphones, TiVo, text messaging, and the Internet. The idea of communicating instantly with people around the world was unimaginable to many people as recently as a decade ago. High-tech industries seem to change every nanosecond, but companies in all industries face greater pressures for innovation today. Bob Jordon, head of technology and strategy at Southwest Airlines, spoke for managers all over the world when he said, "We have to change to survive."

Purpose of This Chapter

This chapter explores how organizations change and how managers direct the innovation and change process. First we look at the forces driving a need for change in today's organizations. The next section describes the four types of change—technology, product, structure, people—occurring in organizations, and how to

369

manage change successfully. The organization structure and management approach for facilitating each type of change is then discussed. Management techniques for influencing both the creation and implementation of change are also covered. The final section of the chapter looks at barriers to change and implementation techniques managers can use to overcome resistance.

THE STRATEGIC ROLE OF CHANGE

If there is one theme or lesson that emerges from previous chapters, it is that organizations must run fast to keep up with changes taking place all around them. Large organizations must find ways to act like small, flexible organizations. Manufacturing firms need to reach out for new, flexible manufacturing technology and service firms for new information technology (IT). Today's organizations must keep themselves open to continuous innovation, not only to prosper but merely to survive in a world of disruptive change and increasingly stiff competition.

Innovate or Perish

As illustrated in Exhibit 10.1, a number of environmental forces drive this need for major organizational change.[2] Powerful forces associated with advancing technology, international economic integration, the maturing of domestic markets, and the shift to capitalism in formerly communist regions have brought about a globalized economy that affects every business, from the largest to the smallest, creating more threats as well as more opportunities. To recognize and manage the threats and take advantage of the opportunities, today's companies are undergoing dramatic changes in all areas of their operations.

Many organizations are responding to global forces by adopting self-directed teams and horizontal structures that enhance communication and collaboration, streamlining supply and distribution channels, and overcoming barriers of time and place through IT and e-business. Others become involved in joint ventures or consortia to exploit opportunities and extend operations or markets internationally. Some adopt structural innovations such as the virtual network approach to focus on their core competencies while outside specialists handle other activities. In addition, today's organizations face a need for major strategic and cultural change and for rapid and continuous innovations in technology, services, products, and processes. For example, when the price of fuel spiked, Southwest Airlines looked for technology innovations to increase efficiency. The company was able to dramatically cut fuel usage by adding efficiency-boosting winglets on its aircraft. FedEx is continually introducing service innovations. It recently launched the Smart Package, used for transporting delicate goods like human organs. The Smart Package is wired so that shippers and recipients can not only track the package every step of the way but also monitor its temperature and humidity and get alerts if it is damaged.[3]

Change, rather than stability, is the norm today. Whereas change once occurred incrementally and infrequently, today it is dramatic and constant. A key element of the success of companies such as FedEx, Southwest Airlines, Apple, and Toyota has been their passion for creating change. On the other hand, U.S. auto companies are in dire straits largely because they have been slow to change.

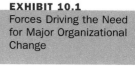

EXHIBIT 10.1
Forces Driving the Need
for Major Organizational
Change

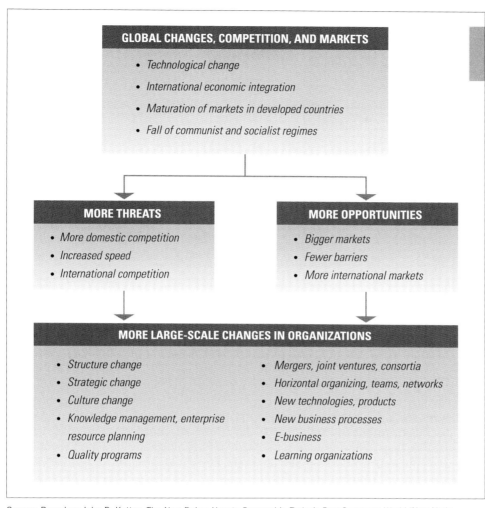

GLOBAL CHANGES, COMPETITION, AND MARKETS

- *Technological change*
- *International economic integration*
- *Maturation of markets in developed countries*
- *Fall of communist and socialist regimes*

MORE THREATS

- *More domestic competition*
- *Increased speed*
- *International competition*

MORE OPPORTUNITIES

- *Bigger markets*
- *Fewer barriers*
- *More international markets*

MORE LARGE-SCALE CHANGES IN ORGANIZATIONS

- *Structure change*
- *Strategic change*
- *Culture change*
- *Knowledge management, enterprise resource planning*
- *Quality programs*

- *Mergers, joint ventures, consortia*
- *Horizontal organizing, teams, networks*
- *New technologies, products*
- *New business processes*
- *E-business*
- *Learning organizations*

Source: Based on John P. Kotter, *The New Rules: How to Succeed in Today's Post-Corporate World* (New York: The Free Press, 1995).

Strategic Types of Change

Managers can focus on four types of change within organizations to achieve strategic advantage. These four types of change are summarized in Exhibit 10.2 as technology, products and services, strategy and structure, and culture. We touched on overall leadership and organizational vision in Chapter 3 and in the previous chapter on corporate culture. These factors provide an overall context within which the four types of change serve as a competitive wedge to achieve an advantage in the international environment. Each company has a unique configuration of products and services, strategy and structure, culture, and technologies that can be focused for maximum impact upon the company's chosen markets.[4]

Technology changes are changes in an organization's production process, including its knowledge and skill base, that enable distinctive competence. These changes are designed to make production more efficient or to produce greater volume. Changes in technology involve the techniques for making products or services. They include work methods, equipment, and workflow. For

Briefcase

As an organization manager, keep this guideline in mind:

Recognize that the four types of change are interdependent and that changes in one area often require changes in others.

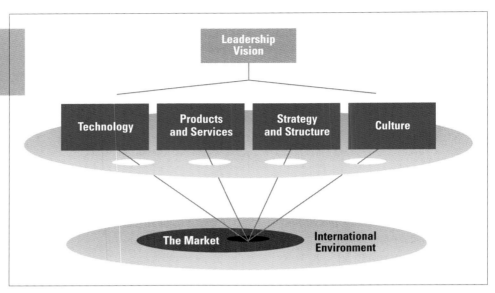

Source: *Academy of Management Executive: The Thinking Manager's Source* by McCann. Copyright 1991 by Academy of Management (NY). Reproduced with permission of Academy of Management (NY) in the format Textbook via Copyright Clearance Center.

example, a technology change at GlaxoSmithKline was the development of software that helps researchers screen potential drugs for possible adverse medical reactions while the drugs are at the earliest stage of development. This means GlaxoSmithKline doesn't spend time and resources on promising drugs only to find out years down the road that they are potentially harmful and can't be marketed.[5]

Product and service changes pertain to the product or service outputs of an organization. New products include small adaptations of existing products or entirely new product lines. New products and services are normally designed to increase the market share or to develop new markets, customers, or clients. Toyota's Hilux truck was a new product designed to increase market share, whereas Apple's iPod was a new product that created a new market for the company. An example of a new service designed to reach new markets and customers comes from India's Tata Consultancy Services. The company's new mKrishi service delivers weather information and crop advice to farmers in rural India via cell phone. The service brings together existing technologies, such as remote sensors, voice-enabled text messaging, and camera phones, in a new way to serve a new market.[6]

Strategy and structure changes pertain to the administrative domain in an organization. The administrative domain involves the supervision and management of the organization. These changes include changes in organization structure, strategic management, policies, reward systems, labor relations, coordination devices, management information and control systems, and accounting and budgeting systems. Structure and system changes are usually top-down, that is, mandated by top management, whereas product and technology changes often come from the bottom up. A system change instituted by top management at 3M was the implementation of a Six Sigma program, a series of management techniques designed to cut defects and increase efficiency. The shift to self-directed teams at ICU Medical Inc. is an example of a top-down structure change. Dr. George Lopez, founder and CEO, made the decision and implemented it, even though some managers and employees at first hated the idea.[7]

Culture changes refer to changes in the values, attitudes, expectations, beliefs, abilities, and behavior of employees. Culture changes pertain to changes in how employees think; these are changes in mind-set rather than technology, structure, or products. Culture was discussed in detail in the previous chapter.

The four types of change in Exhibit 10.2 are interdependent—a change in one often means a change in another. A new product may require changes in the production technology, or a change in structure may require new employee skills. For example, when Shenandoah Life Insurance Company acquired new computer technology to process claims, the technology was not fully utilized until clerks were restructured into teams of five to seven members that were compatible with the technology. The structural change was an outgrowth of the technology change. Organizations are interdependent systems, and changing one part often has implications for other organization elements.

ELEMENTS FOR SUCCESSFUL CHANGE

Regardless of the type or scope of change, there are identifiable stages of innovation, which generally occur as a sequence of events, though innovation stages may overlap.[8] In the research literature on innovation, **organizational change** is considered the adoption of a new idea or behavior by an organization.[9] **Organizational innovation**, in contrast, is the adoption of an idea or behavior that is new to the organization's industry, market, or general environment.[10] The first organization to introduce a new product is considered the innovator, and organizations that copy it are considered to adopt changes. For purposes of managing change, however, the terms *innovation* and *change* will be used interchangeably because the **change process** within organizations tends to be identical whether a change is early or late with respect to other organizations in the environment. Innovations typically are assimilated into an organization through a series of steps or elements. Organization members first become aware of a possible innovation, evaluate its appropriateness, and then evaluate and choose the idea.[11] The required elements of successful change are summarized in Exhibit 10.3. For a change to be successfully implemented, managers must make sure each element occurs in the organization. If one of the elements is missing, the change process will fail.

1. *Ideas.* No company can remain competitive without new ideas; change is the outward expression of those ideas.[12] An idea is a new way of doing things. It may be a new product or service, a new management concept, or a new procedure for working together in the organization. Ideas can come from within or from outside the organization. Internal creativity is a dramatic element of organizational change. **Creativity** is the generation of novel ideas that may meet perceived needs or respond to opportunities. For example, an employee at Boardroom Inc., a publisher of books and newsletters, came up with the idea of cutting the dimensions of the company's books by a quarter inch. Managers learned that the smaller size would reduce postal rates, and implementation of the idea led to annual savings of more than $500,000.[13] Some techniques for spurring internal creativity are to increase the diversity within the organization, make sure employees have plenty of opportunities to interact with people different from themselves, give people time and freedom for experimentation, and support risk taking and making mistakes.[14] Eli Lilly, the Indianapolis-based pharmaceutical company, holds "failure parties," to commemorate brilliant, efficient scientific work that nevertheless resulted in failure. The company's scientists

374

EXHIBIT 10.3
Sequence of Elements
for Successful Change

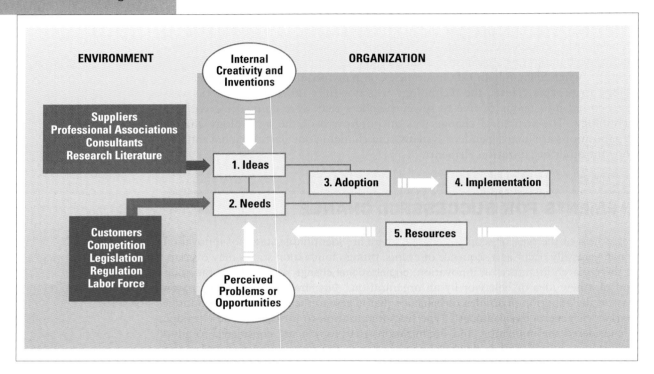

are encouraged to take risks and look for alternative uses for failed drugs. Lilly's osteoporosis drug Evista was a failed contraceptive. Strattera, which treats attention deficit/hyperactivity disorder, had been unsuccessful as an antidepressant. The blockbuster impotence drug Viagra was originally developed to treat severe heart pain.[15]

2. *Need.*   Ideas are generally not seriously considered unless there is a perceived need for change. A perceived need for change occurs when managers see a gap between actual performance and desired performance in the organization. Managers try to establish a sense of urgency so that others will understand the need for change. Sometimes a crisis provides an undoubted sense of urgency. In many cases, however, there is no crisis, so managers have to recognize a need and communicate it to others.[16] A study of innovativeness in industrial firms, for example, suggests that organizations that encourage close attention to customers and market conditions and actively support entrepreneurial activity produce more ideas and are more innovative.[17] Managers at the Walt Disney Company are trying to create those conditions to keep Disney theme parks relevant to a new generation of digitally savvy visitors. They realized the company had lost touch with today's customers, providing ho-hum, passive rides in an era when people expect instant gratification and customized experiences.[18]

3. *Adoption.*   Adoption occurs when decision makers choose to go ahead with a proposed idea. Key managers and employees need to be in agreement to support the change. For a major organizational change, the decision might require the signing of a legal document by the board of directors. For a small change, adoption might occur with informal approval by a middle manager.

4. *Implementation.* Implementation occurs when organization members actually use a new idea, technique, or behavior. Materials and equipment may have to be acquired, and workers may have to be trained to use the new idea. Implementation is a very important step because without it, previous steps are to no avail. Implementation of change is often the most difficult part of the change process. Until people use the new idea, no change has actually taken place.

5. *Resources.* Human energy and activity are required to bring about change. Change does not happen on its own; it requires time and resources, for both creating and implementing a new idea. Employees have to provide energy to see both the need and the idea to meet that need. Someone must develop a proposal and provide the time and effort to implement it. Most innovations go beyond ordinary budget allocations and require special funding. Some companies use task forces, as described in Chapter 2, to focus resources on a change. Others set up seed funds or venture funds that employees with promising ideas can tap into. At Eli Lilly, a "blue sky fund" pays researchers for working on projects that don't appear to make immediate commercial sense.[19]

One point about Exhibit 10.3 is especially important. Needs and ideas are listed simultaneously at the beginning of the change sequence. Either may occur first. Many organizations adopted the computer, for example, because it seemed a promising way to improve efficiency. The search for a vaccine against the HIV virus, on the other hand, was stimulated by a severe need. Whether the need or the idea occurs first, for the change to be accomplished, each of the steps in Exhibit 10.3 must be completed.

Briefcase

As an organization manager, keep these guidelines in mind:

Make sure every change undertaken has a definite need, idea, adoption decision, implementation strategy, and resources. Avoid failure by not proceeding until each element is accounted for.

TECHNOLOGY CHANGE

In today's business world, any company that isn't continually developing, acquiring, or adapting new technology will likely be out of business in a few years. Managers can create the conditions to encourage technology changes. However, organizations face a contradiction when it comes to technology change, because the conditions that promote new ideas are not generally the best for implementing those ideas for routine production. An innovative organization is characterized by flexibility and empowered employees and the absence of rigid work rules.[20] As discussed earlier in this book, an organic, free-flowing organization is typically associated with change and is considered the best organization form for adapting to a chaotic environment. Complete the questionnaire in this chapter's "How Do You Fit the Design?" to see if you have characteristics associated with innovativeness.

The flexibility of an organic organization is attributed to people's freedom to be creative and introduce new ideas. Organic organizations encourage a bottom-up innovation process. Ideas bubble up from middle- and lower-level employees because they have the freedom to propose ideas and to experiment. A mechanistic structure, in contrast, stifles innovation with its emphasis on rules and regulations, but it is often the best structure for efficiently producing routine products. The challenge for managers is to create both organic and mechanistic conditions within the organization to achieve both innovation and efficiency. To attain both aspects of technological change, many organizations use an ambidextrous approach.

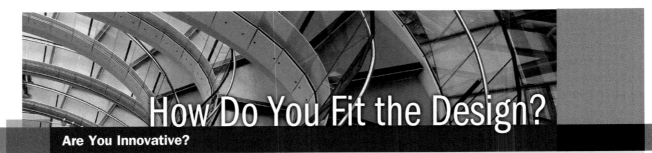

How Do You Fit the Design?

Are You Innovative?

Think about your current life. Indicate whether each of the following items is Mostly True or Mostly False for you.

	Mostly True	Mostly False
1. I am always seeking new ways to do things.		
2. I consider myself creative and original in my thinking and behavior.		
3. I rarely trust new gadgets until I see whether they work for people around me.		
4. In a group or at work I am often skeptical of new ideas.		
5. I typically buy new foods, gear, and other innovations before other people do.		
6. I like to spend time trying out new things.		
7. My behavior influences others to try new things.		
8. Among my co-workers, I will be among the first to try out a new idea or method.		

Scoring: To compute your score on the Personal Innovativeness scale, add the number of Mostly True answers to items 1, 2, 5, 6, 7, 8 and the Mostly False answers to items 3 and 4 for your score.

Interpretation: *Personal Innovativeness* reflects the awareness of a need to innovate and a readiness to try new things. Innovativeness is also thought of as the degree to which a person adopts innovations earlier than other people in the peer group. Innovativeness is considered a positive thing for people in creative companies, creative departments, venture teams, or corporate entrepreneurship. A score of 6–8 indicates that you are very innovative and likely are one of the first people to adopt changes. A score of 4–5 would suggest that you are average or slightly above average in innovativeness compared to others. A score of 0–3 means that you may prefer the tried and true and hence are not excited about new ideas or innovations. As a manager, a high score suggests you will emphasize innovation and change.

Source: Based on H. Thomas Hurt, Katherine Joseph, and Chester D. Cook, "Scales for the Measurement of Innovativeness," *Human Communication Research* 4, no. 1 (1977), 58–65; and John E. Ettlie and Robert D. O'Keefe, "Innovative Attitudes, Values, and Intentions in Organizations," *Journal of Management Studies* 19, no. 2 (1982), 163–182.

The Ambidextrous Approach

Recent thinking has refined the idea of organic versus mechanistic structures with respect to innovation creation versus innovation utilization. Organic characteristics such as decentralization and employee freedom are excellent for initiating ideas; but these same conditions often make it hard to implement a change because employees are less likely to comply. Employees can ignore the innovation because of decentralization and a generally loose structure.

How does an organization solve this dilemma? One remedy is for the organization to use an **ambidextrous approach**—to incorporate structures and management processes that are appropriate to both the creation and the implementation of innovation.[21] Another way to think of the ambidextrous approach is to look at

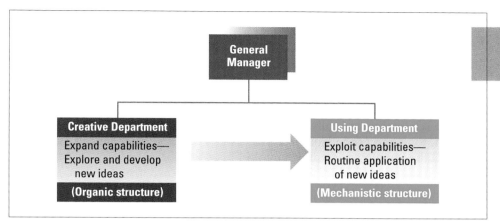

EXHIBIT 10.4
Division of Labor in the Ambidextrous Organization

the organization design elements that are important for *exploring* new ideas versus the design elements that are most suitable for *exploiting* current capabilities.[22] Exploration means encouraging creativity and developing new ideas, whereas exploitation means implementing those ideas to produce routine products. The organization can be designed to behave in an organic way for exploring new ideas and in a mechanistic way to exploit and use the ideas. Exhibit 10.4 illustrates how one department is structured organically to explore and develop new ideas and another department is structured mechanistically for routine implementation of innovations. Research indicates that organizations that use an ambidextrous approach by designing for both exploration and exploitation perform better and are significantly more successful in launching innovative new products or services.[23]

For example, a study of long-established Japanese companies such as Honda and Canon that have succeeded in breakthrough innovations found that these companies use an ambidextrous approach.[24] To develop ideas related to a new technology, the companies assign teams of young staff members who are not entrenched in the "old way of doing things" to work on the project. The teams are headed by an esteemed elder and are charged with doing whatever is needed to develop new ideas and products, even if it means breaking rules that are important in the larger organization for implementing the new ideas.

Techniques for Encouraging Technology Change

Some of the techniques used by companies to maintain an ambidextrous approach are switching structures, separate creative departments, venture teams, corporate entrepreneurship, and collaborative teams.

Switching Structures. **Switching structures** means an organization creates an organic structure when such a structure is needed for the initiation of new ideas.[25] Some of the ways organizations have switched structures to achieve the ambidextrous approach are as follows:

• Philips Corporation, a building materials producer based in Ohio, each year creates up to 150 transient teams—made up of members from various departments—to develop ideas for improving Philips products and work methods. After five days of organic brainstorming and problem solving, the company reverts to a more mechanistic basis to implement the changes.[26]

Briefcase

As an organization manager, keep these guidelines in mind:

Facilitate frequent changes in internal technology by adopting an organic organizational structure. Give technical personnel freedom to analyze problems and develop solutions or create a separate, organically structured department or venture group to conceive and propose new ideas.

- Gardetto's, a family-run snack-food business, sends small teams of workers to Eureka Ranch, where they may engage in a Nerf gun battle to set the tone for fun and freedom and then participate in brainstorming exercises with the idea of generating as many new ideas as possible by the end of the day. After two and a half days, the group returns to the regular organizational structure to put the best of the ideas into action.[27]

- The NUMMI plant, a Toyota subsidiary located in Fremont, California, creates a separate, organically organized, cross-functional subunit, called the Pilot Team, to design production processes for new car and truck models. When the model they are preparing moves into production, workers return to their regular jobs on the shop floor.[28]

Each of these organizations found creative ways to be ambidextrous, establishing organic conditions for developing new ideas in the midst of more mechanistic conditions for implementing and using those ideas.

Creative Departments. In many large organizations the initiation of innovation is assigned to separate **creative departments**.[29] Staff departments, such as research and development (R&D), engineering, design, and systems analysis, create changes for adoption in other departments. Departments that initiate change are organically structured to facilitate the generation of new ideas and techniques. Departments that use those innovations tend to have a mechanistic structure more suitable for efficient production.

One example of a creative department is the research lab at Oksuka Pharmaceutical Company. To get the kind of creative spirit that is willing to try new things and look for the unexpected, Oksuka's president Tatsuo Higuchi says its research labs "put a high value on weird people."[30] However, in the department that manufactures drugs, where routine and precision is important, a pharmaceutical company would prefer to have less-unusual people who are comfortable following rules and standard procedures.

Another type of creative department is the **idea incubator**, an increasingly popular way to facilitate the development of new ideas within the organization. An idea incubator provides a safe harbor where ideas from employees throughout the organization can be developed without interference from company bureaucracy or politics.[31] Companies as diverse as Boeing, Adobe Systems, Yahoo!, Ziff-Davis, and UPS are using incubators to support the development of creative ideas.

Venture Teams. **Venture teams** are a technique used to give free rein to creativity within organizations. Venture teams are often given a separate location and facilities so they are not constrained by organizational procedures. A venture team is like a small company within a large company. Numerous organizations have used the venture team concept to free creative people from the bureaucracy of a large corporation. Texas Instruments (TI) has a loose, informal group of engineers, self-titled the Lunatic Fringe, who are given free rein to follow their curiosity wherever it goes. This approach, according to "lunatic" Gene Frantz, provides a "continuum between total chaos and total order. About 95 percent of the people in TI are total order," he says, "and I thank God for them every day because they create the products that allow me to spend money. I'm down here in total chaos, that total chaos of innovation."[32]

One type of venture team is called a *skunkworks*.[33] A **skunkworks** is a separate, small, informal, highly autonomous, and often secretive group that focuses on breakthrough ideas for the business. The original skunkworks was created by Lockheed Martin more than 50 years ago and is still in operation. The essence of a skunkworks is that highly talented people are given the time and freedom to let creativity reign.

A variation of the venture team concept is the **new-venture fund**, which provides financial resources for employees to develop new ideas, products, or businesses. In order to tap into its employees' entrepreneurial urges, Lockheed Martin allows workers to take up to two years' unpaid leave to explore a new idea, using company labs and equipment and paying company rates for health insurance. If the idea is successful, the corporation's venture fund invests in the start-up company. One successful start-up was Genase, which created an enzyme that "stone-washes" denim.[34]

Corporate Entrepreneurship. Corporate entrepreneurship attempts to develop an internal entrepreneurial spirit, philosophy, and structure that will produce a higher-than-average number of innovations. Corporate entrepreneurship may involve the use of creative departments and new venture teams, but it also attempts to release the creative energy of all employees in the organization. Managers can create systems and structures that encourage entrepreneurship. For example, at the giant oil company BP, top executives establish contracts with the heads of all BP's business units. Unit managers can deliver on the contract in whatever way they see fit, within clearly identified constraints.[35]

An important outcome of corporate entrepreneurship is to facilitate **idea champions**. These go by a variety of names, including *advocate, intrapreneur*, or *change agent*. Idea champions provide the time and energy to make things happen. They fight to overcome natural resistance to change and to convince others of the merit of a new idea.[36] The importance of the idea champion is illustrated by a fascinating fact discovered by Texas Instruments: When TI reviewed fifty successful and unsuccessful technical projects, it discovered that every failure was characterized by the absence of a volunteer champion. There was no one who passionately believed in the idea, who pushed the idea through every obstacle to make it work. TI took this finding so seriously that now its number-one criterion for approving new technical projects is the presence of a zealous champion.[37] Insisting on an idea champion is a guiding rule for many companies that successfully turn ideas into new products and services. Numerous studies support the importance of idea champions as a factor in the success of new products.[38]

Companies encourage idea champions by providing freedom and slack time to creative people. Companies such as IBM, Texas Instruments, General Electric, and 3M allow employees to develop new technologies without company approval. Known as *bootlegging*, the unauthorized research often pays big dividends. The talking educational toy Speak & Spell was developed "under the table" at TI beginning in the 1970s. The product was a hit, but more importantly, it contained TI's first digital-signal processing-chip, which grew into a huge and very profitable business when cell phones and other portable devices came along years later.[39]

Collaborative Teams. Although many individuals have creative ideas, most innovations are created through groups of people working together. Smart companies find

ways to get people communicating and collaborating across boundaries. One large consumer products company, for example, had lots of employees capable of coming up with good ideas, but they still weren't innovating. To kick-start collaboration, the company held an off-site conference designed to get people from different specialties who had complementary skills and talents talking to one another. Everyone was given an electronic name tag which contained information about the person's skills and interests. When an employee approached someone with complementary skills, the badge would light up and flash a welcome such as "Hi Susan. We should be talking about biochemistry."[40] Many of today's successful innovators even bring in people from outside the organization. For example, IBM held an online town-hall style meeting, called the Innovation Jam, inviting employees as well as clients, consultants, and employees' family members to an interactive online brainstorming session about new technology ideas.[41]

NEW PRODUCTS AND SERVICES

Although the concepts just discussed are important to product and service as well as technology changes, other factors also need to be considered. In many ways, new products and services are a special case of innovation because they are used by customers outside the organization. Since new products are designed for sale in the environment, uncertainty about the suitability and success of an innovation is very high.

New Product Success Rate

Research has explored the enormous uncertainty associated with the development and sale of new products.[42] To understand what this uncertainty can mean to organizations, consider such flops as RCA's VideoDisc player, which lost an estimated $500 million, or Time Inc.'s *TV-Cable Week*, which lost $47 million. Pfizer invested more than $70 million in the development and testing of an anti-aging drug before it flopped in the final testing stages.[43] Developing and producing products that fail is a part of business in all industries. U.S. food companies, for example, introduce approximately 5,000 new products into supermarkets each year, but the failure rate of new food products is 70 to 80 percent.[44] Organizations take the risk because product innovation is one of the most important ways companies adapt to changes in markets, technologies, and competition.[45]

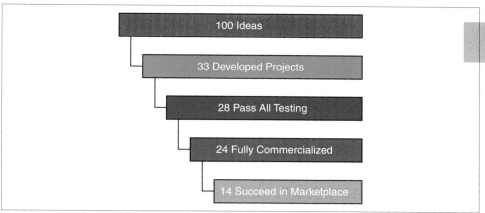

EXHIBIT 10.5
New Product Success
Rates

Source: Based on M. Adams and the Product Development and Management Association, "Comparative Performance Assessment Study 2004," available for purchase at *http://www.pdma.org* (search on CPAS). Results reported in Jeff Cope, "Lessons Learned—Commercialization Success Rates: A Brief Review," RTI Tech Ventures newsletter, 4, no. 4 (December 2007).

Although measuring the success of new products is tricky, a survey by the Product Development and Management Association (PDMA) sheds some light on the commercialization success rates of new products across a variety of industries.[46] PDMA compiled survey results from over 400 PDMA members, most of whom work in new product development in various industries. The findings about success rates are given in Exhibit 10.5. On the average, only 28 percent of all projects undertaken in the R&D laboratories passed the testing stage, which means all technical problems were solved and the projects moved on to production. Less than one-fourth of all product ideas (24 percent) were fully marketed and commercialized, and only 14 percent achieved economic success.[47]

Reasons for New Product Success

The next question to be considered is, Why are some products more successful than others? Other studies indicate that innovation success is related to collaboration between technical and marketing departments. Successful new products and services seem to be technologically sound and also carefully tailored to customer needs.[48] A study called Project SAPPHO examined seventeen pairs of new product innovations, with one success and one failure in each pair, and concluded the following:

1. Successful innovating companies had a much better understanding of customer needs and paid much more attention to marketing.
2. Successful innovating companies made more effective use of outside technology and outside advice, even though they did more work in-house.
3. Top management support in the successful innovating companies was from people who were more senior and had greater authority.

Thus there is a distinct pattern of tailoring innovations to customer needs, making effective use of technology, and having influential top managers support the project. These ideas taken together indicate that the effective design for new product innovation is associated with horizontal coordination across departments.

Horizontal Coordination Model

The organization design for achieving new product innovation involves three components—departmental specialization, boundary spanning, and horizontal coordination. These components are similar to the horizontal coordination mechanisms discussed in Chapter 2, such as teams, task forces, and project managers, and the differentiation and integration ideas discussed in Chapter 6. Exhibit 10.6 illustrates these components in the **horizontal coordination model**.

Specialization. The key departments in new product development are R&D, marketing, and production. The specialization component means that the personnel in all three of these departments are highly competent at their own tasks. The three departments are differentiated from each other and have skills, goals, and attitudes appropriate for their specialized functions.

Boundary Spanning. This component means each department involved with new products has excellent linkage with relevant sectors in the external environment. R&D personnel are linked to professional associations and to colleagues in other R&D departments. They are aware of recent scientific developments. Marketing personnel are closely linked to customer needs. They listen to what customers have to say, and they analyze competitor products and suggestions by distributors. For example, Kimberly-Clark had amazing success with Huggies Pull-Ups because marketing researchers worked closely with customers in their own homes and recognized the emotional appeal of pull-on diapers for toddlers. By the time competitors caught on, Kimberly-Clark was selling $400 million worth of Huggies annually.[49]

EXHIBIT 10.6

Horizontal Coordination Model for New Product Innovations

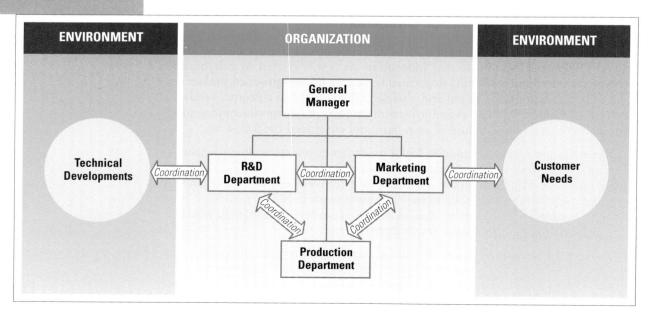

Horizontal Coordination. This component means that technical, marketing, and production people share ideas and information. Research people inform marketing of new technical developments to learn whether the developments are applicable to customers. Marketing people provide customer complaints and information to R&D to use in the design of new products. People from both R&D and marketing coordinate with production because new products have to fit within production capabilities so costs are not exorbitant. The decision to launch a new product is ultimately a joint decision among all three departments. Horizontal coordination, using mechanisms such as cross-functional teams, increases both the amount and the variety of information for new product development, enabling the design of products that meet customer needs and circumventing manufacturing and marketing problems.[50]

Famous innovation failures—such as New Coke, Kellogg's Breakfast Mates, or the Susan B. Anthony Dollar—usually violate the horizontal linkage model. Employees fail to connect with customer needs and market forces or internal departments fail to adequately share needs and coordinate with one another. Research has confirmed a connection between effective boundary spanning that keeps the organization in touch with market forces, smooth coordination among departments, and successful product development.[51]

Many of today's successful companies are including customers, strategic partners, suppliers, and other outsiders directly in the product and service development process. One of the hottest trends is *open innovation*.[52] In the past, most businesses generated their own ideas in-house and then developed, manufactured, marketed, and distributed them, a closed innovation approach. Today, though, forward-looking companies are trying a different method. **Open innovation** means extending the search for and commercialization of new products beyond the boundaries of the organization and even beyond the boundaries of the industry. In a survey conducted by IBM and *Industry Week* magazine, 40 percent of respondents identified collaborating with customers and suppliers as having the most significant impact on product development time-to-market.[53]

Research findings show that collaboration with other firms and with customers can be a significant source of product innovation, and can even stimulate stronger internal coordination. Cooperating with external parties requires the involvement of people from different areas of the company, which in turn necessitates that organizations set up stronger internal coordination mechanisms.[54] Some companies, such as Threadless, dubbed the most innovative small company in America by *Inc.* magazine, take open innovation to the extreme.

IN PRACTICE

Threadless

Threadless, founded by college dropout Jake Nickell and his partner Jacob DeHart, churns out dozens of new T-shirt designs a month and has never produced a flop. How do they do it? By letting potential customers tell them precisely which shirts to make.

Threadless holds design competitions on an online social network, where hundreds of thousands of people socialize, blog, and discuss ideas. Members submit T-shirt designs by the hundreds each week and then vote on which ones they like best. People earn cash prizes for designs that are used, plus reprint fees, but the real appeal to young, unknown designers is the honor of getting their designs printed.

Rather than having the company create products and the customers buy them, the customers essentially *are* the company at Threadless. Threadless employs no professional designers, has no marketing department or sales force, does no advertising, and doesn't distribute through

(continued)

retailers. "[It] was a huge word-of-mouth thing," said one freelance designer. People aren't required to join the social network to buy shirts, but a survey indicates that about 95 percent of people visiting the site participate in talking about and voting on designs. This engagement led to four years of tremendous growth for Threadless, with membership increasing from about 70,000 in 2004 to more than 700,000 in 2008. Sales zoomed to $30 million.

When asked about his company's success, Nickell says it just seems like common sense. "Why wouldn't you want to make the products that people want you to make?" he asks.[55] ∎

Threadless is at the forefront of a movement to drastically rethink relationships with customers. Starbucks is applying a similar idea at MyStarbucks.com, where customers can make suggestions, then discuss and vote on them. Pitney Bowes is building an online social network for direct marketers who use its mail machines.[56] A number of companies have sprung up to help organizations use the Internet to tap into the collective mind-power of a broad public. Web sites such as Kluster, InnoCentive, and Cambrian House let companies post questions or tasks and gather outside ideas.[57] In addition, many major companies such as Procter & Gamble, W. L. Gore, and Boeing routinely turn to customers for advice. Gore worked with physicians to develop its thoracic graft, and with hunters to create Supprescent, a fabric intended to block human odors.[58] During development of new planes, Boeing's engineers work closely with flight attendants, pilots, engineers from major airlines, suppliers, and even banks that finance aircraft purchases, to make sure the plane is designed for maximum functionality and compatibility with suppliers' capabilities and the airlines' needs.[59]

ASSESS YOUR ANSWER

2 **Asking customers what they want is the best way to create new products that will be successful in the marketplace.**

ANSWER: *Agree or disagree.* It depends on the organization. Bringing customers into the product development process has been highly beneficial for many companies. However, many products developed based on what customers say they want do not succeed. In addition, some highly innovative companies, like Apple, believe relying too much on customer input limits the pie-in-the-sky thinking needed to create truly breakthrough products.

Achieving Competitive Advantage: The Need for Speed

Nine out of ten executives say speed and agility have become increasingly urgent concerns for their companies in recent years.[60] In particular, the rapid development of new products and services is becoming a major strategic weapon in an ever-shifting global marketplace.[61] To remain competitive, companies are learning to turn ideas into new products and services incredibly fast.

Time-based competition means delivering products and services faster than competitors, giving companies a competitive edge. Clothing retailer Zara gets new styles into stores twice a week, for example. Russell Stover got a line of low-carb candies, called Net Carb, on store shelves within three months after perfecting the recipe, rather than the twelve months it usually takes candy companies to get a new product to market.[62] Some companies use what are called *fast cycle teams* as a way to support highly important projects and deliver products and services faster than competitors.

A fast cycle team is a multifunctional, and sometimes multinational, team that works under stringent timelines and is provided with high levels of company resources and empowerment to accomplish an accelerated product development project.[63]

Another critical issue is designing products that can compete on a global scale and successfully marketing those products internationally. Companies such as Quaker Oats, Häagen Dazs, and Levi's are trying to improve horizontal communication and collaboration across geographical regions, recognizing that they can pick up winning product ideas from customers in other countries. Many new product development teams today are global teams because organizations have to develop products that will meet diverse needs of consumers all over the world.[64]

STRATEGY AND STRUCTURE CHANGE

The preceding discussion focused on new production processes and products, which are based in the technology of an organization. The expertise for such innovation lies within the technical core and professional staff groups, such as research and engineering. This section turns to an examination of strategy and structure changes.

All organizations need to make changes in their strategies, structures, management processes, and administrative procedures from time to time. In the past, when the environment was relatively stable, most organizations focused on small, incremental changes to solve immediate problems or take advantage of new opportunities. However, over the past decade, companies throughout the world have faced the need to make radical changes in strategy, structure, and management processes to adapt to new competitive demands.[65] Many organizations are cutting out layers of management and decentralizing decision making. There is a strong shift toward more horizontal structures, with teams of front-line workers empowered to make decisions and solve problems on their own. Some companies are breaking totally away from traditional organization forms and shifting toward virtual network strategies and structures. Numerous companies are reorganizing and shifting their strategies to incorporate e-business. These types of changes are the responsibility of the organization's top managers, and the overall process of change is typically different from the process for innovation in technology or new products.

The Dual-Core Approach

The **dual-core approach** to organizational change compares management and technical changes. Management changes pertain to the design and structure of the organization itself, including restructuring, downsizing, teams, control systems, information systems, and departmental grouping. Research into management change suggests two things. First, management changes occur less frequently than do technical changes. Second, management changes occur in response to different environmental sectors and follow a different internal process than do technology-based changes.[66] The dual-core approach to organizational change identifies the unique processes associated with management change.[67]

Organizations—schools, hospitals, city governments, welfare agencies, government bureaucracies, and many business firms—can be conceptualized as having two cores: a *technical core* and a *management core*. Each core has its own employees, tasks, and environmental domain. Innovation can originate in either core.

Briefcase

As an organization manager, keep these guidelines in mind:

Facilitate changes in strategy and structure by adopting a top-down approach. Use a mechanistic structure when the organization needs to adopt frequent management changes in a top-down fashion.

The management core is above the technical core in the hierarchy. The responsibility of the management core includes the structure, control, and coordination of the organization itself and concerns the environmental sectors of government, financial resources, economic conditions, human resources, and competitors. The technical core is concerned with the transformation of raw materials into organizational products and services and involves the environmental sectors of customers and technology.[68]

The point of the dual-core approach is that many organizations—especially nonprofit and government organizations—must adopt frequent management changes and need to be structured differently from organizations that rely on frequent technical and product changes for competitive advantage.

Organization Design for Implementing Management Change

The findings from research comparing management and technical change suggest that a mechanistic organization structure is appropriate for frequent management changes, including changes in goals, strategy, structure, control systems, and human resources.[69] Organizations that successfully adopt many management changes often have a larger administrative ratio, are larger in size, and are centralized and formalized compared with organizations that adopt many technical changes.[70] The reason is the top-down implementation of changes in response to changes in the government, financial, or legal sectors of the environment. If an organization has an organic structure, lower-level employees have more freedom and autonomy and, hence, may resist top-down initiatives.

The innovation approaches associated with management versus technical change are summarized in Exhibit 10.7. Technical change, such as changes in production techniques and innovative technology for new products, is facilitated by an organic

EXHIBIT 10.7
Dual-Core Approach to
Organization Change

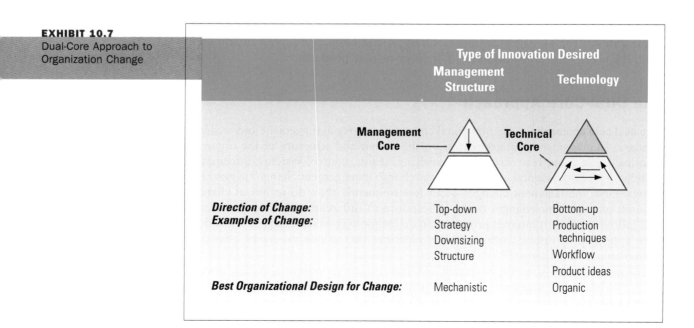

	Type of Innovation Desired	
	Management Structure	**Technology**
	Management Core ——	Technical Core
Direction of Change:	Top-down	Bottom-up
Examples of Change:	Strategy	Production techniques
	Downsizing	Workflow
	Structure	Product ideas
Best Organizational Design for Change:	Mechanistic	Organic

structure, which allows ideas to bubble upward from lower- and middle-level employees. Organizations that must adopt frequent management changes, in contrast, tend to use a top-down process and a mechanistic structure. For example, changes such as implementation of Six Sigma methods, application of the balanced scorecard, decentralization of decision making, or downsizing and restructuring are facilitated by a top-down approach.

Research into civil service reform found that the implementation of management innovation was extremely difficult in organizations that had an organic technical core. The professional employees in a decentralized agency could resist civil service changes. By contrast, organizations that were considered more bureaucratic and mechanistic in the sense of high formalization and centralization adopted management changes readily.[71]

What about business organizations that are normally technologically innovative in bottom-up fashion but suddenly face a crisis and need to reorganize? Or a technically innovative, high-tech firm that must reorganize frequently to accommodate changes in production technology or the environment? Technically innovative firms may suddenly have to restructure, reduce the number of employees, alter pay systems, disband teams, or form a new division.[72] The answer is to use a top-down change process. The authority for strategy and structure change lies with top management, who should initiate and implement the new strategy and structure to meet environmental circumstances. Employee input may be sought, but top managers have the responsibility to direct the change. When Mark Hurd took over as CEO of Hewlett-Packard, he knew that strong, swift top-down change was needed to help the organization get back on track.

IN PRACTICE

Hewlett-Packard

Mark Hurd began hearing complaints about the corporate sales function within weeks of taking over the top job at Hewlett-Packard. Some corporate customers were telling him the company had so many confusing management layers that they never knew who to call. Others were saying they frequently got different price quotes from salespeople in different regions. Inside the company, people were complaining that they were so overwhelmed with administrative tasks that they had little time to spend serving customers.

Hurd took quick action. After digging into H-P's sales structure, he discovered that there were eleven layers of management between him and a customer. In addition, there were too many people assigned to support staff and management roles and too few assigned to work directly with customers, particularly corporate clients that provided 70 percent of the company's revenue. Hurd restructured workers among H-P's PC, printing, and corporate-technology groups so salespeople could master the products they were selling. He fired hundreds of underperformers and cut three layers of sales management. With top corporate clients, Hurd assigned just one salesperson so they would always know whom to contact. The restructuring also included changing the reward system for salespeople, tying commissions to revenue and profitability.

Hurd made a number of other management changes at H-P, including downsizing the overall workforce and giving divisions direct control over about 70 percent of their budgeted costs. Recent years have been tough for computer makers, especially with corporations decreasing their spending. However, H-P has made some impressive gains, significantly increasing its share of both consumer and corporate computer sales.[73] ∎

Some top-down changes, particularly those related to restructuring and downsizing, can be painful for employees, so top managers should move quickly and authoritatively to make them as humane as possible.[74] A study of successful corporate transformations, which frequently involve painful changes, found that managers followed a fast, focused approach. When top managers spread difficult changes such as downsizing over a long time period, employee morale suffers and the change is much less likely to lead to positive outcomes.[75]

Top managers should also remember that top-down change means initiation of the idea occurs at upper levels and is implemented downward. It does not mean that lower-level employees are not educated about the change or allowed to participate in it.

CULTURE CHANGE

Organizations are made up of people and their relationships with one another. Changes in strategy, structure, technologies, and products do not happen on their own, and changes in any of these areas involve changes in people as well. Employees must learn how to use new technologies, or market new products, or work effectively in a team-based structure. Sometimes achieving a new way of thinking requires a focused change in the underlying corporate cultural values and norms. Changing corporate culture fundamentally shifts how work is done in an organization and can lead to renewed commitment and empowerment of employees, as well as a stronger bond between the company and its customers.[76]

However, changing culture can be particularly difficult because it challenges people's core values and established ways of thinking and doing things. Mergers and acquisitions often illustrate how tough culture change can be. For example, the integration of FedEx and Kinko's has been rocky because of wildly disparate cultures. Kinko's always had a somewhat freewheeling culture, captured by a statement made by one former worker: "I had cornrows and green hair and no one seemed to mind." FedEx, on the other hand, has a culture based on structure, uniformity, and discipline. Five years after FedEx bought the copy-center company, managers are still struggling to implement the culture change they feel is needed at Kinko's.[77]

Forces for Culture Change

A number of recent trends have contributed to a need for cultural makeovers at many companies. For example, reengineering and the shift to horizontal forms of organizing, which we discussed in Chapter 2, require greater focus on employee empowerment, collaboration, information sharing, and meeting customer needs, which means managers and employees need a new mind-set. Mutual trust, risk taking, and tolerance for mistakes become key cultural values in the horizontal organization.

Another force for culture change is the diversity of today's workforce. Diversity is a fact of life for today's organizations, and many are implementing new recruiting, mentoring, and promotion methods, diversity training programs, tough policies regarding sexual harassment and racial discrimination, and new benefits programs that respond to a more diverse workforce. However, if the underlying culture of an organization does not change, all other efforts to support diversity will fail.

Finally, a growing emphasis on learning and adaptation in organizations calls for new cultural values. Recall from Chapter 1 that shifting to a learning organization involves changes in a number of areas, such as more horizontal structures with empowered teams working directly with customers. There are few rules and procedures for performing tasks, and knowledge and control of tasks are located with employees rather than supervisors. Information is broadly shared, and employees, customers, suppliers, and partners all play a role in determining the organization's strategic direction. Clearly, all of these changes require new values, new attitudes, and new ways of thinking and working together.

---

3 **Changing a company's culture is probably one of the hardest jobs a manager can undertake.**

ANSWER: *Agree.* Changing people and culture is typically much more difficult than changing any other aspect of the organization. Managers often underestimate the difficulty of changing culture and fail to appreciate that it takes a determined, consciously-planned effort over a long period of time.

ASSESS YOUR ANSWER

Organization Development Culture Change Interventions

Managers use a variety of approaches and techniques for changing corporate culture, some of which we discussed in Chapter 9. One method of quickly bringing about culture change is known as **organization development** (OD), which focuses on the human and social aspects of the organization as a way to improve the organization's ability to adapt and solve problems. OD emphasizes the values of human development, fairness, openness, freedom from coercion, and individual autonomy that allows workers to perform the job as they see fit, within reasonable organizational constraints.[78] In the 1970s, OD evolved as a separate field that applied the behavioral sciences in a process of planned organization-wide change, with the goal of increasing organizational effectiveness. Today, the concept has been enlarged to examine how people and groups can change to an adaptive culture in a complex and turbulent environment. Organization development is not a step-by-step procedure to solve a specific problem but a process of fundamental change in the human and social systems of the organization, including organizational culture.[79]

OD uses knowledge and techniques from the behavioral sciences to create a learning environment through increased trust, open confrontation of problems, employee empowerment and participation, knowledge and information sharing, the design of meaningful work, cooperation and collaboration between groups, and the full use of human potential.

OD interventions involve training of specific groups or of everyone in the organization. For OD interventions to be successful, senior management in the organization must see the need for OD and provide enthusiastic support for the change. Techniques used by many organizations for improving people skills through OD include the following.

Large Group Intervention. Most early OD activities involved small groups and focused on incremental change. However, in recent years, there has been growing

Briefcase

As an organization manager, keep these guidelines in mind:

Work with organization development consultants for large-scale changes in the attitudes, values, or skills of employees, and when trying to change the overall culture toward a more adaptable one.

interest in the application of OD techniques to large group settings, which are more attuned to bringing about radical or transformational change in organizations operating in complex environments.[80] The **large group intervention** approach, sometimes referred to as "whole system in the room,"[81] brings together participants from all parts of the organization—often including key stakeholders from outside the organization as well—in an off-site setting to discuss problems or opportunities and plan for change. A large group intervention might involve 50 to 500 people and last for several days. For example, the global furniture retailer IKEA recently used the large-group intervention approach to completely re-conceptualize how the company operates. During eighteen hours of meetings held over several days, fifty-two stakeholders created a new system for product design, manufacturing, and distribution, which involved cutting layers of hierarchy and decentralizing the organization.[82] All of the departments that had information, resources, or an interest in the design outcome worked together to create and implement the new system.

Using an off-site setting limits interference and distractions, enabling participants to focus on new ways of doing things. General Electric's "Work Out" program, an ongoing process of solving problems, learning, and improving, begins with large-scale off-site meetings that get people talking across functional, hierarchical, and organizational boundaries. Hourly and salaried workers come together from many different parts of the organization and join with customers and suppliers to discuss and solve specific problems.[83] The process forces a rapid analysis of ideas, the creation of solutions, and the development of a plan for implementation. Over time, Work Out creates a culture where ideas are rapidly translated into action and positive business results.[84]

Team Building. **Team building** promotes the idea that people who work together can work as a team. A work team can be brought together to discuss conflicts, goals, the decision-making process, communication, creativity, and leadership. The team can then plan to overcome problems and improve results. Team-building activities are also used in many companies to train task forces, committees, and new product development groups. These activities enhance communication and collaboration and strengthen the cohesiveness of organizational groups and teams.

Interdepartmental Activities. Representatives from different departments are brought together in a mutual location to expose problems or conflicts, diagnose the causes, and plan improvements in communication and coordination. This type of intervention has been applied to union–management conflict, headquarters–field office conflict, interdepartmental conflict, and mergers.[85] One company that stores archived records for other organizations found interdepartmental meetings to be a key means of building a culture based on team spirit and customer focus. People from different departments met for hour-long sessions every two weeks and shared their problems, told stories about their successes, and talked about things they'd observed in the company. The meetings helped people understand the problems faced in other departments and see how everyone depended on each other to do their jobs successfully.[86]

One current area in which OD can provide significant value is in spurring culture change toward valuing diversity.[87] In addition, today's organizations are continuously adapting to environmental uncertainty and increasing global competition, and OD interventions can respond to these new realities as companies strive to create greater capability for learning and growth.[88]

STRATEGIES FOR IMPLEMENTING CHANGE

Managers and employees can think of inventive ways to improve the organization's technology, creative ideas for new products and services, fresh approaches to strategies and structures, or ideas for fostering adaptive cultural values, but until the ideas are put into action, they are worthless to the organization. Implementation is the most crucial part of the change process, but it is also the most difficult. Change is frequently disruptive and uncomfortable for managers as well as employees. Change is complex, dynamic, and messy, and implementation requires strong and persistent leadership. In this final section, we briefly discuss the role of leadership for change, some reasons for resistance to change, and techniques that managers can use to overcome resistance and successfully implement change.

Leadership for Change

A recent survey found that among companies that are successful innovators, 80 percent have top leaders who frequently reinforce the value and importance of innovation. These leaders think about innovation, demonstrate its importance through their actions, and follow through to make sure people are investing time and resources in innovation issues.[89] Philip A. Newbold, chief executive of Memorial Hospital in South Bend, Indiana, illustrates this type of leader.

Sixty-year-old Philip Newbold has been chief of Memorial Hospital for more than twenty years, but he keeps his mind—and his organization—as fresh-thinking as a young Silicon Valley entrepreneur. Newbold regularly visits innovative organizations in all industries, from retailers to furniture makers. He encourages his staff to have fun by making cardboard prototypes of project ideas. He holds regular brainstorming sessions, sometimes requiring everyone to stand for the entire twenty or so minutes to keep them thinking fast on their feet. Memorial was the first community hospital in the United States to have an innovation R&D budget. Part of the money goes for the Innovation Café, a unique teaching laboratory where people learn about the basic ingredients of innovation. "Good Try" rewards honor promising projects that failed, and staff members make presentations to senior executives about lessons learned from failure.

Newbold says he has stayed in one job for so long because of an insatiable interest in new ideas that keeps every day fresh. "In the hospital industry, he's way out front with his emphasis on an innovation culture," said one health industry observer.[90] ■

Memorial Hospital

Executives like Philip Newbold are innovation champions. The leadership style of the top executive sets the tone for how effective the organization is at continuous adaptation and innovation. One style of leadership, referred to as *transformational leadership*, is particularly suited for bringing about change. Top leaders who use a transformational leadership style enhance organizational innovation both directly, by creating a compelling vision, and indirectly, by creating an environment that supports exploration, experimentation, risk taking, and sharing of ideas.[91]

Successful change can happen only when employees are willing to devote the time and energy needed to reach new goals, as well as endure possible stress and hardship. Having a clearly communicated vision that embodies flexibility and openness

EXHIBIT 10.8
Stages of Commitment
to Change

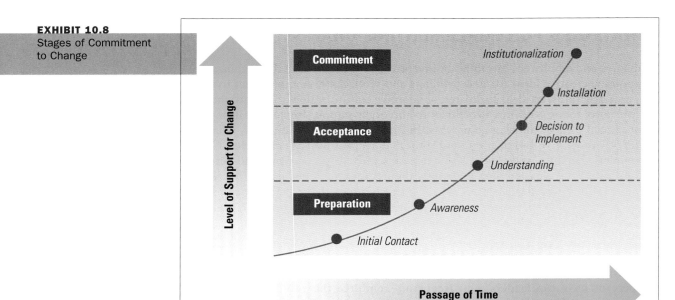

Source: From *Managing at the Speed of Change* by Daryl R. Connor, copyright © 1993 by O.D. Resources, Inc. Used by permission of Villard Books, a division of Random House, Inc. and Margaret McBride Literary Agency.

to new ideas, methods, and styles sets the stage for a change-oriented organization and helps employees cope with the chaos and tension associated with change.[92]

Leaders also build organization-wide commitment by taking employees through three stages of the change commitment process, illustrated in Exhibit 10.8.[93] In the first stage, *preparation*, employees hear about the change through memos, meetings, speeches, or personal contact and become aware that the change will directly affect their work. In the second stage, *acceptance*, leaders help employees develop an understanding of the full impact of the change and the positive outcomes of making the change. When employees perceive the change as positive, the decision to implement is made. In the third stage, the true *commitment* process begins. The commitment stage involves the steps of installation and institutionalization. Installation is a trial process for the change, which gives leaders an opportunity to discuss problems and employee concerns and build commitment to action. In the final step, *institutionalization*, employees view the change not as something new but as a normal and integral part of organizational operations.

The pressures on organizations to change will probably increase over the next few decades. Leaders must develop the personal qualities, skills, and methods needed to help their companies remain competitive. Indeed, some management experts argue that to survive the upheaval of the early twenty-first century, managers must turn their organizations into *change leaders* by using the present to actually create the future—breaking industry rules, creating new market space, and routinely abandoning outmoded products, services, and processes to free up resources to build the future.[94]

Barriers to Change

Visionary leadership is crucial for change; however, leaders should expect to encounter resistance as they attempt to take the organization through the three stages of the change commitment process. It is natural for people to resist change, and many barriers to change exist at the individual and organizational levels.[95]

1. *Excessive focus on costs.* Management may possess the mind-set that costs are all-important and may fail to appreciate the importance of a change that is not focused on costs—for example, a change to increase employee motivation or customer satisfaction.

2. *Failure to perceive benefits.* Any significant change will produce both positive and negative reactions. Education may be needed to help managers and employees perceive more positive than negative aspects of the change. In addition, if the organization's reward system discourages risk taking, a change process might falter because employees think that the risk of making the change is too high.

3. *Lack of coordination and cooperation.* Organizational fragmentation and conflict often result from the lack of coordination for change implementation. Moreover, in the case of new technology, the old and new systems must be compatible.

4. *Uncertainty avoidance.* At the individual level, many employees fear the uncertainty associated with change. Constant communication is needed so that employees know what is going on and understand how it affects their jobs.

5. *Fear of loss.* Managers and employees may fear the loss of power and status—or even their jobs. In these cases, implementation should be careful and incremental, and all employees should be involved as closely as possible in the change process.

Implementation can typically be designed to overcome many of the organizational and individual barriers to change.

Techniques for Implementation

Top leaders articulate the vision and set the tone, but managers and employees throughout the organization are involved in the process of change. A number of techniques can be used to successfully implement change.[96]

1. *Establish a sense of urgency for change.* Once managers identify a true need for change, they thaw resistance by creating a sense of urgency in others that the change is really needed. Organizational crises can help unfreeze employees and make them willing to invest the time and energy needed to adopt new techniques or procedures. When there is no public crisis, managers have to find creative ways to make others aware of the need for change.

2. *Establish a coalition to guide the change.* Effective change managers build a coalition of people throughout the organization who have enough power and influence to steer the change process. For implementation to be successful, there must be a shared commitment to the need and possibilities for change. Top management support is crucial for any major change project, and lack of top management support is one of the most frequent causes of implementation failure.[97] In addition, the coalition should involve lower-level supervisors and middle managers from across the organization. For smaller changes, the support of influential managers in the affected departments is important.

3. *Create a vision and strategy for change.* Leaders who have taken their companies through major successful transformations often have one thing in common: They focus on formulating and articulating a compelling vision and strategy that will guide the change process. Even for a small change, a vision of how the future can be better and strategies to get there are important motivations for change.

4. *Find an idea that fits the need.* Finding the right idea often involves search procedures—talking with other managers, assigning a task force to investigate the problem, sending out a request to suppliers, or asking creative people within the organization to develop a solution. This is a good opportunity to encourage employee participation, because employees need the freedom to think about and explore new options.[98] ALLTEL set up a program called Team Focus to gather input from all employees. In twenty group meetings over a period of two weeks, managers gathered 2,800 suggestions, which they then narrowed down to 170 critical action items that specifically addressed problems affecting employee morale and performance.[99]

5. *Develop plans to overcome resistance to change.* Many good ideas are never used because managers failed to anticipate or prepare for resistance to change by consumers, employees, or other managers. No matter how impressive the performance characteristics of an innovation, its implementation will conflict with some interests and jeopardize some alliances in the organization. To increase the chance of successful implementation, managers acknowledge the conflict, threats, and potential losses perceived by employees. Several strategies can be used by managers to overcome resistance:

   • *Alignment with needs and goals of users.* The best strategy for overcoming resistance is to make sure change meets a real need. Employees in R&D often come up with great ideas that solve nonexistent problems. This happens because initiators fail to consult with the intended users. Resistance can be frustrating for managers, but moderate resistance to change is good for an organization. Resistance provides a barrier to frivolous changes and to change for the sake of change. The process of overcoming resistance to change normally requires that the change be good for its users. When David Zugheri wanted to switch to a primarily paperless system at First Houston Mortgage, he emphasized to employees that storing customer records electronically meant they could now work from home when they needed to care for a sick child, or take a vacation and still keep track of critical accounts. "I could literally see their attitudes change through their body language," Zugheri says.[100]

   • *Communication and training.* Communication means informing users about the need for change and the consequences of a proposed change, preventing rumors, misunderstanding, and resentment. In one study of change efforts, the most commonly cited reason for failure was that employees learned of the change from outsiders. Top managers concentrated on communicating with the public and shareholders but failed to communicate with the people who would be most intimately involved with and most affected by the change—their own employees.[101] Open communication often gives management an opportunity to explain what steps will be taken to ensure that the change will have no adverse consequences for employees. Training is also needed to help employees understand and cope with their role in the change process.

   • *An environment that affords psychological safety.* Psychological safety means that people feel a sense of confidence that they will not be embarrassed or rejected by others in the organization. People need to feel secure and capable of making the changes that are asked of them.[102] Change requires that people be willing to take risks and do things differently, but many people are fearful of trying something new if they think they might be

Briefcase

As an organization manager, keep these guidelines in mind:

Lead employees through the three stages of commitment to change—preparation, acceptance, and commitment—and use techniques to achieve successful implementation. These include obtaining top management support, implementing the change in a series of steps, assigning change teams or idea champions, and overcoming resistance by actively communicating with workers and encouraging their participation in the change process.

embarrassed by mistakes or failure. Managers support psychological safety by creating a climate of trust and mutual respect in the organization. "Not being afraid someone is laughing at you helps you take genuine risks," says Andy Law, one of the founders of St. Luke's, an advertising agency based in London.[103]

- *Participation and involvement.* Early and extensive participation in a change should be part of implementation. Participation gives those involved a sense of control over the change activity. They understand it better, and they become committed to its successful implementation. One study of the implementation and adoption of information technology systems at two companies showed a much smoother implementation process at the company that introduced the new technology using a participatory approach.[104] The team-building and large group intervention activities described earlier can be effective ways to involve employees in a change process.

- *Forcing and coercion.* As a last resort, managers may overcome resistance by threatening employees with the loss of jobs or promotions or by firing or transferring them. In other words, management power is used to overwhelm resistance. In most cases, this approach is not advisable because it leaves people angry at change managers, and the change may be sabotaged. However, this technique may be needed when speed is essential, such as when the organization faces a crisis. It may also be required for needed administrative changes that flow from the top down, such as downsizing the workforce.[105]

6. *Create change teams.* Throughout this chapter the need for resources and energy to make change happen has been discussed. Separate creative departments, new-venture groups, and ad hoc teams or task forces are ways to focus energy on both creation and implementation. A separate department has the freedom to create a new technology that fits a genuine need. A task force can be created to see that implementation is completed. The task force can be responsible for communication, involvement of users, training, and other activities needed for change.

7. *Foster idea champions.* One of the most effective weapons in the battle for change is the idea champion. The most effective champion is a volunteer champion who is deeply committed to a new idea. The idea champion sees that all technical activities are correct and complete. An additional champion, such as a manager sponsor, may also be needed to persuade people about implementation, even using coercion if necessary.

Learning to manage change effectively, including understanding why people resist change and ways to overcome resistance, is crucial, particularly when top-down changes are needed. The failure to recognize and overcome resistance is one of the top reasons managers fail to implement new strategies that can keep their companies competitive.[106] Smart managers approach the change process mindfully and consistently, planning for implementation and preparing for resistance.

DESIGN ESSENTIALS

■ Organizations face a dilemma. Managers prefer to organize day-to-day activities in a predictable, routine manner. However, change—not stability—is the natural order of things in today's global environment. Thus, organizations need to build in change as well as stability, to facilitate innovation as well as efficiency.

■ Four types of change—technology, products and services, strategy and structure, and culture—may give an organization a competitive edge, and managers can make certain each of the necessary ingredients for change is present.

■ For technology innovation, which is of concern to most organizations, an organic structure that encourages employee autonomy works best because it encourages a bottom-up flow of ideas. Other approaches are to establish a separate department charged with creating new technical ideas, establish venture teams or idea incubators, use collaborative teams, and encourage idea champions. New products and services generally require cooperation among several departments, so horizontal linkage is an essential part of the innovation process. The latest trend is open innovation, which brings customers, suppliers, and other outsiders directly into the search for and development of new products.

■ For changes in strategy and structure, a top-down approach is typically best. These innovations are in the domain of top managers who take responsibility for restructuring, for downsizing, and for changes in policies, goals, and control systems.

■ Culture changes are also generally the responsibility of top management. Some recent trends that may create a need for broad-scale culture change in the organization are reengineering, the shift to horizontal forms of organizing, greater organizational diversity, and the learning organization. All of these changes require significant shifts in employee and manager attitudes and ways of working together. One method for bringing about this level of culture change is organization development (OD). OD focuses on the human and social aspects of the organization and uses behavioral science knowledge to bring about changes in attitudes and relationships.

■ Finally, the implementation of change can be difficult. Strong leadership is needed to guide employees through the turbulence and uncertainty and build organization-wide commitment to change. A number of barriers to change exist, including excessive focus on cost, failure to perceive benefits, lack of organizational coordination, and individual uncertainty avoidance and fear of loss. Managers can increase the likelihood of success by thoughtfully planning how to deal with resistance. Implementation techniques are to establish a sense of urgency that change is needed; create a powerful coalition to guide the change; formulate a vision and strategy to achieve the change; and overcome resistance by aligning with the needs and goals of users, including users in the change process, providing psychological safety, and, in rare cases, forcing the innovation if necessary.

Key Concepts

ambidextrous approach	idea incubator	skunkworks
change process	large group intervention	strategy and structure changes
creative departments	new-venture fund	switching structures
creativity	open innovation	team building
culture changes	organization development	technology changes
dual-core approach	organizational change	time-based competition
horizontal coordination model	organizational innovation	venture teams
idea champion	product and service changes	

Discussion Questions

1. "Change requires more coordination than does the performance of normal organizational tasks. Any time you change something, you discover its connections to other parts of the organization, which have to be changed as well." Discuss whether you agree or disagree with this quote, and why.
2. Review the stages of commitment to change illustrated in Exhibit 10.8 and the seven techniques for implementing change discussed at the end of the chapter. At which stage of change commitment would each of the seven techniques most likely be used?
3. Do you think factory employees would typically be more resistant to changes in production methods, changes in structure, or changes in culture? Why? What steps could managers take to overcome this resistance?
4. The manager of R&D for a drug company said that only 5 percent of the company's new products ever achieve market success. She also said the industry average is 10 percent and wondered how her organization might increase its success rate. If you were acting as a consultant, what advice would you give her about designing organization structure to improve market success?
5. What does it mean to say managers should organize for both exploration and exploitation?
6. How do the underlying values of organization development compare to the values underlying other types of change? Why do the values underlying OD make it particularly useful in shifting to an adaptive culture as described in Chapter 9 (Exhibit 9.5)?
7. Describe the dual-core approach. How does the process of management change normally differ from technology change? Discuss.
8. Of the five elements in Exhibit 10.3 required for successful change, which element do you think managers are most likely to overlook? Discuss.
9. Why do you think open innovation has become popular in recent years? What steps might a company take to be more "open" with innovation? What might be some disadvantages of taking an open innovation approach?
10. A noted organization theorist said, "Pressure for change originates in the environment; pressure for stability originates within the organization." Do you agree? Discuss.

Chapter 10 Workbook: Innovation Climate*

In order to examine differences in the level of innovation encouragement in organizations, you will be asked to rate two organizations. The first should be an organization in which you have worked, or the university. The second should be someone else's workplace, that of a family member, a friend, or an acquaintance. You will have to interview that person to answer the following questions. You should put your own answers in column A, your interviewee's answers in column B, and what you think would be the ideal in column C.

Innovation Measures

Item of Measure	A Your Organization	B Other Organization	C Your Ideal
Score items 1–5 on this scale: 1 = *don't agree at all* to 5 = *agree completely*			
1. Creativity is encouraged here.[†]			
2. People are allowed to solve the same problems in different ways.[†]			
3. I get to pursue creative ideas.[†]			
4. The organization publicly recognizes and also rewards those who are innovative.[†]			

5. Our organization is flexible and always open to change.[†]			
Score items 6–10 on the opposite scale: 1 = *agree completely* to 5 = *don't agree at all*			
6. The primary job of people here is to follow orders that come from the top.[†]			
7. The best way to get along here is to think and act like the others.[†]			
8. This place seems to be more concerned with the status quo than with change.[†]			
9. People are rewarded more if they don't rock the boat.[†]			
10. New ideas are great, but we don't have enough people or money to carry them out.[‡]			

[†] These items indicate the organization's innovation climate.

[‡] These items show resource support.

Questions

1. What comparisons in terms of innovation climates can you make between these two organizations?
2. How might productivity differ between a climate that supports innovation and a climate that does not?
3. Where would you rather work? Why?

*Adapted by Dorothy Marcic from Susanne G. Scott and Reginald A. Bruce, "Determinants of Innovative Behavior: A Path Model of Individual Innovation in the Workplace," *Academy of Management Journal* 37, no. 3 (1994), 580–607.

Case for Analysis: Shoe Corporation of Illinois*

Shoe Corporation of Illinois (SCI) produces a line of women's shoes that sell in the lower-price market for $27.99 to $29.99 per pair. Profits averaged 30 cents to 50 cents per pair 10 years ago, but according to the president and the controller, labor and materials costs have risen so much in the intervening period that profits today average only 25 cents to 30 cents per pair.

Production at both the company's plants totals 12,500 pairs per day. The two factories are located within a radius of 60 miles of Chicago: one at Centerville, which produces 4,500 pairs per day, and the other at Meadowvale, which produces 8,000 pairs per day. Company headquarters is located in a building adjacent to the Centerville plant.

It is difficult to give an accurate picture of the number of items in the company's product line. Shoes change in style perhaps more rapidly than any other style product, including garments. This is chiefly because it is possible to change production processes quickly and because, historically, each company, in attempting to get ahead of competitors, gradu-

ally made style changes more frequently. At present, including both major and minor style changes, SCI offers 100 to 120 different products to customers each year.

A partial organizational chart, showing the departments involved in this case, appears in Exhibit 10.9.

Competitive Structure of the Industry

Very large general shoe houses, such as International and Brown, carry a line of women's shoes and are able to undercut prices charged by SCI, principally because of the policy in the big companies of producing large numbers of "stable" shoes, such as the plain pump and the loafer. They do not attempt to change styles as rapidly as their smaller competitors. Thus, without constant changes in production processes and sales presentations, they are able to keep costs substantially lower.

Charles F. Allison, the president of SCI, feels that the only way for a small independent company to be competitive is to change styles frequently, taking advantage of the

EXHIBIT 10.9
Partial Organization Chart of
Shoe Corporation of Illinois

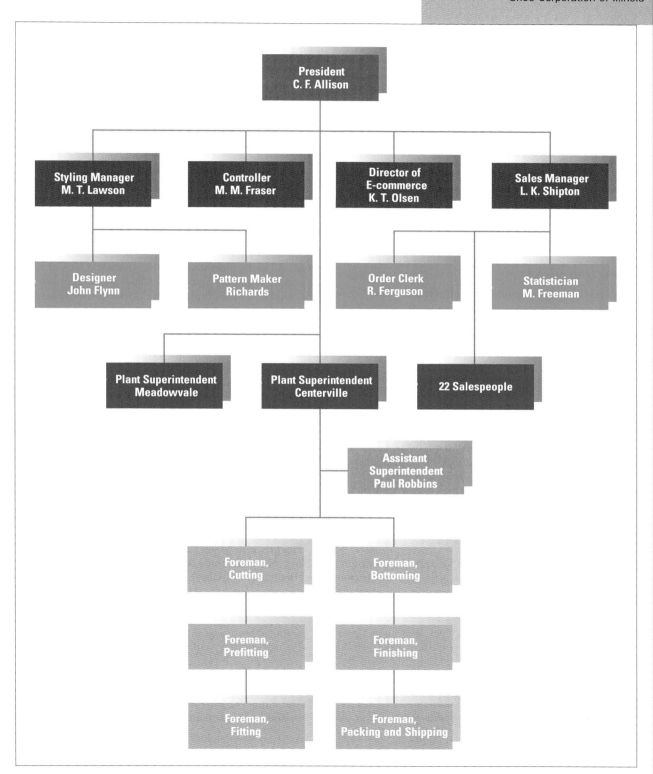

flexibility of a small organization to create designs that appeal to customers. Thus, demand can be created and a price set high enough to make a profit. Allison, incidentally, appears to have an artistic talent in styling and a record of successful judgments in approving high-volume styles over the years.

Regarding how SCI differs from its large competitors, Allison has said:

You see, Brown and International Shoe Company both produce hundreds of thousands of the same pair of shoes. They store them in inventory at their factories. Their customers, the large wholesalers and retailers, simply know their line and send in orders. They do not have to change styles nearly as often as we do. Sometimes I wish we could do that, too. It makes for a much more stable and orderly system. There is also less friction between people inside the company. The salespeople always know what they're selling; the production people know what is expected of them. The plant personnel are not shook up so often by someone coming in one morning and tampering with their machine lines or their schedules. The styling people are not shook up so often by the plant saying, "We can't do your new style the way you want it."

To help SCI be more competitive against larger firms, Allison recently created an e-commerce department. Although his main interest was in marketing over the Internet, he also hoped new technology would help reduce some of the internal friction by giving people an easier way to communicate. He invested in a sophisticated new computer system and hired consultants to set up a company intranet and provide a few days' training to upper and middle managers. Katherine Olsen came on board as director of e-commerce, charged primarily with coordinating Internet marketing and sales. When she took the job, she had visions of one day offering consumers the option of customized shoe designs. However, Olsen was somewhat surprised to learn that most employees still refused to use the intranet even for internal communication and coordination. The process for deciding on new styles, for example, had not changed since the 1970s.

Major Style Changes

The decision about whether to put a certain style into production requires information from a number of different people. Here is what typically happens in the company. It may be helpful to follow the organization chart (see Exhibit 10.9) tracing the procedure.

M. T. Lawson, the styling manager, and his designer, John Flynn, originate most of the ideas about shape, size of heel, use of flat sole or heels, and findings (the term used for ornaments attached to, but not part of, the shoes— bows, straps, and so forth). They get their ideas principally from reading style and trade magazines or by copying top-flight designers. Lawson corresponds with publications and friends in large stores in New York, Rome, and Paris to obtain pictures and samples of up-to-the-minute style innovations. Although he uses e-mail occasionally, Lawson prefers telephone contact and receiving drawings or samples by overnight mail. Then, he and Flynn discuss various ideas and come up with design options.

When Lawson decides on a design, he takes a sketch to Allison, who either approves or disapproves it. If Allison approves, he (Allison) then passes the sketch on to L. K. Shipton, the sales manager, to find out what lasts (widths) should be chosen. Shipton, in turn, forwards the design to Martin Freeman, a statistician in the sales department, who maintains summary information on customer demand for colors and lasts.

To compile this information, Freeman visits salespeople twice a year to get their opinions on the colors and lasts that are selling best, and he keeps records of shipments by color and by last. For these needs, he simply totals data that are sent to him by the shipping foreman in each of the two plants.

When Freeman has decided on the lasts and colors, he sends Allison a form that lists the colors and lasts in which the shoe should be produced. Allison, if he approves this list, forwards the information to Lawson, who passes it on to Jenna Richards, an expert pattern maker. Richards makes a paper pattern and then constructs a prototype in leather and paper. She sends this to Lawson, who in turn approves or disapproves it. He forwards any approved prototype to Allison. Allison, if he, too, approves, notifies Lawson, who takes the prototype to Paul Robbins, assistant to the superintendent of the Centerville plant. Only this plant produces small quantities of new or experimental shoe styles. This is referred to as a "pilot run" by executives at the plant.

Robbins then literally carries the prototype through the six production departments of the plant—from cutting to finishing—discussing it with each foreman, who in turn works with employees on the machines in having a sample lot of several thousand pairs made. When the finished lot is delivered by the finishing foreman to the shipping foreman (because of the importance of styling, Allison has directed that each foreman personally deliver styling goods in process to the foreman of the next department), the latter holds the inventory in storage and sends one pair each to Allison and Lawson. If they approve of the finished product, Allison instructs the shipping foreman to mail samples to each of the company's twenty-two salespeople throughout the country. Olsen also receives samples, photos, and drawings to post on the Web page and gauge customer interest.

Salespeople have instructions to take the samples immediately (within one week) to at least ten customers. Orders for already-established shoes are normally sent to Ralph Ferguson, a clerk in Shipton's office, who records them and forwards them to the plant superintendents for production. However, salespeople have found by experience that Martin Freeman has a greater interest in the success of new "trials," so they rush these orders to him by overnight mail, and he in turn places the first orders for a new style in the interoffice mail to the plant superintendents. He then sends off a duplicate of the order, mailed in by the salespeople, to Ferguson for entering in his statistical record of all orders received by the company.

Three weeks after the salespeople receive samples, Allison requires Ralph Ferguson to give him a tabulation of orders. At that time, he decides whether the salespeople and the Web page should push the item and the superintendents should produce large quantities, or whether he will tell them that although existing orders will be produced, the item will be discontinued in a short time.

The procedures outlined here have, according to Allison,

worked reasonably well. The average time from when Lawson decides on a design until we notify the Centerville plant to produce the pilot run is two weeks to a month. Of course, if we could speed that up, it would make the company just that much more secure in staying in the game against the big companies, and in taking sales away from our competitors. There seems to be endless bickering among people around here involved in the styling phase of the business. That's to be expected when you have to move fast—there isn't much time to stop and observe all of the social amenities. I have never thought that a formal organization chart would be good in this company—we've worked out a customary system here that functions well.

M. T. Lawson, manager of styling, said that within his department all work seems to get out in minimum time; he also stated that both Flynn and Richards are good employees and skilled in their work. He mentioned that Flynn had been in to see him twice in the last year

to inquire about his [Flynn's] future in the company. He is 33 years old and has three children. I know that he is eager to make money, and I assured him that over the years we can raise him right along from the $60,000 we are now paying. Actually, he has learned a lot about shoe styles since we hired him from the design department of a fabric company six years ago.

John Flynn revealed:

I was actually becoming dissatisfied with this job. All shoe companies copy styles—it's a generally accepted practice within the industry. But I've picked up a real feel for designs, and several times I've suggested that the company make all its own original styles. We could make SCI a style leader and also increase our volume. When I ask Lawson about this, he says it takes too much time for the designer to create originals—that we have all we can handle to do

research in trade magazines and maintain contracts feeding us the results of experts. Beside, he says our styles are standing the test of the marketplace.

Projects X and Y

Flynn also said that he and Martin Freeman had frequently talked about the styling problem. They felt that

Allison is really a great president, and the company surely would be lost without him. However, we've seen times when he lost a lot of money on bad judgments in styles. Not many times—perhaps six or seven times in the last eighteen months. Also, he is, of course, extremely busy as president of the corporation. He must look after everything from financing from the banks to bargaining with the union. The result is that he is sometimes unavailable to do his styling approvals for several days, or even two weeks. In a business like this, that kind of delay can cost money. It also makes him slightly edgy. It tends, at times when he has many other things to do, to make him look quickly at the styles we submit, or the prototypes Richards makes, or even the finished shoes that are sent for approval by the shipping foreman. Sometimes I worry that he makes two kinds of errors. He simply rubber-stamps what we've done, which makes sending these things to him a waste of time. At other times he makes snap judgments of his own, overruling those of us who have spent so much time and expertise on the shoe. We do think he has good judgment, but he himself has said at times that he wishes he had more time to concentrate on styling and approval of prototypes and final products.

Flynn further explained (and this was corroborated by Freeman) that the two had worked out two plans, which they referred to as "project X" and "project Y." In the first, Flynn created an original design that was not copied from existing styles. Freeman then gave special attention to color and last research for the shoe and recommended a color line that didn't exactly fit past records on consumer purchases—but one he and Flynn thought would have "great consumer appeal." This design and color recommendation was accepted by Lawson and Allison; the shoe went into production and was one of the three top sellers during the calendar year. The latter two men did not know that the shoe was styled in a different way from the usual procedure.

The result of a second, similar project (Y) was put into production the next year, but this time sales were discontinued after three weeks.

Problem between Lawson and Robbins

Frequently, perhaps ten to twelve times a year, disagreement arises between Mel Lawson, manager of styling, and Paul Robbins, assistant to the superintendent of the Centerville plant. Robbins said,

The styling people don't understand what it means to produce a shoe in the quantities that we do, and to make the changes in production that we have to. They dream up a style quickly, out of thin air. They do not realize that we have a lot of machines that have to be adjusted and that some things they dream up take much longer on certain machines than others, thus creating a bottleneck in the production line. If they put a bow or strap in one position rather than another, it may mean we have to keep people idle on later machines while there is a pileup on the sewing machines on which this complicated little operation is performed. This costs the plant money. Furthermore, there are times when they get the prototype here late, and either the foremen and I work overtime or the trial run won't get through in time to have new production runs on new styles, to take the plant capacity liberated by our stopping production on old styles. Lawson doesn't know much about production and sales and the whole company. I think all he does is to bring shoes down here to the plant, sort of like a messenger boy. Why should he be so hard to get along with? He isn't getting paid any more than I am, and my position in the plant is just as important as his.

Lawson, in turn, said that he has a difficult time getting along with Robbins:

There are many times when Robbins is just unreasonable. I take prototypes to him five or six times a month, and other minor style changes to him six or eight times. I tell him every time that we have problems in getting these ready, but he knows only about the plant, and telling him doesn't seem to do any good. When we first joined the company, we got along all right, but he has gotten harder and harder to get along with.

Other Problems

Ralph Ferguson, the clerk in the sales department who receives orders from salespeople and forwards totals for production schedules to the two plant superintendents, has complained that the salespeople and Freeman are bypassing him in their practice of sending experimental shoe orders to Freeman. He insisted that his job description (one of only two written descriptions in the company) gives him responsibility for receiving all orders throughout the company and for maintaining historical statistics on shipments.

Both the salespeople and Freeman, on the other hand, said that before they started the new practice (that is, when Ferguson still received the experimental shoe orders), there were at least eight or ten instances a year when these were delayed from one to three days on Ferguson's desk. They

reported that Ferguson just wasn't interested in new styles, so the salespeople "just started sending them to Freeman." Ferguson acknowledged that there were times of short delay, but said that there were good reasons for them:

They [the salespeople and Freeman] are so interested in new designs, colors, and lasts that they can't understand the importance of a systematic handling of the whole order procedure, including both old and new shoe styles. There must be accuracy. Sure, I give some priority to experimental orders, but sometimes when rush orders for existing company products are piling up, and when there's a lot of planning I have to do to allocate production between Centerville and Meadowvale, I decide which comes first—processing of these, or processing the experimental shoe orders. Shipton is my boss, not the salespeople or Freeman. I'm going to insist that these orders come to me.

The Push for New Technology

Katherine Olsen believes many of these problems could be solved through better use of technology. She has approached Charles Allison several times about the need to make greater use of the expensive and sophisticated computer information systems he had installed. Although Allison always agrees with her, he has so far done nothing to help solve the problem. Olsen thinks the new technology could dramatically improve coordination at SCI.

Everyone needs to be working from the same data at the same time. As soon as Lawson and Flynn come up with a new design, it should be posted on the intranet so all of us can be informed. And everyone needs access to sales and order information, production schedules, and shipping deadlines. If everyone—from Allison down to the people in the production plants—was kept up to date throughout the entire process, we wouldn't have all this confusion and bickering. But no one around here wants to give up any control—they all have their own little operations and don't want to share information with anyone else. For example, I sometimes don't even know there's a new style in the works until I get finished samples and photos. No one seems to recognize that one of the biggest advantages of the Internet is to help stay ahead of changing styles. I know that Flynn has a good feel for design, and we're not taking advantage of his abilities. But I also have information and ideas that could help this company keep pace with changes and really stand out from the crowd. I don't know how long we expect to remain competitive using this cumbersome, slow-moving process and putting out shoes that are already behind the times.

*Written by Charles E. Summer. Copyright 1978.

Case for Analysis: Southern Discomfort*

Jim Malesckowski remembered the call of two weeks ago as if he had just put down the telephone receiver: "I just read your analysis and I want you to get down to Mexico right away," Jack Ripon, his boss and chief executive officer, had blurted in his ear. "You know we can't make the plant in Oconomo work anymore—the costs are just too high. So go down there, check out what our operational costs would be if we move, and report back to me in a week."

As president of the Wisconsin Specialty Products Division of Lamprey Inc., Jim knew quite well the challenge of dealing with high-cost labor in a third-generation, unionized, U.S. manufacturing plant. And although he had done the analysis that led to his boss's knee-jerk response, the call still stunned him. There were 520 people who made a living at Lamprey's Oconomo facility, and if it closed, most of them wouldn't have a chance of finding another job in the town of 9,900 people.

Instead of the $16-per-hour average wage paid at the Oconomo plant, the wages paid to the Mexican workers—who lived in a town without sanitation and with an unbelievably toxic effluent from industrial pollution—would amount to about $1.60 an hour on average. That would be a savings of nearly $15 million a year for Lamprey, to be offset in part by increased costs for training, transportation, and other matters.

After two days of talking with Mexican government representatives and managers of other companies in the town, Jim had enough information to develop a set of comparative figures of production and shipping costs. On the way home, he started to outline the report, knowing full well that unless some miracle occurred, he would be ushering in a blizzard of pink slips for people he had come to appreciate.

The plant in Oconomo had been in operation since 1921, making special apparel for people suffering from injuries and other medical conditions. Jim had often talked with employees who would recount stories about their fathers or grandfathers working in the same Lamprey company plant—the last of the original manufacturing operations in town.

But friendship aside, competitors had already edged past Lamprey in terms of price and were dangerously close to overtaking it in product quality. Although both Jim and the plant manager had tried to convince the union to accept lower wages, union leaders resisted. In fact, on one occasion when Jim and the plant manager tried to discuss a cell manufacturing approach, which would cross-train employees to perform up to three different jobs, local union leaders could barely restrain their anger. Jim thought he sensed an underlying fear, meaning the union reps were aware of at least some of the problems, but he had been unable to get them to acknowledge this and move on to open discussion.

A week passed and Jim had just submitted his report to his boss. Although he didn't specifically bring up the point, it was apparent that Lamprey could put its investment dollars in a bank and receive a better return than what its Oconomo operation was currently producing.

The next day, he would discuss the report with the CEO. Jim didn't want to be responsible for the plant's dismantling, an act he personally believed would be wrong as long as there was a chance its costs can be lowered. "But Ripon's right," he said to himself. "The costs are too high, the union's unwilling to cooperate, and the company needs to make a better return on its investment if it's to continue at all. It sounds right but feels wrong. What should I do?"

*Doug Wallace, "What Would You Do?" *Business Ethics* (March/April 1996), 52–53. Reprinted with permission from *Business Ethics*, PO Box 8439, Minneapolis, MN 55408; phone: 612-879-0695.

Integrative Case 5.0
Dick Spencer*

After the usual banter when old friends meet for cocktails, the conversation between a couple of university professors and Dick Spencer, who was now a successful businessman, turned to Dick's life as a vice president of a large manufacturing firm.

"I've made a lot of mistakes, most of which I could live with, but this one series of incidents was so frustrating that I could have cried at the time," Dick said in response to a question. "I really have to laugh at how ridiculous it is now, but at the time I blew my cork."

Spencer was plant manager of Modrow Company, a Canadian branch of the Tri-American Corporation. Tri-American was a major producer of primary aluminum with integrated operations ranging from the mining of bauxite through the processing to fabrication of aluminum into a variety of products. The company had also made and sold refractories and industrial chemicals. The parent company had wholly-owned subsidiaries in five separate United States locations and had foreign affiliates in fifteen different countries.

Tri-American mined bauxite in the Jamaican West Indies and shipped the raw material by commercial vessels to two plants in Louisiana where it was processed into alumina. The alumina was then shipped to reduction plants in one of three locations for conversion into primary aluminum. Most of the primary aluminum was then moved to the companies' fabricating plants for further processing. Fabricated aluminum items included sheet, flat, coil, and corrugated products; siding; and roofing.

Tri-American employed approximately 22,000 employees in the total organization. The company was governed by a board of directors, which included the chairman, vice chairman, president, and twelve vice presidents. However, each of the subsidiaries and branches functioned as independent units. The board set general policy, which was then interpreted and applied by the various plant managers. In a sense, the various plants competed with one another as though they were independent companies. This decentralization in organizational structure increased the freedom and authority of the plant managers, but increased the pressure for profitability.

The Modrow branch was located in a border town in Canada. The total work force in Modrow was 1,000. This Canadian subsidiary was primarily a fabricating unit. Its main products were foil and building products such as roofing and siding. Aluminum products were gaining in importance in architectural plans, and increased sales were predicted for this branch. Its location and its stable work force were the most important advantages it possessed.

In anticipation of estimated increases in building product sales, Modrow had recently completed a modernization and expansion project. At the same time, their research and art departments combined talents in developing a series of twelve new patterns of siding which were being introduced to the market. Modernization and pattern development had been costly undertakings, but the expected return on investment made the project feasible. However, the plant manager, who was a Tri-American vice president, had instituted a campaign to cut expenses wherever possible. In this introductory notice of the campaign, he emphasized that cost reduction would be the personal aim of every employee at Modrow.

Salesman

The plant manager of Modrow, Dick Spencer, was an American who had been transferred to this Canadian branch two years previously, after the start of the modernization plan. Dick had been with the Tri-American Company for fourteen years, and his progress within the organization was considered spectacular by those who knew him well. Dick had received a master's degree in Business Administration from a well-known university at the age of twenty-two. Upon graduation he had accepted a job as salesman for Tri-American. During his first year as a salesman, he succeeded in landing a single, large contract, which put him near the top of the sales-volume leaders. In discussing this phenomenal rise in the sales volume, several of his fellow salesmen concluded that his looks, charm, and ability on the golf course contributed as much to his success as his knowledge of the business or his ability to sell the products.

The second year of his sales career, he continued to set a fast pace. Although his record set difficult goals for the other salesmen, he was considered a "regular guy" by them, and both he and they seemed to enjoy the few occasions when they socialized. However, by the end of the second year of constant traveling and selling, Dick began to experience some doubt about his future.

*This case was developed and prepared by Professor Margaret E. Fenn, Graduate School of Business Administration, University of Washington. Reprinted by permission.

His constant involvement in business affairs disrupted his marital life, and his wife divorced him during the second year with Tri-American. Dick resented her action at first, but gradually seemed to recognize that his career at present depended on his freedom to travel unencumbered. During that second year, he ranged far and wide in his sales territory, and successfully closed several large contracts. None of them was as large as his first year's major sale, but in total volume he again was well up near the top of salesmen for the year. Dick's name became well known in the corporate headquarters, and he was spoken of as "the boy to watch."

Dick had met the president of Tri-American during his first year as a salesman at a company conference. After three days of golfing and socializing they developed a relaxed camaraderie considered unusual by those who observed the developing friendship. Although their contacts were infrequent after the conference, their easy relationship seemed to blossom the few times they did meet. Dick's friends kidded him about his ability to make use of his new friendship to promote himself in the company, but Dick brushed aside their jibes and insisted that he'd make it on his own abilities, not someone's coattails.

By the time he was twenty-five, Dick began to suspect that he did not look forward to a life as a salesman for the rest of his career. He talked about his unrest with his friends, and they suggested that he groom himself for sales manager. "You won't make the kind of money you're making from commissions," he was told, "but you will have a foot in the door from an administrative standpoint, and you won't have to travel quite as much as you do now." Dick took their suggestions lightly, and continued to sell the product, but was aware that he felt dissatisfied and did not seem to get the satisfaction out of his job that he had once enjoyed.

By the end of his third year with the company Dick was convinced that he wanted a change in direction. As usual, he and the president spent quite a bit of time on the golf course during the annual company sales conference. After their match one day, the president kidded Dick about his game. The conversation drifted back to business, and the president, who seemed to be in a jovial mood, started to kid Dick about his sales ability. In a joking way, he implied that anyone could sell a product as good as Tri-American's, but that it took real "guts and know-how" to make the products. The conversation drifted to other things, but the remark stuck with Dick.

Sometime later, Dick approached the president formally with a request for a transfer out of the sales division. The president was surprised and hesitant about this change in career direction for Dick. He recognized the superior sales ability that Dick seemed to possess, but was unsure that Dick was willing or able to assume responsibilities in any other division of the organization. Dick sensed the hesitancy, but continued to push his request. He later remarked that it seemed that the initial hesitancy of the president convinced Dick that he needed an opportunity to prove himself in a field other than sales.

Troubleshooter

Dick was finally transferred back to the home office of the organization and indoctrinated into production and administrative roles in the company as a special assistant to the senior vice president of production. As a special assistant, Dick was assigned several troubleshooting jobs. He acquitted himself well in this role, but in the process succeeded in gaining a reputation as a ruthless headhunter among the branches where he had performed a series of amputations. His reputation as an amiable, genial, easygoing guy from the sales department was the antithesis of the reputation of a cold, calculating headhunter which he earned in his troubleshooting role. The vice president, who was Dick's boss, was aware of the reputation which Dick had earned but was pleased with the results that were obtained. The faltering departments that Dick had worked in seemed to bloom with new life and energy after Dick's recommended amputations. As a result, the vice president began to sing Dick's praises, and the president began to accept Dick in his new role in the company.

Management Responsibility

About three years after Dick's switch from sales, he was given an assignment as assistant plant manager of an English branch of the company. Dick, who had remarried, moved his wife and family to London, and they attempted to adapt to their new routine. The plant manager was English, as were most of the other employees. Dick and his family were accepted with reservations into the community life as well as into the plant life. The difference between British and American philosophy and performance within the plant was marked for Dick, who was imbued with modern managerial concepts and methods. Dick's directives from headquarters were to update and upgrade performance in this branch. However, his power and authority were less than those of his superiors, so he constantly found himself in the position of having to soft pedal or withhold suggestions that he would have liked to make, or innovations that he would have liked to introduce. After a frustrating year and a half, Dick was suddenly made plant manager of an old British company which had just been purchased by Tri-American. He left his first English assignment with mixed feelings and moved from London to Birmingham.

As the new plant manager, Dick operated much as he had in his troubleshooting job for the first couple of years of his change from sales to administration. Training and reeducation programs were instituted for all supervisors and managers who survived the initial purge. Methods were studied and simplified or redesigned whenever possible, and new attention was directed toward production which better met the needs of the sales organization. A strong controller helped to straighten out the profit picture through stringent cost control; and by the end of the third year, the company showed a small profit for the first time in many years. Because he felt that this battle was won, Dick requested transfer back to the United States. The request was partially granted when nine months later he was awarded a junior vice president title, and was made manager of a subsidiary Canadian plant, Modrow.

Modrow Manager

Prior to Dick's appointment as plant manager at Modrow, extensive plans for plant expansion and improvement had been approved and started. Although he had not been in on the original discussions and plans, he inherited all the problems that accompany large-scale changes in any organization. Construction was slower in completion than originally planned, equipment arrived before the building was finished, employees were upset about the extent of change expected in their work routines with the installation of additional machinery, and, in general, morale was at a low ebb.

Various versions of Dick's former activities had preceded him, and on his arrival he was viewed with dubious eyes. The first few months after his arrival were spent in a frenzy of catching up. This entailed constant conferences and meetings, volumes of reading of past reports, becoming acquainted with the civic leaders of the area, and a plethora of dispatches to and from the home office. Costs continued to climb unabated.

By the end of his first year at Modrow, the building program had been completed, although behind schedule, the new equipment had been installed, and some revamping of cost procedures had been incorporated. The financial picture at this time showed a substantial loss, but since it had been budgeted as a loss, this was not surprising. All managers of the various divisions had worked closely with their supervisors and accountants in planning the budget for the following year, and Dick began to emphasize his personal interest in cost reduction.

As he worked through his first year as plant manager, Dick developed the habit of strolling around the organization. He was apt to leave his office and appear anywhere on the plant floor, in the design offices, at the desk of a purchasing agent or accountant, in the plant cafeteria rather than the executive dining room, or wherever there was activity concerned with Modrow. During his strolls he looked, listened, and became acquainted. If he observed activities which he wanted to talk about, or heard remarks that gave him clues to future action, he did not reveal these

at the time. Rather he had a nod, a wave, a smile, for the people near him, but a mental note to talk to his supervisors, managers, and foremen in the future. At first his presence disturbed those who noted him coming and going, but after several exposures to him without any noticeable effect, the workers came to accept his presence and continue their usual activities. Supervisors, managers, and foremen, however, did not feel as comfortable when they saw him in the area.

Their feelings were aptly expressed by the manager of the siding department one day when he was talking to one of his foremen: "I wish to hell he'd stay up in the front office where he belongs. Whoever heard of a plant manager who has time to wander around the plant all the time? Why doesn't he tend to his paper work and let us tend to our business?"

"Don't let him get you down," joked the foreman. "Nothing ever comes of his visits. Maybe he's just lonesome and looking for a friend. You know how these Americans are."

"Well, you may feel that nothing ever comes of his visits, but I don't. I've been called into his office three separate times within the last two months. The heat must really be on from the head office. You know these conferences we have every month where he reviews our financial progress, our building progress, our design progress, etc.? Well, we're not really progressing as fast as we should be. If you ask me we're in for continuing trouble."

In recalling his first year at Modrow, Dick had felt constantly pressured and badgered. He always sensed that the Canadians he worked with resented his presence since he was brought in over the heads of the operating staff. At the same time he felt this subtle resistance from his Canadian work force, he believed that the president and his friends in the home office were constantly on the alert, waiting for Dick to prove himself or fall flat on his face. Because of the constant pressures and demands of the work, he had literally dumped his family into a new community and had withdrawn into the plant. In the process, he built up a wall of resistance toward the demands of his wife and children who, in turn, felt as though he was abandoning them.

During the course of the conversation with his university friends, he began to recall a series of incidents that probably had resulted from the conflicting pressures. When describing some of these incidents, he continued to emphasize the fact that his attempt to be relaxed and casual had backfired. Laughingly, Dick said, "As you know, both human relations and accounting were my weakest subjects during the master's program, and yet they are two fields I felt I needed the most at Modrow at this time." He described some of the cost procedures that he would have liked to incorporate. However, without the support and knowledge furnished by his former controller, he busied himself with details that were unnecessary. One day, as he describes it, he overheard a conversation between two of the accounting staff members with whom he had been working very closely. One of them commented to the other, "For a guy who's a vice president, he sure spends a lot of time breathing down our necks. Why doesn't he simply tell us the kind of systems he would like to try, and let us do the experimenting and work out the budget?" Without commenting on the conversation he overheard, Dick then described himself as attempting to spend less time and be less directive in the accounting department.

Another incident he described, which apparently had real meaning for him, was one in which he had called a staff conference with his top-level managers. They had been going "hammer and tongs" for better than an hour in his private office, and in the process of heated conversation had loosened ties, taken off coats, and really rolled up their sleeves. Dick himself had slipped out of his shoes. In the midst of this, his secretary reminded him of an appointment with public officials. Dick had rapidly finished up his conference with his managers, straightened his tie, donned his coat, and had wandered out into the main office in his stocking feet.

Dick fully described several incidents when he had disappointed, frustrated, or confused his wife and family by forgetting birthdays, appointments, dinner engagements, etc. He seemed to be describing a pattern of behavior which resulted from continuing pressure and frustration. He was setting the scene to describe his baffling and humiliating position in the siding department. In looking back and recalling his activities during this first year, Dick commented on the fact that his frequent wanderings throughout the plant had resulted in a nodding acquaintance with the workers, but probably had also resulted in foremen and supervisors spending more time getting ready for his visits and reading meaning into them afterwards than attending to their specific duties. His attempts to know in detail the accounting procedures being used required long hours of concentration and detailed conversations with the accounting staff, which were time consuming and very frustrating for him, as well as for them. His lack of attention to his family life resulted in continued pressure from both wife and family.

The Siding Department Incident

Siding was the product which had been budgeted as a large profit item of Modrow. Aluminum siding was gaining in popularity among both architects and builders, because of its possibilities in both decorative and practical uses. Panel sheets of siding were shipped in standard sizes to order; large sheets of the coated siding were cut to specifications in the trim department, packed, and shipped. The trim shop was located near the loading platforms, and Dick often cut through the trim shop on his wanderings through the plant. On one of his frequent trips through the area, he suddenly became aware of the fact that several workers responsible for the disposal function were spending countless hours at high-speed saws cutting scraps into specified lengths to fit into scrap barrels. The narrow bands of scrap which resulted from the trim process varied in length from seven to twenty-seven feet and had to be reduced in size to fit into disposal barrels. Dick, in his concentration on cost reduction, picked up one of the thin strips, bent it several times and fitted it into the barrel. He tried this with another piece, and it bent very easily. After assuring himself that bending was possible, he walked over to a worker at the saw and asked why he was using the saw when material could easily be bent and fitted into the barrels, resulting in saving time and equipment. The worker's response was, "We've never done it that way, sir. We've always cut it."

Following his plan of not commenting or discussing matters on the floor, but distressed by the reply, Dick returned to his office and asked the manager of the siding department if he could speak to the foreman in the scrap division. The manager said, "Of course, I'll send him up to you in just a minute."

After a short time, the foreman, very agitated at being called to the plant manager's office, appeared. Dick began questioning him about the scrap disposal process and received the standard answer: "We've always done it that way." Dick then proceeded to review cost-cutting objectives. He talked about the pliability of the strips of scrap. He called for a few pieces of scrap to demonstrate the ease with which it could be bent, and ended what he thought was a satisfactory conversation by requesting the foreman to order heavy-duty gloves for his workers and use the bending process for a trial period of two weeks to check the cost savings possible.

The foreman listened throughout most of this hour's conference, offered several reasons why it wouldn't work, raised some questions about the record-keeping process for cost purposes, and finally left the office with the forced agreement to try the suggested new method of bending, rather than cutting, for disposal. Although he was immersed in many other problems, his request was forcibly brought home one day as he cut through the scrap area. The workers were using power saws to cut scraps. He called the manager of the siding department and questioned him about the process. The manager explained that each foreman was responsible for his own processes, and since Dick had already talked to the foreman, perhaps he had better talk to him again. When the foreman arrived, Dick began to question him. He received a series of excuses, and some explanations of the kinds of problems they were meeting by attempting to bend the scrap material. "I don't care what the problems are," Dick nearly shouted, "when

I request a cost-reduction program instituted, I want to see it carried through."

Dick was furious. When the foreman left, Dick phoned the maintenance department and ordered the removal of the power saws from the scrap area immediately. A short time later the foreman of the scrap department knocked on Dick's door reporting his astonishment at having maintenance men step into his area and physically remove the saws. Dick reminded the foreman of his request for a trial at cost reduction to no avail, and ended the conversation by saying that the power saws were gone and would not be returned, and the foreman had damned well better learn to get along without them. After a stormy exit by the foreman, Dick congratulated himself on having solved a problem and turned his attention to other matters.

A few days later Dick cut through the trim department and literally stopped to stare. As he described it, he was completely nonplussed to discover gloved workmen using hand shears to cut each strip of scrap.

5.0

Integrative Case 6.0
"Ramrod" Stockwell*

The Benson Metal Company employs about 1,500 people, is listed on the stock exchange, and has been in existence for many decades. It makes a variety of metals that are purchased by manufacturers or specialized metal firms. It is one of the five or six leading firms in the specialty steel industry. This industry produces steels in fairly small quantities with a variety of characteristics. Orders tend to be in terms of pounds rather than tons, although a 1,000-pound order is not unusual. For some of the steels, 100 pounds is an average order.

The technology for producing specialty steels in the firm is fairly well established, but there is still a good deal of guesswork, skill, and even some "black magic" involved. Small changes are made in the ingredients going into the melting process, often amounting to the addition of a tiny bit of expensive alloying material in order to produce varieties of specialty steels. Competitors can analyze one another's products and generally produce the same product without too much difficulty, although there are some secrets. There are also important variations stemming from the type of equipment used to melt, cog, roll, and finish the steel.

In the period that we are considering, the Benson Company and some of its competitors were steadily moving into more sophisticated and technically more difficult steels, largely for the aerospace industry. The aerospace products were far more difficult to make, required more research skills and metallurgical analysis, and required more "delicate" handling in all stages of production, even though the same basic equipment was involved. Furthermore, they were marketed in a different fashion. They were produced to the specifications of government subcontractors, and government inspectors were often in the plant to watch all stages of production. One firm might be able to produce a particular kind of steel that another firm could not produce even though it had tried. These steels were considerably more expensive than the specialty steels, and failures to meet specifications resulted in more substantial losses for the company. At the time of the study about 20 percent of the cash value output was in aerospace metals.

The chairman, Fred Benson, had been president (managing director) of the company for two decades before moving up to this position. He is an elderly man but has a strong will and is much revered in the company for having built it up to its present size and influence. The president, Tom Hollis, has been in office for about four years; he was formerly the sales director and has worked closely with Fred Benson over many years. Hollis has three or four years to go before expected retirement. His assistant, Joe Craig, had been a sales manager in one of the smaller offices. It is the custom of this firm to pick promising people from middle-management and put them in the "assistant-to" position for perhaps a year to groom them for higher offices in their division. For some time these people had come from sales, and they generally went back as managers of large districts, from whence they might be promoted to a sales manager position in the main office.

Dick Benson, the executive vice president (roughly, general manager), is the son of Fred Benson. He is generally regarded as being willing, fairly competent, and decent, but weak and still much under his father's thumb. Traditionally, the executive vice president became president. Dick is not thought to be up to that job, but it is believed that he will get it anyway.

Ramsey Stockwell, vice president of production, had come into the organization as an experienced engineer about six years before. He rose rather rapidly to his present position. Rob Bronson, vice president of sales, succeeded Dick Benson after Benson had a rather short term as vice president of sales. Alan Carswell, the vice president of research, has a doctorate in metallurgy and some patents in his name, but he is not considered an aggressive researcher or an aggressive in-fighter in the company.

The Problem

When the research team studied Benson Metal, there were the usual problems of competition and price-cutting, the difficulties with the new aerospace metals, and inadequate plant facilities for a growing industry and company. However, the problem that particularly interests us here concerned the vice president of production, Ramsey Stockwell. He was regarded as a very competent production man. His loyalty to the company was unquestioned. He managed to keep outdated facilities operating and still had been able to push through the construction of quite modern facilities in the finishing phases of the production process. But he was in trouble with his own staff and with other divisions of the company, principally sales.

It was widely noted that Stockwell failed to delegate authority to his subordinates. A steady stream of people came into his office asking for permission for this and that or bringing questions to him. People who took some action

*Charles Perrow, Yale University. Reprinted with permission.

6.0

on their own could be bawled out unmercifully at times. At other times they were left on their own because of the heavy demands on Stockwell's time, given his frequent attention to details in some matters, particularly those concerning schedules and priorities. He "contracted" the lines of authority by giving orders directly to a manager or even to a head foreman rather than by working through the intermediate levels. This violated the chain of command, left managers uninformed, and reduced their authority. It was sometimes noted that he had good people under him but did not always let them do their jobs.

The key group of production people rarely met in a group unless it was to be bawled out by Stockwell. Coordinating committees and the like existed mainly on paper.

More serious perhaps than this was the relationship to sales. Rob Bronson was widely regarded as an extremely bright, capable, likable, and up-and-coming manager. The sales division performed like a well-oiled machine but also had the enthusiasm and flashes of brilliance that indicated considerable adaptability. Morale was high, and identification with the company was complete. However, sales personnel found it quite difficult to get reliable information from production as to delivery dates or even what stage in the process a product was in.

Through long tradition, they were able to get special orders thrust into the work flow when they wanted to, but they often could not find out what this was going to do to normal orders, or even how disruptive this might be. The reason was that Stockwell would not allow production people to give any but the most routine information to sales personnel. In fact, because of the high centralization of authority and information in production, production personnel often did not know themselves. "Ramrod" Stockwell knew, and the only way to get information out of him was to go up the sales line to Rob Bronson. The vice president of sales could get the information from the vice president of production.

But Bronson had more troubles than just not wanting to waste his time by calling Stockwell about status reports. At the weekly top-management meeting, which involved all personnel from the vice presidential level and above, and frequently a few from below that level, Bronson would continually ask Stockwell whether something or other could be done. Stockwell always said that he thought it could be. He could not be pressed for any better estimations, and he rarely admitted that a job was, in fact, not possible. Even queries from President Tom Hollis could not evoke accurate forecasts from Stockwell. Consequently, planning on the part of sales and other divisions was difficult, and failures on the part of production were many because it always vaguely promised so much. Stockwell was willing to

try anything, and worked his head off at it, but the rest of the group knew that many of these attempts would fail.

While the people under Stockwell resented the way he took over their jobs at times and the lack of information available to them about other aspects of production, they were loyal to him. They admired his ability and they knew that he fought off the continual pressure of sales to slip in special orders, change schedules, or blame production for rejects. "Sales gets all the glory here" said one. "At the semiannual company meeting last week, the chairman of the board and the managing director of the company couldn't compliment sales enough for their good work, but there was only the stock 'well done' for production; 'well done given the trying circumstances.' Hell, Sales is what is trying us." The annual reports over the years credited sales for the good years and referred to equipment failures, crowded or poor production facilities, and the like in bad years. But it was also true that problems still remained even after Stockwell finally managed to pry some new production facilities out of the board of directors.

Stockwell was also isolated socially from the right group of top personnel: He tended to work later than most, had rougher manners, was less concerned with cultural activities, and rarely played golf. He occasionally relaxed with the manager of aerospace sales, who, incidentally, was the only high-level sales person who tended to defend Stockwell. "Ramrod's a rough diamond; I don't know that we ought to try to polish him," he sometimes said.

But polishing was in the minds of many. "Great production man—amazing what he gets out of that mill. But he doesn't know how to handle people. He won't delegate; he won't tell us when he is in trouble with something; he builds a fence around his people, preventing easy exchange," said the president. "Bullheaded as hell—he was good a few years ago, but I would never give him the job again," said the chairman of the board. He disagreed with the president that Stockwell could change. "You can't change people's personalities, least of all production men." "He's in a tough position," said the vice president of sales, "and he has to be able to get his people to work with him, not against him, and we all have to work together in today's market. I just wish he would not be so uptight."

A year or so before, the president had approached Stockwell about taking a couple of weeks off and joining a leadership training session. Stockwell would have nothing to do with it and was offended. The president waited a few months, then announced that he had arranged for the personnel manager and each of the directors to attend successive four-day T-group sessions run by a well-known organization. This had been agreed on at one of the directors' meetings, though no one had taken it very seriously. One by one, the directors came back with marked enthusiasm for the program. "It's almost as if they had our company in mind when they designed it," said one. Some started having evening and weekend sessions with their staff, occasionally using the personnel manager, who had had more experience with this than the others. Stockwell was scheduled to be the last one to attend the four-day session, but he canceled at the last minute—there were too many crises in the plant, he said, to go off that time. In fact, several had developed over the previous few weeks.

That did it, as far as the other vice presidents were concerned. They got together themselves, then with the president and executive vice president, and said that they had to get to the bottom of the problem. A top-level group session should be held to discuss the tensions that were accumulating. The friction between production and sales was spilling over into other areas as well, and the morale of management in general was suffering. They acknowledged that they put a lot of pressure on production, and were probably at fault in this or that matter, and thus a session would do all the directors good, not just Stockwell. The president hesitated. Stockwell, he felt, would just ride it out. Besides, he added, the "Old Man" (chairman of the board) was skeptical of such techniques. The executive vice president was quite unenthusiastic. It was remarked later that Stockwell had never recognized his official authority, and thus young Dick feared any open confrontation.

But events overtook the plan of the vice presidents. A first-class crisis had developed involving a major order for their oldest and best customer, and an emergency top-management meeting was called, which included several of their subordinates. Three in particular were involved: Joe Craig, assistant to the president, who knows well the problems at the plant in his role as troubleshooter for the managing director; Sandy Falk, vice president of personnel, who is sophisticated about leadership training programs and in a position to watch a good bit of the bickering at the middle and lower levels between sales and production; Bill Bletchford, manager of finishing, who is loyal to Stockwell and who has the most modern-equipped phase of the production process and the most to do with sales. It was in his department that the jam had occurred, due to some massive scheduling changes at the rolling phase and to the failure of key equipment.

In the meeting, the ground is gone over thoroughly. With their backs to the wall, the two production men, behaving somewhat uncharacteristically in an open meeting, charge sales with devious tactics for introducing special orders and for acting on partial and misinterpreted information from a foreman. Joe Craig knows, and admits, that the specialty A sales manager made promises to the customer without checking with the vice president of sales, who could have checked with Stockwell. "He was right," says Vice President Bronson. "I can't spend all my time calling Ramsey about status reports; if Harrison can't find out from production on an official basis, he has to do the best he can." Ramsey Stockwell, after his forceful outburst about misleading information through devious tactics, falls into a hardened silence, answering only direct questions, and then briefly. The manager of finishing and the specialty A sales manager start working on each other. Sandy Falk, of personnel, knows they have been enemies for years, so he intervenes as best he can. The vice president of research, Carswell, a reflective man, often worried about elusive dimensions of company problems, then calls a halt with the following speech:

You're all wrong and you're all right. I have heard bits and pieces of this fracas a hundred times over the last two or three years, and it gets worse each year. The facts of this damn case don't matter unless all you want is to score points with your opponents. What is wrong is something with the whole team here. I don't know what it is, but I know that we have to radically rethink our relations with one another. Three years ago this kind of thing rarely happened; now it is starting to happen all the time. And it is a time when we can't afford it. There is no more growth in our bread-and-butter line, specialty steels. The money, and the growth, is in aerospace; we all know that. Without aerospace we will just stand still. Maybe that's part of it. But maybe Ramsey's part of it too; this crisis is over specialty steel, and more of them seem to concern that than aerospace, so it can't be the product shift or that only. Some part of it has to be people, and you're on the hot seat, Ramsey.

Carswell let that sink in, then went on.

Or maybe it's something more than even these. . . . It is not being pulled together at the top, or maybe, the old way of pulling it together won't work anymore. I'm talking about you, Tom [Hollis], as well as Fred [Benson, the chairman of the board, who did not attend these meetings] and Dick [the executive vice president, and heir apparent]. I don't know what it is, here are Ramsey and Rob at loggerheads; neither of them are fools, and both of them are working their heads off. Maybe the problem is above their level.

There is a long silence. Assume you break the silence with your own analysis. What would that be?

Part 5

Internal Factors and Design

xyno.fotenizen

Chapter 11
Information and
Control Processes

Chapter 12
Organization Size
and Life Cycle

Chapter 13
Workplace Technology
and Design

415

Chapter 11

Information and Control Processes

xyno lorenzen

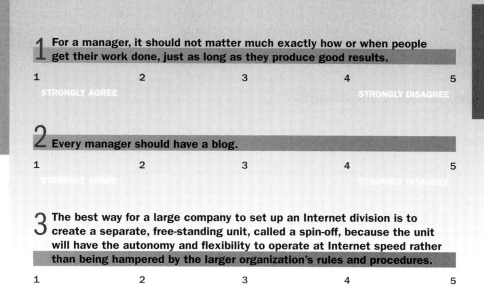

Before reading this chapter, please circle your
opinion below for each of the following statements:

Managing
by Design
Questions

1 For a manager, it should not matter much exactly how or when people
get their work done, just as long as they produce good results.

1	2	3	4	5
STRONGLY AGREE			STRONGLY DISAGREE	

2 Every manager should have a blog.

1	2	3	4	5
STRONGLY AGREE			STRONGLY DISAGREE	

3 The best way for a large company to set up an Internet division is to
create a separate, free-standing unit, called a spin-off, because the unit
will have the autonomy and flexibility to operate at Internet speed rather
than being hampered by the larger organization's rules and procedures.

1	2	3	4	5

Wood Flooring International (WFI), based in Delran, New Jersey, uses a sophisti-cated Internet-based system to manage every link of its supply chain, from vendors all the way through to its customers' customers. The small company buys exotic wood overseas, mostly from small, family-owned mills in Latin America, turns the wood into floorboards, and sells the flooring to distributors. Whenever WFI takes an order, the vendor can see an update instantly on the website and adjust its production levels accordingly. The mills can also check real-time reports of their sales histories, check whether their shipments have arrived, and ensure that WFI's accounting squares with their own.[1] Olive Garden, a restaurant chain, uses comput-erized systems to measure and control everything from bathroom cleanliness to food preparation time. And Memorial Health Services in Long Beach, California, uses medical identification cards (available over the Internet) that can be swiped into a computer to speed registration and give emergency room personnel immediate access to vital patient information, which means better care and fewer errors.[2]

As these examples illustrate, many organizations have been transformed by infor-mation technology (IT). Effectively using IT in knowledge-based firms such as consult-ing firm KPMG, Amerex Energy, a brokerage firm specializing in energy resources, and Business Wire, which provides business and corporate information, has long been fundamental. Today, IT has become a crucial factor helping companies in all indus-tries maintain a competitive edge in the face of growing global competition and rising customer demands for speed, convenience, quality, and value. The primary benefits of IT for organizations include its potential for improving decision making as well as for enhancing coordination and control of the organization internally and with external partners and customers. Some organization theorists argue that IT is gradually replac-ing the traditional hierarchy in coordinating and controlling organizational activities.[3]

Even fast-food franchisees are finding highly creative uses for IT. If you've ever ordered a Big Mac at the McDonald's off Interstate 55 near Cape Girardeau,

Missouri, you probably had no idea that the order taker was located in a call center more than 900 miles away, in Colorado Springs, Colorado. A customer's order traverses two states and bounces back to Cape Girardeau over high-speed data lines before the customer even pulls up to the pickup window. In a business where time is money, shaving even 5 seconds off order processing time makes a difference. The call center approach cuts order time in most restaurants that use it by 30 seconds to 1 minute, as well as improves the accuracy of orders.[4]

Purpose of This Chapter

Managers spend at least 80 percent of their time actively exchanging information. They need this information to hold the organization together. For example, the vertical and horizontal information linkages described in Chapter 2 are designed to provide managers with relevant information for decision making, coordination, evaluation, and control. It isn't just facilities, equipment, or even products and services that define organization success, but rather the information managers have and how they use it. Highly successful organizations today are typically those that most effectively apply information technology.

This chapter examines the evolution of IT. The chapter begins by looking at IT systems applied to organizational operations and then examines how IT is used for decision making and control of the organization. The next sections consider how IT can add strategic value through the use of internal coordination applications such as intranets, enterprise resource planning, and knowledge management systems, as well as applications for external coordination and collaboration, such as extranets, customer-relationship systems, e-business, and the integrated enterprise. The final section of the chapter presents an overview of how IT affects organization design and interorganizational relationships.

INFORMATION TECHNOLOGY EVOLUTION

Exhibit 11.1 illustrates the evolution of IT. First-line management is typically concerned with well-defined problems about operational issues and past events. Top management, by contrast, deals mostly with uncertain, ambiguous issues, such as strategy and planning. As computer-based IT systems have grown increasingly sophisticated, applications have grown to support effective management coordination, control, and decision making about complex and uncertain problems.

Initially, IT systems in organizations were applied to operations. These initial applications were based on the notion of machine-room efficiency—that is, current operations could be performed more efficiently with the use of computer technology. The goal was to reduce labor costs by having computers take over some tasks. These systems became known as **transaction processing systems** (TPS), which automate the organization's routine, day-to-day business transactions. A TPS collects data from transactions such as sales, purchases from suppliers, and inventory changes, and stores them in a database. For example, at Enterprise Rent-a-Car, a computerized system keeps track of the 1.4 million transactions the company logs every hour. The system can provide front-line employees with up-to-the-minute information on car availability and other data, enabling them to provide exceptional customer service.[5]

In recent years, the use of data warehousing and business intelligence software has expanded the usefulness of these accumulated data. **Data warehousing** is the use

EXHIBIT 11.1
Evolution of
Organizational
Applications of IT

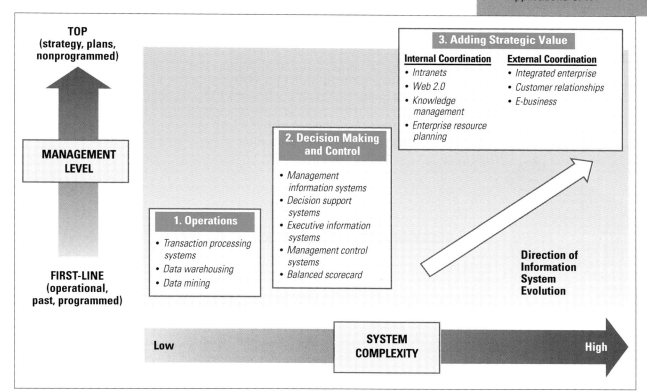

of huge databases that combine all of a company's data and allow users to access the data directly, create reports, and obtain responses to what-if questions. Building a database at a large corporation is a huge undertaking that includes defining hundreds of gigabytes of data from many existing systems, providing a means of continually updating the data, making it all compatible, and linking it to software that makes it possible for users to search and analyze the data and produce helpful reports. Software for business intelligence helps users make sense of all these data. **Business intelligence** refers to the high-tech analysis of a company's data in order to make better strategic decisions.[6] Sometimes referred to as *data mining*, business intelligence means searching out and analyzing data from multiple sources across the enterprise, and sometimes from outside sources as well, to identify patterns and relationships that might be significant.

By collecting the right data and using business intelligence software to analyze it and spot trends and patterns, managers can make smarter decisions. Thus, IT has evolved to more complex systems for managerial decision making and control of the organization, the second stage illustrated in Exhibit 11.1. Further advancements have led to the use of IT to add strategic value by providing tight coordination both internally and with external customers, suppliers, and partners, the highest level of application shown in Exhibit 11.1. The remainder of this chapter will focus on these two higher-level stages in the evolution of IT.

INFORMATION FOR DECISION MAKING AND CONTROL

Through the application of more sophisticated computer-based systems, managers have tools to improve the performance of departments and the organization as a whole. These applications use information stored in corporate databases to help managers control the organization and make important decisions. Exhibit 11.2 illustrates the various elements of information systems used for decision making and control. Management information systems—including information reporting systems, decision support systems, and executive information systems—facilitate rapid and effective decision making. Elements for control include various management control systems, including executive dashboards, and a procedure known as the balanced scorecard. In an organization, these systems are interconnected, as illustrated by the dashed lines in Exhibit 11.2. The systems for decision making and control often share the same basic data, but the data and reports are designed and used for a primary purpose of decision making versus control.

Organizational Decision-Making Systems

A **management information system** (MIS) is a computer-based system that provides information and support for managerial decision making. The MIS is supported by the organization's transaction processing systems and by organizational and external databases. The **information reporting system**, the most common form of MIS, provides mid-level managers with reports that summarize data and support day-to-day decision making. For example, when managers need to make decisions about production scheduling, they can review data on the anticipated number of orders within the next month, inventory levels, and availability of human resources.

At Harrah's casinos, an information reporting system keeps track of detailed information on each player and uses quantitative models to predict each customer's potential long-term value. The information helps managers create customized marketing plans, as well as provide customers just the right combination of services and rewards to keep them coming back rather than moving on to another casino. "Almost everything we do in marketing and decision making is influenced by technology," says Harrah's CEO Gary Loveman.[7]

An **executive information system** (EIS) is a higher-level application that facilitates decision making at the highest levels of management. These systems are typically based on software that can convert large amounts of complex data into pertinent information and provide that information to top managers in a timely fashion. For example, Motorola's Semiconductor Products Sector, based in Austin, Texas, had massive amounts of stored data, but managers couldn't find what they needed. The company implemented an EIS using online analytical processing software so that more than a thousand senior executives, as well as managers and project analysts in finance, marketing, sales, and accounting departments around the world, could quickly and easily get information about customer buying trends, manufacturing, and so forth, right from their desktop computers, without having to learn complex and arcane search commands.[8]

A **decision support system** (DSS) provides specific benefits to managers at all levels of the organization. These interactive, computer-based systems rely on decision models

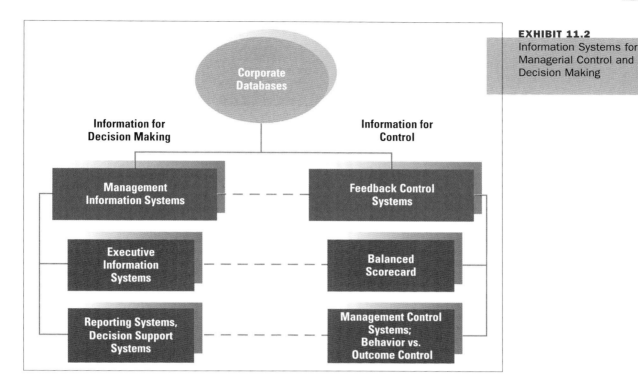

and integrated databases. Using decision-support software, users can pose a series of what-if questions to test possible alternatives. Based on assumptions used in the software or specified by the user, managers can explore various alternatives and receive information to help them choose the alternative that will likely have the best outcome.

Wal-Mart uses an EIS and a DSS that rely on a massive database to make decisions about what to stock, how to price and promote it, and when to reorder. Information about what products are selling and what items are often purchased together is obtained at checkout scanners. Wireless handheld units operated by clerks and department managers help keep close tabs on inventory levels. All these data are sent to Wal-Mart's data warehouse in Bentonville, Arkansas, which has more than 460 terabytes of data. Wal-Mart uses its mountain of data to push for greater efficiency at all levels, as well as to forecast trends and do more business. For example, Wal-Mart managers in Florida know to have plenty of beer and Pop-Tarts stocked in the days preceding a hurricane. Managers might expect beer to sell out quickly, but why Pop-Tarts? By analyzing data with a decision support system using predictive technology, Wal-Mart learned that sales of strawberry Pop-Tarts zoom seven times their normal sales rate in the days ahead of a hurricane.[9]

Feedback Control Model

Another primary use of information in organizations is for control. Effective control systems involve the use of feedback to determine whether organizational performance meets established standards to help the organization attain its goals. Managers set up systems for organizational control that consist of the four key steps in the **feedback control model** illustrated in Exhibit 11.3.

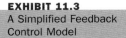

EXHIBIT 11.3
A Simplified Feedback
Control Model

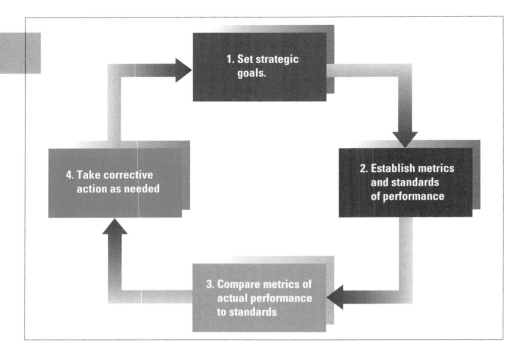

1. Set strategic goals.

2. Establish metrics and standards of performance

3. Compare metrics of actual performance to standards

4. Take corrective action as needed

The cycle of control includes setting strategic goals for departments or the organization as a whole, establishing metrics and standards of performance, comparing metrics of actual performance to standards, and correcting or changing activities as needed. Feedback control helps managers make needed adjustments in work activities, standards of performance, or goals to help the organization be successful. Complete the questionnaire in the "How Do You Fit the Design?" box to see how effective you are at setting goals.

Managers carefully assess what they will measure and how they define it. British Airways, for example, measures its performance in key areas of customer service because its strategy is to compete on superior service in an industry dominated by companies that compete on price. Thus, British Airways measures and controls areas of service that have the greatest impact on a customer's experience, including in-flight service, meal rating, baggage claim, and executive club membership.[10] For pharmaceutical companies such as Wyeth, getting more productivity from research and development is a top priority, so Wyeth sets firm targets and measures how many compounds move forward at each stage of the drug development process. Most companies, like Wyeth and British Airways, use a number of different operational metrics to track performance and control the organization, rather than relying on financial measures alone. Managers track metrics in such areas as customer satisfaction, product quality, employee commitment and turnover, operational performance, innovation, and corporate social responsibility, for example, as well as financial results.

Management Control Systems

Management control systems are broadly defined as the formal routines, reports, and procedures that use information to maintain or alter patterns in organizational

How Do You Fit the Design?

Is Goal-Setting Your Style?

How do your work habits fit with making plans and setting goals? Answer the following questions as they apply to your work or study behavior. Please answer whether each item is Mostly True or Mostly False for you.

	Mostly True	Mostly False
1. I set clear, specific goals in more than one area of my work and life.	_____	_____
2. I have a definite outcome in life I want to achieve.	_____	_____
3. I prefer general to specific goals.	_____	_____
4. I work better without specific deadlines.	_____	_____
5. I set aside time each day or week to plan my work.	_____	_____
6. I am clear about the measures that indicate when I have achieved a goal.	_____	_____
7. I work better when I set more challenging goals for myself.	_____	_____
8. I help other people clarify and define their goals.	_____	_____
9. Trying for specific goals makes life more fun than being without goals.	_____	_____

Scoring: Give yourself one point for each item you marked as Mostly True, except items 3 and 4. For items 3 and 4 give yourself one point for each one you marked Mostly False. If you scored 4 or less, goal-setting behavior may not be natural for you. A score of 6 or above suggests a positive level of goal-setting behavior and better preparation for a managerial role in an organization.

Interpretation: An important part of organization life is setting goals, measuring results, and reviewing progress for people and departments. Most organizations have goal-setting and review systems. The preceding questions indicate the extent to which you have already adopted the disciplined use of goals in your life and work. Research indicates that setting clear, specific, and challenging goals in key areas will produce better performance. Not everyone thrives under a disciplined goal-setting system, but as an organization manager, setting goals, assessing results, and holding people accountable will enhance your impact. Goal-setting can be learned.

activities.[11] These feedback control systems include the formalized information-based activities for planning, budgeting, performance evaluation, resource allocation, and employee rewards. Targets are set in advance, outcomes compared to targets, and variances reported to managers for corrective action. Exhibit 11.4 lists four control system elements that are often considered the core of management control systems: the budget and financial reports; periodic nonfinancial statistical reports; reward systems; and quality-control systems.[12]

The *budget* is typically used to set targets for the organization's expenditures for the year and then report actual costs on a monthly or quarterly basis. As a means of control, budgets report actual as well as planned expenditures for cash, assets, raw materials, salaries, and other resources so that managers can take action to correct variances. Sometimes, the variance between budgeted and actual amounts for each

EXHIBIT 11.4
Management Control
Systems

Subsystem	Content and Frequency
Budget, financial reports	Financial, resource expenditures, profit and loss; monthly
Statistical reports	Nonfinancial outputs; weekly or monthly, often computer-based
Reward systems	Evaluation of managers based on department goals and performance, set rewards; yearly
Quality control systems	Participation, benchmarking guidelines, Six Sigma goals; continuous

Source: Based on Richard L. Daft and Norman B. Macintosh, "The Nature and Use of Formal Control Systems for Management Control and Strategy Implementation," *Journal of Management* 10 (1984), 43–66.

line item is listed as a part of the budget. Managers also rely on a variety of other financial reports. The *balance sheet* shows a firm's financial position with respect to assets and liabilities at a specific point in time. An *income statement*, sometimes called a *profit and loss statement (P&L)*, summarizes the company's financial performance for a given time interval, such as for the week, month, or year. This statement shows revenues coming into the organization from all sources and subtracts all expenses, such as cost of goods sold, interest, taxes, and depreciation. The *bottom line* indicates the net income—profit or loss—for the given time period.

Managers use periodic statistical reports to evaluate and monitor nonfinancial performance, such as customer satisfaction, employee performance, or rate of staff turnover. For e-commerce organizations, important measurements of nonfinancial performance include metrics such as *stickiness* (how much attention a site gets over time), the *conversion rate*, the ratio of buyers to site visitors, and *site performance data*, such as how long it takes to load a page or how long it takes to place an order.[13] E-commerce managers regularly review reports on conversion rates, customer drop-off, and other metrics to identify problems and improve their business. For all organizations, nonfinancial reports typically are computer based and may be available daily, weekly, or monthly. The online auction company eBay provides a good illustration of using both financial and nonfinancial statistical reports for feedback control.

eBay

When Meg Whitman was CEO of eBay, her guiding mantra was "If you can't measure it, you can't control it." Whitman has moved on to other pursuits, but eBay is still a company that is obsessed with performance measurement. Top executives monitor performance metrics such as number of site visitors, percentage of new users, and time spent on the site, as well as profit and loss statements and the ratio of eBay's revenues to the value of goods traded. Managers throughout the company also monitor performance regularly. Category managers, for example, have clear standards of performance for their auction categories (such as sports memorabilia, jewelry and watches, health and beauty, etc.). They continuously measure, tweak, and promote their categories to meet or outperform their targets.

Having a firm grip on performance measurement helps managers know where to spend money, where to assign more personnel, and which projects to promote or abandon. The more statistics that are available, the more early warnings managers have about problems and opportunities. But performance isn't just about numbers at eBay. Measuring customer (user) satisfaction requires a mix of methods, such as surveys, monitoring eBay discussion boards, and personal contact with customers at regular live conferences.

By defining standards and effectively using financial and statistical reports, eBay managers can identify trouble spots and move quickly to take corrective action when and where it is needed.[14] ▪

Managers at companies such as eBay, Oracle, Verizon, General Electric, and Microsoft often track both nonfinancial and financial data by means of an executive dashboard. Forrester Research Inc. estimated that 40 percent of the 2,000 largest companies were using dashboard technology by 2006, and that number has continued to grow.[15] An **executive dashboard**, sometimes called a *business performance dashboard*, is a software program that presents key business information in graphical, easy-to-interpret form and alerts managers to any deviations or unusual patterns in the data. Dashboards pull data from a variety of organizational systems and databases; gauge the data against key performance metrics; and pull out the right nuggets of information to deliver to managers' laptops or PCs for analysis and action.[16] Exhibit 11.5 shows an example of an executive dashboard. Managers can see at a glance key control indicators such as sales in relation to targets, fill rates on orders, number of products on back-order, production status, or percentage of customer service calls resolved, and then drill down for additional details.[17]

Dashboard systems coordinate, organize, and display the metrics that managers consider most important to monitor on a regular basis, with software automatically updating the figures. Managers at Erickson Retirement Communities use a dashboard to monitor and control costs in areas such as salaries and resident meals. At Verizon Communications, a dashboard system keeps track of more than 300 different measures of business performance in three broad categories: market pulse (including daily sales numbers and market share); customer service (for example, call center wait times and problems resolved on the first call); and cost drivers (such as number of repair trucks in the field). Managers in the various units choose which metrics their dashboard will display, based on what relates most to their unit.[18]

Other elements of the overall control system listed in Exhibit 11.4 are reward systems and quality control systems. Reward systems offer incentives for managers and employees to improve performance and meet departmental goals. Managers and employees evaluate how well previous goals were met, set new goals, and establish rewards for meeting the new targets. Rewards are often tied to the annual performance appraisal process, during which managers assess employee performance and provide feedback to help people improve performance and obtain rewards.

Quality-control systems involve training employees in quality-control methods, setting targets for employee participation, establishing benchmarking guidelines, and assigning and measuring *Six Sigma* goals. **Benchmarking** means the process of persistently measuring products, services, and practices against tough competitors or other organizations recognized as industry leaders.[19] **Six Sigma** specifically means a highly ambitious quality standard that specifies a goal of no more than 3.4 defects per million parts. However, it has deviated from that precise meaning to refer to a whole set of control procedures that emphasize the relentless pursuit of higher quality and

Briefcase

As an organization manager, keep these guidelines in mind:

Devise control systems that consist of the four essential steps of the feedback control model: set goals, establish standards of performance, measure actual performance, and correct or change activities as needed. Use executive dashboards so managers can keep tabs on important performance metrics.

EXHIBIT 11.5
An Executive Dashboard

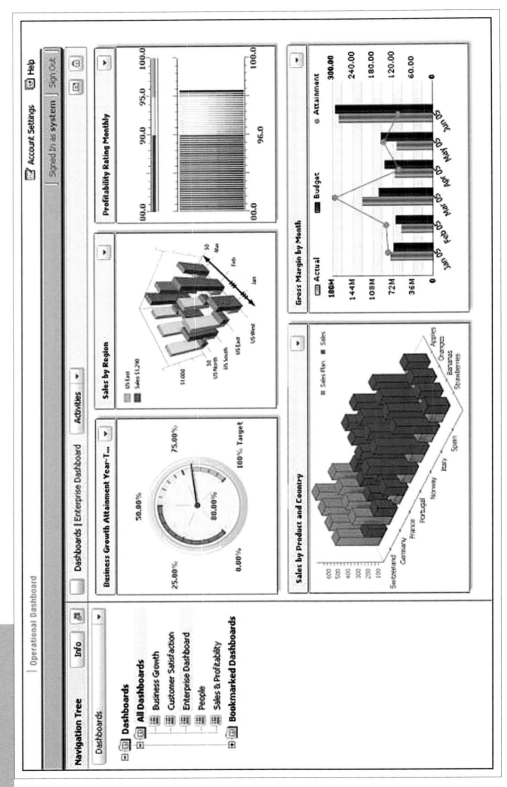

Source: IBM Cognos BI and Performance Management Software; *http://www.cognos.com/products/now/images/master_dashboard.jpg* (accessed on November 12, 2008).

lower costs.[20] The discipline is based on a methodology referred to as DMAIC (Define, Measure, Analyze, Improve, and Control, pronounced de-MAY-ick), which provides a structured way for organizations to approach and solve problems.[21] Companies such as General Electric, ITT Industries, Dow Chemical, ABB Ltd., and 3M have saved millions of dollars by rooting out inefficiencies and waste through Six Sigma processes.[22]

One finding from research into management control systems is that each of the four control systems listed in Exhibit 11.4 focuses on a different aspect of the production process. These four systems thus form an overall management control system that provides middle managers with control information about resource inputs, process efficiency, and outputs.[23] Moreover, the specific use of control systems depends on the strategic targets set by top management.

The budget is used primarily to allocate resource inputs. Managers use the budget for planning the future and reducing uncertainty about the availability of human and material resources needed to perform department tasks. Computer-based statistical reports are used to control outputs. These reports contain data about output volume and quality and other indicators that provide feedback to middle management about departmental results. The reward system and quality control system are directed at the production process. Quality control systems specify standards for employee participation, teamwork, and problem solving. Reward systems provide incentives to meet goals and can help guide and correct employee behavior. Managers may also use direct supervision to keep departmental work activities within desired limits.

THE LEVEL AND FOCUS OF CONTROL SYSTEMS

Managers consider both control of the overall organization and control of departments, teams, and individuals. Some control strategies apply to the top levels of an organization, where the concern is for the entire organization or major divisions. There are five key principles top executives at winning organizations apply for effective performance management and control. Control is also an issue at the lower, operational level, where department managers and supervisors focus on the performance of teams and individual employees.

Organization Level: The Balanced Scorecard

As discussed earlier, most companies use a combination of metrics for measuring organizational performance and effectively controlling the organization. A recent control system innovation, introduced in Chapter 3, is to integrate internal financial measurements and statistical reports with a concern for markets and customers as well as employees. The **balanced scorecard (BSC)** is a comprehensive management control system that balances traditional financial measures with operational measures relating to a company's critical success factors.[24] A balanced scorecard contains four major perspectives, as illustrated in Exhibit 11.6: financial performance, customer service, internal business processes, and the organization's capacity for learning and growth.[25] Within these four areas, managers identify key performance indicators the organization will track. The *financial perspective* reflects a concern that the organization's activities contribute to improving short- and long-term financial performance. It includes traditional measures such as net income and return on

Briefcase

As an organization manager, keep these guidelines in mind:

Use a balanced scorecard to integrate various control dimensions and get a more complete picture of organizational performance. Select indicators in the areas of financial performance, customer service, internal processes, and learning and growth, and consider a strategy map to visualize how outcomes are linked.

investment. *Customer service indicators* measure such things as how customers view the organization, as well as customer retention and satisfaction. *Business process indicators* focus on production and operating statistics, such as order fulfillment or cost per order. The final component looks at the organization's *potential for learning and growth*, focusing on how well resources and human capital are being managed for the company's future. Measurements include such things as employee retention, business process improvements, and the introduction of new products. The components of the scorecard are designed in an integrative manner so that they reinforce one another and link short-term actions with long-term strategic goals, as illustrated in Exhibit 11.6. Managers can use the scorecard to set goals, allocate resources, plan budgets, and determine rewards.

EXHIBIT 11.6
Major Perspectives of the Balanced Scorecard

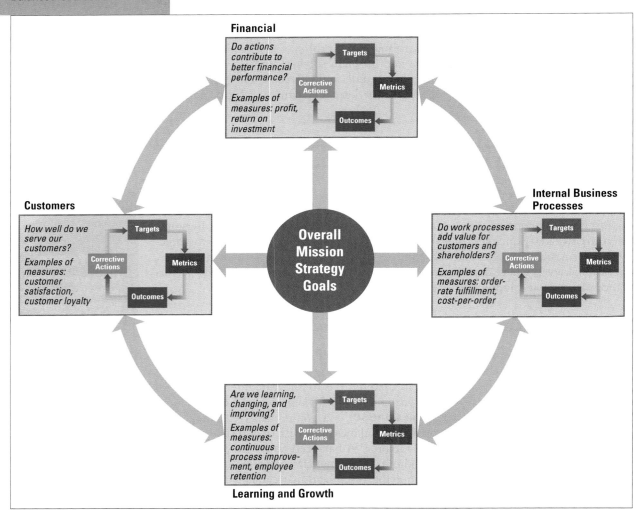

Source: Based on Robert S. Kaplan and David P. Norton, "Using the Balanced Scorecard as a Strategic Management System," *Harvard Business Review* (January–February 1996), 75–85; Chee W. Chow, Kamal M. Haddad, and James E. Williamson, "Applying the Balanced Scorecard to Small Companies," *Management Accounting* 79, no. 2 (August 1997), 21–27; and Cathy Lazere, "All Together Now," *CFO* (February 1998), 28–36.

Executive information systems and dashboards facilitate use of the balanced scorecard by enabling top managers to easily track metrics in multiple areas, rapidly analyze the data, and convert huge amounts of data into clear information reports. The scorecard has become the core management control system for many organizations, including Hilton Hotels, Allstate, British Airways, and Cigna Insurance. British Airways clearly ties its use of the balanced scorecard to the feedback control model shown earlier in Exhibit 11.3. Scorecards serve as the agenda for monthly management meetings, where managers evaluate performance, discuss what corrective actions need to be taken, and set new targets for the various BSC categories.[26]

In recent years, the balanced scorecard has evolved into a system that helps managers see how organizational performance results from cause-effect relationships among these four mutually supportive areas. Overall effectiveness is a result of how well these four elements are aligned, so that individuals, teams, and departments are working in concert to attain specific goals that cause high organizational performance.[27]

The cause-effect control technique is the strategy map. A **strategy map** provides a visual representation of the key drivers of an organization's success and shows how specific outcomes in each area are linked.[28] The strategy map is a powerful way for managers to see the cause-and-effect relationships among various performance metrics. The simplified strategy map in Exhibit 11.7 illustrates the four key areas that contribute to a firm's long-term success—learning and growth, internal processes, customer service, and financial performance—and how the various outcomes in one area link directly to performance in another area. The idea is that effective performance in terms of learning and growth serves as a foundation to help achieve excellent internal business processes. Excellent business processes, in turn, enable the organization to achieve high customer service and satisfaction, which enables the organization to reach its financial goals and optimize its value to all stakeholders.

In the strategy map shown in Exhibit 11.7, the organization has learning and growth goals that include employee training and development, continuous learning and knowledge sharing, and building a culture of innovation. Achieving these will help the organization build efficient internal business processes that promote good relationships with suppliers and partners, improve the quality and flexibility of operations, and excel at developing innovative products and services. Accomplishing internal process goals, in turn, enables the organization to maintain strong relationships with customers, be a leader in quality and reliability, and provide innovative solutions to emerging customer needs. At the top of the strategy map, the accomplishment of these lower-level goals helps the organization increase revenues in existing markets, reduce costs through better productivity and efficiency, and grow by selling new products and services in new market segments.

In a real-life organization, the strategy map would typically be more complex and would state concrete, specific goals, desired outcomes, and metrics relevant to the particular business. However, the generic map in Exhibit 11.7 gives an idea of how managers can use strategy maps to set goals, track metrics, assess performance, and make changes as needed.

Department Level: Behavior versus Outcome Control

The balanced scorecard and strategy map are techniques used primarily by top and upper-level managers. Lower level managers focus on the performance of people at the department level, who must meet goals and standards if the organization is to attain its overall goals. Although lower-level managers may use any of the control

Briefcase

As an organization manager, keep these guidelines in mind:

Don't overdo the use of behavior control. Set some reasonable guidelines for behavior and work activities, but emphasize outcome control by focusing on results and allowing employees some discretion and autonomy about how they accomplish outcomes.

EXHIBIT 11.7
A Strategy Map
for Performance
Management

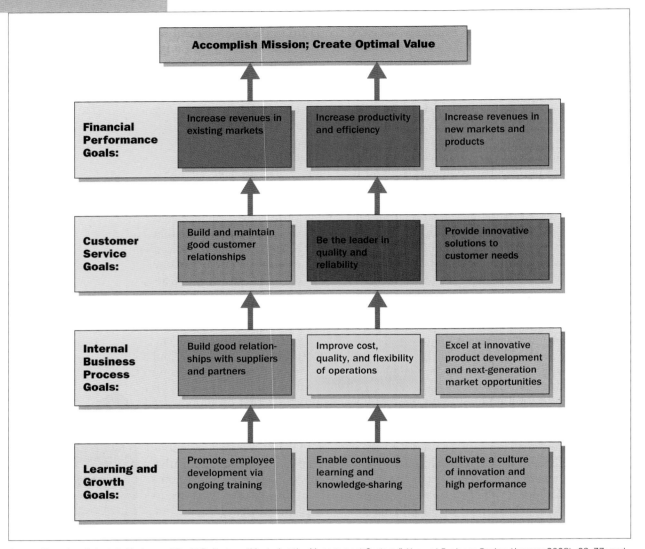

Source: Based on Robert S. Kaplan and David P. Norton, "Mastering the Management System," *Harvard Business Review* (January 2008), 63–77; and R. S. Kaplan and D. P. Norton, "Having Trouble with Your Strategy? Then Map It," *Harvard Business Review* (September–October 2000), 167–176.

systems listed earlier in Exhibit 11.4, the reward system is often of paramount concern at the supervisory level.

There are two different approaches to evaluating and controlling team or individual performance and allocating rewards. One approach focuses primarily on *how* people do their jobs, whereas the other focuses primarily on the *outcomes* people produce.[29] **Behavior control** is based on manager observation of employee actions to see whether the individual follows desired procedures and performs tasks as instructed. Do people get to work on time? Do they stay

focused on their tasks or spend a lot of time socializing with colleagues? Do they dress appropriately for the job? Do they perform their jobs according to established methods or supervisor instructions? With behavior control, managers provide heavy supervision and monitoring, pay attention to the methods people use to accomplish their jobs, and evaluate and reward people based on specific criteria, which might include areas such as appearance, punctuality, skills, activities, and so forth.

Information technology has increased the potential for managers to use behavior control. Managers in many companies monitor employees' e-mail and other online activities, for example. Retailers such as Saks and Sunglass Hut use cash-register management software that monitors cashiers' activities in real-time. Managers at Verizon call centers screen representatives' interactions with customers to make sure they hit on the dozens of different points that are required for every customer contact. Some trucking companies track trucks by computer to monitor driver behavior.[30]

A second approach to control is to pay less attention to what people *do* than to what they *accomplish*. **Outcome control** is based on monitoring and rewarding results, and managers might pay little attention to how those results are obtained. With outcome control, managers don't supervise employees in the traditional sense. People have a great deal of autonomy in terms of how they do their jobs—and sometimes in terms of where and when they do their jobs—as long as they produce desired outcomes. Rather than monitoring how many hours an employee works, for example, managers focus on how much work the employee accomplishes. The Results-Only Work Environment program at Best Buy provides an illustration of outcome control carried to the extreme.

Best Buy

When Best Buy managers noticed an alarming increase in turnover of headquarters employees, they began looking for ways to reverse the trend. They realized that the Best Buy culture that emphasized long hours, mandatory procedures, and managers "acting like hall monitors" was no longer working. So, what was the best approach to keep talented people from reaching burnout?

The answer turned out to be an innovative initiative known as ROWE (Results-Only Work Environment), which lets people work when and where they want as long as they get the job done. The experiment started in one department, where morale had reached a dismal low. Under the ROWE system, claims processors and data entry clerks now focus on how many forms they can process in a week rather than how many hours they put in each day or how many keystrokes it takes to complete a form. The program worked so well that it quickly spread to other departments.

The results? From 2005 to 2007, the turnover rate in departments using ROWE decreased nearly 90 percent, while productivity shot up 41 percent. Managers have now implemented ROWE throughout corporate headquarters. There are no set working hours, no mandatory meetings, and no managers keeping tabs on employees' activities. Senior vice-president John Thompson, who was at first skeptical of ROWE, became a strong believer when he saw the results. "For years I had been focused on the wrong currency," Thompson says. "I was always looking to see if people were here. I should have been looking at what they were getting done."[31] ■

Switching from behavior control to outcome control had significant positive effects at Best Buy headquarters, and managers are now trying to implement a form of the ROWE system in the retail stores. However, outcome control is not necessarily the best for all situations. In some cases, behavior control is more appropriate and effective, but in general, managers in successful organizations are moving away from closely monitoring and controlling behavior toward allowing employees more discretion and autonomy in how they do their jobs. In most organizations, managers use both behavior and outcome control.

ASSESS YOUR ANSWER

1 For a manager, it should not matter much exactly how or when people get their work done, just as long as they produce good results.

ANSWER: *Agree.* Focusing on results, or outcomes, can be a highly effective approach to department level control in many organizations. Employees resent being micromanaged and don't like being treated like children. Most managers find it necessary to set some reasonable boundaries for correct behavior, with most control emphasis placed on outcome control to achieve highest performance.

With outcome control, IT is used not to monitor and control individual employee behavior but rather to assess performance outcomes. For example, at Best Buy, the manager of the online orders department can use IT to measure how many orders per hour his team processes, even if one team member is working down the hall, one working from home, one taking the afternoon off, and another working from her vacation cabin 400 miles away.[32] Good performance metrics are key to making an outcome control system work effectively.

ADDING STRATEGIC VALUE: STRENGTHENING INTERNAL COORDINATION

Following the use of information systems for managerial decision making and control, IT has evolved further as a strategic tool for both internal and external coordination. This is the highest level of application, as illustrated in Exhibit 11.1 at the beginning of the chapter. Primary IT applications for internal coordination are intranets, Web 2.0 tools, knowledge-management systems, and enterprise resource planning (ERP). Coordination with external parties will be discussed in the next section.

Intranets

Networking, which links people and departments within a particular building or across corporate offices, enabling them to share information and cooperate on projects, has become an important strategic tool for many companies. For example, an online database called CareWeb that medical professionals access via a network at Beth Israel Deaconess Medical Center in Boston contains records of more than 9 million patients. Emergency room doctors can instantly review a patient's past medical history, saving seconds that could make a difference between life and death. By managing information and making it available to anyone who needs it across the organization, CareWeb enables Beth Israel to provide better care as well as maintain better cost control.[33]

One prevalent form of corporate networking is an **intranet**, a private, company-wide information system that uses the communications protocols and standards of the Internet and the World Wide Web but is accessible only to people within the company. To view files and information, users simply navigate the site with a standard Web browser, clicking on links.[34] Today, most companies with intranets have moved their management information systems, executive information systems, and so forth over to the intranet so they are accessible to anyone who needs them. In addition, having these systems as part of the intranet means new features and applications can easily be added and accessed through a standard browser. Intranets can improve internal communications and unlock hidden information. They enable employees to keep in touch with what's going on around the organization, quickly and easily find information they need, share ideas, and work on projects collaboratively.

Web 2.0 Tools

Companies are also tapping into the power of new IT applications such as Web services, group blogs, wikis, and social networking as powerful collaboration tools within organizations. These second-generation Internet technologies are often referred to collectively as Web 2.0. *Web services* refers to a variety of software that makes it easier for people to exchange information and conduct business transactions via the Internet.[35] A **blog** is a running Web log that allows an individual to post opinions and ideas about anything from work projects and processes to the weather and dating relationships. The simplicity and informality of blogs make them an easy and comfortable medium for people to communicate and share ideas. A **wiki** is similar to a blog and uses software to create a website that allows people to create, share, and edit content through a browser-based interface. Rather than simply sharing opinions and ideas as with a blog, wikis are free-form, allowing people to edit what they find on the site and add content.[36] **Social networking**, also referred to as *social media* or *user generated content*, is an extension of blogs and wikis.[37] Social networking sites provide an unprecedented peer-to-peer communication channel, where people interact in an online community, sharing personal data and photos, producing and sharing all sorts of information and opinions. Work networks on Facebook and MySpace are exploding, and some companies, including Dow Chemical, JPMorgan Chase, and Lockheed Martin, have started their own in-house social networks as a way to facilitate information sharing and collaboration.[38]

A 2008 survey by *The McKinsey Quarterly* sheds some light on organizations' use of Web 2.0 technologies. Fifty-eight percent of responding companies said they are using Web services software, 34 percent report the use of blogs, 32 percent the use of wikis, and 28 percent the use of social networking. According to the survey, the top reasons organizations use these new technologies are to foster internal collaboration and to enhance knowledge management.[39]

Knowledge Management

Knowledge management is a new way to think about organizing and sharing an organization's intellectual and creative resources. It refers to the efforts to systematically find, organize, and make available a company's intellectual capital and to foster a culture of

Briefcase

As an organization manager, keep these guidelines in mind:

Improve internal coordination and information sharing with intranets, enterprise resource planning (ERP) systems, and knowledge management systems. Give people a way to easily communicate and collaborate through blogs, wikis, and social networking.

continuous learning and knowledge sharing so that organizational activities build on what is already known.[40] The company's **intellectual capital** is the sum of its knowledge, experience, understanding, relationships, processes, innovations, and discoveries.

Companies need ways to transfer both explicit knowledge and implicit, or tacit, knowledge across the organization.[41] **Explicit knowledge** is formal, systematic knowledge that can be codified, written down, and passed on to others in documents or general instructions. Tacit knowledge, on the other hand, is often difficult to put into words. **Tacit knowledge** is based on personal experience, rules of thumb, intuition, and judgment. It includes professional know-how and expertise, individual insight and experience, and creative solutions that are difficult to communicate and pass on to others. Explicit knowledge can easily be captured and shared in documents and through IT systems, but as much as 80 percent of an organization's valuable knowledge may be tacit knowledge that is not easily captured and transferred.[42]

Two distinct approaches to knowledge management are outlined in Exhibit 11.8. The first approach deals primarily with the collection and sharing of explicit knowledge, largely through the use of sophisticated IT systems.[43] Explicit knowledge may include intellectual properties such as patents and licenses; work processes such as policies and procedures; specific information on customers, markets, suppliers, or competitors; competitive intelligence reports; benchmark data; and so forth. When an organization uses this approach, the focus is on collecting and codifying knowledge and storing it in databases where it can easily be accessed and reused by anyone in the organization. With this "people-to-documents" approach, knowledge is gathered from the individuals who possess it and is organized into documents that others can access and reuse.

The second approach focuses on leveraging individual expertise and know-how—tacit knowledge—by connecting people face-to-face or through interactive media. Tacit knowledge includes professional know-how, individual insights and creativity, and personal experience and intuition. With this approach, managers concentrate on developing personal networks that link people together for the sharing of tacit

EXHIBIT 11.8
Two Approaches to Knowledge Management

Explicit	Tacit
Provide high-quality, reliable, and fast information systems for access of codified, reusable knowledge	Channel individual expertise to provide creative advice on strategic problems
People-to-documents approach	**Person-to-person approach**
Develop an electronic document system that codifies, stores, disseminates, and allows reuse of knowledge	Develop networks for linking people so that tacit knowledge can be shared

Knowledge Management Strategy

Invest heavily in information technology, with a goal of connecting people with reusable, codified knowledge	Invest moderately in information technology, with a goal of facilitating conversations and the personal exchange of tacit knowledge

Information Technology Approach

Source: Based on Morten T. Hansen, Nitin Nohria, and Thomas Tierney, "What's Your Strategy for Managing Knowledge?" *Harvard Business Review* (March–April 1999), 106–116.

knowledge. The organization uses IT systems primarily for facilitating conversation and person-to-person sharing of experience, insight, and ideas. For example, intranets and other collaboration tools are important for helping employees, especially those who are geographically dispersed, share ideas and tap into expert knowledge throughout the organization.

Organizations typically combine several methods and technologies to facilitate the sharing and transfer of both explicit and tacit knowledge. Here's how ExactTarget Inc. hopes to handle the knowledge management challenge.

ExactTarget Inc.

The problem started when sales began to zoom. That's when sales-support staff at software company ExactTarget became overwhelmed with requests from sales representatives for technical details or other information about products. Managers realized that the best source for some of the information people were seeking was often other salespeople who had dealt with the issues before.

The solution was to set up a knowledge management system that provides not only a way to search out explicit knowledge but also to encourage the more informal sharing of tacit knowledge among employees. Sales representatives use the system to answer each other's questions, share insights, or offer advice. All the questions and answers remain in the system so that people can easily search for them at a later date, and some reps subscribe to get e-mail alerts each time a new question is posted. In addition, sales reps post useful documents or helpful information they find in the field, and support staff post tools such as product details, online case studies, or training videos. The system allows people to rate each others' answers, identify the most useful posts, and flag inaccuracies.

Managers say there are still some kinks to work out in the system, but the early results seem to be paying off. For example, when Andy Skirvin, marketing development manager, was asked by a client how ExactTarget's product would work in connection with another customer-management technology, Skirvin was able to find an answer on the spot, rather than having to send a query to support staff and perhaps wait days for a response.[44] ∎

Enterprise Resource Planning

Another recent approach to information and knowledge management pulls together various types of information to see how decisions and actions in one part of the organization affect other parts of the firm. A growing number of companies are using broad-scale information systems that take a comprehensive view of the organization's activities. These **enterprise resource planning** (ERP) systems collect, process, and provide information about a company's entire enterprise, including order processing, product design, purchasing, inventory, manufacturing, distribution, human resources (HR), receipt of payments, and forecasting of future demand.[45] ERP systems can be expensive and difficult to implement, but when applied successfully, an ERP system can serve as the backbone for an entire organization by integrating and optimizing all the various business processes across the entire firm.[46]

Such a system links all of these areas of activity into a network, as illustrated in Exhibit 11.9. When a salesperson takes an order, the ERP system checks to see how the order affects inventory levels, scheduling, HR, purchasing, and distribution. The system replicates organizational processes in software, guides employees through the processes step by step, and automates as many of them as possible. For example,

EXHIBIT 11.9
Example of an ERP
Network

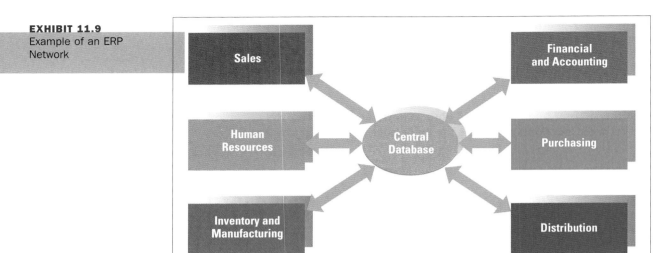

ERP software can automatically cut an accounts payable check as soon as a clerk confirms that goods have been received in inventory, send an online purchase order immediately after a manager has authorized a purchase, or schedule production at the most appropriate plant after an order is received.[47] In addition, because the system integrates data about all aspects of operations, managers and employees at all levels can see how decisions and actions in one part of the organization affect other parts, using this information to make better decisions. ERP can provide the kind of information furnished by transaction processing systems, as well as that provided by information reporting systems, decision support systems, or executive information systems. The key is that ERP weaves all of these systems together so people can see the big picture and act quickly, helping the organization be smarter and more effective. More recently, ERP has incorporated tools for supply chain management, so that coordination across organizational boundaries is strengthened as well.[48]

ADDING STRATEGIC VALUE: STRENGTHENING EXTERNAL COORDINATION

Briefcase

As an organization manager, keep this guideline in mind:

Use IT applications such as extranets, supply chain management systems, and e-business systems to strengthen relationships with customers, suppliers, and business partners.

External applications of IT for strengthening coordination with customers, suppliers, and partners include systems for supply chain management and the integrated enterprise, tools for enhancing customer relationships, and e-business organization design. One basic approach is to extend the corporate intranet to include customers and partners. An **extranet** is an external communications system that uses the Internet and is shared by two or more organizations. Each organization moves certain data outside of its private intranet, but makes the data available only to the other companies sharing the extranet.

The Integrated Enterprise

Extranets play a critical role in today's integrated enterprise. The **integrated enterprise** is an organization that uses advanced IT to enable close coordination within the company as well as with suppliers, customers, and partners. An important aspect of the integrated enterprise is using *supply chain management systems*, which manage the sequence of suppliers and purchasers covering all stages of processing from obtaining raw materials to distributing finished goods to consumers.[49]

Information Linkages. Applying supply chain management systems enables organizations to achieve the right balance of low inventory levels and customer responsiveness. Exhibit 11.10 illustrates horizontal information linkages in the integrated enterprise. By establishing electronic linkages between the organization and key partners for the sharing and exchange of data, the integrated enterprise creates a seamless, integrated line stretching from end consumers to raw materials suppliers.[50] For example, in the exhibit, as consumers purchase products in retail stores, the data are automatically fed into the retail chain's information system. In turn, the chain gives access to this constantly updated data to the manufacturing company through a secure extranet. With knowledge of this demand data, the manufacturer can produce and ship products when needed. As products are made by the manufacturer, data about raw materials used in the production process, updated inventory information, and updated forecasted demand are electronically provided to the manufacturer's suppliers, and the suppliers automatically replenish the manufacturer's raw materials inventory as needed.

Horizontal Relationships. The purpose of integrating the supply chain is for everyone to work closely together, moving in lockstep to meet customers' product and time demands. Honeywell Garrett Engine Boosting Systems, which makes turbochargers for cars, trucks, and light aircraft, uses an extranet to give suppliers access to its inventory and production data so they can respond rapidly to the manufacturer's need for parts. Honeywell is also working with big customers such as Ford and Volkswagen to integrate their systems so the company will have better information about turbocharger demands from customers as well. "Our goal," says Honeywell's Paul Hopkins, "is seamless value-chain connectivity from customer demand to suppliers."[51] Another organization that has made superb use of technology to forge integrated horizontal relationships is Corrugated Supplies.

Briefcase

As an organization manager, keep these guideline in mind:

Transform your organization into an integrated enterprise by establishing horizontal information linkages between the organization and key outsiders. Create a seamless, integrated line stretching from end consumers to raw materials suppliers that will meet customers' product and time demands.

EXHIBIT 11.10
The Integrated Enterprise

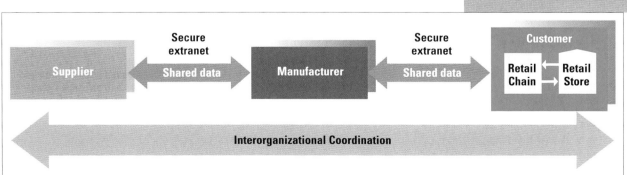

Source: Based on Jim Turcotte, Bob Silveri, and Tom Jobson, "Are You Ready for the E-Supply Chain?" *APICS–The Performance Advantage* (August 1998), 56–59.

IN PRACTICE

Corrugated Supplies

You might not expect a cardboard manufacturer to be on the cutting edge of information technology, but Rick Van Horne transformed Corrugated Supplies into one of the world's first completely Web-based production plants. The plant's equipment continually feeds data to the Internet, where the rest of the company, as well as suppliers and customers, can keep track of what's happening on the factory floor in real time. Using a password, customers call up Corrugated's production schedules to see exactly where their orders are in the process and when they will arrive. Suppliers tap into the system to manage inventory.

Exhibit 11.11 illustrates how the system works for a customer placing an order: The customer logs onto the website and types in an order for corrugated paper precisely cut and folded for 20,000 boxes. The order is downloaded into the database and computers at Corrugated's factory determine the best way to blend that order with numerous other orders ranging from a few dozen boxes to 50,000. The computer comes up with the optimum schedule—that is, the one that gets the most orders out of a single roll with little leftover paper. A human operator checks the schedule on one of the numerous linked computer screens scattered around the plant and hits the *Send* button. Computer software directs the massive corrugators, trimmers, slitters, and other equipment, which begin spewing out paper orders at 800 feet per minute. Computer-controlled conveyor belts carry the order to

EXHIBIT 11.11
Corrugated Supplies
System in Action

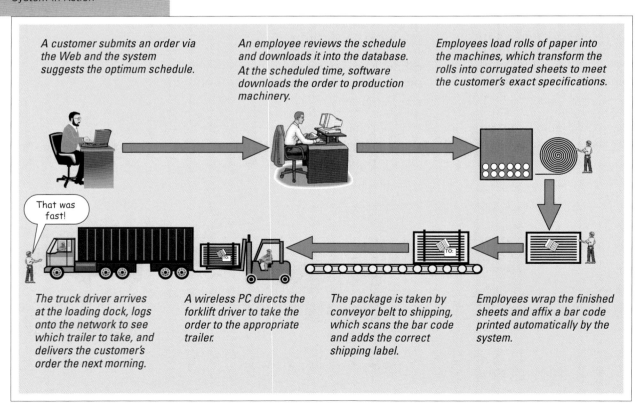

A customer submits an order via the Web and the system suggests the optimum schedule.

An employee reviews the schedule and downloads it into the database. At the scheduled time, software downloads the order to production machinery.

Employees load rolls of paper into the machines, which transform the rolls into corrugated sheets to meet the customer's exact specifications.

That was fast!

The truck driver arrives at the loading dock, logs onto the network to see which trailer to take, and delivers the customer's order the next morning.

A wireless PC directs the forklift driver to take the order to the appropriate trailer.

The package is taken by conveyor belt to shipping, which scans the bar code and adds the correct shipping label.

Employees wrap the finished sheets and affix a bar code printed automatically by the system.

Source: Adapted from Bill Richards, "Superplant," *eCompany* (November 2000), 182–196.

the loading dock, where forklifts equipped with wireless PCs take the load to the designated trailer. Truck drivers log on to the website and are told which trailer to haul to maximize their trip's efficiency. The order is usually delivered to the customer the very next day.

About 70 percent of Corrugated's orders are submitted via the Internet and routed electronically to the plant floor. The system saves time and money for Corrugated by automatically scheduling special-order details and cutting out paper waste. For customers, it means faster service and fewer mix-ups. One customer, Gene Mazurek, co-owner of Suburban Corrugated Box Co., says it is "the best thing that's ever happened. . . . It's like Rick put his corrugating machine right inside my plant."[52] ∎

For the integrated enterprise to work, horizontal relationships such as those between Corrugated and its suppliers and customers get more emphasis than vertical relationships. Enterprise integration can create a level of cooperation not previously imaginable if managers approach the practice with an attitude of trust and partnership, as in the interorganizational relationships described in Chapter 4.

Customer Relationships

Strengthening customer relationships is of particular concern to many organizations, and managers apply a variety of IT tools to this purpose. One approach is the use of **customer relationship management** (CRM) systems. These systems help companies track customers' interactions with the firm and allow employees to call up a customer's past sales and service records, outstanding orders, or unresolved problems.[53] CRM stashes in a database all the customer information that a small-town store owner would keep in his or her head—the names of customers, what they bought, what problems they've had with purchases, and so forth. The system helps coordinate sales, marketing, and customer service departments so that all are smoothly working together. Companies are also applying Web 2.0 technologies such as Web services, blogs, wikis, and social networking, as described earlier, to enhance customer relationships. In McKinsey's survey, respondents say they use these new Web 2.0 tools for improving customer service, developing new markets, getting customer participation in product development, and offering opportunities for customers to interact with one another.[54] Disney, for example, revamped its website with a goal of making it a social networking destination for kids and preteens.[55]

2 **Every manager should have a blog.**

ANSWER: *Disagree.* Blogs are an increasingly popular way for managers to communicate, both with employees and with customers. Many people think that within a few years blogging will be as common for managers as using e-mail is today. But blogs are not yet appropriate for many managers in many work environments.

ASSESS
YOUR
ANSWER

Blogs in particular are an increasingly popular customer-facing technology. One estimate is that around 12 percent of *Fortune* 500 companies, including General

Electric, Boeing, Marriott, and Wal-Mart, use blogs to keep in touch with stake-holders, and the number is growing fast.[56] Blogs give organizations a human voice, enable companies to influence opinion, and provide an easy way to share company news directly with outsiders. "When I blog, I'm talking to the world," says Jonathan Schwartz, CEO of Sun Microsystems. Schwartz believes that, within ten years, most CEOs "will communicate directly with customers, employees, and the broader business community through blogs. For executives, having a blog is not going to be a matter of choice, any more than email is today."[57]

E-BUSINESS ORGANIZATION DESIGN

E-business can be defined as any business that takes place by digital processes over a computer network rather than in physical space. Thus, all of the computer-based technologies we have discussed so far are aspects of e-business. However, e-business most commonly refers to electronic linkages over the Internet with customers, partners, suppliers, employees, or other key constituents.

Many traditional organizations have set up Internet operations to strengthen and improve these external relationships, but managers have to make a decision about how best to integrate *bricks and clicks*—that is, how to blend their traditional operations with an Internet initiative. In the early days of e-business, many companies set up dot-com initiatives with little understanding of how those activities could and should be integrated with the overall business. As the reality of e-business has evolved, companies have gained valuable lessons in how to merge online and offline activities.[58]

The range of basic strategies for setting up an Internet operation is illustrated in Exhibit 11.12. At one end of the spectrum, companies can set up an in-house division

EXHIBIT 11.12
The Range of Strategies for Integrating Bricks and Clicks

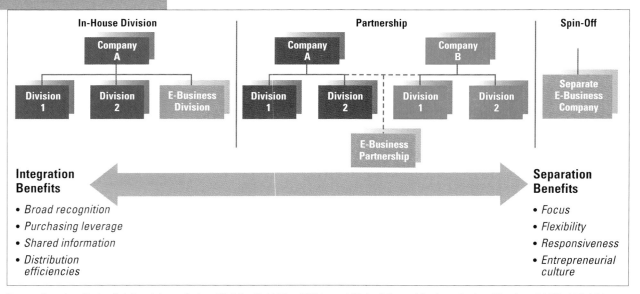

Source: Based on Ranjay Gulati and Jason Garino, "Get the Right Mix of Bricks and Clicks," *Harvard Business Review* (May–June 2000), 107–114.

that is closely integrated with the traditional business. The opposite approach is to create a spin-off company that is totally separate from the traditional organization. Many companies take a middle road by forging strategic partnerships with other organizations for their Internet initiative. Each of these options presents distinct advantages and disadvantages.[59]

In-House Division

An in-house division offers tight integration between the Internet operation and the organization's traditional operation. The organization creates a separate unit within the company that functions within the structure and guidance of the traditional organization. For example, WalMart.com is totally operated and controlled by Wal-Mart, and Disney.com is a division under the guidance and control of the Walt Disney Company. *The New York Times* embraced the Web early on with an in-house division that today provides a growing percentage of the newspaper outfit's business and advertising revenue.[60] The in-house approach gives the new division several advantages by piggybacking on the established company. These include brand recognition, purchasing leverage with suppliers, shared customer information and marketing opportunities, and distribution efficiencies. A potential problem with an in-house division, however, is that the new operation doesn't have the flexibility needed to move quickly in the Internet world.

Spin-Off

To give the Internet operation greater autonomy, flexibility, and focus, some organizations choose to create a separate spin-off company. Advantages of a spin-off include faster decision making, increased flexibility and responsiveness to changing market conditions, an entrepreneurial culture, and management that is totally focused on the success of the online operation. Potential disadvantages are the loss of brand recognition and marketing opportunities, higher start-up costs, and loss of leverage with suppliers. For example, CVS.com was launched in August 1999 as a spin-off of drug store retailer CVS and gained an early advantage over competitors such as Walgreens. However, Walgreens' in-house division eventually overtook CVS because the in-house approach enabled greater efficiencies. CVS managers began re-integrating online operations so that functions such as marketing, merchandising, and purchasing could be handled more efficiently in-house. The autonomy, flexibility, and focus of the spin-off was an advantage during the start-up phase, but the organization later on gained efficiencies by bringing the Web business back in-house for better coordination with other departments.[61]

Strategic Partnership

Partnerships offer a middle ground, enabling organizations to attain some of the advantages and overcome some of the disadvantages of the purely in-house or spin-off options. For example, when J&R Electronics, a Manhattan store with limited national reach, decided to go online, managers quickly realized that J&R didn't have the resources needed to build a solid online business. The company partnered with Amazon.com to capitalize on the advantages of both integration and separation. Amazon invests around $200 million a year in technology and site content, something that a small retailer like J&R simply couldn't do. The partnership approach gave J&R access to Amazon's millions of customers and allowed the firm to build its online identity and reputation. Managers at J&R agree with the advice of Drew Sharma, managing director of Internet marketing agency Mindfire Interactive, for smaller companies going online: "If you can stand on the shoulders of giants, then why not?"[62] The biggest disadvantages of partnerships include the time required to manage relationships, potential conflicts between partners, and a possibility that one company will fail to deliver as promised or go out of business. For example, if Amazon.com should fail, it would take J&R's online business with it and damage the company's reputation with Internet customers.

ASSESS YOUR ANSWER

3 The best way for a large company to set up an Internet division is to create a separate, free-standing unit, called a spin-off, because the unit will have the autonomy and flexibility to operate at Internet speed rather than being hampered by the larger organization's rules and procedures.

ANSWER: *Disagree.* Each approach to creating an e-business operation has advantages and disadvantages. Creating a free-standing spin-off can give the new unit greater autonomy and flexibility, but it can also reduce efficiency and require higher start-up costs. Managers carefully consider whether to use an in-house division, a spin-off, or a strategic partnership, any of which may work out best depending on the organization's circumstances.

IT IMPACT ON ORGANIZATION DESIGN

Managers and organization theorists have been studying the relationship between technology and organization design and functioning for more than half a century. In recent years, the advances in information technology have had the greatest impact in most organizations.[63] Some specific implications of these advances for organization design are smaller organizations, decentralized structures, improved internal and external coordination, and new network organization structures.

Briefcase

As an organization manager, keep this guideline in mind:

With greater use of IT, consider smaller organizational units, decentralized structures, improved internal coordination, and greater interorganizational collaboration, including the possibility of outsourcing or a network structure.

1. *Smaller organizations.*   Some Internet-based businesses exist almost entirely in cyberspace; there is no formal organization in terms of a building with offices, desks, and so forth. One or a few people may maintain the site from their homes or a rented work space. Even for traditional businesses, new IT enables the organization to do more work with fewer people. Customers can buy insurance, clothing, tools and equipment, and practically anything else over the Internet without ever speaking to an agent or salesperson. In addition, ERP and other IT systems automatically handle many administrative duties within organizations, reducing the need for clerical staff. The Michigan Department of Transportation (MDOT) used to need an army of workers to verify contractors' work. Large projects often required as many as twenty inspectors on-site every day to keep track of thousands of work items. Today, MDOT rarely sends more than one field technician to a site. The employee enters data into a laptop computer using road construction management software tied to computers at headquarters. The system can automatically generate payment estimates and handle other administrative

processes that used to take hours of labor.[64] Thanks to IT, today's companies can also outsource many functions and thus use fewer in-house resources.

2. *Decentralized organization structures.* Although management philosophy and corporate culture have a substantial impact on whether IT is used to decentralize information and authority or to reinforce a centralized authority structure,[65] most organizations today use technology to further decentralization. With IT, information that may have previously been available only to top managers at headquarters can be quickly and easily shared throughout the organization, even across great geographical distances. Managers in varied business divisions or offices have the information they need to make important decisions quickly rather than waiting for decisions from headquarters. Technologies that enable people to meet, coordinate, and collaborate online facilitate communication and decision making among distributed, autonomous groups of workers, such as in virtual teams. In addition, technology allows for telecommuting, whereby individual workers can perform work that was once done in the office from their computers at home or other remote locations. Margaret Hooshmand moved to Texas, but she still works as an executive assistant to Cisco Senior Vice President Marthin De Beer in California. Hooshmand reports to work virtually, appearing each morning on a 65-inch high-definition plasma screen that faces De Beer's office. She fields his calls, arranges meeting, and can see and hear what's going on in the Silicon Valley hallways.[66]

3. *Improved horizontal coordination.* Perhaps one of the greatest outcomes of IT is its potential to improve coordination and communication within the firm. IT applications can connect people even when their offices, factories, or stores are scattered around the world. IBM, for example, makes extensive use of virtual teams, whose members use a wide variety of IT tools to easily communicate and collaborate. One team made up of members in the United States, Germany, and the United Kingdom used collaboration software as a virtual meeting room to solve a client's technical problem resulting from Hurricane Katrina within the space of just a few days.[67] Siemens uses a global intranet that connects 450,000 employees around the world to share knowledge and collaborate on projects.[68] Xerox set up a knowledge management system to connect 25,000 field service representatives as if they were gathered around a virtual water cooler. The ability of service reps to share "war stories" and repair tips cut average repair time by 50 percent.[69]

4. *Improved interorganizational relationships.* IT can also improve horizontal coordination and collaboration with external parties such as suppliers, customers, and partners. Exhibit 11.13 shows differences between traditional interorganizational relationship characteristics and emerging relationship characteristics. Traditionally, organizations had an arm's-length relationship with suppliers. However, as we discussed in Chapter 4, suppliers are becoming closer partners, tied electronically to the organization for orders, invoices, and payments.

Studies have shown that interorganizational information networks tend to heighten integration, blur organizational boundaries, and create shared strategic contingencies among firms.[70] One good example of interorganizational collaboration is the PulseNet alliance, sponsored by the Centers for Disease Control and Prevention (CDC). The PulseNet information network uses collaborative technology to help U.S. state and federal agencies anticipate, identify, and prevent food-borne disease outbreaks. Through more frequent communication and real-time information sharing, rich relationships among the various agencies have evolved. State health labs and the CDC once had

EXHIBIT 11.13

Key Characteristics
of Traditional
versus Emerging
Interorganizational
Relationships

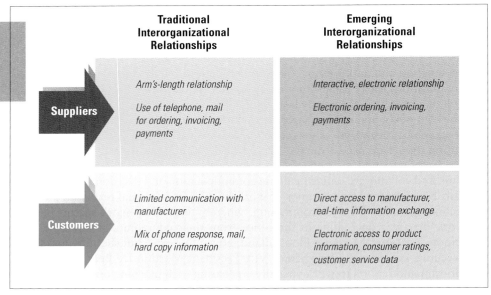

Source: Based on Charles V. Callahan and Bruce A. Pasternack, "Corporate Strategy in the Digital Age," *Strategy & Business*, Issue 15 (Second Quarter 1999), 10–14.

infrequent contact but are now involved in joint strategic planning regarding the PulseNet project.[71]

5. *Enhanced network structures.* The high level of interorganizational collaboration needed in a network organization structure, described in Chapter 2, would not be possible without the use of advanced IT. In the business world, these are also sometimes called *modular structures* or *virtual organizations*. Outsourcing has become a major trend, thanks to computer technology that can tie companies together into a seamless information flow. For example, Hong Kong's Li & Fung is one of the biggest providers of clothing for retailers such as Abercrombie & Fitch, Guess, Ann Taylor, the Limited, and Disney, but the company doesn't own any factories, machines, or fabrics. Li & Fung specializes in managing information, relying on an electronically connected web of 7,500 partners in thirty-seven countries to provide raw materials and assemble the clothes. Using an extranet allows Li & Fung to stay in touch with worldwide partners and move items quickly from factories to retailers. It also lets retailers track orders as they move through production and make last-minute changes and additions.[72] With a network structure, most activities are outsourced, so that different companies perform the various functions needed by the organization. The speed and ease of electronic communication makes the network structure a viable option for companies that want to keep costs low but expand activities or market presence.

DESIGN ESSENTIALS

■ Today's most successful organizations are generally those that most effectively apply information technology. IT systems have evolved to a variety of applications to meet organizations' information needs. Operations applications are applied to well-defined tasks at lower organization levels and help improve efficiency. These include transaction processing systems, data warehousing, and data mining.

▪ Advanced computer-based systems are also used for better decision making, coordination, and control of the organization. Decision-making systems include management information systems, reporting systems, decision support systems, and executive information systems, which are typically used at middle and upper levels of the organization. Management control systems include budgets and financial reports, periodic nonfinancial statistical reports, reward systems, and quality control systems.

▪ At the organization level of control, an innovation called the *balanced scorecard* provides managers with a balanced view of the organization by integrating traditional financial measurements and statistical reports with a concern for markets, customers, and employees. Managers also use strategy maps to see the cause-effect relationships among these critical success factors. At the department level, managers use behavior control or outcome control. Behavior control involves close monitoring of employee activities, whereas outcome control measures and rewards results. Most managers use a combination of behavior and outcome control, with a greater emphasis on outcome control because it leads to better performance and higher motivation.

▪ Today, all the various computer-based systems have begun to merge into an overall IT system that adds strategic value by enabling close coordination internally and with outside parties. Intranets, Web 2.0 tools, knowledge management systems, and ERP are used primarily to support greater internal coordination and flexibility. Systems that support and strengthen external relationships include extranets and supply chain management systems, customer relationship systems, and e-business. The integrated enterprise uses advanced IT to enable close coordination among a company and its suppliers, partners, and customers. To establish an e-business, companies can choose among an in-house division, a spin-off, or a strategic partnership. Each has strengths and weaknesses.

▪ Advanced IT is having a significant impact on organization design, and some experts suggest that it will eventually replace traditional hierarchy as a primary means of coordination and control. Technology has enabled creation of the network organization structure, in which a company subcontracts most of its major functions to separate companies. In addition, most other organizations are also rapidly evolving toward greater interorganizational collaboration. Other specific implications of advanced IT for organization design include smaller organizations, decentralized organization structures, and improved internal and external coordination.

Key Concepts

balanced scorecard
behavior control
benchmarking
blog
business intelligence
customer relationship management
data warehousing
decision support system
e-business
enterprise resource planning

executive dashboard
executive information system
explicit knowledge
extranet
feedback control model
information reporting system
integrated enterprise
intellectual capital
intranet
knowledge management

management control systems
management information system
networking
outcome control
Six Sigma
social networking
strategy map
tacit knowledge
transaction processing systems
wiki

Discussion Questions

1. Describe how the four balanced scorecard components discussed in the chapter might be used for feedback control within organizations. Which of these components is more similar to outcome control? Behavior control?
2. Why does the application of advanced IT typically lead to greater decentralization? Could it also be used for greater centralization in some organizations? Explain.
3. Discuss some ways a large insurance company such as Allstate, Progressive, or State Farm might use Web 2.0 tools such as blogs, wikis, or social networking. Do you think these tools are more applicable to a service company than to a manufacturing organization? Discuss.
4. What are some competitive issues that might lead a company to take a partnership approach to e-business rather than setting up an in-house Internet division? What are the advantages and disadvantages of each approach?
5. How might an enterprise resource planning system be used to improve the management of a manufacturing organization?
6. What is meant by the *integrated enterprise*? Describe how organizations can use extranets to extend and enhance horizontal relationships required for enterprise integration.
7. What types of information technology do you as a student use on a regular basis? How might your life be different if this technology were not available to you?
8. Why is knowledge management particularly important to a company that wants to learn and change continuously rather than operate at a stable state?
9. Do you think technology will eventually enable top managers to do their jobs with little face-to-face communication? Discuss.
10. Describe your use of explicit knowledge when you research and write a term paper. Do you also use tacit knowledge regarding this activity? Discuss.

Chapter 11 Workbook: Balanced Scorecard Exercise

Read the measures and objectives listed below for a business firm and a healthcare organization. Make a check for each objective/measure in the correct balanced scorecard column. If you think an objective/measure fits into two balanced scorecard categories, write the numbers 1 and 2 for your first vs. second preference.

	Financial	Customers	Business Processes	Learning & Growth
Business Firm				
Return on capital employed (ROCE)				
Build employee recreation venue by December 2012				
Develop new products within a time period of 8 months				
Provide team leader training program by July 2010				
Achieve 98% customer satisfaction by December 2012				
Number of monthly customer complaints				
Reduce cost per unit sold by 10%				
Increase customer retention by 15%				
Improve employee satisfaction scores by 20%				
Lead market in speed of delivery by 2011				
Lowest industry cost by 2012				
Improve profits by 12% over next year				
Budget forecast accuracy				
Introduce three new products by December 2011				
Percent training completed				
Number of leaders ready for promotion				
Completed succession plan				

	Financial	Customers	Business Processes	Learning & Growth
Percentage of employees part-time				
Sales growth to increase 1% monthly				
Number of employee grievances				
Employee engagement scores				
Number of employee terminations				
Policy implementation time lag				
Vendor on-time delivery rate				
Total annual revenues				
Utility consumption costs				
Workers compensation claims				
EBITDA				
Healthcare Organization				
Fundraising targets				
Patient satisfaction				
Appointments accomodated on time				
Percentage of patients restored to full functioning				
Number of patients wanting service				
Percentage clinical support staff				
Nurse satisfaction				
Length of physician employment				
Patient satisfaction with scheduling				
Wait time satisfaction				
Patient perception of quality				
Cost of patient care				
Profitability				
Staff compliance with privacy regulations				
Bed utilization rate				
Falls per 100 patients				
Percentage of nurse master's degrees				
Speed of patient admissions & discharge				
Education for family member care giving				
Quality of pain control				
Percentage of medicines filled accurately				
Nurse turnover rate				
Nurse shortage rate				
Completion rate of prescribed services				
Total labor costs				
Operating margins				
Amount of charity care				
Unpaid cost of public programs				
Smoking cessation program effectiveness				
Medicare reimbursement audit results				
Education completion rate				

Case for Analysis: Century Medical*

Sam Nolan clicked the mouse for one more round of solitaire on the computer in his den. He'd been at it for more than an hour, and his wife had long ago given up trying to persuade him to join her for a movie or a rare Saturday night on the town. The mind-numbing game seemed to be all that calmed Sam enough to stop thinking about work and how his job seemed to get worse every day.

Nolan was chief information officer at Century Medical, a large medical products company based in Connecticut. He had joined the company four years ago, and since that time Century had made great progress integrating technology into its systems and processes. Nolan had already led projects to design and build two highly successful systems for Century. One was a benefits-administration system for the company's HR department. The other was a complex Web-based purchasing system that streamlined the process of purchasing supplies and capital goods. Although the system had been up and running for only a few months, modest projections were that it would save Century nearly $2 million annually.

Previously, Century's purchasing managers were bogged down with shuffling paper. The purchasing process would begin when an employee filled out a materials request form. Then the form would travel through various offices for approval and signatures before eventually being converted into a purchase order. The new Web-based system allowed employees to fill out electronic request forms that were automatically e-mailed to everyone whose approval was needed. The time for processing request forms was cut from weeks to days or even hours. When authorization was complete, the system would automatically launch a purchase order to the appropriate supplier. In addition, because the new system had dramatically cut the time purchasing managers spent shuffling paper, they now had more time to work collaboratively with key stakeholders to identify and select the best suppliers and negotiate better deals.

Nolan thought wearily of all the hours he had put in developing trust with people throughout the company and showing them how technology could not only save time and money but also support team-based work and give people more control over their own jobs. He smiled briefly as he recalled one long-term HR employee, 61-year-old Ethel Moore. She had been terrified when Nolan first began showing her the company's intranet, but she was now one of his biggest supporters. In fact, it had been Ethel who had first approached him with an idea about a Web-based job posting system. The two had pulled together a team and developed an idea for linking Century managers, internal recruiters, and job applicants using artificial intelligence software on top of an integrated Web-based system. When Nolan had presented the idea to his boss, executive vice president Sandra Ivey, she had enthusiastically endorsed it, and within a few weeks the team had authorization to proceed with the project.

But everything began to change when Ivey resigned her position six months later to take a plum job in New York. Ivey's successor, Tom Carr, seemed to have little interest in the project. During their first meeting, Carr had openly referred to the project as a waste of time and money. He immediately disapproved several new features suggested by the company's internal recruiters, even though the project team argued that the features could double internal hiring and save millions in training costs. "Just stick to the original plan and get it done. All this stuff needs to be handled on a personal basis anyway," Carr countered. "You can't learn more from a computer than you can talking to real people—and as for internal recruiting, it shouldn't be so hard to talk to people if they're already working right here in the company." Carr seemed to have no understanding of how and why technology was being used. He became irritated when Ethel Moore referred to the system as "Web-based." He boasted that he had never visited Century's intranet site and suggested that "this Internet fad" would eventually blow over anyway. Even Ethel's enthusiasm couldn't get through to him. She tried to show him some of the HR resources available on the intranet and explain how it had benefited the department and the company, but he waved her away. "Technology is for those people in the IT department. My job is people, and yours should be too." Ethel was crushed, and Nolan realized it would be like beating his head against a brick wall to try to persuade Carr to the team's point of view. Near the end of the meeting, Carr even jokingly suggested that the project team should just buy a couple of filing cabinets and save everyone some time and money.

Just when the team thought things couldn't get any worse, Carr dropped the other bomb. They would no longer be allowed to gather input from users of the new system. Nolan feared that without the input of potential users, the system wouldn't meet their needs, or even that users would boycott the system because they hadn't been allowed to participate. No doubt that would put a great big "I told you so" smile right on Carr's face.

Nolan sighed and leaned back in his chair. The project had begun to feel like a joke. The vibrant and innovative HR

Chapter 11: Information and Control Processes

449

department his team had imagined now seemed like nothing more than a pipe dream. But despite his frustration, a new thought entered Nolan's mind: "Is Carr just stubborn and narrow-minded or does he have a point that HR is a people business that doesn't need a high-tech job-posting system?"

*Based on Carol Hildebrand, "New Boss Blues," *CIO Enterprise*, Section 2 (November 15, 1998), 53–58; and Megan Santosus, "Advanced Micro Devices' Web-Based Purchasing System," *CIO*, Section 1 (May 15, 1998), 84.

Case for Analysis: Product X*

Several years ago the top management of a multibillion-dollar corporation decided that Product X was a failure and should be disbanded. The losses involved exceeded $100 million. At least five people knew that Product X was a failure six years before the decision was made to stop producing it. Three of those people were plant managers who lived daily with the production problems. The other two were marketing officials who realized that the manufacturing problems were not solvable without expenditures that would raise the price of the product to the point where it would no longer be competitive in the market.

There are several reasons why this information did not get to the top sooner. At first, the subordinates believed that with exceptionally hard work they might turn the errors into successes. But the more they struggled, the more they realized the massiveness of the original error. The next task was to communicate the bad news upward so that it would be heard. They knew that in their company bad news would not be well received at the upper levels if it was not accompanied with suggestions for positive action. They also knew that the top management was enthusiastically describing Product X as a new leader in its field. Therefore, they spent much time composing memos that would communicate the realities without shocking top management.

Middle management read the memos and found them too open and forthright. Since they had done the production and marketing studies that resulted in the decision to produce Product X, the memos from lower-level management questioned the validity of their analysis. They wanted time to really check these gloomy predictions and, if they were accurate, to design alternative corrective strategies. If the pessimistic information was to be sent upward, middle management wanted it accompanied with optimistic action alternatives. Hence further delay.

Once middle management was convinced that the gloomy predictions were valid, they began to release some of the bad news to the top—but in carefully measured doses. They managed the releases carefully to make certain they were covered if top management became upset. The tactic they used was to cut the memos drastically and summarize the findings. They argued that the cuts were necessary because top management was always complaining about receiving long memos; indeed, some top executives had let it be known that good memos were memos of one page or less. The result was that top management received fragmented information underplaying the intensity of the problem (not the problem itself) and overplaying the degree to which middle management and the technicians were in control of the problem.

Top management therefore continued to speak glowingly about the product, partially to ensure that it would get the financial backing it needed from within the company. Lower-level management became confused and eventually depressed because they could not understand this continued top management support, nor why studies were ordered to evaluate the production and marketing difficulties that they had already identified. Their reaction was to reduce the frequency of their memos and the intensity of their alarm, while simultaneously turning over the responsibility for dealing with the problem to middle-management people. When local plant managers, in turn, were asked by their foremen and employees what was happening, the only response they gave was that the company was studying the situation and continuing its support. This information bewildered the foremen and led them to reduce their own concern.

*Excerpted from C. Argyris and D. Schon, *Organizational Learning: A Theory of Action Perspective*. Argyris/Schon, *Organizational Learning*, © 1978, Addison-Wesley Publishing Co., Inc., Reading, Massachusetts. Pages 1–2. Reprinted with permission. Case appeared in Gareth Morgan, *Creative Organization Theory* (1989), Sage Publications.

Chapter 12

Organization Size and Life Cycle

xyno lorenzen

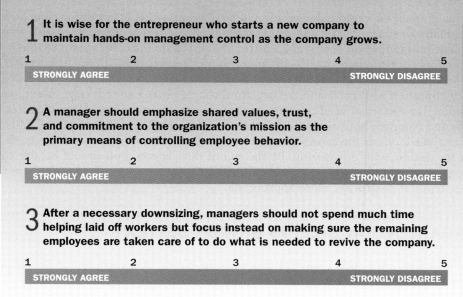

1 It is wise for the entrepreneur who starts a new company to maintain hands-on management control as the company grows.

1	2	3	4	5
STRONGLY AGREE				STRONGLY DISAGREE

2 A manager should emphasize shared values, trust, and commitment to the organization's mission as the primary means of controlling employee behavior.

1	2	3	4	5
STRONGLY AGREE				STRONGLY DISAGREE

3 After a necessary downsizing, managers should not spend much time helping laid off workers but focus instead on making sure the remaining employees are taken care of to do what is needed to revive the company.

1	2	3	4	5
STRONGLY AGREE				STRONGLY DISAGREE

In the world of advertising, Crispin Porter & Bogusky is a bit of a maverick. The agency's unusual ads and innovative techniques have been successful in an environment in which consumers are viewing media and looking at advertising in new ways. But Crispin managers now face a challenge: how to make sure the hotshot agency stays hot as it copes with rapid growth and huge international accounts. They know that many creative upstarts have faltered, failed, or been swallowed up by larger firms as they try to make the transition to ad industry titans.[1] As organizations like Crispin Porter & Bogusky grow large and complex, they need more complex systems and procedures for guiding and controlling the organization. Many entrepreneurs have trouble taking their companies through the growing pains. Moreover, the addition of more complex systems and procedures can also cause problems of inefficiency, rigidity, and slow response time, meaning the company has a hard time adapting quickly to client or customer needs.

Every organization—from locally owned restaurants and auto body shops to large international firms such as Coca-Cola and law-enforcement agencies such as the CIA and Interpol—wrestles with questions about organizational size, bureaucracy, and control. During the twentieth century, large organizations became widespread, and bureaucracy has become a major topic of study in organization theory.[2] Most large organizations have bureaucratic characteristics, which can be very effective. These organizations provide us with abundant goods and services and accomplish astonishing feats—explorations of Mars, overnight delivery of packages to any location in the world, the scheduling and coordination of thousands of airline flights a day—that are testimony to their effectiveness. On the other hand, bureaucracy is also accused of many sins, including inefficiency, rigidity, and demeaning routinized work that alienates both employees and the customers an organization tries to serve.

Purpose of This Chapter

In this chapter, we explore the question of large versus small organizations and how size relates to structure and control. Organization size is a contextual variable that influences organization design and functioning just as do the contextual variables—technology, environment, goals—discussed in previous chapters. In the first section, we look at the advantages of large versus small size. Then, we explore what is called an organization's life cycle and the structural characteristics at each stage. Next, we examine the historical need for bureaucracy as a means to control large organizations and compare bureaucratic control to various other control strategies. Finally, the chapter looks at the causes of organizational decline and discusses some methods for dealing with downsizing. By the end of this chapter, you should be able to recognize when bureaucratic control can make an organization effective and when other types of control are more appropriate.

ORGANIZATION SIZE: IS BIGGER BETTER?

The question of big versus small begins with the notion of growth and the reasons so many organizations feel the need to grow large.

Pressures for Growth

Briefcase

As an organization manager, keep these guidelines in mind:

Decide whether your organization should act like a large or small company. To the extent that economies of scale, global reach, and complexity are important, introduce greater bureaucratization as the organization increases in size. As it becomes necessary, add rules and regulations, written documentation, job specialization, technical competence in hiring and promotion, and decentralization.

Do you ever dream of starting a small company? Many people do, and entrepreneurial start-ups are the lifeblood of the U.S. economy. Yet the hope of practically every entrepreneur is to have his or her company grow fast and grow large, maybe even to eventually make the *Fortune* 500 list.[3] Sometimes this goal is more urgent than to make the best products or show the greatest profits. However, there are some thriving companies where managers have resisted the pressure for endless growth to focus instead on different goals.

Recent economic woes and layoffs at many large firms have spurred budding entrepreneurs to take a chance on starting their own company or going it alone in a sole proprietorship. Yet despite the proliferation of new, small organizations, the giants such as Procter & Gamble, General Electric, Toyota, and Wal-Mart have continued to grow. For example, Wal-Mart's employee base is almost as big as the population of the city of Houston, Texas. The combined square footage of Home Depot's retail stores is about the same as 92,564 average-sized U.S. homes. Verizon's fiber-optic cable for its Internet network would reach around the world 18 times.[4]

Companies in all industries, from retail, to aerospace, to media, strive for growth to acquire the size and resources needed to compete on a global scale, to invest in new technology, and to control distribution channels and guarantee access to markets.[5] There are a number of other pressures for organizations to grow. Many executives have found that firms must grow to stay economically healthy. To stop growing is to stagnate. To be stable means that customers may not have their demands fully met or that competitors will increase market share at the expense of your company. At Wal-Mart, managers have vowed to continue an emphasis on growth even though it means a decreasing return on investment (ROI). They are ingrained with the idea that to stop growing is to stagnate and die. As chief financial officer Tom Schoewe put it, even if the ROI could "come down a bit and we could grow faster, that would be just fine by me."[6]

Large size enables companies to take risks that could ruin smaller firms, and scale is crucial to economic health in some industries. For marketing-intensive companies such as Coca-Cola, Procter & Gamble, and Anheuser-Busch, greater size provides power in the marketplace and thus increased revenues.[7] Companies striving to develop renewable-energy technology have found that "the biggest bang for the buck is to go large," as entrepreneur Mark Rogers of the Cape Wind project in Massachusetts said. Many of the development costs for wind turbine and solar energy projects vary little whether the project is very large or very small, so increasing the size of the project makes it more cost-effective.[8] In addition, growing organizations are vibrant, exciting places to work, which enables these companies to attract and keep quality employees. When the number of employees is expanding, the company can offer many challenges and opportunities for advancement.

Dilemmas of Large Size

Organizations feel compelled to grow, but how much and how large? What size organization is better poised to compete in a fast-changing global environment? The arguments are summarized in Exhibit 12.1.

EXHIBIT 12.1
Differences between Large and Small Organizations

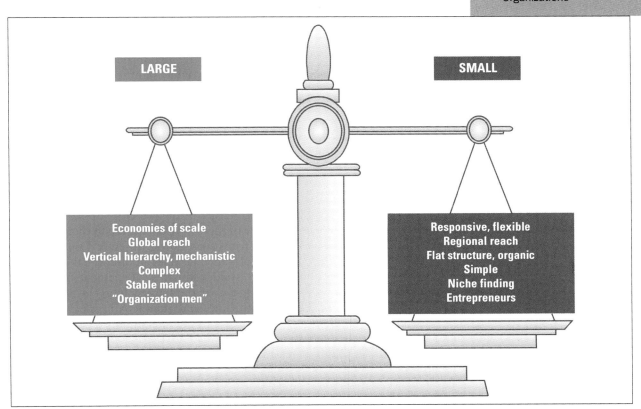

Source: Based on John A. Byrne, "Is Your Company Too Big?" *BusinessWeek* (March 27, 1989), 84–94.

Large. Huge resources and economies of scale are needed for many organizations to compete globally. Only large organizations can build a massive pipeline in Alaska. Only a large corporation like General Electric can afford to build ultra-efficient $2 million wind turbines that contain 8,000 different parts.[9] Only a large Johnson & Johnson can invest hundreds of millions in new products such as bifocal contact lenses and a patch that delivers contraceptives through the skin. In addition, large organizations have the resources to be a supportive economic and social force in difficult times. In 2005, after Hurricane Katrina wiped out New Orleans and much of the Gulf Coast, Wal-Mart gave thousands of employees $1,000 for emergency assistance, offered residents of the affected areas a free seven-day emergency supply of prescription drugs, shipped more than 100 truckloads of supplies to evacuation centers, and donated millions to relief organizations.[10] Similarly, following the 2001 terrorist attacks in the United States, American Express had the resources to help stranded customers get home and waive delinquent fees on late payments.[11] Large organizations also are able to get back to business more quickly following a disaster, giving employees a sense of security and belonging during an uncertain time.

Large companies are standardized, often mechanistically run, and complex. The complexity offers hundreds of functional specialties within the organization to perform multifaceted tasks and to produce varied and complicated products. Moreover, large organizations, once established, can be a presence that stabilizes a market for years. Managers can join the company and expect a career reminiscent of the "organization men" of the 1950s and 1960s. The organization can provide longevity, raises, and promotions.

Small. The competing argument says small is beautiful because the crucial requirements for success in a global economy are responsiveness and flexibility in fast-changing markets. Small scale can provide significant advantages in terms of quick reaction to changing customer needs or shifting environmental and market conditions.[12] In addition, small organizations often enjoy greater employee commitment because it is easier for people to feel like part of a community. Employees typically work on a variety of tasks rather than narrow, specialized jobs. For many people, working in a small company is more exciting and fulfilling than working in a huge organization. Where would you be happier as a manager? Complete the questionnaire in this chapter's "How Do You Fit the Design?" box for some insight.

Many large companies have grown even larger through merger or acquisition in recent years, yet research indicates that few of these mergers live up to their expected performance levels. Studies by consulting firms such as McKinsey & Company, the Hay Group, and others suggest that performance declines in almost 20 percent of acquired companies after acquisition. By some estimates, 90 percent of mergers never live up to expectations.[13] A look at ten of the biggest mergers of all time, including AOL/Time Warner, Glaxo/SmithKline, and Daimler/Chrysler, showed a significant decline in shareholder value for eight of the ten combined companies, as illustrated in Exhibit 12.2. Only two, Exxon/Mobil and Travelers/Citicorp, actually increased in value.[14] Although there are numerous factors involved in the decline in value, many researchers and analysts agree that, frequently, bigness just doesn't add up to better performance.[15]

Despite the increasing size of many companies, the economic vitality of the United States, as well as most of the rest of the developed world, is tied to small

How Do You Fit the Design?

What Size Organization for You?

How do your work preferences fit organization size? Answer the following questions as they reflect your likes and dislikes. Please answer whether each item is Mostly True or Mostly False for you.

	Mostly True	Mostly False
1. I value stability and predictability in the organization I work for.	_____	_____
2. Rules are meant to be broken.	_____	_____
3. Years of service should be an important determinant of pay and promotion.	_____	_____
4. I generally prefer to work on lots of different things rather than specialize in a few things.	_____	_____
5. Before accepting a job, I would want to make sure the company had good benefits.	_____	_____
6. I would rather work on a team where managerial responsibility is shared than work in a department with a single manager.	_____	_____
7. I would like to work for a large, well-known company.	_____	_____
8. I would rather earn $90,000 a year as a VP in a small company than earn $100,000 a year as a middle manager in a big company.	_____	_____

Scoring: Give yourself one point for each odd-numbered item you marked as Mostly True and one point for each even-numbered item you marked Mostly False.

Interpretation: Working in a large organization is a very different experience from working in a small organization. The large organization is well-established, has good benefits, is stable, and has rules, well-defined jobs, and a clear management hierarchy of authority. A small organization may be struggling to survive, has excitement, multitasking, risk, and sharing of responsibility. If you scored 6 or more, a large organization may be for you. If you scored 3 or less, you may be happier in a smaller, less structured organization.

and mid-sized businesses. There are an estimated 25 to 26 million small businesses in the United States, which account for a tremendous portion of goods and services provided.[16] In addition, a large percentage of exporters are small businesses. The growth of the Internet and other information technologies has made it easier for small companies to compete with larger firms. And the growing service sector also contributes to a decrease in average organization size, as many service companies remain small to better serve customers.

Small organizations have a flat structure and an organic, free-flowing management style that encourages entrepreneurship and innovation. Today's leading

EXHIBIT 12.2
Effect of Ten
Mega-Mergers on
Shareholder Wealth

Merger	Year of Deal	Value Created or Destroyed As of July 1, 2002
AOL/Time Warner	2001	−$148 billion
Vodafone/Mannesmann	2000	−$299 billion
Pfizer/Warner-Lambert	2000	−$78 billion
Glaxo/SmithKline	2000	−$40 billion
Chase/J.P. Morgan	2000	−$26 billion
Exxon/Mobil	1999	+$8 billion
SBC/Ameritech	1999	−$68 billion
WorldCom/MCI	1998	−$94 billion
Travelers/Citicorp	1998	+$109 billion
Daimler/Chrysler	1998	−$36 billion

Source: Reported in Keith Hammonds, "Size Is Not a Strategy," *Fast Company* (September 2002), 78–86.

biotechnology drugs, for example, were all discovered by small firms, such as Gilead Sciences, which developed anti-retroviral drugs to treat HIV, rather than by huge pharmaceutical companies such as Merck.[17] Moreover, the personal involvement of employees in small firms encourages motivation and commitment because employees personally identify with the company's mission. Based on studies of primitive societies, religious sects, military organizations, and some businesses, anthropologist Robin Dunbar proposed that 150 is the optimum size for any group trying to achieve a goal. Dunbar says beyond that size, the group's effectiveness wanes because of too many rules, procedures, and red tape that slows things down and saps group morale, enthusiasm, and commitment.[18]

Big-Company/Small-Company Hybrid. The paradox is that the advantages of small companies sometimes enable them to succeed and, hence, grow large. Small companies can become victims of their own success as they grow, shifting to a mechanistic structure emphasizing vertical hierarchy and spawning "organization men" rather than entrepreneurs. Giant companies are "built for optimization, not innovation."[19] Big companies become committed to their existing products and technologies and have a hard time supporting innovation for the future.

The solution is what Jack Welch, retired chairman and CEO of General Electric, called the "big-company/small-company hybrid" that combines a large corporation's resources and reach with a small company's simplicity and flexibility. Full-service global firms need a strong resource base and sufficient complexity and hierarchy to serve clients around the world. Size is not necessarily at odds with speed and flexibility, but managers must find ways to encourage innovation and adapt quickly. The divisional structure, described in Chapter 2, is one way some large organizations attain a big-company/small-company hybrid. By reorganizing into groups of small companies, huge corporations such as Johnson & Johnson capture the mindset and advantages of smallness. Johnson & Johnson is actually a group of 250 separate companies operating in fifty-seven countries.[20]

Briefcase

As an organization manager, keep these guidelines in mind:

If responsiveness, flexibility, simplicity, and niche finding are important, subdivide the organization into simple, autonomous divisions that have freedom and a small-company approach.

The development of new organizational forms, with an emphasis on decentralizing authority and cutting out layers of the hierarchy, combined with the increasing use of information technology described in Chapter 11, is making it easier than ever for companies to be simultaneously large and small, thus capturing the advantages of each. The shift can even be seen in the U.S. military. Unlike World War II, for example, which was fought with large masses of soldiers guided by decisions made at top levels, today's "war on terrorism" depends on decentralized decision making and smaller forces of highly skilled soldiers with access to up-to-the-minute information.[21] Big companies also find a variety of ways to act both large and small. Retail giant Lowe's, for example, uses the advantage of size in areas such as advertising, purchasing, and raising capital; however, executives give each individual store the autonomy needed to serve customers as if it were a small, hometown shop. To avoid the problem of isolated top managers, mutual fund manager Vanguard requires everyone—even the CEO—to spend some time each month manning the phones and talking directly to customers.[22] The giant corporation Royal Dutch/Shell encourages innovation in its exploration-and-production division by setting aside 10 percent of the division's research budget for "crazy" ideas. Anyone can apply for the funds, and decisions are made not by managers but by a small group of nonconformist employees.[23] Small companies that are growing can also use these ideas to help their organizations retain the flexibility and customer focus that fueled their growth.

ORGANIZATIONAL LIFE CYCLE

A useful way to think about organizational growth and change is the concept of an organizational **life cycle**,[24] which suggests that organizations are born, grow older, and eventually die. Organization structure, leadership style, and administrative systems follow a fairly predictable pattern through stages in the life cycle. Stages are sequential and follow a natural progression.

Stages of Life Cycle Development

Research on organizational life cycle suggests that four major stages characterize organizational development.[25] Exhibit 12.3 illustrates these four stages along with the problems associated with transition to each stage. Growth is not easy. Each time an organization enters a new stage in the life cycle, it enters a whole new ball game with a new set of rules for how the organization functions internally and how it relates to the external environment.[26] For technology companies today, life cycles are getting shorter; to stay competitive, companies like eBay, Google, and MySpace have to successfully progress through stages of the cycle faster.

1. *Entrepreneurial stage.*   When an organization is born, the emphasis is on creating a product or service and surviving in the marketplace. The founders are entrepreneurs, and they devote their full energies to the technical activities of production and marketing. The organization is informal and nonbureaucratic. The hours of work are long. Control is based on the owners' personal supervision. Growth is from a creative new product or service. For example, Jimmy Wales and Larry Sanger co-founded *Wikipedia* in 2001 based on the idea of an open source, collaborative encyclopedia, open to contributions by ordinary people. They personally provided oversight of the project during its early years, with Wales acting as

Briefcase

As an organization manager, keep this guideline in mind:

Grow when possible. With growth, you can provide opportunities for employee advancement and greater profitability and effectiveness. Apply new management systems and structural configurations at each stage of an organization's development. Interpret the needs of the growing organization and respond with the management and internal systems that will carry the organization through to the next stage of development.

EXHIBIT 12.3
Organizational Life Cycle

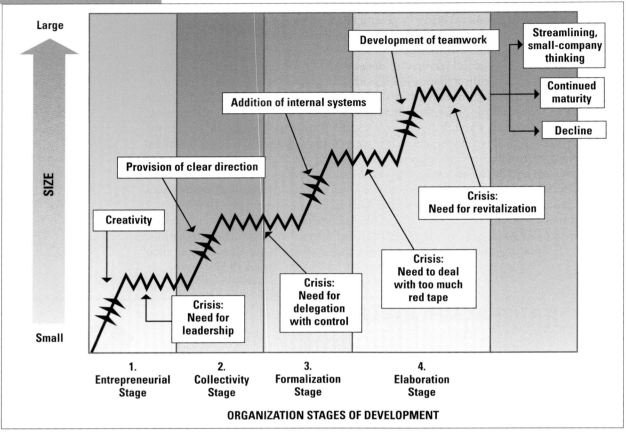

Source: Adapted from Robert E. Quinn and Kim Cameron, "Organizational Life Cycles and Shifting Criteria of Effectiveness: Some Preliminary Evidence," *Management Science* 29 (1983), 33–51; and Larry E. Greiner, "Evolution and Revolution as Organizations Grow," *Harvard Business Review* 50 (July–August 1972), 37–46.

visionary leader and Sanger focused primarily on developing the new service.[27] Apple (originally Apple Computer) was in the **entrepreneurial stage** when it was created by Steve Jobs and Stephen Wozniak in Wozniak's parents' garage.

Crisis: Need for leadership. As the organization starts to grow, the larger number of employees causes problems. The creative and technically oriented owners are confronted with management issues, but they may prefer to focus their energies on making and selling the product or inventing new products and services. At this time of crisis, entrepreneurs must either adjust the structure of the organization to accommodate continued growth or else bring in strong managers who can do so. When Apple began a period of rapid growth, A. C. Markkula was brought in as a leader because neither Jobs nor Wozniak was qualified or cared to manage the expanding company.

2. *Collectivity stage.* If the leadership crisis is resolved, strong leadership is obtained and the organization begins to develop clear goals and direction. Departments are established along with a hierarchy of authority, job assignments,

and a beginning division of labor. Social networking company Facebook moved quickly from the entrepreneurial to the collectivity stage. Twenty-three-year-old founder Mark Zuckerberg knows his company has to "grow up at Internet speed," so he recruited a top Google executive, Sheryl Sandberg, to serve as chief operating officer. Facebook also hired other skilled executives to manage various functions such as marketing, legal, communications and public relations, and finance.[28] In the collectivity stage, employees identify with the mission of the organization and spend long hours helping the organization succeed. Members feel part of a collective. Communication and control are mostly informal although a few formal systems begin to appear. Apple was in the **collectivity stage** during the rapid growth years from 1978 to 1981. Jobs remained as CEO and visionary leader, although Markkula and other executives handled most of the management responsibilities. Employees threw themselves into the business as the major product line was established and more than 2,000 dealers signed on.

Crisis: Need for delegation. If the new management has been successful, lower-level employees gradually find themselves restricted by the strong top-down leadership. Lower-level managers begin to acquire confidence in their own functional areas and want more discretion. An autonomy crisis occurs when top managers, who were successful because of their strong leadership and vision, do not want to give up responsibility. Top managers want to make sure that all parts of the organization are coordinated and pulling together. The organization needs to find mechanisms to control and coordinate departments without direct supervision from the top.

---

1 **It is wise for the entrepreneur who starts a new company to maintain hands-on management control as the company grows.**

ANSWER: *Disagree.* Entrepreneurs typically enjoy using their creativity for making and selling a new product or service. Many stay hands-on too long because they have a hard time shifting to the role of managing other people and setting up procedures and systems the company needs as it grows. In most cases, successful entrepreneurs bring in skilled managers to run the business and take the organization to the next level.

ASSESS YOUR ANSWER

---

3. *Formalization stage.* The **formalization stage** involves the installation and use of rules, procedures, and control systems. Communication is less frequent and more formal. Engineers, human resource specialists, and other staff may be added. Top management becomes concerned with issues such as strategy and planning and leaves the operations of the firm to middle management. Product groups or other decentralized units may be formed to improve coordination. Incentive systems based on profits may be implemented to ensure that managers work toward what is best for the overall company. When effective, the new coordination and control systems enable the organization to continue growing by establishing linkage mechanisms between top management and field units. Apple was in the formalization stage in the late 1980s.

Crisis: Too much red tape. At this point in the organization's development, the proliferation of systems and programs may begin to strangle middle-level executives. The organization seems bureaucratized. Middle management may resent the intrusion of staff. Innovation may be restricted. The organization seems too large and complex to be managed through formal programs. It was at this stage of Apple's growth that Jobs resigned from the company and a new CEO took control to face his own management challenges.

4. *Elaboration stage.* The solution to the red tape crisis is a new sense of collaboration and teamwork. Throughout the organization, managers develop skills for confronting problems and working together. Bureaucracy may have reached its limit. Social control and self-discipline reduce the need for additional formal controls. Managers learn to work within the bureaucracy without adding to it. Formal systems may be simplified and replaced by manager teams and task forces. To achieve collaboration, teams are often formed across functions or divisions of the company. The organization may also be split into multiple divisions to maintain a small-company philosophy. Apple is currently in the **elaboration stage** of the life cycle, as are such large companies as General Electric, Caterpillar, and Motorola.

Crisis: Need for revitalization. After the organization reaches maturity, it may enter periods of temporary decline.[29] A need for renewal may occur every ten to twenty years. The organization shifts out of alignment with the environment or perhaps becomes slow moving and overbureaucratized and must go through a stage of streamlining and innovation. Top managers are often replaced during this period. At Apple, the top spot changed hands a number of times as the company struggled to revitalize. CEOs John Sculley, Michael Spindler, and Gilbert Amelio were each ousted by the board as Apple's problems deepened. Steve Jobs returned in mid-1997 to run the company he had founded nearly twenty-five years earlier. Jobs quickly reorganized the company, weeded out inefficiencies, and refocused Apple on innovative products for the consumer market. Jobs brought the entrepreneurial spirit back to Apple and moved the company into a whole new direction with the iPod music system and the iPhone. Sales and profits began to zoom.[30] In the years since he had left Apple, Jobs had gained management skills and experience, but he was also smart enough to bring in other skilled managers. For instance, Timothy D. Cook, hired by Jobs in 1998, has been referred to as "the story behind the story." Jobs provides vision and entrepreneurial spirit, but Cook, as chief operating officer and second-in-command, makes sure things run smoothly behind the scenes.[31] Apple is hot right now, but it faces the problems all mature organizations deal with. All mature organizations have to go through periods of revitalization or they will decline, as shown in the last stage of Exhibit 12.3.

Summary. Eighty-four percent of businesses that make it past the first year still fail within five years because they can't make the transition from the entrepreneurial stage.[32] The transitions become even more difficult as organizations progress through future stages of the life cycle. Organizations that do not successfully resolve the problems associated with these transitions are restricted in their growth and may even fail. From within an organization, the life cycle crises are very real. For example, some former employees as well as Wall Street analysts worry that Amazon CEO Jeff Bezos's leadership style has the company stuck at early stages of the life cycle.

Few people who know him deny that Jeff Bezos is brilliant. One former manager calls the Amazon.com founder and CEO "the smartest, best entrepreneur I've ever met in my life." Others talk about his intelligence, his enthusiasm, and his ability to lead and inspire others.

Amazon

Yet most of those people also admit that Bezos has a hard time delegating. He wants to be involved in every detail of the business and every decision that's made. One top technologist who worked with Amazon said Bezos wanted to have a say in everything, even if it was just changing the color of a tab on the website. The CEO's inability to delegate might be responsible for a high rate of manager turnover at the company. Bezos knew he needed to bring in experienced managers as Amazon grew, because he had little interest in dealing with issues such as human resources, legal, and accounting. However, his reluctance to share power doesn't sit well with many managers. When it comes to operations, Bezos seems to have a particularly hard time giving up control. Joseph Galli, hired as president and chief operations officer in 1999, lasted only thirteen months. Since then, Bezos himself has retained the title of president, CEO, and chairman, and the company has made do without a chief operations officer.

Bezos typically laughs at criticisms of his management style and points out that Amazon continues to grow and succeed. The CEO says he believes in focusing relentlessly on the customer, but observers say someone also needs to be focused on running the business.[33] ■

Can Amazon.com continue to progress successfully through the stages of the life cycle, or will Jeff Bezos's inability to delegate keep it stuck in a prolonged adolescence? Amazon.com might be considered as entering the formalization stage. By continuing to run Amazon like a young, entrepreneurial firm, Bezos might be hurting the company's ability to keep good managers and grow successfully.

Organizational Characteristics during the Life Cycle

As organizations evolve through the four stages of the life cycle, changes take place in structure, control systems, innovation, and goals. The organizational characteristics associated with each stage are summarized in Exhibit 12.4.

Entrepreneurial. Initially, the organization is small, nonbureaucratic, and a one-person show. The top manager provides the structure and control system. Organizational energy is devoted to survival and the production of a single product or service.

Collectivity. This is the organization's youth. Growth is rapid, and employees are excited and committed to the organization's mission. The structure is still mostly informal, although some procedures are emerging. Strong charismatic leaders like Jeff Bezos at Amazon.com provide direction and goals for the organization. Continued growth is a major goal.

Formalization. At this point, the organization is entering midlife. Bureaucratic characteristics emerge. The organization adds staff support groups, formalizes procedures, and establishes a clear hierarchy and division of labor. At the formalization

EXHIBIT 12.4
Organization
Characteristics during
Four Stages of Life Cycle

Characteristic	1. Entrepreneurial Nonbureaucratic	2. Collectivity Prebureaucratic	3. Formalization Bureaucratic	4. Elaboration Very Bureaucratic
Structure	Informal, one-person show	Mostly informal, some procedures	Formal procedures, division of labor, new specialties added	Teamwork within bureaucracy, small-company thinking
Products or services	Single product or service	Major product or service, with variations	Line of products or services	Multiple product or service lines
Reward and control systems	Personal, paternalistic	Personal, contribution to success	Impersonal, formalized systems	Extensive, tailored to product and department
Innovation	By owner-manager	By employees and managers	By separate innovation group	By institutionalized R&D department
Goal	Survival	Growth	Internal stability, market expansion	Reputation, complete organization
Top management style	Individualistic, entrepreneurial	Charismatic, direction-giving	Delegation with control	Team approach, attack bureaucracy

Source: Adapted from Larry E. Greiner, "Evolution and Revolution as Organizations Grow," *Harvard Business Review* 50 (July–August 1972), 37–46; G. L. Lippitt and W. H. Schmidt, "Crises in a Developing Organization," *Harvard Business Review* 45 (November–December 1967), 102–112; B. R. Scott, "The Industrial State: Old Myths and New Realities," *Harvard Business Review* 51 (March–April 1973), 133–148; and Robert E. Quinn and Kim Cameron, "Organizational Life Cycles and Shifting Criteria of Effectiveness," *Management Science* 29 (1983), 33–51.

stage, organizations may also develop complementary products to offer a complete product line. Innovation may be achieved by establishing a separate research and development (R&D) department. Major goals are internal stability and market expansion. Top management delegates, but it also implements formal control systems. This is the stage where Jeff Bezos of Amazon is having trouble managing the transition because he doesn't want to give up personal control.

Elaboration. The mature organization is large and bureaucratic, with extensive control systems, rules, and procedures. Organization managers attempt to develop a team orientation within the bureaucracy to prevent further bureaucratization. Top managers are concerned with establishing a complete organization. Organizational stature and reputation are important. Innovation is institutionalized through an R&D department. Management may attack the bureaucracy and streamline it.

Summary. Growing organizations move through stages of a life cycle, and each stage is associated with specific characteristics of structure, control systems, goals, and innovation. The life cycle phenomenon is a powerful concept used for understanding problems facing organizations and how managers can respond in a positive way to move an organization to the next stage.

ORGANIZATIONAL SIZE, BUREAUCRACY, AND CONTROL

As organizations progress through the life cycle, they usually take on bureaucratic characteristics as they grow larger and more complex. The systematic study of bureaucracy was launched by Max Weber, a sociologist who studied government organizations in Europe and developed a framework of administrative characteristics that would make large organizations rational and efficient.[34] Weber wanted to understand how organizations could be designed to play a positive role in the larger society.

What Is Bureaucracy?

Although Weber perceived **bureaucracy** as a threat to basic personal liberties, he also recognized it as the most efficient possible system of organizing. He predicted the triumph of bureaucracy because of its ability to ensure more efficient functioning of organizations in both business and government settings. Weber identified a set of organizational characteristics, listed in Exhibit 12.5, that could be found in successful bureaucratic organizations.

Rules and standard procedures enabled organizational activities to be performed in a predictable, routine manner. Specialized duties meant that each employee had a clear task to perform. Hierarchy of authority provided a sensible mechanism for supervision

EXHIBIT 12.5
Weber's Dimensions of Bureaucracy

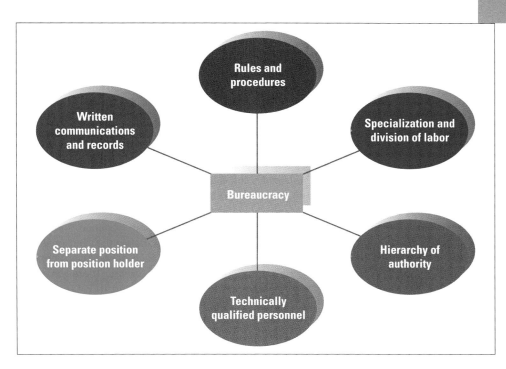

and control. Technical competence was the basis by which people were hired rather than friendship, family ties, and favoritism. The separation of the position from the position holder meant that individuals did not own or have an inherent right to the job, which promoted efficiency. Written records provided an organizational memory and continuity over time.

Although bureaucratic characteristics carried to an extreme are widely criticized today, the rational control introduced by Weber was a significant idea and a new form of organization. Bureaucracy provided many advantages over organization forms based on favoritism, social status, family connections, or graft. Consider the situation in many Latin American countries, where graft, corruption, and nepotism are rampant throughout government and business institutions. In Brazil, for example, government officials have been accused of paying bribes to legislators for their support, favoring contractors who made clandestine campaign contributions, and using their influence to gain jobs or favorable circumstances for family members.[35] In China, the tradition of giving government posts to relatives is still widespread, but China's emerging class of educated people doesn't like seeing the best jobs going to children and other relatives of officials.[36] The United States, as well, sees its share of corruption, as evidenced by the recent case of Illinois Governor Rod Blagojevich, accused of a wide-ranging corruption that included trying to sell the Senate seat vacated by President Barack Obama.[37] By comparison with these examples, the logical and rational form of organization described by Weber allows work to be conducted fairly, efficiently, and according to established rules.

A recent study of empirical organization research over four decades confirms the validity and persistence of Weber's model of bureaucracy, showing positive relationships among elements such as specialization, formalization, and standardization, as shown in Exhibit 12.5.[38] Bureaucratic characteristics can have a positive effect for many large organizations. Consider United Parcel Service (UPS), one of today's most efficient large organizations.

IN PRACTICE

United Parcel Service (UPS)

UPS, sometimes called *Big Brown* for the color of delivery trucks and employee uniforms, is the largest package-distribution company in the world, delivering over 15 million packages a day, and a global leader in supply chain, logistics, and information services. The company operates in more than 200 countries and territories around the world.

How did UPS become so successful? Many efficiencies were realized through adoption of the bureaucratic model of organization. UPS operates according to a mountain of rules and regulations. It teaches drivers an astounding 340 precise steps to correctly deliver a package. For example, it tells them how to load their trucks, how to fasten their seat belts, how to step off the truck, how to walk, and how to carry their keys. Strict dress codes are enforced—clean uniforms (called *browns*) every day, black or brown polished shoes with nonslip soles, no shirt unbuttoned below the first button, no hair below the shirt collar, no beards, no tattoos visible during deliveries, and so on. Before each shift, drivers conduct a "Z-scan," a Z-shaped inspection of the sides and front of their vehicles. There are safety rules for drivers, loaders, clerks, and managers. Employees are asked to clean off their desks at the end of each day so they can start fresh the next morning. Managers are given copies of policy books with the expectation that they will use them regularly, and memos on various policies and rules circulate by the hundreds every day.

Despite the strict rules and numerous policies, employees are satisfied and UPS has a high employee retention rate. Employees are treated well and paid well, and the company has maintained a sense of equality and fairness. Everyone is on a first-name basis. The policy book states, "A leader does not have to remind others of his authority by use of a title. Knowledge, performance, and capacity should be adequate evidence of position and leadership." Technical qualification, not favoritism, is the criterion for hiring and promotion. Top executives started at the bottom—former CEO James Kelly began his career as a temporary holiday-rush driver, and the recently retired CEO Michael Eskew started off at UPS by redesigning a parking lot to accommodate more trucks. The emphasis on equality, fairness, and a promote-from-within mentality inspires loyalty and commitment throughout the ranks.[39] ∎

UPS illustrates how bureaucratic characteristics increase with large size. UPS is so productive and dependable that it dominates the small package delivery market. As it expands and transitions into a global, knowledge-based logistics business, UPS managers may need to find effective ways to reduce the bureaucracy. New technology and new services place more demands on workers, who may need more flexibility and autonomy to perform well. Now, let's look at some specific ways size affects organization structure and control.

Size and Structural Control

In the field of organization theory, organization size has been described as an important variable that influences structural design and methods of control. Should an organization become more bureaucratic as it grows larger? In what size organizations are bureaucratic characteristics most appropriate? More than 100 studies have attempted to answer these questions.[40] Most of these studies indicate that large organizations are different from small organizations along several dimensions of bureaucratic structure, including formalization, centralization, and personnel ratios.

Formalization and Centralization. Formalization, as described in Chapter 1, refers to rules, procedures, and written documentation, such as policy manuals and job descriptions, that prescribe the rights and duties of employees.[41] The evidence supports the conclusion that large organizations are more formalized, as at UPS. The reason is that large organizations rely on rules, procedures, and paperwork to achieve standardization and control across their large numbers of employees and departments, whereas top managers can use personal observation to control a small organization.[42] For example, a locally-owned coffee shop in a small town doesn't need the detailed manuals, policies, and procedures that Starbucks uses to standardize and control its operations around the world.

Centralization refers to the level of hierarchy with authority to make decisions. In centralized organizations, decisions tend to be made at the top. In decentralized organizations, similar decisions would be made at a lower level.

Decentralization represents a paradox because, in the perfect bureaucracy, all decisions would be made by the top administrator, who would have perfect control. However, as an organization grows larger and has more people and departments, decisions cannot be passed to the top because senior managers would be overloaded. Thus, the research on organization size indicates that larger organizations permit greater decentralization.[43] In small start-up organizations, on the other

Briefcase

As an organization manager, keep this guideline in mind:

As the organization grows, provide greater formalization to achieve standardization and control. Guard against excessive overhead by keeping administrative, clerical, and support staff costs low.

hand, the founder or top executive can effectively be involved in every decision, large and small.

Personnel Ratios. Another characteristic of bureaucracy relates to **personnel ratios** for administrative, clerical, and professional support staff. The most frequently studied ratio is the administrative ratio.[44] Two patterns have emerged. The first is that the ratio of top administration to total employees is actually smaller in large organizations,[45] indicating that organizations experience administrative economies as they grow larger. The second pattern concerns clerical and professional support staff ratios.[46] These groups tend to *increase* in proportion to organization size. The clerical ratio increases because of the greater communication and reporting requirements needed as organizations grow larger. The professional staff ratio increases because of the greater need for specialized skills in larger, complex organizations.

Exhibit 12.6 illustrates administrative and support ratios for small and large organizations. As organizations increase in size, the administrative ratio declines and the ratios for other support groups increase.[47] The net effect for direct workers is that they decline as a percentage of total employees. In summary, whereas top administrators do not make up a disproportionate number of employees in large organizations, the idea that proportionately greater overhead is required in large organizations is supported. Although large organizations reduced overhead during

EXHIBIT 12.6
Percentage of
Personnel Allocated
to Administrative and
Support Activities

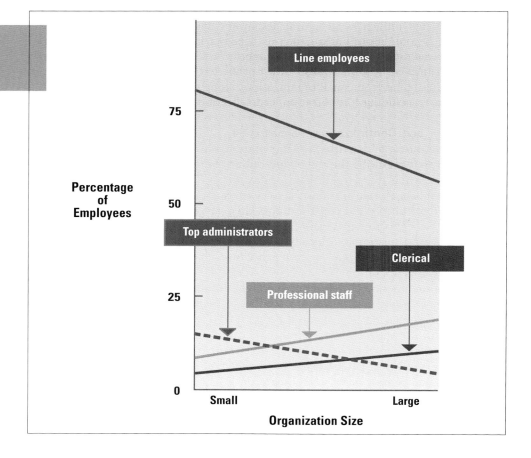

the difficult economic years of the 1980s, overhead costs for many American corporations began creeping back up again as revenues soared during the late 1990s.[48] With the declining U.S. economy, many companies have again been struggling to cut overhead costs. Keeping costs for administrative, clerical, and professional support staff low represents an ongoing challenge for large organizations.

BUREAUCRACY IN A CHANGING WORLD

Weber's prediction of the triumph of bureaucracy proved accurate. Bureaucratic characteristics have many advantages and have worked extremely well for many of the needs of the industrial age.[49] By establishing a hierarchy of authority and specific rules and procedures, bureaucracy provided an effective way to bring order to large groups of people and minimize abuses of power. Impersonal relationships based on roles rather than people reduced the favoritism and nepotism characteristic of many preindustrial organizations. Bureaucracy also provided for systematic and rational ways to organize and manage tasks too complex to be understood and handled by a few individuals, thus greatly improving the efficiency and effectiveness of large organizations.

Today's world is in constant flux, however, and the machinelike bureaucratic system of the industrial age no longer works so well as organizations face new challenges and need to respond quickly. Consider Microsoft, which some current and former employees complain has become slow and muscle-bound by heavy bureaucracy in recent years. Almost every significant action requires a lawyer's signature, they say, and getting approval for even routine matters can take weeks. One employee left the company because he was tired of being inundated with paperwork. "The smallest issue would balloon into a nightmare of a thousand e-mails," he says.[50] Managers are trying to find ways to cut the bureaucracy so people can do their jobs more effectively and help Microsoft stay competitive against nimbler rivals such as Google. Like Microsoft, many organizations are fighting against increasing formalization and professional staff ratios. ConAgra Foods, for instance, implemented an initiative called RoadMap, which brings together people from all across the company to simplify and streamline processes for reporting, planning, performance management, and so forth. The simplified processes cut overhead costs as well as improved the quality and speed of communication and decision making.[51]

The problems caused by over-bureaucratization are evident in the inefficiencies of some large U.S. government organizations. Some agencies have so many clerical staff members and confusing job titles that no one is really sure who does what. Richard Cavanagh, once an aide to President Jimmy Carter, reports his favorite federal title as the "administrative assistant to the assistant administrator for administration of the General Services Administration."[52] Some critics have blamed government bureaucracy for intelligence, communication, and accountability failures related to the 2001 terrorist attacks, the Columbia space shuttle disaster, the abuses at Abu Ghraib prison, and a slow response to the 2005 Hurricane Katrina devastation. "Every time you add a layer of bureaucracy, you delay the movement of information up the chain of command . . . And you dilute the information because at each step some details are taken out," says Richard A. Posner, a federal appeals court judge who has written a book on intelligence reform.[53] Many business organizations, too, need to reduce formalization and bureaucracy. Narrowly defined job descriptions and excessive rules, for example, tend to limit the creativity, flexibility, and rapid response needed in today's knowledge-based organizations.

Organizing Temporary Systems

How can organizations overcome the problems of bureaucracy in rapidly changing environments? Some are implementing innovative structural solutions. One structural concept is to use temporary systems or structures to respond to an emergency or crisis situation. This approach is often used by organizations such as police and fire departments or other emergency management agencies to maintain the efficiency and control benefits of bureaucracy yet prevent the problem of slow response.[54] The approach is being adapted by other types of organizations to help them respond quickly to new opportunities, unforeseen competitive threats, or organizational crises.

The basic idea is that the organization can glide smoothly between a highly formalized, hierarchical structure that is effective during times of stability and a more flexible, loosely structured one needed to respond well to unexpected and demanding environmental conditions. The hierarchical side with its rules, procedures, and chain of command helps maintain control and ensure adherence to rules that have been developed and tested over many years to cope with well-understood problems and situations. However, during times of high uncertainty, the most effective structure is one that loosens the lines of command and enables people to work across departmental and hierarchical lines to anticipate, avoid, and solve unique problems within the context of a clearly understood mission and guidelines. The approach can be seen in action at the Salvation Army, which has been called "the most effective organization in the world."

IN PRACTICE

Salvation Army

The Salvation Army provides day-to-day assistance to the homeless and economically disadvantaged. In addition, the organization rushes in whenever there is a major disaster—whether it be a tornado, flood, hurricane, airplane crash, or terrorist attack—to network with other agencies to provide disaster relief. The Army's management realizes that emergencies demand high flexibility. At the same time, the organization must have a high level of control and accountability to ensure its continued existence and meet its day-to-day responsibilities. As a former national commander puts it, "We have to have it both ways. We can't choose to be flexible and reckless or to be accountable and responsive . . . We have to be several different kinds of organization at the same time."

In the early emergency moments of a crisis, the Salvation Army deploys a temporary organization that has its own command structure. People need to have a clear sense of who's in charge to prevent the rapid response demands from degenerating into chaos. For example, if the Army responds to a flood in Tennessee or a tornado in Oklahoma, manuals clearly specify in advance who is responsible for talking to the media, who is in charge of supply inventories, who liaises with other agencies, and so forth. This model for the temporary organization keeps the Salvation Army responsive and consistent. However, in the later recovery and rebuilding phases of a crisis, supervisors frequently give people general guidelines and allow them to improvise the best solutions. There isn't time for supervisors to review and sign off on every decision that needs to be made to get families and communities reestablished.

Thus, the Salvation Army actually has people simultaneously working in all different types of structures, from traditional vertical command structures, to horizontal teams, to a sort of network form that relies on collaboration with other agencies. Operating in such a fluid way enables the organization to accomplish amazing results. In one year, the Army assisted more than 2.3 million people caught in disasters in the United States, in addition to many more served by regular day-to-day programs. It has been recognized as a leader in putting money to maximal use, meaning donors are willing to give because they trust the organization to be responsible and accountable at the same time it is flexible and innovative in meeting human needs.[55] ■

Other Approaches to Busting Bureaucracy

Organizations are taking a number of other, less dramatic steps to reduce bureaucracy. Many are cutting layers of the hierarchy, keeping headquarters staff small, and giving lower-level workers greater freedom to make decisions rather than burdening them with excessive rules and regulations. Consider the following examples:

- Executives at Sun Microsystems found that after a period of rapid growth, the organization had become too top-heavy, with too many hierarchical layers impeding communication and slowing decision making. They reorganized to a flatter, more streamlined organization, with typically no more than three or four levels between any employee and the CEO.[56]
- Centex Corporation, which has annual revenues of about $3.8 billion, is run from a modest headquarters in Dallas by a staff of less than 100. Centex decentralizes authority and responsibility to the operating divisions.[57] The point is to not overload headquarters with lawyers, accountants, and financial analysts who inhibit the flexibility and autonomy of divisions.
- At the London-based pharmaceuticals company GlaxoSmithKline PLC, frontline scientists, not top executives or a research committee, set priorities and allocate resources for drugs in development. The shift in who decides which drug research projects to fund has brought an entrepreneurial spirit to the giant firm similar to that of a small biotechnology company.[58]

Another attack on bureaucracy is from the increasing professionalism of employees. *Professionalism* is defined as the length of formal training and experience of employees. More employees need college degrees, MBAs, and other professional degrees to work as attorneys, researchers, or doctors at Nortel, Zurich Financial Services, or GlaxoSmithKline. In addition, Internet-based companies may be staffed entirely by well-educated knowledge workers. Studies of professionals show that formalization is not needed because professional training regularizes a high standard of behavior for employees, which acts as a substitute for bureaucracy.[59] Companies enhance this trend when they provide ongoing training for *all* employees, from the front office to the shop floor, in a push for continuous individual and organizational learning. Increased training substitutes for bureaucratic rules and procedures that can constrain the creativity of employees in solving problems, in addition to enhancing individual and organizational capability.

A form of organization called the *professional partnership* has emerged that is made up completely of professionals.[60] These organizations include accounting firms, medical practices, law firms, and consulting firms. The general finding concerning professional partnerships is that branches have substantial autonomy and decentralized authority to make necessary decisions. They work with a consensus orientation rather than the top-down direction typical of traditional business and government organizations. Thus, the trend of increasing professionalism combined with rapidly changing environments is leading to less bureaucracy in corporate North America.

BUREAUCRACY VERSUS OTHER FORMS OF CONTROL

Even though many organizations are trying to reduce bureaucracy and streamline rules and procedures that constrain employees, every organization needs systems for guiding and controlling the organization. Employees may have more freedom in today's companies, but control is still a major responsibility of management.

Managers at the top and middle levels of an organization can choose among three overall control strategies. These strategies come from a framework for organizational control proposed by William Ouchi of the University of California at Los Angeles. Ouchi suggested three control strategies that organizations could adopt—bureaucratic, market, and clan.[61] Each form of control uses different types of information. However, all three types may appear simultaneously in an organization. The requirements for each control strategy are given in Exhibit 12.7.

Bureaucratic Control

Bureaucratic control is the use of rules, policies, hierarchy of authority, written documentation, standardization, and other bureaucratic mechanisms to standardize behavior and assess performance. Bureaucratic control uses the bureaucratic characteristics defined by Weber and illustrated in the UPS case. The primary purpose of bureaucratic rules and procedures is to standardize and control employee behavior.

Recall that as organizations progress through the life cycle and grow larger, they become more formalized and standardized. Within a large organization, thousands of work behaviors and information exchanges take place both vertically and horizontally. Rules and policies evolve through a process of trial and error to regulate these behaviors. Some degree of bureaucratic control is used in virtually every organization. Rules, regulations, and directives contain information about a range of behaviors.

To make bureaucratic control work, managers must have the authority to maintain control over the organization. Weber argued that legitimate, rational authority granted to managers was preferred over other types of control (e.g., favoritism or payoffs) as the basis for organizational decisions and activities. Within the larger society, however, Weber identified three types of authority that could explain the creation and control of a large organization.[62]

Rational-legal authority is based on employees' belief in the legality of rules and the right of those elevated to positions of authority to issue commands. Rational-legal authority is the basis for both creation and control of most government orga-

EXHIBIT 12.7
Three Organizational
Control Strategies

Type	Requirements
Bureaucracy	Rules, standards, hierarchy, legitimate authority
Market	Prices, competition, exchange relationship
Clan	Tradition, shared values and beliefs, trust

Source: Based on William G. Ouchi, "A Conceptual Framework for the Design of Organizational Control Mechanisms," *Management Science* 25 (1979), 833–848.

nizations and is the most common base of control in organizations worldwide. **Traditional authority** is the belief in traditions and in the legitimacy of the status of people exercising authority through those traditions. Traditional authority is the basis for control for monarchies, churches, and some organizations in Latin America and the Persian Gulf. **Charismatic authority** is based on devotion to the exemplary character or to the heroism of an individual person and the order defined by him or her. Revolutionary military organizations are often based on the leader's charisma, as are North American organizations led by charismatic individuals such as Steve Jobs of Apple, Tom Anderson of MySpace, or Oprah Winfrey of Harpo Productions. The organization reflects the personality and values of the leader.

More than one type of authority—such as long tradition and the leader's special charisma—may exist in organizations, but rational-legal authority is the most widely used form to govern internal work activities and decision making, particularly in large organizations.

Market Control

Market control occurs when price competition is used to evaluate the output and productivity of an organization or its major departments and divisions. The idea of market control originated in economics.[63] A dollar price is an efficient form of control, because managers can compare prices and profits to evaluate the efficiency of their corporation. Top managers nearly always use the price mechanism to evaluate performance in their corporations. Corporate sales and costs are summarized in a profit-and-loss statement that can be compared against performance in previous years or with that of other corporations.

The use of market control requires that outputs be sufficiently explicit for a price to be assigned and that competition exist. Without competition, the price does not accurately reflect internal efficiency. Even some government and traditionally nonprofit organizations are turning to market control. For example, the U.S. Federal Aviation Administration took bids to operate its payroll computers. The Department of Agriculture beat out IBM and two other private companies to win the bid.[64] The city of Indianapolis requires all its departments to bid against private companies. When the transportation department was underbid by a private company on a contract to fill potholes, the city's union workers made a counterproposal that involved eliminating most of the department's middle managers and reengineering union jobs to save money. Eighteen supervisors were laid off, costs were cut by 25 percent, and the department won the bid.[65]

Market control was once used primarily at the level of the entire organization, but it is increasingly used in product divisions or individual departments. Profit centers are self-contained product divisions, such as those described in Chapter 2. Each division contains resource inputs needed to produce a product. Each division can be evaluated on the basis of profit or loss compared with other divisions. Asea Brown Boveri (ABB), a multinational electrical contractor and manufacturer of electrical equipment, includes three different types of profit centers, all operating according to their own bottom line and all interacting through buying and selling with one another and with outside customers.[66] The network organization, also described in Chapter 2, illustrates market control as well. Different companies compete on price to provide the functions and services required by the hub organization. The organization typically contracts with the company that offers the best price and value.

Clan Control

Clan control is the use of social characteristics, such as shared values, commitment, traditions, and beliefs, to control behavior. Organizations that use clan control have strong cultures that emphasize shared values and trust among employees.[67] Clan control is important when ambiguity and uncertainty are high. High uncertainty means the organization cannot put a price on its services, and things change so fast that rules and regulations are not able to specify every correct behavior. Under clan control, people may be hired because they are committed to the organization's purpose, such as in a religious organization or an organization focused on a social mission. New employees are typically subjected to a long period of socialization to gain acceptance by colleagues. There is strong pressure to conform to group norms, which govern a wide range of employee behaviors. Managers act primarily as mentors, role models, and agents for transmitting values.[68]

ASSESS YOUR ANSWER

2 **A manager should emphasize shared values, trust, and commitment to the organization's mission as the primary means of controlling employee behavior.**

ANSWER: *Agree or disagree.* Clan control, which relies on culture, trust, commitment, and shared values and traditions, can be highly effective and is particularly useful in departments or organizations experiencing high uncertainty or environmental turbulence. However, other forms of control, such as bureaucratic or market control, are also effective and appropriate under the right circumstances.

Traditional control mechanisms based on strict rules and close supervision are ineffective for controlling behavior in conditions of high uncertainty and rapid change.[69] In addition, the growing use of computer networks and the Internet, which often leads to a democratic spread of information throughout the organization, is influencing companies to depend less on bureaucratic control and more on shared values that guide individual actions for the corporate good.[70] Clan control is most often used in small, informal organizations where people are strongly committed to the organization's purpose, or in certain departments or divisions of larger organizations. One company that has succeeded with clan control even as it grew large is Southwest Airlines.

IN PRACTICE

Southwest Airlines

In a tough environment of exorbitant fuel costs and declining business, Southwest was one of the few airlines that didn't ask for wage and benefit concessions from employees. At Southwest, people are viewed as the airline's "greatest competitive weapon," says CEO Gary Kelly. Employees have sometimes voluntarily given up vacation pay or contributed in other ways to help the airline pay for rising costs. When founder and former CEO Herb Kelleher asked employees several years ago to find a way to help the company save $5 a day, one employee began taking the stairs instead of the elevator to save electricity. Loyalty, commitment, and

peer pressure are strong components of control at Southwest Airlines, where a "we're all family" culture spurs employees to give their best and make sure others do too.

New hires are selected carefully to fit in with the culture, and each employee goes through a long period of socialization and training. The peer pressure to work hard and help the company cut costs and boost productivity is powerful. Employees routinely challenge each other on matters such as questionable sick-day calls or overuse of office supplies. People frequently go above and beyond the call of duty. Flight attendants who are traveling off-duty pitch in to help clean planes. Pilots help ramp agents load bags to keep flights on time.

The strong culture and clan control helped Southwest grow into the world's third largest airline and remain profitable for thirty-five consecutive years. In 2007, Southwest was tops among the ten biggest carriers in on-time arrivals, had the fewest customer complaints, and posted the biggest profits. However, as the company grows larger and faces new competitive pressures, the culture is showing signs of strain. Revenues have slowed, costs have mounted, new low-cost carriers are snatching business, and larger rivals have grown leaner and more competitive. Southwest has lost its underdog status and the motivation it provided for employees to work hard and conquer new territory. Labor negotiations with unions have been significantly less amicable than in the past as well.[71] ■

Despite these tensions, clan control still works at Southwest. Leaders are trying to reinforce the family-like culture to ensure that heavy bureaucratic controls are not needed. Southwest's story illustrates that large size increases the demands on managers to maintain strong cultural values that support this type of control. Today's companies that are trying to become learning organizations often use clan control or *self-control* rather than relying on rules and regulations. Self-control is similar to clan control, but whereas clan control is a function of being socialized into a group, self-control stems from individual values, goals, and standards. The organization attempts to induce a change such that individual employees' own internal values and work preferences are brought in line with the organization's values and goals.[72] With self-control, employees generally set their own goals and monitor their own performance, yet companies relying on self-control need strong leaders who can clarify boundaries within which people exercise their own knowledge and discretion.

Clan control or self-control may also be used in some departments, such as strategic planning, where uncertainty is high and performance is difficult to measure. Managers of departments that rely on these informal control mechanisms must not assume that the absence of written, bureaucratic control means no control is present. Clan control is invisible yet very powerful. One study found that the actions of employees were controlled even more powerfully and completely with clan control than with a bureaucratic hierarchy.[73] When clan control works, bureaucratic control is not needed.

ORGANIZATIONAL DECLINE AND DOWNSIZING

Earlier in the chapter, we discussed the organizational life cycle, which suggests that organizations are born, grow older, and eventually die. Size can become a burden for many organizations. For example, General Motors is collapsing under its own weight. Not only is the company laboring under a financial burden of huge pension and health care obligations, but its cumbersome bureaucracy has made it hard for GM to connect with the needs of consumers. Regional managers say their ideas and suggestions for product changes or advertising approaches never reach decision makers or fall on deaf ears.[74] Every organization goes through periods of temporary decline. Even the storied General Electric is facing problems related to huge size, which have been compounded by the global financial crisis. By the time GE decided to sell off its private-label credit card business and the lightbulb division, for instance, no one was buying.[75] In addition, a reality in today's environment is that for some companies, continual growth and expansion may not be possible.

All around, we see evidence that some organizations have stopped growing, and many are declining. Huge financial services firms, such as Lehman Brothers and Bear Stearns, collapsed partly as a result of unfettered growth and ineffective control. Starbucks had to bring its period of rampant expansion to an end when it became clear that it was cannibalizing sales and threatening the chain's success. In mid-2008, Starbucks announced that it would close 500 of its U.S. stores.[76] Local governments have been forced to close schools and lay off teachers as tax revenues have declined. Many big organizations, including Siemens, Sprint, American Airlines, Nissan, Yahoo!, and even the American Red Cross, have had significant job cuts in recent years.

In this section, we examine the causes and stages of organizational decline and then discuss how leaders can effectively manage the downsizing that is a reality in today's companies.

Definition and Causes

The term **organizational decline** is used to define a condition in which a substantial, absolute decrease in an organization's resource base occurs over time.[77] Organizational decline is often associated with environmental decline in the sense that an organizational domain experiences either a reduction in size (such as shrinkage in customer demand or erosion of a city's tax base) or a reduction in shape (such as a shift in customer demand). In general, three factors are considered to cause organizational decline.

1. *Organizational atrophy.* Atrophy occurs when organizations grow older and become inefficient and overly bureaucratized. The organization's ability to adapt to its environment deteriorates. Often, atrophy follows a long period of success, because an organization takes success for granted, becomes attached to practices and structures that worked in the past, and fails to adapt to changes in the environment.[78] Some warning signals for organizational atrophy include excess administrative and support staff, cumbersome administrative procedures, lack of effective communication and coordination, and outdated organizational structure.[79]

2. *Vulnerability.* Vulnerability reflects an organization's strategic inability to prosper in its environment. This often happens to small organizations that are not yet fully established. They are vulnerable to shifts in consumer tastes or in the economic health of the larger community. Small e-commerce companies that had not yet become established were the first to go out of business when the technology sector began to decline. Some organizations are vulnerable because they are unable to define the correct strategy to fit the environment. Vulnerable organizations typically need to redefine their environmental domain to enter new industries or markets.

3. *Environmental decline or competition.* Environmental decline refers to reduced energy and resources available to support an organization. When the environment has less capacity to support organizations, the organization has to either scale

down operations or shift to another domain.[80] This is the problem managers face at the American Red Cross. The 126-year-old organization has struggled with fund-raising for several years and now finds itself in a position of spending more than it is bringing in. Steep drops in the stock market, rising prices, and general pessimism about the U.S. economy are creating a tough fund-raising environment for all nonprofits.[81] New competition can also be a problem, especially for small organizations. Consider what's happening to U.S. toolmakers, the companies that make the dies, molds, jigs, fixtures, and gauges used on factory floors to manufacture everything from car doors to laser-guided bombs. Hundreds of these companies—including one of only two firms in the United States capable of making tools used to build components of stealth aircraft—have gone out of business in recent years, unable to compete with the super-low prices their counterparts in China are offering. As more and more toolmakers go out of business, the National Tooling and Machining Association has urged Congress to pass legislation that would "level the playing field" and enable these small firms to stay competitive with Chinese companies.[82]

A Model of Decline Stages

Based on an extensive review of organizational decline research, a model of decline stages has been proposed and is summarized in Exhibit 12.8. This model suggests that decline, if not managed properly, can move through five stages resulting in organizational dissolution.[83]

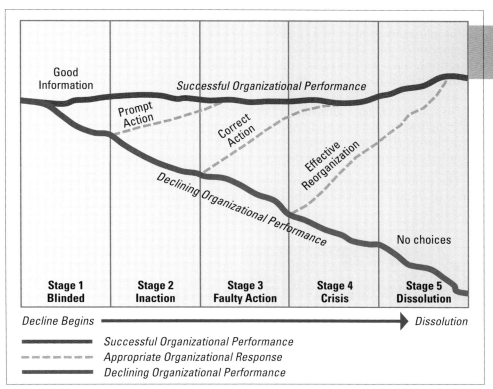

EXHIBIT 12.8
Stages of Decline and the Widening Performance Gap

Source: *American Science Quarterly.* "Decline in Organizations: A Literature Integration and Extension," by William Weitzel and Ellen Jonsson, vol. 34, pp. 99–109, March 1989. Reprinted by permission.

1. *Blinded stage.* The first stage of decline is the internal and external change that threatens long-term survival and may require the organization to tighten up. The organization may have excess personnel, cumbersome procedures, or lack of harmony with customers. Leaders often miss the signals of decline at this point, and the solution is to develop effective scanning and control systems that indicate when something is wrong. With timely information, alert executives can bring the organization back to top performance.

2. *Inaction stage.* The second stage of decline is called *inaction* in which denial occurs despite signs of deteriorating performance. Leaders may try to persuade employees that all is well. "Creative accounting" may make things look fine during this period. The solution is for leaders to acknowledge decline and take prompt action to realign the organization with the environment. Leadership actions may include new problem-solving approaches, increasing decision-making participation, and encouraging expression of dissatisfaction to learn what is wrong.

3. *Faulty action stage.* In the third stage, the organization is facing serious problems, and indicators of poor performance cannot be ignored. Failure to adjust to the declining spiral at this point can lead to organizational failure. Leaders are forced by severe circumstances to consider major changes. Actions may involve retrenchment, including downsizing personnel. Leaders should reduce employee uncertainty by clarifying values and providing information. A major mistake at this stage decreases the organization's chance for a turnaround.

4. *Crisis stage.* In the fourth stage, the organization still has not been able to deal with decline effectively and is facing a panic. The organization may experience chaos, efforts to go back to basics, sharp changes, and anger. It is best for managers to prevent a stage-4 crisis; at this stage, the only solution is major reorganization. The social fabric of the organization is eroding, and dramatic actions, such as replacing top administrators and revolutionary changes in structure, strategy, and culture, are necessary. Workforce downsizing may be severe.

5. *Dissolution stage.* This stage of decline is irreversible. The organization is suffering loss of markets and reputation, the loss of its best personnel, and capital depletion. The only available strategy is to close down the organization in an orderly fashion and reduce the separation trauma of employees.

The following example shows how good managers take action to reverse the course of decline and position the organization for future success.

Herman Miller

It was late 2001 when Brian Walker confronted Herman Miller CEO Michael Volkema and the rest of the top executive team. Walker (who was then president of Herman Miller North America and today serves as CEO of the company) told the team they needed to stop hoping for a quick turnaround and start planning for brutal cutbacks to help the company survive. After years of success, the maker of office furniture such as the stylish, ergonomically engineered Aeron chair was suffering "an industry heart attack," with sales dropping drastically after the collapse of the dot-com boom.

Managers noticed the decline, but they kept thinking it would be short-lived. Walker, though, believed it was just the beginning of a long and painful downturn. He was right; by 2003, the company's business had dropped 45 percent. Fortunately, the executive team had listened and taken action. The plan involved some painful decisions and some risky ones. First, the team cut 4,500 jobs—nearly 38 percent of the workforce, sold off more than a million square feet of prime real estate, and slashed some promising new businesses, such as a ready-to-assemble line of furniture sold over the Internet. However, managers knew that cutting back wasn't enough to ensure that the company would survive over the long term. Looking at the industry environment, the economy, and international competition, the team believed volatility in their business would increase rather than decrease in the future. Therefore, they made a risky decision to invest millions in research and development of highly innovative ideas that might not pay off for years—if ever.

The decisions about what to cut and what to fund were made thoughtfully after much debate and discussion. With the current economic environment, Herman Miller is still facing challenges, but the most recent fiscal year's profits exceeded forecasts and new products, such as a new-generation cubicle that promises a sense of privacy with openness, are showing promise. The company began hiring more workers in mid-2008, and a $1,595 "environmentally friendly" executive chair named the Embody was touted by *Fortune* magazine as "the new throne of the techie." Moreover, the company is building business by creating innovative hospital furniture, such as a chair designed to help patients recovering from surgery.[84] ■

Properly managing organizational decline is necessary if an organization is to avoid dissolution. Leaders have a responsibility to detect the signs of decline, acknowledge them, implement necessary action, and reverse course. Some of the most difficult decisions pertain to **downsizing**, which refers to intentionally reducing the size of a company's workforce.

Downsizing Implementation

The economic downturn has made downsizing a common practice in America's corporations. In addition, downsizing is a part of many change initiatives in today's organizations.[85] Reengineering projects, mergers and acquisitions, global competition, and the trend toward outsourcing have all led to job reductions.[86]

Some researchers have found that massive downsizing has often not achieved the intended benefits and in some cases has significantly harmed the organization.[87] Nevertheless, there are times when downsizing is a necessary part of managing organizational decline. A number of techniques can help smooth the downsizing process and ease tensions for employees who leave and for those who remain.[88]

1. *Communicate more, not less.* Some managers seem to think the less that's said about a pending layoff, the better. Not so. Rumors can be much more damaging than open communication. At 3Com Corporation, managers drew up a three-stage plan as they prepared for layoffs. First, they warned employees several months ahead that layoffs were inevitable. Soon thereafter, they held on-site presentations at all locations to explain to employees why the layoffs were needed and to provide as much information as they could about what employees should expect. Employees being cut were given a full sixty

Briefcase

As an organization manager, keep this guideline in mind:

When layoffs are necessary, handle them with care. Treat departing employees humanely, communicate with employees and provide as much information as possible, provide assistance to displaced workers, and remember the emotional needs of remaining employees.

days' notice (now required by U.S. regulations).[89] Managers should remember that it is impossible to "overcommunicate" during turbulent times. Remaining employees need to know what is expected of them, whether future layoffs are a possibility, and what the organization is doing to help co-workers who have lost their jobs.

2. *Provide assistance to displaced workers.* The organization has a responsibility to help displaced workers cope with the loss of their jobs and get reestablished in the job market. The organization can provide training, severance packages, extended benefits, and outplacement assistance. Ford Motor Company runs internal job fairs for laid-off employees. Kaiser-Hill, a company running the cleanup and dismantling of the Rocky Flats nuclear site in Colorado, set up a Workforce Transition Program, sponsors an online job bank, and funds grants for entrepreneurs. Because Kaiser-Hill has to motivate employees to work themselves out of a job in a couple of years, it knows people need the security of feeling that they can provide for their families when the job is over.[90] In addition, counseling services for both employees and their families can ease the trauma associated with a job loss. A growing number of companies are giving laid-off workers continued access to employee assistance programs to help them cope with stress, depression, and other problems.[91] Another key step is to allow employees to leave with dignity, giving them an opportunity to say goodbye to colleagues and meet with leaders to express their hurt and anger.

3. *Help the survivors thrive.* There has been much research on the "layoff survivor syndrome."[92] Many people experience guilt, anger, confusion, and sadness after the loss of colleagues, and leaders should acknowledge these feelings. Survivors also might be concerned about losing their own jobs, lose confidence in company management, and grow depressed and cynical. People sometimes have difficulty adapting to the changes in job duties, responsibilities, and reporting relationships after a downsizing. The state of Oregon hired consultant Al Siebert to help employees adapt following the elimination of more than a thousand jobs. Most people "just aren't emotionally prepared to handle major disruptions," Siebert says. Through a series of workshops, Siebert helped people acknowledge their anger and unhappiness and then helped them become "change-resilient" by developing coping skills such as flexibility, curiosity, and optimism.[93]

ASSESS YOUR ANSWER

3 After a necessary downsizing, managers should not spend much time helping laid-off workers but focus instead on making sure the remaining employees are taken care of to do what is needed to revive the company.

ANSWER: *Disagree.* The way to take care of remaining employees after a downsizing is to take care of the people who were laid off. Helping laid-off employees sends a signal to remaining workers that the organization cares about the departed co-workers and friends, which helps get the company going again. Managing downsizing means providing assistance to both departing and remaining workers.

Even the best-managed organizations may sometimes need to lay off employees in a turbulent environment or to revitalize the organization and reverse decline. Leaders can attain positive results if they handle downsizing in a way that lets departing employees leave with dignity and enables remaining organization members to be motivated, productive, and committed to a better future.

DESIGN ESSENTIALS

- Organizations experience many pressures to grow, and large size is crucial to economic health in some industries. Size enables economies of scale, provides a wide variety of opportunities for employees, and allows companies to invest in expensive and risky projects. However, large organizations have a hard time adapting to rapid changes in the environment. Large organizations are typically standardized, mechanistically run, and complex. Small organizations typically have a flatter structure and an organic, free-flowing management. They can respond more quickly to environmental changes and are more suited to encouraging innovation and entrepreneurship. Managers in large or growing firms try to find mechanisms to make their organizations more flexible and responsive.

- Organizations evolve through distinct life-cycle stages as they grow and mature. Organization structure, internal systems, and management issues are different for each stage of development. Growth creates crises and revolutions along the way toward large size. A major task of managers is to guide the organization through the entrepreneurial, collectivity, formalization, and elaboration stages of development.

- As organizations progress through the life cycle and grow larger and more complex, they generally take on bureaucratic characteristics, such as rules, division of labor, written records, hierarchy of authority, and impersonal procedures. Bureaucracy is a logical form of organizing that lets firms use resources efficiently. However, in many large corporate and government organizations, bureaucracy has come under attack with attempts to decentralize authority, flatten organization structure, reduce rules and written records, and create a small-company mindset. These companies are willing to trade economies of scale for responsive, adaptive organizations. Many companies are subdividing to gain small-company advantages. Another approach to overcoming the problems of bureaucracy is to use temporary systems, enabling the organization to glide smoothly between a highly formalized, hierarchical style that is effective during times of stability and a more flexible, loosely structured one needed to respond to unexpected or volatile environmental conditions.

- All organizations, large and small, need systems for control. Managers can choose among three overall control strategies: market, bureaucratic, and clan. Bureaucratic control relies on standard rules and the rational-legal authority of managers. Market control is used where product or service outputs can be priced and competition exists. Clan control, and more recently self-control, are associated with uncertain and rapidly changing organization processes. They rely on commitment, tradition, and shared values for control. Managers may use a combination of control approaches to meet the organization's needs.

■ Many organizations have stopped growing, and some are declining. Organizations go through stages of decline, and it is the responsibility of managers to detect the signs of decline, implement necessary action, and reverse course. One of the most difficult decisions pertains to downsizing the workforce. To smooth the downsizing process, managers can communicate with employees and provide as much information as possible, provide assistance to displaced workers, and remember to address the emotional needs of those who remain with the organization.

Key Concepts

bureaucracy
bureaucratic control
centralization
charismatic authority
clan control
collectivity stage

downsizing
elaboration stage
entrepreneurial stage
formalization
formalization stage
life cycle

market control
organizational decline
personnel ratios
rational-legal authority
traditional authority

Discussion Questions

1. Look through several recent issues of a business magazine such as *Fortune*, *BusinessWeek*, or *Fast Company* and find examples of two companies that are using approaches to busting bureaucracy. Discuss the techniques these companies are applying.
2. Do you think a "no growth" philosophy of management should be taught in business schools? Discuss.
3. Describe the three bases of authority identified by Weber. Is it possible for each of these types of authority to function at the same time within an organization? Discuss.
4. Numerous large financial institutions, including Lehman Brothers and Merrill Lynch, experienced significant decline or dissolution in recent years. Which of the three causes of organizational decline described in the chapter seems to apply most clearly to these firms?
5. Why do you think organizations feel pressure to grow?
6. How does the Salvation Army manage to be "several different kinds of organization at the same time"? Does the Salvation Army's approach seem workable for a large media company like Time Warner or Disney that wants to reduce bureaucracy?
7. Apply the concept of life cycle to an organization with which you are familiar, such as a local business. What stage is the organization in now? How did the organization handle or pass through its life cycle crises?
8. Government organizations often seem more bureaucratic than for-profit organizations. Could this partly be the result of the type of control used in government organizations? Explain.
9. Why do large organizations tend to have larger ratios of clerical and administrative support staff? Why are they typically more formalized than small organizations?
10. In writing about types of control, William Ouchi said, "The Market is like the trout and the Clan like the salmon, each a beautiful highly specialized species which requires uncommon conditions for its survival. In comparison, the bureaucratic method of control is the catfish—clumsy, ugly, but able to live in the widest range of environments and ultimately, the dominant species." Discuss what Ouchi meant with that analogy.

Chapter 12 Workbook: Control Mechanisms*

Think of two situations in your life: your work and your school experiences. How is control exerted? Fill out the tables.

On the Job

Your job responsibilities	How your boss controls	Positives of this control	Negatives of this control	How you would improve control
1.				
2.				
3.				
4.				

At the University

Items	How professor A (small class) controls	How professor B (large class) controls	How these controls influence you	What you think is a better control
1. Exams				
2. Assignments/ papers				
3. Class participation				
4. Attendance				
5. Other				

Questions

1. What are the advantages and disadvantages of the various controls?
2. What happens when there is too much control? Too little?
3. Does the type of control depend on the situation and the number of people involved?
4. *Optional:* How do the control mechanisms in your tables compare to those of other students?

*Copyright 1996 Dorothy Marcic. All rights reserved.

Case for Analysis: Sunflower Incorporated*

Sunflower Incorporated is a large distribution company with more than 5,000 employees and gross sales of more than $550 million (2003). The company purchases salty snack foods and liquor and distributes them to independent retail stores throughout the United States and Canada. Salty snack foods include corn chips, potato chips, cheese curls, tortilla chips, pretzels, and peanuts. The United States and Canada are divided into twenty-two regions, each with its own central warehouse, salespeople, finance department, and purchasing department. The company distributes national and local brands and packages some items under private labels. Competition in this industry is intense. The demand for liquor has been declining, and competitors like Procter & Gamble and Frito-Lay have developed new snack foods and low-carb options to gain market share from smaller companies like Sunflower. The head office encourages each region to be autonomous because of local tastes and practices. In the northeastern United States, for example, people consume a greater percentage of Canadian whiskey and American bourbon, whereas in the West, they consume more light liquors, such as vodka, gin, and rum. Snack foods in the Southwest are often seasoned to reflect Mexican tastes, and customers in the Northeast buy a greater percent of pretzels.

Early in 1998, Sunflower began using a financial reporting system that compared sales, costs, and profits across company regions. Each region was a profit center, and top management was surprised to learn that profits varied widely. By 2001, the differences were so great that management decided some standardization was necessary. Managers believed highly profitable regions were sometimes using lower-quality items, even seconds, to boost profit margins. This practice could hurt Sunflower's image. Most regions were facing cutthroat price competition to hold market share. Triggered by price cuts by Anheuser-Busch Company's Eagle Snacks division, national distributors, such as Frito-Lay, Borden, Nabisco, Procter & Gamble (Pringles), and Standard Brands (Planters Peanuts), were pushing to hold or increase market share by cutting prices and launching new products. Independent snack food distributors had a tougher and tougher time competing, and many were going out of business.

As these problems accumulated, Joe Steelman, president of Sunflower, decided to create a new position to monitor pricing and purchasing practices. Loretta Williams was hired from the finance department of a competing organization. Her new title was director of pricing and purchasing, and she reported to the vice president of finance, Peter Langly. Langly gave Williams great latitude in organizing her job and encouraged her to establish whatever rules and procedures were necessary. She was also encouraged to gather information from each region. Each region was notified of her appointment by an official memo sent to the twenty-two regional directors. A copy of the memo was posted on each warehouse bulletin board. The announcement was also made in the company newspaper.

After three weeks on the job, Williams decided two problems needed her attention. Over the long term, Sunflower should make better use of information technology. Williams believed information technology could provide more information to headquarters for decision making. Top managers in the divisions were connected to headquarters by an intranet, but lower-level employees and salespeople were not connected. Only a few senior managers in about half the divisions used the system regularly.

In the short term, Williams decided fragmented pricing and purchasing decisions were a problem and these decisions should be standardized across regions. This should be undertaken immediately. As a first step, she wanted the financial executive in each region to notify her of any change in local prices of more than 3 percent. She also decided that all new contracts for local purchases of more than $5,000 should be cleared through her office. (Approximately 60 percent of items distributed in the regions were purchased in large quantities and supplied from the home office. The other 40 percent were purchased and distributed within the region.) Williams believed the only way to standardize operations was for each region to notify the home office in advance of any change in prices or purchases. She discussed the proposed policy with Langly. He agreed, so they submitted a formal proposal to the president and board of directors, who approved the plan. The changes represented a complicated shift in policy procedures, and Sunflower was moving into peak holiday season, so Williams wanted to implement the new procedures right away. She decided to send an e-mail message followed by a fax to the financial and purchasing executives in each region notifying them of the new procedures. The change would be inserted in all policy and procedure manuals throughout Sunflower within four months.

Williams showed a draft of the message to Langly and invited his comments. Langly said the message was a good idea but wondered if it was sufficient. The regions handled hundreds of items and were accustomed to decentralized decision making. Langly suggested that Williams ought to visit the regions and discuss purchasing and pricing policies with the executives. Williams refused, saying that such trips would be expensive and time consuming. She had so many things to do at headquarters that trips were impossible. Langly also suggested waiting to implement the procedures until after the annual company meeting in three months, when Williams could meet the regional directors personally. Williams said this would take too long, because the procedures would then not take effect until after the peak sales season. She believed the procedures were needed now. The messages went out the next day.

During the next few days, e-mail replies came in from seven regions. The managers said they were in agreement and were happy to cooperate.

Eight weeks later, Williams had not received notices from any regions about local price or purchase changes. Other executives who had visited regional warehouses indicated to her that the regions were busy as usual. Regional executives seemed to be following usual procedures for that time of year. She telephoned one of the regional managers and discovered that he did not know who she was and had never heard of her position. Besides, he said, "we have enough to worry about reaching profit goals without additional procedures from headquarters." Williams was chagrined that her position and her suggested changes in procedure had no impact. She wondered whether field managers were disobedient or whether she should have used another communication strategy.

*This case was inspired by "Frito-Lay May Find Itself in a Competition Crunch," BusinessWeek (July 19, 1982), 186; Jim Bohman, "Mike-Sells Works to Remain on Snack Map," Dayton Daily News (February 27, 2005) D; "Dashman Company" in Paul R. Lawrence and John A. Seiler, Organizational Behavior and Administration: Cases, Concepts, and Research Findings (Homewood, Ill: Irwin and Dorsey, 1965), 16–17; and Laurie M. Grossman, "Price Wars Bring Flavor to Once Quiet Snack Market," The Wall Street Journal (May 23, 1991), B1, B3.

Chapter 12 Workshop: Windsock Inc.*

1. *Introduction.* Class is divided into four groups: Central Office, Product Design, Marketing/Sales, and Production. Central Office is a slightly smaller group. If groups are large enough, assign observers to each one. Central Office is given 500 straws and 750 pins. Each person reads *only* the role description relevant to that group. *Materials needed:* plastic milk straws (500) and a box of straight pins (750).
2. *Perform task.* Depending on length of class, step 2 may take 30 to 60 minutes. Groups perform functions and prepare for a 2-minute report for stockholders.
3. *Group reports.* Each group gives a 2-minute presentation to stockholders.
4. *Observers' reports (optional).* Observers share insights with subgroups.
5. Class discussion.
   a. What helped or blocked intergroup cooperation and coordination?
   b. To what extent was there open versus closed communication? What impact did that have?
   c. What styles of leadership were exhibited?
   d. What types of team interdependencies emerged?

Roles

Central Office

Your team is the central management and administration of Windsock Inc. You are the heart and pulse of the organization, because without your coordination and resource allocation, the organization would go under. Your task is to manage the operations of the organization, which is not an easy responsibility because you have to coordinate the activities of three distinct groups of personnel: the Marketing/Sales group, the Production group, and the Product Design group. In addition, you have to manage resources including materials (pins and straws), time deadlines, communications, and product requirements.

In this exercise, you are to do whatever is necessary to accomplish the mission and to keep the organization operating harmoniously and efficiently.

Windsock Inc. has a total of 30 minutes (more if instructor assigns) to design an advertising campaign and ad copy, to design the windmill, and to produce the first windmill prototypes for delivery. Good luck to you all.

Product Design

Your team is the research and product design group of Windsock Inc. You are the brain and creative aspect of the operation, because without an innovative and successfully designed product, the organization would go under. Your duties are to design products that compete favorably in the marketplace, keeping in mind function, aesthetics, cost, ease of production, and available materials.

In this exercise, you are to come up with a workable plan for a product that will be built by your production team. Your windmill must be light, portable, easy to assemble, and aesthetically pleasing. Central Office controls the budget and allocates material for your division.

Windsock Inc. as an organization has a total of 30 minutes (more if instructor assigns) to design an advertising campaign, to design the windmill (your group's task), and to produce the first windmill prototypes for delivery. Good luck to you all.

Marketing/Sales

Your team is the marketing/sales group of Windsock Inc. You are the backbone of the operation, because without customers and sales the organization would go under. Your task is to determine the market, develop an advertising campaign to promote your company's unique product, produce ad copy, and develop a sales force and sales procedures for both potential customers and the public at large.

For the purpose of this exercise, you may assume that a market analysis has been completed. Your team is now in a position to produce an advertising campaign and ad copy for the product. To be effective, you have to become very familiar with the characteristics of the product and how it is different from those products already on the market. The Central Office controls your budget and allocates materials for use by your division.

Windsock Inc. has a total of 30 minutes (more if instructor assigns) to design an advertising campaign and ad (your group's task), to design the windmill, and to produce the first windmill prototypes for delivery. Good luck to you all.

Production

Your team is the production group of Windsock Inc. You are the heart of the operation, because without a group to produce the product, the organization would go under. You have the responsibility to coordinate and produce the product for delivery. The product involves an innovative design for a windmill that is cheaper, lighter, more portable, more flexible, and more aesthetically pleasing than other designs currently available in the marketplace. Your task is to build windmills within cost guidelines, according to specifications, and within a prescribed period, using predetermined materials.

For the purpose of this exercise, you are to organize your team, set production schedules, and build the windmills. Central Office controls your budget, materials, and specifications.

Windsock Inc. has a total of 30 minutes (more if instructor assigns) to design an advertising campaign, to design the windmill, and to produce the first windmill prototypes (your group's task) for delivery. Good luck to you all.

*Adapted by Dorothy Marcic from Christopher Taylor and Saundra Taylor in "Teaching Organizational Team-Building through Simulations," Organizational Behavior Teaching Review XI(3), 86–87.

xyno lorenzen

Chapter 13

Workplace Technology and Design

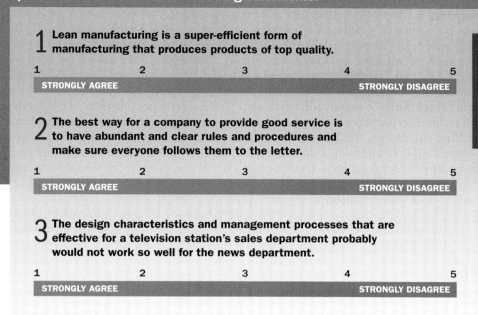

Before reading this chapter, please circle your opinion below for each of the following statements:

Managing by Design Questions

1. Lean manufacturing is a super-efficient form of manufacturing that produces products of top quality.

1	2	3	4	5
STRONGLY AGREE				STRONGLY DISAGREE

2. The best way for a company to provide good service is to have abundant and clear rules and procedures and make sure everyone follows them to the letter.

1	2	3	4	5
STRONGLY AGREE				STRONGLY DISAGREE

3. The design characteristics and management processes that are effective for a television station's sales department probably would not work so well for the news department.

1	2	3	4	5
STRONGLY AGREE				STRONGLY DISAGREE

An auto parts factory sends engineers around the world to learn about new production methods. A team of airline employees studies the pit stop techniques used by NASCAR racing crews. A small clothing manufacturer in New York invests in a computerized German-made knitting machine. What do all these organizations have in common? They are looking for ways to provide goods and services more efficiently and effectively.

For many manufacturers in the United States, it's a do-or-die situation. Manufacturing has been on the decline in the United States and other developed countries for years, with services becoming an increasingly greater part of the economy. A report from the U.S. Business and Industry Council indicates that more than 100 U.S.-based manufacturing industries lost a significant percentage of their domestic market to imports between 1997 and 2004, and nineteen industries lost more than half of their U.S. market during that time period.[1] However, some manufacturing companies are applying new technology to gain a new competitive edge. For example, by integrating computerized production equipment and sophisticated information systems, American Axle & Manufacturing (AAM) dramatically improved efficiency and productivity to the point where it began winning contracts to make components in Detroit that a competitor had previously been making in China.[2] Service companies also need to keep pace with changing technology and continually strive for better approaches. Many service firms are fighting for their lives as global competition intensifies, and the cost of ineffective or outdated technology and procedures can be organizational decline and failure.

This chapter explores both service and manufacturing technologies. **Technology** refers to the work processes, techniques, machines, and actions used to transform organizational inputs (materials, information, ideas) into outputs (products and services).[3] Technology is an organization's production process and includes work procedures as well as machinery.

One important theme in this chapter is how core technology influences organization structure. Understanding core technology provides insight into how an

487

organization can be structured for efficient performance.[4] An organization's **core technology** is the work process that is directly related to the organization's mission, such as teaching in a high school, medical services in a health clinic, or manufacturing at AAM. For example, at AAM, the core technology begins with raw materials (e.g., steel, aluminum, and composite metals). Employees take action on the raw material to make a change in it (they cut and forge metals and assemble parts), thus transforming the raw material into the output of the organization (axles, drive shafts, crankshafts, transmission parts, etc.). For a service organization like UPS, the core technology includes the production equipment (e.g., sorting machines, package handling equipment, trucks, airplanes) and procedures for delivering packages and overnight mail. In addition, as at companies like UPS and AAM, computers and new information technology have revolutionized work processes in both manufacturing and service organizations. The specific impact of new information technology on organizations was described in Chapter 11.

Exhibit 13.1 features an example of core technology for a manufacturing plant. Note how the core technology consists of raw material inputs, a transformation work process (milling, inspection, assembly) that changes and adds value to the raw material and produces the ultimate product or service output that is sold to consumers in the environment. In today's large, complex organizations, core work processes vary widely and sometimes can be hard to pinpoint. A core technology can be partly understood by examining the raw materials flowing into the organization,[5] the variability of work activities,[6] the degree to which the production process is mechanized,[7] the extent to which one task depends on another in the workflow,[8] or the number of new product or service outputs.[9]

EXHIBIT 13.1
Core Transformation
Process for a
Manufacturing Company

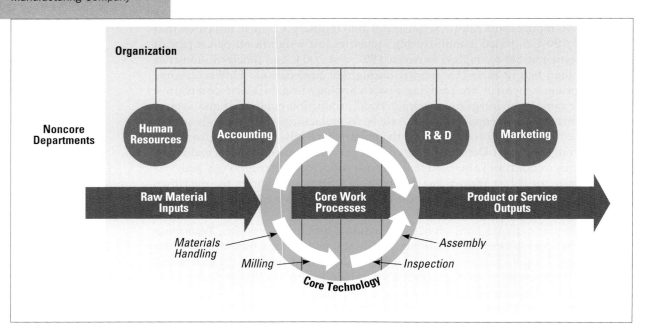

EXHIBIT 13.2
Pressures Affecting
Organization Design

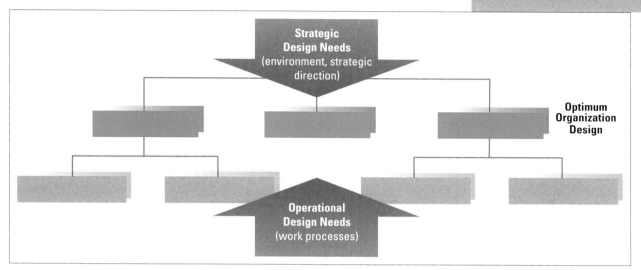

Source: Based on David A. Nadler and Michael L. Tushman, with Mark B. Nadler, *Competing by Design: The Power of Organizational Architecture* (New York: Oxford University Press, 1997), 54.

Organizations are also made up of many departments, each of which may use a different work process (technology) to provide a good or service within an organization. A **non-core technology** is a department work process that is important to the organization but is not directly related to its primary mission. In Exhibit 13.1, non-core work processes are illustrated by the departments of human resources (HR), accounting, research and development (R&D), and marketing. Thus, R&D transforms ideas into new products, and marketing transforms inventory into sales, each using a somewhat different work process. The output of the HR department is people to work in the organization, and accounting produces accurate statements about the organization's financial condition.

Purpose of This Chapter

In this chapter, we will discuss both core and non-core work processes and their relationship to designing organization structure. The nature of the organization's work processes must be considered in designing the organization for maximum efficiency and effectiveness. The optimum organization design is based on a variety of elements. Exhibit 13.2 illustrates that forces affecting organization design come from both outside and inside the organization. External strategic needs, such as environmental conditions, strategic direction, and organizational goals, create top-down pressure for designing the organization in such a way as to fit the environment and accomplish goals. These pressures on design have been discussed in previous chapters. However, decisions about design should also take into consideration pressures from the bottom up—from the work processes that are performed to produce the organization's

products or services. The operational work processes will influence the structural design associated with both the core technology and non-core departments. Thus, the subject with which this chapter is concerned is, "How should the organization be designed to accommodate and facilitate its operational work processes?"

The remainder of the chapter will unfold as follows. First, we examine how the technology for the organization as a whole influences organization structure and design. This discussion includes both manufacturing and service technologies. Next, we examine differences in departmental technologies and how the technologies influence the design and management of organizational subunits. Third, we explore how interdependence—flow of materials and information—among departments affects structure.

CORE ORGANIZATION MANUFACTURING TECHNOLOGY

Manufacturing technologies include traditional manufacturing processes and contemporary applications, such as flexible manufacturing and lean manufacturing.

Manufacturing Firms

Briefcase

As an organization manager, keep these guidelines in mind:

Use the categories developed by Woodward to diagnose whether the production technology in a manufacturing firm is small batch, mass production, or continuous process. Use a more organic structure with small-batch or continuous-process technologies and with new flexible manufacturing systems. Use a mechanistic structure with mass-production technologies.

The first and most influential study of manufacturing technology was conducted by Joan Woodward, a British industrial sociologist. Her research began as a field study of management principles in south Essex. The prevailing management wisdom at the time (1950s) was contained in what were known as universal principles of management. These principles were "one best way" prescriptions that effective organizations were expected to adopt. Woodward surveyed 100 manufacturing firms firsthand to learn how they were organized.[10] She and her research team visited each firm, interviewed managers, examined company records, and observed the manufacturing operations. Her data included a wide range of structural characteristics (span of control, levels of management), dimensions of management style (written versus verbal communications, use of rewards), and the type of manufacturing process. Data were also obtained that reflected commercial success of the firms.

Woodward developed a scale and organized the firms according to technical complexity of the manufacturing process. **Technical complexity** represents the extent of mechanization of the manufacturing process. High technical complexity means most of the work is performed by machines. Low technical complexity means workers play a larger role in the production process. Woodward's scale of technical complexity originally had ten categories, as summarized in Exhibit 13.3. These categories were further consolidated into three basic technology groups:

- *Group I: Small-batch and unit production.* These firms tend to be job shop operations that manufacture and assemble small orders to meet specific needs of customers. Custom work is the norm. **Small-batch production** relies heavily on the human operator; it is thus not highly mechanized. One example of small-batch production is Hermes International's Kelly handbag, named for the late actress Grace Kelly. Craftsmen stitch the majority of each $7,000 bag by hand and sign it when they finish.[11] Another example comes from Rockwell Collins, which makes electronic equipment for airplanes. Although sophisticated computerized machinery is used for part of the production process, final assembly requires highly skilled human operators to ensure absolute reliability of products used

EXHIBIT 13.3
Woodward's Classification of 100 British Firms According to Their Systems of Production

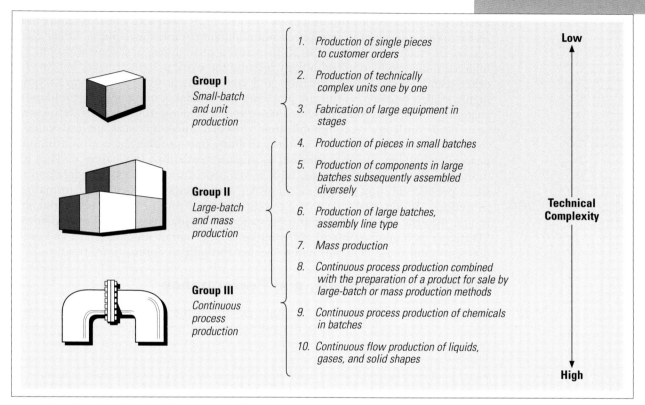

Source: Adapted from Joan Woodward, *Management and Technology* (London: Her Majesty's Stationery Office, 1958). Used with permission of Her Britannic Majesty's Stationery Office.

by aerospace companies, defense contractors, and the U.S. military. The company's workforce is divided into manufacturing cells, some of which produce only ten units a day. In one plant, 140 workers build Joint Tactical Information Distribution Systems, for managing battlefield communications from a circling plane, at a rate of ten a month.[12]

- *Group II: Large-batch and mass production.* **Large-batch production** is a manufacturing process characterized by long production runs of standardized parts. Output often goes into inventory from which orders are filled, because customers do not have special needs. Examples include traditional assembly lines, such as for automobiles.

- *Group III: Continuous-process production.* In **continuous-process production**, the entire process is mechanized. There is no starting and stopping. This represents mechanization and standardization one step beyond those in an assembly line. Automated machines control the continuous process, and outcomes are highly predictable. Examples would include chemical plants, oil refineries, liquor producers, pharmaceuticals, and nuclear power plants.

Using this classification of technology, Woodward's data made sense. A few of her key findings are given in Exhibit 13.4. The number of management levels and the manager-to-total personnel ratio, for example, show definite increases as technical complexity increases from unit production to continuous process. This indicates that greater management intensity is needed to manage complex technology. The direct-to-indirect labor ratio decreases with technical complexity because more indirect workers are required to support and maintain complex machinery. Other characteristics, such as span of control, formalized procedures, and centralization, are high for mass-production technology because the work is standardized, but low for other technologies. Unit-production and continuous-process technologies require highly skilled workers to run the machines and verbal communication to adapt to changing conditions. Mass production is standardized and routinized, so few exceptions occur, little verbal communication is needed, and employees are less skilled.

Overall, the management systems in both unit-production and continuous-process technology are characterized as organic, as defined in Chapter 6. They are more free-flowing and adaptive, with fewer procedures and less standardization. Mass production, however, is mechanistic, with standardized jobs and formalized procedures. Woodward's discovery about technology thus provided substantial new insight into the causes of organization structure. In Joan Woodward's own words, "Different technologies impose different kinds of demands on individuals and organizations, and those demands had to be met through an appropriate structure."[13]

Strategy, Technology, and Performance

Another portion of Woodward's study examined the success of the firms along dimensions such as profitability, market share, stock price, and reputation. As indicated in Chapter 3, the measurement of effectiveness is not simple or precise, but Woodward was able to rank firms on a scale of commercial success according to whether they displayed above-average, average, or below-average performance on strategic objectives.

EXHIBIT 13.4

Relationship between Technical Complexity and Structural Characteristics

	Technology		
Structural Characteristic	**Unit Production**	**Mass Production**	**Continuous Process**
Number of management levels	3	4	6
Supervisor span of control	23	48	15
Direct/indirect labor ratio	9:1	4:1	1:1
Manager/total personnel ratio	Low	Medium	High
Workers' skill level	High	Low	High
Formalized procedures	Low	High	Low
Centralization	Low	High	Low
Amount of verbal communication	High	Low	High
Amount of written communication	Low	High	Low
Overall structure	Organic	Mechanistic	Organic

Source: Joan Woodward, *Industrial Organization: Theory and Practice* (London: Oxford University Press, 1965). Used with permission.

Woodward compared the structure–technology relationship against commercial success and discovered that successful firms tended to be those that had complementary structures and technologies. Many of the organizational characteristics of the successful firms were near the average of their technology category, as shown in Exhibit 13.4. Below-average firms tended to depart from the structural characteristics for their technology type. Another conclusion was that structural characteristics could be interpreted as clustering into organic and mechanistic management systems, as defined in Chapter 6. Successful small-batch and continuous process organizations had organic structures, and successful mass-production organizations had mechanistic structures. Subsequent research has replicated her findings.[14]

What this illustrates for today's companies is that strategy, structure, and technology need to be aligned, especially when competitive conditions change.[15] For example, some years ago, when Dell created a business model to build personal computers faster and cheaper, other computer manufacturers had to realign strategy, structure, and technology to stay competitive. Dell made PCs to order for each customer and sold most of them directly to consumers without the expense of distributors or retailers. Manufacturers such as IBM that once tried to differentiate their products and charge a premium price switched to a low-cost strategy, adopted new technology to enable them to customize PCs, revamped supply chains, and began outsourcing manufacturing to other companies that could do the job more efficiently.

Today, many U.S. manufacturers farm production out to other companies. Printronix, a publicly owned company in Irvine, California, however, has gone in the opposite direction and achieved success by carefully aligning technology, structure, and management processes to achieve strategic objectives.

Briefcase

As an organization manager, keep this guideline in mind:

When adopting a new technology, realign strategy, structure, and management processes to achieve top performance.

IN PRACTICE

Printronix

Printronix makes 60 percent of the electro-mechanical line printers used in the world's factories and warehouses. To maintain the reliability that makes Printronix products worth $2,600 to $26,000 each, the company does almost everything in-house—from design, to making hundreds of parts, to final assembly, to research on new materials. Printronix began in the 1970s by making a high-speed line printer that could run with the minicomputers then being used on factory floors.

The company started as a traditional mass-production operation, but managers faced a tremendous challenge in the late 1980s when factories began switching from minicomputers to personal computers and servers. Within two years, sales and profits plunged, and founder and CEO Robert A. Kleist realized Printronix needed new ideas, new technology, and new methods to adapt to a world where printers were no longer stand-alone products but parts of emerging enterprise networks. One change Kleist made was to switch from mass producing printers that were kept in inventory to a small-batch or unit production system that built printers to order. Products were redesigned and assembly work reorganized so that small groups of workers could configure each printer to a customer's specific needs. Many employees had to be trained in new skills and to take more responsibility than they had on the traditional assembly line. Highly skilled workers were needed to make some of the precision parts needed in the new machines as well. Besides internal restructuring, Kleist decided to pick up on the outsourcing trend and go after the computer industry's factory printer business, winning orders to produce under the labels of IBM, Hewlett-Packard, and Siemens. Kleist doubled the research and development (R&D) budget to be sure the company kept pace with

(continued)

new technological developments. In 2000, Printronix began building thermal printers as well as specialized laser printers that print adhesive bar-code labels at lightning speed.

By making changes in technology, design, and management methods, Printronix has continued to meet its strategic objective of differentiating its products from the competition. "The restructuring made us a stronger company in both manufacturing and engineering," says Kleist.[16] ■

Failing to adopt appropriate new technologies to support strategy, or adopting a new technology and failing to realign strategy to match it, can lead to poor performance. Today's increased global competition means more volatile markets, shorter product life cycles, and more sophisticated and knowledgeable consumers; and flexibility to meet these new demands has become a strategic imperative for many companies.[17] Manufacturing companies can adopt new technologies to support the strategy of flexibility. However, organization structures and management processes must also be realigned, as a highly mechanistic structure hampers flexibility and prevents the company from reaping the benefits of the new technology.[18] Managers should always remember that the technological and human systems of an organization are intertwined.

CONTEMPORARY APPLICATIONS

In the years since Woodward's research, new developments have occurred in manufacturing technology. The factory of today is far different from the industrial firms Woodward studied in the 1950s. In particular, computers have revolutionized all types of manufacturing—small batch, large batch, and continuous process. At the Marion, North Carolina, plant of Rockwell Automation's Power Systems Division, for example, highly trained employees can quickly handle a build-on-demand unit of one thanks to computers, wireless technology, and radio-frequency identification (RFID) systems. In one instance, the Marion plant built, packaged, and delivered a replacement bearing for installation in an industrial air conditioning unit in Texas only 15 hours after the customer called for help.[19] An example in continuous process manufacturing comes from BP's Texas City, Texas, petrochemical plant. Technicians who once manually monitored hundreds of complex processes now focus their energy on surveying long-term production trends. Controlling the continuous production of petrochemicals today is handled faster, smarter, more precisely, and more economically by computer. Productivity at the Texas City plant has increased 55 percent. The plant uses 3 percent less electricity and 10 percent less natural gas, which amounts to millions of dollars in savings and fewer CO_2 emissions.[20]

Mass production manufacturing has seen similar transformations. Two significant contemporary applications of manufacturing technology are flexible manufacturing systems and lean manufacturing.

Flexible Manufacturing Systems

Most of today's factories use a variety of new manufacturing technologies, including robots, numerically controlled machine tools, RFID, wireless technology, and computerized software for product design, engineering analysis, and remote control of machinery. The ultimate automated factories are referred to as **flexible manufacturing systems** (FMS).[21] Also called *computer-integrated manufacturing*, *smart factories*, *advanced manufacturing technology, agile manufacturing*, or *the factory of the future*, FMS links together manufacturing components that previously stood alone. Thus, robots, machines, product design, and engineering analysis are coordinated by a single computer system.

The result has revolutionized the shop floor, enabling large factories to deliver a wide range of custom-made products at low mass-production costs.[22] Flexible manufacturing is typically the result of three subcomponents:

- *Computer-aided design (CAD).* Computers are used to assist in the drafting, design, and engineering of new parts. Designers guide their computers to draw specified configurations on the screen, including dimensions and component details. Hundreds of design alternatives can be explored, as can scaled-up or scaled-down versions of the original.[23]
- *Computer-aided manufacturing (CAM).* Computer-controlled machines in materials handling, fabrication, production, and assembly greatly increase the speed at which items can be manufactured. CAM also permits a production line to shift rapidly from producing one product to any variety of other products by changing the instruction tapes or software codes in the computer. CAM enables the production line to quickly honor customer requests for changes in product design and product mix.[24]
- *Integrated information network.* A computerized system links all aspects of the firm—including accounting, purchasing, marketing, inventory control, design, production, and so forth. This system, based on a common data and information base, enables managers to make decisions and direct the manufacturing process in a truly integrated fashion.

The combination of CAD, CAM, and integrated information systems means that a new product can be designed on the computer and a prototype can be produced untouched by human hands. The ideal factory can switch quickly from one product to another, working fast and with precision, without paperwork or record keeping to bog down the system.[25]

Some advanced factories have moved to a system called *product life-cycle management* (PLM). PLM software can manage a product from idea through development, manufacturing, testing, and even maintenance in the field. The PLM software provides three primary advantages for product innovation. PLM (1) stores data on ideas and products from all parts of the company; (2) links product design to all departments (and even outside suppliers) involved in new product development; and (3) provides three-dimensional images of new products for testing and maintenance. PLM has been used to coordinate people, tools, and facilities around the world for the design, development, and manufacture of products as diverse as roller skates produced by GID of Yorba Linda, California, product packaging for Procter & Gamble consumer products, and Boeing's new 787 Dreamliner passenger jet.[26]

Automakers provide good examples of the benefits of flexible manufacturing. Ford's Kansas City, Missouri, plant, one of the largest manufacturing facilities in the world, produces around 490,000 F-150s, Ford Escapes, and Mazda Tributes a year. With just a little tweaking, the assembly lines can be programmed to manufacture any kind of car or truck Ford makes. Robots in wire cages do most of the work, while people act as assistants, taking measurements, refilling parts, and altering the system if something goes wrong. Assembly is synchronized by computers, right down to the last rearview mirror. Ford's flexible manufacturing system is projected to save the company $2 billion over the next 10 years.[27] Honda has achieved an even greater degree of flexibility at its plant in East Liberty, Ohio. Considered the most flexible auto manufacturer in North America, the Honda plant can switch from making Civic compacts to making the longer, taller CR-V crossover in as little as five minutes. Most of the company's vehicles are designed to be put together the same way, even if their parts are different. All that's needed to switch assembly from one type of vehicle to another is to put different "hands" on the robots to handle different parts. The ability to quickly adjust inventory levels of different types of vehicles has been a key strategic advantage for Honda in an era of volatile gasoline prices and shifting vehicle popularity.[28]

Lean Manufacturing

Flexible manufacturing reaches its ultimate level to improve quality, customer service, and cost cutting when all parts are used interdependently and combined with flexible management processes in a system referred to as lean manufacturing. **Lean manufacturing** uses highly trained employees at every stage of the production process, who take a painstaking approach to details and problem solving to cut waste and improve quality. In a recent survey by *Industry Week* and the Manufacturing Performance Institute asking 745 manufacturers which improvement programs they used, lean manufacturing was by far the most common answer, with more than 40 percent reporting the use of lean manufacturing techniques.[29]

Lean manufacturing incorporates technological elements, such as CAD/CAM and PLM, but the heart of lean manufacturing is not machines or software, but people. Lean manufacturing requires changes in organizational systems, such as decision-making processes and management processes, as well as an organizational culture that supports active employee participation, a quality perspective, and focus on the customer. Employees are trained to attack waste and strive for continuous improvement in all areas.[30] One lesson of lean manufacturing is that there is always room for improvement. Consider the example of Matsushita Electric Industrial Company's factory in Saga, Japan.

IN PRACTICE

Matsushita Electric Industrial Company

To an outsider, Matsushita Electric Company's Saga plant looked pretty lean. Over a four-year period, the facility had doubled productivity and could pump out cordless phones, security cameras, and fax machines in record time. But for plant managers Hitoshi Hirata and Hirofumi Tsuru, that wasn't good enough.

So, the plant recently ripped out miles of conveyor belts and replaced them with clusters of robots, controlled by software that synchronizes production so that there's no downtime. If one robot breaks down, work can quickly be routed to another. One outcome is a dramatic increase in speed. "It used to be 2½ days into a production run before we had our first finished product. But now the first is done in 40 minutes," says Hirata. The Saga plant can churn out 500 phones, for example, every eight-hour shift, which means it produces twice as many phones per week as it could before the changes. That also significantly cuts inventory costs because components spend less time in the factory waiting to be used.

Are Saga's plant managers satisfied with the reinvention? Well, sort of. They know their factory is at the forefront of Matsushita's efforts to counter low-cost rivals by doing things better, faster, and cheaper. But they're also continually striving to take efficiency to new heights. "Next year," says Hirata, "we'll try to shorten the cycle even more."[31] ■

Japanese companies such as Matsushita have long been global leaders in lean manufacturing. Another Japanese company, Toyota Motor Corporation, is often considered the premier manufacturing organization in the world. The famed Toyota Production System combines techniques such as just-in-time inventory, product life-cycle management, continuous-flow production, quick changeover of assembly lines, continuous improvement, and preventive maintenance with a management system that encourages employee involvement and problem solving. Any employee can stop the production line at any time to solve a problem. In addition, designing equipment to stop automatically so that a defect can be fixed is a key element of the system.[32]

Many North American organizations have studied the Toyota Production System and seen dramatic improvements in productivity, inventory reduction, and quality. "We're not trying to be Toyota," says Kristen Workman, manufacturing engineering manager at Schneider Electric's Peru, Indiana, facility, "but we can take their ideas and try to make them work in our own way." Since implementing lean ideas, Schneider's Peru operations have reduced waste significantly and increased productivity by 30 percent. Even with 85 percent of the 2,200 or so lighting and power panelboards the plant assembles and ships each day being custom orders, the facility has a 97 percent on-time delivery rate.[33]

Lean manufacturing and flexible manufacturing systems have paved the way for **mass customization**, which refers to using mass-production technology to quickly and cost-effectively assemble goods that are uniquely designed to fit the demands of individual customers.[34] Mass customization has been applied to products as diverse as farm machinery, water heaters, clothing, computers, and industrial detergents.[35] Oshkosh Truck Company has thrived during an industrywide slump in sales by offering customized fire, cement, garbage, and military trucks. Firefighters often travel to the plant to watch their new vehicle take shape, sometimes bringing paint chips to customize the color of their fleet.[36] Auto manufacturers, too, are moving toward mass customization. Sixty percent of the cars BMW sells in Europe are built to order.[37]

Performance and Structural Implications

The awesome advantage of flexible manufacturing is that products of different sizes, types, and customer requirements freely intermingle on the assembly line. Computerized machines can make instantaneous changes—such as putting a larger screw in a different location—without slowing the production line. A manufacturer can turn out an infinite variety of products in unlimited batch sizes, as illustrated in Exhibit 13.5. In traditional manufacturing systems studied by Woodward, choices were limited to the diagonal. Small batch allowed for high product flexibility and custom orders, but because of the "craftsmanship" involved in custom-making products, batch size was necessarily small. Mass production could have large batch size, but offered limited product flexibility. Continuous process could produce a single standard product in unlimited quantities. Flexible manufacturing systems allow plants to break free of this diagonal and to increase both batch size and product

EXHIBIT 13.5

Relationship of Flexible Manufacturing
Technology to Traditional Technologies

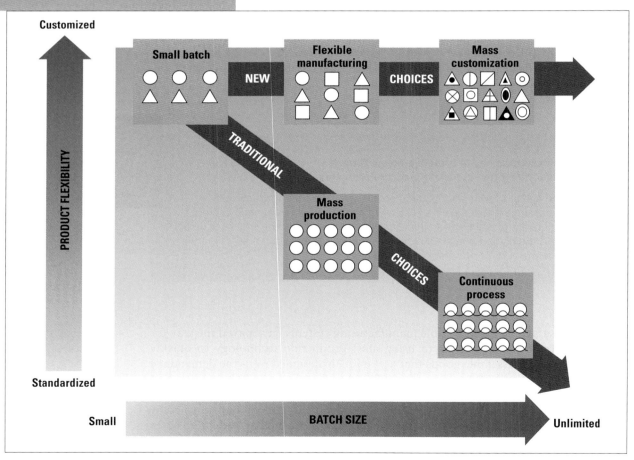

Source: Based on Jack Meredith, "The Strategic Advantages of New Manufacturing Technologies for Small Firms," *Strategic Management Journal* 8 (1987), 249–258; Paul Adler, "Managing Flexible Automation," *California Management Review* (Spring 1988), 34–56; and Otis Port, "Custom-made Direct from the Plant," *BusinessWeek/*21st Century Capitalism (November 18, 1994), 158–159.

flexibility at the same time. When taken to its ultimate level, FMS allows for mass customization, with each specific product tailored to customer specification. This high-level use of FMS has been referred to as *computer-aided craftsmanship*.[38]

Studies suggest that with FMS, machine utilization is more efficient, labor productivity increases, scrap rates decrease, and product variety and customer satisfaction increase.[39] Many U.S. manufacturing companies are reinventing the factory using FMS and lean manufacturing systems to increase productivity.

Research into the relationship between FMS and organizational characteristics has discovered the organizational patterns summarized in Exhibit 13.6. Compared with traditional mass-production technologies, FMS has a narrow span of control, few hierarchical levels, adaptive tasks, low specialization, and decentralization, and the overall environment is characterized as organic and self-regulative. Employees need the skills to participate in teams; training is broad (so workers are not overly specialized) and frequent (so workers are up to date). Expertise tends to be cognitive so workers can process abstract ideas and solve problems. Interorganizational relationships in FMS firms are characterized by changing demand from customers—which is easily handled with the new technology—and close relationships with a few suppliers that provide top-quality raw materials.[40]

Technology alone cannot give organizations the benefits of flexibility, quality, increased production, and greater customer satisfaction. Research suggests that FMS can become a competitive burden rather than a competitive advantage unless organizational structures and management processes are redesigned to take advantage of the new technology.[41] When top managers make a commitment to

EXHIBIT 13.6
Comparison of Organizational Characteristics Associated with Mass Production and Flexible Manufacturing Systems

Characteristic	Mass Production	FMS
Structure		
Span of control	Wide	Narrow
Hierarchical levels	Many	Few
Tasks	Routine, repetitive	Adaptive, craftlike
Specialization	High	Low
Decision making	Centralized	Decentralized
Overall	Bureaucratic, mechanistic	Self-regulating, organic
Human Resources		
Interactions	Standalone	Teamwork
Training	Narrow, one time	Broad, frequent
Expertise	Manual, technical	Cognitive, social
		Solve problems
Interorganizational		
Customer demand	Stable	Changing
Suppliers	Many, arm's length	Few, close relationships

Source: Based on Patricia L. Nemetz and Louis W. Fry, "Flexible Manufacturing Organizations: Implications for Strategy Formulation and Organization Design," *Academy of Management Review* 13 (1988), 627–638; Paul S. Adler, "Managing Flexible Automation," *California Management Review* (Spring 1988), 34–56; and Jeremy Main, "Manufacturing the Right Way," *Fortune* (May 21, 1990) 54–64.

implement new structures and processes that empower workers and support a learning and knowledge-creating environment, FMS can help companies be more competitive.[42]

CORE ORGANIZATION SERVICE TECHNOLOGY

Another big change occurring in the technology of organizations is the growing service sector. A large percentage of the U.S. workforce is employed in services, such as hospitals, hotels, package delivery, online services, or telecommunications. Service technologies are different from manufacturing technologies and, in turn, require a different organization design.

Service Firms

Definition. Whereas manufacturing organizations achieve their primary purpose through the production of products, service organizations accomplish their primary purpose through the production and provision of services, such as education, health care, transportation, banking, and hospitality. Studies of service organizations have focused on the unique dimensions of service technologies. The characteristics of **service technology** are compared to those of manufacturing technology in Exhibit 13.7.

EXHIBIT 13.7
Differences between Manufacturing and Service Technologies

Service Technology
1. Intangible output
2. Production and consumption take place simultaneously
3. Labor- and knowledge-intensive
4. Customer interaction generally high
5. Human element very important
6. Quality is perceived and difficult to measure
7. Rapid response time is usually necessary
8. Site of facility is extremely important

Manufacturing Technology
1. Tangible product
2. Products can be inventoried for later consumption
3. Capital asset-intensive
4. Little direct customer interaction
5. Human element may be less important
6. Quality is directly measured
7. Longer response time is acceptable
8. Site of facility is moderately important

Service	Product and Service	Product
Airlines	Fast-food outlets	Soft drink companies
Hotels	Cosmetics	Steel companies
Consultants	Real estate	Automobile manufacturers
Health care	Stockbrokers	Mining corporations
Law firms	Retail stores	Food processing plants

Source: Based on F. F. Reichheld and W. E. Sasser, Jr., "Zero Defections: Quality Comes to Services," *Harvard Business Review* 68 (September–October 1990), 105–111; and David E. Bowen, Caren Siehl, and Benjamin Schneider, "A Framework for Analyzing Customer Service Orientations in Manufacturing," *Academy of Management Review* 14 (1989), 75–95.

The most obvious difference is that service technology produces an *intangible output*, rather than a tangible product, such as a refrigerator produced by a manufacturing firm. A service is abstract and often consists of knowledge and ideas rather than a physical product. Thus, whereas manufacturers' products can be inventoried for later sale, services are characterized by *simultaneous production and consumption*. A client meets with a doctor or attorney, for example, and students and teachers come together in the classroom or over the Internet. A service is an intangible product that does not exist until it is requested by the customer. It cannot be stored, inventoried, or viewed as a finished good. If a service is not consumed immediately upon production, it disappears.[43] This typically means that service firms are *labor and knowledge intensive*, with many employees needed to meet the needs of customers, whereas manufacturing firms tend to be *capital intensive*, relying on mass production, continuous process, and flexible manufacturing technologies.[44]

Direct interaction between customer and employee is generally very high with services, while there is little direct interaction between customers and employees in the technical core of a manufacturing firm. This direct interaction means that the *human element* (employees) becomes extremely important in service firms. Whereas most people never meet the workers who manufactured their cars, they interact directly with the salesperson who sold them their Honda Civic or Ford F-150. The treatment received from the salesperson—or from a doctor, lawyer, or hairstylist—affects the perception of the service received and the customer's level of satisfaction. The *quality of a service is perceived* and cannot be directly measured and compared in the same way that the quality of a tangible product can. Another characteristic that affects customer satisfaction and perception of quality service is *rapid response time*. A service must be provided when the customer wants and needs it. When you take a friend to dinner, you want to be seated and served in a timely manner; you would not be very satisfied if the host or manager told you to come back tomorrow when there would be more tables or servers available to accommodate you.

The final defining characteristic of service technology is that *site selection is often much more important* than with manufacturing. Because services are intangible, they have to be located where the customer wants to be served. Services are dispersed and located geographically close to customers. For example, fast-food franchises usually disperse their facilities into local stores. Most towns of even moderate size today have two or more McDonald's restaurants rather than one large one, for example, in order to provide service where customers want and need it.

In reality, it is difficult to find organizations that reflect 100 percent service or 100 percent manufacturing characteristics. Some service firms take on characteristics of manufacturers, and vice versa. Many manufacturing firms are placing a greater emphasis on customer service to differentiate themselves and be more competitive. In addition, manufacturing organizations have departments such as purchasing, HR, and marketing that are based on service technology. On the other hand, organizations such as gas stations, stockbrokers, retail stores, and restaurants belong to the service sector, but the provision of a product is a significant part of the transaction. The vast majority of organizations involve some combination of products and services. The important point is that all organizations can be classified along a continuum that includes both manufacturing and service characteristics, as illustrated in Exhibit 13.7. This chapter's "How Do You Fit the Design?" questionnaire will give you some insight into whether you are better suited to be a manager in a service organization or a manufacturing firm.

Briefcase

As an organization manager, keep this guideline in mind:

Use the concept of service technology to evaluate the production process in non-manufacturing firms. Service technologies are intangible and must be located close to the customer. Hence, service organizations may have an organization structure with fewer boundary roles, greater geographical dispersion, decentralization, highly skilled employees in the technical core, and generally less control than in manufacturing organizations.

How Do You Fit the Design?

Manufacturing vs. Service

The questions that follow ask you to describe your behavior. For each question, check the answer that best describes you.

1. I am usually running late for class or other appointments:
   a. Yes
   b. No

2. When taking a test I prefer:
   a. Subjective questions (discussion or essay)
   b. Objective questions (multiple choice)

3. When making decisions, I typically:
   a. Go with my gut—what feels right
   b. Carefully weigh each option

4. When solving a problem, I would more likely:
   a. Take a walk, mull things over, then discuss
   b. Write down alternatives, prioritize them, then pick the best

5. I consider time spent daydreaming as:
   a. A viable tool for planning my future
   b. A waste of time.

6. To remember directions, I typically:
   a. Visualize the information
   b. Make notes

7. My work style is mostly:
   a. Juggle several things at once.
   b. Concentrate on one task at a time until complete

8. My desk, work area, or laundry area are typically:
   a. Cluttered
   b. Neat and organized

Scoring: Count the number of checked "a" items and "b" items. Each "a" represents right-brain processing, and each "b" represents left-brain processing. If you scored 6 or higher on either, you have a distinct processing style. If you checked fewer than 6 for either, you probably have a balanced style.

Interpretation: People have two thinking processes—one visual and intuitive in the right half of the brain, and the other verbal and analytical in the left half of the brain. The thinking process you prefer predisposes you to certain types of knowledge and information—technical reports, analytical information, and quantitative data (left brain) vs. talking to people, thematic impressions, and personal intuition (right brain)—as effective input to your thinking and decision making. Manufacturing organizations typically use left-brain processing to handle data based on physical, measurable technology. Service organizations typically use right-brain processing to interpret less tangible situations and serve people in a direct way. Left-brain processing has been summarized as based on logic; right-brain processing has been summarized as based on love.

Source: Adapted from Carolyn Hopper, *Practicing Management Skills* (Houghton Mifflin, 2003); and Jacquelyn Wonder and Priscilla Donovan, "Mind Openers," *Self* (March 1984).

New Directions in Services. Service firms have always tended toward providing *customized output*—that is, providing exactly the service each customer wants and needs. When you visit a hairstylist, you don't automatically get the same cut the stylist gave the three previous clients. The stylist cuts your hair the way you request it. However, customer expectations of what constitutes good service are rising. Service companies such as the Ritz-Carlton Hotels, Vanguard, and Progressive Insurance use new technology to keep customers coming back. All Ritz-Carlton hotels are linked to a database filled with the preferences of half a million guests, allowing any desk clerk or bellhop to find out what your favorite wine is, whether you're allergic to feather pillows, and how many extra towels you want in your room.[45] At Vanguard, customer service reps teach customers how to effectively use the company's website. That means customers needing simple information now get it quickly and easily over the Web, and reps have more time to help clients with complicated questions. The new approach has had a positive impact on Vanguard's customer retention rate.[46]

The expectation for better service has also pushed service firms in industries from package delivery to health care to take a lesson from manufacturing.[47] Japan Post, under pressure to cut a $191 million loss on operations, hired Toyota's Toshihiro Takahashi to help apply the Toyota Production System to the collection, sorting, and delivery of mail. In all, Takahashi's team came up with 370 improvements and reduced the post office's person-hours by 20 percent. The waste reduction is expected to cut costs by around $350 million a year.[48] Numerous other service firms, in the United States as well as in other countries, have also applied lean principles in recent years.

Designing the Service Organization

The feature of service technologies with a distinct influence on organizational structure and control systems is the need for technical core employees to be close to the customer.[49] The differences between service and product organizations necessitated by customer contact are summarized in Exhibit 13.8.

The impact of customer contact on organization structure is reflected in the use of boundary roles and structural disaggregation.[50] Boundary roles are used extensively in manufacturing firms to handle customers and to reduce disruptions for the technical core. They are used less in service firms because a service is intangible and cannot be passed along by boundary spanners, so service customers must interact directly with technical employees, such as doctors or brokers.

A service firm deals in information and intangible outputs and does not need to be large. Its greatest economies are achieved through disaggregation into small units that can be located close to customers. Stockbrokers, doctors' clinics, consulting firms, and banks disperse their facilities into regional and local offices. Manufacturing firms, on the other hand, tend to aggregate operations in a single

EXHIBIT 13.8

Configuration and Structural Characteristics of Service Organizations versus Product Organizations

Structural Characteristic	Service	Product
1. Separate boundary roles	Few	Many
2. Geographical dispersion	Much	Little
3. Decision making	Decentralized	Centralized
4. Formalization	Lower	Higher
Human Resources		
1. Employee skill level	Higher	Lower
2. Skill emphasis	Interpersonal	Technical

area that has raw materials and an available workforce. A large manufacturing firm can take advantage of economies derived from expensive machinery and long production runs.

Service technology also influences internal organization characteristics used to direct and control the organization. For one thing, the skills of technical core employees typically need to be higher. These employees need enough knowledge and awareness to handle customer problems rather than just enough to perform mechanical tasks. Employees need social and interpersonal skills as well as technical skills.[51] Because of higher skills and structural dispersion, decision making often tends to be decentralized in service firms, and formalization tends to be low. Although some service organizations, such as many fast-food chains, have set rules and procedures for customer service, employees in service organizations typically have more freedom and discretion on the job. Managers at Home Depot have learned that how employees are managed has a great deal to do with the success of a service organization.

Home Depot Inc.

Home Depot grew to the world's largest home improvement retailer largely on the strength of its employees. Many people hired to work in the stores were former plumbers, carpenters, or other skilled tradesmen who understood the products and took pride in helping do-it-yourselfers find the right tools and supplies and know how to use them.

However, to cut costs in recent years, the company began hiring more part-time employees and instituted a salary cap that made jobs less appealing to experienced workers. As a further way to reduce costs, managers began measuring every aspect of the stores' productivity, such as how long it took to unload shipments of goods or how many extended warranties each employee sold per week. What got overlooked, though, was how well employees were providing service. Customers began complaining that they could never find anyone to assist them—and even when they did, many employees didn't have the knowledge and experience to be of much help. Some customers took their business elsewhere, even if it meant going to small shops where they would pay higher prices but get better service.

Now managers are working hard to get things back on track. The stores are hiring more full-timers again, instituting new training programs, and looking for other ways to make sure employees are knowledgeable and helpful. The CEO even reached out to the company's founders, Bernie Marcus and Arthur Blank, for advice on how to put the shine back on Home Depot's customer service reputation.[52] ■

Managers at Home Depot can use an understanding of the nature of service technology to help them align strategy, structure, and management processes and make the retailer more effective. Service technologies require structures and systems that are quite different from those for a traditional manufacturing technology. For example, the concept of separating complex tasks into a series of small jobs and exploiting economies of scale is a cornerstone of traditional manufacturing, but researchers have found that applying it to service organizations often does not work so well.[53] Some service firms have redesigned jobs to separate low– and high–customer-contact activities, with more rules and standardization in the low-contact jobs. High-touch service jobs, like those on the Home Depot sales floor, need more freedom and less control to satisfy customers.

2 **The best way for a company to provide good service is to have abundant and clear rules and procedures and make sure everyone follows them to the letter.**

ANSWER: *Disagree.* Service employees need good interpersonal skills and a degree of autonomy to be able to satisfy each customer's specific needs. Although many service organizations have some standard procedures for serving customers, service firms are typically low on both centralization and formalization. Abundant rules can take away both personal autonomy and the personal touch.

Now let's turn to another perspective on technology, that of production activities within specific organizational departments. Departments often have characteristics similar to those of service technology, providing services to other departments within the organization.

NON-CORE DEPARTMENTAL TECHNOLOGY

This section shifts to the department level of analysis for departments not necessarily within the technical core. Each department in an organization has a production process that consists of a distinct technology. A company such as Tenneco, a maker of auto parts, for example, might have departments for engineering, research and development, human resources, marketing, quality control, finance, and dozens of other functions. This section analyzes the nature of departmental technology and its relationship with departmental structure.

The framework that has had the greatest impact on the understanding of departmental technologies was developed by Charles Perrow.[54] Perrow's model has been useful for a broad range of technologies, which made it ideal for research into departmental activities.

Variety

Perrow specified two dimensions of departmental activities that were relevant to organization structure and process. The first is the number of exceptions in the work. This refers to task **variety**, which is the frequency of unexpected and novel events that occur in the conversion process. Task variety concerns whether work processes are performed the same way every time or differ from time to time as employees transform the organization's inputs into outputs.[55] When individuals encounter a large number of unexpected situations, with frequent problems, variety is considered high. When there are few problems, and when day-to-day job requirements are repetitive, technology contains little variety. Variety in departments can range from repeating a single act, such as on a traditional assembly line, to working on a series of unrelated problems, such as in a hospital emergency room.

Analyzability

The second dimension of technology concerns the **analyzability** of work activities. When the conversion process is analyzable, the work can be reduced to mechanical steps and participants can follow an objective, computational procedure to solve problems. Problem solution may involve the use of standard procedures, such as instructions and manuals, or technical knowledge, such as that in a textbook or handbook. On the other hand, some work is not analyzable. When problems arise, it is difficult to identify the correct solution. There is no store of techniques or procedures to tell a person exactly what to do. The cause of or solution to a problem is not clear, so employees rely on accumulated experience, intuition, and judgment. The final solution to a problem is often the result of wisdom and experience and not the result of standard procedures. For example, Philippos Poulos, a tone regulator at Steinway & Sons, has an unanalyzable technology. Tone regulators carefully check each piano's hammers to ensure they produce the proper "Steinway sound."[56] These quality-control tasks require years of experience and practice. Standard procedures will not tell a person how to do such tasks.

Framework

The two dimensions of technology and examples of departmental activities on Perrow's framework are shown in Exhibit 13.9. The dimensions of variety and analyzability form the basis for four major categories of technology: routine, craft, engineering, and nonroutine.

Categories of Technology. Routine technologies are characterized by little task variety and the use of objective, computational procedures. The tasks are formalized and standardized. Examples include an automobile assembly line and a bank teller department.

Craft technologies are characterized by a fairly stable stream of activities, but the conversion process is not analyzable or well understood. Tasks require extensive training and experience because employees respond to intangible factors on the basis of wisdom, intuition, and experience. Although advances in machine technologies seem to have reduced the number of craft technologies in organizations, craft technologies are still important. For example, steel furnace engineers continue to mix steel based on intuition and experience, pattern makers at fashion houses such as Louis Vuitton, Zara, or H&M convert rough designers' sketches into salable garments, and teams of writers for television series such as *House* or *Grey's Anatomy* convert ideas into story lines.

Engineering technologies tend to be complex because there is substantial variety in the tasks performed. However, the various activities are usually handled on the basis of established formulas, procedures, and techniques. Employees normally refer to a well-developed body of knowledge to handle problems. Engineering and accounting tasks usually fall in this category.

Nonroutine technologies have high task variety, and the conversion process is not analyzable or well understood. In nonroutine technology, a great deal of effort is devoted to analyzing problems and activities. Several equally acceptable options typically can be found. Experience and technical knowledge are used to solve problems and perform the work. Basic research, strategic planning, and other work that involves new projects and unexpected problems are nonroutine. The blossoming

EXHIBIT 13.9
Framework for
Department Technologies

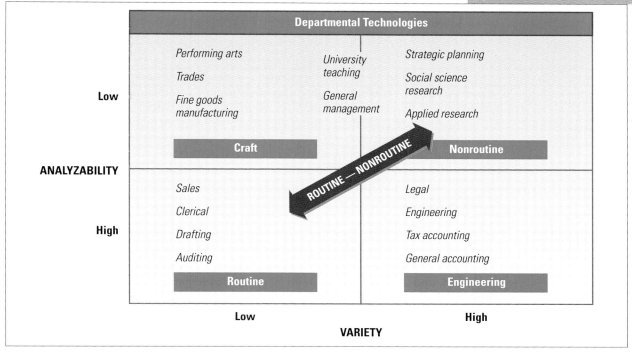

Source: *California Management Review* by Daft and Macintosh. Copyright 1978 by California Management Review. Reproduced with permission of California Management Review via Copyright Clearance Center.

biotechnology industry also represents a nonroutine technology. Breakthroughs in understanding metabolism and physiology at a cellular level depend on highly trained employees who use their experience and intuition as well as scientific knowledge.[57]

Routine versus Nonroutine. Exhibit 13.9 also illustrates that variety and analyzability can be combined into a single dimension of technology. This dimension is called *routine versus nonroutine technology*, and it is the diagonal line in Exhibit 13.9. The analyzability and variety dimensions are often correlated in departments, meaning that technologies high in variety tend to be low in analyzability, and technologies low in variety tend to be analyzable. Departments can be evaluated along a single dimension of routine versus nonroutine that combines both analyzability and variety, which is a useful shorthand measure for analyzing departmental technology.

The following questions show how departmental technology can be analyzed for determining its placement on Perrow's technology framework in Exhibit 13.9.[58] Employees normally circle a number from 1 to 7 in response to each question.

Variety:
1. To what extent would you say your work is routine?
2. Does most everyone in this unit do about the same job in the same way most of the time?
3. Are unit members performing repetitive activities in doing their jobs?

Analyzability:

1. To what extent is there a clearly known way to do the major types of work you normally encounter?
2. To what extent is there an understandable sequence of steps that can be followed in doing your work?
3. To do your work, to what extent can you actually rely on established procedures and practices?

If answers to the preceding questions indicate high scores for analyzability and low scores for variety, the department would have a routine technology. If the opposite occurs, the technology would be nonroutine. Low variety and low analyzability indicate a craft technology, and high variety and high analyzability indicate an engineering technology. As a practical matter, most departments fit somewhere along the diagonal and can be most easily characterized as routine or nonroutine.

DEPARTMENT DESIGN

Once the nature of a department's technology has been identified, the appropriate structure can be determined. Department technology tends to be associated with a cluster of departmental characteristics, such as the skill level of employees, formalization, and methods of communication. Definite patterns exist in the relationship between work unit technology and structural characteristics, which are associated with departmental performance.[59] Key relationships between technology and other dimensions of departments are described in this section and are summarized in Exhibit 13.10.

The overall structure of departments may be characterized as either organic or mechanistic. Routine technologies are associated with a mechanistic structure and processes, with formal rules and rigid management processes. Nonroutine technologies are associated with an organic structure, and department management is more flexible and free-flowing. The specific design characteristics of formalization, centralization, worker skill level, span of control, and communication and coordination vary, depending on work unit technology.

ASSESS YOUR ANSWER

3 The design characteristics and management processes that are effective for a television station's sales department probably would not work so well for the news department.

ANSWER: *Agree.* The news department has a nonroutine technology compared to the sales department. No one knows what newsworthy events are going to happen during the day, when or where they will happen, or how they will need to be covered. Sales tasks, particularly telephone sales to repeat customers involving standard rates for advertising, can be performed using standard procedures, but gathering and reporting news events can't be standardized. A sales department would be characterized as routine because there is little variety and tasks are well understood.

EXHIBIT 13.10
Relationship of
Department Technology
to Structural and
Management
Characteristics

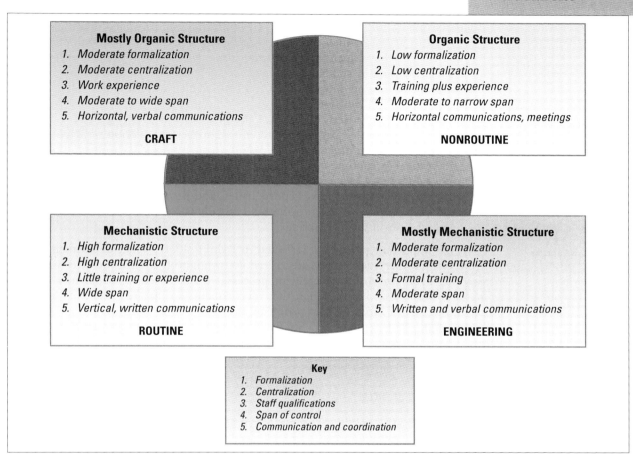

Mostly Organic Structure
1. *Moderate formalization*
2. *Moderate centralization*
3. *Work experience*
4. *Moderate to wide span*
5. *Horizontal, verbal communications*

CRAFT

Organic Structure
1. *Low formalization*
2. *Low centralization*
3. *Training plus experience*
4. *Moderate to narrow span*
5. *Horizontal communications, meetings*

NONROUTINE

Mechanistic Structure
1. *High formalization*
2. *High centralization*
3. *Little training or experience*
4. *Wide span*
5. *Vertical, written communications*

ROUTINE

Mostly Mechanistic Structure
1. *Moderate formalization*
2. *Moderate centralization*
3. *Formal training*
4. *Moderate span*
5. *Written and verbal communications*

ENGINEERING

Key
1. *Formalization*
2. *Centralization*
3. *Staff qualifications*
4. *Span of control*
5. *Communication and coordination*

1. *Formalization.* Routine technology is characterized by standardization and division of labor into small tasks that are governed by formal rules and procedures. For nonroutine tasks, the structure is less formal and less standardized. When variety is high, as in a research department, fewer activities are covered by formal procedures.[60]
2. *Decentralization.* In routine technologies, most decision making about task activities is centralized to management.[61] In engineering technologies, employees with technical training tend to acquire moderate decision authority because technical knowledge is important to task accomplishment. Production employees who have years of experience obtain decision authority in craft technologies because they know how to respond to problems. Decentralization to employees is greatest in nonroutine settings, where many decisions are made by employees.
3. *Worker skill level.* Work staff in routine technologies typically require little education or experience, which is congruent with repetitious work activities.

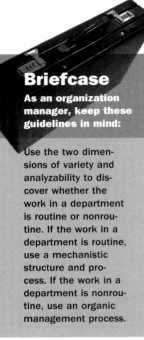

In work units with greater variety, staff are more skilled and often have formal training in technical schools or universities. Training for craft activities, which are less analyzable, is more likely to be through job experience. Nonroutine activities require both formal education and job experience.[62]

4. *Span of control.* Span of control is the number of employees who report to a single manager or supervisor. This characteristic is normally influenced by departmental technology. The more complex and nonroutine the task, the more problems arise in which the supervisor becomes involved. Although the span of control may be influenced by other factors, such as skill level of employees, it typically should be smaller for complex tasks because on such tasks the supervisor and subordinate must interact frequently.[63]

5. *Communication and coordination.* Communication activity and frequency increase as task variety increases.[64] Frequent problems require more information sharing to solve problems and ensure proper completion of activities. The direction of communication is typically horizontal in nonroutine work units and vertical in routine work units.[65] The form of communication varies by task analyzability.[66] When tasks are highly analyzable, statistical and written forms of communication (memos, reports, rules, and procedures) are frequent. When tasks are less analyzable, information typically is conveyed face-to-face, over the telephone, or in group meetings.

Two important points are reflected in Exhibit 13.10. First, departments differ from one another and can be categorized according to their workflow technology.[67] Second, structural and management processes differ based on departmental technology. Managers should design their departments so that requirements based on technology can be met. Design problems are most visible when the design is clearly inconsistent with technology. Studies have found that when structure and communication characteristics did not reflect technology, departments tended to be less effective.[68] Employees could not communicate with the frequency needed to solve problems.

WORKFLOW INTERDEPENDENCE AMONG DEPARTMENTS

So far, this chapter has explored how organization and department technologies influence structural design. The final characteristic of technology that influences structure is called interdependence. **Interdependence** means the extent to which departments depend on each other for resources or materials to accomplish their tasks. Low interdependence means that departments can do their work independently of each other and have little need for interaction, consultation, or exchange of materials. High interdependence means departments must constantly exchange resources.

Types

James Thompson defined three types of interdependence that influence organization structure.[69] These interdependencies are illustrated in Exhibit 13.11 and are discussed in the following sections.

Form of Interdependence	Demands on Horizontal Communication, Decision Making	Type of Coordination Required	Priority for Locating Units Close Together
Pooled (bank) Clients	Low communication	Standardization, rules, procedures Divisional structure	Low
Sequential (assembly line) Client	Medium communication	Plans, schedules, feedback Task forces	Medium
Reciprocal (hospital) Client	High communication	Mutual adjustment, cross-departmental meetings, teamwork Horizontal structure	High

EXHIBIT 13.11

Thompson's Classification of Interdependence and Management Implications

Pooled. **Pooled interdependence** is the lowest form of interdependence among departments. In this form, work does not flow between units. Each department is part of the organization and contributes to the common good of the organization, but works independently. Subway restaurants or Bank of America branches are examples of pooled interdependence. An outlet in Chicago need not interact with an outlet in Urbana. Pooled interdependence may be associated with the relationships within a *divisional structure*, defined in Chapter 2. Divisions or branches share financial resources from a common pool, and the success of each division contributes to the success of the overall organization.

Thompson proposed that pooled interdependence would exist in firms with what he called a mediating technology. A **mediating technology** provides products or services that mediate or link clients from the external environment and, in so doing, allows each department to work independently. Banks, brokerage firms, and real estate offices all mediate between buyers and sellers, but the offices work independently within the organization.

The management implications associated with pooled interdependence are quite simple. Thompson argued that managers should use rules and procedures to standardize activities across departments. Each department should use the same procedures and financial statements so the outcomes of all departments can be measured and pooled. Very little day-to-day coordination is required among units.

Sequential. When interdependence is of serial form, with parts produced in one department becoming inputs to another department, it is called **sequential interdependence**.

Briefcase

As an organization manager, keep these guidelines in mind:

Evaluate the interdependencies among organizational departments. Use the general rule that, as interdependencies increase, mechanisms for coordination must also increase. Consider a divisional structure for pooled interdependence. For sequential interdependence, use task forces and integrators for greater horizontal coordination. At the highest level of interdependence (reciprocal interdependence), a horizontal structure may be appropriate.

The first department must perform correctly for the second department to perform correctly. This is a higher level of interdependence than pooled interdependence, because departments exchange resources and depend on others to perform well. Sequential interdependence creates a greater need for horizontal mechanisms such as integrators or task forces.

Sequential interdependence occurs in what Thompson called **long-linked technology**, which "refers to the combination in one organization of successive stages of production; each stage of production uses as its inputs the production of the preceding stage and produces inputs for the following stage."[70] An example of sequential interdependence comes from the shipbuilding industry. Until recently, ship designers made patterns and molds out of paper and plywood, which were passed on to assembly. The cutting department depended on accurate measurements from the designers, and the assembly department depended on accurate parts from the cutting department. This sequential interdependence meant that mistakes in measurements or pattern mix-ups often caused errors in the cutting and assembly process, leading to delays and increased costs. Naval architect Filippo Cali created a complex software program that computerizes the process of making patterns and molds, thus eliminating many of the problems between design and assembly.[71] Another example of sequential interdependence would be an automobile assembly line, which must have all the parts it needs, such as engines, steering mechanisms, and tires, to keep production rolling.

The management requirements for sequential interdependence are more demanding than those for pooled interdependence. Coordination among the linked plants or departments is required. Since the interdependence implies a one-way flow of materials, extensive planning and scheduling are generally needed. Department B needs to know what to expect from Department A so both can perform effectively. Some day-to-day communication among plants or departments is also needed to handle unexpected problems and exceptions that arise.

Reciprocal. The highest level of interdependence is **reciprocal interdependence**. This exists when the output of operation A is the input to operation B, and the output of operation B is the input back again to operation A. The outputs of departments influence those departments in reciprocal fashion.

Reciprocal interdependence tends to occur in organizations with what Thompson called **intensive technologies**, which provide a variety of products or services in combination to a client. A firm developing new products provides an example of reciprocal interdependence. Intense coordination is needed between design, engineering, manufacturing, and marketing to combine all their resources to suit the customer's product need. Hospitals are also an excellent example because they provide coordinated services to patients, as illustrated by the following story.

IN PRACTICE

Great Ormond Street Hospital for Children

The Great Ormond Street Hospital is known for its expertise in infant heart surgery, where a lot can go wrong. One of the most dangerous phases of the procedure comes during the "handoff," that is, transferring the patient from surgery to intensive care. If an infant is transferred to ICU and the ventilator isn't ready, for instance, it could be disastrous. Thousands of similar handoffs occur in hospitals all over the world every day, and devastating mistakes can happen if coordination is sloppy or weak. Studies have found that 70 percent of preventable hospital mistakes occur because of communication breakdowns, and at least half of those breakdowns come during the critical handoff phase—transferring a patient from one department to another or to a new team during a shift change.

Hospitals all over the world are borrowing ideas from other industries skilled in the process of high-risk handoffs. Great Ormond's smooth handoff system is based partly on the pit-stop techniques of Italy's Ferrari racing team. Kaiser Permanente of California uses a handoff procedure based on the change-of-command system developed for nuclear submarines. A Saint Joseph's Health System facility has a handoff system called "Ticket to Ride," which is a series of questions about the patient's medications, infections, and other medical issues that have to be asked of a person transferring a patient from one department to another. Health care providers and hospital managers are looking for any approach that will improve coordination between departments and prevent deadly mistakes.[72] ■

Reciprocal interdependence such as that at hospitals like Great Ormond requires that departments work together intimately and be tightly coordinated. A recent study of top management teams confirms that effective performance of teams characterized by high interdependence depends on good communication and close coordination.[73] With reciprocal interdependence, the structure must allow for frequent horizontal communication and adjustment, perhaps using cross-functional teams or a horizontal structure. Extensive planning is required, but plans will not anticipate or solve all problems. Daily interaction and mutual adjustment among departments are required. Managers from several departments are jointly involved in face-to-face coordination, teamwork, and decision making. Reciprocal interdependence is the most complex interdependence for organizations to handle and the most challenging for managers in designing the organization.

Structural Priority

As indicated in Exhibit 13.11, because decision making, communication, and coordination problems are greatest for reciprocal interdependence, reciprocal interdependence should receive first priority in organization structure. New product development is one area of reciprocal interdependence that is of growing concern to managers as companies face increasing pressure to get new products to market fast. Many firms are revamping the design–manufacturing relationship by closely integrating CAD and CAM technologies discussed earlier in this chapter.[74] Activities that are reciprocally interdependent should be grouped close together in the organization so managers have easy access to one another for mutual adjustment. These units should report to the same person on the organization chart and should be physically close so the time and effort for coordination can be minimized. A horizontal structure, with linked sets of teams working on core processes, can provide the close coordination needed to support reciprocal interdependence. Poor coordination will result in poor performance for the organization. If reciprocally interdependent units are not located close together, the organization should design mechanisms for coordination, such as daily meetings between departments or an intranet to facilitate communication. The next priority is given to sequential interdependencies, and finally to pooled interdependencies.

This strategy of organizing keeps the communication channels short where coordination is most critical to organizational success. For example, Boise Cascade Corporation experienced poor service to customers because customer-service reps located in New York City were not coordinating with production planners in Oregon plants. Customers couldn't get delivery as needed. Boise was reorganized, and the two groups were consolidated under one roof, reporting to the same supervisor at division headquarters. Now customer needs are met because customer-service reps work with production planning to schedule customer orders.

Structural Implications

Most organizations experience various levels of interdependence, and structure can be designed to fit these needs, as illustrated in Exhibit 13.12.[75] In a manufacturing firm, new product development entails reciprocal interdependence among the design, engineering, purchasing, manufacturing, and sales departments. Perhaps a horizontal structure or cross-functional teams could be used to handle the back-and-forth flow of information and resources. Once a product is designed, its actual manufacture would be sequential interdependence, with a flow of goods from one department to another, such as among purchasing, inventory, production control, manufacturing, and assembly. The actual ordering and delivery of products is pooled interdependence, with warehouses working independently. Customers could place an order with the nearest facility, which would not require coordination among warehouses, except in unusual cases such as a stock outage.

The three levels of interdependence are illustrated by a study of athletic teams that examined interdependency among players and how it influences other aspects of baseball, football, and basketball teams.

EXHIBIT 13.12
Primary Means to
Achieve Coordination for
Different Levels of Task
Interdependence in a
Manufacturing Firm

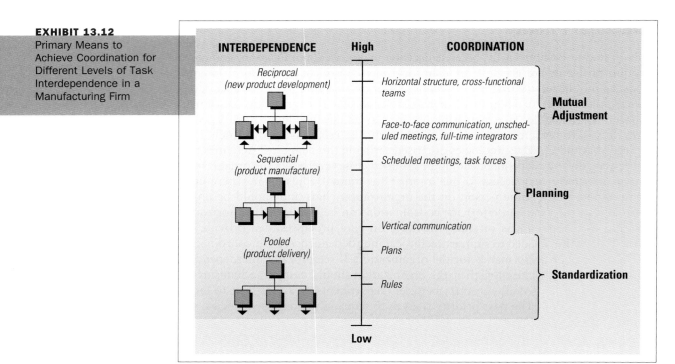

Source: Adapted from Andrew H. Van de Ven, Andre Delbecq, and Richard Koenig, "Determinants of Communication Modes within Organizations," *American Sociological Review* 41 (1976), 330.

IN PRACTICE

Athletic Teams

A major difference among baseball, football, and basketball is the interdependence among players. Baseball is low in interdependence, football is medium, and basketball represents the highest player interdependence. The relationships among interdependence and other characteristics of team play are illustrated in Exhibit 13.13.

Pete Rose said, "Baseball is a team game, but nine men who reach their individual goals make a nice team." In baseball, interdependence among team players is low and can be defined as pooled. Each member acts independently, taking a turn at bat and playing his or her own position. When interaction does occur, it is between only two or three players, as in a double play. Players are physically dispersed, and the rules of the game are the primary means of coordinating players. Players practice and develop their skills individually, such as by taking batting practice and undergoing physical conditioning. Management's job is to select good players. If each player is successful as an individual, the team should win.

In football, interdependence among players is higher and tends to be sequential. The line first blocks the opponents to enable the backs to run or pass. Plays are performed sequentially from first down to fourth down. Physical dispersion is medium, which allows players to operate as a coordinated unit. The primary mechanism for coordinating players is developing a game plan along with rules that govern the behavior of team members. Each player has an assignment that fits with other assignments, and management designs the game plan to achieve victory.

In basketball, interdependence tends to be reciprocal. The game is free-flowing, and the division of labor is less precise than in other sports. Each player is involved in both offense and defense, handles the ball, and attempts to score. The ball flows back and forth among players. Team members interact in a dynamic flow to achieve victory. Management skills involve the ability to influence this dynamic process, either by substituting players or by working the ball into certain areas. Players must learn to adapt to the flow of the game and to one another as events unfold.

Interdependence among players is a primary factor explaining the difference among the three sports. Baseball is organized around an autonomous individual, football around groups that are sequentially interdependent, and basketball around the free flow of reciprocal players.[76] ■

EXHIBIT 13.13

Relationships among Interdependence and Other Characteristics of Team Play

	Baseball	Football	Basketball
Interdependence	Pooled	Sequential	Reciprocal
Physical dispersion of players	High	Medium	Low
Coordination	Rules that govern the sport	Game plan and position roles	Mutual adjustment and shared responsibility
Key management job	Select players and develop their skills	Prepare and execute game	Influence flow of game

Source: Based on William Pasmore, Carol E. Francis, and Jeffrey Haldeman, "Sociotechnical Systems: A North American Reflection on the Empirical Studies of the 70s," *Human Relations* 35 (1982), 1179–1204.

IMPACT OF TECHNOLOGY ON JOB DESIGN

So far, this chapter has described models for analyzing how manufacturing, service, and department technologies influence structure and management processes. The relationship between a new technology and the organization seems to follow a pattern, beginning with immediate effects on the content of jobs followed (after a longer period) by impact on design of the organization. The ultimate impact of technology on employees can be partially understood through the concepts of job design and sociotechnical systems.

Job Design

Job design includes the assignment of goals and tasks to be accomplished by employees. Managers may consciously change job design to improve productivity or worker motivation. However, managers may also unconsciously influence job design through the introduction of new technologies, which can change how jobs are done and the very nature of jobs.[77] Managers should understand how the introduction of a new technology may affect employees' jobs. The common theme of new technologies in the workplace is that they in some way substitute machinery for human labor in transforming inputs into outputs. Automated teller machines (ATMs) have replaced thousands of human bank tellers, for example. Robots used in flexible manufacturing systems are replacing laborers on the production line.

In addition to actually replacing human workers, technology may have several different effects on the human jobs that remain. Research has indicated that mass-production technologies tend to produce **job simplification**, which means that the variety and difficulty of tasks performed by a single person are reduced. The consequence is boring, repetitive jobs that generally provide little satisfaction. Sometimes, managers introduce **job rotation**, which means moving employees from job to job to give them a greater variety of tasks. More advanced technology, on the other hand, tends to cause **job enrichment**, meaning that the job provides greater responsibility, recognition, and opportunities for growth and development. Advanced technologies create a greater need for employee training and education because workers need higher-level skills and greater competence to master their tasks. For example, ATMs took most of the routine tasks (deposits and withdrawals) away from bank tellers and left them with the more complex tasks that require higher-level skills. Studies of flexible manufacturing found that it produces three noticeable results for employees: more opportunities for intellectual mastery and enhanced cognitive skills for workers; more worker responsibility for results; and greater interdependence among workers, enabling more social interaction and the development of teamwork and coordination skills.[78] Flexible manufacturing technology may also contribute to **job enlargement**, which is an expansion of the number of different tasks performed by an employee. Fewer workers are needed with the new technology, and each employee has to be able to perform a greater number and variety of tasks.

With advanced technology, workers have to keep learning new skills because technology changes so rapidly. Advances in *information technology*, to be discussed in detail in the next chapter, are having a significant effect on jobs in the service industry, including doctors' offices and medical clinics, law firms, financial planners, and libraries. Workers may find that their jobs change almost daily because of new

Briefcase

As an organization manager, keep these guidelines in mind:

Be aware that the introduction of a new technology has significant impact on job design. Consider using the sociotechnical systems approach to balance the needs of workers with the requirements of the new technological system.

software programs, changes in use of the Internet, and other advances in information technology.

Advanced technology does not always have a positive effect on employees, but research findings in general are encouraging, suggesting that jobs for workers are enriched rather than simplified, engaging their higher mental capacities, offering opportunities for learning and growth, and providing greater job satisfaction.

Sociotechnical Systems

The **sociotechnical systems approach** recognizes the interaction of technical and human needs in effective job design, combining the needs of people with the organization's need for technical efficiency. The *socio* portion of the approach refers to the people and groups that work in organizations and how work is organized and coordinated. The *technical* portion refers to the materials, tools, machines, and processes used to transform organizational inputs into outputs.

Exhibit 13.14 illustrates the three primary components of the sociotechnical systems model.[79] The *social system* includes all human elements—such as individual and team behaviors, organizational culture, management practices, and degree of communication openness—that can influence the performance of work. The *technical system* refers to the type of production technology, the level of interdependence, the complexity of tasks, and so forth. The goal of the sociotechnical systems approach is to design the organization for **joint optimization**, which means that an organization functions best when the social and technical systems are designed to fit the needs of one another. Designing the organization to meet human needs while ignoring the technical systems, or changing technology to improve efficiency while ignoring human needs, may inadvertently cause performance problems. The sociotechnical systems approach attempts to find a balance between what workers want and need and the technical requirements of the organization's production system.[80]

EXHIBIT 13.14
Sociotechnical Systems Model

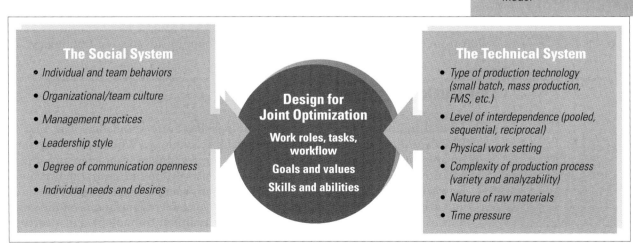

Sources: Based on T. Cummings, "Self-Regulating Work Groups: A Socio-Technical Synthesis," *Academy of Management Review* 3 (1978), 625–634; Don Hellriegel, John W. Slocum, and Richard W. Woodman, *Organizational Behavior*, 8th ed. (Cincinnati, Ohio: South-Western, 1998), 492; and Gregory B. Northcraft and Margaret A. Neale, *Organizational Behavior: A Management Challenge*, 2nd ed. (Fort Worth, Tex.: The Dryden Press, 1994), 551.

One example comes from a museum that installed a closed-circuit television system. Rather than having several guards patrolling the museum and grounds, the television could easily be monitored by a single guard. Although the technology saved money because only one guard was needed per shift, it led to unexpected performance problems. Guards had previously enjoyed the social interaction provided by patrolling; monitoring a closed-circuit television led to alienation and boredom. When a federal agency did an 18-month test of the system, only 5 percent of several thousand experimental covert intrusions were detected by the guard.[81] The system was inadequate because human needs were not taken into account.

Sociotechnical principles evolved from the work of the Tavistock Institute, a research organization in England, during the 1950s and 1960s.[82] Examples of organizational change using sociotechnical systems principles have occurred in numerous organizations, including General Motors, Volvo, the Tennessee Valley Authority (TVA), and Procter & Gamble.[83] Although there have been failures, in many of these applications, the joint optimization of changes in technology and structure to meet the needs of people as well as efficiency improved performance, safety, quality, absenteeism, and turnover. In some cases, work design was not the most efficient based on technical and scientific principles, but worker involvement and commitment more than made up for the difference. Thus, once again research shows that new technologies need not have a negative impact on workers, because the technology often requires higher-level mental and social skills and can be organized to encourage the involvement and commitment of employees, thereby benefiting both the employee and the organization.

The sociotechnical systems principle that people should be viewed as resources and provided with appropriate skills, meaningful work, and suitable rewards becomes even more important in today's world of growing technological complexity.[84] One study of paper manufacturers found that organizations that put too much faith in machines and technology and pay little attention to the appropriate management of people do not achieve advances in productivity and flexibility. Today's most successful companies strive to find the right mix of machines, computer systems, and people and the most effective way to coordinate them.[85]

Although many principles of sociotechnical systems theory are still valid, current scholars and researchers are also arguing for an expansion of the approach to capture the dynamic nature of today's organizations, the chaotic environment, and the shift from routine to nonroutine jobs brought about by advances in technology.[86]

DESIGN ESSENTIALS

■ Several important ideas in the technology literature stand out. The first is Woodward's research into manufacturing technology. Woodward went into organizations and collected practical data on technology characteristics, organization structure, and management systems. She found clear relationships between technology and structure in high-performing organizations. Her findings are so clear that managers can analyze their own organizations on the same dimensions of technology and structure. In addition, technology and structure can be co-aligned with organizational strategy to meet changing needs and provide new competitive advantages.

■ The second important idea is that service technologies differ in a systematic way from manufacturing technologies. Service technologies are characterized by intangible outcomes and direct client involvement in the production process. Service firms do not have the fixed, machine-based technologies that appear in manufacturing organizations; hence, organization design often differs as well.

■ A third significant idea is Perrow's framework applied to department technologies. Understanding the variety and analyzability of a technology tells one about the management style, structure, and process that should characterize that department. Routine technologies are characterized by mechanistic structure and nonroutine technologies by organic structure. Applying the wrong management system to a department will result in dissatisfaction and reduced efficiency.

■ The fourth important idea is interdependence among departments. The extent to which departments depend on each other for materials, information, or other resources determines the amount of coordination required between them. As interdependence increases, demands on the organization for coordination increase. Organization design must allow for the correct amount of communication and coordination to handle interdependence across departments.

■ The fifth idea is that new flexible manufacturing systems and lean manufacturing are being adopted by organizations and having impact on organization design. For the most part, the impact is positive, with shifts toward more organic structures both on the shop floor and in the management hierarchy. These technologies replace routine jobs, give employees more autonomy, produce more challenging jobs, encourage teamwork, and let the organization be more flexible and responsive. The new technologies are enriching jobs to the point where organizations are happier places to work.

■ Several principles of sociotechnical systems theory, which attempts to design the technical and human aspects of an organization to fit one another, are increasingly important as advances in technology alter the nature of jobs and social interaction in today's companies.

Key Concepts

analyzability
continuous-process production
core technology
craft technologies
engineering technologies
flexible manufacturing systems
intensive technologies
interdependence
job design
job enlargement
job enrichment

job rotation
job simplification
joint optimization
large-batch production
lean manufacturing
long-linked technology
mass customization
mediating technology
non-core technology
nonroutine technologies
pooled interdependence

reciprocal interdependence
routine technologies
sequential interdependence
service technology
small-batch production
sociotechnical systems approach
technical complexity
technology
variety

Discussion Questions

1. What is a service technology? Are different types of service technologies likely to be associated with different structures? Explain.
2. Describe the sociotechnical systems model. Why might some managers oppose a sociotechnical systems approach?
3. How do flexible manufacturing and lean manufacturing differ from other manufacturing technologies? Why are these new approaches needed in today's environment?
4. To what extent does the development of new technologies simplify and routinize the jobs of employees? Can you give an example? How can new technology lead to job enlargement? Discuss.
5. What relationships did Woodward discover between supervisor span of control and technological complexity?
6. A top executive claimed that top-level management is a craft technology because the work contains intangibles, such as handling personnel, interpreting the environment, and coping with unusual situations that have to be learned through experience. If this is true, is it appropriate to teach management in a business school? Does teaching management from a textbook assume that the manager's job is analyzable, and hence that formal training rather than experience is most important?
7. Explain Thompson's levels of interdependence. What is the level of interdependence among departments (finance, marketing) in a business school? What kinds of coordination mechanisms might be used to handle that interdependence?
8. In what primary ways does the design of service firms typically differ from that of product firms? Why?
9. Where would your university or college department be located on Perrow's technology framework? Would a department devoted exclusively to teaching be in a different quadrant from a department devoted exclusively to research?
10. Mass customization of products has become a common approach in manufacturing organizations. Discuss ways in which mass customization can be applied to service firms as well.

Chapter 13 Workbook: Bistro Technology*

You will be analyzing the technology used in three different restaurants—McDonald's, Subway, and a typical family restaurant. Your instructor will tell you whether to do this assignment as individuals or in a group.

You must visit all three restaurants and infer how the work is done, according to the following criteria. You are not allowed to interview any employees, but instead you will be an observer. Take lots of notes when you are there.

	McDonald's	Subway	Family Restaurant
Organization goals: Speed, service, atmosphere, etc.			
Authority structure			
Type of technology using Woodward's model			
Organization structure: Mechanistic or organic?			
Team versus individual: Do people work together or alone?			
Interdependence: How do employees depend on each other?			

	McDonald's	Subway	Family Restaurant
Tasks: Routine versus nonroutine			
Specialization of tasks by employees			
Standardization: How varied are tasks and products?			
Expertise required: Technical versus social			
Decision making: Centralized versus decentralized			

Questions

1. Is the technology used the best one for each restaurant, considering its goals and environment?
2. From the preceding data, determine if the structure and other characteristics fit the technology.
3. If you were part of a consulting team assigned to improve the operations of each organization, what recommendations would you make?

*Adapted loosely by Dorothy Marcic from "Hamburger Technology," in Douglas T. Hall et al., *Experiences in Management and Organizational Behavior*, 2nd ed. (New York: Wiley, 1982), 244–247, as well as "Behavior, Technology, and Work Design" in A. B. Shani and James B. Lau, *Behavior in Organizations* (Chicago: Irwin, 1996), M16–23 to M16–26.

Case for Analysis: Acetate Department*

The acetate department's product consisted of about twenty different kinds of viscous liquid acetate used by another department to manufacture transparent film to be left clear or coated with photographic emulsion or iron oxide.

Before the change: The department was located in an old four-story building as in Exhibit 13.15. The workflow was as follows:

1. Twenty kinds of powder arrived daily in 50-pound paper bags. In addition, storage tanks of liquid would be filled weekly from tank trucks.
2. Two or three acetate helpers would jointly unload pallets of bags into the storage area using a lift truck.
3. Several times during a shift, the helpers would bring the bagged material up in the elevator to the third floor, where it would be temporarily stored along the walls.
4. Mixing batches was under the direction of the group leader and was rather like baking a cake. Following a prescribed formula, the group leader, mixers, and helpers operated valves to feed in the proper solvent and manually dump in the proper weight and mixture of solid material. The glob would be mixed by giant eggbeaters and heated according to the recipe.

5. When the batch was completed, it was pumped to a finished-product storage tank.
6. After completing each batch, the crew would thoroughly clean the work area of dust and empty bags, because cleanliness was extremely important to the finished product.

To accomplish this work, the department was structured as in Exhibit 13.16.

The helpers were usually young men 18 to 25 years of age; the mixers, 25 to 40; and the group leaders and foremen, 40 to 60. Foremen were on salary; group leaders, mixers, and helpers were on hourly pay.

To produce 20 million pounds of product per year, the department operated 24 hours a day, 7 days a week. Four crews rotated shifts: for example, shift foreman A and his two group leaders and crews would work two weeks on the day shift (8:00 A.M. to 4:00 P.M.), then two weeks on the evening shift (4:00 P.M. to midnight), then two weeks on the night shift (midnight to 8:00 A.M.). There were two days off between shift changes.

During a typical shift, a group leader and his crew would complete two or three batches. A batch would

EXHIBIT 13.15
Elevation View of Acetate
Department before Change

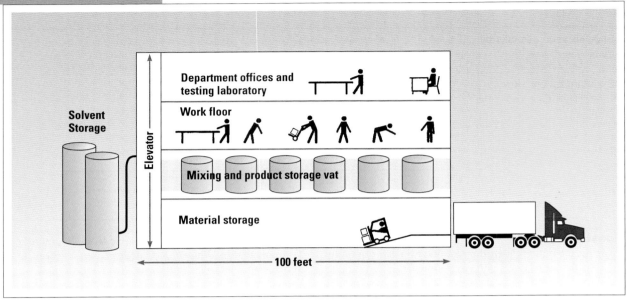

Source: *Hampton, Organizational Behavior Practice Management,* 4th Edition, Copyright 1982. pp. 751–755. Reprinted by permission of Pearson Education, Inc., Upper Saddle River, NJ.

EXHIBIT 13.16
Organizational Chart of Acetate
Department before Change

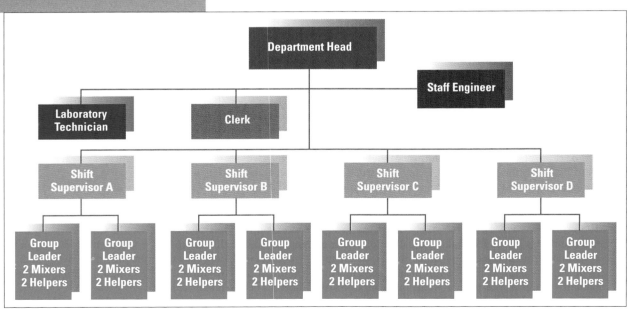

frequently be started on one shift and completed by the next shift crew. There was slightly less work on the evening and night shifts because no deliveries were made, but these crews engaged in a little more cleaning. The shift foreman would give instructions to the two group leaders at the beginning of each shift as to the status of batches in process, batches to be mixed, what deliveries were expected, and what cleaning was to be done. Periodically throughout the shift, the foreman would collect samples in small bottles, which he would leave at the laboratory technicians' desk for testing.

The management and office staff (department head, staff engineer, lab technician, and department clerk) worked only on the day shift, although if an emergency arose on the other shifts, the foreman might call.

All in all, the department was a pleasant place in which to work. The work floor was a little warm, but well lit, quiet, and clean. Substantial banter and horseplay occurred when the crew wasn't actually loading batches, particularly on the evening and night shifts. The men had a dartboard in the work area and competition was fierce and loud. Frequently a crew would go bowling right after work, even at 1:00 A.M., because the community's alleys were open 24 hours a day. Department turnover and absenteeism were low. Most employees spent their entire career with the company, many in one department. The corporation was large, paternalistic, and well paying and offered attractive fringe benefits including large, virtually automatic bonuses for all. Then came the change.

The new system: To improve productivity, the acetate department was completely redesigned; the technology changed from batches to continuous processing. The basic building was retained but substantially modified as in Exhibit 13.17. The modified workflow is as follows:
1. Most solid raw materials are delivered via trucks in large aluminum bins holding 500 pounds.
2. One handler (formerly helper) is on duty at all times on the first floor to receive raw materials and to dump the bins into the semiautomatic screw feeder.
3. The head operator (former group leader) directs the mixing operations from his control panel on the fourth floor located along one wall across from the department offices. The mixing is virtually an automatic operation once the solid material has been sent up the screw feed; a tape program opens and closes the necessary valves to add solvent, heat, mix, and so on. Sitting at a table before his panel, the head operator monitors the process to see that everything is operating within specified temperatures and pressures.

This technical change allowed the department to greatly reduce its workforce. The new structure is illustrated in Exhibit 13.18. One new position was created, that of a pump operator who is located in a small, separate shack about 300 feet from the main building. He operates the pumps and valves that move the finished product among various storage tanks.

Under the new system, production capacity was increased to 25 million pounds per year. All remaining

EXHIBIT 13.17

Elevation View of Acetate Department after Change

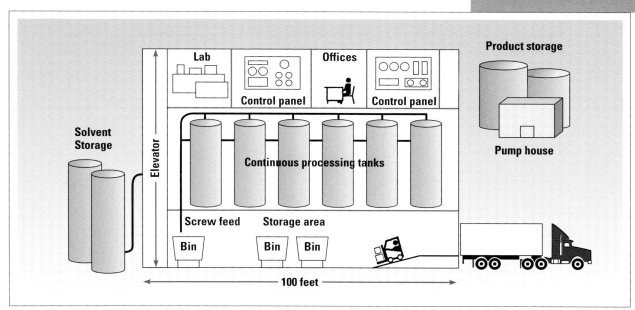

EXHIBIT 13.18
Organizational Chart of Acetate
Department after Change

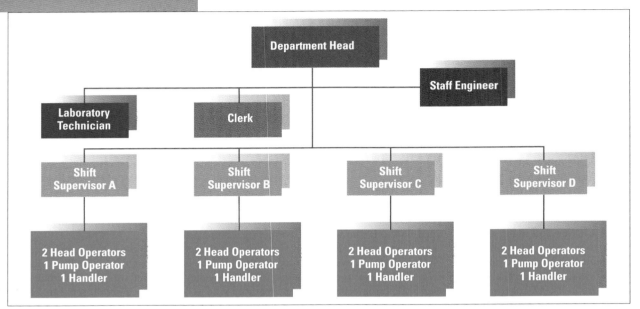

employees received a 15 percent increase in pay. Former personnel not retained in the acetate department were transferred to other departments in the company. No one was dismissed.

Unfortunately, actual output has lagged well below capacity in the several months since the construction work and technical training were completed. Actual production is virtually identical with that under the old technology.

Absenteeism has increased markedly, and several judgmental errors by operators have resulted in substantial losses.

*From "Redesigning the Acetate Department," by David L. Hampton, Charles E. Summer, and Ross A. Webber, *Organizational Behavior and the Practice of Management* (Glenview, Ill.: Scott Foresman and Co., 1982), 751–755. Used with permission.

Introduction

It was 7:50 on Monday morning. Frank Questin, product engineering manager at Custom Chip, Inc., was sitting in his office making a TO DO list for the day. From 8:00 to 9:30 a.m., he would have his weekly meeting with his staff of engineers. After the meeting, Frank thought he would begin developing a proposal for solving what he called "Custom Chip's manufacturing documentation problem"—inadequate technical information regarding the steps to manufacture many of the company's products. Before he could finish his TO DO list, he answered a phone call from Custom Chip's human resource manager, who asked him about the status of two overdue performance appraisals and reminded him that this day marked Bill Lazarus's fifth-year anniversary with the company. Following this call, Frank hurried off to the Monday morning meeting with his staff.

Frank had been product engineering manager at Custom Chip for fourteen months. This was his first management position, and he sometimes questioned his effectiveness as a manager. Often he could not complete the tasks he set out for himself due to interruptions and problems brought to his attention by others. Even though he had not been told exactly what results he was supposed to accomplish, he had a nagging feeling that he should have achieved more after these fourteen months. On the other hand, he thought maybe he was functioning pretty well in some of his areas of responsibility given the complexity of the problems his group handled and the unpredictable changes in the semiconductor industry—changes caused not only by rapid advances in technology, but also by increased foreign competition and a recent downturn in demand.

Company Background

Custom Chip, Inc., was a semiconductor manufacturer specializing in custom chips and components used in radars, satellite transmitters, and other radio frequency devices. The company had been founded in 1977 and had grown rapidly with sales exceeding $25 million in 1986. Most of the company's 300 employees were located in the main plant in Silicon Valley, but overseas manufacturing facilities in Europe and the Far East were growing in size and importance. These overseas facilities assembled the less complex, higher-volume products. New products and the more complex ones were assembled in the main plant. Approximately one-third of the assembly employees were in overseas facilities.

While the specialized products and markets of Custom Chip provided a market niche that had thus far shielded the company from the major downturn in the semiconductor industry, growth had come to a standstill. Because of this, cost reduction had become a high priority.

The Manufacturing Process

Manufacturers of standard chips have long production runs of a few products. Their cost per unit is low and cost control is a primary determinant of success. In contrast, manufacturers of custom chips have extensive product lines and produce small production runs of special applications. Custom Chip, Inc., for example, had manufactured over 2,000 different products in the last five years. In any one quarter the company might schedule 300 production runs for different products, as many as one-third of which might be new or modified products that the company had not made before. Because they must be efficient in designing and manufacturing many product lines, all custom chip manufacturers are highly dependent on their engineers. Customers are often first concerned with whether Custom Chip can design and manufacture the needed product *at all*; second, with whether they can deliver it on time; and only third, with cost.

After a product is designed, there are two phases to the manufacturing process. (See Exhibit 1.) The first is wafer fabrication. This is a complex process in which circuits are etched onto the various layers added to a silicon wafer. The number of steps that the wafer goes through plus inherent problems in controlling various chemical processes make it very difficult to meet the exacting specifications required for the final wafer. The wafers, which are typically "just a few" inches in diameter when the fabrication process is complete, contain hundreds, sometimes thousands, of tiny identical die. Once the wafer has been tested and sliced up to produce these die, each die will be used as a circuit component.

If the completed wafer passes the various quality tests, it moves on to the assembly phase. In assembly, the die from the wafers, very small wires, and other components are attached to a circuit in a series of precise operations. This finished circuit is the final product of Custom Chip, Inc.

Each product goes through many independent and delicate operations, and each step is subject to operator

EXHIBIT 1
Manufacturing Process

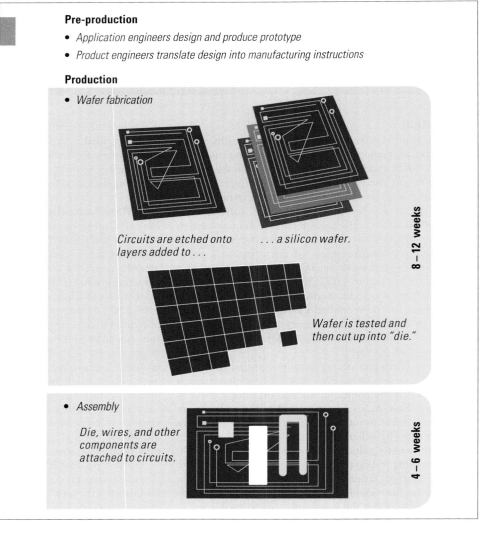

Pre-production

- *Application engineers design and produce prototype*
- *Product engineers translate design into manufacturing instructions*

Production

- *Wafer fabrication*

Circuits are etched onto layers added to . . .

. . . a silicon wafer.

Wafer is tested and then cut up into "die."

8 – 12 weeks

- *Assembly*

Die, wires, and other components are attached to circuits.

4 – 6 weeks

or machine error. Due to the number of steps and tests involved, the wafer fabrication takes eight to twelve weeks and the assembly process takes four to six weeks. Because of the exacting specifications, products are rejected for the slightest flaw. The likelihood that every product starting the run will make it through all of the processes and still meet specifications is often quite low. For some products, average yield[1] is as low as 40 percent, and actual yields can vary considerably from one run to another. At Custom Chip, the average yield for all products is in the 60 to 70 percent range.

Because it takes so long to make a custom chip, it is especially important to have some control of these yields. For

---

[1]Yield refers to the ratio of finished products that meet specifications relative to the number that initially entered the manufacturing process.

example, if a customer orders one thousand units of a product and typical yields for that product average 50 percent, Custom Chip will schedule a starting batch of 2,200 units. With this approach, even if the yield falls as low as 45.4 percent (45.4 percent of 2,200 is 1,000) the company can still meet the order. If the actual yield falls below 45.4 percent, the order will not be completed in that run, and a very small, costly run of the item will be needed to complete the order. The only way the company can effectively control these yields and stay on schedule is for the engineering groups and operations to cooperate and coordinate their efforts efficiently.

Role of the Product Engineer

The product engineer's job is defined by its relationship to applications engineering and operations. The applications engineers are responsible for designing and developing prototypes when incoming orders are for new or modified products. The product engineer's role is to translate the applications engineering group's design into a set of manufacturing instructions and then to work alongside manufacturing to make sure that engineering-related problems get solved. The product engineers' effectiveness is ultimately measured by their ability to control yields on their assigned products. The organization chart in Exhibit 2 shows the engineering and operations departments. Exhibit 3 summarizes the roles and objectives

7.0

EXHIBIT 2
Custom Chip, Inc., Partial Organization Chart

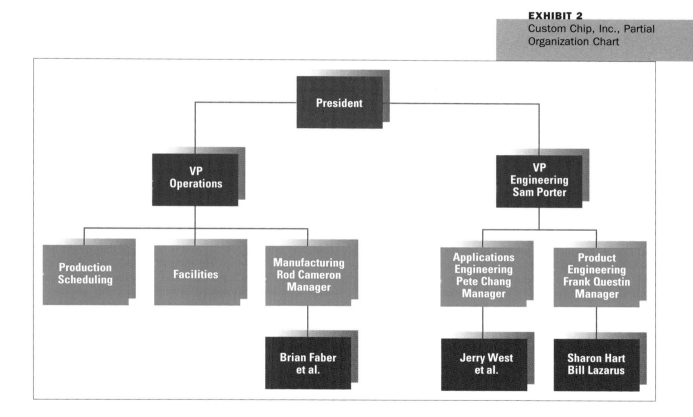

EXHIBIT 3
Departmental Roles and Objectives

Department	Role	Primary Objective
Applications Engineering	Designs and develops prototypes for new or modified products	Satisfy customer needs through innovative designs
Product Engineering	Translates designs into manufacturing instructions and works alongside manufacturing to solve "engineering-related" problems	Maintain and control yields on assigned products
Manufacturing	Executes designs	Meet productivity standards and time schedules

7.0

of manufacturing, applications engineering, and product engineering.

The product engineers estimate that 70 to 80 percent of their time is spent in solving day-to-day manufacturing problems. The product engineers have cubicles in a room directly across the hall from the manufacturing facility. If a manufacturing supervisor has a question regarding how to build a product during a run, that supervisor will call the engineer assigned to that product. If the engineer is available, he or she will go to the manufacturing floor to help answer the question. If the engineer is not available, the production run may be stopped and the product put aside so that other orders can be manufactured. This results in delays and added costs. One reason that product engineers are consulted is that documentation—the instructions for manufacturing the product—is unclear or incomplete.

The product engineer will also be called if a product is tested and fails to meet specifications. If a product fails to meet test specifications, production stops, and the engineer must diagnose the problem and attempt to find a solution. Otherwise, the order for that product may be only partially met. Test failures are a very serious problem, which can result in considerable cost increases and schedule delays for customers. Products do not test properly for many reasons, including operator errors, poor materials, a design that is very difficult to manufacture, a design that provides too little margin for error, or a combination of these.

On a typical day, the product engineers may respond to half a dozen questions from the manufacturing floor, and two to four calls to the testing stations. When interviewed, the engineers expressed a frustration with this situation. They thought they spent too much time solving short-term problems, and, consequently, they were neglecting other important parts of their jobs. In particular, they felt they had little time in which to:

- *Coordinate with applications engineers during the design phase.* The product engineers stated that their knowledge of manufacturing could provide valuable input to the applications engineers. Together they could improve the manufacturability and thus, the yields of the new or modified products.
- *Engage in yield improvement projects.* This would involve an in-depth study of the existing process for a specific product in conjunction with an analysis of past product failures.
- *Accurately document the manufacturing steps for their assigned products, especially for those that tend to have large or repeat orders.* They said that the current state of the documentation is very poor. Operators often have to build products using only a drawing showing the final circuit, along with a few notes scribbled in the margins. While experienced operators and supervisors

may be able to work with this information, they often make incorrect guesses and assumptions. Inexperienced operators may not be able to proceed with certain products because of this poor documentation.

Weekly Meeting

As manager of the product engineering group, Frank Questin had eight engineers reporting to him, each responsible for a different set of Custom Chip products. According to Frank:

When I took over as manager, the product engineers were not spending much time together as a group. They were required to handle operations problems on short notice. This made it difficult for the entire group to meet due to constant requests for assistance from the manufacturing area.

I thought that my engineers could be of more assistance and support to each other if they all spent more time together as a group, so one of my first actions as a manager was to institute a regularly scheduled weekly meeting. I let the manufacturing people know that my staff would not respond to requests for assistance during the meeting.

The meeting on this particular Monday morning followed the usual pattern. Frank talked about upcoming company plans, projects, and other news that might be of interest to the group. He then provided data about current yields for each product and commended those engineers who had maintained or improved yields on most of their products. This initial phase of the meeting lasted until about 8:30 a.m. The remainder of the meeting was a meandering discussion of a variety of topics. Since there was no agenda, engineers felt comfortable in raising issues of concern to them.

The discussion started with one of the engineers describing a technical problem in the assembly of one of his products. He was asked a number of questions and given some advice. Another engineer raised the topic of a need for new testing equipment and described a test unit he had seen at a recent demonstration. He claimed the savings in labor and improved yields from this machine would allow it to pay for itself in less than nine months. Frank immediately replied that budget limitations made such a purchase unfeasible, and the discussion moved into another area. They briefly discussed the increasing inaccessibility of the applications engineers and then talked about a few other topics.

In general, the engineers valued these meetings. One commented that:

The Monday meetings give me a chance to hear what's on everyone's mind and to find out about and discuss company-wide news. It's hard to reach any conclusions because the meeting is a freewheeling discussion. But I really appreciate the friendly atmosphere with my peers.

Coordination with Applications Engineers

Following the meeting that morning, an event occurred that highlighted the issue of the inaccessibility of the applications engineers. An order of 300 units of custom chip 1210A for a major customer was already overdue. Because the projected yield of this product was 70 percent, they had started with a run of 500 units. A sample tested at one of the early assembly points indicated a major performance problem that could drop the yield to below 50 percent. Bill Lazarus, the product engineer assigned to the 1210A, examined the sample and determined that the problem could be solved by redesigning the wiring. Jerry West, the applications engineer assigned to that product category, was responsible for revising the design. Bill tried to contact Jerry, but he was not immediately available, and didn't get back to Bill until later in the day. Jerry explained that he was on a tight schedule trying to finish a design for a customer who was coming into town in two days, and could not get to "Bill's problem" for a while.

Jerry's attitude that the problem belonged to product engineering was typical of the applications engineers. From their point of view there were a number of reasons for making the product engineers' needs for assistance a lower priority. In the first place, applications engineers were rewarded and acknowledged primarily for satisfying customer needs through designing new and modified products. They got little recognition for solving manufacturing problems. Second, applications engineering was perceived to be more glamorous than product engineering because of opportunities to be credited with innovative and groundbreaking designs. Finally, the size of the applications engineering group had declined over the past year, causing the workload on each engineer to increase considerably. Now they had even less time to respond to the product engineers' requests.

When Bill Lazarus told Frank about the situation, Frank acted quickly. He wanted this order to be in process again by tomorrow, and he knew manufacturing was also trying to meet this goal. He walked over to see Pete Chang, head of applications engineering (see the organizational chart in Exhibit 2). Meetings like this with Pete to discuss and resolve interdepartmental issues were common.

Frank found Pete at a workbench talking with one of his engineers. He asked Pete if he could talk to him in private, and they walked to Pete's office.

Frank: We've got a problem in manufacturing in getting out an order of 1210As. Bill Lazarus is getting little or no assistance from Jerry West. I'm hoping you can get Jerry to pitch in and help Bill. It should take no more than a few hours of his time.

Pete: I do have Jerry on a short leash trying to keep him focused on getting out a design for Teletronics.

We can't afford to show up empty-handed at our meeting with them in two days.

Frank: Well, we are going to end up losing one customer in trying to please another. Can't we satisfy everyone here?

Pete: Do you have an idea?

Frank: Can't you give Jerry some additional support on the Teletronics design?

Pete: Let's get Jerry in here to see what we can do.

Pete brought Jerry back to the office, and together they discussed the issues and possible solutions. When Pete made it clear to Jerry that he considered the problem with the 1210As a priority, Jerry offered to work on the 1210A problem with Bill. He said, "This will mean I'll have to stay a few hours past 5:00 this evening, but I'll do what's required to get the job done."

Frank was glad he had developed a collaborative relationship with Pete. He had always made it a point to keep Pete informed about activities in the product engineering group that might affect the applications engineers. In addition, he would often chat with Pete informally over coffee or lunch in the company cafeteria. This relationship with Pete made Frank's job easier. He wished he had the same rapport with Rod Cameron, the manufacturing manager.

Coordination with Manufacturing

The product engineers worked closely on a day-to-day basis with the manufacturing supervisors and workers. The problems between these two groups stemmed from an inherent conflict between their objectives (see Exhibit 3). The objective of the product engineers was to maintain and improve yields. They had the authority to stop production of any run that did not test properly. Manufacturing, on the other hand, was trying to meet productivity standards and time schedules. When a product engineer stopped a manufacturing run, he or she was possibly preventing the manufacturing group from reaching its objectives.

Rod Cameron, the current manufacturing manager, had been promoted from his position as a manufacturing supervisor a year ago. His views on the product engineers:

The product engineers are perfectionists. The minute a test result looks a little suspicious they want to shut down the factory. I'm under a lot of pressure to get products out the door. If they pull a few $50,000 orders off the line when they are within a few days of reaching shipping, I'm liable to miss my numbers by $100,000 that month.

Besides that, they are doing a lousy job of documenting the manufacturing steps. I've got a lot of turnover, and my new operators need to be told or shown exactly what to do for each product. The instructions for a lot of our products are a joke.

7.0

At first, Frank found Rod very difficult to deal with. Rod found fault with the product engineers for many problems and sometimes seemed rude to Frank when they talked. For example, Rod might tell Frank to "make it quick; I haven't got much time." Frank tried not to take Rod's actions personally, and through persistence was able to develop a more amicable relationship with him. According to Frank:

Sometimes, my people will stop work on a product because it doesn't meet test results at that stage of manufacturing. If we study the situation, we might be able to maintain yields or even save an entire run by adjusting the manufacturing procedures. Rod tries to bully me into changing my engineers' decisions. He yells at me or criticizes the competence of my people, but I don't allow his temper or ravings to influence my best judgment in a situation. My strategy in dealing with Rod is to try not to respond defensively to him. Eventually he cools down, and we can have a reasonable discussion of the situation.

Despite this strategy, Frank could not always resolve his problems with Rod. On these occasions, Frank took the issue to his own boss, Sam Porter, the vice president in charge of engineering. However, Frank was not satisfied with the support he got from Sam. Frank said:

Sam avoids confrontations with the operations VP. He doesn't have the influence or clout with the other VPs or the president to do justice to engineering's needs in the organization.

Early that afternoon, Frank again found himself trying to resolve a conflict between engineering and manufacturing. Sharon Hart, one of his most effective product engineers, was responsible for a series of products used in radars—the 3805A–3808A series. Today she had stopped a large run of 3806As. The manufacturing supervisor, Brian Faber, went to Rod Cameron to complain about the impact of this stoppage on his group's productivity. Brian felt that yields were low on that particular product because the production instructions were confusing to his operators, and that even with clearer instructions, his operators would need additional training to build it satisfactorily. He stressed that the product engineer's responsibility was to adequately document the production instructions and provide training. For these reasons, Brian asserted that product engineering, and not manufacturing, should be accountable for the productivity loss in the case of these 3806As.

Rod called Frank to his office, where he joined the discussion with Sharon, Brian, and Rod. After listening to the issues, Frank conceded that product engineering had responsibility for documenting and training. He also explained, even though everyone was aware of it, that

the product engineering group had been operating with reduced staff for over a year now, so training and documentation were lower priorities. Because of this staffing situation, Frank suggested that manufacturing and product engineering work together and pool their limited resources to solve the documentation and training problem. He was especially interested in using a few of the long-term experienced workers to assist in training newer workers. Rod and Brian opposed his suggestion. They did not want to take experienced operators off of the line because it would decrease productivity. The meeting ended when Brian stormed out, saying that Sharon had better get the 3806As up and running again that morning.

Frank was particularly frustrated by this episode with manufacturing. He knew perfectly well that his group had primary responsibility for documenting the manufacturing steps for each product. A year ago he told Sam Porter that the product engineers needed to update and standardize all of the documentation for manufacturing products. At that time, Sam told Frank that he would support his efforts to develop the documentation, but would not increase his staff. In fact, Sam had withheld authorization to fill a recently vacated product engineering slot. Frank was reluctant to push the staffing issue because of Sam's adamance about reducing costs. "Perhaps," Frank thought, "if I develop a proposal clearly showing the benefits of a documentation program in manufacturing and detailing the steps and resources required to implement the program, I might be able to convince Sam to provide us with more resources." But Frank could never find the time to develop that proposal. And so he remained frustrated.

Later in the Day

Frank was reflecting on the complexity of his job when Sharon came to the doorway to see if he had a few moments. Before he could say "Come in," the phone rang. He looked at the clock. It was 4:10 P.M. Pete was on the other end of the line with an idea he wanted to try out on Frank, so Frank said he could call him back shortly. Sharon was upset, and told him that she was thinking of quitting because the job was not satisfying for her.

Sharon said that although she very much enjoyed working on yield improvement projects, she could find no time for them. She was tired of the applications engineers acting like "prima donnas," too busy to help her solve what they seemed to think were mundane day-to-day manufacturing problems. She also thought that many of the day-to-day problems she handled wouldn't exist if there was enough time to document manufacturing procedures to begin with.

Frank didn't want to lose Sharon, so he tried to get into a frame of mind where he could be empathetic to her. He listened to her and told her that he could understand her frustration in this situation. He told her the situation would change as industry conditions improved. He told her that he was pleased that she felt comfortable in venting her frustrations with him, and he hoped she would stay with Custom Chip.

After Sharon left, Frank realized that he had told Pete that he would call back. He glanced at the TO DO list he had never completed, and realized that he hadn't spent time on his top priority—developing a proposal relating to solving the documentation problem in manufacturing. Then, he remembered that he had forgotten to acknowledge Bill Lazarus's fifth-year anniversary with the company. He thought to himself that his job felt like a roller coaster ride, and once again he pondered his effectiveness as a manager.

7.0

8.0

Integrative Case 8.0
Dowling Flexible Metals*

Background

In 1960, Bill Dowling, a "machine-tool set-up-man" for a large auto firm, became so frustrated with his job that he quit to form his own business. The manufacturing operation consisted of a few general purpose metal working machines that were set up in Dowling's garage. Space was such a constraint that it controlled the work process. For example, if the cutting press was to be used with long stock, the milling machines would have to be pushed back against the wall and remain idle. Production always increased on rain-free, summer days since the garage doors could be opened and a couple of machines moved out onto the drive. Besides Dowling, who acted as salesman, accountant, engineer, president, manufacturing representative, and working foreman, members of the original organization were Eve Sullivan, who began as a part-time secretary and payroll clerk; and Wally Denton, who left the auto firm with Bill. The workforce was composed of part-time "moonlighters," full-time machinists for other firms, who were attracted by the job autonomy which provided experience in setting up jobs and job processes, where a high degree of ingenuity was required.

The first years were touch and go with profits being erratic. Gradually the firm began to gain a reputation for being ingenious at solving unique problems and for producing a quality product on, or before, deadlines. The "product" consisted of fabricating dies for making minor component metal parts for automobiles and a specified quantity of the parts. Having realized that the firm was too dependent on the auto industry and that sudden fluctuations in auto sales could have a drastic effect on the firm's survival, Dowling began marketing their services toward manufacturing firms not connected with the auto industry. Bids were submitted for work that involved legs for vending machines, metal trim for large appliances, clamps and latches for metal windows, and display racks for small power hand tools.

As Dowling Flexible Metals became more diversified, the need for expansion forced the company to borrow building funds from the local bank, which enabled construction of a small factory on the edge of town. As new markets and products created a need for increasingly more versatile equipment and a larger workforce, the plant has since expanded twice until it is now three times its original size.

In 1980, Dowling Flexible Metals hardly resembles the garage operation of the formative years. The firm now employs approximately 30 full-time journeymen and apprentice machinists, a staff of 4 engineers that were hired

about three years ago, and a full-time office secretary subordinate to Eve Sullivan, the Office Manager. (See Exhibit 1.) Their rapid growth has created problems that in 1980 have not been resolved. Bill Dowling, realizing his firm is suffering from growing pains, has asked you to "take a look at the operation and make recommendations as to how things could be run better." You begin the consulting project by interviewing Dowling, other key people in the firm, and workers out in the shop who seem willing to express their opinions about the firm.

Bill Dowling, Owner-President

"We sure have come a long way from that first set-up in my garage. On a nice day we would get everything all spread out in the drive and then it would start pouring cats and dogs—so we would have to move back inside. It was just like a one-ring circus. Now it seems like a three-ring circus. You would think that with all that talent we have here and all the experience, things would run smoother. Instead, it seems I am putting in more time than ever and accomplishing a whole lot less in a day's time.

"It's not like the old days. Everything has gotten so complicated and precise in design. When you go to a customer to discuss a job you have to talk to six kids right out of engineering school. Every one of them has a calculator—they don't even carry slide rules anymore—and all they can talk is fancy formulas and how we should do our job. It just seems I spend more time with customers and less time around the shop than I used to. That's why I hired the engineering staff—to interpret specifications, solve engineering problems, and draw blueprints. It still seems all the problems are solved out on the shop floor by guys like Walt and Tom, just like always. Gene and the other engineers are necessary, but they don't seem to be working as smoothly with the guys on the floor as they should.

"One of the things I would like to see us do in the future is to diversify even more. Now that we have the capability, I am starting to bid jobs that require the computerized milling machine process tape. This involves devising a work process for milling a part on a machine and then making a computer process tape of it. We can then sell copies of the tape just like we do dies and parts. These tapes allow less skilled operators to operate complicated milling machines without

*This case was prepared by Floyd G. Willoughby, Oakland University, Rochester, MI. © 1980 by Floyd G. Willoughby. Reprinted by permission.

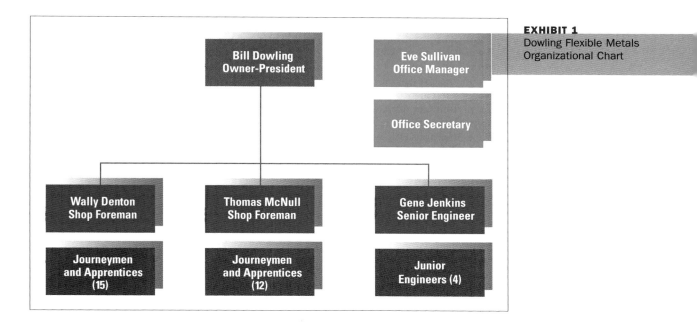

EXHIBIT 1
Dowling Flexible Metals
Organizational Chart

the long apprenticeship of a tradesman. All they have to do is press buttons and follow the machine's instructions for changing the milling tools. Demand is increasing for the computerized process tapes.

"I would like to see the firm get into things like working with combinations of bonded materials such as plastics, fiberglass, and metals. I am also starting to bid jobs involving the machining of plastics and other materials beside metals."

Wally Denton, Shop Foreman, First Shift

"Life just doesn't seem to be as simple as when we first started in Bill's garage. In those days he would bring a job back and we would all gather 'round and decide how we were going to set it up and who would do it. If one of the 'moonlighters' was to get the job either Bill or I would lay the job out for him when he came in that afternoon. Now, the customers' ideas get processed through the engineers and we, out here in the shop, have to guess just exactly what the customer had in mind.

"What some people around here don't understand is that I am a partner in this business. I've stayed out here in the shop because this is where I like it and it's where I feel most useful. When Bill isn't here, I'm always around to put out fires. Between Eve, Gene, and myself we usually make the right decision.

"With all this diversification and Bill spending a lot of time with customers, I think we need to get somebody else out there to share the load."

Thomas McNull, Shop Foreman, Second Shift

"In general, I agree with Wally that things aren't as simple as they used to be, but I think, given the amount of jobs we are handling at any one time, we run the shop pretty smoothly. When the guys bring problems to me that require major job changes, I get Wally's approval before making the changes. We haven't had any difficulty in that area.

"Where we run into problems is with the engineers. They get the job when Bill brings it back. They decide how the part should be made and by what process, which in turn pretty much restricts what type of dies we have to make. Therein lies the bind. Oftentimes we run into a snag following the engineers' instructions. If it's after five o'clock, the engineers have left for the day. We, on the second shift, either have to let the job sit until the next morning or solve the problem ourselves. This not only creates bad feelings between the shop personnel and the engineers, but it makes extra work for the engineers because they have to draw up new plans.

"I often think we have the whole process backwards around here. What we should be doing is giving the job to the journeymen—after all, these guys have a lot of experience and know-how—then give the finished product to the engineers to draw up. I'll give you an example. Last year we got a job from a vending machine manufacturer. The job consisted of fabricating five sets of dies for making those stubby little legs for vending machines, plus five hundred of the finished legs. Well, the engineers figured the job all out, drew up the plans, and sent it out to us. We made the first die to specs, but when we tried to punch out the leg on the press, the metal tore. We took the problem back to the engineers, and after the preliminary accusations of who was responsible for the screw up, they changed the raw material specifications. We waited two weeks for delivery of the new steel, then tried again. The metal still tore. Finally, after two months of hassle, Charlie Oakes and I worked on the die for two days and finally came up with a solution. The problem was that the shoulders of the die were too steep for forming the leg in just one punch. We had to use two punches (see Exhibit 2). The problem was the production process, not the raw materials. We spent four months on that job and ran over our deadline. Things like that shouldn't happen."

Charlie Oakes, Journeyman Apprentice

"Really, I hate to say anything against this place because it is a pretty good place to work. The pay and benefits are pretty good and because it is a small shop our hours can be somewhat flexible. If you have a doctor's appointment you can either come in late or stay until you get your time in or punch out and come back. You can work as much overtime as you want to.

"The thing I'm kind of disappointed about is that I thought the work would be more challenging. I'm just an apprentice, but I've only got a year to go in my program before I can get my journeyman's card, and I think I should be handling more jobs on my own. That's why I came to work here. My Dad was one of the original 'moonlighters' here. He told me about how interesting it was when he was here. I guess I just expected the same thing."

Gene Jenkins, Chief Engineer

"I imagine the guys out in the shop already have told you about 'The Great Vending Machine Fiasco.' They'll never let us forget that. However, it does point out the need for better coordination around here. The engineers were hired as engineers, not as draftsmen, which is just about all we do. I'm not saying we should have the final say on how the job is designed, because there is a lot of practical experience out in that shop; but just as we haven't their expertise neither do they have ours. There is a need for both, the technical skill of the engineers and the practical experience of the shop.

"One thing that would really help is more information from Bill. I realize Bill is spread pretty thin but there are a lot of times he comes back with a job, briefs us, and we still have to call the customer about details because Bill hasn't been specific enough or asked the right questions of the customer. Engineers communicate best with other engineers. Having an engineering function gives us a competitive advantage over our competition. In my opinion, operating as we do now, we are not maximizing that advantage.

"When the plans leave here we have no idea what happens to those plans once they are out in the shop. The next thing we know, we get a die or set of dies back that doesn't even resemble the plans we sent out in the shop. We then have to draw up new plans to fit the dies. Believe me, it is not only discouraging, but it really makes you wonder what your job is around here. It's embarrassing when a customer calls to check on the status of a job and I have to run out in the shop, look up the guy handling the job, and get his best estimate of how the job is going."

Eve Sullivan, Office Manager

"One thing is for sure, life is far from dull around here. It seems Bill is either dragging in a bunch of plans or racing off with the truck to deliver a job to a customer.

EXHIBIT 2
Two Stage Production
Process

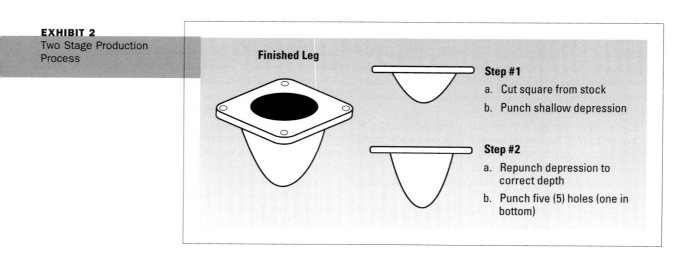

"Really, Wally and I make all the day-to-day decisions around here. Of course, I don't get involved in technical matters. Wally and Gene take care of those, but if we are short-handed or need a new machine, Wally and I start the ball rolling by getting together the necessary information and talking to Bill the first chance we get. I guess you could say that we run things around here by consensus most of the time. If I get a call from a customer asking about the status of a job, I refer the call to Gene because Wally is usually out in the shop.

"I started with Bill and Wally 20 years ago, on a part-time basis, and somehow the excitement has turned into work. Joan, the office secretary, and I handle all correspondence, bookkeeping, payroll, insurance forms, and everything else besides run the office. It's just getting to be too hectic—I just wish the job was more fun, the way it used to be."

Having listened to all concerned, you returned to Bill's office only to find him gone. You tell Eve and Wally that you will return within one week with your recommendations.

8.0

Chapter 1

1. This case is based on Anthony Bianco and Pamela L. Moore, "Downfall: The Inside Story of the Management Fiasco at Xerox," *BusinessWeek* (March 5, 2001), 82–92; Robert J. Grossman, "HR Woes at Xerox," *HR Magazine* (May 2001), 34–45; Jeremy Kahn, "The Paper Jam from Hell," *Fortune* (November 13, 2000), 141–146; Pamela L. Moore, "She's Here to Fix the Xerox," *BusinessWeek* (August 6, 2001), 47–48; Claudia H. Deutsch, "At Xerox, the Chief Earns (Grudging) Respect," *The New York Times* (June 2, 2002), section 3, 1, 12; Olga Kharif, "Anne Mulcahy Has Xerox by the Horns," *BusinessWeek Online* (May 29, 2003); Amy Yee, "Xerox Comeback Continues to Thrive," *Financial Times* (January 26, 2005), 30; "Developing Vision for an Organization," *The Bangkok Post* (February 11, 2008), 1; George Anders, "Corporate News; Business: At Xerox, Jettisoning Dividend Helped Company Out of a Crisis," *The Asian Wall Street Journal* (November 28, 2007), 6; Andrew Davidson, "Xerox Saviour in the Spotlight," *Sunday Times* (June 1, 2008), 6; Betsy Morris, "The Accidental CEO," *Fortune* (June 23, 2003), 58–67; Matt Hartley, "Copy That: Xerox Tries Again to Rebound," *The Globe and Mail* (January 7, 2008), B1; "Anne Mulcahy Becomes the First Woman CEO to Receive *Chief Executive* Magazine's 'CEO of the Year' Award," *PR Newswire* (June 3, 2008); and "Xerox Marks Human Rights and Environmental Progress in Annual Citizenship Report," *Canada Newswire* (November 12, 2007), 1.

2. Matthew Karnitschnig, Carrick Mollenkamp, and Dan Fitzpatrick, "Bank of America Eyes Merrill," *The Wall Street Journal* (September 15, 2008), A1; Carrick Mollenkamp and Mark Whitehouse, "Old-School Banks Emerge Atop New World of Finance," *The Wall Street Journal* (September 16, 2008), A1, A10.

3. Janet Adamy, "Man Behind Burger King Turnaround," *The Wall Street Journal* (April 2, 2008), B1; Phred Dvorak, "Theory & Practice: Experts Have a Message for Managers: Shake It Up," *The Wall Street Journal* (June 16, 2008), B8; Justin Scheck and Ben Worthen, "Hewlett-Packard Takes Aim at IBM," *The Wall Street Journal* (May 14, 2008), B1.

4. Harry G. Barkema, Joel A. C. Baum, and Elizabeth A. Mannix, "Management Challenges in a New Time," *Academy of Management Journal* 45, no. 5 (2002), 916–930.

5. Darrell Rigby and Barbara Bilodeau, "Bain's Global 2007 Management Tools and Trends Survey," *Strategy & Leadership* 35, no. 5 (2007), 9–16.

6. Hammonds, "Smart, Determined, Ambitious, Cheap: The New Face of Global Competition," *Fast Company* (February 2003), 91–97.

7. Jason Dean, "Upgrade Plan: Long a Low-Tech Player, China Sets Its Sights on Chip Making," *The Wall Street Journal* (February 17, 2004), A1.

8. Hammonds, "Smart, Determined, Ambitious, Cheap"; Pete Engardio, Aaron Bernstein, and Manjeet Kripalani, "Is Your Job Next?" *BusinessWeek* (February 3, 2003), 50–60.

9. Pete Engardio, "Can the U.S. Bring Jobs Back from China?" *BusinessWeek* (June 30, 2008), 38ff.

10. Janet Adamy, "McDonald's Tests Changes in $1 Burger As Costs Rise," *The Wall Street Journal* (August 4, 2008), B1.

11. Lavonne Kuykendall, "Auto Insurers Paying Up to Compete for Drivers," *The Wall Street Journal* (April 9, 2008), B5.

12. Chris Serres, "As Shoppers Cut Back, Grocers Feel the Squeeze," *Star Tribune* (July 23, 2008), D1.

13. Bethany McLean, "Why Enron Went Bust," *Fortune* (December 24, 2001), 58–68; survey results reported in Patricia Wallington, "Honestly?!" *CIO* (March 15, 2003), 41–42.

14. Mike Esterl, "Executive Derision: In Germany, Scandals Tarnish Business Elite," *The Wall Street Journal* (March 4, 2008), A1.

15. John Hechinger, "Financial-Aid Directors Received Payments from Preferred Lender; Student Loan Xpress Puts Three Managers on Leave Amid Multiple Inquiries," *The Wall Street Journal* (April 10, 2007), A3; and Kathy Chu, "3 Top Financial Aid Chiefs Suspended," *USA Today* (April 6, 2007), B1.

16. Kuykendall, "Auto Insurers Paying Up to Compete."

17. Bernard Wysocki Jr., "Corporate Caveat: Dell or Be Delled," *The Wall Street Journal* (May 10, 1999), A1.

18. Andy Reinhardt, "From Gearhead to Grand High Pooh-Bah," *BusinessWeek* (August 28, 2000), 129–130.

19. G. Pascal Zachary, "Mighty Is the Mongrel," *Fast Company* (July 2000), 270–284.

20. Russ Wiles, "Businesses Encourage Employees to Learn Spanish," *USA Today*, December 7, 2008, http://www.usatoday.com/money/workplace/2007-12-08-spanish_n.htm?loc=interstitialskip, accessed on March 17, 2008.

21. Steven Greenhouse, N.Y. Times News Service, "Influx of Immigrants Having Profound Impact on Economy," *Johnson City Press* (September 4, 2000), 9; Richard W. Judy and Carol D'Amico, *Workforce 2020: Work and Workers in the 21st Century* (Indianapolis, Ind.: Hudson Institute, 1997); statistics reported in Jason Forsythe, "Diversity Works," special advertising supplement to *The New York Times Magazine* (September 14, 2003), 75–100.

22. Howard Aldrich, *Organizations and Environments* (Englewood Cliffs, N.J.: Prentice-Hall, 1979), 3.

23. This section is based largely on Peter F. Drucker, *Managing the Non-Profit Organization: Principles and Practices* (New York: HarperBusiness, 1992); and Thomas Wolf, *Managing a Nonprofit Organization* (New York: Fireside/Simon & Schuster, 1990).

24. Christine W. Letts, William P. Ryan, and Allen Grossman, *High Performance Nonprofit Organizations* (New York: John Wiley & Sons, Inc., 1999), 30–35.

25. Lisa Bannon, "Dream Works: As Make-a-Wish Expands Its Turf, Local Groups Fume," *The Wall Street Journal* (July 8, 2002), A1, A8.

26. Robert N. Stern and Stephen R. Barley, "Organizations and Social Systems: Organization Theory's Neglected Mandate," *Administrative Science Quarterly* 41 (1996), 146–162.

27. Philip Siekman, "Build to Order: One Aircraft Carrier," *Fortune* (July 22, 2002), 180[B]–180[J].

28. Brent Schlender, "The New Soul of a Wealth Machine," *Fortune* (April 5, 2004), 102–110.

29. Schlender, "The New Soul of a Wealth Machine," and Keith H. Hammonds, "Growth Search," *Fast Company* (April 2003), 75–80.

30. Christopher Lawton, Yukari Iwatani Kane, and Jason Dean, "Picture Shift: U.S. Upstart Takes on TV Giants in Price War," *The Wall Street Journal* (April 15, 2008), A1.

31. The following discussion was heavily influenced by Richard H. Hall, *Organizations: Structures, Processes, and Outcomes* (Englewood Cliffs, N.J.: Prentice-Hall, 1991); D. S. Pugh, "The Measurement of Organization Structures: Does Context Determine Form?" *Organizational Dynamics* 1 (Spring 1973), 19–34; and D. S. Pugh, D. J. Hickson, C. R. Hinings, and C. Turner, "Dimensions of Organization Structure," *Administrative Science Quarterly* 13 (1968), 65–91.

32. Jaclyne Badal, "Can a Company Be Run As a Democracy? *The Wall Street Journal* (April 23, 2007), B1; John Huey, "Wal-Mart: Will It Take Over the World?" *Fortune* (January 30, 1989), 52–61; http://www.walmartstores.com, accessed on August 28, 2002.

33. Steve Lohr, "Who Pays for Efficiency?" *The New York Times* (June 11, 2007) H1.

34. T. Donaldson and L. E. Preston, "The Stakeholder Theory of the Corporation: Concepts, Evidence, and Implications," *Academy of Management Review* 20 (1995), 65–91; Anne S. Tusi, "A Multiple-Constituency Model of Effectiveness: An Empirical Examination at the Human Resource Subunit Level," *Administrative Science Quarterly* 35 (1990), 458–483; Charles Fombrun and Mark Shanley, "What's in a Name? Reputation Building and Corporate Strategy," *Academy of Management Journal* 33 (1990), 233–258; Terry Connolly, Edward J. Conlon, and Stuart Jay Deutsch, "Organizational Effectiveness: A Multiple-Constituency Approach," *Academy of Management Review* 5 (1980), 211–217.

35. Charles Fishman, "The Wal-Mart You Don't Know—Why Low Prices Have a High Cost," *Fast Company* (December 2003), 68–80.

36. Tusi, "A Multiple-Constituency Model of Effectiveness."

37. Fombrun and Shanley, "What's in a Name?"

38. Gary Fields and John R. Wilke, "The Ex-Files: FBI's New Focus Places Big Burden on Local Police," *The Wall Street Journal* (June 30, 2003), A1, A12; and Susan Schmidt, Gary Fields, Elizabeth Williamson, and Evan Perez, "FBI Used DNA to Link Anthrax to Suspect," *The Wall Street Journal* (August 4, 2008), A1.

39. Roger L. M. Dunbar and William H. Starbuck, "Learning to Design Organizations and Learning from Designing Them," *Organization Science* 17, no. 2 (March–April 2006), 171–178.

40. Cynthia Crossen, "Early Industry Expert Soon Realized a Staff Has Its Own Efficiency," *The Wall Street Journal* (November 6, 2006), B1.

41. Robert Kanigel, *The One Best Way: Frederick Winslow Taylor and the Enigma of Efficiency* (New York: Viking, 1997); Alan Farnham, "The Man Who Changed Work Forever," *Fortune* (July 21, 1997), 114; and Charles D. Wrege and Ann Marie Stoka, "Cooke Creates a Classic: The Story Behind F. W. Taylor's Principles of Scientific Management," *Academy of Management Review* (October 1978), 736–749. For a discussion of the impact of scientific management on American industry, government, and nonprofit organizations, also see Mauro F. Guillèn, "Scientific Management's Lost Aesthetic: Architecture, Organization, and the Taylorized Beauty of the Mechanical," *Administrative Science Quarterly* 42 (1997), 682–715.

42. Gary Hamel, "The Why, What, and How of Management Innovation," *Harvard Business Review* (February 2006), 72–84.

43. Amanda Bennett, *The Death of the Organization Man* (New York: William Morrow, 1990).

44. Ralph Sink, "My Unfashionable Legacy," *Strategy + Business* (Autumn 2007), http://www.strategy-business.com/press/enewsarticle/enews122007?pg=0, accessed on August 7, 2008.

45. Dunbar and Starbuck, "Learning to Design Organizations."

46. Johannes M. Pennings, "Structural Contingency Theory: A Reappraisal," *Research in Organizational Behavior* 14 (1992), 267–309.

47. Henry Mintzberg, *The Structuring of Organizations: The Synthesis of the Research* (Englewood Cliffs, N.J.: Prentice-Hall, 1979), 215–297; Henry Mintzberg, "Organization Design: Fashion or Fit?" *Harvard Business Review* 59 (January–February 1981), 103–116; and Henry Mintzberg, *Mintzberg on Management: Inside Our Strange World of Organizations* (New York: The Free Press, 1989).

48. This discussion is based in part on Toby J. Tetenbaum, "Shifting Paradigms: From Newton to Chaos," *Organizational Dynamics* (Spring 1998), 21–32.

49. William Bergquist, *The Postmodern Organization* (San Francisco: Jossey-Bass, 1993).

50. Based on Tetenbaum, "Shifting Paradigms: From Newton to Chaos," and Richard T. Pascale, "Surfing the Edge of Chaos," *Sloan Management Review* (Spring 1999), 83–94.

51. Greg Jaffe, "Trial by Fire: On Ground in Iraq, Capt. Ayers Writes His Own Playbook," *The Wall Street Journal* (September 22, 2004), A1.

52. David K. Hurst, *Crisis and Renewal: Meeting the Challenge of Organizational Change* (Boston, Mass.: Harvard Business School Press, 1995), 32–52.

53. Alan Deutschman, "Open Wide; The Traditional Business Organization Meets Democracy," *Fast Company* (March 2007), 40–41.

54. Ann Harrington, note on QuikTrip, in Robert Levering and Milton Moskowitz, "100 Best Companies to Work For," *Fortune* (January 20, 2003), 127–152.

55. Thomas Petzinger, *The New Pioneers: The Men and Women Who Are Transforming the Workplace and Marketplace* (New York: Simon & Schuster, 1999), 91–93; idem, "In Search of the New World of Work," *Fast Company* (April 1999), 214–220; Peter Katel, "Bordering on Chaos," *Wired* (July 1997), 98–107; Oren Harari, "The Concrete Intangibles," *Management Review* (May 1999), 30–33; "Mexican Cement Maker on Verge of a Deal," *The New York Times* (September 27, 2004), A8 and Joel Millman, "Hard Times for Cement Man," *The Wall Street Journal* (December 11, 2008), A1.

56. Robert House, Denise M. Rousseau, and Melissa Thomas-Hunt, "The Meso Paradigm: A Framework for the Integration of Micro and Macro Organizational Behavior," *Research in Organizational Behavior* 17 (1995), 71–114.

Chapter 2

1. Pete Engardio with Michael Arndt and Dean Foust, "The Future of Outsourcing," *BusinessWeek* (January 30, 2006), 50–58; and "Working with Wyeth to Establish a High-Performance Drug Discovery Capability," Accenture, *http://www.accenture.com/NR/rdonlyres/8266D49F-3BFB-4937-AD6F-FCC5095CA02A/0/wyeth.pdf*, accessed on August 15, 2008.

2. Carol Hymowitz, "Have Advice, Will Travel; Lacking Permanent Offices, Accenture's Executives Run 'Virtual' Company on the Fly," *The Wall Street Journal* (June 5, 2006), B1.

3. John Child, *Organization* (New York: Harper & Row, 1984).

4. Stuart Ranson, Bob Hinings, and Royston Greenwood, "The Structuring of Organizational Structures," *Administrative Science Quarterly* 25 (1980), 1–17; and Hugh Willmott, "The Structuring of Organizational Structure: A Note," *Administrative Science Quarterly* 26 (1981), 470–474.

5. This section is based on Frank Ostroff, *The Horizontal Organization: What the Organization of the Future Looks Like and How It Delivers Value to Customers* (New York: Oxford University Press, 1999).

6. Stephen Salsbury, *The State, the Investor, and the Railroad: The Boston & Albany, 1825–1867* (Cambridge: Harvard University Press, 1967), 186–187.

7. David Nadler and Michael Tushman, *Strategic Organization Design* (Glenview, Ill.: Scott Foresman, 1988).

8. William C. Ouchi, "Power to the Principals: Decentralization in Three Large School Districts," *Organization Science* 17, no. 2 (March–April 2006), 298–307.

9. William Newman, "Management of Subways to Be Split," *The New York Times* (December 6, 2007), B1.

10. Brian Hindo, "Making the Elephant Dance," *BusinessWeek* (May 1, 2006), 88–90.

11. "Country Managers: From Baron to Hotelier," *The Economist* (May 11, 2002), 55–56.

12. Based on Jay R. Galbraith, *Designing Complex Organizations* (Reading, Mass.: Addison-Wesley, 1973), and *Organization Design* (Reading, Mass.: Addison-Wesley, 1977), 81–127.

13. George Anders, "Overseeing More Employees—With Fewer Managers," *The Wall Street Journal* (March 24, 2008), B6.

14. Lee Iacocca with William Novak, *Iacocca: An Autobiography* (New York: Phantom Books, 1984), 152–153.

15. Based on Galbraith, *Designing Complex Organizations*.

16. "Mandate 2003: Be Agile and Efficient," *Microsoft Executive Circle* (Spring 2003), 46–48.

17. Jay Galbraith, Diane Downey, and Amy Kates, "How Networks Undergird the Lateral Capability of an Organization—Where the Work Gets Done," *Journal of Organizational Excellence* (Spring 2002), 67–78.

18. Amy Barrett, "Staying on Top," *BusinessWeek* (May 5, 2003), 60–68.

19. Walter Kiechel III, "The Art of the Corporate Task Force," *Fortune* (January 28, 1991), 104–105; and William J. Altier, "Task Forces: An Effective Management Tool," *Management Review* (February 1987), 52–57.

20. Neal E. Boudette, "Marriage Counseling; At DaimlerChrysler, A New Push to Make Its Units Work Together," *The Wall Street Journal* (March 12, 2003), A1, A15.

21. Paul R. Lawrence and Jay W. Lorsch, "New Managerial Job: The Integrator," *Harvard Business Review* (November–December 1967), 142–151.

22. Laurianne McLaughlin, "Project Collaboration: How One Company Got a Diverse Team on the Same Page," *CIO* (August 13, 2007), *http://www.cio.com/article/130300/Project_Collaboration_How_One_Company_Got_A_Diverse_Team_on_the_Same_Page?contentId=130300&slug=&*, accessed on August 20, 2008.

23. Thomas L. Legare, "How Hewlett-Packard Used Virtual Cross-Functional Teams to Deliver Healthcare Industry

Solutions," *Journal of Organizational Excellence* (Autumn 2001), 29–37.

24. Anthony M. Townsend, Samuel M. DeMarie, and Anthony R. Hendrickson, "Virtual Teams: Technology and the Workplace of the Future," *Academy of Management Executive* 12, no. 3 (August 1998), 17–29.

25. Erin White, "How a Company Made Everyone a Team Player," *The Wall Street Journal* (August 13, 2007), B1.

26. Thom Shanker, "Edging Away from Air Force, Army Is Starting Its Own Aviation Unit," *The New York Times* (June 22, 2008), A6.

27. Henry Mintzberg, *The Structuring of Organizations* (Englewood Cliffs, N.J.: Prentice-Hall, 1979).

28. Frank Ostroff, "Stovepipe Stomper," *Government Executive* (April 1999), 70.

29. Based on Robert Duncan, "What Is the Right Organization Structure?" *Organizational Dynamics* (Winter 1979), 59–80; and W. Alan Randolph and Gregory G. Dess, "The Congruence Perspective of Organization Design: A Conceptual Model and Multivariate Research Approach," *Academy of Management Review* 9 (1984), 114–127.

30. R. W. Apple, Jr., "Making Texas Cows Proud," *The New York Times* (May 31, 2006), F1; Lynn Cook, "How Sweet It Is," *Forbes* (March 1, 2004), 90ff; David Kaplan, "Cool Commander; Brenham's Little Creamery Gets New Leader in Low-Key Switch," *Houston Chronicle* (May 1, 2004), 1; Toni Mack, "The Ice Cream Man Cometh," *Forbes* (January 22, 1990), 52–56; David Abdalla, J. Doehring, and Ann Windhager, "Blue Bell Creameries, Inc.: Case and Analysis" (unpublished manuscript, Texas A&M University, 1981); Jorjanna Price, "Creamery Churns Its Ice Cream into Cool Millions," *Parade* (February 21, 1982), 18–22; and Art Chapman, "Lone Star Scoop—Blue Bell Ice Cream Is a Part of State's Culture," *http://www.bluebell.com/press/FtWorthStar-july2002.htm*.

31. Timothy Galpin, Rod Hilpirt, and Bruce Evans, "The Connected Enterprise: Beyond Division of Labor," *Journal of Business Strategy* 28, no. 2 (2007), 38–47.

32. Rahul Jacob, "The Struggle to Create an Organization for the 21st Century," *Fortune* (April 3, 1995), 90–99.

33. N. Anand and Richard L. Daft, "What Is the Right Organization Design?" *Organizational Dynamics* 36, no. 4 (2007), 329–344.

34. Johnson & Johnson website, *http://www.jnj.com/connect/about-jnj/company-structure/?flash=true*, accessed on August 18, 2008; and Joseph Weber, "A Big Company That Works," *BusinessWeek* (May 4, 1992), 124–132.

35. Eliza Newlin Carney, "Calm in the Storm," *Government Executive* (October 2003), 57–63; and Brian Friel, "Hierarchies and Networks," *Government Executive* (April 2002), 31–39.

36. Based on Duncan, "What Is the Right Organization Structure?"

37. Weber, "A Big Company That Works."

38. Phred Dvorak and Merissa Marr, "Stung by iPod, Sony Addresses a Digital Lag," *The Wall Street Journal* (December 30, 2004), B1.

39. Maisie O'Flanagan and Lynn K. Taliento, "Nonprofits: Ensuring That Bigger Is Better," *McKinsey Quarterly*, Issue 2 (2004), 112ff.

40. John Markoff, "John Sculley's Biggest Test," *The New York Times* (February 26, 1989), sec. 3, 1, 26.

41. David Enrich and Carrick Mollenkamp, "Citi's Focus: Out with Old, In with Profit Drivers," *The Wall Street Journal* (February 20, 2008), C3.

42. Stanley M. Davis and Paul R. Lawrence, *Matrix* (Reading, Mass.: Addison-Wesley, 1977), 11–24.

43. Erik W. Larson and David H. Gobeli, "Matrix Management: Contradictions and Insight," *California Management Review* 29 (Summer 1987), 126–138.

44. Davis and Lawrence, *Matrix*, 155–180.

45. Robert C. Ford and W. Alan Randolph, "Cross-Functional Structures: A Review and Integration of Matrix Organizations and Project Management," *Journal of Management* 18 (June 1992), 267–294; and Duncan, "What Is the Right Organization Structure?"

46. Lawton R. Burns, "Matrix Management in Hospitals: Testing Theories of Matrix Structure and Development," *Administrative Science Quarterly* 34 (1989), 349–368.

47. Carol Hymowitz, "Managers Suddenly Have to Answer to a Crowd of Bosses" (In the Lead column), *The Wall Street Journal* (August 12, 2003), B1; and Michael Goold and Andrew Campbell, "Making Matrix Structures Work: Creating Clarity on Unit Roles and Responsibilities," *European Management Journal* 21, no. 3 (June 2003), 351–363.

48. Christopher A. Bartlett and Sumantra Ghoshal, "Matrix Management: Not a Structure, a Frame of Mind," *Harvard Business Review* (July–August 1990), 138–145.

49. This case was inspired by John E. Fogerty, "Integrative Management at Standard Steel" (unpublished manuscript, Latrobe, Pennsylvania, 1980); Stanley Reed with Adam Aston, "Steel: The Mergers Aren't Over Yet," *BusinessWeek* (February 21, 2005), 6; Michael Arndt, "Melting Away Steel's Costs," *BusinessWeek* (November 8, 2004), 48; and "Steeling for a Fight," *The Economist* (June 4, 1994), 63.

50. Michael Hammer, "Process Management and the Future of Six Sigma," *Sloan Management Review* (Winter 2002), 26–32; and Michael Hammer and Steve Stanton, "How Process Enterprises *Really* Work," *Harvard Business Review* 77 (November–December 1999), 108–118.

51. Hammer, "Process Management and the Future of Six Sigma."

52. Based on Ostroff, *The Horizontal Organization*, and Anand and Daft, "What Is the Right Organization Design?."

53. Julia Moskin, "Your Waiter Tonight . . . Will Be the Chef," *The New York Times* (March 12, 2008), F1.

54. Frank Ostroff, *The Horizontal Organization*, 102–114.

55. See Anand and Daft, "What Is the Right Organization Design?"; Pete Engardio, "The Future of Outsourcing," *BusinessWeek* (January 30, 2006), 50–58; Jane C. Linder, "Transformational Outsourcing," *MIT Sloan Management Review* (Winter 2004), 52–58; and Denis Chamberland, "Is It Core or Strategic? Outsourcing as a Strategic Management Tool," *Ivey Business Journal* (July–August 2003), 1–5.

56. Raymund Flandez, "Firms Tackle Government Chores," *The Wall Street Journal* (June 17, 2008), B7.

57. Anand and Daft, "What Is the Right Organization Design?"; Engardio, "The Future of Outsourcing"; Chamberland,

"Is It Core or Strategic?"; Keith H. Hammonds, "Smart, Determined, Ambitious, Cheap: The New Face of Global Competition," *Fast Company* (February 2003), 91–97; Giuseppe Bonazzi and Cristiano Antonelli, "To Make or to Sell? The Case of In-House Outsourcing at Fiat Auto," *Organization Studies* 24, no. 4 (2003), 575–594.

58. David Nadler, quoted in "Partners in Wealth: The Ins and Outs of Collaboration," *The Economist* (January 21–27, 2006), 16–17.

59. Ranjay Gulati, "Silo Busting: How to Execute on the Promise of Customer Focus," *Harvard Business Review* (May 2007), 98–108.

60. The discussion of virtual networks is based on Anand and Daft, "What Is the Right Organization Design?"; Melissa A. Schilling and H. Kevin Steensma, "The Use of Modular Organizational Forms: An Industry-Level Analysis," *Academy of Management Journal* 44, no. 6 (2001), 1149–1168; Raymond E. Miles and Charles C. Snow, "The New Network Firm: A Spherical Structure Built on a Human Investment Philosophy," *Organizational Dynamics* (Spring 1995), 5–18; and R. E. Miles, C. C. Snow, J. A. Matthews, G. Miles, and H. J. Coleman Jr., "Organizing in the Knowledge Age: Anticipating the Cellular Form," *Academy of Management Executive* 11, no. 4 (1997), 7–24.

61. Paul Engle, "You *Can* Outsource Strategic Processes," *Industrial Management* (January–February 2002), 13–18.

62. Don Tapscott, "Rethinking Strategy in a Networked World," *Strategy & Business* 24 (Third Quarter, 2001), 34–41.

63. Based on the story of TiVo as described in Jane C. Linder, "Transformational Outsourcing," *MIT Sloan Management Review* (Winter 2004), 52–58; with additional information from Alison Neumer, "I Want My TiVo; Subscriptions Hike as Nation Gets Hooked," *Chicago Tribune* (February 22, 2005), 8; Carolyn Y. Johnson, "In Strategic Shift, Comcast, TiVo Team Up; Move Is 1st Step Toward a More Open Platform," *Boston Globe* (January 22, 2008), C6; and David Lieberman, "TiVo Expands Its Reach with YouTube Videos," *USA Today* (March 13, 2008), B3.

64. This discussion of strengths and weaknesses is based on Miles and Snow, "The New Network Firm"; Gregory G. Dess, Abdul M. A. Rasheed, Kevin J. McLaughlin, and Richard L. Priem, "The New Corporate Architecture," *Academy of Management Executive* 9, no. 2 (1995), 7–20; Engle, "You *Can* Outsource Strategic Processes"; Anand and Daft, "What Is the Right Organization Structure?"; and Henry W. Chesbrough and David J. Teece, "Organizing for Innovation: When Is Virtual Virtuous?" *Harvard Business Review* (August 2002), 127–134.

65. Linda S. Ackerman, "Transition Management: An In-depth Look at Managing Complex Change," *Organizational Dynamics* (Summer 1982), 46–66.

66. Based on Ostroff, *The Horizontal Organization*, 29–44.

67. Based on Child, *Organization*, Ch. 1; and Jonathan D. Day, Emily Lawson, and Keith Leslie, "When Reorganization Works," *The McKinsey Quarterly*, 2003 Special Edition: The Value in Organization, 21–29.

Chapter 3

1. Brian Stelter, "Plenty of Users, Too Few Dollars; Trying to Turn Popularity Into Gold, MySpace Gets a New Look," *International Herald Tribune* (June 16, 2008), 10; and Ellen McGirt, "MySpace, the Sequel," *Fortune* (September 2008), 92–102.

2. Amitai Etzioni, *Modern Organizations* (Englewood Cliffs, N.J.: Prentice-Hall, 1964), 6.

3. John P. Kotter, "What Effective General Managers Really Do," *Harvard Business Review* (November December 1982), 156–167; and Henry Mintzberg, *The Nature of Managerial Work* (New York: Harper & Row, 1973).

4. Charles C. Snow and Lawrence G. Hrebiniak, "Strategy, Distinctive Competence, and Organizational Performance," *Administrative Science Quarterly* 25 (1980), 317–335; and Robert J. Allio, " Strategic Thinking: The Ten Big Ideas," *Strategy & Leadership* 34, no. 4 (2006), 4–13.

5. Jeffrey A. Trachtenberg, "Borders Business Plan Gets a Rewrite; It Will Reopen Web Site, Give Up Most Stores Abroad, Close Many Waldenbooks," *The Wall Street Journal* (March 22, 2007), B1; and "Research and Markets: Borders' Strategy for 2008 Includes Development of an E-Commerce Platform," press release, Yahoo! Finance Website, *http://biz.yahoo.com/bw/081016/20081016005779.html?.v=1*, accessed on October 30, 2008.

6. Gary Hamel and C. K. Prahalad, "Strategic Intent," *Harvard Business Review* (July–August 2005), 148–161.

7. Hamel and Prahalad, "Strategic Intent."

8. Barbara Bartkus, Myron Glassman, and R. Bruce McAfee, "Mission Statements: Are They Smoke and Mirrors?" *Business Horizons* (November–December 2000), 23–28.

9. Mark C. Suchman, "Managing Legitimacy: Strategic and Institutional Approaches," *Academy of Management Review* 20, no. 3 (1995), 571–610.

10. Ian Wilson, "The Agenda for Redefining Corporate Purpose: Five Key Executive Actions," *Strategy & Leadership* 32, no. 1 (2004), 21–26.

11. Bill George, "The Company's Mission Is the Message," *Strategy & Business*, Issue 33 (Winter 2003), 13–14; Jim Collins and Jerry Porras, *Built to Last: Successful Habits of Visionary Companies* (New York: HarperBusiness, 1994).

12. Hamel and Prahalad, "Strategic Intent."

13. Amy Merrick, "How Walgreen Changes Its Prescription for Growth," *The Wall Street Journal* (March 19, 2008), B1.

14. Arthur A. Thompson, Jr., and A. J. Strickland III, *Strategic Management: Concepts and Cases*, 6th ed. (Homewood, Ill.: Irwin, 1992); and Briance Mascarenhas, Alok Baveja, and Mamnoon Jamil, "Dynamics of Core Competencies in Leading Multinational Companies," *California Management Review* 40, no. 4 (Summer 1998), 117–132.

15. Michael V. Copeland, "Stitching Together an Apparel Power-house," *Business 2.0* (April 2005), 52–54.

16. "Gaylord Says Hotels Prosper by Becoming Destinations," *The Tennessean* (July 24, 2005), *http://www.tennessean.com.*

17. Chris Woodyard, "Big Dreams for Small Choppers Paid Off," *USA Today* (September 11, 2005), *http://www.usatoday.com.*

18. Charles Perrow, "The Analysis of Goals in Complex Organizations," *American Sociological Review* 26 (1961), 854–866.

19. Johannes U. Stoelwinder and Martin P. Charns, "The Task Field Model of Organization Analysis and Design," *Human Relations* 34 (1981), 743–762; and Anthony Raia, *Managing by Objectives* (Glenview, Ill.: Scott Foresman, 1974).

20. Kate Murphy, "Not Just Another Jelly Bean," *The New York Times* (June 26, 2008), C5.

21. Joseph Pereira and Christopher J. Chipello, "Battle of the Block Makers," *The Wall Street Journal* (February 4, 2004), B1.

22. Reed Abelson, "Managing Outcomes Helps a Children's Hospital Climb in Renown," *The New York Times* (September 15, 2007), C1.

23. Kevin E. Joyce, "Lessons for Employers from *Fortune's* '100 Best,'" *Business Horizons* (March–April 2003), 77–84; Ann Harrington, "The 100 Best Companies to Work for Hall of Fame," *Fortune* (January 24, 2005), 94; and Robert Levering and Milton Moskowitz, "100 Best Companies to Work For: The Rankings," *Fortune* (February 4, 2008), 75–94.

24. Kim Cross, "Does Your Team Measure Up?" *Business2.com* (June 12, 2001), 22–28.

25. Larry Huston and Nabil Sakkab, "Connect and Develop; Inside Procter & Gamble's New Model for Innovation," *Harvard Business Review* (March 2006), 58–66.

26. Studies reported in Gary P. Latham and Edwin A. Locke, "Enhancing the Benefits and Overcoming the Pitfalls of Goal Setting," *Organizational Dynamics* 35, no. 4 (2006), 332–340.

27. Paul Sloan, "The Sales Force That Rocks," *Business 2.0* (July 2005), 102–107.

28. James D. Thompson, *Organizations in Action* (New York: McGraw-Hill, 1967), 83–98.

29. Michael E. Porter, "What Is Strategy?" *Harvard Business Review* (November–December 1996), 61–78.

30. Michael E. Porter, "The Five Competitive Forces That Shape Strategy," *Harvard Business Review* (January 2008), 78–93.

31. Sean Gregory, "Under Armour's Big Step Up," *Time* (May 26, 2008), 44–45.

32. Bill Carter, "Nielsen Tells TV Clients It Is Working on Ending Delays in Ratings," *The New York Times* (February 9, 2008), C3; and Stephanie Kang, "NBC to Use TiVo's TV Viewership Data," *The Wall Street Journal* (November 27, 2007), B8.

33. Peter Loftus, "Drug Firms Employ Strategy Masters," *The Wall Street Journal* (April 14, 2008), B5.

34. Geoffrey A. Fowler and Betsy McKay, "Coke Pins China Hopes on Blitz in Beijing," *The Wall Street Journal* (August 19, 2008), A1, A13.

35. Michael E. Porter, *Competitive Strategy: Techniques for Analyzing Industries and Competitors* (New York: Free Press, 1980).

36. Tom Krazit, "Apple's iPhone Price Cuts Leave Mixed Feelings," CNet News.com, *http://business2-cnet.com/Apples +iPhone+price+cuts+leave+mixed+feelings/ 2100-1041_ 3-6206367.html*, accessed on August 13, 2008; Nick Wingfield, "Apple Positions iPhone As Rival to the BlackBerry," *The Wall Street Journal* (March 7, 2008), B1; Laura M. Holson, "Even AT&T Is Startled By Cost of iPhone Partnership," *The New York Times* (October 23, 2008), B2; and Brad Stone, "BlackBerry's Quest: Fend Off the iPhone," *The New York Times* (April 27, 2008), BU1.

37. Rob Walker, "Branching Out," *New York Times Magazine* (September 24, 2006), 21.

38. Alan Ruddock, "Keeping Up with O'Leary," *Management Today* (September 2003), 48–55; Jane Engle, "Flying High for Pocket Change; Regional Carriers Offer Inexpensive Travel Alternative," *South Florida Sun Sentinel* (February 13, 2005), 5.

39. Richard Teitelbaum, "The Wal-Mart of Wall Street," *Fortune* (October 13, 1997), 128–130.

40. Kevin J. O'Brien, "Focusing on Armchair Athletes, Puma Becomes a Leader," *The New York Times* (March 12, 2004), W1.

41. Michael E. Porter, "Strategy and the Internet," *Harvard Business Review* (March 2001), 63–78; and John Magretta, "Why Business Models Matter," *Harvard Business Review* (May 2002), 86.

42. Raymond E. Miles and Charles C. Snow, *Organizational Strategy, Structure, and Process* (New York: McGraw-Hill, 1978).

43. Nicholas Casey, "New Nike Sneaker Targets Jocks, Greens, Wall Street," *The Wall Street Journal* (February 15, 2008), B1.

44. Geraldine Fabrikant, "The Paramount Team Puts Profit Over Splash," *The New York Times* (June 30, 2002), Section 3, 1, 15.

45. Mylene Mangalindan, "Slow Slog for Amazon's Digital Media—Earnings Today May Provide Data on What Works," *The Wall Street Journal* (April 23, 2008), B1.

46. Nanette Byrnes and Peter Burrows, "Where Dell Went Wrong," *BusinessWeek* (February 19, 2007), 62–63.

47. "On the Staying Power of Defenders, Analyzers, and Prospectors: Academic Commentary by Donald C. Hambrick," *Academy of Management Executive* 17, no. 4 (2003), 115–118.

48. Etzioni, Modern Organizations, 8.

49. Etzioni, Modern Organizations, 8; and Gary D. Sandefur, "Efficiency in Social Service Organizations," *Administration and Society* 14 (1983), 449–468.

50. Richard M. Steers, *Organizational Effectiveness: A Behavioral View* (Santa Monica, Calif.: Goodyear, 1977), 51.

51. Michael Hammer, "The 7 Deadly Sins of Performance Measurement (and How to Avoid Them)," *MIT Sloan Management Review* 48, no. 3 (Spring 2007), 19–28.

52. Karl E. Weick and Richard L. Daft, "The Effectiveness of Interpretation Systems," in Kim S. Cameron and David A. Whetten, eds., *Organizational Effectiveness: A Comparison of Multiple Models* (New York: Academic Press, 1982).

53. David L. Blenkhorn and Brian Gaber, "The Use of 'Warm Fuzzies' to Assess Organizational Effectiveness," *Journal of General Management,* 21, no. 2 (Winter 1995), 40–51; and Scott Leibs, "Measuring Up," *CFO* (June 2007), 63–66.

54. James L. Price, "The Study of Organizational Effectiveness," *Sociological Quarterly* 13 (1972), 3–15; and Steven Strasser, J. D. Eveland, Gaylord Cummins, O. Lynn Deniston, and John H. Romani, "Conceptualizing the Goal and Systems

Models of Organizational Effectiveness—Implications for Comparative Evaluation Research," *Journal of Management Studies* 18 (1981), 321–340.

55. Lucy McCauley, ed., "Unit of One: Measure What Matters," *Fast Company* (May 1999), 97.

56. Richard H. Hall and John P. Clark, "An Ineffective Effectiveness Study and Some Suggestions for Future Research," *Sociological Quarterly* 21 (1980), 119–134; Price, "The Study of Organizational Effectiveness"; and Perrow, "Analysis of Goals."

57. The discussion of the resource-based approach is based in part on Michael V. Russo and Paul A. Fouts, "A Resource-Based Perspective on Corporate Environmental Performance and Profitability," *Academy of Management Journal* 40, no. 3 (June 1997), 534–559; and Jay B. Barney, J. L. "Larry" Stempert, Loren T. Gustafson, and Yolanda Sarason, "Organizational Identity within the Strategic Management Conversation: Contributions and Assumptions," in David A. Whetten and Paul C. Godfrey, eds., *Identity in Organizations: Building Theory through Conversations* (Thousand Oaks, Calif.: Sage Publications, 1998), 83–98.

58. Chris Argyris, *Integrating the Individual and the Organization* (New York: Wiley, 1964); Warren G. Bennis, *Changing Organizations* (New York: McGraw-Hill, 1966); Rensis Likert, *The Human Organization* (New York:

McGraw-Hill, 1967); and Richard Beckhard, *Organization Development Strategies and Models* (Reading, Mass.: Addison-Wesley, 1969).

59. Cheri Ostroff and Neal Schmitt, "Configurations of Organizational Effectiveness and Efficiency," *Academy of Management Journal* 36 (1993), 1345–1361.

60. J. Barton Cunningham, "Approaches to the Evaluation of Organizational Effectiveness," *Academy of Management Review* 2 (1977), 463–474; Beckhard, *Organization Development.*

61. "On Balance," a CFO Interview with Robert Kaplan and David Norton, *CFO* (February 2001), 73–78; Chee W. Chow, Kamal M. Haddad, and James E. Williamson, "Applying the Balanced Scorecard to Small Companies," *Management Accounting* 79, no. 2 (August 1997), 21–27; and Robert Kaplan and David Norton, "The Balanced Scorecard: Measures That Drive Performance," *Harvard Business Review* (January-February 1992), 71–79.

62. Scott Leibs, "Measuring Up," *CFO* (June 2007), 63–66.

63. Geary A. Rummler and Kimberly Morrill, "The Results Chain," *TD* (February 2005), 27–35; and John C. Crotts, Duncan R. Dickson, and Robert C. Ford, "Aligning Organizational Processes with Mission: The Case of Service Excellence," *Academy of Management Executive* 19, no. 3 (August 2005), 54–68.

Chapter 4

1. "SAP and Microsoft Tighten Bonds," *IT Week* (November 20, 2006), 1; Miguel Helft, "Yahoo Is Joining An Alliance That Has Google As Leader," *The New York Times* (March 26, 2008), C7.

2. Douglas Quenqua, "The Force Lives On, As Do the Toys," *The New York Times* (July 1, 2008), C2; "Star Wars: The Clone Wars and McDonald's Join Forces for an Intergalactic Happy Meal Experience," *PR Newswire* (August 14, 2008); and Mike Scott, "'Clone Wars' Is More Marketing Than Movie," *Times-Picayune* (August 15, 2008), 5.

3. Christine Oliver, "Determinants of Interorganizational Relationships: Integration and Future Directions," *Academy of Management Review* 15 (1990), 241–265.

4. James Moore, *The Death of Competition: Leadership and Strategy in the Age of Business Ecosystems* (New York: HarperCollins, 1996).

5. John Jurgensen, "The Family Guy Goes Online," *The Wall Street Journal* (September 5, 2006), W1.

6. Jonathan Hughes and Jeff Weiss, "Simple Rules for Making Alliances Work," *Harvard Business Review* (November 2007), 122–131; Howard Muson, "Friend? Foe? Both? The Confusing World of Corporate Alliances," *Across the Board* (March–April 2002), 19–25; and Devi R. Gnyawali and Ravindranath Madhavan, "Cooperative Networks and Competitive Dynamics: A Structural Embeddedness Perspective," *Academy of Management Review* 26, no. 3 (2001), 431–445.

7. Thomas Petzinger, Jr., *The New Pioneers: The Men and Women Who Are Transforming the Workplace and Marketplace* (New York: Simon & Schuster, 1999), 53–54.

8. James Moore, "The Death of Competition," *Fortune* (April 15, 1996), 142–144.

9. Brian Goodwin, *How the Leopard Changed Its Spots: The Evolution of Complexity* (New York: Touchstone, 1994), 181, quoted in Petzinger, *The New Pioneers,* 53.

10. Phred Dvorak and Evan Ramstad, "TV Marriage: Behind Sony-Samsung Rivalry, An Unlikely Alliance Develops," *The Wall Street Journal* (January 3, 2006), A1.

11. Sumantra Ghoshal and Christopher A. Bartlett, "Changing the Role of Top Management: Beyond Structure and Process," *Harvard Business Review* (January–February 1995), 86–96.

12. "Toward a More Perfect Match: Building Successful Leaders by Effectively Aligning People and Roles," Hay Group Working Paper (2004); and "Making Sure the Suit Fits," *Hay Group Research Brief* (2004). Available from Hay Group, The McClelland Center, 116 Huntington Avenue, Boston, MA 02116, or at *http://www.haygroup.com.*

13. Hughes and Weiss, "Simple Rules for Making Alliances Work."

14. Susan Greco and Kate O'Sullivan, "Independents' Day," *Inc.* (August 2002), 76–83.

15. J. Pfeffer and G. R. Salancik, *The External Control of Organizations: A Resource Dependence Perspective* (New York: Harper & Row, 1978).

16. Definition based on Steven A. Melnyk and David R. Denzler, *Operations Management: A Value Driven Approach* (Burr Ridge, Ill.: Irwin, 1996): 613.

17. Patricia J. Daugherty, R. Glenn Richey, Anthony S. Roath, Soonhong Min, Haozhe Chen, Aaron D. Arndt, and Stefan E. Gencehv, "Is Collaboration Paying Off for Firms?" *Business Horizons* 49, no. 2 (January–February 2006), 61–70.

18. Jim Turcotte, Bob Silveri, and Tom Jobson, "Are You Ready for the E-Supply Chain?" *APICS–The Performance Advantage* (August 1998): 56–59.

19. "The AMR Research Supply Chain Top 25 for 2008," *http://www.amrresearch.com/supplychaintop25/#, accessed on May 30, 2008.*

20. This discussion is based on Matthew Schifrin, "The Big Squeeze," *Forbes* (March 11, 1996), 45–46; Wendy Zellner with Marti Benedetti, "CLOUT!" *BusinessWeek* (December 21, 1992), 62–73; Kevin Kelly and Zachary Schiller with James B. Treece, "Cut Costs or Else," *BusinessWeek* (March 22, 1993), 28–29; and Lee Berton, "Push from Above," *The Wall Street Journal* (May 23, 1996), R24.

21. Doreen Carvajal, "Small Publishers Feel Power of Amazon's 'Buy' Button," *The New York Times* (June 16, 2008), C7.

22. Mitchell P. Koza and Arie Y. Lewin, "The Co-Evolution of Network Alliances: A Longitudinal Analysis of an International Professional Service Network," Center for Research on New Organizational Forms, Working Paper 98–09–02; and Kathy Rebello with Richard Brandt, Peter Coy, and Mark Lewyn, "Your Digital Future," *BusinessWeek* (September 7, 1992), 56–64.

23. Amol Sharma and Vishesh Kumar, "Big Tech Firms to Invest in Wireless," *The Wall Street Journal* (May 7, 2008), B1.

24. Christine Oliver, "Determinants of Inter-organizational Relationships: Integration and Future Directions," *Academy of Management Review*, 15 (1990), 241–265; Ken G. Smith, Stephen J. Carroll, and Susan Ashford, "Intra- and Interorganizational Cooperation: Toward a Research Agenda," *Academy of Management Journal*, 38 (1995), 7–23; and Ken G. Smith, Stephen J. Carroll, and Susan Ashford, "Intra- and Interorganizational Cooperation: Toward a Research Agenda," *Academy of Management Journal* 38 (1995), 7–23.

25. Timothy M. Stearns, Alan N. Hoffman, and Jan B. Heide, "Performance of Commercial Television Stations as an Outcome of Interorganizational Linkages and Environmental Conditions," *Academy of Management Journal* 30 (1987), 71–90; and David A. Whetten and Thomas K. Kueng, "The Instrumental Value of Interorganizational Relations: Antecedents and Consequences of Linkage Formation," *Academy of Management Journal* 22 (1979), 325–344.

26. Martin Fackler, "Nintendo Changes Direction, and It Appears to Be Paying Off," *The New York Times* (June 8, 2007), C1.

27. Alice Dragoon, "A Travel Guide to Collaboration," *CIO* (November 15, 2004), 68–75.

28. Elizabeth Olson, "OMG! Cute Boys, Kissing Tips and Lots of Pics, As Magazines Find a Niche," *The New York Times* (May 28, 2007): C1.

29. Keith G. Provan and H. Brinton Milward, "A Preliminary Theory of Interorganizational Network Effectiveness: A Comparative of Four Community Mental Health Systems," *Administrative Science Quarterly* 40 (1995), 1–33.

30. Peter Smith Ring and Andrew H. Van de Ven, "Developmental Processes of Corporate Interorganizational Relationships," *Academy of Management Review* 19 (1994), 90–118; Jeffrey H. Dyer, "How Chrysler Created an American *Keiretsu*," *Harvard Business Review* (July–August 1996), 42–56; Peter Grittner, "Four Elements of Successful Sourcing Strategies" *Management Review* (October 1995), 41–45; Myron Magnet, "The New Golden Rule of Business," *Fortune* (February 21, 1994), 60–64; and Mick Marchington and Steven Vincent, "Analysing the Influence of Institutional, Organizational and Interpersonal Forces in Shaping Inter-Organizational Relationships," *Journal of Management Studies* 41, no. 6 (September 2004), 1029–1056.

31. Nick Bunkley, "Chrysler and Nissan Agree to Vehicle-Building Pact," *The New York Times* (April 15, 2008), C5.

32. Dan Mankin and Susan G. Cohen, "Business Without Boundaries: Collaboration Across Organizations," *Journal of Organizational Excellence* (Spring 2006), 63–78.

33. Philip Siekman, "The Snap-Together Business Jet," *Fortune* (January 21, 2002), 104[A]–104[H].

34. This section draws from Joel A. C. Baum, "Organizational Ecology," in Stewart R. Clegg, Cynthia Hardy, and Walter R. Nord, eds., *Handbook of Organization Studies* (Thousand Oaks, Calif.: Sage, 1996); Jitendra V. Singh, *Organizational Evolution: New Directions* (Newbury Park, Calif.: Sage, 1990); Howard Aldrich, Bill McKelvey, and Dave Ulrich, "Design Strategy from the Population Perspective," *Journal of Management* 10 (1984), 67–86; Howard E. Aldrich, *Organizations and Environments* (Englewood Cliffs, N.J.: Prentice Hall, 1979); Michael Hannan and John Freeman, "The Population Ecology of Organizations," *American Journal of Sociology* 82 (1977), 929–964; Dave Ulrich, "The Population Perspective: Review, Critique, and Relevance," *Human Relations* 40 (1987), 137–152; Jitendra V. Singh and Charles J. Lumsden, "Theory and Research in Organizational Ecology," *Annual Review of Sociology* 16 (1990), 161–195; Howard E. Aldrich, "Understanding, Not Integration: Vital Signs from Three Perspectives on Organizations," in Michael Reed and Michael D. Hughes, eds., *Rethinking Organizations: New Directions in Organizational Theory and Analysis* (London: Sage, 1992); Jitendra V. Singh, David J. Tucker, and Robert J. House, "Organizational Legitimacy and the Liability of Newness," *Administrative Science Quarterly* 31 (1986), 171–193; and Douglas R. Wholey and Jack W. Brittain, "Organizational Ecology: Findings and Implications," *Academy of Management Review* 11 (1986), 513–533.

35. Derek S. Pugh and David J. Hickson, *Writers on Organizations* (Thousand Oaks, Calif.: Sage, 1996); and Lex Donaldson, *American Anti-Management Theories of Organization* (New York: Cambridge University Press, 1995).

36. Jim Collins, "The Secret of Enduring Greatness," *Fortune* (May 5, 2008), 72–76.

37. Hannan and Freeman, "The Population Ecology of Organizations."

38. Gary McWilliams, "Wal-Mart Era Wanes Amid Big Shifts in Retail," *The Wall Street Journal* (October 3, 2007), A1.

39. Ashby Jones, "Corporate News—Legal Beat: Newcomer Law Firms Are Creating Niches with Blue-Chip Clients," *The Wall Street Journal* (July 2, 2008), B4.

40. David Stires, "Fallen Arches," *Fortune* (April 29, 2002), 74–76.

41. David J. Tucker, Jitendra V. Singh, and Agnes G. Meinhard, "Organizational Form, Population Dynamics, and Institutional Change: The Founding Patterns of Voluntary Organizations," *Academy of Management Journal* 33 (1990), 151–178; Glenn R. Carroll and Michael T. Hannan, "Density Delay in the Evolution of Organizational Populations: A Model and Five Empirical Tests," *Administrative Science Quarterly* 34 (1989), 411–430; Jacques Delacroix and Glenn R. Carroll, "Organizational Foundings: An Ecological Study of the Newspaper Industries of Argentina and Ireland," *Administrative Science Quarterly* 28 (1983), 274–291; Johannes M. Pennings, "Organizational Birth Frequencies: An Empirical Investigation," *Administrative Science Quarterly* 27 (1982), 120–144; David Marple, "Technological Innovation and Organizational Survival: A Population Ecology Study of Nineteenth-Century American Railroads," *Sociological Quarterly* 23 (1982), 107–116; and Thomas G. Rundall and John O. McClain, "Environmental Selection and Physician Supply," *American Journal of Sociology* 87 (1982), 1090–1112.

42. Robert D. Hof and Linda Himelstein, "eBay vs. Amazon. com," *BusinessWeek* (May 31, 1999), 128–132; and Maria Mallory with Stephanie Anderson Forest, "Waking Up to a Major Market," *BusinessWeek* (March 23, 1992), 70–73.

43. Arthur G. Bedeian and Raymond F. Zammuto, *Organizations: Theory and Design* (Orlando, Fla.: Dryden Press, 1991); and Richard L. Hall, *Organizations: Structure, Process and Outcomes* (Englewood Cliffs, N.J.: Prentice-Hall, 1991).

44. M. Tina Dacin, Jerry Goodstein, and W. Richard Scott, "Institutional Theory and Institutional Change: Introduction to the Special Research Forum," *Academy of Management Journal* 45, no. 1 (2002), 45–47. Thanks to Tina Dacin for her material and suggestions for this section of the chapter.

45. J. Meyer and B. Rowan, "Institutionalized Organizations: Formal Structure as Myth and Ceremony," *American Journal of Sociology* 83 (1990), 340–363.

46. Mark C. Suchman, "Managing Legitimacy: Strategic and Institutional Approaches," *Academy of Management Review* 20 (1995), 571–610.

47. Anne Fisher, "America's Most Admired Companies," *Fortune* (March 17, 2008), 665–67; and Survey Results from Harris Interactive and the Reputation Institute, reported in Ronald Alsop, "In Business Ranking, Some Icons Lose Luster," *The Wall Street Journal* (November 15, 2004), B1.

48. Richard J. Martinez and Patricia M. Norman, "Whither Reputation? The Effects of Different Stakeholders," *Business Horizons* 47, no. 5 (September–October 2004), 25–32.

49. Pamela S. Tolbert and Lynne G. Zucker, "The Institutionalization of Institutional Theory," in Stewart R. Clegg, Cynthia Hardy, and Walter R. Nord, eds., *Handbook of Organization Studies* (Thousand Oaks, Calif.: Sage, 1996).

50. Pugh and Hickson, *Writers on Organizations;* and Paul J. DiMaggio and Walter W. Powell, "The Iron Cage Revisited: Institutional Isomorphism and Collective Rationality in Organizational Fields," *American Sociological Review* 48 (1983), 147–160.

51. This section is based largely on DiMaggio and Powell, "The Iron Cage Revisited"; Pugh and Hickson, *Writers on Organizations;* and W. Richard Scott, *Institutions and Organizations* (Thousand Oaks, Calif.: Sage, 1995).

52. Ellen R. Auster and Mark L. Sirower, "The Dynamics of Merger and Acquisition Waves," *The Journal of Applied Behavioral Science* 38, no. 2 (June 2002), 216–244; and Monica Yang and Mary Anne Hyland, "Who Do Firms Imitate? A Multilevel Approach to Examining Sources of Imitation in Choice of Mergers and Acquisitions," *Journal of Management* 32, no. 3 (June 2006), 381–399.

53. Barry M. Staw and Lisa D. Epstein, "What Bandwagons Bring: Effects of Popular Management Techniques on Corporate Performance, Reputation, and CEO Pay," *Administrative Science Quarterly* 45, no. 3 (September 2000), 523–560.

54. Karen Donovan, "Pushed by Clients, Law Firms Step Up Diversity Efforts," *The New York Times* (July 21, 2006), C6.

Chapter 5

1. Vanessa O'Connell, "Department Stores: Tough Sell Abroad," *The Wall Street Journal* (May 22, 2008), B1; James Bandler and Matthew Karnitschnig, "Lost in Translation; European Giant in Magazines Finds U.S. a Tough Read," *The Wall Street Journal* (August 19, 2004), A1, A6; David Carr, "The Decline and Fall of Business Magazines," *International Herald Tribune* (May 31, 2005), 11; and Barbara Whitaker, "The Web Makes Going Global Easy, Until You Try to Do It," *The New York Times* (September 2000), 20.

2. Choe Sang-Hun, "Wal-Mart Selling Stores and Leaving South Korea," *The New York Times* (May 23, 2006), C5.

3. Louise Story, "Seeking Leaders, U.S. Companies Think Globally," *The New York Times* (December 12, 2007), A1.

4. Phred Dvorak and Merissa Marr, "In Surprise Move, Sony Plans to Hand Reins to a Foreigner," *The Wall Street Journal* (March 7, 2005), A1; Carol Hymowitz, "More American Chiefs Are Taking Top Posts at Overseas Concerns," *The Wall Street Journal* (October 17, 2005), B1; Justin Martin, "The Global CEO: Overseas Experience Is Becoming

a Must on Top Executives' Resumes," *Chief Executive* (January–February 2004), 24.

5. Richard Gibson, "U.S. Restaurants Push Abroad," *The Wall Street Journal* (June 18, 2008), B5.

6. Steve Hamm, "IBM vs. Tata: Which Is More American?" *BusinessWeek* (May 5, 2008), 28.

7. Jenny Mero, "Power Shift," *Fortune* (July 21, 2008), 161; Paola Hject, "The Fortune Global 500," *Fortune* (July 26, 2004), 159–180; and *http://money.cnn.com/magazines/fortune/global500/2008/*, accessed on September 22, 2008.

8. This discussion is based heavily on Christopher A. Bartlett and Sumantra Ghoshal, *Transnational Management: Text, Cases, and Readings in Cross-Border Management,* 3rd ed. (Boston: Irwin McGraw-Hill, 2000), 94–96; and Anil K. Gupta and Vijay Govindarajan, "Converting Global Presence into Global Competitive Advantage," *Academy of Management Executive* 15, no. 2 (2001), 45–56.

9. Neil King Jr., "A Whole New World: Competition from China and India Is Changing the Way Businesses Operate Everywhere," *The Wall Street Journal* (September 27, 2004), R1.

10. Jim Carlton, "Branching Out; New Zealanders Now Shear Trees Instead of Sheep," *The Wall Street Journal* (May 29, 2003), A1, A10.

11. "Little Trouble in Big China," *FSB* (March 2004), 56–61; "Trade Gap," sidebar in *Fast Company* (June 2004), 42; Chris Hawley, "Aircraft Makers Flock to Mexico," *USA Today* (April 6, 2008), *http://www.usatoday.com/money/industries/manufacturing/2008-04-06-aerospace_N.htm?loc=interstitialskip*, accessed on April 7, 2008; Dan Morse, "Cabinet Decisions; In North Carolina, Furniture Makers Try to Stay Alive," *The Wall Street Journal* (February 20, 2004), A1.

12. Keith H. Hammonds, "Smart, Determined, Ambitious, Cheap: The New Face of Global Competition," *Fast Company* (February 2003), 91–97.

13. James Flanigan, "Now, High-Tech Work Is Going Abroad," *The New York Times* (November 17, 2005), C6; and Sheridan Prasso, "Google Goes to India," *Fortune* (October 29, 2007), 160–166.

14. Todd Zaun, Gregory L. White, Norihiko Shirouzu, and Scott Miller, "More Mileage: Auto Makers Look for Another Edge Farther from Home," *The Wall Street Journal* (July 31, 2002), A1, A8.

15. Alison Stein Wellner, "Turning the Tables," *Inc.* (May 2006), 55–57.

16. Ken Belson, "Outsourcing, Turned Inside Out," *The New York Times* (April 11, 2004), Section 3, 1.

17. Based on Nancy J. Adler, *International Dimensions of Organizational Behavior,* 4th ed. (Cincinnati, Ohio: South-Western, 2002); Theodore T. Herbert, "Strategy and Multinational Organizational Structure: An Interorganizational Relationships Perspective," *Academy of Management Review* 9 (1984), 259–271; and Laura K. Rickey, "International Expansion—U.S. Corporations: Strategy, Stages of Development, and Structure" (unpublished manuscript, Vanderbilt University, 1991).

18. Julia Boorstin, "Exporting Cleaner Air," segment of "Small and Global," *FSB* (June 2004), 36–48.

19. Geraldo Samor, Cecilie Rohwedder, and Ann Zimmerman, "Innocents Abroad? Wal-Mart's Global Sales Rise As It Learns from Mistakes," *The Wall Street Journal* (May 16, 2006), B1.

20. Michael E. Porter, "Changing Patterns of International Competition," *California Management Review* 28 (Winter 1986), 9–40.

21. William J. Holstein, "The Stateless Corporation," *BusinessWeek* (May 14, 1990), 98–115.

22. Phred Dvorak, "Why Multiple Headquarters Multiply," *The Wall Street Journal* (November 19, 2007), B1.

23. Debra Sparks, "Partners," *BusinessWeek,* Special Report: Corporate Finance (October 25, 1999), 106–112.

24. David Lei and John W. Slocum, Jr., "Global Strategic Alliances: Payoffs and Pitfalls," *Organizational Dynamics* (Winter 1991), 17–29.

25. O'Connell, "Department Stores: Tough Sell Abroad."

26. Stratford Sherman, "Are Strategic Alliances Working?" *Fortune* (September 21, 1992), 77–78; and David Lei, "Strategies for Global Competition," *Long-Range Planning* 22 (1989), 102–109.

27. Cyrus F. Freidheim, Jr., *The Trillion-Dollar Enterprise: How the Alliance Revolution Will Transform Global Business* (New York: Perseus Books, 1998).

28. Pete Engardio, "Emerging Giants," *BusinessWeek* (July 31, 2006), 40–49.

29. Eric Bellman and Kris Hudson, "Wal-Mart to Enter India in Venture," *The Wall Street Journal* (November 28, 2006), A3; and *http://walmartstores.com/AboutUs/276.aspx?p=251*, accessed on September 22, 2008.

30. Sparks, "Partners."

31. Kenichi Ohmae, "Managing in a Borderless World," *Harvard Business Review* (May–June 1989), 152–161.

32. Choe Sang-Hun, "Wal-Mart Selling Stores and Leaving South Korea"; Constance L. Hays, "From Bentonville to Beijing and Beyond," *The New York Times* (December 6, 2004), C6.

33. Conrad de Aenlle, "Famous Brands Can Bring Benefit, or a Backlash," *The New York Times* (October 19, 2003), Section 3, 7.

34. Cesare R. Mainardi, Martin Salva, and Muir Sanderson, "Label of Origin: Made on Earth," *Strategy & Business* 15 (Second Quarter 1999), 42–53; and Joann S. Lublin, "Place vs. Product: It's Tough to Choose a Management Model," *The Wall Street Journal* (June 27, 2001), A1, A4.

35. Mainardi, Salva, and Sanderson, "Label of Origin."

36. Julie Jargon, "Kraft Reformulated Oreo, Scores in China," *The Wall Street Journal* (May 1, 2008), B1, B7.

37. José Pla-Barber, "From Stopford and Wells's Model to Bartlett and Ghoshal's Typology: New Empirical Evidence," *Management International Review* 42, no. 2 (2002), 141–156.

38. Sumantra Ghoshal and Nitin Nohria, "Horses for Courses: Organizational Forms for Multinational Corporations," *Sloan Management Review* (Winter 1993), 23–35; and Roderick E. White and Thomas A. Poynter, "Organizing for Worldwide Advantage," *Business Quarterly* (Summer 1989), 84–89.

39. Robert J. Kramer, *Organizing for Global Competitiveness: The Country Subsidiary Design* (New York: The Conference Board, 1997), 12.

40. Laura B. Pincus and James A. Belohlav, "Legal Issues in Multinational Business: To Play the Game, You Have to Know the Rules," *Academy of Management Executive* 10, no. 3 (1996), 52–61.

41. John D. Daniels, Robert A. Pitts, and Marietta J. Tretter, "Strategy and Structure of U.S. Multinationals: An Exploratory Study," *Academy of Management Journal* 27 (1984), 292–307.

42. Hay Group Study, reported in Mark A. Royal and Melvyn J. Stark, "Why Some Companies Excel at Conducting Business Globally," *Journal of Organizational Excellence* (Autumn 2006), 3–10.

43. Robert J. Kramer, *Organizing for Global Competitiveness: The Product Design* (New York: The Conference Board, 1994).

44. Robert J. Kramer, *Organizing for Global Competitiveness: The Business Unit Design* (New York: The Conference Board, 1995), 18–19.

45. Carol Matlack, "Nestlé Is Starting to Slim Down at Last; But Can the World's No. 1 Food Colossus Fatten Up Its Profits As It Slashes Costs?" *BusinessWeek* (October 27, 2003), 56.

46. Based on Robert J. Kramer, *Organizing for Global Competitiveness: The Geographic Design* (New York: The Conference Board, 1993).

47. William M. Bulkeley, "Spinning a Global Plan," *The Wall Street Journal* (February 14, 2008), B1.

48. Kramer, *Organizing for Global Competitiveness: The Geographic Design*, 29–31.

49. William Taylor, "The Logic of Global Business: An Interview with ABB's Percy Barnevik," *Harvard Business Review* (March–April 1991), 91–105; Carla Rappaport, "A Tough Swede Invades the U.S.," *Fortune* (January 29, 1992), 76–79; Raymond E. Miles and Charles C. Snow, "The New Network Firm: A Spherical Structure Built on a Human Investment Philosophy," *Organizational Dynamics* (Spring 1995), 5–18; and Manfred F. R. Kets de Vries, "Making a Giant Dance," *Across the Board* (October 1994), 27–32.

50. Matthew Karnitschnig, "Identity Question; For Siemens, Move into U.S. Causes Waves Back Home," *The Wall Street Journal* (September 8, 2003), A1.

51. Gupta and Govindarajan, "Converting Global Presence into Global Competitive Advantage."

52. Robert Frank, "Withdrawal Pains: In Paddies of Vietnam, Americans Once Again Land in a Quagmire," *The Wall Street Journal* (April 21, 2000), A1, A6.

53. The discussion of these challenges is based on Bartlett and Ghoshal, *Transnational Management.*

54. Dvorak, "Why Multiple Headquarters Multiply."

55. Gibson, "U.S. Restaurants Push Abroad," and Peter Gumbel, "Big Mac's Local Flavor," *Fortune* (May 5, 2008), 114–121.

56. Peter Koudal and Gary C. Coleman, "Coordinating Operations to Enhance Innovation in the Global Corporation," *Strategy & Leadership* 33, no. 4 (2005), 20–32; and Steven D. Eppinger and Anil R. Chitkara, "The New Practice of Global Product Development," *MIT Sloan Management* (Summer 2006), 22–30.

57. Steve Hamm, "Big Blue Shift," *BusinessWeek* (June 5, 2006), 108–110.

58. P. Ingrassia, "Industry Is Shopping Abroad for Good Ideas to Apply to Products," *The Wall Street Journal* (April 29, 1985), A1.

59. Benson Rosen, Stacie Furst, and Richard Blackburn, "Overcoming Barriers to Knowledge Sharing in Virtual Teams," *Organizational Dynamics* 36, no. 3 (2007), 259–273.

60. Based on Gupta and Govindarajan, "Converting Global Presence into Global Competitive Advantage" and Giancarlo Ghislanzoni, Risto Penttinen, and David Turnbull, "The Multilocal Challenge: Managing Cross-Border Functions," *The McKinsey Quarterly* (March 2008); *http://www.mckinseyquarterly.com*, accessed on April 1, 2008.

61. Vijay Govindarajan and Anil K. Gupta, "Building an Effective Global Business Team," *MIT Sloan Management Review* 42, no. 4 (Summer 2001), 63–71.

62. Charlene Marmer Solomon, "Building Teams across Borders," *Global Workforce* (November 1998), 12–17.

63. Charles C. Snow, Scott A. Snell, Sue Canney Davison, and Donald C. Hambrick, "Use Transnational Teams to Globalize Your Company," *Organizational Dynamics* 24, no. 4 (Spring 1996), 50–67.

64. Carol Saunders, Craig Van Slyke, and Douglas R. Vogel, "My Time or Yours? Managing Time Visions in Global Virtual Teams," *Academy of Management Executive* 18, no. 1 (2004), 19–31.

65. Snow et al., "Use Transnational Teams to Globalize Your Company."

66. Gupta and Govindarajan, "Converting Global Presence into Global Competitive Advantage"; and Nadine Heintz, "In Spanish, It's *Un Equipo*; In English, It's a Team; Either Way, It's Tough to Build," *Inc.* (April 2008), 41–42.

67. Richard Pastore, "Global Team Management: It's a Small World After All," *CIO* (January 23, 2008), *http://www.cio.com/article/174750/Global_Team_Management_It_s_a_Small_World_After_All*, accessed on May 20, 2008).

68. Pete Engardio, "A Guide for Multinationals: One of the Greatest Challenges for a Multinational Is Learning How to Build a Productive Global Team," *BusinessWeek* (August 20, 2007), 48–51; and Lynda Gratton, "Working Together … When Apart," *The Wall Street Journal* (June 18, 2007), R1.

69. Robert J. Kramer, *Organizing for Global Competitiveness: The Corporate Headquarters Design* (New York: The Conference Board, 1999).

70. Ghislanzoni et al., "The Multilocal Challenge."

71. Based on Christopher A. Bartlett and Sumantra Ghoshal, *Managing across Borders: The Transnational Solution*, 2nd ed. (Boston: Harvard Business School Press, 1998), Chapter 11, 231–249.

72. See Jay Galbraith, "Building Organizations around the Global Customer," *Ivey Business Journal* (September–October 2001), 17–24, for a discussion of both formal and informal lateral networks used in multinational companies.

73. This section and the BP examples are based on Morten T. Hansen and Nitin Nohria, "How to Build Collaborative Advantage," *MIT Sloan Management Review* (Fall 2004), 22ff.

74. Gumbel, "Big Mac's Local Flavor."

75. Geert Hofstede, "The Interaction between National and Organizational Value Systems," *Journal of Management Studies* 22 (1985), 347–357; and Geert Hofstede, *Cultures and Organizations: Software of the Mind* (London: McGraw-Hill, 1991).

76. See Mansour Javidan and Robert J. House, "Cultural Acumen for the Global Manager: Lessons from Project GLOBE," *Organizational Dynamics* 29, no. 4 (2001), 289–305; and R. J. House, M. Javidan, Paul Hanges, and Peter Dorfman, "Understanding Cultures and Implicit Leadership Theories across the Globe: An Introduction to Project GLOBE," *Journal of World Business* 37 (2002), 3–10.

77. Mansour Javidan, Peter W. Dorfman, Mary Sully de Luque, and Robert J. House, "In the Eye of the Beholder: Cross Cultural Lessons in Leadership from Project GLOBE," *Academy of Management Perspectives* (February 2006), 67–90.

78. This discussion is based on "Culture and Organization," Reading 2–2 in Christopher A. Bartlett and Sumantra Ghoshal, *Transnational Management*, 3rd ed. (Boston: Irwin McGraw-Hill, 2000), 191–216, excerpted from Susan Schneider and Jean-Louis Barsoux, *Managing across Cultures* (London: Prentice-Hall, 1997).

79. Based on Bartlett and Ghoshal, *Managing across Borders*, 181–201.

80. Martin Hemmert, "International Organization of R&D and Technology Acquisition Performance of High-Tech Business Units," *Management International Review* 43, no. 4 (2003), 361–382.

81. Jean Lee, "Culture and Management—A Study of a Small Chinese Family Business in Singapore," *Journal of Small Business Management* 34, no. 3 (July 1996), 63ff; Olivier Blanchard and Andrei Shleifer, "Federalism with and without Political Centralization: China versus Russia," *IMF Staff Papers* 48 (2001), 171ff; and Javidan et al., "In the Eye of the Beholder."

82. Nailin Bu, Timothy J. Craig, and T. K. Peng, "Reactions to Authority," *Thunderbird International Business Review* 43, no. 6 (November–December 2001), 773–795.

83. Phred Dvorak and Leila Abboud, "Difficult Upgrade: SAP's Plan to Globalize Hits Cultural Barriers; Software Giant's Shift Irks German Engineers," *The Wall Street Journal* (May 11, 2007), A1.

84. Sumantra Ghoshal and Christopher Bartlett, "The Multinational Corporation as an Inter-organizational Network," *Academy of Management Review* 15 (1990), 603–625.

85. Claudia H. Deutsch, "As Sales Go Abroad for U.S. Firms, So Do Managers," *International Herald Tribune* (February 15, 2008), 14.

86. The description of the transnational organization is based on Bartlett and Ghoshal, *Transnational Management and Managing across Borders*.

87. Phred Dvorak, "How Irdeto Split Headquarters—Move to Run Dutch Firm From Beijing Means Meeting Challenges," *The Wall Street Journal* (January 7, 2008), B3; and Dvorak, "Why Multiple Headquarters Multiply."

88. Royal and Stark, "Why Some Companies Excel at Conducting Business Globally."

Chapter 6

1. Justin Lahart and Conor Dougherty, "U.S. Retools Economy, Curbing Thirst for Oil," *The Wall Street Journal* (August 12, 2008), A1, A18.

2. Amy Costello, "No Economic Slowdown For Reusable Bags," NPR Morning Edition (August 22, 2008); http://www.npr.org/templates/story/story.php?storyId=93866215, accessed on August 22, 2008.

3. Gary McWilliams, "Wal-Mart Era Wanes Amid Big Shifts in Retail," *The Wall Street Journal* (October 3, 2007), A1, A17.

4. Dana Milbank, "Aluminum Producers, Aggressive and Agile, Outfight Steelmakers," *The Wall Street Journal* (July 1, 1992), A1.

5. Michel Marriott, "PC Games, Once Down, Show Signs of Rebound," *The New York Times* (April 23, 2007), C1.

6. Jennifer Pellet, "Top 10 Enterprise Risks: What Potential Threats Keep CEOs Up at Night?" *Chief Executive* (October–November 2007), 48–53.

7. Nicholas Zamiska, "U.S. Opens the Door to Chinese Pills," *The Wall Street Journal* (October 9, 2007), B1.

8. Brian Grow, "Hispanic Nation," *BusinessWeek* (March 15, 2004), 58–70.

9. Jeffrey McCracken and John D. Stoll, "Auto Industry Skid Imperils Parts Makers," *The Wall Street Journal* (August 29, 2008), A1, A14.

10. "A Virtual Roundtable: Seven Thought Leaders Sound Off on How Connectivity Is Changing the Planet," *Fortune* (July 10, 2006), 103–106.

11. Jane J. Kim, "Where Either a Borrower or a Lender Can Be," *The Wall Street Journal* (March 12, 2008), D1, D3.

12. Alex Salkever, "Anatomy of a Business Decision; Case Study: A Chocolate Maker Is Buffeted by Global Forces Beyond His Control," *Inc.* (April 2008), 59–63.

13. Scott Kilman, "Consumers Feel Impact of Rising Grain Costs," *The Wall Street Journal* (August 8, 2008), A1, A11.

14. Joseph B. White, "There Are No German or U.S. Companies, Only Successful Ones," *The Wall Street Journal* (May 7, 1998), A1.

15. Adam Lashinsky, "Intel Outside," and Patricia Sellers, "Blowing in the Wind," segments of a special supplement titled "Fortune 500: The World of Ideas," *Fortune* (July 25, 2005), 127–138.

16. Mireya Navarro, "Changing U.S. Audience Poses Test for a Giant of Spanish TV," *The New York Times* (March 10, 2006), A1.

17. Randall D. Harris, "Organizational Task Environments: An Evaluation of Convergent and Discriminant Validity," *Journal of Management Studies* 41, no. 5 (July 2004), 857–882; Allen C. Bluedorn, "Pilgrim's Progress: Trends

and Convergence in Research on Organizational Size and Environment," *Journal of Management* 19 (1993), 163–191; Howard E. Aldrich, *Organizations and Environments* (Englewood Cliffs, N.J.: Prentice-Hall, 1979); and Fred E. Emery and Eric L. Trist, "The Casual Texture of Organizational Environments," *Human Relations* 18 (1965), 21–32.

18. Gregory G. Dess and Donald W. Beard, "Dimensions of Organizational Task Environments," *Administrative Science Quarterly* 29 (1984), 52–73; Ray Jurkovich, "A Core Typology of Organizational Environments," *Administrative Science Quarterly* 19 (1974), 380–394; Robert B. Duncan, "Characteristics of Organizational Environments and Perceived Environmental Uncertainty," *Administrative Science Quarterly* 17 (1972), 313–327.

19. Christine S. Koberg and Gerardo R. Ungson, "The Effects of Environmental Uncertainty and Dependence on Organizational Structure and Performance: A Comparative Study," *Journal of Management* 13 (1987), 725–737; and Frances J. Milliken, "Three Types of Perceived Uncertainty about the Environment: State, Effect, and Response Uncertainty," *Academy of Management Review* 12 (1987), 133–143.

20. Jon Swartz, "MySpace Cranks Up Heat in Turf War with Facebook," *USA Today* (December 21, 2007), B1; and Ellen McGirt, "MySpace, The Sequel," *Fortune* (September 2008), 92–102.

21. Heather Green, The Big Shots of Blogdom, *BusinessWeek* (May 7, 2007), 66; David Kirkpatrick and Daniel Roth, "Why There's No Escaping the Blog," *Fortune* (January 10, 2005), 44–50

22. J. A. Litterer, *The Analysis of Organizations,* 2nd ed. (New York: Wiley, 1973), 335.

23. Constance L. Hays, "More Gloom on the Island of Lost Toy Makers," *The New York Times* (February 23, 2005), C1; and Nicholas Casey, "Fisher-Price Game Plan: Pursue Toy Sales in Developing Markets," *The Wall Street Journal* (May 29, 2008), B1, B2.

24. Rosalie L. Tung, "Dimensions of Organizational Environments: An Exploratory Study of Their Impact on Organizational Structure," *Academy of Management Journal* 22 (1979), 672–693.

25. Joseph E. McCann and John Selsky, "Hyper-turbulence and the Emergence of Type 5 Environments," *Academy of Management Review* 9 (1984), 460–470.

26. Susan Carey and Melanie Trottman, "Airlines Face New Reckoning as Fuel Costs Take Big Bite," *The Wall Street Journal* (March 20, 2008), A1, A15.

27. Barney Gimbel, "Attack of the Wal-Martyrs," *Fortune* (December 11, 2006), 125–130; and Michael Barbaro, "Wal-Mart Begins Quest for Generals in P. R. War," *The New York Times* (March 30, 2006), C3.

28. James D. Thompson, *Organizations in Action* (New York: McGraw-Hill, 1967), 20–21.

29. Kevin Kelly, "The New Soul of John Deere," *BusinessWeek* (January 31, 1994), 64–66; Laura M. Holson, "Hoping to Make Phone Buyers Flip," *The New York Times* (February 29, 2008), C1.

30. David B. Jemison, "The Importance of Boundary Spanning Roles in Strategic Decision-Making," *Journal of Management Studies* 21 (1984), 131–152; and Mohamed Ibrahim Ahmad

at-Twaijri and John R. Montanari, "The Impact of Context and Choice on the Boundary-Spanning Process: An Empirical Extension," *Human Relations* 40 (1987), 783–798.

31. Michelle Cook, "The Intelligentsia," *Business 2.0* (July 1999), 135–136.

32. Robert C. Schwab, Gerardo R. Ungson, and Warren B. Brown, "Redefining the Boundary-Spanning Environment Relationship," *Journal of Management* 11 (1985), 75–86.

33. Tom Duffy, "Spying the Holy Grail," *Microsoft Executive Circle* (Winter 2004), 38–39.

34. Julie Schlosser, "Looking for Intelligence in Ice Cream," *Fortune* (March 17, 2003), 114–120.

35. Ken Western, "Ethical Spying," *Business Ethics* (September/October 1995), 22–23; Stan Crock, Geoffrey Smith, Joseph Weber, Richard A. Melcher, and Linda Himelstein, "They Snoop to Conquer," *BusinessWeek* (October 28, 1996), 172–176; and Kenneth A. Sawka, "Demystifying Business Intelligence," *Management Review* (October 1996), 47–51.

36. Liam Fahey and Jan Herring, "Intelligence Teams," *Strategy & Leadership* 35, no. 1 (2007), 13–20.

37. Edwin M. Epstein, "How to Learn from the Environment about the Environment—A Prerequisite for Organizational Well-Being," *Journal of General Management* 29, no. 1 (Autumn 2003), 68–80.

38. "Snooping on a Shoestring," *Business 2.0* (May 2003), 64–66.

39. Jay W. Lorsch, "Introduction to the Structural Design of Organizations," in Gene W. Dalton, Paul R. Lawrence, and Jay W. Lorsch, eds., *Organizational Structure and Design* (Homewood, Ill.: Irwin and Dorsey, 1970), 5.

40. Paul R. Lawrence and Jay W. Lorsch, *Organization and Environment* (Homewood, Ill.: Irwin, 1969).

41. Lorsch, "Introduction to the Structural Design of Organizations," 7.

42. Jay W. Lorsch and Paul R. Lawrence, "Environmental Factors and Organizational Integration," in J. W. Lorsch and Paul R. Lawrence, eds., *Organizational Planning: Cases and Concepts* (Homewood, Ill.: Irwin and Dorsey, 1972), 45.

43. Tom Burns and G. M. Stalker, *The Management of Innovation* (London: Tavistock, 1961).

44. John A. Courtright, Gail T. Fairhurst, and L. Edna Rogers, "Interaction Patterns in Organic and Mechanistic Systems," *Academy of Management Journal* 32 (1989), 773–802.

45. Dennis K. Berman, "Crunch Time," *BusinessWeek Frontier* (April 24, 2000), F28–F38.

46. Thomas C. Powell, "Organizational Alignment as Competitive Advantage," *Strategic Management Journal* 13 (1992), 119–134; Mansour Javidan, "The Impact of Environmental Uncertainty on Long-Range Planning Practices of the U.S. Savings and Loan Industry," *Strategic Management Journal* 5 (1984), 381–392; Tung, "Dimensions of Organizational Environments," 672–693; and Thompson, *Organizations in Action.*

47. Peter Brews and Devavrat Purohit, "Strategic Planning in Unstable Environments," *Long Range Planning* 40 (2007), 64–83; and Darrell Rigby and Barbara Bilodeau, "A Growing Focus on Preparedness," *Harvard Business Review* (July–August 2007), 21–22.

48. Ribgy and Bilodeau, "A Growing Focus on Preparedness."

49. Ian Wylie, "There Is No Alternative To . . .," *Fast Company* (July 2002), 106–110.

50. General Colin Powell, quoted in Oren Harari, "Good/Bad News About Strategy," *Management Review* (July 1995), 29–31.

51. David Ulrich and Jay B. Barney, "Perspectives in Organizations: Resource Dependence, Efficiency, and Population," *Academy of Management Review* 9 (1984), 471–481; and Jeffrey Pfeffer and Gerald Salancik, *The External Control of Organizations: A Resource Dependent Perspective* (New York: Harper & Row, 1978).

52. Andrew H. Van de Ven and Gordon Walker, "The Dynamics of Interorganizational Coordination," *Administrative Science Quarterly* (1984), 598–621; and Huseyin Leblebici and Gerald R. Salancik, "Stability in Interorganizational Exchanges: Rulemaking Processes of the Chicago Board of Trade," *Administrative Science Quarterly* 27 (1982), 227–242.

53. Mike Esterl and Corey Dade, "DHL Sends an SOS to UPS in $1 Billion Parcel Deal," *The Wall Street Journal* (May 29, 2008), B1.

54. Judith A. Babcock, *Organizational Responses to Resource Scarcity and Munificence: Adaptation and Modification in Colleges within a University* (Ph.D. diss., Pennsylvania State University, 1981).

55. Peter Smith Ring and Andrew H. Van de Ven, "Developmental Processes of Corporative Interorganizational Relationships," *Academy of Management Review* 19 (1994), 90–118; Jeffrey Pfeffer, "Beyond Management and the Worker: The Institutional Function of Management," *Academy of Management Review* 1 (April 1976), 36–46; and John P. Kotter, "Managing External Dependence," *Academy of Management Review* 4 (1979), 87–92.

56. Bryan Borys and David B. Jemison, "Hybrid Arrangements as Strategic Alliances: Theoretical Issues in Organizational Combinations," *Academy of Management Review* 14 (1989), 234–249.

57. Roger O. Crockett with Brian Grow and Spencer Ante, "Lord of the Rings," *BusinessWeek* (March 20, 2006), 30ff; AT&T Corporate Profile: Company History, http://www.att.com/gen/investor-relations?pid=5711, accessed on September 2, 2008; and Amol Sharma, "Phone Giants to Roll Out 'Three Screen' Strategy; Video Programming and Ads to Be Served on TV, Cellphones, Web," *The Wall Street Journal* (June 26, 2008), B7.

58. Julie Cohen Mason, "Strategic Alliances: Partnering for Success," *Management Review* (May 1993), 10–15.

59. Teri Agins and Alessandra Galloni, "After Gianni; Facing a Squeeze, Versace Struggles to Trim the Fat," *The Wall Street Journal* (September 30, 2003), A1, A10; John F. Love, *McDonald's: Behind the Arches* (New York: Bantam Books, 1986).

60. Borys and Jemison, "Hybrid Arrangements as Strategic Alliances."

61. Donald Palmer, "Broken Ties: Interlocking Directorates and Intercorporate Coordination," *Administrative Science Quarterly* 28 (1983), 40–55; F. David Shoorman, Max H. Bazerman, and Robert S. Atkin, "Interlocking Directorates: A Strategy for Reducing Environmental Uncertainty," *Academy of Management Review* 6 (1981), 243–251; and

Ronald S. Burt, *Toward a Structural Theory of Action* (New York: Academic Press, 1982).

62. James R. Lang and Daniel E. Lockhart, "Increased Environmental Uncertainty and Changes in Board Linkage Patterns," *Academy of Management Journal* 33 (1990), 106–128; and Mark S. Mizruchi and Linda Brewster Stearns, "A Longitudinal Study of the Formation of Interlocking Directorates," *Administrative Science Quarterly* 33 (1988), 194–210.

63. Claudia H. Deutsch, "Companies and Critics Try Collaboration," *The New York Times* (May 17, 2006), G1.

64. Keith J. Winstein and Suzanne Vranica, "Drug Ads' Impact Questioned," *The Wall Street Journal* (September 3, 2008), B7; and Jon Kamp, "Pfizer Drops Celebrity Pitch in New Lipitor Spots," *The Wall Street Journal* (September 2, 2008), B8.

65. Stanley Holmes, "Into the Wild Blog Yonder," *BusinessWeek* (May 22, 2006), 84–86.

66. Kotter, "Managing External Dependence."

67. Quentin Hardy and Evan Hessel, "GooTube," *Forbes* (June 16, 2008), 50ff.

68. Katherine Q. Seelye, "Time Inc. Cutting Almost 300 Magazine Jobs to Focus More on Web Sites," *The New York Times* (January 19, 2007), C4.

69. Amy Schartz, "Net Firms Raise Capitol Hill Profile," *The Wall Street Journal* (January 28, 2006), A4.

70. Katie Hafner, "Going Once, Going Twice, Gone! How eBay Makes Regulations Disappear," *The New York Times* (June 4, 2006), 3.1.

71. David B. Yoffie, "How an Industry Builds Political Advantage," *Harvard Business Review* (May–June 1988), 82–89; and Jeffrey H. Birnbaum, "Chief Executives Head to Washington to Ply the Lobbyist's Trade," *The Wall Street Journal* (March 19, 1990), A1, A16.

72. David Whitford, "Built by Association," *Inc.* (July 1994), 71–75.

73. Anthony J. Daboub, Abdul M. A. Rasheed, Richard L. Priem, and David A. Gray, "Top Management Team Characteristics and Corporate Illegal Activity," *Academy of Management Review* 20, no. 1 (1995), 138–170.

74. Barry M. Staw and Eugene Szwajkowski, "The Scarcity-Munificence Component of Organizational Environments and the Commission of Illegal Acts," *Administrative Science Quarterly* 20 (1975), 345–354; and Kimberly D. Elsbach and Robert I. Sutton, "Acquiring Organizational Legitimacy through Illegitimate Actions: A Marriage of Institutional and Impression Management Theories," *Academy of Management Journal* 35 (1992), 699–738.

75. Russell Gold, "Halliburton Ex-Official Pleads Guilty in Bribe Case," *The Wall Street Journal* (September 4, 2005), A1, A15.

76. G. Thomas Sims, "German Industry Would Alter Law Requiring Labor Seats on Boards," *The New York Times* (April 6, 2007), C3.

Chapter 7

1. Richard Pérez-Peña, "For Publisher in Los Angeles, Cuts and Worse," *The New York Times* (February 19, 2008), A1; R. Pérez-Peña, "Los Angeles Editor Ousted After Resisting Job Cuts," *The New York Times* (January 21, 2008), A15; and Emily Steel, "Why *Los Angeles Times* Can't Keep an Editor," *The Wall Street Journal* (January 22, 2008), B1.

2. Lee G. Bolman and Terrence E. Deal, *Reframing Organizations: Artistry, Choice, and Leadership* (San Francisco: Jossey-Bass, 1991).

3. Michael Oneal and Phil Rosenthal, "Tribune Company Files for Bankruptcy Protection," *The Chicago Tribune* (December 10, 2008), http://www.chicagotribune.com/business/chi-081208tribune-bankruptcy,0,3718621.story, accessed December 11, 2008; and Andrew Ross Sorkin, "Workers Pay for Debacle at Tribune," *The New York Times* (December 9, 2008), A1.

4. Paul M. Terry, "Conflict Management," *The Journal of Leadership Studies* 3, no. 2 (1996), 3–21; and Kathleen M. Eisenhardt, Jean L. Kahwajy, and L. J. Bourgeois III, "How Management Teams Can Have a Good Fight," *Harvard Business Review* (July–August 1997), 77–85.

5. Clayton T. Alderfer and Ken K. Smith, "Studying Intergroup Relations Imbedded in Organizations," *Administrative Science Quarterly* 27 (1982), 35–65.

6. Muzafer Sherif, "Experiments in Group Conflict," *Scientific American* 195 (1956), 54–58; and Edgar H. Schein, *Organizational Psychology*, 3d ed. (Englewood Cliffs, N.J.: Prentice-Hall, 1980).

7. M. Afzalur Rahim, "A Strategy for Managing Conflict in Complex Organizations," *Human Relations* 38 (1985), 81–89; Kenneth Thomas, "Conflict and Conflict Management," in M. D. Dunnette, ed., *Handbook of Industrial and Organizational Psychology* (Chicago: Rand McNally, 1976); and Stuart M. Schmidt and Thomas A. Kochan, "Conflict: Toward Conceptual Clarity," *Administrative Science Quarterly* 13 (1972), 359–370.

8. L. David Brown, "Managing Conflict among Groups," in David A. Kolb, Irwin M. Rubin, and James M. McIntyre, eds., *Organizational Psychology: A Book of Readings* (Englewood Cliffs, N.J.: Prentice-Hall, 1979), 377–389; and Robert W. Ruekert and Orville C. Walker, Jr., "Interactions between Marketing and R&D Departments in Implementing Different Business Strategies," *Strategic Management Journal* 8 (1987), 233–248.

9. Joseph B. White, Lee Hawkins, Jr., and Karen Lundegaard, "UAW Is Facing Biggest Battles in Two Decades," *The Wall Street Journal* (June 10, 2005), B1; Amy Barrett, "Indigestion at Taco Bell," *BusinessWeek* (December 14, 1994), 66–67; and Greg Burns, "Fast-Food Fight," *BusinessWeek* (June 2, 1997), 34–36.

10. Nanette Byrnes, with Mike McNamee, Ronald Grover, Joann Muller, and Andrew Park, "Auditing Here, Consulting Over There," *BusinessWeek* (April 8, 2002), 34–36.

11. Victoria L. Crittenden, Lorraine R. Gardiner, and Antonie Stam, "Reducing Conflict between Marketing and Manufacturing," *Industrial Marketing Management* 22 (1993), 299–309; and Benson S. Shapiro, "Can Marketing and Manufacturing Coexist?" *Harvard Business Review* 55 (September–October 1977), 104–114.

12. Ben Worthen, "Cost-Cutting versus Innovation: Reconcilable Differences," *CIO* (October 1, 2004), 89–94.

13. Thomas A. Kochan, George P. Huber, and L. L. Cummings, "Determinants of Intraorganizational Conflict in Collective Bargaining in the Public Sector," *Administrative Science Quarterly* 20 (1975), 10–23.

14. Suzanne Sataline, "Veneration Gap: A Popular Strategy for Church Growth Splits Congregants," *The Wall Street Journal* (September 5, 2006), A1; and Laurie Goodstein, "Episcopal Split as Conservatives Form New Group," *The New York Times* (December 4, 2008), A1.

15. Eric H. Neilsen, "Understanding and Managing Intergroup Conflict," in Jay W. Lorsch and Paul R. Lawrence, eds., *Managing Group and Intergroup Relations* (Homewood, Ill.: Irwin and Dorsey, 1972), 329–343; and Richard E. Walton and John M. Dutton, "The Management of Interdepartmental Conflict: A Model and Review," *Administrative Science Quarterly* 14 (1969), 73–84.

16. Jay W. Lorsch, "Introduction to the Structural Design of Organizations," in Gene W. Dalton, Paul R. Lawrence, and Jay W. Lorsch, eds., *Organization Structure and Design* (Homewood, Ill.: Irwin and Dorsey, 1970), 5.

17. James D. Thompson, *Organizations in Action* (New York: McGraw-Hill, 1967), 54–56.

18. Walton and Dutton, "The Management of Interdepartmental Conflict."

19. Joseph McCann and Jay R. Galbraith, "Interdepartmental Relations," in Paul C. Nystrom and William H. Starbuck, eds., *Handbook of Organizational Design*, vol. 2 (New York: Oxford University Press, 1981), 60–84.

20. Roderick M. Cramer, "Intergroup Relations and Organizational Dilemmas: The Role of Categorization Processes," in L. L. Cummings and Barry M. Staw, eds., *Research in Organizational Behavior*, vol. 13 (New York: JAI Press, 1991), 191–228; Neilsen, "Understanding and Managing Intergroup Conflict"; and Louis R. Pondy, "Organizational Conflict: Concepts and Models," *Administrative Science Quarterly* 12 (1968), 296–320.

21. Jeffrey Pfeffer, *Power in Organizations* (Marshfield, Mass.: Pitman, 1981).

22. Alan Deutschman, "The Mind of Jeff Bezos," *Fast Company* (August 2004), 53–58.

23. Robert A. Dahl, "The Concept of Power," *Behavioral Science* 2 (1957), 201–215.

24. W. Graham Astley and Paramijit S. Sachdeva, "Structural Sources of Intraorganizational Power: A Theoretical Synthesis," *Academy of Management Review* 9 (1984), 104–113; and Abraham Kaplan, "Power in Perspective," in Robert L. Kahn and Elise Boulding, eds., *Power and Conflict in Organizations* (London: Tavistock, 1964), 11–32.

25. Gerald R. Salancik and Jeffrey Pfeffer, "The Bases and Use of Power in Organizational Decision-Making: The Case of

the University," *Administrative Science Quarterly* 19 (1974), 453–473.

26. Rosabeth Moss Kanter, "Power Failure in Management Circuits," *Harvard Business Review* (July–August 1979), 65–75.

27. Richard M. Emerson, "Power-Dependence Relations," *American Sociological Review* 27 (1962), 31–41.

28. Sharon Waxman, "Squabbling and Spiraling Costs Dissolve a Comedy Mill," *The New York Times* (September 25, 2006), C1.

29. Examples are Robert Greene and Joost Elffers, *The 48 Laws of Power* (New York: Viking, 1999); and Jeffrey J. Fox, *How to Become CEO* (New York: Hyperion, 1999).

30. John R. P. French, Jr., and Bertram Raven, "The Bases of Social Power," in D. Cartwright and A. F. Zander, eds. *Group Dynamics* (Evanston, Ill.: Row Peterson, 1960), 607–623.

31. Ran Lachman, "Power from What? A Reexamination of Its Relationships with Structural Conditions," *Administrative Science Quarterly* 34 (1989), 231–251; and Daniel J. Brass, "Being in the Right Place: A Structural Analysis of Individual Influence in an Organization," *Administrative Science Quarterly* 29 (1984), 518–539.

32. Michael Warshaw, "The Good Guy's Guide to Office Politics," *Fast Company* (April–May 1998), 157–178.

33. A. J. Grimes, "Authority, Power, Influence, and Social Control: A Theoretical Synthesis," *Academy of Management Review* 3 (1978), 724–735.

34. Astley and Sachdeva, "Structural Sources of Intraorganizational Power."

35. Robert A. Guth, "Gates-Ballmer Clash Shaped Microsoft's Coming Handover," *The Wall Street Journal* (June 5, 2008), A1.

36. Jeffrey Pfeffer, *Managing with Power: Politics and Influence in Organizations* (Boston: Harvard Business School Press, 1992).

37. Monica Langley, "Columbia Tells Doctors at Hospital to End Their Outside Practice," *The Wall Street Journal* (May 2, 1997), A1, A6.

38. Richard S. Blackburn, "Lower Participant Power: Toward a Conceptual Integration," *Academy of Management Review* 6 (1981), 127–131.

39. Kanter, "Power Failure in Management Circuits," 70.

40. Pfeffer, *Power in Organizations.*

41. Erik W. Larson and Jonathan B. King, "The Systemic Distortion of Information: An Ongoing Challenge to Management," *Organizational Dynamics* 24, no. 3 (Winter 1996), 49–61; and Thomas H. Davenport, Robert G. Eccles, and Laurence Prusak, "Information Politics," *Sloan Management Review* (Fall 1992), 53–65.

42. Andrew M. Pettigrew, *The Politics of Organizational Decision-Making* (London: Tavistock, 1973).

43. Warshaw, "The Good Guy's Guide to Office Politics."

44. Astley and Sachdeva, "Structural Sources of Intraorganizational Power"; and Noel M. Tichy and Charles Fombrun, "Network Analysis in Organizational Settings," *Human Relations* 32 (1979), 923–965.

45. Greg Ip, Kate Kelly, Susanne Craig, and Ianthe Jeanne Dugan, "A Bull's Market; Dick Grasso's NYSE Legacy: Buffed Image, Shaky Foundation," *The Wall Street Journal* (December 30, 2003), A1, A6; and Yochi J. Dreazen and

Christopher Cooper, "Lingering Presence; Behind the Scenes, U.S. Tightens Grip on Iraq's Future," *The Wall Street Journal* (May 13, 2004), A1.

46. Edwin P. Hollander and Lynn R. Offermann, "Power and Leadership in Organizations," *American Psychologist* 45 (February 1990), 179–189.

47. Jay A. Conger and Rabindra N. Kanungo, "The Empowerment Process: Integrating Theory and Practice," *Academy of Management Review* 13 (1988), 471–482.

48. David E. Bowen and Edward E. Lawler III, "The Empowerment of Service Workers: What, Why, How, and When," *Sloan Management Review* (Spring 1992), 31–39; and Ray W. Coye and James A. Belohav, "An Exploratory Analysis of Employee Participation," *Group and Organization Management* 20, no. 1, (March 1995), 4–17.

49. Robert C. Ford and Myron D. Fottler, "Empowerment: A Matter of Degree," *Academy of Management Executive* 9, no. 3 (1995), 21–31.

50. Ricardo Semler, "Out of This World: Doing Things the Semco Way," *Global Business and Organizational Excellence* (July–August 2007), 13–21.

51. Charles Perrow, "Departmental Power and Perspective in Industrial Firms," in Mayer N. Zald, ed., *Power in Organizations* (Nashville, Tenn.: Vanderbilt University Press, 1970), 59–89.

52. Dionne Searcey, Kevin J. Delaney, and Dennis K. Berman, "New Numbers; As Power Shifts, AT&T May Alter Yahoo Pact," *The Wall Street Journal* (March 9, 2007), A1.

53. D. J. Hickson, C. R. Hinings, C. A. Lee, R. E. Schneck, and J. M. Pennings, "A Strategic Contingencies Theory of Intraorganizational Power," *Administrative Science Quarterly* 16 (1971), 216–229; and Gerald R. Salancik and Jeffrey Pfeffer, "Who Gets Power—and How They Hold onto It: A Strategic-Contingency Model of Power," *Organizational Dynamics* (Winter 1977), 3–21.

54. William C. Rhoden, "The N.F.L. Backed Down for All the World to See," *The New York Times* (December 30, 2007), Sunday Sports section, 1, 3.

55. Pfeffer, *Managing with Power*; Salancik and Pfeffer, "Who Gets Power"; C. R. Hinings, D. J. Hickson, J. M. Pennings, and R. E. Schneck, "Structural Conditions of Intraorganizational Power," *Administrative Science Quarterly* 19 (1974), 22–44.

56. Carol Stoak Saunders, "The Strategic Contingencies Theory of Power: Multiple Perspectives," *Journal of Management Studies* 27 (1990), 1–18; Warren Boeker, "The Development and Institutionalization of Sub-Unit Power in Organizations," *Administrative Science Quarterly* 34 (1989), 388–510; and Irit Cohen and Ran Lachman, "The Generality of the Strategic Contingencies Approach to Sub-Unit Power," *Organizational Studies* 9 (1988), 371–391.

57. Emerson, "Power-Dependence Relations."

58. Jeffrey Pfeffer and Gerald Salancik, "Organizational Decision-Making as a Political Process: The Case of a University Budget," *Administrative Science Quarterly* (1974), 135–151.

59. Salancik and Pfeffer, "Bases and Use of Power in Organizational Decision-Making," 470.

60. Hickson et al., "A Strategic Contingencies Theory."

61. Pettigrew, *The Politics of Organizational Decision-Making.*

62. Robert Levine, "For Some Music, It Has to Be Wal-Mart and Nowhere Else," *The New York Times* (June 9, 2008), C1.

63. Hickson et al., "A Strategic Contingencies Theory."

64. Ibid.

65. John Carreyrou, "Nonprofit Hospitals Flex Pricing Power—In Roanoke, Va., Carilion's Fees Exceed Those of Competitors," *The Wall Street Journal* (August 28, 2008), A1.

66. Jeffrey Gantz and Victor V. Murray, "Experience of Workplace Politics," *Academy of Management Journal* 23 (1980), 237–251; and Dan L. Madison, Robert W. Allen, Lyman W. Porter, Patricia A. Renwick, and Bronston T. Mayes, "Organizational Politics: An Exploration of Managers' Perception," *Human Relations* 33 (1980), 79–100.

67. Gerald R. Ferris and K. Michele Kacmar, "Perceptions of Organizational Politics," *Journal of Management* 18 (1992), 93–116; Parmod Kumar and Rehana Ghadially, "Organizational Politics and Its Effects on Members of Organizations," *Human Relations* 42 (1989), 305–314; Donald J. Vredenburgh and John G. Maurer, "A Process Framework of Organizational Politics," *Human Relations* 37 (1984), 47–66; and Gerald R. Ferris, Dwight D. Frink, Maria Carmen Galang, Jing Zhou, Michele Kacmar, and Jack L. Howard, "Perceptions of Organizational Politics: Prediction, Stress-Related Implications, and Outcomes," *Human Relations* 49, no. 2 (1996), 233–266.

68. Ferris et al., "Perceptions of Organizational Politics: Prediction, Stress-Related Implications, and Outcomes"; John J. Voyer, "Coercive Organizational Politics and Organizational Outcomes: An Interpretive Study," *Organization Science* 5, no. 1 (February 1994), 72–85; and James W. Dean, Jr., and Mark P. Sharfman, "Does Decision Process Matter? A Study of Strategic Decision-Making Effectiveness," *Academy of Management Journal* 39, no. 2 (1996), 368–396.

69. Jeffrey Pfeffer, *Managing with Power: Politics and Influence in Organizations* (Boston: Harvard Business School Press, 1992).

70. Amos Drory and Tsilia Romm, "The Definition of Organizational Politics: A Review," *Human Relations* 43 (1990), 1133–1154; Vredenburgh and Maurer, "A Process Framework of Organizational Politics"; and Lafe Low, "It's Politics, As Usual," *CIO* (April 1, 2004), 87–90.

71. "Questioning Authority; Mario Moussa Wants You to Win Your Next Argument" (Mario Moussa interviewed by Vadim Liberman), *The Conference Board Review* (November–December 2007), 25–26.

72. Pfeffer, *Power in Organizations*, 70.

73. Madison et al., "Organizational Politics"; and Jay R. Galbraith, *Organizational Design* (Reading, Mass.: Addison-Wesley, 1977).

74. Gantz and Murray, "Experience of Workplace Politics"; and Pfeffer, *Power in Organizations*.

75. Daniel J. Brass and Marlene E. Burkhardt, "Potential Power and Power Use: An Investigation of Structure and Behavior," *Academy of Management Journal* 38 (1993), 441–470.

76. Gerald R. Ferris, Darren C. Treadway, Pamela L. Perrewé, Robyn L. Brouer, Ceasar Douglas, and Sean Lux, "Political Skill in Organizations," *Journal of Management* (June 2007), 290–320; "Questioning Authority; Mario Moussa Wants You to Win Your Next Argument"; and Samuel B. Bacharach, "Politically Proactive," *Fast Company* (May 2005), 93.

77. Harvey G. Enns and Dean B. McFarlin, "When Executives Influence Peers, Does Function Matter?" *Human Resource Management* 4, no. 2 (Summer 2003), 125–142.

78. Hickson et al., "A Strategic Contingencies Theory."

79. Pfeffer, *Power in Organizations*.

80. Robert B. Cialdini, *Influence: Science and Practice*, 4th ed. (Boston: Allyn & Bacon, 2001); R. B. Cialdini, "Harnessing the Science of Persuasion," *Harvard Business Review* (October 2001), 72–79; Allan R. Cohen and David L. Bradford, "The Influence Model: Using Reciprocity and Exchange to Get What You Need," *Journal of Organizational Excellence* (Winter 2005), 57–80; and Jared Sandberg, "People Can't Resist Doing a Big Favor—Or Asking for One," (Cubicle Culture column), *The Wall Street Journal* (December 18, 2007), B1.

81. Ferris et al., "Political Skill in Organizations"; and Pfeffer, *Power in Organizations*.

82. V. Dallas Merrell, *Huddling: The Informal Way to Management Success* (New York: AMACON, 1979).

83. Ceasar Douglas and Anthony P. Ammeter, "An Examination of Leader Political Skill and Its Effect on Ratings of Leader Effectiveness," *The Leadership Quarterly* 15 (2004), 537–550.

84. Vredenburgh and Maurer, "A Process Framework of Organizational Politics."

85. Pfeffer, *Power in Organizations*.

86. Ibid.

87. Ibid.

88. Ibid.

89. Damon Darlin, "Using the Web to Get the Boss to Pay More," *The New York Times* (March 3, 2007), C1

90. Steven R. Weisman, "How Battles at Bank Ended 'Second Chance' at a Career," *The New York Times* (May 18, 2007), A14.

91. Kanter, "Power Failure in Management Circuits"; and Pfeffer, *Power in Organizations*.

92. Robert R. Blake and Jane S. Mouton, "Overcoming Group Warfare," *Harvard Business Review* (November–December 1984), 98–108.

93. Blake and Mouton, "Overcoming Group Warfare"; Paul R. Lawrence and Jay W. Lorsch, "New Management Job: The Integrator," *Harvard Business Review* 45 (November–December 1967), 142–151.

94. John S. McClenahen, "Culture of Cooperation," (*Industry Week's Best Plants* series: Magee Rieter Automotive Systems), *Industry Week* (October 2006), 38.

95. Ibid.

96. Robert R. Blake, Herbert A. Shepard, and Jane S. Mouton, *Managing Intergroup Conflict in Industry* (Houston: Gulf Publishing, 1964); and Doug Stewart, "Expand the Pie before You Divvy It Up," *Smithsonian* (November 1997), 78–90.

97. Patrick S. Nugent, "Managing Conflict: Third-Party Interventions for Managers," *Academy of Management Executive* 16, no. 1 (2002), 139–155.

98. Blake and Mouton, "Overcoming Group Warfare"; Schein, *Organizational Psychology*; Blake, Shepard, and Mouton,

"Managing Intergroup Conflict in Industry; and Richard E. Walton, *Interpersonal Peacemaking: Confrontation and Third-Party Consultations* (Reading, Mass.: Addison-Wesley, 1969).

99. Neilsen, "Understanding and Managing Intergroup Conflict"; and McCann and Galbraith, "Interdepartmental Relations."

100. Ibid.

101. Dean Tjosvold, Valerie Dann, and Choy Wong, "Managing Conflict between Departments to Serve Customers," *Human Relations* 45 (1992), 1035–1054.

Chapter 8

1. Gretchen Morgenson, "How the Thundering Herd Faltered and Fell," *The New York Times* (November 9, 2008), BU1.

2. Brad Stone, "The Empire of Excess; Lax Real Estate Decisions Hurt Starbucks," *The New York Times* (July 4, 2008), C1.

3. Betsy Morris, "What Makes Apple Golden?" *Fortune* (March 17, 2008), 68–74.

4. "World's Most Admired Companies: Cereal Cost Cutters" (Top Performers series), *Fortune* (November 10, 2008), 24.

5. Charles Lindblom, "The Science of 'Muddling Through,'" *Public Administration Review* 29 (1954), 79–88.

6. Herbert A. Simon, *The New Science of Management Decision* (Englewood Cliffs, N.J.: Prentice-Hall, 1960), 1–8.

7. Paul J. H. Schoemaker and J. Edward Russo, "A Pyramid of Decision Approaches," *California Management Review* (Fall 1993), 9–31.

8. Justin Scheck, "Dell's Revival Strategy Runs Into Trouble," *The Wall Street Journal* (November 28, 2008), A1, A12.

9. Michael Pacanowsky, "Team Tools for Wicked Problems," *Organizational Dynamics* 23, no. 3 (Winter 1995), 36–51.

10. The idea of a good decision potentially producing a bad outcome under uncertain conditions is attributed to Robert Rubin, reported in David Leonhardt, "This Fed Chief May Yet Get a Honeymoon," *The New York Times* (August 23, 2006), C1.

11. Doug Wallace, "What Would You Do? Southern Discomfort," *Business Ethics* (March/April 1996), 52–53; and Renee Elder, "Apparel Plant Closings Rip Fabric of Community's Employment," *The Tennessean* (November 3, 1996), 1E.

12. Karen Dillon, "The Perfect Decision" (an interview with John S. Hammond and Ralph L. Keeney), *Inc.* (October 1998), 74–78; and John S. Hammond and Ralph L. Keeney, *Smart Choices: A Practical Guide to Making Better Decisions* (Boston: Harvard Business School Press, 1998).

13. Earnest R. Archer, "How to Make a Business Decision: An Analysis of Theory and Practice," *Management Review* 69 (February 1980), 54–61; and Boris Blai, "Eight Steps to Successful Problem Solving," *Supervisory Management* (January 1986), 7–9.

14. Francine Schwadel, "Christmas Sales' Lack of Momentum Tests Store Manager's Mettle," *The Wall Street Journal* (December 16, 1987), 1.

15. Noel M. Tichy and Warren G. Bennis, "Making Judgment Calls: The Ultimate Act of Leadership," *Harvard Business Review* (October 2007), 94–102.

16. Adapted from Archer, "How to Make a Business Decision," 59–61.

17. James W. Dean, Jr., and Mark P. Sharfman, "Procedural Rationality in the Strategic Decision-Making Process," *Journal of Management Studies* 30 (1993), 587–610.

18. Michael R. Gordon, "Fateful Choice on Iraq Army Bypassed Washington Debate," *The New York Times* (March 17, 2008), A1; and Farnaz Fassihi, Greg Jaffe, Yaroslav Trofimov, Carla Anne Robbins, and Yochi J. Dreazen, "Winning the Peace; Early U.S. Decisions on Iraq Now Haunt American Efforts," *The Wall Street Journal* (April 19, 2004), A1, A14.

19. Art Kleiner, "Core Group Therapy," *Strategy & Business*, Issue 27 (Second Quarter, 2002), 26–31.

20. Irving L. Janis, *Crucial Decisions: Leadership in Policymaking and Crisis Management* (New York: The Free Press, 1989); and Paul C. Nutt, "Flexible Decision Styles and the Choices of Top Executives," *Journal of Management Studies* 30 (1993), 695–721.

21. Herbert A. Simon, "Making Management Decisions: The Role of Intuition and Emotion," *Academy of Management Executive* 1 (February 1987), 57–64; and Daniel J. Eisenberg, "How Senior Managers Think," *Harvard Business Review* 62 (November–December 1984), 80–90.

22. Kurt Matzler, Franz Bailom, and Todd A. Mooradian, "Intuitive Decision Making," *MIT Sloan Management Review* 49, no. 1 (Fall 2007), 13–15; Stefan Wally and J. Robert Baum, "Personal and Structural Determinants of the Pace of Strategic Decision Making," *Academy of Management Journal* 37, no. 4 (1994), 932–956; and Orlando Behling and Norman L. Eckel, "Making Sense Out of Intuition," *Academy of Management Executive* 5, no. 1 (1991), 46–54.

23. Eric Dane and Michael G. Pratt, "Exploring Intuition and Its Role in Managerial Decision Making," *Academy of Management Review* 32, no. 1 (2007), 33–54; Gary Klein, *Intuition at Work: Why Developing Your Gut Instincts Will Make You Better at What You Do* (New York: Doubleday, 2002); Milorad M. Novicevic, Thomas J. Hench, and Daniel A. Wren, "'Playing By Ear … In an Incessant Din of Reasons': Chester Barnard and the History of Intuition in Management Thought," *Management Decision* 40, no. 10 (2002), 992–1002; Alden M. Hayashi, "When to Trust Your Gut," *Harvard Business Review* (February 2001), 59–65; Brian R. Reinwald, "Tactical Intuition," *Military Review* 80, no. 5 (September–October 2000), 78–88; Thomas A. Stewart, "How to Think with Your Gut," *Business 2.0* (November 2002), *http://www.business2.com/articles,* accessed on November 7, 2002; Henry Mintzberg and Frances Westley, "Decision Making: It's Not What You

Think," *MIT Sloan Management Review* (Spring 2001), 89–93; and Carlin Flora, "Gut Almighty," *Psychology Today* (May–June 2007), 68–75.

24. Thomas F. Issack, "Intuition: An Ignored Dimension of Management," *Academy of Management Review* 3 (1978), 917–922.

25. Marjorie A. Lyles, "Defining Strategic Problems: Subjective Criteria of Executives," *Organizational Studies* 8 (1987), 263–280; and Marjorie A. Lyles and Ian I. Mitroff, "Organizational Problem Formulation: An Empirical Study," *Administrative Science Quarterly* 25 (1980), 102–119.

26. Marjorie A. Lyles and Howard Thomas, "Strategic Problem Formulation: Biases and Assumptions Embedded in Alternative Decision-Making Models," *Journal of Management Studies* 25 (1988), 131–145.

27. Ross Stagner, "Corporate Decision-Making: An Empirical Study," *Journal of Applied Psychology* 53 (1969), 1–13.

28. Reported in Eric Bonabeau, "Don't Trust Your Gut," *Harvard Business Review* (May 2003), 116–123.

29. Matzler et al., "Intuitive Decision Making."

30. Bonabeau, "Don't Trust Your Gut."

31. Ann Langley, "Between 'Paralysis by Analysis' and 'Extinction by Instinct,'" *Sloan Management Review* (Spring 1995), 63–76.

32. W. A. Agor, "The Logic of Intuition: How Top Executives Make Important Decisions," *Organizational Dynamics* 14, no. 3 (1986), 5–18; and Paul C. Nutt, "Types of Organizational Decision Processes," *Administrative Science Quarterly* 29 (1984), 414–450.

33. Nandini Rajagopalan, Abdul M. A. Rasheed, and Deepak K. Datta, "Strategic Decision Processes: Critical Review and Future Decisions," *Journal of Management* 19 (1993), 349–384; Paul J. H. Schoemaker, "Strategic Decisions in Organizations: Rational and Behavioral Views," *Journal of Management Studies* 30 (1993), 107–129; Charles J. McMillan, "Qualitative Models of Organizational Decision Making," *Journal of Management Studies* 5 (1980), 22–39; and Paul C. Nutt, "Models for Decision Making in Organizations and Some Contextual Variables Which Stimulate Optimal Use," *Academy of Management Review* 1 (1976), 84–98.

34. Hugh J. Miser, "Operations Analysis in the Army Air Forces in World War II: Some Reminiscences," *Interfaces* 23 (September–October 1993), 47–49; and Harold J. Leavitt, William R. Dill, and Henry B. Eyring, *The Organizational World* (New York: Harcourt Brace Jovanovich, 1973), chap. 6.

35. Stephen J. Huxley, "Finding the Right Spot for a Church Camp in Spain," *Interfaces* 12 (October 1982), 108–114; and James E. Hodder and Henry E. Riggs, "Pitfalls in Evaluating Risky Projects," *Harvard Business Review* (January–February 1985), 128–135.

36. Edward Baker and Michael Fisher, "Computational Results for Very Large Air Crew Scheduling Problems," *Omega* 9 (1981), 613–618; and Jean Aubin, "Scheduling Ambulances," *Interfaces* 22 (March–April, 1992), 1–10.

37. Susan Carey, "Calculating Costs in the Clouds; How Flight-Planning Software Helps Airlines Balance Fuel, Distance, Wind, 'Overfly' Fees," *The Wall Street Journal* (March 6, 2007), B1.

38. Stephen Baker, "Math Will Rock Your World," *BusinessWeek* (January 23, 2006), 54–60; Julie Schlosser, "Markdown Lowdown," *Fortune* (January 12, 2004), 40; Laura Landro, "The Informed Patient: Cutting Waits at the Doctor's Office—New Programs Reorganize Practices to Be More Efficient," *The Wall Street Journal* (April 19, 2006), D1.

39. Richard L. Daft and John C. Wiginton, "Language and Organization," *Academy of Management Review* (1979), 179–191.

40. Based on Richard M. Cyert and James G. March, *A Behavioral Theory of the Firm* (Englewood Cliffs, N.J.: Prentice-Hall, 1963); and James G. March and Herbert A. Simon, *Organizations* (New York: Wiley, 1958).

41. William B. Stevenson, Joan L. Pearce, and Lyman W. Porter, "The Concept of 'Coalition' in Organization Theory and Research," *Academy of Management Review* 10 (1985), 256–268.

42. Cyert and March, *A Behavioral Theory of the Firm*, 120–222.

43. Michael R. Gordon, "Troop 'Surge' in Iraq Took Place Amid Doubt and Intense Debate," *The New York Times* (August 31, 2008), A1; and Fred Barnes, "How Bush Decided on the Surge," *The Weekly Standard* (February 4, 2008), 20–27.

44. Lawrence G. Hrebiniak, "Top-Management Agreement and Organizational Performance," *Human Relations* 35 (1982), 1139–1158; and Richard P. Nielsen, "Toward a Method for Building Consensus during Strategic Planning," *Sloan Management Review* (Summer 1981), 29–40.

45. Based on Henry Mintzberg, Duru Raisinghani, and Théorêt, André, "The Structure of 'Unstructured' Decision Processes," *Administrative Science Quarterly* 21 (1976), 246–275.

46. Lawrence T. Pinfield, "A Field Evaluation of Perspectives on Organizational Decision Making," *Administrative Science Quarterly* 31 (1986), 365–388.

47. Mintzberg et al., "The Structure of 'Unstructured' Decision Processes."

48. Ibid., 270.

49. William C. Symonds with Carol Matlack, "Gillette's Edge," *BusinessWeek* (January 19, 1998), 70–77; William C. Symonds, "Would You Spend $1.50 for a Razor Blade?" *BusinessWeek* (April 27, 1998), 46; and Peter J. Howe, "Innovative; For the Past Half Century, 'Cutting Edge' Has Meant More at Gillette Co. Than a Sharp Blade," *Boston Globe* (January 30, 2005), D1.

50. Michael D. Cohen, James G. March, and Johan P. Olsen, "A Garbage Can Model of Organizational Choice," *Administrative Science Quarterly* 17 (March 1972), 1–25; and Michael D. Cohen and James G. March, *Leadership and Ambiguity: The American College President* (New York: McGraw-Hill, 1974).

51. Michael Masuch and Perry LaPotin, "Beyond Garbage Cans: An AI Model of Organizational Choice," *Administrative Science Quarterly* 34 (1989), 38–67.

52. Sharon Waxman, "The Nudist Buddhist Borderline-Abusive Love-In," *The New York Times* (September 19, 2004), Section 2, 1; and V. A. Musetto, "Crix Pick Best Pix," *The New York Post* (May 29, 2005), 93.

53. Thomas R. King, "Why 'Waterworld,' with Costner in Fins, Is Costliest Film Ever," *The Wall Street Journal* (January 31, 1995), A1.

54. Adapted from James D. Thompson, *Organizations in Action* (New York: McGraw-Hill, 1967), chap. 10; McMillan, "Qualitative Models of Organizational Decision Making," 25; and Clayton M. Christensen, Matt Marx, and Howard H. Stevenson, "The Tools of Cooperation and Change," *Harvard Business Review* (October 2006), 73–80.
55. Louise Lee, "Courts Begin to Award Damages to Victims of Parking-Area Crime," *The Wall Street Journal* (April 23, 1997), A1, A8.
56. Beth Dickey, "NASA's Next Step," *Government Executive* (April 15, 2004), 34–42; and Jena McGregor, "Gospels of Failure," *Fast Company* (February 2005), 61–67.
57. Mintzberg and Westley, "Decision Making: It's Not What You Think."
58. Paul C. Nutt, "Selecting Decision Rules for Crucial Choices: An Investigation of the Thompson Framework," *The Journal of Applied Behavioral Science* 38, no. 1 (March 2002), 99–131; and Paul C. Nutt, "Making Strategic Choices," *Journal of Management Studies* 39, no. 1 (January 2002), 67–95.
59. George T. Doran and Jack Gunn, "Decision Making in High-Tech Firms: Perspectives of Three Executives," *Business Horizons* (November–December 2002), 7–16.
60. L. J. Bourgeois III and Kathleen M. Eisenhardt, "Strategic Decision Processes in High Velocity Environments: Four Cases in the Microcomputer Industry," *Management Science* 34 (1988), 816–835.
61. Kathleen M. Eisenhardt, "Speed and Strategic Course: How Managers Accelerate Decision Making," *California Management Review* (Spring 1990), 39–54.
62. David A. Garvin and Michael A. Roberto, "What You Don't Know about Making Decisions," *Harvard Business Review* (September 2001), 108–116.
63. Karl Weick, *The Social Psychology of Organizing*, 2nd ed. (Reading, Mass.: Addison-Wesley, 1979), 243.
64. Jena McGregor, "How Failure Breeds Success," *BusinessWeek* (July 10, 2006), 42–52.
65. Ibid.
66. For discussions of various cognitive biases, see John S. Hammond, Ralph L. Keeney, and Howard Raiffa, *Smart Choices: A Practical Guide to Making Better Decisions* (Boston: Harvard Business School Press, 1999); Max H. Bazerman and Dolly Chugh, "Decisions Without Blinders," *Harvard Business Review* (January 2006), 88–97; J. S. Hammond, R.L. Keeney, and H. Raiffa, "The Hidden Traps in Decision Making," *Harvard Business Review* (September–October 1998), 47–58; Oren Harari, "The Thomas Lawson Syndrome," *Management Review* (February 1994), 58–61; and Max H. Bazerman, *Judgment in Managerial Decision Making*, 5th ed. (New York: John Wiley & Sons, 2002).
67. Helga Drummond, "Too Little Too Late: A Case Study of Escalation in Decision Making," *Organization Studies* 15, no. 4 (1994), 591–607; Joel Brockner, "The Escalation of Commitment to a Failing Course of Action: Toward Theoretical Progress," *Academy of Management Review* 17 (1992), 39–61; Barry M. Staw and Jerry Ross, "Knowing When to Pull the Plug," *Harvard Business Review* 65 (March–April 1987), 68–74; and Barry M. Staw, "The Escalation of Commitment to a Course of Action," *Academy of Management Review* 6 (1981), 577–587.
68. Daniel Kahneman and Amos Tversky, "Prospect Theory: An Analysis of Decision Under Risk," *Econometrica* 47 (1979), 263–292.
69. Irving L. Janis, *Groupthink: Psychological Studies of Policy Decisions and Fiascoes*, 2nd ed. (Boston: Houghton Mifflin, 1982).
70. This section is based on Jeffrey Pfeffer and Robert I. Sutton, "Evidence-Based Management," *Harvard Business Review* (January 2006), 62–74; Rosemary Stewart, *Evidence-based Decision Making* (Radcliffe Publishing, 2002); and Joshua Klayman, Richard P. Larrick, and Chip Heath, "Organizational Repairs," *Across the Board* (February 2000), 26–31.
71. Michael A. Roberto, "Making Difficult Decisions in Turbulent Times," *Ivey Business Journal* (May–June 2003), 1–7; Kathleen M. Eisenhardt, "Strategy as Strategic Decision Making," *Sloan Management Review* (Spring 1999), 65–72; and Garvin and Roberto, "What You Don't Know About Making Decisions."
72. Roberto, "Making Difficult Decisions in Turbulent Times."
73. David M. Schweiger and William R. Sandberg, "The Utilization of Individual Capabilities in Group Approaches to Strategic Decision Making," *Strategic Management Journal* 10 (1989), 31–43; and "The Devil's Advocate," *Small Business Report* (December 1987), 38–41.
74. "Tools for Managing in a Complex Context," sidebar in David J. Snowden and Mary E. Boone, "A Leader's Framework for Decision Making," *Harvard Business Review* (November 2007), 69–76.

Chapter 9

1. Steve Hamm, "A Passion For the Planet," *BusinessWeek* (August 21–28, 2006), 92–94; Geoff Colvin, "The Defiant One," *Fortune* (April 30, 2007), 86–92.
2. Julia Boorstin, "Secret Recipe: J. M. Smucker," *Fortune* (January 12, 2004), 58–59.
3. Anita Raghavan, Kathryn Kranhold, and Alexei Barrionuevo, "Full Speed Ahead: How Enron Bosses Created a Culture of Pushing Limits," *The Wall Street Journal* (August 26, 2002), A1, A7.
4. Mark C. Bolino, William H. Turnley, and James M. Bloodgood, "Citizenship Behavior and the Creation of Social Capital in Organizations," *Academy of Management Review* 27, no. 4 (2002), 505–522; and Don Cohen and Laurence Prusak, *In Good Company: How Social Capital Makes Organizations Work* (Boston: Harvard Business School Press, 2001), 3–4.
5. W. Jack Duncan, "Organizational Culture: 'Getting a Fix' on an Elusive Concept," *Academy of Management Executive*

3 (1989), 229–236; Linda Smircich, "Concepts of Culture and Organizational Analysis," *Administrative Science Quarterly* 28 (1983), 339–358; and Andrew D. Brown and Ken Starkey, "The Effect of Organizational Culture on Communication and Information," *Journal of Management Studies* 31, no. 6 (November 1994), 807–828.

6. Edgar H. Schein, "Organizational Culture," *American Psychologist* 45 (February 1990), 109–119.

7. James H. Higgins and Craig McAllaster, "Want Innovation? Then Use Cultural Artifacts That Support It," *Organizational Dynamics* 31, no. 1 (2002), 74–84.

8. Harrison M. Trice and Janice M. Beyer, "Studying Organizational Cultures through Rites and Ceremonials," *Academy of Management Review* 9 (1984), 653–669; Janice M. Beyer and Harrison M. Trice, "How an Organization's Rites Reveal Its Culture," *Organizational Dynamics* 15 (Spring 1987), 5–24; Steven P. Feldman, "Management in Context: An Essay on the Relevance of Culture to the Understanding of Organizational Change," *Journal of Management Studies* 23 (1986), 589–607; and Mary Jo Hatch, "The Dynamics of Organizational Culture," *Academy of Management Review* 18 (1993), 657–693.

9. This discussion is based on Edgar H. Schein, *Organizational Culture and Leadership*, 2nd ed. (Homewood, Ill.: Richard D. Irwin, 1992); and John P. Kotter and James L. Heskett, *Corporate Culture and Performance* (New York: Free Press, 1992).

10. Chip Jarnagan and John W. Slocum, Jr., "Creating Corporate Cultures Through Mythopoetic Leadership," *Organizational Dynamics* 36, no. 3 (2007), 288–302.

11. Larry Mallak, "Understanding and Changing Your Organization's Culture," *Industrial Management* (March–April 2001), 18–24.

12. For an expanded list of various elements that can be used to assess or interpret corporate culture, see "10 Key Cultural Elements," sidebar in Micah R. Kee, "Corporate Culture Makes a Fiscal Difference," *Industrial Management* (November–December 2003), 16–20.

13. Charlotte B. Sutton, "Richness Hierarchy of the Cultural Network: The Communication of Corporate Values" (unpublished manuscript, Texas A&M University, 1985); and Terrence E. Deal and Allan A. Kennedy, "Culture: A New Look through Old Lenses," *Journal of Applied Behavioral Science* 19 (1983), 498–505.

14. Jarnagan and Slocum, "Creating Corporate Culture Through Mythopoetic Leadership."

15. Don Hellriegel and John W. Slocum, Jr., *Management*, 7th ed. (Cincinnati, Ohio: South-Western, 1996), 537.

16. Trice and Beyer, "Studying Organizational Cultures through Rites and Ceremonials."

17. Jarnagan and Slocum, "Creating Cultures Through Mythopoetic Leadership."

18. Joanne Martin, *Organizational Culture: Mapping the Terrain* (Thousand Oaks, Calif.: Sage Publications, 2002), 71–72.

19. Joann S. Lublin, "Theory & Practice: Keeping Clients by Keeping Workers; Unique Efforts to Encourage Employee Loyalty Pay Off for U.K. Ad Shop Mother," *The Wall Street Journal* (November 20, 2006), B3.

20. Raghavan, Kranhold, and Barrionuevo, "Full Speed Ahead."

21. "FYI," *Inc.* (April 1991), 14.

22. Nanette Byrnes, "The Art of Motivation," *BusinessWeek* (May 1, 2006), 57–62.

23. Gary Hamel with Bill Breen, *The Future of Management* (Boston: Harvard Business School Press, 2007).

24. Matt Moffett, "At InBev, a Gung-Ho Culture Rules; American Icon Anheuser, A Potential Target, Faces Prospect of Big Changes," *The Wall Street Journal* (May 28, 2008), B1; and Matt Moffett, "InBev's Chief Built Competitive Culture," *The Wall Street Journal* (June 13, 2008), B6.

25. Michelle Conlin, "Netflix: Flex to the Max," *BusinessWeek* (September 24, 2007), 72–74.

26. Gerry Johnson, "Managing Strategic Change—Strategy, Culture, and Action," *Long Range Planning* 25, no. 1 (1992), 28–36.

27. Jennifer A. Chatman and Sandra Eunyoung Cha, "Leading by Leveraging Culture," *California Management Review* 45, no. 4 (Summer 2003), 20–34; and Abby Ghobadian and Nicholas O'Regan, "The Link between Culture, Strategy, and Performance in Manufacturing SMEs," *Journal of General Management* 28, no. 1 (Autumn 2002), 16–34.

28. James R. Detert, Roger G. Schroeder, and John J. Mauriel, "A Framework for Linking Culture and Improvement Initiatives in Organizations," *Academy of Management Review* 25, no. 4 (2000), 850–863.

29. Based on Daniel R. Denison, *Corporate Culture and Organizational Effectiveness* (New York: Wiley, 1990), 11–15; Daniel R. Denison and Aneil K. Mishra, "Toward a Theory of Organizational Culture and Effectiveness," *Organization Science* 6, no. 2 (March–April 1995), 204–223; R. Hooijberg and F. Petrock, "On Cultural Change: Using the Competing Values Framework to Help Leaders Execute a Transformational Strategy," *Human Resource Management* 32 (1993), 29–50; and R. E. Quinn, *Beyond Rational Management: Mastering the Paradoxes and Competing Demands of High Performance* (San Francisco: Jossey-Bass, 1988).

30. Sara Kehaulani Goo, "Building a 'Googley' Workforce; Corporate Culture Breeds Innovation," *The Washington Post* (October 21, 2006), D1; Adam Lashinsky, "Chaos by Design," *Fortune* (October 2, 2006), 86ff; and Adam Lashinsky, "Search and Enjoy," part of "The 100 Best Companies to Work For, 2007," *Fortune* (January 22, 2007), 70–82.

31. Elizabeth Montalbano, "Growing Pains for Google," *Computerworld* (October 20, 2008), 28–31; Adam Lashinsky, "Where Does Google Go Next?" *Fortune* (May 26, 2008), 104–110; and Jessica E. Vascellaro and Scott Morrison, "Google Gears Down for Tougher Times," *The Wall Street Journal* (December 3, 2008), A1, A13.

32. Moffett, "InBev's Chief Built Competitive Culture."

33. Matthew Boyle, "The Wegmans Way," *Fortune* (January 24, 2005), 62–68; and Robert Levering and Milton Moskowitz, "100 Best Companies to Work For: The Rankings," *Fortune* (February 4, 2008), 75–94.

34. Rekha Balu, "Pacific Edge Projects Itself," *Fast Company* (October 2000), 371–381.

35. Bernard Arogyaswamy and Charles M. Byles, "Organizational Culture: Internal and External Fits," *Journal of Management* 13 (1987), 647–659.

36. Paul R. Lawrence and Jay W. Lorsch, *Organization and Environment* (Homewood, Ill.: Irwin, 1969).

37. Scott Kirsner, "Designed for Innovation," *Fast Company* (November 1998), 54, 56.

38. Chatman and Cha, "Leading by Leveraging Culture"; and Jeff Rosenthal and Mary Ann Masarech, "High-Performance Cultures: How Values Can Drive Business Results," *Journal of Organizational Excellence* (Spring 2003), 3–18.

39. Ghobadian and O'Regan, "The Link between Culture, Strategy and Performance"; G. G. Gordon and N. DiTomaso, "Predicting Corporate Performance from Organisational Culture," *Journal of Management Studies* 29, no. 6 (1992), 783–798; and G. A. Marcoulides and R. H. Heck, "Organizational Culture and Performance: Proposing and Testing a Model," *Organization Science* 4 (1993), 209–225.

40. Kee, "Corporate Culture Makes a Fiscal Difference."

41. Tressie Wright Muldrow, Timothy Buckley, and Brigitte W. Schay, "Creating High-Performance Organizations in the Public Sector," *Human Resource Management* 41, no. 3 (Fall 2002), 341–354.

42. John P. Kotter and James L. Heskett, *Corporate Culture and Performance* (New York: The Free Press, 1992).

43. Betsy Morris, "The Best Place to Work Now (100 Best Companies to Work For 2006)," *Fortune* (January 23, 2006), 79–86.

44. Robert W. Clement, "Just How Unethical Is American Business?" *Business Horizons* 49 (2006), 313–327.

45. Mike Esterl, "Executive Decision: In Germany, Scandals Tarnish Business Elite," *The Wall Street Journal* (March 4, 2008), A1; and Martin Fackler, "The Salaryman Accuses," *The New York Times* (June 7, 2008), C1.

46. Gordon F. Shea, *Practical Ethics* (New York: American Management Association, 1988); Linda K. Treviño, "Ethical Decision Making in Organizations: A Person–Situation Interactionist Model," *Academy of Management Review* 11 (1986), 601–617; and Linda Klebe Treviño and Katherine A. Nelson, *Managing Business Ethics: Straight Talk about How to Do It Right*, 2nd ed. (New York: John Wiley & Sons Inc., 1999).

47. This discussion of the sources of individual ethics is based on Susan H. Taft and Judith White, "Ethics Education: Using Inductive Reasoning to Develop Individual, Group, Organizational, and Global Perspectives," *Journal of Management Education* 31, no. 5 (October 2007), 614–646.

48. Dawn-Marie Driscoll, "Don't Confuse Legal and Ethical Standards," *Business Ethics* (July–August 1996), 44.

49. LaRue Tone Hosmer, *The Ethics of Management*, 2nd ed. (Homewood, Ill.: Irwin, 1991).

50. Some of these incidents are from Hosmer, *The Ethics of Management*.

51. Linda K. Treviño and Katherine A. Nelson, *Managing Business Ethics: Straight Talk about How to Do It Right* (New York: John Wiley & Sons, Inc., 1995), 4.

52. N. Craig Smith, "Corporate Social Responsibility: Whether or How?" *California Management Review* 45, no. 4 (Summer 2003), 52–76; and Eugene W. Szwajkowski, "The Myths and Realities of Research on Organizational Misconduct," in James E. Post, ed., *Research in Corporate Social Performance and Policy*, vol. 9 (Greenwich, Conn.: JAI Press, 1986), 103–122.

53. Reported in Beckey Bright, "How More Companies Are Embracing Social Responsibility as Good Business," *The Wall Street Journal* (March 10, 2008), R3.

54. Sarah E. Needleman, "The Latest Office Perk: Getting Paid to Volunteer," *The Wall Street Journal* (April 29, 2008), D1; Andrew Martin, "Burger King Shifts Policy on Animals," *The New York Times* (March 23, 2007), C1; Kate O'Sullivan, "Virtue Rewarded," *CFO* (October 2006), 46–52.

55. O'Sullivan, "Virtue Rewarded"; Bright, "How More Companies Are Embracing Social Responsibility as Good Business"; and Oliver Falck and Stephan Heblich, "Corporate Social Responsibility: Doing Well By Doing Good," *Business Horizons* 50 (2007): 247–254.

56. Curtis C. Verschoor and Elizabeth A. Murphy, "The Financial Performance of Large U.S. Firms and Those with Global Prominence: How Do the Best Corporate Citizens Rate?" *Business and Society Review* 107, no. 2 (Fall 2002), 371–381; Homer H. Johnson, "Does It Pay to Be Good? Social Responsibility and Financial Performance," *Business Horizons* (November–December 2003), 34–40; Quentin R. Skrabec, "Playing By the Rules: Why Ethics Are Profitable," *Business Horizons* (September–October 2003), 15–18; Marc Gunther, "Tree Huggers, Soy Lovers, and Profits," *Fortune* (June 23, 2003), 98–104; and Dale Kurschner, "5 Ways Ethical Business Creates Fatter Profits," *Business Ethics* (March–April 1996), 20–23. Also see various studies reported in Lori Ioannou, "Corporate America's Social Conscience," *Fortune*, special advertising section (May 26, 2003), S1–S10.

57. Verschoor and Murphy, "The Financial Performance of Large U.S. Firms."

58. Phred Dvorak, "Theory & Practice: Finding the Best Measure of 'Corporate Citizenship,'" *The Wall Street Journal* (July 2, 2007), B3; and Gretchen Morgenson, "Shares of Corporate Nice Guys Can Finish First," *The New York Times* (April 27, 2003), Section 3, 1.

59. Daniel W. Greening and Daniel B. Turban, "Corporate Social Performance as a Competitive Advantage in Attracting a Quality Workforce," *Business and Society* 39, no. 3 (September 2000), 254.

60. Needleman, "The Latest Office Perk."

61. Christopher Marquis, "Doing Well and Doing Good," *The New York Times* (July 13, 2003), Section 3, 2; and Joseph Pereira, "Career Journal: Doing Good and Doing Well at Timberland," *The Wall Street Journal* (September 9, 2003), B1.

62. Reported in Needleman, "The Latest Office Perk."

63. "The Socially Correct Corporate Business," segment in Leslie Holstrom and Simon Brady, "The Changing Face of Global Business," *Fortune*, special advertising section (July 24, 2000), S1–S38.

64. Remi Trudel and June Cotte, "Does Being Ethical Pay?" *The Wall Street Journal* (May 12, 2008), R4.

65. *Corporate Ethics: A Prime Business Asset* (New York: The Business Round Table, February 1988).

66. Treviño and Nelson, *Managing Business Ethics*, 201.

67. Gary R. Weaver, Linda Klebe Treviño, and Bradley Agle, "'Somebody I Look Up To': Ethical Role Models in Organizations," *Organizational Dynamics* 34, no. 4 (2005), 313–330; Andrew W. Singer, "The Ultimate Ethics Test," *Across the Board* (March 1992), 19–22; Ronald B.

Morgan, "Self and Co-Worker Perceptions of Ethics and Their Relationships to Leadership and Salary," *Academy of Management Journal* 36, no. 1 (February 1993), 200–214; and Joseph L. Badaracco Jr., and Allen P. Webb, "Business Ethics: A View from the Trenches," *California Management Review* 37, no. 2 (Winter 1995), 8–28.

68. This definition is based on Robert J. House, Andre Delbecq, and Toon W. Taris, "Value Based Leadership: An Integrated Theory and an Empirical Test" (working paper).

69. Michael Barrier, "Doing the Right Thing," *Nation's Business* (March 1998), 33–38.

70. Thomas J. Peters and Robert H. Waterman, Jr., *In Search of Excellence* (New York: Harper & Row, 1982).

71. Carol Hymowitz, "CEOs Must Work Hard to Maintain Faith in the Corner Office" (In the Lead column), *The Wall Street Journal* (July 9, 2002), B1.

72. Richard Osborne, "Kingston's Family Values," *Industry Week* (August 13, 2001), 51–54.

73. Weaver, Treviño, and Agle, "'Somebody I Look Up To': Ethical Role Models in Organizations."

74. Based on Weaver et al., "'Somebody I Look Up To.'"

75. Alan Yuspeh, "Do the Right Thing," *CIO* (August 1, 2000), 56–58.

76. Reported in Cheryl Rosen, "A Measure of Success? Ethics After Enron," *Business Ethics* (Summer 2006), 22–26.

77. Treviño and Nelson, *Managing Business Ethics*, 212.

78. Beverly Geber, "The Right and Wrong of Ethics Offices," *Training* (October 1995), 102–118.

79. Janet P. Near and Marcia P. Miceli, "Effective Whistle-Blowing," *Academy of Management Review* 20, no. 3 (1995), 679–708.

80. Jene G. James, "Whistle-Blowing: Its Moral Justification," in Peter Madsen and Jay M. Shafritz, eds., *Essentials of Business Ethics* (New York: Meridian Books, 1990), 160–190; and Janet P. Near, Terry Morehead Dworkin, and Marcia P. Miceli, "Explaining the Whistle-Blowing Process: Suggestions from Power Theory and Justice Theory," *Organization Science* 4 (1993), 393–411.

81. Martin Fackler, "Loyalty No Longer Blind for Salarymen in Japan; Whistle-Blowers a Sign of Changing Times," *International Herald Tribune* (June 7, 2008), 1.

82. "Setting the Standard," Lockheed Martin's Web site, *http://www.lockheedmartin.com/exeth/html/code/code.html*, accessed August 7, 2001.

83. Carl Anderson, "Values-Based Management," *Academy of Management Executive* 11, no. 4 (1997), 25–46.

84. Ronald E. Berenbeim, *Corporate Ethics Practices* (New York: The Conference Board, 1992).

85. Rosen, "A Measure of Success? Ethics After Enron."

86. James Weber, "Institutionalizing Ethics into Business Organizations: A Model and Research Agenda," *Business Ethics Quarterly* 3 (1993), 419–436.

87. Landon Thomas Jr. "On Wall Street, a Rise in Dismissals over Ethics," *The New York Times* (March 29, 2005), A1.

88. Mark Henricks, "Ethics in Action," *Management Review* (January 1995), 53–55; Dorothy Marcic, *Management and the Wisdom of Love* (San Francisco: Jossey-Bass, 1997); and Beverly Geber, "The Right and Wrong of Ethics Offices," *Training* (October 1995), 102–118.

89. Susan J. Harrington, "What Corporate America Is Teaching about Ethics," *Academy of Management Executive* 5 (1991), 21–30.

90. Jerry G. Kreuze, Zahida Luqmani, and Mushtaq Luqmani, "Shades of Gray," *Internal Auditor* (April 2001), 48.

91. David Scheer, "For Your Eyes Only; Europe's New High-Tech Role: Playing Privacy Cop to the World," *The Wall Street Journal* (October 10, 2003), A1, A16.

92. S. C. Schneider, "National vs. Corporate Culture: Implications for Human Resource Management," *Human Resource Management* (Summer 1988), 239; and Terence Jackson, "Cultural Values and Management Ethics: A 10-Nation Study," *Human Relations* 54, no. 10 (2001), 1267–1302.

93. Vijay Govindarajan, reported in Gail Dutton, "Building a Global Brain," *Management Review* (May 1999), 34–38.

94. Homer H. Johnson, "Corporate Social Audits—This Time Around," *Business Horizons* (May–June 2001), 29–36.

95. Cassandra Kegler, "Holding Herself Accountable," *Working Woman* (May 2001), 13; and Louisa Wah, "Treading the Sacred Ground," *Management Review* (July–August 1998), 18–22.

Chapter 10

1. Ellen Byron, "A New Odd Couple: Google, P&G Swap Workers to Spur Innovation," *The Wall Street Journal* (November 19, 2008), A1, A18.

2. Based on John P. Kotter, *Leading Change* (Boston: Harvard Business School Press, 1996), 18–20.

3. Anne Fisher, "America's Most Admired Companies," *Fortune* (March 17, 2008), 65–67.

4. Joseph E. McCann, "Design Principles for an Innovating Company," *Academy of Management Executive* 5 (May 1991), 76–93.

5. Michael Totty, "The Wall Street Journal 2008 Technology Innovation Awards," *The Wall Street Journal* (September 29, 2008), R1, R4, R6.

6. Ibid.

7. Brian Hindo, "At 3M, A Struggle Between Efficiency and Creativity," *BusinessWeek* (June 11, 2007), 8–14; Erin White, "How a Company Made Everyone a Team Player," *The Wall Street Journal* (August 13, 2007), B1, B7.

8. Richard A. Wolfe, "Organizational Innovation: Review, Critique and Suggested Research Directions," *Journal of Management Studies* 31, no. 3 (May 1994), 405–431.

9. John L. Pierce and Andre L. Delbecq, "Organization Structure, Individual Attitudes and Innovation," *Academy of Management Review* 2 (1977), 27–37; and Michael Aiken and Jerald Hage, "The Organic Organization and Innovation," *Sociology* 5 (1971), 63–82.

10. Richard L. Daft, "Bureaucratic versus Non-bureaucratic Structure in the Process of Innovation and Change," in Samuel B. Bacharach, ed., *Perspectives in Organizational Sociology: Theory and Research* (Greenwich, Conn.: JAI Press, 1982), 129–166.

11. Alan D. Meyer and James B. Goes, "Organizational Assimilation of Innovations: A Multilevel Contextual Analysis," *Academy of Management Journal* 31 (1988), 897–923.

12. Richard W. Woodman, John E. Sawyer, and Ricky W. Griffin, "Toward a Theory of Organizational Creativity," *Academy of Management Review* 18 (1993), 293–321.

13. John Grossman, "Strategies: Thinking Small," *Inc.* (August 2004), 34–36.

14. Robert I. Sutton, "Weird Ideas That Spark Innovation," *MIT Sloan Management Review* (Winter 2002), 83–87; Robert Barker, "The Art of Brainstorming," *BusinessWeek* (August 26, 2002), 168–169; Gary A. Steiner, ed., *The Creative Organization* (Chicago: University of Chicago Press, 1965), 16–18; and James Brian Quinn, "Managing Innovation: Controlled Chaos," *Harvard Business Review* (May–June 1985), 73–84.

15. Thomas M. Burton, "Flop Factor: By Learning from Failures, Lilly Keeps Drug Pipeline Full," *The Wall Street Journal* (April 21, 2004), A1, A12.

16. Kotter, *Leading Change*, 20–25; and John P. Kotter, "Leading Change," *Harvard Business Review* (March–April 1995), 59–67.

17. G. Tomas M. Hult, Robert F. Hurley, and Gary A. Knight, "Innovativeness: Its Antecedents and Impact on Business Performance," *Industrial Marketing Management* 33 (2004), 429–438.

18. Brooks Barnes, "Will Disney Keep Us Amused?" *The New York Times* (February 10, 2008), BU1.

19. Burton, "Flop Factor."

20. D. Bruce Merrifield, "Intrapreneurial Corporate Renewal," *Journal of Business Venturing* 8 (September 1993), 383–389; Linsu Kim, "Organizational Innovation and Structure," *Journal of Business Research* 8 (1980), 225–245; and Tom Burns and G. M. Stalker, *The Management of Innovation* (London: Tavistock Publications, 1961).

21. Charles A. O'Reilly III and Michael L. Tushman, "The Ambidextrous Organization," *Harvard Business Review* (April 2004), 74–81; M. L. Tushman and C. A. O'Reilly III, "Building an Ambidextrous Organization: Forming Your Own 'Skunk Works,'" *Health Forum Journal* 42, no. 2 (March–April 1999), 20–23; J. C. Spender and Eric H. Kessler, "Managing the Uncertainties of Innovation: Extending Thompson (1967)," *Human Relations* 48, no. 1 (1995), 35–56; and Robert B. Duncan, "The Ambidextrous Organization: Designing Dual Structures for Innovation," in Ralph H. Killman, Louis R. Pondy, and Dennis Slevin, eds., *The Management of Organization*, vol. 1 (New York: North-Holland, 1976), 167–188.

22. J. G. March, "Exploration and Exploitation in Organizational Learning," *Organization Science* 2 (1991), 71–87. For a review of the research on exploration and exploitation since March's pioneering article, see A. K. Gupta, K. G. Smith, and C. E. Shalley, "The Interplay Between Exploration and Exploitation," *Academy of Management Journal* 49, no. 4 (2006), 693–706.

23. M. H. Lubatkin, Z. Simsek, Y. Ling, and J. F. Veiga, "Ambidexterity and Performance in Small- to Medium-Sized Firms: The Pivotal Role of Top Management Team Behavioral Integration," *Journal of Management* 32, no. 5 (October 2006), 646–672; and C. A. O'Reilly III and M. L. Tushman, "The Ambidextrous Organization."

24. Tushman and O'Reilly, "Building an Ambidextrous Organization."

25. Edward F. McDonough III and Richard Leifer, "Using Simultaneous Structures to Cope with Uncertainty," *Academy of Management Journal* 26 (1983), 727–735.

26. John McCormick and Bill Powell, "Management for the 1990s," *Newsweek* (April 25, 1988), 47–48.

27. Todd Datz, "Romper Ranch," *CIO Enterprise* Section 2 (May 15, 1999), 39–52.

28. Paul S. Adler, Barbara Goldoftas, and David I. Levine, "Ergonomics, Employee Involvement, and the Toyota Production System: A Case Study of NUMMI's 1993 Model Introduction," *Industrial and Labor Relations Review* 50, no. 3 (April 1997), 416–437.

29. Judith R. Blau and William McKinley, "Ideas, Complexity, and Innovation," *Administrative Science Quarterly* 24 (1979), 200–219.

30. Peter Landers, "Back to Basics; With Dry Pipelines, Big Drug Makers Stock Up in Japan," *The Wall Street Journal* (November 24, 2003), A1, A7.

31. Sherri Eng, "Hatching Schemes," *The Industry Standard* (November 27–December 4, 2000), 174–175.

32. Peter Lewis, "Texas Instruments' Lunatic Fringe," *Fortune* (September 4, 2006), 120–128.

33. Christopher Hoenig, "Skunk Works Secrets," *CIO* (July 1, 2000), 74–76.

34. Phaedra Hise, "New Recruitment Strategy: Ask Your Best Employees to Leave," *Inc.* (July 1997), 2.

35. Daniel F. Jennings and James R. Lumpkin, "Functioning Modeling Corporate Entrepreneurship: An Empirical Integrative Analysis," *Journal of Management* 15 (1989), 485–502; and Julian Birkinshaw, "The Paradox of Corporate Entrepreneurship," *Strategy & Business*, Issue 30 (Spring 2003), 46–57.

36. Jane M. Howell and Christopher A. Higgins, "Champions of Technology Innovation," *Administrative Science Quarterly* 35 (1990), 317–341; and Jane M. Howell and Christopher A. Higgins, "Champions of Change: Identifying, Understanding, and Supporting Champions of Technology Innovations," *Organizational Dynamics* (Summer 1990), 40–55.

37. Thomas J. Peters and Robert H. Waterman, Jr., *In Search of Excellence* (New York: Harper & Row, 1982).

38. See Lionel Roure, "Product Champion Characteristics in France and Germany," *Human Relations* 54, no. 5 (2001), 663–682, for a review of the literature related to product champions.

39. Lewis, "Texas Instruments' Lunatic Fringe."

40. Rob Cross, Andrew Hargadon, Salvatore Parise, and Robert J. Thomas, "Business Insight (A Special Report); Together We Innovate: How Can Companies Come Up With New Ideas? By Getting Employees Working with

One Another," *The Wall Street Journal* (September 15, 2007), R6.

41. Jessi Hempel, "Big Blue Brainstorm," *BusinessWeek* (August 7, 2006), 70.

42. G. A. Stevens and J. Burley, "3,000 Raw Ideas = 1 Commercial Success!" *Research Technology Management* 40, no. 3 (May–June 1997), 16–27; R. P. Morgan, C. Kruytbosch, and N. Kannankutty, "Patenting and Invention Activity of U.S. Scientists and Engineers in the Academic Sector: Comparisons with Industry," *Journal of Technology Transfer* 26 (2001), 173–183; Edwin Mansfield, J. Rapaport, J. Schnee, S. Wagner, and M. Hamburger, *Research and Innovation in Modern Corporations* (New York: Norton, 1971); Christopher Power with Kathleen Kerwin, Ronald Grover, Keith Alexander, and Robert D. Hof, "Flops," *BusinessWeek* (August 16, 1993), 76–82; and Modesto A. Maidique and Billie Jo Zirger, "A Study of Success and Failure in Product Innovation: The Case of the U.S. Electronics Industry," *IEEE Transactions in Engineering Management* 31 (November 1984), 192–203.

43. Scott Hensley, "Bleeding Cash: Pfizer 'Youth Pill' Ate Up $71 Million Before It Flopped," *The Wall Street Journal* (May 2, 2002), A1, A8.

44. Linton, Matysiak & Wilkes Inc. study results reported in "Market Study Results Released: New Product Introduction Success, Failure Rates Analyzed," *Frozen Food Digest* (July 1, 1997).

45. Deborah Dougherty and Cynthia Hardy, "Sustained Product Innovation in Large, Mature Organizations: Overcoming Innovation-to-Organization Problems," *Academy of Management Journal* 39, no. 5 (1996), 1120–1153.

46. M. Adams and the Product Development and Management Association, "Comparative Performance Assessment Study 2004," available for purchase at *http://www.pdma.org*. Results reported in Jeff Cope, "Lessons Learned—Commercialization Success Rates: A Brief Review," *RTI Tech Ventures* newsletter, 4, no. 4 (December 2007).

47. Ibid.

48. Shona L. Brown and Kathleen M. Eisenhardt, "Product Development: Past Research, Present Findings, and Future Directions," *Academy of Management Review* 20, no. 2 (1995), 343–378; F. Axel Johne and Patricia A. Snelson, "Success Factors in Product Innovation: A Selective Review of the Literature," *Journal of Product Innovation Management* 5 (1988), 114–128; Antonio Bailetti and Paul F. Litva, "Integrating Customer Requirements into Product Designs," *Journal of Product Innovation Management* 12 (1995), 3–15; and Science Policy Research Unit, University of Sussex, *Success and Failure in Industrial Innovation* (London: Centre for the Study of Industrial Innovation, 1972).

49. Dorothy Leonard and Jeffrey F. Rayport, "Spark Innovation through Empathic Design," *Harvard Business Review* (November–December 1997), 102–113.

50. Brown and Eisenhardt, "Product Development"; and Dan Dimancescu and Kemp Dwenger, "Smoothing the Product Development Path," *Management Review* (January 1996), 36–41.

51. Kenneth B. Kahn, "Market Orientation, Interdepartmental Integration, and Product Development Performance," *The Journal of Product Innovation Management* 18 (2001), 314–323; and Ali E. Akgün, Gary S. Lynn, and John C. Byrne, "Taking the Guesswork Out of New Product Development: How Successful High-Tech Companies Get That Way," *Journal of Business Strategy* 25, no. 4 (2004), 41–46.

52. The discussion of open innovation is based on Henry Chesbrough, "The Era of Open Innovation," *MIT Sloan Management Review* (Spring 2003), 35–41; Julian Birkinshaw and Susan A. Hill, "Corporate Venturing Units: Vehicles for Strategic Success in the New Europe," *Organizational Dynamics* 34, no. 3 (2005), 247–257; Amy Muller and Liisa Välikangas, "Extending the Boundary of Corporate Innovation," *Strategy & Leadership* 30, no. 3 (2002), 4–9; Navi Radjou, "Networked Innovation Drives Profits," *Industrial Management* (January–February 2005), 14–21; Darrell Rigby and Barbara Bilodeau, "The Bain 2005 Management Tool Survey," *Strategy & Leadership* 33, no. 4 (2005), 4–12; Ian Mount, "The Return of the Lone Inventor," *FSB (Fortune Small Business)* (March 2005), 18; and Henry Chesbrough, "The Logic of Open Innovation: Managing Intellectual Property," *California Management Review* 45, no. 3 (Spring 2003), 33–58.

53. Reported in Jill Jusko, "A Team Effort," *Industry Week* (January 2007), 42, 45.

54. Bettina von Stamm, "Collaboration with Other Firms and Customers: Innovation's Secret Weapon," *Strategy & Leadership* 32, no. 3 (2004), 16–20"; and Bas Hillebrand and Wim G. Biemans, "Links between Internal and External Cooperation in Product Development: An Exploratory Study," *The Journal of Product Innovation Management* 21 (2004), 110–122.

55. Max Chafkin, "The Customer Is the Company," *Inc.* (June 2008), 88–96.

56. Jeff Jarvis, "The Buzz From Starbucks Customers," *BusinessWeek* (April 28, 2008), 106; Chafkin, "The Customer Is the Company."

57. Bob Tedeschi, "Putting Innovation in the Hands of a Crowd," *The New York Times* (March 3, 2008), C6.

58. Ann Harrington, "Who's Afraid of a New Product?" *Fortune* (November 10, 2003), 189–192.

59. Melissa A. Schilling and Charles W. L. Hill, "Managing the New Product Development Process," *Academy of Management Executive* 12, no. 3 (1998), 67–81; and J. Lynn Lunsford and Daniel Michaels, "New Orders; After Four Years in the Rear, Boeing Is Set to Jet Past Airbus," *The Wall Street Journal* (June 10, 2005), A1, A5.

60. McKinsey survey, reported in Gloria Macias-Lizaso Miranda and Kiko Thiel, "Improving Organizational Speed and Agility," *The McKinsey Quarterly* Issue 1 (2007).

61. John A. Pearce II, "Speed Merchants," *Organizational Dynamics* 30, no. 3 (2002), 191–205; Kathleen M. Eisenhardt and Behnam N. Tabrizi, "Accelerating Adaptive Processes: Product Innovation in the Global Computer Industry," *Administrative Science Quarterly* 40 (1995), 84–110; Dougherty and Hardy, "Sustained Product Innovation in Large, Mature Organizations"; and Karne Bronikowski, "Speeding New Products to Market," *Journal of Business Strategy* (September–October 1990), 34–37.

62. Cecilie Rohwedder and Keith Johnson, "Pace-Setting Zara Seeks More Speed to Fight Its Rising Cheap-Chic Rivals," *The Wall Street Journal* (February 20, 2008), B1; Janet Adamy, "Leadership (A Special Report); Catch the Wave: Russell Stover Candies Wanted to Get a Piece of the Low-Carb Craze; But to Do So It Had to Be Quick—and Smart," *The Wall Street Journal* (October 25, 2004), R8.

63. V. K. Narayanan, Frank L. Douglas, Brock Guernsey, and John Charnes, "How Top Management Steers Fast Cycle Teams to Success," *Strategy & Leadership* 30, no. 3 (2002), 19–27.

64. Edward F. McDonough III, Kenneth B. Kahn, and Gloria Barczak, "An Investigation of the Use of Global, Virtual, and Colocated New Product Development Teams," *The Journal of Product Innovation Management* 18 (2001), 110–120.

65. Raymond E. Miles, Henry J. Coleman, Jr., and W. E. Douglas Creed, "Keys to Success in Corporate Redesign," *California Management Review* 37, no. 3 (Spring 1995), 128–145.

66. Fariborz Damanpour and William M. Evan, "Organizational Innovation and Performance: The Problem of 'Organizational Lag,'" *Administrative Science Quarterly* 29 (1984), 392–409; David J. Teece, "The Diffusion of an Administrative Innovation," *Management Science* 26 (1980), 464–470; John R. Kimberly and Michael J. Evaniski, "Organizational Innovation: The Influence of Individual, Organizational and Contextual Factors on Hospital Adoption of Technological and Administrative Innovation," *Academy of Management Journal* 24 (1981), 689–713; Michael K. Moch and Edward V. Morse, "Size, Centralization, and Organizational Adoption of Innovations," *American Sociological Review* 42 (1977), 716–725; and Mary L. Fennell, "Synergy, Influence, and Information in the Adoption of Administrative Innovation," *Academy of Management Journal* 27 (1984), 113–129.

67. Richard L. Daft, "A Dual-Core Model of Organizational Innovation," *Academy of Management Journal* 21 (1978), 193–210.

68. Daft, "Bureaucratic versus Nonbureaucratic Structure"; and Robert W. Zmud, "Diffusion of Modern Software Practices: Influence of Centralization and Formalization," *Management Science* 28 (1982), 1421–1431.

69. Daft, "A Dual-Core Model of Organizational Innovation"; and Zmud, "Diffusion of Modern Software Practices."

70. Fariborz Damanpour, "The Adoption of Technological, Administrative, and Ancillary Innovations: Impact of Organizational Factors," *Journal of Management* 13 (1987), 675–688.

71. Gregory H. Gaertner, Karen N. Gaertner, and David M. Akinnusi, "Environment, Strategy, and the Implementation of Administrative Change: The Case of Civil Service Reform," *Academy of Management Journal* 27 (1984), 525–543.

72. Claudia Bird Schoonhoven and Mariann Jelinek, "Dynamic Tension in Innovative, High Technology Firms: Managing Rapid Technology Change through Organization Structure," in Mary Ann Von Glinow and Susan Albers Mohrman, eds., *Managing Complexity in High Technology Organizations* (New York: Oxford University Press, 1990), 90–118.

73. Pui-Wing Tam, "System Reboot—Hurd's Big Challenge at H-P: Overhauling Corporate Sales," *The Wall Street Journal*

(April 3, 2006), A1; and Don Clark, "PC Market Sends Conflicting Signals; Shift Toward Portables, Consumer Purchases Aid Only Some Makers," *The Wall Street Journal* (April 19, 2007), B3.

74. David Ulm and James K. Hickel, "What Happens after Restructuring?" *Journal of Business Strategy* (July–August 1990), 37–41; and John L. Sprague, "Restructuring and Corporate Renewal: A Manager's Guide," *Management Review* (March 1989), 34–36.

75. Stan Pace, "Rip the Band-Aid Off Quickly," *Strategy & Leadership* 30, no. 1 (2002), 4–9.

76. Benson L. Porter and Warrington S. Parker, Jr., "Culture Change," *Human Resource Management* 31 (Spring–Summer 1992), 45–67.

77. Claudia H. Deutsch, "Paper Jam at FedEx Kinko's," *The New York Times* (May 5, 2007), C1.

78. W. Warner Burke, "The New Agenda for Organization Development," in Wendell L. French, Cecil H. Bell, Jr., and Robert A. Zawacki, *Organization Development and Transformation: Managing Effective Change* (Burr Ridge, Ill.: Irwin McGraw-Hill, 2000), 523–535.

79. W. Warner Burke, *Organization Development: A Process of Learning and Changing*, 2nd ed. (Reading, Mass.: Addison-Wesley, 1994); and Wendell L. French and Cecil H. Bell, Jr., "A History of Organization Development," in French, Bell, and Zawacki, *Organization Development and Transformation*, 20–42.

80. French and Bell, "A History of Organization Development."

81. The information on large group intervention is based on Kathleen D. Dannemiller and Robert W. Jacobs, "Changing the Way Organizations Change: A Revolution of Common Sense," *The Journal of Applied Behavioral Science* 28, no. 4 (December 1992), 480–498; Barbara B. Bunker and Billie T. Alban, "Conclusion: What Makes Large Group Interventions Effective?" *The Journal of Applied Behavioral Science* 28, no. 4 (December 1992), 570–591; and Marvin R. Weisbord, "Inventing the Future: Search Strategies for Whole System Improvements," in French, Bell, and Zawacki, *Organization Development and Transformation*, 242–250.

82. Marvin Weisbord and Sandra Janoff, "Faster, Shorter, Cheaper May Be Simple; It's Never Easy," *The Journal of Applied Behavioral Science* 41, no. 1 (March 2005), 70–82.

83. J. Quinn, "What a Workout!" *Performance* (November 1994), 58–63; and Bunker and Alban, "Conclusion: What Makes Large Group Interventions Effective?"

84. Dave Ulrich, Steve Kerr, and Ron Ashkenas, with Debbie Burke and Patrice Murphy, *The GE Work Out: How to Implement GE's Revolutionary Method for Busting Bureaucracy and Attacking Organizational Problems—Fast!* (New York: McGraw-Hill, 2002).

85. Paul F. Buller, "For Successful Strategic Change: Blend OD Practices with Strategic Management," *Organizational Dynamics* (Winter 1988), 42–55.

86. Norm Brodsky, "Everybody Sells," (Street Smarts column), *Inc.* (June 2004), 53–54.

87. Richard S. Allen and Kendyl A. Montgomery, "Applying an Organizational Development Approach to Creating Diversity," *Organizational Dynamics* 30, no. 2 (2001), 149–161.

88. Jyotsna Sanzgiri and Jonathan Z. Gottlieb, "Philosophic and Pragmatic Influences on the Practice of Organization Development, 1950–2000," *Organizational Dynamics* (Autumn 1992), 57–69.

89. Pierre Loewe and Jennifer Dominiquini, "Overcome the Barriers to Effective Innovation," *Strategy & Leadership* 34, no. 1 (2006), 24–31.

90. Joann S. Lublin, "Career Journal; Managing Your Career: A CEO's Recipe for Fresh Ideas," *The Wall Street Journal* (September 2, 2008), D4.

91. Bernard M. Bass, "Theory of Transformational Leadership Redux," *Leadership Quarterly* 6, no. 4 (1995), 463–478; and Dong I. Jung, Chee Chow, and Anne Wu, "The Role of Transformational Leadership in Enhancing Organizational Innovation: Hypotheses and Some Preliminary Findings," *The Leadership Quarterly* 14 (2003), 525–544.

92. Ronald Recardo, Kathleen Molloy, and James Pellegrino, "How the Learning Organization Manages Change," *National Productivity Review* (Winter 1995/96), 7–13.

93. Based on Daryl R. Conner, *Managing at the Speed of Change* (New York: Villard Books, 1992), 146–160.

94. Peter Drucker, *Management Challenges for the 21st Century* (New York: HarperBusiness, 1999); Tushman and O'Reilly, "Ambidextrous Organizations"; Gary Hamel and C. K. Prahalad, "Seeing the Future First," *Fortune* (September 4, 1994), 64–70; and Linda Yates and Peter Skarzynski, "How Do Companies Get to the Future First?" *Management Review* (January 1999), 16–22.

95. Based in part on Carol A. Beatty and John R. M. Gordon, "Barriers to the Implementation of CAD/CAM Systems," *Sloan Management Review* (Summer 1988), 25–33.

96. These techniques are based on John P. Kotter's eight-stage model of planned organizational change, Kotter, *Leading Change*, 20–25.

97. Everett M. Rogers and Floyd Shoemaker, *Communication of Innovations: A Cross Cultural Approach*, 2nd ed. (New York: Free Press, 1971); and Stratford P. Sherman, "Eight Big Masters of Innovation," *Fortune* (October 15, 1984), 66–84.

98. Richard L. Daft and Selwyn W. Becker, *Innovation in Organizations* (New York: Elsevier, 1978); and John P. Kotter and Leonard A. Schlesinger, "Choosing Strategies for Change," *Harvard Business Review* 57 (1979), 106–114.

99. Jim Cross, "Back to the Future," *Management Review* (February 1999), 50–54.

100. Darren Dahl, "Trust Me: You're Gonna Love This; Getting Employees to Embrace New Technology," *Inc.* (November 2008), 41.

101. Peter Richardson and D. Keith Denton, "Communicating Change," *Human Resource Management* 35, no. 2 (Summer 1996), 203–216.

102. Edgar H. Schein and Warren Bennis, *Personal and Organizational Change via Group Methods* (New York: Wiley, 1965); and Amy Edmondson, "Psychological Safety and Learning Behavior in Work Teams," *Administrative Science Quarterly* 44 (1999), 350–383.

103. Diane L. Coutu, "Creating the Most Frightening Company on Earth; An Interview with Andy Law of St. Luke's," *Harvard Business Review* (September–October 2000), 143–150.

104. Philip H. Mirvis, Amy L. Sales, and Edward J. Hackett, "The Implementation and Adoption of New Technology in Organizations: The Impact on Work, People, and Culture," *Human Resource Management* 30 (Spring 1991), 113–139; Arthur E. Wallach, "System Changes Begin in the Training Department," *Personnel Journal* 58 (1979), 846–848, 872; and Paul R. Lawrence, "How to Deal with Resistance to Change," *Harvard Business Review* 47 (January–February 1969), 4–12, 166–176.

105. Dexter C. Dunphy and Doug A. Stace, "Transformational and Coercive Strategies for Planned Organizational Change: Beyond the O.D Model," *Organizational Studies* 9 (1988), 317–334; and Kotter and Schlesinger, "Choosing Strategies for Change."

106. Lawrence G. Hrebiniak, "Obstacles to Effective Strategy Implementation," *Organizational Dynamics* 35, no. 1 (2006), 12–31.

Chapter 11

1. Leigh Buchanan, "Working Wonders on the Web," *Inc. Magazine* (November 2003), 76–84, 104.

2. James Cox, "Changes at Olive Garden Have Chain Living 'La Dolce Vita,'" *USA Today*, (December 18, 2000), B1; Bernard Wysocki Jr., "Hospitals Cut ER Waits," *The Wall Street Journal* (July 3, 2002), D1, D3.

3. Raymond F. Zammuto, Terri L. Griffith, Ann Majchrzak, Deborah J. Dougherty, and Samer Faraj, "Information Technology and the Changing Fabric of Organization," *Organization Science* 18, no. 5 (September–October 2007), 749–762.

4. Michael Fitzgerald, "A Drive-Through Lane to the Next Time Zone," *The New York Times* (July 18, 2004), Section 3, 3.

5. Erik Berkman, "How to Stay Ahead of the Curve," *CIO* (February 1, 2002), 72–80; and Heather Harreld, "Pick-Up Artists," *CIO* (November 1, 2000), 148–154.

6. "Business Intelligence," special advertising section, *Business 2.0* (February 2003), S1–S4; and Alice Dragoon, "Business Intelligence Gets Smart," *CIO* (September 15, 2003), 84–91.

7. Gary Loveman, "Diamonds in the Data Mine," *Harvard Business Review* (May 2003), 109–113; Joe Ashbrook Nickell, "Welcome to Harrah's," *Business 2.0* (April 2002), 48–54; and Meridith Levinson, "Harrah's Knows What You Did Last Night," *Darwin Magazine* (May 2001), 61–68.

8. Megan Santosus, "Motorola's Semiconductor Products Sector's EIS," Working Smart column, *CIO*, Section 1 (November 15, 1998), 84.

9. Constance L. Hays, "What They Know About You; Wal-Mart—An Obsessive Monitor of Customer Behavior," *The New York Times* (November 14, 2004), Section 3, 1.

10. Andy Neely and Mohammed Al Najjar, "Management Learning, Not Management Control: The True Role of

Performance Measurement," *California Management Review*
48, no. 3 (Spring, 2006), 105.

11. Robert Simons, "Strategic Organizations and Top
Management Attention to Control Systems," *Strategic
Management Journal* 12 (1991), 49–62.

12. Richard L. Daft and Norman B. Macintosh, "The Nature
and Use of Formal Control Systems for Management Control
and Strategy Implementation," *Journal of Management* 10
(1984), 43–66.

13. Susannah Patton, "Web Metrics That Matter," *CIO*
(November 14, 2002), 84–88; and Ramin Jaleshgari,
"The End of the Hit Parade," *CIO* (May 14, 2000),
183–190.

14. Adam Lashinsky, "Meg and the Machine," *Fortune*
(September 1, 2003), 68–78.

15. Reported in Spencer E. Ante, "Giving the Boss the Big
Picture," *BusinessWeek* (February 13, 2006), 48–51.

16. Ante, "Giving the Boss the Big Picture"; Doug Bartholomew,
"Gauging Success," *CFO-IT* (Summer 2005), 17–19; and
Russ Banham, "Seeing the Big Picture: New Data Tools
Are Enabling CEOs to Get a Better Handle on Performance
Across Their Organizations," *Chief Executive* (November
2003), 46.

17. Kevin Ferguson, "Mission Control," *Inc. Magazine* (November
2003), 27–28; and Banham, "Seeing the Big Picture."

18. Carol Hymowitz, "Dashboard Technology: Is It a Helping
Hand or a New Big Brother?" *The Wall Street Journal*
(September 26, 2005), B1; Christopher Koch, "How Verizon
Flies by Wire," *CIO* (November 1, 2004), 94–96.

19. Howard Rothman, "You Need Not Be Big to Benchmark,"
Nation's Business (December 1992), 64–65.

20. Tom Rancour and Mike McCracken, "Applying 6 Sigma
Methods for Breakthrough Safety Performance," *Professional
Safety* 45, no. 10 (October 2000), 29–32; and Lee Clifford,
"Why You Can Safely Ignore Six Sigma," *Fortune*
(January 22, 2001), 140.

21. Michael Hammer and Jeff Goding, "Putting Six Sigma in
Perspective," *Quality* (October 2001), 58–62; and Michael
Hammer, "Process Management and the Future of Six
Sigma," *Sloan Management Review* (Winter 2002), 26–32.

22. Michael Arndt, "Quality Isn't Just for Widgets,"
BusinessWeek (July 22, 2002), 72–73.

23. Daft and Macintosh, "The Nature and Use of Formal
Control Systems for Management Control and Strategy
Implementation"; Scott S. Cowen and J. Kendall
Middaugh II, "Matching an Organization's Planning and
Control System to Its Environment," *Journal of General
Management* 16 (1990), 69–84.

24. "On Balance," a CFO Interview with Robert Kaplan and
David Norton, *CFO* (February 2001), 73–78; Chee W.
Chow, Kamal M. Haddad, and James E. Williamson,
"Applying the Balanced Scorecard to Small Companies,"
Management Accounting 79, no. 2 (August 1997), 21–27;
and Robert Kaplan and David Norton, "The Balanced
Scorecard: Measures That Drive Performance," *Harvard
Business Review* (January–February 1992), 71–79.

25. Based on Kaplan and Norton, "The Balanced Scorecard";
Chow, Haddad, and Williamson, "Applying the Balanced
Scorecard"; and Cathy Lazere, "All Together Now," *CFO*
(February 1998), 28–36.

26. Nils–Göran Olve, Carl-Johan Petri, Jan Roy, and Sofie Roy,
"Twelve Years Later: Understanding and Realizing the Value
of Balanced Scorecards," *Ivey Business Journal* (May–June
2004), 1–7.

27. Geary A. Rummler and Kimberly Morrill, "The Results
Chain," *TD* (February 2005), 27–35; and John C. Crotts,
Duncan R. Dickson, and Robert C. Ford, "Aligning
Organizational Processes with Mission: The Case of Service
Excellence," *Academy of Management Executive* 19, no. 3
(August 2005), 54–68.

28. This discussion is based on Robert S. Kaplan and
David P. Norton, "Mastering the Management System,"
Harvard Business Review (January 2008), 63–77; and
Robert S. Kaplan and David P. Norton, "Having Trouble
with Your Strategy? Then Map It," *Harvard Business
Review* (September–October 2000), 167–176.

29. This discussion of behavior versus outcome control is based
on Erin Anderson and Vincent Onyemah, "How Right
Should the Customer Be?" *Harvard Business Review*
(July–August 2006), 59–67.

30. Pui-Wing Tam, Erin White, Nick Wingfield, and Kris Maher,
"Snooping E-Mail by Software Is Now a Workplace Norm,"
The Wall Street Journal (March 9, 2005), B1; Jennifer S. Lee,
"Tracking Sales and the Cashiers," *The New York Times*
(July 11, 2001), C1, C6; Kris Maher, "At Verizon Call
Center, Stress Is Seldom on Hold," *The Wall Street Journal*
(January 16, 2001), B1, B12; Anna Wilde Matthews, "New
Gadgets Track Truckers' Every Move," *The Wall Street
Journal* (July 14, 1997), B1, B10.

31. Bill Ward, "Power to the People: Thanks to a Revolutionary
Program Called ROWE, Best Buy Employees Can Lead
Lives—Professional and Personal—On Their Own Terms,"
Star Tribune (June 1, 2008), E1; Michelle Conlin, "Smashing
the Clock," *BusinessWeek* (December 11, 2006), 60ff; and
Jyoti Thottam, "Reworking Work," *Time* (July 25, 2005),
50–55.

32. Conlin, "Smashing the Clock."

33. Melanie Warner, "Under the Knife," *Business 2.0* (January–
February 2004), 84–89.

34. Wayne Kawamoto, "Click Here for Efficiency," *BusinessWeek
Enterprise* (December 7, 1998), Ent. 12–Ent. 14.

35. "Building the Web 2.0 Enterprise: McKinsey Global Survey
Results," *The McKinsey Quarterly* (July 2008) http://
www.mckinseyquarterly.com.

36. Cindy Waxer, "Workers of the World—Collaborate," *FSB*
(April 2005), 57–58.

37. Based on Anya Kamenetz, "The Network Unbound" *Fast
Company* (June 2006), 68–73.

38. Brad Stone, "Facebook Goes Off the Campus," *The New
York Times* (May 25, 2007), C1; and Heather Green,
"The Water Cooler Is Now on the Web," *BusinessWeek*
(October 1, 2007), 78.

39. "Building the Web 2.0 Enterprise: McKinsey Global Survey
Results."

40. Based on Andrew Mayo, "Memory Bankers" *People
Management* (January 22, 1998), 34–38; William Miller,
"Building the Ultimate Resource," *Management Review*
(January 1999), 42–45; and Todd Datz, "How to Speak
Geek," *CIO Enterprise*, Section 2 (April 15, 1999),
46–52.

41. The discussion of explicit versus tacit knowledge is based on Ikujiro Nonaka and Hirotaka Takeuchi, *The Knowledge-Creating Company: How Japanese Companies Create the Dynamics of Innovation* (New York: Oxford University Press, 1995), 8–9; Robert M. Grant, "Toward a Knowledge-Based Theory of the Firm," *Strategic Management Journal* 17 (Winter 1996), 109–122; and Martin Schulz, "The Uncertain Relevance of Newness: Organizational Learning and Knowledge Flows," *Academy of Management Journal* 44, no. 4 (2001), 661–681.

42. C. Jackson Grayson, Jr., and Carla S. O'Dell, "Mining Your Hidden Resources," *Across the Board* (April 1998), 23–28.

43. Based on Morten T. Hansen, Nitin Nohria, and Thomas Tierney, "What's Your Strategy for Managing Knowledge?" *Harvard Business Review* (March–April 1999), 106–116.

44. Kelly K. Spors, "Getting Workers to Share Their Know-How with Peers," *The Wall Street Journal* (April 3, 2008), B6.

45. Derek Slater, "What Is ERP?" *CIO Enterprise*, Section 2 (May 15, 1999), 86; and Jeffrey Zygmont, "The Ties That Bind," *Inc. Tech* no. 3 (1998), 70–84.

46. Vincent A. Mabert, Ashok Soni, and M. A. Venkataramanan, "Enterprise Resource Planning: Common Myths versus Evolving Reality," *Business Horizons* (May–June 2001), 69–76.

47. Slater, "What Is ERP?"

48. Zammuto et al., "Information Technology and the Changing Fabric of Organization."

49. Steven A. Melnyk and David R. Denzler, *Operations Management: A Value-Driven Approach* (Burr Ridge, Ill.: Richard D. Irwin, 1996), 613.

50. Jim Turcotte, Bob Silveri, and Tom Jobson, "Are You Ready for the E-Supply Chain?" *APICS–The Performance Advantage* (August 1998), 56–59.

51. Sandra Swanson, "Get Together," *Information Week* (July 1, 2002), 47–48.

52. Bill Richards, "Superplant," *eCompany* (November 2000), 182–196.

53. Brian Caulfield, "Facing Up to CRM," *Business 2.0* (August–September 2001), 149–150; and "Customer Relationship Management: The Good, The Bad, The Future," special advertising section, *BusinessWeek* (April 28, 2003), 53–64.

54. "Building the Web 2.0 Enterprise: McKinsey Global Survey Results."

55. Merissa Marr, "Updated Disney.com Offers Networking for Kids; Web Site's Strategic Revamp Encourages More Interaction—But Parents Will Be in Charge," *The Wall Street Journal* (January 2, 2007), B1.

56. Fortune 500 Business Blogging Wiki, *http://www.socialtext.net/bizblogs/index.cgi*, accessed on October 20, 2008.

57. Interview with Jonathan Schwartz by Oliver Ryan, "Blogger in Chief," *Fortune* (November 13, 2006), 51.

58. Christopher Barnatt, "Embracing E-Business," *Journal of General Management* 30, no. 1 (Autumn 2004), 79–96.

59. This discussion is based on Ranjay Gulati and Jason Garino, "Get the Right Mix of Bricks and Clicks," *Harvard Business Review* (May–June 2000), 107–114.

60. Bob Tedeschi, "Retailer's Shortcut from Desktop to Store," *The New York Times* (September 24, 2007), C6; Marr, "Updated Disney.com Offers Networking for Kids"; John Heilemann, "All the News That's Fit for Bits," *Business 2.0* (September 2006), 40–43.

61. George Westerman, F. Warren McFarlan, and Marco Iansiti, "Organization Design and Effectiveness Over the Innovation Life Cycle," *Organization Science* 17, no. 2 (March–April 2006), 230–238.

62. Andrew Blackman, "A Strong Net Game," *The Wall Street Journal* (October 25, 2004), R1, R11.

63. Zammuto et al., "Information Technology and the Changing Fabric of Organization."

64. Stephanie Overby, "Paving over Paperwork," *CIO* (February 1, 2002), 82–86.

65. Siobhan O'Mahony and Stephen R. Barley, "Do Digital Telecommunications Affect Work and Organization? The State of Our Knowledge," *Research in Organizational Behavior* 21 (1999), 125–161.

66. Robert D. Hof, "The End of Work As You Know It," (The Future of Work: Technology on the March section), *BusinessWeek* (August 20, 2007), 80–83.

67. "Big and No Longer Blue," *The Economist* (January 21–27, 2006), *http://www.economist.com*.

68. "Mandate 2003: Be Agile and Efficient," *Microsoft Executive Circle* (Spring 2003), 46–48.

69. Jenny C. McCune, "Thirst for Knowledge," *Management Review* (April 1999), 10–12.

70. O'Mahony and Barley, "Do Digital Telecommunications Affect Work and Organization?"

71. Michael A. Fontaine, Salvatore Parise, and David Miller, "Collaborative Environments: An Effective Tool for Transforming Business Processes," *Ivey Business Journal* (May–June 2004).

72. Joanne Lee-Young and Megan Barnett, "Furiously Fast Fashions," *The Industry Standard* (June 11, 2001), 72–79.

Chapter 12

1. Julie Bosman, "Will Size Spoil a Cheeky Ad Agency?" *The New York Times* (November 7, 2005), C1.

2. James Q. Wilson, *Bureaucracy* (New York: Basic Books, 1989); and Charles Perrow, *Complex Organizations: A Critical Essay* (Glenview, Ill.: Scott, Foresman, 1979), 4.

3. Tom Peters, "Rethinking Scale," *California Management Review* (Fall 1992), 7–29.

4. These analogies are from Jerry Useem, "The Big … Get Bigger," *Fortune* (April 30, 2007), 81–84.

5. Donald V. Potter, "Scale Matters," *Across the Board* (July–August 2000), 36–39.

6. Kris Hudson, "Wal-Mart Sticks with Fast Pace of Expansion Despite Toll on Sales," *The Wall Street Journal* (April 13, 2006), A1.

7. James B. Treece, "Sometimes, You Still Gotta Have Size," *BusinessWeek* (October 22, 1993), 200–201.

8. Matthew L. Wald, "What's So Bad About Big?" *The New York Times* (March 7, 2007), H1.

9. Nelson D. Schwartz, "Is G.E. Too Big for Its Own Good?" *The New York Times* (July 22, 2007), Section 3, 1.

10. Alan Murray, "The Profit Motive Has a Limit: Tragedy," *The Wall Street Journal* (September 7, 2005), A2.

11. John A. Byrne and Heather Timmons, "Tough Times for a New CEO," *BusinessWeek* (October 29, 2001), 64–70; and Patrick McGeehan, "Sailing Into a Sea of Trouble," *The New York Times* (October 5, 2001), C1, C4.

12. Frits K. Pil and Matthias Holweg, "Exploring Scale: The Advantages of Thinking Small," *MIT Sloan Management Review* (Winter 2003), 33–39; and David Sadtler, "The Problem with Size," *Management Today* (November 2007), 52–55.

13. Chip Jarnagan and John W. Slocum, Jr., "Creating Corporate Cultures Through Mythopoetic Leadership," *Organizational Dynamics* 36, no. 3 (2007), 288–302.

14. Keith H. Hammonds, "Size Is Not a Strategy," *Fast Company* (September 2002), 78–86.

15. See Hammonds, "Size Is Not a Strategy"; David Henry, "Mergers: Why Most Big Deals Don't Pay Off," *BusinessWeek* (October 14, 2002), 60–70; and Tom Brown, "How Big Is Too Big?" *Across the Board* (July–August 1999), 15–20, for a discussion.

16. Leslie Taylor, "Number of Small Businesses Reaches All-Time High," *Inc.*, http://www.inc.com/news/articles/200612/sba.html, accessed on October 24, 2008.

17. "The Hot 100," *Fortune* (September 5, 2005), 75–80.

18. Sadtler, "The Problem with Size."

19. Gary Hamel, quoted in Hammonds, "Size Is Not a Strategy."

20. "Company Structure," Johnson & Johnson website; http://www.jnj.com/connect/about-jnj/company-structure/, accessed on October 24, 2008.

21. Michael Barone, "Not a Victory for Big Government," *The Wall Street Journal* (January 15, 2002), A16.

22. Useem, "The Big ... Get Bigger."

23. Hammonds, "Size Is Not a Strategy."

24. John R. Kimberly, Robert H. Miles, and associates, *The Organizational Life Cycle* (San Francisco: Jossey-Bass, 1980); Ichak Adices, "Organizational Passages—Diagnosing and Treating Lifecycle Problems of Organizations," *Organizational Dynamics* (Summer 1979), 3–25; Danny Miller and Peter H. Friesen, "A Longitudinal Study of the Corporate Life Cycle," *Management Science* 30 (October 1984), 1161–1183; and Neil C. Churchill and Virginia L. Lewis, "The Five Stages of Small Business Growth," *Harvard Business Review* 61 (May–June 1983), 30–50.

25. Larry E. Greiner, "Evolution and Revolution as Organizations Grow," *Harvard Business Review* 50 (July–August 1972), 37–46; and Robert E. Quinn and Kim Cameron, "Organizational Life Cycles and Shifting Criteria of Effectiveness: Some Preliminary Evidence," *Management Science* 29 (1983), 33–51.

26. George Land and Beth Jarman, "Moving beyond Breakpoint," in Michael Ray and Alan Rinzler, eds., *The New Paradigm* (New York: Jeremy P. Tarcher/Perigee Books, 1993), 250–266; and Michael L. Tushman,

William H. Newman, and Elaine Romanelli, "Convergence and Upheaval: Managing the Unsteady Pace of Organizational Evolution," *California Management Review* 29 (1987), 1–16.

27. Peter Meyers, "Fact-Driven? Collegial? This Site Wants You," *The New York Times* (September 20, 2001), G2; "Jimmy Wales" biography, *Wikipedia* http://en.wikipedia.org/wiki/Jimmy_Wales, accessed on October 24, 2008; and Noam Cohen, "Open-Source Trouble in Wiki World," *The New York Times* (March 17, 2008), C1.

28. Vauhini Vara, "Facebook CEO Seeks Help as Site Grows—Google Veteran to Be Zuckerberg's No. 2," *The Wall Street Journal* (March 5, 2008), A1.

29. David A. Whetten, "Sources, Responses, and Effects of Organizational Decline," in Kimberly, Miles, and associates, *The Organizational Life Cycle*, 342–374.

30. Brent Schlender, "How Big Can Apple Get?" *Fortune* (February 21, 2005), 67–76; and Josh Quittner with Rebecca Winters, "Apple's New Core—Exclusive: How Steve Jobs Made a Sleek Machine That Could Be the Home-Digital Hub of the Future," *Time* (January 14, 2002), 46.

31. Nick Wingfield, "Apple's No. 2 Has Low Profile, High Impact," *The Wall Street Journal* (October 16, 2006), B1, B9.

32. Land and Jarman, "Moving beyond Breakpoint."

33. Gary Rivlin, "A Retail Revolution Turns 10," *The New York Times* (July 10, 2005), Section 3, 1.

34. Max Weber, *The Theory of Social and Economic Organizations*, translated by A. M. Henderson and T. Parsons (New York: Free Press, 1947).

35. Larry Rohter and Juan Forero, "Unending Graft Is Threatening Latin America," *The New York Times* (July 30, 2005), A1.

36. John Crewdson, "Corruption Viewed as a Way of Life," *Bryan College Station Eagle* (November 28, 1982), 13A; Barry Kramer, "Chinese Officials Still Give Preference to Kin, Despite Peking Policies," *The Wall Street Journal* (October 29, 1985), 1, 21.

37. John Chase, "Delay Requested for Indictment; 3 More Months Sought in Case against Governor," *The Chicago Tribune* (January 1, 2009), 4.

38. Eric J. Walton, "The Persistence of Bureaucracy: A Meta-analysis of Weber's Model of Bureaucratic Control," *Organization Studies* 26, no. 4 (2005), 569–600.

39. Nadira A. Hira, "The Making of a UPS Driver," *Fortune* (November 12, 2007), 118–129; David J. Lynch, "Thanks to Its CEO, UPS Doesn't Just Deliver," *USA Today* (July 24, 2006), http://www.usatoday.com/money/companies/management/2006-07-23-ups_x.htm?tab1=t2, accessed on July 24, 2006; Kelly Barron, "Logistics in Brown," *Forbes* (January 10, 2000), 78–83; Scott Kirsner, "Venture Vèritè: United Parcel Service," *Wired* (September 1999), 83–96; Kathy Goode, Betty Hahn, and Cindy Seibert, *United Parcel Service: The Brown Giant* (unpublished manuscript, Texas A&M University, 1981); and "About UPS," UPS Corporate Website, http://www.ups.com/content/corp/about/index.html?WT.svl=SubNav, accessed on October 27, 2008.

40. Allen C. Bluedorn, "Pilgrim's Progress: Trends and Convergence in Research on Organizational Size and

Environment," *Journal of Management Studies* 19 (Summer 1993), 163–191; John R. Kimberly, "Organizational Size and the Structuralist Perspective: A Review, Critique, and Proposal," *Administrative Science Quarterly* (1976), 571–597; and Richard L. Daft and Selwyn W. Becker, "Managerial, Institutional, and Technical Influences on Administration: A Longitudinal Analysis," *Social Forces* 59 (1980), 392–413.

41. James P. Walsh and Robert D. Dewar, "Formalization and the Organizational Life Cycle," *Journal of Management Studies* 24 (May 1987), 215–231.

42. Nancy M. Carter and Thomas L. Keon, "Specialization as a Multidimensional Construct," *Journal of Management Studies* 26 (1989), 11–28; Cheng-Kuang Hsu, Robert M. March, and Hiroshi Mannari, "An Examination of the Determinants of Organizational Structure," *American Journal of Sociology* 88 (1983), 975–996; Guy Geeraerts, "The Effect of Ownership on the Organization Structure in Small Firms," *Administrative Science Quarterly* 29 (1984), 232–237; Bernard Reimann, "On the Dimensions of Bureaucratic Structure: An Empirical Reappraisal," *Administrative Science Quarterly* 18 (1973), 462–476; Richard H. Hall, "The Concept of Bureaucracy: An Empirical Assessment," *American Journal of Sociology* 69 (1963), 32–40; and William A. Rushing, "Organizational Rules and Surveillance: A Proposition in Comparative Organizational Analysis," *Administrative Science Quarterly* 10 (1966), 423–443.

43. Jerald Hage and Michael Aiken, "Relationship of Centralization to Other Structural Properties," *Administrative Science Quarterly* 12 (1967), 72–91.

44. Peter Brimelow, "How Do You Cure Injelitance?" *Forbes* (August 7, 1989), 42–44; Jeffrey D. Ford and John W. Slocum, Jr., "Size, Technology, Environment and the Structure of Organizations," *Academy of Management Review* 2 (1977), 561–575; and John D. Kasarda, "The Structural Implications of Social System Size: A Three-Level Analysis," *American Sociological Review* 39 (1974), 19–28.

45. Graham Astley, "Organizational Size and Bureaucratic Structure," *Organization Studies* 6 (1985), 201–228; Spyros K. Lioukas and Demitris A. Xerokostas, "Size and Administrative Intensity in Organizational Divisions," *Management Science* 28 (1982), 854–868; Peter M. Blau, "Interdependence and Hierarchy in Organizations," *Social Science Research* 1 (1972), 1–24; Peter M. Blau and R. A. Schoenherr, *The Structure of Organizations* (New York: Basic Books, 1971); A. Hawley, W. Boland, and M. Boland, "Population Size and Administration in Institutions of Higher Education," *American Sociological Review* 30 (1965), 252–255; Richard L. Daft, "System Influence on Organization Decision-Making: The Case of Resource Allocation," *Academy of Management Journal* 21 (1978), 6–22; and B. P. Indik, "The Relationship between Organization Size and the Supervisory Ratio," *Administrative Science Quarterly* 9 (1964), 301–312.

46. T. F. James, "The Administrative Component in Complex Organizations," *Sociological Quarterly* 13 (1972), 533–539; Daft, "System Influence on Organization Decision Making"; E. A. Holdaway and E. A. Blowers, "Administrative Ratios and Organization Size: A Longitudinal Examination,"

American Sociological Review 36 (1971), 278–286; and John Child, "Parkinson's Progress: Accounting for the Number of Specialists in Organizations," *Administrative Science Quarterly* 18 (1973), 328–348.

47. Richard L. Daft and Selwyn Becker, "School District Size and the Development of Personnel Resources," *Alberta Journal of Educational Research* 24 (1978), 173–187.

48. Thomas A. Stewart, "Yikes! Deadwood Is Creeping Back," *Fortune* (August 18, 1997), 221–222.

49. Based on Gifford and Elizabeth Pinchot, *The End of Bureaucracy and the Rise of the Intelligent Organization* (San Francisco: Berrett-Koehler Publishers, 1993), 21–29.

50. Victoria Murphy, "Microsoft's Midlife Crisis," *Forbes* (October 3, 2005), 88.

51. Ron Ashkenas, "Simplicity-Minded Management," *Harvard Business Review* (December 2007), 101–109.

52. Jack Rosenthal, "Entitled: A Chief for Every Occasion, and Even a Chief Chief," *New York Times Magazine* (August 26, 2001), 16.

53. Scott Shane, "The Beast That Feeds on Boxes: Bureaucracy," *The New York Times* (April 10, 2005), Section 4, 3.

54. Gregory A. Bigley and Karlene H. Roberts, "The Incident Command System: High-Reliability Organizing for Complex and Volatile Task Environments," *Academy of Management Journal* 44, no. 6 (2001), 1281–1299.

55. Robert A. Watson and Ben Brown, *The Most Effective Organization in the U.S.: Leadership Secrets of the Salvation Army* (New York: Crown Business, 2001), 159–181.

56. Capt. (Sel) Adam S. Levitt, USN, "Final Report: Sun Microsystems, Inc.," Secretary of Defense Corporate Fellows Program (June 2003).

57. Cathy Lazere, "Resisting Temptation: The Fourth Annual SG&A Survey," *CFO* (December 1997), 64–70.

58. Jeanne Whalen, "Bureaucracy Buster? Glaxo Lets Scientists Choose Its New Drugs," *The Wall Street Journal* (March 27, 2006), B1.

59. Philip M. Padsakoff, Larry J. Williams, and William D. Todor, "Effects of Organizational Formalization on Alienation among Professionals and Nonprofessionals," *Academy of Management Journal* 29 (1986), 820–831.

60. Royston Greenwood, C. R. Hinings, and John Brown, "'P2-Form' Strategic Management: Corporate Practices in Professional Partnerships," *Academy of Management Journal* 33 (1990), 725–755; and Royston Greenwood and C. R. Hinings, "Understanding Strategic Change: The Contribution of Archetypes," *Academy of Management Journal* 36 (1993), 1052–1081.

61. William G. Ouchi, "Markets, Bureaucracies, and Clans," *Administrative Science Quarterly* 25 (1980), 129–141; idem, "A Conceptual Framework for the Design of Organizational Control Mechanisms," *Management Science* 25 (1979), 833–848.

62. Weber, *The Theory of Social and Economic Organizations*, 328–340.

63. Oliver A. Williamson, *Markets and Hierarchies: Analyses and Antitrust Implications* (New York: Free Press, 1975).

64. David Wessel and John Harwood, "Capitalism Is Giddy with Triumph: Is It Possible to Overdo It?" *The Wall Street Journal* (May 14, 1998), A1, A10.

65. Anita Micossi, "Creating Internal Markets," *Enterprise* (April 1994), 43–44.

66. Raymond E. Miles, Henry J. Coleman, Jr., and W. E. Douglas Creed, "Keys to Success in Corporate Redesign," *California Management Review* 37, no. 3 (Spring 1995), 128–145.

67. Ouchi, "Markets, Bureaucracies, and Clans."

68. Jeffrey Kerr and John W. Slocum, Jr., "Managing Corporate Culture Through Reward Systems," *Academy of Management Executive* 19, no. 4 (2005), 130–138.

69. Richard Leifer and Peter K. Mills, "An Information Processing Approach for Deciding upon Control Strategies and Reducing Control Loss in Emerging Organizations," *Journal of Management* 22, no. 1 (1996), 113–137.

70. Stratford Sherman, "The New Computer Revolution," *Fortune* (June 14, 1993), 56–80.

71. Melanie Trottman, "New Atmosphere Inside Southwest Airlines; Storied Culture Feels Strain," *The Wall Street Journal* (July 11, 2003), A1, A6; Scott McCartney, "The Middle Seat: The Airline Champ of 2007; In Dismal Year, Southwest Scored; American Struggled," *The Wall Street Journal* (February 5, 2008), D4; Melanie Trottman, "New Route: As Competition Rebounds, Southwest Faces Squeeze; Growth Hits Turbulence for Low-Cost Pioneer," *The Wall Street Journal* (June 27, 2007), A1; "Major Airlines of the World; The World's Biggest Airlines," *http://www.nationsonline.org/oneworld/major_airlines.htm*, accessed on October 29, 2008; and "Southwest Airlines Reports Fourth Quarter Earnings and 35th Consecutive Year of Profitability," *Smart Brief* (January 23, 2008), *http://www.smartbrief.com/news/aia/industryPR-detail.jsp?id=B276A381-7625-4A27-B63E-A6064AC065CE*, accessed on October 29, 2008.

72. Leifer and Mills, "An Information Processing Approach for Deciding upon Control Strategies"; and Laurie J. Kirsch, "The Management of Complex Tasks in Organizations: Controlling the Systems Development Process," *Organization Science* 7, no. 1 (January–February 1996), 1–21.

73. James R. Barker, "Tightening the Iron Cage: Concertive Control in Self-Managing Teams," *Administrative Science Quarterly* 38 (1993), 408–437.

74. Lee Hawkins Jr., "Lost in Transmission – Behind GM's Slide: Bosses Misjudged New Urban Tastes; Local Dealers, Managers Tried Alerting Staid Bureaucracy," *The Wall Street Journal* (March 8, 2006), A1.

75. Geoff Colvin and Katie Benner, "GE Under Siege," *Fortune* (October 27, 2008), 84–94.

76. Claudia H. Deutsch, "In 2007, Some Giants Went Smaller," *The New York Times* (January 1, 2008), C1; Janet Adamy, "Starbucks to Shut 500 More Stores, Cut Jobs," *The Wall Street Journal* (July 2, 2008), B1.

77. Kim S. Cameron, Myung Kim, and David A. Whetten, "Organizational Effects of Decline and Turbulence," *Administrative Science Quarterly* 32 (1987), 222–240.

78. Danny Miller, "What Happens after Success: The Perils of Excellence," *Journal of Management Studies* 31, no. 3 (May 1994), 325–358.

79. Leonard Greenhalgh, "Organizational Decline," in Samuel B. Bacharach, ed., *Research in the Sociology of Organizations* 2 (Greenwich, Conn.: JAI Press, 1983), 231–276; and Peter Lorange and Robert T. Nelson, "How to Recognize—and Avoid—Organizational Decline," *Sloan Management Review* (Spring 1987), 41–48.

80. Kim S. Cameron and Raymond Zammuto, "Matching Managerial Strategies to Conditions of Decline," *Human Resources Management* 22 (1983), 359–375; and Leonard Greenhalgh, Anne T. Lawrence, and Robert I. Sutton, "Determinants of Workforce Reduction Strategies in Organizations," *Academy of Management Review* 13 (1988), 241–254.

81. Stephanie Strom, "Short on Fund-Raising, Red Cross Will Cut Jobs," *The New York Times* (January 16, 2008), A15.

82. Timothy Aeppel, "Die Is Cast; Toolmakers Know Precisely What's the Problem: Price," *The Wall Street Journal* (November 21, 2003), A1, A6; "NTMA Urges Congress to Level the Playing Field for U.S. Manufacturers," National Tooling and Machining Association press release (June 21, 2007), *https://www.ntma.org/eweb/Dynamicpage.aspx?webcode=PRTemplate&wps_key=17e03068-0ad9-4-ef5-ae50-779610c5f025&post_year=2007&post_month_name=Jun*, accessed on October 29, 2008.

83. William Weitzel and Ellen Jonsson, "Reversing the Downward Spiral: Lessons from W. T. Grant and Sears Roebuck," *Academy of Management Executive* 5 (1991), 7–21; and William Weitzel and Ellen Jonsson, "Decline in Organizations: A Literature Integration and Extension," *Administrative Science Quarterly* 34 (1989), 91–109.

84. Linda Tischler, "Herman Miller's Leap of Faith," *Fast Company* (June 2006), 52–57; Paul Keegan, "Behold, the New Throne of the Techie," *Fortune* (October 13, 2008), 62, 64; Reena Jana, "Herman Miller's Clinical Trials," *BusinessWeek* (June 16, 2008); 60ff; and Julia Bauer, "Herman Miller Keeps It Upbeat; Sales, Profits Exceed Forecast for Quarter, Fiscal Year," *The Grand Rapids Press* (June 26, 2008), C1.

85. William McKinley, Carol M. Sanchez, and Allen G. Schick, "Organizational Downsizing: Constraining, Cloning, Learning," *Academy of Management Executive* 9, no. 3 (1995), 32–42.

86. Gregory B. Northcraft and Margaret A. Neale, *Organizational Behavior: A Management Challenge*, 2nd ed. (Fort Worth, Tex: The Dryden Press, 1994), 626; and A. Catherine Higgs, "Executive Commentary" on McKinley, Sanchez, and Schick, "Organizational Downsizing: Constraining, Cloning, Learning," *Academy of Management Executive* 9, no. 3 (1995), 43–44.

87. Wayne Cascio, "Strategies for Responsible Restructuring," *Academy of Management Executive* 16, no. 3 (2002), 80–91; James R. Morris, Wayne F. Cascio, and Clifford E. Young, "Downsizing after All These Years: Questions and Answers about Who Did It, How Many Did It, and Who Benefited from It," *Organizational Dynamics* (Winter 1999), 78–86; Stephen Doerflein and James Atsaides, "Corporate Psychology: Making Downsizing Work," *Electrical World* (September–October 1999), 41–43; and Brett C. Luthans and Steven M. Sommer, "The Impact of Downsizing on Workplace Attitudes," *Group and Organization Management* 2, no. 1 (1999), 46–70.

88. These techniques are based on Mitchell Lee Marks and Kenneth P. De Meuse, "Resizing the Organization: Maximizing the Gain While Minimizing the Pain of Layoffs,

Divestitures, and Closings," *Organizational Dynamics* 34, no. 2 (2005), 19–35; Bob Nelson, "The Care of the Un-Downsized," *Training and Development* (April 1997), 40–43; Shari Caudron, "Teach Downsizing Survivors How to Thrive," *Personnel Journal* (January 1996), 38; Joel Brockner, "Managing the Effects of Layoffs on Survivors," *California Management Review* (Winter 1992), 9–28; Ronald Henkoff, "Getting beyond Downsizing," *Fortune* (January 10, 1994), 58–64; Kim S. Cameron, "Strategies for Successful Organizational Downsizing," *Human Resource Management* 33, no. 2 (Summer 1994), 189–211; and Doerflein and Atsaides, "Corporate Psychology: Making Downsizing Work."

89. Matt Murray, "Stress Mounts as More Firms Announce Large Layoffs, But Don't Say Who or When" (Your Career Matters column), *The Wall Street Journal* (March 13, 2001), B1, B12.

90. Bill Vlasic, "Ford Is Pushing Buyout Offers to Its Workers," *The New York Times* (February 26, 2008), A1; and Jena McGregor, "Rocky Mountain High," and sidebar, "Downsizing Decently," *Fast Company* (July 2004), 58ff.

91. Joann S. Lublin, "Theory & Practice: Employers See Value in Helping Those Laid Off; Some Firms Continue Access to Programs That Assist Workers," *The Wall Street Journal* (September 24, 2007), B3.

92. Marks and De Meuse, "Resizing the Organization."

93. Example from Caudron, "Teach Downsizing Survivors How to Thrive."

Chapter 13

1. Reported in Dale Buss, "The New Look of American Manufacturing," *Chief Executive* (June 2006), 22–27.

2. Gene Bylinsky, "Heroes of Manufacturing," *Fortune* (March 8, 2004), 190[B]–190[H].

3. Charles Perrow, "A Framework for the Comparative Analysis of Organizations," *American Sociological Review* 32 (1967), 194–208; and R. J. Schonberger, *World Class Manufacturing: The Next Decade* (New York: The Free Press, 1996).

4. Wanda J. Orlikowski, "The Duality of Technology: Rethinking the Concept of Technology in Organizations," *Organization Science* 3 (1992), 398–427.

5. Linda Argote, "Input Uncertainty and Organizational Coordination in Hospital Emergency Units," *Administrative Science Quarterly* 27 (1982), 420–434; Charles Perrow, *Organizational Analysis: A Sociological Approach* (Belmont, Calif.: Wadsworth, 1970); and William Rushing, "Hardness of Material as Related to the Division of Labor in Manufacturing Industries," *Administrative Science Quarterly* 13 (1968), 229–245.

6. Lawrence B. Mohr, "Organizational Technology and Organization Structure," *Administrative Science Quarterly* 16 (1971), 444–459; and David Hickson, Derek Pugh, and Diana Pheysey, "Operations Technology and Organization Structure: An Empirical Reappraisal," *Administrative Science Quarterly* 14 (1969), 378–397.

7. Joan Woodward, *Industrial Organization: Theory and Practice* (London: Oxford University Press, 1965); and Joan Woodward, *Management and Technology* (London: Her Majesty's Stationery Office, 1958).

8. Hickson, Pugh, and Pheysey, "Operations Technology and Organization Structure"; and James D. Thompson, *Organizations in Action* (New York: McGraw-Hill, 1967).

9. Edward Harvey, "Technology and the Structure of Organizations," *American Sociological Review* 33 (1968), 241–259.

10. Based on Woodward, *Industrial Organization* and *Management and Technology*.

11. Christina Passariello, "Brand-New Bag: Louis Vuitton Tried Modern Methods on Factory Lines—For Craftsmen, Multitasking Replaces Specialization," *The Wall Street Journal* (October 9, 2006), A1.

12. Philip Siekman, "A Big Maker of Tiny Batches," *Fortune* (May 27, 2002), 152[A]–152[H].

13. Woodward, *Industrial Organization*, vi.

14. William L. Zwerman, *New Perspectives on Organizational Theory* (Westport, Conn.: Greenwood, 1970); and Harvey, "Technology and the Structure of Organizations."

15. Dean M. Schroeder, Steven W. Congden, and C. Gopinath, "Linking Competitive Strategy and Manufacturing Process Technology," *Journal of Management Studies* 32, no. 2 (March 1995), 163–189.

16. Gene Bylinsky, "Heroes of U.S. Manufacturing," *Fortune* (March 18, 2002), 130[A]–130[L].

17. Fernando F. Suarez, Michael A. Cusumano, and Charles H. Fine, "An Empirical Study of Flexibility in Manufacturing," *Sloan Management Review* (Fall 1995), 25–32.

18. Raymond F. Zammuto and Edward J. O'Connor, "Gaining Advanced Manufacturing Technologies' Benefits: The Roles of Organization Design and Culture," *Academy of Management Review* 17, no. 4 (1992), 701–728; and Schroeder, Congden, and Gopinath, "Linking Competitive Strategy and Manufacturing Process Technology."

19. John S. McClenahen, "Bearing Necessitites," *Industry Week* (October 2004), 63–65.

20. Gene Bylinsky, "Elite Factories," *Fortune*, special section, "Industrial Management and Technology" (September 1, 2003), 154[B]–154[J].

21. Jack R. Meredith, "The Strategic Advantages of the Factory of the Future," *California Management Review* 29 (Spring 1987), 27–41; Jack Meredith, "The Strategic Advantages of the New Manufacturing Technologies for Small Firms," *Strategic Management Journal* 8 (1987), 249–258; and Althea Jones and Terry Webb, "Introducing Computer Integrated Manufacturing," *Journal of General Management* 12 (Summer 1987), 60–74.

22. Zammuto and O'Connor, "Gaining Advanced Manufacturing Technologies' Benefits."

23. Paul S. Adler, "Managing Flexible Automation," *California Management Review* (Spring 1988), 34–56.

24. Bela Gold, "Computerization in Domestic and International Manufacturing," *California Management Review* (Winter 1989), 129–143.

25. Graham Dudley and John Hassard, "Design Issues in the Development of Computer Integrated Manufacturing (CIM)," *Journal of General Management* 16 (1990), 43–53.

26. Ibid; and Tom Massung, "Manufacturing Efficiency," *Microsoft Executive Circle* (Winter 2004), 28–29.

27. Grainger David, "One Truck a Minute," *Fortune* (April 5, 2004), 252-258; and Scott McMurray, "Ford F-150: Have It Your Way," *Business 2.0* (March 2004), 53–55.

28. Kate Linebaugh, "Honda's Flexible Plants Provide Edge; Company Can Rejigger Vehicle Output to Match Consumer Demand Faster Than Its Rivals," *The Wall Street Journal* (September 23, 2008), B1.

29. 2006 Census of Manufacturers, reported in "Lean Choices," sidebar in Jonathan Katz, "Back to School," *Industry Week* (May 2007), 14.

30. Jeffrey K. Liker and James M. Morgan, "The Toyota Way in Services: The Case of Lean Product Development," *Academy of Management Perspectives* (May 2006), 5–20; and Brian Heymans, "Leading the Lean Enterprise," *Industrial Management* (September–October 2002), 28–33.

31. Kenji Hall, "No One Does Lean Like the Japanese," *BusinessWeek* (July 10, 2006), 40–41.

32. Peter Strozniak, "Toyota Alters Face of Production," *IndustryWeek* (August 13, 2001), 46–48.

33. Jonathan Katz, "Back to School," *Industry Week* (May 2007), 14; and Jonathan Katz, "A Plant's Grand Vision," *Industry Week* (October 2006), 43.

34. B. Joseph Pine II, *Mass Customization: The New Frontier in Business Competition* (Boston: Harvard Business School Press, 1999).

35. Barry Berman, "Should Your Firm Adopt a Mass Customization Strategy?" *Business Horizons* (July–August 2002), 51–60.

36. Mark Tatge, "Red Bodies, Black Ink," *Forbes* (September 18, 2000), 114–115.

37. Erick Schonfeld, "The Customized, Digitized, Have-It-Your-Way Economy," *Fortune* (September 28, 1998), 115–124.

38. Joel D. Goldhar and David Lei, "Variety Is Free: Manufacturing in the Twenty-First Century," *Academy of Management Executive* 9, no. 4 (1995), 73–86.

39. Meredith, "The Strategic Advantages of the Factory of the Future."

40. Patricia L. Nemetz and Louis W. Fry, "Flexible Manufacturing Organizations: Implementations for Strategy Formulation and Organization Design," *Academy of Management Review* 13 (1988), 627–638; Paul S. Adler, "Managing Flexible Automation," *California Management Review* (Spring 1988), 34–56; Jeremy Main, "Manufacturing the Right Way," *Fortune* (May 21, 1990), 54–64; and Frank M. Hull and Paul D. Collins, "High-Technology Batch Production Systems: Woodward's Missing Type," *Academy of Management Journal* 30 (1987), 786–797.

41. Goldhar and Lei, "Variety Is Free: Manufacturing in the Twenty-First Century"; P. Robert Duimering, Frank Safayeni, and Lyn Purdy, "Integrated Manufacturing: Redesign the Organization before Implementing Flexible Technology," *Sloan Management Review* (Summer 1993), 47–56; and Zammuto and O'Connor, "Gaining Advanced Manufacturing Technologies' Benefits."

42. Goldhar and Lei, "Variety Is Free: Manufacturing in the Twenty-First Century."

43. Byron J. Finch and Richard L. Luebbe, *Operations Management: Competing in a Changing Environment* (Fort Worth, Tex.: The Dryden Press, 1995), 51.

44. David E. Bowen, Caren Siehl, and Benjamin Schneider, "A Framework for Analyzing Customer Service Orientations in Manufacturing," *Academy of Management Review* 14 (1989), 79–95; Peter K. Mills and Newton Margulies, "Toward a Core Typology of Service Organizations," *Academy of Management Review* 5 (1980), 255–265; and Peter K. Mills and Dennis J. Moberg, "Perspectives on the Technology of Service Operations," *Academy of Management Review* 7 (1982), 467–478.

45. Erick Schonfeld, "The Customized, Digitized, Have-It-Your-Way Economy," *Fortune* (September 28, 1998), 115–124.

46. Duff McDonald, "Customer, Support Thyself," *Business 2.0* (April 2004), 56.

47. Liker and Morgan, "The Toyota Way in Services."

48. Paul Migliorato, "Toyota Retools Japan," *Business 2.0* (August 2004), 39–41.

49. Richard B. Chase and David A. Tansik, "The Customer Contact Model for Organization Design," *Management Science* 29 (1983), 1037–1050.

50. Ibid.

51. David E. Bowen and Edward E. Lawler III, "The Empowerment of Service Workers: What, Why, How, and When," *Sloan Management Review* (Spring 1992), 31–39: Gregory B. Northcraft and Richard B. Chase, "Managing Service Demand at the Point of Delivery," *Academy of Management Review* 10 (1985), 66–75; and Roger W. Schmenner, "How Can Service Businesses Survive and Prosper?" *Sloan Management Review* 27 (Spring 1986), 21–32.

52. Ann Zimmerman, "Home Depot Tries to Make Nice to Customers," *The Wall Street Journal* (February 20, 2007), D1.

53. Richard Metters and Vincente Vargas, "Organizing Work in Service Firms," *Business Horizons* (July–August 2000), 23–32.

54. Perrow, "A Framework for the Comparative Analysis of Organizations" and *Organizational Analysis*.

55. Brian T. Pentland, "Sequential Variety in Work Processes," *Organization Science* 14, no. 5 (September–October 2003), 528–540.

56. Jim Morrison, "Grand Tour. Making Music: The Craft of the Steinway Piano," *Spirit* (February 1997), 42–49, 100.

57. Stuart F. Brown, "Biotech Gets Productive," *Fortune*, special section, "Industrial Management and Technology" (January 20, 2003), 170[A]–170[H].

58. Michael Withey, Richard L. Daft, and William C. Cooper, "Measures of Perrow's Work Unit Technology: An Empirical Assessment and a New Scale," *Academy of Management Journal* 25 (1983), 45–63.

59. Christopher Gresov, "Exploring Fit and Misfit with Multiple Contingencies," *Administrative Science Quarterly* 34 (1989), 431–453; and Dale L. Goodhue and Ronald L. Thompson, "Task-Technology Fit and Individual Performance," *MIS Quarterly* (June 1995), 213–236.

60. Gresov, "Exploring Fit and Misfit with Multiple Contingencies"; Charles A. Glisson, "Dependence of Technological Routinization on Structural Variables in Human Service Organizations," *Administrative Science Quarterly* 23 (1978), 383–395; and Jerald Hage and Michael Aiken, "Routine Technology, Social Structure and Organizational Goals," *Administrative Science Quarterly* 14 (1969), 368–379.

61. Gresov, "Exploring Fit and Misfit with Multiple Contingencies"; A. J. Grimes and S. M. Kline, "The Technological Imperative: The Relative Impact of Task Unit, Modal Technology, and Hierarchy on Structure," *Academy of Management Journal* 16 (1973), 583–597; Lawrence G. Hrebiniak, "Job Technologies, Supervision and Work Group Structure," *Administrative Science Quarterly* 19 (1974), 395–410; and Jeffrey Pfeffer, *Organizational Design* (Arlington Heights, Ill.: AHM, 1978), Chapter 1.

62. Patrick E. Connor, *Organizations: Theory and Design* (Chicago: Science Research Associates, 1980); Richard L. Daft and Norman B. Macintosh, "A Tentative Exploration into Amount and Equivocality of Information Processing in Organizational Work Units," *Administrative Science Quarterly* 26 (1981), 207–224.

63. Paul D. Collins and Frank Hull, "Technology and Span of Control: Woodward Revisited," *Journal of Management Studies* 23 (1986), 143–164; Gerald D. Bell, "The Influence of Technological Components of Work upon Management Control," *Academy of Management Journal* 8 (1965), 127–132; and Peter M. Blau and Richard A. Schoenherr, *The Structure of Organizations* (New York: Basic Books, 1971).

64. W. Alan Randolph, "Matching Technology and the Design of Organization Units," *California Management Review* 22–23 (1980–81), 39–48; Daft and Macintosh, "Tentative Exploration into Amount and Equivocality of Information Processing"; and Michael L. Tushman, "Work Characteristics and Subunit Communication Structure: A Contingency Analysis," *Administrative Science Quarterly* 24 (1979), 82–98.

65. Andrew H. Van de Ven and Diane L. Ferry, *Measuring and Assessing Organizations* (New York: Wiley, 1980); and Randolph, "Matching Technology and the Design of Organization Units."

66. Richard L. Daft and Robert H. Lengel, "Information Richness: A New Approach to Managerial Behavior and Organization Design," in Barry Staw and Larry L. Cummings, eds., *Research in Organizational Behavior*, vol. 6 (Greenwich, Conn.: JAI Press, 1984), 191–233; Richard L. Daft and Norman B. Macintosh, "A New Approach into Design and Use of Management Information," *California Management Review* 21 (1978), 82–92; Daft and Macintosh, "A Tentative Exploration into Amount and Equivocality of Information Processing"; W. Alan Randolph, "Organizational Technology and the Media and Purpose Dimensions of Organizational Communication," *Journal of Business Research* 6 (1978), 237–259; Linda

Argote, "Input Uncertainty and Organizational Coordination in Hospital Emergency Units," *Administrative Science Quarterly* 27 (1982), 420–434; and Andrew H. Van de Ven and Andre Delbecq, "A Task Contingent Model of Work Unit Structure," *Administrative Science Quarterly* 19 (1974), 183–197.

67. Peggy Leatt and Rodney Schneck, "Criteria for Grouping Nursing Subunits in Hospitals," *Academy of Management Journal* 27 (1984), 150–165; and Robert T. Keller, "Technology-Information Processing," *Academy of Management Journal* 37, no. 1 (1994), 167–179.

68. Gresov, "Exploring Fit and Misfit with Multiple Contingencies"; Michael L. Tushman, "Technological Communication in R&D Laboratories: The Impact of Project Work Characteristics," *Academy of Management Journal* 21 (1978), 624–645; and Robert T. Keller, "Technology-Information Processing Fit and the Performance of R&D Project Groups: A Test of Contingency Theory," *Academy of Management Journal* 37, no. 1 (1994), 167–179.

69. James Thompson, *Organizations in Action* (New York: McGraw-Hill, 1967).

70. Ibid., 40.

71. Gene Bylinsky, "Shipmaking Gets Modern," *Fortune*, special section, "Industrial Management and Technology" (January 20, 2003), 170[K]–170[L].

72. Gautam Naik, "New Formula: A Hospital Races to Learn Lessons of Ferrari Pit Stop," *The Wall Street Journal* (November 14, 2006), A1.

73. Murray R. Barrick, Bret H. Bradley, Amy L. Kristof-Brown, and Amy E. Colbert, "The Moderating Role of Top Management Team Interdependence: Implications for Real Teams and Working Groups," *Academy of Management Journal* 50, no. 3 (2007), 544–557.

74. Paul S. Adler, "Interdepartmental Interdependence and Coordination: The Case of the Design/Manufacturing Interface," *Organization Science* 6, no. 2 (March–April 1995), 147–167.

75. Christopher Gresov, "Effects of Dependence and Tasks on Unit Design and Efficiency," *Organization Studies* 11 (1990), 503–529; Andrew H. Van de Ven, Andre Delbecq, and Richard Koenig, "Determinants of Coordination Modes within Organizations," *American Sociological Review* 41 (1976), 322–338; Argote, "Input Uncertainty and Organizational Coordination in Hospital Emergency Units"; Jack K. Ito and Richard B. Peterson, "Effects of Task Difficulty and Interdependence on Information Processing Systems," *Academy of Management Journal* 29 (1986), 139–149; and Joseph L. C. Cheng, "Interdependence and Coordination in Organizations: A Role-System Analysis," *Academy of Management Journal* 26 (1983), 156–162.

76. Robert W. Keidel, "Team Sports Models as a Generic Organizational Framework," *Human Relations* 40 (1987), 591–612; Robert W. Keidel, "Baseball, Football, and Basketball: Models for Business," *Organizational Dynamics* (Winter 1984), 5–18; and Nancy Katz, "Sports Teams as a Model for Workplace Teams: Lessons and Liabilities," *Academy of Management Executive* 15, no. 3 (2001), 56–67.

77. Michele Liu, Héléne Denis, Harvey Kolodny, and Benjt Stymne, "Organization Design for Technological Change," *Human Relations* 43 (January 1990), 7–22.

78. Gerald I. Susman and Richard B. Chase, "A Sociotechnical Analysis of the Integrated Factory," *Journal of Applied Behavioral Science* 22 (1986), 257–270; and Paul Adler, "New Technologies, New Skills," *California Management Review* 29 (Fall 1986), 9–28.

79. Based on Don Hellriegel, John W. Slocum, Jr., and Richard W. Woodman, *Organizational Behavior*, 8th ed. (Cincinnati, Ohio: South-Western, 1998), 491–495; and Gregory B. Northcraft and Margaret A. Neale, *Organizational Behavior: A Management Challenge*, 2nd ed. (Fort Worth, Tex.: The Dryden Press, 1994), 550–553.

80. F. Emery, "Characteristics of Sociotechnical Systems," Tavistock Institute of Human Relations, document 527, 1959; William Pasmore, Carol Francis, and Jeffrey Haldeman, "Sociotechnical Systems: A North American Reflection on Empirical Studies of the 70s," *Human Relations* 35 (1982), 1179–1204; and William M. Fox, "Sociotechnical System Principles and Guidelines: Past and Present," *Journal of Applied Behavioral Science* 31, no. 1 (March 1995), 91–105.

81. W. S. Cascio, *Managing Human Resources* (New York: McGraw-Hill, 1986), 19.

82. Eric Trist and Hugh Murray, eds., *The Social Engagement of Social Science: A Tavistock Anthology*, vol. II (Philadelphia: University of Pennsylvania Press, 1993); and William A. Pasmore, "Social Science Transformed: The Socio-Technical Perspective," *Human Relations* 48, no. 1 (1995), 1–21.

83. R. E. Walton, "From Control to Commitment in the Workplace," *Harvard Business Review* 63, no. 2 (1985), 76–84; E. E. Lawler, III, *High Involvement Management* (London: Jossey-Bass, 1986), 84; and Hellriegel, Slocum, and Woodman, *Organizational Behavior*, 491.

84. William A. Pasmore, "Social Science Transformed: The Socio-Technical Perspective," *Human Relations* 48, no. 1 (1995), 1–21.

85. David M. Upton, "What Really Makes Factories Flexible?" *Harvard Business Review* (July–August 1995), 74–84.

86. Pasmore, "Social Science Transformed: The Socio-Technical Perspective"; H. Scarbrough, "Review Article: *The Social Engagement of Social Science: A Tavistock Anthology*, Vol. II," *Human Relations* 48, no. 1 (1995), 23–33.

A

adaptability culture a culture characterized by strategic focus on the external environment through flexibility and change to meet customer needs.

adhocracy an organization form that develops in a complex, rapidly changing environment and is designed to support innovation and change.

administrative principles a management perspective that focuses on the design and functioning of the organization as a whole.

ambidextrous approach a design approach that incorporates structures and management processes that are appropriate to both the creation and the implementation of innovation.

analyzability a dimension of technology in which work can be reduced to mechanical steps and participants can follow an objective, computational procedure to solve problems.

analyzer a business strategy based on maintaining a stable business while innovating on the periphery.

authority a force for achieving desired outcomes that is prescribed by the formal hierarchy and reporting relationships.

B

balanced scorecard a comprehensive management control system that balances traditional financial measures with operational measures relating to a company's critical success factors.

behavior control manager observation of employee actions to see whether the individual follows desired procedures and performs tasks as instructed.

benchmarking the process of continually measuring products, services, and practices against tough competitors or other organizations recognized as industry leaders.

blog a running Web log that allows an individual to post opinions and ideas.

boundary-spanning roles activities that link and coordinate an organization with key elements in the external environment.

bounded rationality perspective a perspective that describes how decisions are made when problems are ill-defined, numerous factors affect the decision, and time is limited.

buffering roles activities that absorb uncertainty from the environment.

bureaucracy an organizational framework marked by rules and procedures, specialization and division of labor, hierarchy of authority, emphasis on technically qualified personnel, and written communications and records.

bureaucratic control the use of rules, policies, hierarchy of authority, written documentation, standardization, and other bureaucratic mechanisms to standardize behavior and assess performance.

bureaucratic culture a culture with an internal focus and a consistency orientation for a stable environment.

bureaucratic organizations organizations that emphasize designing and managing on an impersonal, rational basis through such elements as clearly defined authority and responsibility, formal recordkeeping, and uniform application of standard rules.

business intelligence high-tech analysis of large amounts of internal and external data to spot patterns and relationships that might be significant in helping managers make better strategic decisions.

C

Carnegie model organization decision making that involves many managers making a final choice based on a coalition among those managers.

centrality a source of horizontal power for a department that is engaged in the primary activity of an organization.

centralization refers to the level of hierarchy with authority to make decisions.

Bettina Anzeletti

centralized decision making decision making in which problems and decisions are funneled to top levels of the hierarchy for resolution.

change process the way in which changes occur in an organization.

chaos theory a theory that suggests that relationships in complex, adaptive systems—including organizations—are nonlinear and made up of numerous interconnections and divergent choices that create unintended effects and render the whole unpredictable.

charismatic authority authority based on devotion to the exemplary character or to the heroism of an individual person and the order defined by him or her.

chief ethics officer a high-level company executive who oversees all aspects of ethics.

clan control the use of social characteristics, such as shared cultural values, commitment, traditions, and beliefs, to control behavior.

clan culture a culture with a primary focus on the involvement and participation of the organization's members and on rapidly changing expectations from the external environment.

coalition an alliance among several managers who agree about organizational goals and problem priorities.

code of ethics a formal statement of the organization's values concerning ethics and social responsibility.

coercive forces the external pressures exerted on an organization to adopt structures, techniques, or behaviors similar to other organizations.

cognitive biases severe errors in judgment that all humans are prone to and that typically lead to bad choices.

collaborative network a perspective whereby organizations join together to become more competitive and to share scarce resources to increase value and productivity for all.

collective bargaining the negotiation of an agreement between management and workers.

collectivity stage the life cycle phase in which an organization has strong leadership and begins to develop clear goals and direction.

competition rivalry among groups in the pursuit of a common prize.

competitive advantage what sets the organization apart from others and provides it with a distinctive edge for meeting customer or client needs in the marketplace.

confrontation a situation in which parties in conflict directly engage one another and try to work out their differences.

consortia groups of independent companies (suppliers, customers, and possibly competitors) that join together to share skills, resources, costs, and access to one another's markets.

contextual dimensions traits that characterize the whole organization, including its size, technology, environment, and goals.

contingency theory meaning that one thing depends on other things; for organizations to be effective, there must be a "goodness of fit" between their structure and the conditions in their external environment.

contingency decision-making framework a perspective that brings together the two organizational dimensions of problem consensus and technical knowledge about solutions.

continuous-process production a completely mechanized manufacturing process in which there is no starting or stopping.

cooptation occurs when leaders from important sectors in the environment are made part of an organization and thus are more engaged in that organization's interests.

coping with uncertainty a source of horizontal power for a department that reduces uncertainty for other departments by obtaining prior information, prevention, or absorption.

core competence describes what the organization does especially well in comparison to its competitors.

core technology the work process that is directly related to the organization's mission.

corporate social responsibility (CSR) the concept of management's obligation to make choices and take action so that the organization contributes to the welfare and interest of all organizational stakeholders.

craft technology technology characterized by a fairly stable stream of activities, but the conversion process is not analyzable or well understood.

creative departments departments that initiate change, such as research and development, engineering, design, and systems analysis.

creativity the generation of novel ideas that may meet perceived needs or respond to opportunities.

culture the set of values, norms, guiding beliefs, and understandings that is shared by members of an organization and taught to new members as the correct way to think, feel, and behave.

culture change change in the values, attitudes, expectations, beliefs, and behavior of employees.

culture strength the degree of agreement among members of an organization about the importance of specific values.

customer relationship management (CRM) systems that help companies track customers' interactions with the firm and allow employees to call up a customer's past sales and service records, outstanding orders, or unresolved problems.

D

data warehousing the use of huge databases that combine all of a company's data and allow users to access the data directly, create reports, and obtain responses to what-if questions.

decentralized decision making decision making in which authority is pushed down to lower organizational levels.

decision learning a process of recognizing and admitting mistakes that allows managers to acquire sufficient experience and knowledge to perform more effectively in the future.

decision premises constraining frames of reference and guidelines placed by top managers on decisions made at lower levels.

decision support system (DSS) an interactive, computer-based system that relies on decision models and integrated databases.

defender a business strategy that is concerned with stability or even retrenchment.

departmental grouping a grouping in which employees share a common supervisor and common resources, are jointly responsible for performance, and tend to identify and collaborate with one another.

dependency an aspect of horizontal power, in which one department is dependent on another and the latter is in a position of greater power.

devil's advocate the role of challenging the assumptions and assertions made by the group.

differentiation the cognitive and emotional differences among managers in various functional departments of an organization and formal structure differences among these departments.

differentiation strategy a business strategy that attempts to distinguish an organization's products or services from others in the industry.

direct interlock occurs when one individual is the link between two companies, such as when a member of one company's board also sits on the board of another company.

diversified form an organization form that occurs when large, mature firms are subdivided into product or market groups.

divisional grouping a grouping in which employees are organized according to what the organization produces.

divisional structure structure in which divisions can be organized according to individual products, services, product groups, major projects or programs, divisions, businesses, or profit centers; sometimes called a *product structure* or *strategic business units*.

domain the chosen environmental field of action; the territory an organization stakes out for itself with respect to products, services, and markets served.

domains of political activity areas in which politics plays a role. Three domains in organizations are structural change, management succession, and resource allocation.

domestic stage the first stage of international development in which a company is domestically oriented while managers are aware of the global environment.

downsizing intentionally reducing the size of a company's workforce by laying off employees.

dual-core approach an organizational change perspective that identifies the unique processes associated with administrative change compared to those associated with technical change.

E

e-business any business that takes place by digital processes over a computer network rather than in physical space.

economies of scale achieving lower costs through large volume production; often made possible by global expansion.

economies of scope achieving economies by having a presence in many product lines, technologies, or geographic areas.

effectiveness the degree to which an organization achieves its goals.

efficiency the amount of resources used to achieve an organization's goals; based on the quantity of raw materials, money, and employees necessary to produce a given level of output.

elaboration stage a mature stage of the life cycle in which a red tape crisis is resolved through the development of a new sense of teamwork and collaboration.

empowerment the delegation of power or authority to subordinates in an organization, also known as *power sharing*.

engineering technology technology that tends to be complex because there is substantial variety in the tasks performed, but activities are usually handled on the basis of established formulas, procedures, and techniques.

enterprise resource planning (ERP) a system that collects, processes, and provides information about a company's entire enterprise.

entrepreneurial stage the life cycle stage in which an organization is born and its emphasis is on creating a product and surviving in the marketplace.

entrepreneurial structure an organization form that consists mainly of a top manager and workers in the technical core; occurs typically in small start-up companies.

escalating commitment persisting to invest time and money in a solution despite strong evidence that it is not working.

ethical dilemma the result of when each alternative choice or behavior seems undesirable because of a potentially negative ethical consequence.

ethics the code of moral principles and values that governs the behaviors of a person or group with respect to what is right or wrong.

ethics committee a cross-functional group of executives who oversee company ethics.

ethics hotline a telephone number employees can call to seek guidance as well as report questionable behavior.

evidence-based management a commitment to make more informed and intelligent decisions based on the best available facts and evidence.

executive dashboard a software program that presents key business information in graphical, easy-to-interpret form and alerts managers to any deviations or unusual patterns in the data; sometimes called a *business performance dashboard*.

executive information system (EIS) a higher-level application that facilitates decision making at the highest levels of management, these systems are typically based on software that can convert large amounts of complex data into pertinent information and provide that information to top managers in a timely fashion.

explicit knowledge formal, systematic knowledge that can be codified, written down, and passed on to others in documents or general instructions.

external adaptation the manner in which an organization meets goals and deals with outsiders.

extranet an external communications system that uses the Internet and is shared by two or more organizations.

F

factors of production resources necessary for production, such as land, raw materials, and labor.

feedback control model a control cycle that involves setting goals, establishing standards of performance, measuring actual performance and comparing it to standards, and changing activities as needed based on the feedback.

financial resources a source of horizontal power when a person or department has control over money in an organization.

flexible manufacturing systems (FMS) using computers to link together manufacturing components such as robots, machines, product design, and engineering analysis to enable fast switching from one product to another.

focus strategy a business strategy that concentrates on a specific regional market or buyer group.

formalization the degree to which an organization has rules, procedures, and written documentation.

formalization stage the life cycle stage that involves the installation and use of rules, procedures, and control systems.

functional grouping a grouping that consists of employees who perform similar functions or work processes or who bring similar knowledge and skills to bear.

functional matrix type of matrix structure in which the functional bosses have primary authority and the project or product managers simply coordinate product activities.

functional structure organization structure in which activities are grouped together by common function from the bottom to the top of the organization.

G

garbage can model decision-making model that describes the pattern or flow of multiple decisions within an organization.

general environment those sectors that might not have a direct impact on the daily operations of a firm but will indirectly influence it.

generalist an organization that offers a broad range of products or services or serves a broad market.

global companies companies that no longer think of themselves as having a single home country; sometimes called *stateless corporations*.

global geographic structure structure that divides the world into geographic regions, with each geographic division reporting to the CEO.

global matrix structure a form of horizontal linkage in an international organization in which both product and geographical structures are implemented simultaneously to achieve a balance between standardization and globalization.

global product structure structure in which the product divisions take responsibility for global operations in their specific product area.

global stage the stage of international development in which the company transcends any one country.

global teams cross-border work groups made up of multiskilled, multinational members whose activities span multiple countries; also called *transnational teams*.

globalization strategy the standardization of product design, manufacturing, and marketing strategy throughout the world.

goal approach an approach to effectiveness that is concerned with an organization's outputs and how well the organization has met its output goals.

groupthink the tendency of people in groups to suppress contrary opinions for the sake of group harmony.

H

Hawthorne studies a series of experiments on worker productivity begun in 1924 at the Hawthorne plant of Western Electric Company in Illinois; attributed employees' increased output to managers' better treatment of them during the study.

heroes organization members who serve as models or ideals that illustrate and support desired cultural norms and values.

high-velocity environments industries in which competitive and technological change is so extreme that market data is either unavailable or obsolete, strategic windows open and shut quickly, and decisions must be make quickly with limited information.

horizontal coordination model a model of the three components of organizational design needed to achieve new product innovation: departmental specialization, boundary spanning, and horizontal linkages.

horizontal grouping a grouping in which employees are organized around core work processes, the end-to-end work, information, and material flows that provide value directly to customers.

horizontal linkage communication and coordination horizontally across organizational departments.

horizontal structure organization structure that organizes employees around core processes rather than by function, product, or geography.

hybrid structure structure that combines characteristics of various structural approaches tailored to specific strategic needs.

I

idea champions organization members who provide the time and energy to make change happen; sometimes called *advocates, intrapreneurs,* and *change agents.*

idea incubator a safe harbor in which ideas from employees throughout the organization can be developed without interference from company bureaucracy or politics.

imitation the act of adopting a decision tried elsewhere in the hope that it will work in this situation.

incremental decision model decision-making model that describes the structured sequence of activities undertaken from the discovery of a problem to its solution.

indirect interlock occurs when a director of company A and a director of company B are both directors of company C.

information reporting system the most common form of management information system, this type of system provides mid-level managers with reports that summarize data and support day-to-day decision making.

inspiration an innovative, creative solution that is not reached by logical means.

institutional environment norms, values, and expectations from stakeholders (customers, investors, boards, government, community, etc.).

institutional perspective the view of how organizations survive and succeed through congruence between an organization and the expectations from its institutional environment.

institutional similarity the emergence of a common structure and approach among organizations in the same field; called *institutional isomorphism* in the academic literature.

integrated enterprise an organization that uses advanced IT to enable close coordination within the company as well as with suppliers, customers, and partners.

integration the quality of collaboration among departments or organizations.

integrator a position or department created solely to coordinate several departments.

intellectual capital the sum of an organization's knowledge, experience, understanding, relationships, processes, innovations, and discoveries.

intelligence team cross-functional group of managers and employees, usually led by a competitive intelligence professional, who work together to gain a deep understanding of a specific competitive issue.

intensive technology technology that provides a variety of products or services in combination to a client.

interdependence the extent to which departments depend on each other for resources or materials to accomplish their tasks.

intergroup conflict the behavior that occurs among organizational groups when participants identify with one group and perceive that other groups may block their group's goal achievement or expectations.

interlocking directorate formal linkage that occurs when a member of the board of directors of one company sits on the board of directors of another company.

internal integration a state in which members develop a collective identity and know how to work together effectively.

internal process approach an approach that looks at internal activities and assesses effectiveness by indicators of internal health and efficiency.

international division a division organized to handle business in other countries.

international stage the second stage of international development, in which the company takes exports seriously and begins to think multidomestically.

interorganizational relationships the relatively enduring resource transactions, flows, and linkages that occur among two or more organizations.

intranet a private, companywide information system that uses the communications protocols and standards of the Internet and the World Wide Web but is accessible only to people within the company.

intuitive decision making decision making based on experience and judgment rather than sequential logic or explicit reasoning.

J

job design the assignment of goals and tasks to be accomplished by employees.

job enlargement an expansion of the number of different tasks performed by an employee in a job.

job enrichment designing a job to provide greater responsibility, recognition, and opportunities for growth and development.

job rotation moving employees from job to job to give them a greater variety of tasks.

job simplification the variety and difficulty of tasks performed by a single person are reduced.

joint optimization the goal of the sociotechnical systems approach, which states that an organization functions best when the social and technical systems are designed to fit the needs of one another.

joint venture a separate entity created with two or more active firms as sponsors.

K

knowledge a conclusion drawn from information that has been linked to other information and compared to what is already known.

knowledge management the ability to systematically find, organize, and make available a company's intellectual capital and to foster a culture of continuous learning and knowledge sharing so that organizational activities build on what is already known.

L

labor–management teams a cooperative approach designed to increase worker participation and provide a cooperative model for union-management problems.

large group intervention an approach that brings together participants from all parts of the organization, often including key stakeholders from outside the organization as well, in an off-site setting to discuss problems or opportunities and plan for change.

large-batch production a manufacturing process characterized by long production runs of standardized parts.

lean manufacturing a process that uses highly trained employees at every stage of the production process, who take a painstaking approach to details and problem solving to cut waste and improve quality.

learning organization an organization that promotes communication and collaboration so that everyone is engaged in identifying and solving problems, enabling the organization to continuously experiment, improve, and increase its capability.

legends stories of historic events that may have been embellished with fictional details.

legitimacy the general perception that an organization's actions are desirable, proper, and appropriate within the environment's system of norms, values, and beliefs.

level of analysis in systems theory, the subsystem on which the primary focus is placed; four levels of analysis normally characterize organizations.

liaison role a role in which a person is located in one department but has the responsibility for communicating and achieving coordination with another department.

life cycle the concept that organizations are born, grow older, and eventually die.

long-linked technology the combination within one organization of successive stages of production, with each stage using as its inputs the production of the preceding stage.

low-cost leadership strategy a strategy of increasing market share by keeping costs low compared to competitors.

M

machine bureaucracy an organization form suited to a simple, stable environment, in which there is extensive formalization and specialization, a tall hierarchy, a goal of efficiency, and a technical core typically oriented to mass production.

management champion a manager who acts as a supporter and sponsor of a technical champion to shield and promote an idea within the organization.

management control systems broadly defined as the formal routines, reports, and procedures that use information to maintain or alter patterns in organizational activities.

management information system (MIS) a computer-based system that provides information and support for managerial decision making.

management science approach organization decision making that uses quantitative models to analyze numerous variables and arrive at the best solution; the analog to the rational approach by individual managers.

managerial ethics principles that guide the decisions and behaviors of managers with regard to whether they are right or wrong.

market control the use of price competition to evaluate the output and productivity of an organization or its major departments and divisions.

mass customization using mass-production technology to quickly and cost-effectively assemble goods that are uniquely designed to fit the demands of individual customers.

matrix structure organization structure in which both product division and functional structures (horizontal and vertical) are implemented simultaneously.

mechanistic an organization system marked by rules, procedures, a clear hierarchy of authority, and centralized decision making.

mediating technology technology that allows each department to work independently by virtue of providing products or services that mediate or link clients from the external environment.

meso theory an approach to organization studies that concerns the integration of both micro and macro levels of analysis.

mimetic forces the pressure to copy or model other organizations that appear to be successful.

mission the organization's reason for existence; describes the organization's shared values and beliefs and its reason for being.

mission culture a culture characterized by emphasis on a clear vision of the organization's purpose and on the achievement of goals, such as sales growth, profitability, or market share, to help achieve the purpose.

multidomestic manager mindset in which competitive issues in each country are viewed independently of other countries; the company deals with each country individually.

multidomestic strategy strategy in which competition in each country is handled independently of competition in other countries.

multifocused grouping a grouping in which the organization embraces two or more structural grouping alternatives simultaneously, often called *matrix* or *hybrid*.

multinational stage the stage of international development in which a company has marketing and production facilities in many countries and more than one-third of its sales outside its home country.

myths stories that are consistent with the values and beliefs of the organization but are not supported by facts.

N

negotiation the bargaining process that often occurs during confrontation and that enables the parties to systematically reach a solution.

network centrality a source of power based on being centrally located in the organization and having access to information and people that are critical to the company's success.

networking electronically linking people and departments within a particular building or across corporate offices, enabling them to share information and cooperate on projects.

new-venture fund a fund that provides financial resources for employees to develop new ideas, products, or businesses.

niche a domain of unique environmental resources and needs.

non-core technology a department work process that is important to the organization but is not directly related to its primary mission.

nonprogrammed decision novel and poorly defined, these decisions are required when no procedure exists for solving a problem.

nonroutine technology technology characterized by high task variety, and the conversion process is not analyzable or well understood.

nonsubstitutability a source of horizontal power when a department's function cannot be performed by other readily available resources.

normative forces pressures to achieve standards of professionalism and to adopt techniques that are considered by the professional community to be up to date and effective.

O

official goals formally stated definition of business scope and outcomes the organization is trying to achieve.

open innovation an approach that extends the search for and commercialization of new products beyond the boundaries of the organization.

operative goals goals stated in terms of outcomes sought through the actual operating procedures of the organization.

organic an organization system marked by free-flowing, adaptive processes, an unclear hierarchy of authority, and decentralized decision making.

organization development (OD) a behavioral science field devoted to improving performance through trust, open confrontation of problems, employee empowerment and participation, the design of meaningful work, cooperation between groups, and the full use of human potential.

organization structure designates formal reporting relationships, including the number of levels in the hierarchy and the span of control of managers and supervisors; identifies the grouping together of individuals into departments and of departments into the total organization; and includes the design of systems to ensure effective communication, coordination, and integration of efforts across departments.

organization theory a macro examination of organizations that analyzes the whole organization as a unit.

organizational behavior a micro approach to organizations that focuses on the individuals within organizations as the relevant units of analysis.

organizational change the adoption of a new idea or behavior by an organization.

organizational decision making the process of identifying and solving problems.

organizational decline a condition in which a substantial, absolute decrease in an organization's resource base occurs over a period of time.

organizational ecosystem a system formed by the interaction of a community of organizations and their environment.

organizational environment all elements that exist outside the boundary of the organization and have the potential to affect all or part of the organization.

organizational form an organization's specific technology, structure, products, goals, and personnel.

organizational goal a desired state of affairs that the organization attempts to reach.

organizational innovation the adoption of an idea or behavior that is new to the organization's industry, market, or general environment.

organizational politics the activities of acquiring, developing, and using power and other resources to influence others and obtain the preferred outcome when there is uncertainty or disagreement about choices.

organizations social entities that are goal-directed, designed as deliberately structured and coordinated activity systems, and are linked to the external environment.

organized anarchy extremely organic organizations characterized by highly uncertain conditions.

outcome control a management focus on monitoring and rewarding results rather than on how those results are obtained.

outsourcing contracting out certain functions or tasks, such as manufacturing or credit processing, to other companies.

P

personnel ratios the proportions of administrative, clerical, and professional support staff.

point–counterpoint a decision-making technique that divides decision makers into two groups and assigns them different, often competing responsibilities.

political model a definition of an organization as being made up of groups that have separate interests, goals, and values in which power and influence are needed to reach decisions.

political tactics for using power these include building coalitions, expanding networks, controlling decision premises, enhancing legitimacy and expertise, and making a direct appeal.

pooled interdependence the lowest form of interdependence, in which work does not flow between departments.

population a set of organizations engaged in similar activities with similar patterns of resource utilization and outcomes.

population-ecology perspective focuses on organizational diversity and adaptation within a population of organizations.

power the potential ability of one person (or department) to influence other people (or departments) to carry out orders or to do something they would not otherwise have done.

power distance the level of inequality people are willing to accept in an organization.

power sources the five sources of horizontal power in organizations are dependency, financial resources, centrality, nonsubstitutability, and the ability to cope with uncertainty.

problem consensus the level of agreement among managers about the nature of a problem or opportunity and about which goals and outcomes to pursue.

problem identification the decision-making stage during which information about environmental and organizational conditions is monitored to determine if performance is satisfactory and to diagnose the cause of shortcomings.

problem solution the decision-making stage during which alternative courses of action are considered and one alternative is selected and implemented.

problemistic search search that occurs when managers look around in the immediate environment for a solution to quickly resolve a problem.

process an organized group of related tasks and activities that work together to transform inputs into outputs that create value for customers.

professional bureaucracy a form of organization made up primarily of highly skilled professionals, such as in hospitals, universities, law firms, and consulting firms.

product and service change change that pertains to the product or service outputs of an organization.

product matrix type of matrix structure in which the project or product managers have primary authority and functional managers simply assign technical personnel to projects and provide advisory expertise as needed.

programmed decisions repetitive and well defined, these decisions are used when procedures exist for resolving the problem.

prospect theory theory that suggests that the threat of a loss has a greater impact on a decision than the possibility of an equivalent gain.

prospector a business strategy of innovating, taking risks, seeking out new opportunities, and growing.

R

rational approach decision-making process based on systematic analysis of a problem followed by choice and implementation in a logical sequence.

rational model a model of organization characterized by rational decision processes, clear goals and choices, centralized power and control, an efficiency orientation, and little conflict among groups; an ideal not fully achievable in the real world.

rational–legal authority authority based on employees' belief in the legality of rules and the right of those elevated to positions of authority to issue commands.

reactor a response to environmental threats and opportunities in an ad hoc rather than strategic fashion.

reciprocal interdependence the highest level of interdependence, in which the output of one operation is the input of a second, and the output of the second operation is the input of the first (for example, a hospital).

reengineering the redesign of a vertical organization along its horizontal workflows and processes.

resource dependence a situation in which organizations depend on the environment but strive to acquire control over resources to minimize their dependence.

resource-based approach an organizational perspective that assesses effectiveness by observing how successfully the organization obtains, integrates, and manages valued resources.

resource-dependence theory theory that organizations try to minimize their dependence on other organizations for the supply of important resources and try to influence the environment to make resources available.

retention the preservation and institutionalization of selected organizational forms.

rites and ceremonies the elaborate, planned activities that make up a special event and are often conducted for the benefit of an audience.

role a part in a dynamic social system that allows an employee to use his or her discretion and ability to achieve an outcome or meet a goal.

routine technology technology characterized by little task variety and the use of objective, computational procedures.

rule of law that which arises from a set of codified principles and regulations that describe how people are required to act, that are generally accepted in society, and that are enforceable in the courts.

S

satisficing the acceptance of a satisfactory rather than a maximum level of performance, enabling an organization to achieve several goals simultaneously.

scientific management emphasizes scientifically determined jobs and management practices as the way to improve efficiency and labor productivity.

sectors subdivisions of the external environment that contain similar elements.

selection the process by which a new organizational form is determined to suit the environment and survive, or is "selected out" and fails.

sequential interdependence a serial form of interdependence in which the output of one operation becomes the input to another operation.

service technology technology characterized by simultaneous production and consumption, customized output, customer participation, intangible output, and being labor intensive.

simple–complex dimension the number and dissimilarity of external elements relevant to an organization's operations.

Six Sigma a highly ambitious quality standard that specifies a goal of no more than 3.4 defects per million parts; also, a set of control procedures that emphasizes the relentless pursuit of quality.

skunkworks a separate, small, informal, highly autonomous, and often secretive group that focuses on breakthrough ideas for the business.

small-batch production a manufacturing process, often custom work, that relies heavily on the human operator and is not highly mechanized.

social audit measures and reports the ethical, social, and environmental impact of an organization's operations.

social capital the quality of interactions among people and the degree to which they share a common perspective.

social networking a peer-to-peer communication channel, where people interact in an online community, share personal data and photos, and produce and share a variety of information and opinions.

sociotechnical systems approach an approach that combines the needs of people with the organization's need for technical efficiency.

sources of intergroup conflict factors that generate conflict, including goal incompatibility, differentiation, task interdependence, and limited resources.

specialist an organization that provides a narrower range of goods or services or that serves a narrower market.

stable–unstable dimension refers to whether elements in the environment are dynamic.

stakeholder any group within or outside of an organization that has a stake in the organization's performance.

stakeholder approach integrates and balances diverse organizational activities by looking at various organizational stakeholders and what they want from the organization.

standardization policies that ensure all branches of the company at all locations operate in the same way.

stories narratives based on true events that are frequently shared among organizational employees and told to new employees to inform them about an organization.

strategic contingencies events and activities both inside and outside an organization that are essential for attaining organizational goals.

strategic intent a situation in which all the organization's energies and resources are directed toward a focused, unifying, and compelling overall goal.

strategy a plan for interacting with the competitive environment to achieve organizational goals.

strategy and structure change change that pertains to the administrative domain in an organization.

strategy map a visual representation of the key drivers of an organization's success that shows how specific outcomes in each area are linked.

structural dimensions describe the internal characteristics of an organization, and create a basis for measuring and comparing organizations.

structure the formal reporting relationships, groupings, and systems of an organization.

struggle for existence the concept that organizations and populations of organizations are engaged in a competitive struggle over resources, and each organizational form is fighting to survive.

subcultures cultures that develop within an organization that reflect the common problems, goals, and experiences that members of a team, department, or other unit share.

supply chain management managing the sequence of suppliers and purchasers, covering all stages of processing from obtaining raw materials to distributing finished goods to consumers.

switching structures an organization creates an organic structure when such a structure is needed for the initiation of new ideas and reverts to a more mechanistic structure to implement the ideas.

symbol something that represents another thing.

symptoms of structural deficiency signs that the organization structure is out of alignment, including delayed or poor-quality decision making, failure to respond innovatively to environmental changes, and too much conflict.

T

tacit knowledge knowledge based on personal experience, rules of thumb, intuition, and judgment; knowledge that is difficult to put into writing.

tactics for enhancing collaboration these include techniques such as integration devices, confrontation and negotiation, intergroup consultation, member rotation, and shared mission and superordinate goals that enable groups to overcome differences and work together.

tactics for increasing power these include entering areas of high uncertainty, creating dependencies, providing resources, and satisfying strategic contingencies.

task a narrowly defined piece of work assigned to a person.

task environment sectors with which the organization interacts directly and that have a direct impact on the organization's ability to achieve its goals.

task force a temporary committee composed of representatives from each organizational unit affected by a problem.

team building activities that promote the idea that people who work together can work as a team.

teams permanent task forces, often used in conjunction with a full-time integrator.

technical complexity the extent of mechanization of the manufacturing process.

technical knowledge the degree of understanding and agreement about how to solve problems and reach organizational goals.

technology the work processes, techniques, machines, and actions used to transform organizational inputs into outputs.

technology change change in an organization's production process, including its knowledge and skill base, that enables distinctive competence.

time-based competition competition based on delivering products and services faster than competitors, giving companies a competitive edge.

traditional authority authority based on a belief in traditions and in the legitimacy of the status of people exercising authority through those traditions.

transaction processing system (TPS) a system that automates the organization's routine, day-to-day business transactions.

transnational model a form of horizontal organization that has multiple centers, subsidiary managers who initiate strategy and innovations for the company as a whole, and unity and coordination achieved through corporate culture and shared vision and values.

U

uncertainty condition that exists when decision makers do not have sufficient information about environmental factors, and they have a difficult time predicting external changes.

uncertainty avoidance within a cultural group, the degree to which members are uncomfortable with uncertainty and ambiguity and thus support beliefs that promise certainty.

V

values-based leadership a relationship between a leader and followers that is based on shared, strongly internalized values that are advocated and acted upon by the leader.

variation the appearance of new, diverse forms in a population of organizations.

variety in terms of tasks, the frequency of unexpected and novel events that occur in the conversion process.

venture teams a technique used to foster creativity within an organization by setting up a small team as its own company to pursue innovations.

vertical information system a strategy for increasing vertical information capacity.

vertical linkages communication and coordination activities connecting the top and bottom of an organization.

virtual network grouping a loosely connected cluster of separate components.

virtual network structure the firm subcontracts many or most of its major processes to separate companies and coordinates their activities from a small headquarters organization, sometimes called a *modular structure*.

virtual team a team made up of organizationally or geographically dispersed members who are linked primarily through advanced information and communications technologies.

W

whistle-blowing employee disclosure of illegal, immoral, or illegitimate practices on the part of the organization.

wiki a Web page or collection of pages designed to allow people to freely create, share, and edit content using any Web browser.

Name Index

Page numbers followed by the letter n indicate the note in which the entry is located.

A

Abboud, Leila, 548n83
Abdalla, David, 540n30
Abelson, Reed, 542n22
Ackerman, Linda S., 88, 541n65
Ackerman, Val, 120
Adams, M., 480, 561n46
Adamy, Janet, 537n3, 537n10, 562n62, 568n76
Adices, Ichak, 566n24
Adler, Nancy J., 184, 546n17
Adler, Paul S., 499, 500, 560n28, 570n23, 570n40, 571n74, 572n78
Aenlle, Conrad de, 546n33
Aeppel, Timothy, 568n82
Agins, Teri, 550n59
Agle, Bradley, 320, 558n67, 559n72, 559n73, 559n74
Agor, W. A., 555n32
Aiken, Michael, 567n43, 567n44, 559n9, 571n60
Aiken, Paul, 155
Akgün, Ali E., 561n51
Akinnusi, David M., 562n71
Al Najjar, Mohammed, 563n10
Alban, Billie T., 562n81, 562n83
Alderfer, Clayton T., 551n5
Aldrich, Howard E., 538n22, 544n34, 549n17
Alexander, Keith, 561n42
Allair, Paul, 4
Allen, Richard S., 562n87
Allen, Robert W., 553n66, 533n73
Allio, Robert J., 541n4
Allison, Charles F., 399, 401–402, 403

Alsop, Ronald, 545n47
Altier, William J., 539n19
Amdt, Michael, 540n49
Amelio, Gilbert, 461
Ammeter, Anthony P., 553n83
Anand, N., 54n33, 540n52, 540n55, 540n57, 541n60, 541n64
Anders, George, 537n1, 539n13
Anderson, Carl, 559n83
Anderson, Erin, 564n29
Anderson, Tom, 101, 471
Aniston, Jennifer, 320
Ante, Spencer E., 550n57, 564n15, 564n16
Antonelli, Cristiano, 541n57
Antonette, Sara, 318
Appel, Frank, 236
Apple, R. W., Jr., 540n30
Archer, Earnest R., 554n13, 554n16
Argote, Linda, 569n5, 571n66, 571n75
Argyris, Chris, 121, 449, 543n58
Arndt, Aaron D., 544n17
Arndt, Michael, 564n22, 593n1
Arnold, Rick, 291, 292
Arogyaswamy, Bernard, 557n35
Ashbrook, Joe, 563n7
Ashford, Susan, 544n24
Ashkenas, Ron, 562n84, 567n51
Astley, W. Graham, 551n24, 552n34, 552n44, 567n45
Aston, Adam, 540n49
At-Twaijri, Mohamed Ibrahim Ahmad, 549n30
Atkin, Robert S., 550n61

Atsaides, James, 568n87, 569n88
Aubin, Jean, 555n36
Auster, Ellen R., 545n52
Austin, Nancy, 43
Avolio, B., 235

B

Babcock, Judith A., 550n54
Bacharach, Samuel B., 553n76, 560n10, 568n79
Badal, Jaclyne, 538n32
Badaracco, Joseph L., Jr., 559n67
Bailetti, Antonio, 561n48
Bailom, Franz, 554n22, 554n29
Baker, Edward, 555n36
Baker, Steven, 555n38
Ballmer, Steven, 171
Balu, Rekha, 557n34
Bandler, James, 545n1
Banham, Russ, 564n16
Bannon, Lisa, 538n25
Barbaro, Michael, 549n27
Barczak, Gloria, 562n64
Barkema, Harry G., 537n4
Barker, James R., 568n73
Barker, Robert, 560n14
Barley, Stephen R., 538n26, 565n65, 565n70
Barnard, Chester, 554n23
Barnatt, Christopher, 565n58
Barnes, Brooks, 560n18
Barnes, Fred, 555n43
Barnett, Megan, 565n72
Barnevik, Percy, 547n49
Barney, Jay B., 543n57, 550n51
Barnum, Cynthia, 204
Barone, Michael, 566n21

Barrett, Amy, 539n18, 551n9
Barrick, Murray R., 571n73
Barrier, Michael, 559n69
Barrionuevo, Alexei, 556n3, 557n20
Barron, Kelly, 566n39
Barsoux, Jean-Louis, 548n78
Bartholomew, Doug, 564n16
Bartkus, Barbara, 541n8
Bartlett, Christopher A., 207, 208, 543n11, 546n8, 546n48, 546n37, 547n53, 547n71, 548n78, 548n79, 548n84
Baseler, Randy, 242
Bass, Bernard M., 235, 563n91
Bauer, Julia, 568n84
Baum, J. Robert, 554n22
Baum, Joel A. C., 537n4, 544n34
Baveja, Alok, 541n14
Bazerman, Max H., 550n61, 556n66
Beard, Donald W., 549n18
Beatty, Carol A., 563n95
Becker, Selwyn W., 563n98, 567n40, 567n47,
Beckhard, Richard, 121, 543n58, 543n60
Bedeian, Arthur G., 545n43
Behling, Orlando, 554n22
Bell, Cecil H., Jr., 562n78, 562n79, 562n80, 562n81
Bell, Gerald D., 571n63
Bellman, Eric, 546n29
Belohlav, James A., 547n40, 552n48
Belson, Ken, 546n16
Benedetti, Marti, 544n20
Benitz, Linda E., 330, 331
Benner, Katie, 568n75

Corporate Name Index

Change (*continued*)
strategic types of, 371–373
strategic types of, *exhibit,* 372
strategy and structure, 372, 386–388
technology, 371–372, 375–381
Change agents. *See* Idea champions
Change leaders, 393
Change process, 373
Change teams, 396
Chaos theory, 30
Charismatic authority, 471
Chief ethics officers, 321
China
centralized coordination, 205–206
companies on *Fortune* Global 500 list, 181–182
corruption, 465
cost of goods from, 8
in international sector, 222
strategic partnering with firms in, 8
Choice opportunities, 318
Church schisms, 263
CI (competitive intelligence), 231
Clan control, 472–474
Clan culture, 309
Clerical ratio, 466
Coalitions, 283, 310
Codes of ethics, 322
Coercion, 395–396
Coercive forces, 167–168
Coercive power, 266
Cognitive biases, 327–329
Collaboration, 285–288
exhibit, 281
Collaborative networks, 155–160
from adversaries to partners, 157–160
from adversaries to partners, *exhibit,* 158
defined, 155
reasons for, 155–157
Collaborative roles, 151–152
Collaborative strategy, 33
Collaborative teams, 379–381
Collective bargaining, 286
Collectivity stage, 459–460, 462
exhibit, 463
Colleges and universities, 9, 225
Columbia space shuttle, 321–322

Commitment stage, 392
Communication, 395, 478, 511
Company, The (Micklethwait and Wooldridge), 13
Competition. *See also* Porter's competitive forces and strategies
conflict versus, 261
as current challenge, 8
organizational decline and, 475–476
organizational ecosystems and, 149, 151
in population ecology, 163–164
time-based, 385
Competitive advantage, 105–106, 385–386
Competitive forces, 109–111
Competitive intelligence (CI), 230
Competitive strategy, 33
Competitors, rivalry among existing, 111
Complex, stable environment, 227
exhibit, 228
Complex, unstable environment, 227, 228–229
exhibit, 227
Complexity, 197–198
Computer-aided craftsmanship, 499
Computer-aided design (CAD), 495–496
Computer-aided manufacturing (CAM), 469
Computer game industry, 221–222
Computer-integrated manufacturing. *See* Flexible manufacturing systems
Conflict questionnaire, 290–291. *See also* Intergroup conflict
Confrontation, 286
Confronting Reality (Bossidy and Charan), 226
Consortia, 186
Contextual dimensions of organization design, 15, 17–20
Contingency, 26
Contingency decision-making framework, 321–323
contingency framework, 321–323

exhibit, 322
problem consensus, 320–321
technical knowledge, 321
Continuous-process production, 491
Continuous value creation, 380
Control, cultural differences in, 203–206
Control strategies, 369
Control systems, 470–474 *See also* Information for decision making and control
balanced scorecard, 426–428
balanced scorecard, *exhibit,* 427
behavior versus outcome control, 428–432
bureaucratic control, 471–472
clan control, 472–474
level and focus of, 426–432
market control, 472
organizational culture and, 305–306
Conversion rate, 423
Cooptation, 241, 283–284
Coordination
cultural differences in, 203–206
external, 436–439
global, 200–203
horizontal, 383–385, 443
internal, 432–436
lack of, 393
routine versus nonroutine technology, 511
Coordination roles, 201–203
Core competence, 106
Core organization manufacturing technology, 490–495
manufacturing firms, 492–492
manufacturing firms, *exhibit,* 491
strategy, technology, and performance, 492–495
technical complexity and structural characteristics, *exhibit,* 492
Core organization service technology, 500–505
designing service organizations, 504–505
designing service organizations, *exhibit,* 505

service firms, 501–505
service firms, *exhibit,* 501
Core technology, 488
exhibit, 488
Corporate entrepreneurship, 379
Corporate social responsibility (CSR), 317–318. *See also* Ethical values
Cost savings, 202
Costs, excessive focus on, 393
Country managers, 202
CPM officers, 427
Craft technologies, 507–508
Creative departments, 378
Creativity, 373
Crisis stage, 477
CRM (customer relationship management), 439
CSR. *See* Corporate social responsibility
Cultural differences in coordination and control, 203–206
China, 205–206
Europe, 205, 206
Japan, 205
national value systems, 203–205
United States, 206
Culture, 18, 33–34, 299–300. *See also* Organizational culture
Culture change, 373, 389–390
Culture strength, 310
Customer relationship management (CRM), 439
Customer service indicators, 122, 427
exhibit, 122, 428
Customized output, 502

D

Dashboards. *See* Executive dashboards
Data mining, 418
Data warehousing, 417–418
Decentralization, 59–60
divisional structure and, 72
Europe, 205, 206
Germany, 205, 206
information technology and, 442–443
routine versus nonroutine technology, 510
Decision interrupts, 312
Decision learning, 326–327